Mastering
SQL Server® 2008

Mastering
SQL Server® 2008

Michael Lee

Gentry Bieker

WILEY

Wiley Publishing, Inc.

Acquisitions Editor: Agatha Kim

Development Editor: Laurene Sorensen

Technical Editor: Acey Bunch

Production Editor: Christine O'Connor

Copy Editor: Kathy Grider-Carlyle

Production Manager: Tim Tate

Vice President and Executive Group Publisher: Richard Swadley

Vice President and Publisher: Neil Edde

Book Designer: Maureen Forys, Happenstance Type-O-Rama; Judy Fung

Compositor: Jeffrey Lytle, Happenstance Type-O-Rama

Proofreader: Scott Klemp, Word One

Cover Designer: Ryan Sneed

Cover Image: © Pete Gardner / Digital Vision / Getty Images

Library of Congress Cataloging-in-Publication Data

Lee, Michael.
  Mastering SQL server 2008 / Michael Lee, Gentry Bieker. — 1st ed.
    p. cm.
  Includes index.
  ISBN 978-0-470-28904-4 (paper/website)
  1. Client/server computing. 2. SQL server. 3. Relational databases. I. Bieker, Gentry. II. Title.
  QA76.9.C55L45 2009
  005.75'85—dc22

                    2008042924

10 9 8 7 6 5 4 3 2 1

Dear Reader,

Thank you for choosing *Mastering SQL Server 2008*. This book is part of a family of premium-quality Sybex books, all of which are written by outstanding authors who combine practical experience with a gift for teaching.

Sybex was founded in 1976. More than thirty years later, we're still committed to producing consistently exceptional books. With each of our titles we're working hard to set a new standard for the industry. From the paper we print on, to the authors we work with, our goal is to bring you the best books available.

I hope you see all that reflected in these pages. I'd be very interested to hear your comments and get your feedback on how we're doing. Feel free to let me know what you think about this or any other Sybex book by sending me an email at nedde@wiley.com, or if you think you've found a technical error in this book, please visit http://sybex.custhelp.com. Customer feedback is critical to our efforts at Sybex.

Best regards,

Neil Edde
Vice President and Publisher
Sybex, an Imprint of Wiley

To our students, who forced us to
continually improve.

Acknowledgments

Every project of this size is always an intense collaboration. This was certainly no exception. It all starts with the wonderful team at Sybex. This is the seventh project that I have worked on with the Sybex team, and I am always impressed by the work that they do. Special thanks to Neil Edde, Pete Gaughan, and Agatha Kim for their magnificent work on managing this process. Thanks also to our editor, Laurene Sorensen, who was able to merge our ideas together and help us to make the technical content actually readable. And thanks to the production team of Christine O'Connor, Kathy Grider-Carlyle, and Scott Klemp. Acey Bunch was a spectacular technical editor; an accomplished author in his own right, he provided many insights on the content that proved invaluable and substantially improved the quality of the content. Gentry Bieker, my coauthor on this project, was able to really capture the essence of SQL Server in the real world, something with which he has extensive experience. The production team at Sybex is superb. They were even able to take my hand drawings and turn them into real graphics, a true feat if you have ever seen my handwriting.

Finally, on a personal note, my career in training and technology would never have taken off had it not been for a former mentor, Bob Taylor. Other colleagues including Jon Hansen, Dale Byrd, Bryan Bechtoldt, Ken Sandlin, and Mike Mansfield have contributed so much to my career and given me amazing support over the years. Additionally, most of this work was written while I was employed at Aristocrat Technologies in Las Vegas, and I need to thank my colleagues and the management there for their support and input. And of course, I need to offer special thanks to my family, my wife and son, who always pay the highest price for these projects as I lock myself into the office every weekend to write. They have been incredibly supportive as the process continued week after week, and I could not have done it without them.

Most importantly, thanks to you, the reader. You are the reason for this project in the first place. I hope that you find value in the pages. Without you, we would not have had this incredible opportunity. Your feedback is invaluable and will help make any future projects better and more relevant. Good luck in your undertakings with SQL Server 2008. I wish you the best in your endeavors.

—*Michael Lee*

I'm incredibly thankful for the level of support I've received from everyone while writing my portion of this book. Thanks to Jennifer Hanner for all of the sacrifices she made, and the trips she allowed me to miss in order to complete this book, helping to keep me sane, and encouraging me to keep going through the process. To Samantha and Joel, my children, who went on many trips and outings without me through during the writing process. They made me smile, and reminded me that there is more to life than just a book. To Joel: "Yes, I'm finally done with my chapter!" To Michael Lee, who gave me this fantastic opportunity and introduced me to the process, and has always been patient and understanding in my learning about what it takes to put together a book of this size. Thanks to the entire book team: Laurene Sorensen, Acey Bunch, Pete Gaughan, Agatha Kim, and Neil Edde. I had an incredible amount of help and support from everyone I've encountered at Sybex and Wiley. You have all given me a ton of respect for the process that goes into creating a book. And to every one of my students (especially the difficult ones), who helped me to make it to where I am today.

—*Gentry Bieker*

About the Authors

Michael Lee (MCT, MCPD, MCITP, SCJP) has spent the last 15 years in technology training and consulting. Most of his career has been spent working with companies and helping them ease the transition to new technologies and practices. With a degree in Business Finance from the University of Utah, Michael discovered early that he enjoyed the IT aspects of business and built a career bringing together businesses and IT professionals, helping them understand each other and improve communication.

His beginnings in IT were a bit dubious, having worked as an intern with IBM in 1988 on the FAA modernization project (AAS), which has been dubbed one of the greatest project failures in IT history. A lot was learned from that experience, and since then, his focus has been bringing together business and technology interests. As a former Microsoft Regional Director, he was heavily involved in the rollout of Visual Studio 6.0 in 1997 and has made a career out of melding business and technology into a unified strategic front.

Currently, Michael is employed with the Clark County Court System in Las Vegas, Nevada where he still gets a chance to get his hands dirty with all kinds of technology, applying his passion to the public sector. When he is not coding, writing, or spending time with family, you can usually find him on his Harley, looking for that next great American Road.

Gentry Bieker is a certified trainer, consultant, and mentor who has focused on SQL Server and related technologies for the last decade. His experience spans from database design and tuning to application development and enterprise application integration. He has developed numerous presentations, classes, and sessions on SQL Server and many of the other Microsoft technologies that work with SQL Server. In addition to SQL Server, he also focuses on SharePoint and Microsoft CRM. He has worked with customers in many industries, spanning from health care and insurance to casino gaming and manufacturing.

As an energetic and passionate individual, he has found that turning massive amounts of data into useful information is what gets him up in the morning. He's provided training, mentoring, and consulting services for many companies, large and small, including Microsoft, Unisys, and Kimberly-Clark. In his spare time, he enjoys spending time with his children, jumping out of perfectly good airplanes, and gaming.

Contents at a Glance

Contents

Introduction

Database technology is constantly evolving. The interplay among major database vendors such as Microsoft and Oracle, as well as the inevitable pressure of the open-source community, has demanded that database systems continue to push forward in both features and scalability. This fact means that the everyday database professional is constantly in a "catch up" mode. This book is an attempt to simplify that process by distilling the flood of information available.

The very nature of a book like this, where the subject matter is so broad, is to ensure that the important points get included, but we can't possibly include everything that SQL Server 2008 supports. In fact, the authors had numerous long conversations, not about what we had to put into the book, but the trade-offs of what we had to leave out. We tried to find a balance, providing at least general coverage of the most important topics. This meant that we had to sacrifice the "deep dive" in some situations to ensure that we could address as much as possible without overloading the reader.

The other victim to this approach was an extensive coverage of the basics. Although we have included some introductory material, we had to make the assumption that this is not the first SQL Server book that you, the reader, have ever picked up. Although this is not an upgrader's guide, it does assume that you have had some prior experience with SQL Server and are looking to get a firm understanding about the capabilities and mechanics of the tool. We also put a focus on addressing the important new features as much as we could, so that you can quickly add these to your toolbelt. Hopefully, we have hit the mark we were aiming for.

We have also attempted to create a work that could be valuable as a reference as well as being read from cover to cover. The chapters address major topic areas so you should be able to drill into the information that you need. This book can, therefore, act as a roadmap, but we would encourage you to consult the SQL Server Books Online as well. There is a wealth of information there and some good code examples.

Finally, we hope that this book will be an easy and entertaining read. Our biggest complaint about technical books over the years is that they are far too sterile and take themselves too seriously. We have been teaching this stuff for years and have found that you can't take yourself or the subject matter too seriously if you want to engage your audience, so enjoy. We have had a wonderful time putting this together for you.

Who Should Read This Book

Our target audience is the database professional with some SQL Server experience who is either:

◆ Trying to ramp up skills on SQL Server 2008, or

◆ Transitioning from another RDBMS to SQL Server

If you have read through the Microsoft marketing materials on SQL Server 2008 and would like to see what is under the hype, then this book is for you. Also, if you have some experience with database systems and SQL Server and you are ready to take your skills to the next step, this might also be a good match.

We have tried to include information for both the SQL Server developer and administrator. In some organizations, these two roles are separate and distinct. In others, the same individual or team fills both roles. No matter what your perspective, you will find content related to your work. This does mean, however, that some of the chapters may be more meaningful than others.

Although there is some information in this book related to client programming, this is not a book on ADO.NET. We have included an overview of client programming, including the Entity Framework and LINQ, but have done so from the perspective of the SQL Server professional, not the client developer. A client developer who needs to become more familiar with the data-server tier might well find the discussion helpful, however.

The *Mastering* Series

The *Mastering* series from Sybex provides outstanding instruction for readers with intermediate and advanced skills, in the form of top-notch training and development for those already working in their field and clear, serious education for those aspiring to become pros. Every *Mastering* book features:

◆ The Sybex "by professionals for professionals" commitment. *Mastering* authors are themselves practitioners, with plenty of credentials in their areas of specialty.

◆ A practical perspective for a reader who already knows the basics—someone who needs solutions, not a primer.

◆ Real-World Scenarios, ranging from case studies to interviews, that show how the tool, technique, or knowledge presented is applied in actual practice.

◆ Skill-based instruction, with chapters organized around real tasks rather than abstract concepts or subjects.

◆ Self-review test "Master It" problems and questions, so you can be certain you're equipped to do the job right.

What Is Covered in This Book

Mastering SQL Server 2008 is organized to provide you with the following information:

Chapter 1: Overview of Microsoft SQL Server 2008 is a general introduction to SQL Server, its features, and the installation process.

Chapter 2: Understanding SQL Server Architecture contains an overview of the architecture of SQL Server with the intent of using this information to better control and optimize SQL Server performance.

Chapter 3: Databases, Files, and Resource Management discusses creating and maintaining databases and filegroups, including the new FILESTREAM feature.

Chapter 4: Tables and CRUD Operations covers table DDL and an overview of standard data modification statements, including the new MERGE keyword supported in SQL Server 2008.

Chapter 5: Procedural Programming addresses creating views, stored procedures, user-defined functions, and synonyms.

Chapter 6: Managing Data Integrity explains the options for managing data integrity in a database, and covers constraints and DML triggers.

Chapter 7: SQL Server and XML addresses the integration of XML technology into SQL Server and provides coverage of the toolset that manipulates XML data inside the SQL Server environment.

Chapter 8: Managing User Security explains the security structure built into SQL Server and provides instructions on how to implement this system to secure your data resources.

Chapter 9: Data Recovery covers the transaction architecture of SQL Server, as well as the supported backup and restore operations available, including new features such as backup compression.

Chapter 10: Monitoring SQL Server Activity explains the various tools available for monitoring different types of SQL Server activity, including performance counters, SQL Profiler, DDL triggers, and event notifications. An introduction to the Performance Data Warehouse/ Data Collector feature of SQL Server 2008 is also covered.

Chapter 11: Using the SQL Server Agent Service addresses creating jobs, alerts, and operators using the SQL Server Agent service.

Chapter 12: Data Availability and Distribution covers the different options that you have for moving data throughout your enterprise and making data reliably available to data consumers.

Chapter 13: SQL Server Data Security shows the encryption and key management features of SQL Server 2008 including certificates, symmetric keys, and asymmetric keys. This chapter also covers the new Transparent Data Encryption feature of SQL Server 2008.

Chapter 14: Indexing Strategies for Query Optimization discusses the workings of the query optimizer and explains how to create index architectures that will provide the highest level of benefit at the lowest maintenance cost.

Chapter 15: Transactions and Locking provides an overview of the SQL Server locking architecture and explains its interaction with transaction processing. An overview of transaction management is also provided.

Chapter 16: Using the Resource Governor and Policy-Based Management introduces two new features of SQL Server 2008 that allow detailed resource management of different types of workloads, as well as a new method for defining, evaluating, and enforcing nearly every aspect of SQL Server configuration through the use of policies.

Chapter 17: SQL Server and the .NET Client offers the reader a SQL Server professional's perspective on client programming, including traditional ADO.NET development, LINQ, and the entity framework.

Chapter 18: SQL Server and the Common Language Runtime explains the integration of the .NET Common Language Runtime in SQL Server and provides examples of implementing CLR objects in SQL Server applications.

Chapter 19: Using Spatial Data addresses the new geometry and geography datatypes in SQL Server 2008 and provides examples of their use and relevance in today's organizations.

Chapter 20: Service-Oriented Architecture and the Service Broker gives the reader an overview of service-oriented architecture and shows how the SQL Server Service Broker can provide asynchronous services to the enterprise.

Chapter 21: Full-Text Search Services illustrates the process of implementing a text search infrastructure in SQL Server using full-text indexes and queries designed to target those indexes.

Appendix A: The Bottom Line Gathers together all the Master It problems from every chapter and provides a solution for each.

Appendix B: SQL Server Analysis Services Overview provides a high-level overview of the data warehousing and multidimensional tools in SQL Server 2008.

Appendix C: SQL Server Reporting Services Overview provides a high-level overview of the business intelligence reporting tools included in SQL Server 2008.

How to Contact the Authors

We welcome feedback from you about this book or about books you'd like to see from us in the future. You can reach us by using the following email addresses:

Michael Lee: feedback@LeeTechEd.com

Gentry Bieker: feedback@GentryB.com

Sybex strives to keep you supplied with the latest tools and information you need for your work. Please check their website at www.sybex.com, where we'll post additional content and updates that supplement this book if the need arises. Enter the book's ISBN—**9780470289044**—and click Go to get to the book's update page.

Chapter 1

Overview of Microsoft SQL Server 2008

SQL Server 2008 is a very complex product. It definitely deserves a little bit of introduction. Even if you have been working with SQL Server for quite some time, you might find some new features and nuances in the product that may catch you off guard, but they might delight you as well. In this chapter, we will focus on where SQL Server fits into the grand scheme of Microsoft architecture as well as its placement in your own computing enterprise.

In this chapter, you will learn to:

- ◆ Use Architect SQL Server services in the typical IT environment
- ◆ Install SQL Server 2008
- ◆ Use the Microsoft SQL Server toolset
- ◆ Implement other useful third-party tools

SQL Server in the Enterprise World

The authors of this book have been working with SQL Server for over a combined 28 years. Back in the early days, it was a struggle to defend the product. We came to SQL Server with the same background as many other PC developers of our age, having worked with Clipper, Access, and other similar products. But SQL Server was different, and it required a change of perspective from the older tools with which we worked. Because Mike had worked for IBM, he had some previous experience with mainframes. Both Mike and Gentry also did some work with Oracle. However, SQL Server was definitely new territory compared to some of these older tools.

We quickly discovered, by playing with the product and trying to put it through its paces, that SQL Server had a lot of potential, but it still had a long way to go. Part of the problem was developer education. Many of the problems that we came across were the result of developers trying to build applications with SQL Server using the same mindset and techniques that served them well during the Clipper days. Obviously, SQL Server was not Clipper. Some things had to change.

SQL Server 2008 has come a very long way since those days when we first started to kick the tires, but one thing has not changed: the need to understand the big picture. SQL Server is a "big picture" product. Somewhat like an aspen grove where all of the trees share a common root system, SQL Server is integrated tightly with many other services and layers in the typical Microsoft-based IT environment. It is not strictly for storing user data any more. The sooner you grasp that, the better you will understand the logic behind the product, its architecture, and the direction that Microsoft is going with SQL Server.

The Need for an Enterprise System

Most people reading this book should have some prior experience with SQL Server. To that end, we do not need to explain the rationale for enterprise data access. Our data is the lifeblood of our business. Some of the authors' work has been done in heavily regulated industries such as insurance and casino gaming. In those environments, the need for data archival, the types of reports produced, and other data requirements are often dictated by governmental and other regulatory bodies. Without the data and programmatic resources to support those requirements, the organization cannot function.

As we stated previously, in the early days of SQL Server, it was somewhat difficult to defend it as a truly enterprise product, but starting with the 2005 release, SQL Server started to challenge that perception. The key, though, is to effectively match your business's enterprise-level requirements with the features that SQL Server brings to the table. The job is always easier if you are using the right tool. Some of the typical enterprise data requirements of an organization include:

Interoperability   In many cases, SQL Server data must be available to applications outside of your Microsoft Windows infrastructure. With the strong presence of mainframe systems, UNIX and Linux environments, Java platforms, etc., data interoperability requirements may be extensive.

Performance   Performance often means different things to different people. To the end user, it is typically about how fast they can get their data. For an administrator, the primary concern is maximizing overall throughput. These are often conflicting goals, and the database system must be able to balance them.

Security   The integrity of your data is only as good as your ability to secure it, but security these days goes beyond the typical authentication/authorization issues of the past. We must also be able to manage encryption processes, backup security, etc., while at the same time being proactive to prevent the security exposures of tomorrow.

High Availability   What good is having the data if it is not available to the people who need it when they need it? A good enterprise framework must ensure that we have adequate redundancy and the means to minimize downtime. Every second that the data system is not available can mean lost revenue, and in some cases, legal repercussions.

Automation   The more complex and larger a system becomes, the more important it is to be able to automate routine tasks and proactive maintenance to ensure that data availability and integrity is maintained. Otherwise, the typical database administrator (DBA) will be completely overwhelmed with day to day maintenance.

Centralized Reporting   Storing data isn't much use if you can't get data out when you need it in the formats that you need. A number of reporting environments are available. Whichever one you use, it is essential that the reporting tier be efficient, be flexible, and have the lowest possible footprint in terms of resource consumption.

This is a pretty short list. Off the top of your head, you could probably double this list right now. In order to be of any real value, a database system must be "enterprise ready" and not just a data engine with a collection of unrelated supporting services. That won't work in today's IT environment.

So, if SQL Server 2008 is our enterprise solution, how does it address these and other issues?

SQL Server Features

All right, we know that this sounds like a marketing speech, but we really do have a rationale for covering features. It is important to have a good understanding of what a system can do if you want to design effective solutions. Besides, some of the features are new, and you have to have some justification for upgrading to the 2008 version when the accountants knock on your door.

SQL Server Editions

Be aware that much of this information is available electronically in SQL Server Books Online, either locally installed or web-based, as well as a variety of other good Internet and published resources. The goal here is to synthesize it for your convenience. You may want to check other online resources, though.

Let's begin by looking at the different editions of SQL Server 2008. SQL Server 2008 is available in a number of different versions. The primary distributions are the Standard and Enterprise editions. Additionally, Microsoft has release four specialized editions of SQL Server, namely Workgroup, Web, Compact, Developer, and Express. Each has its advantages and disadvantages. Because the Compact version specifically targets embedded systems, we will not discuss it here. All of the following editions come in 32-bit and 64-bit versions, although only Enterprise and Developer versions support IA64.

SQL Server Express Edition

- Intended for embeddable, lightweight, and standalone solutions
- Supports one CPU
- 1GB maximum addressable memory
- 4GB maximum database size
- Free download and distribution

SQL Server Workgroup Edition

- Intended for small user loads, low-use web applications, etc.
- Supports two CPUs
- 4GB maximum addressable memory on 64-bit. OS Maximum on 32-bit
- No maximum database size

Web Edition

- Intended for larger traffic web applications
- Supports four CPUs
- OS maximum memory support

Standard Edition

◆ Intended for most applications

◆ Supports four CPUs

◆ Memory up to OS maximum

Enterprise Edition

◆ Provides the highest level of scalability and enterprise features

◆ Unlimited CPUs to OS maximum

◆ Memory up to OS maximum

◆ Numerous enterprise features not found in the Standard Edition such as:

  ◆ Database mirroring

  ◆ Database snapshots

  ◆ Online indexing

  ◆ Online page restores

  ◆ Distributed partitioned views

◆ Numerous business intelligence (BI) features not found in the Standard Edition, such as:

  ◆ Scale-out report servers

  ◆ Infinite click-through reports

  ◆ Text mining

  ◆ OLAP dimension and cell writeback

Developer Edition

◆ Functionally equivalent to Enterprise Edition

◆ Licensed only for development environments, not to be used in production

Choosing the right edition is important. It needs to satisfy your current needs as well as your projected ones. You need to make sure that your database will support your performance and scalability requirements. You must also consider database size and the need for enterprise data and BI features.

SQL SERVER SERVICES AND FEATURES

The feature list for SQL Server is extensive. Because we didn't want to fill these pages with redundant information, we ask you to refer to the SQL Server Books Online. There you will be able to find a great deal of information regarding the essential and expanded features of SQL Server.

A few specific features are worth mentioning. These are the big ones. Not all of them will fit into your enterprise plan, but some may, and the fact that they all are bundled with SQL Server can be incredibly convenient and cost-effective.

Support for Unstructured Data   For the average database administrator (DBA), there are two kinds of data: the data in the database (structured data) and everything else (unstructured data). Unfortunately, most organizations have a significant amount of unstructured data that they must manage ranging from documents to pictures to proprietary data. Through FILESTREAM data, large binary data streams can be stored in the file system without sacrificing the transactional integrity of the database system.

Policy-Based Management   Policies make it easier to enforce best practices and standards. You can configure policies such as naming conventions, configuration standards, and coding standards. You can enforce these centrally for the entire organization. Not only does this simplify enforcement of standards, it also allows central modification of policies as needed.

SQL Server Integration Services (SSIS)   SQL Server Integration Services (SSIS) provide exchange/transform/load (ETL) functionality for SQL Server 2008. SQL 2005 took a significant step forward from DTS when it was released, providing not only more intuitive designers, but also a native .NET execution environment. SQL Server 2008 continues that process with significant pipeline scalability improvements as well as the ability to provide persistent lookups, which is a significant data warehousing enhancement.

SQL Server Reporting Services (SSRS)   Although not a new feature, this is, in our opinion, one of the most important enterprise features that SQL Server provides. The tight integration with SQL Server and the exposure of the reporting engine through a standard web services interface make Reporting Services one of the most compelling reporting solutions available for SQL Server 2008. Enterprise features such as web report distribution, subscriptions, and infinite click-through make this one feature you should definitely evaluate for inclusion in your enterprise data architecture.

Full-Text Search Services   Full-text indexing and special query syntax let you effectively search large text blocks for patterns, word forms, proximities, and other elements. SQL Server 2008 provides some compelling enhancements to the full-text set of services. They include features such as improved full-text index management and performance enhancements. If you haven't at least played with Full-Text Search, you owe it to yourself to spend a few minutes getting cozy with it.

Business Intelligence   Business Intelligence (BI) content is critical to the success of SQL Server 2008. The BI agenda for SQL Server 2008 was very aggressive. One of the reasons that the schedule slipped for SQL Server 2008 was that the BI features needed a bit more polishing.

The cornerstone of this version's BI functionality is SQL Server Analysis Services. Supporting data warehousing through multidimensional data models (data cubes), Analysis Services provides mechanisms for analyzing and mining the large data volumes that most organizations have collected over the years. It is also highly integrated with other services, relying on SSIS for warehouse loading and SSRS for reporting on multidimensional data, including ad hoc reporting through the report builder.

This is another list that we could extend significantly, but our objective here was to give you a taste for the services available in SQL Server 2008, show you where some of the major enhancements fit, and provide a better framework for your own investigation and research. We strongly recommend that you take the time to review the SQL Server 2008 feature documentation in the SQL Server Books Online. As a system architect, you will not be able to design components into your system if you do not know what is available and how it works.

SQL Server's Place Within Microsoft Architecture

To say that Microsoft's enterprise strategy relies on SQL Server is an understatement. Many of the products in Microsoft's enterprise line are dependent on, or have significant integration with, SQL Server at some level. Data services are required everywhere, and SQL Server is the glue that holds many of them together. Among the Microsoft products with SQL Server dependencies or integrations are

- Team Foundation Server
- Systems Management Server/System Center Configuration Manager
- Office SharePoint Server
- Office Project Server
- Operations Manager Server
- BizTalk Server
- ADO.NET

The logic is sound. Microsoft has already created a very compelling data engine, and when you need data services, there is no sense in reinventing the wheel. Of course, different tools require different levels of service support. For example, it is very common for SharePoint Server to be installed with SQL Server Express Edition, but a utility like Team Foundation Server might require real enterprise scalability.

We added the ADO.NET to this list, and at first glance it might seem a little out of place. The rest of the elements listed are Server components, but ADO.NET is a .NET API, used to provide data access support for .NET applications. We've included it because although ADO.NET can provide connectivity to a wide variety of different database systems through their own .NET Data Providers, the SQL Server Native Client is specifically and tightly integrated with the ADO.NET API itself, providing API-level support for features such as SQL notifications and automatic failover with database mirroring.

The lesson to learn from this discussion on Microsoft integration, however, is that sometimes it's a good idea to expand our definition of what we consider "data services." Especially now that to SQL Server 2008 supports unstructured data, the SQL Server Data Engine may play an ever more expansive role whenever and wherever any data is needed in any format and for any purpose. If we remember that and learn to take full advantage of the services that SQL Server provides, we will be able to design more comprehensive architectures, comfortable that SQL Server will provide data services at any level necessary, from embedded to enterprise.

Real World Scenario

SQL SERVER INTEGRATION WITH TEAM FOUNDATION SERVER

One of the most extreme real-world examples of SQL Server integration in the Microsoft Architecture is Team Foundation Server. This is a perfect case study in the prevalence of data and how SQL Server can provide data services whenever and wherever they are needed.

When author Mike Lee teaches classes on Team Foundation Server, he frequently uses a diagram similar to the one shown here to illustrate the architecture of Team Foundation Server. Note the extensive use of SQL Server services in the diagram.

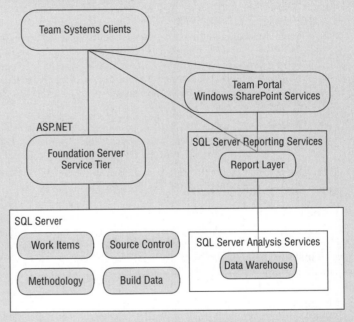

To do its work, Team Foundation Server requires significant data services. Rather than provide the data tier as part of the Team Foundation Server product itself, the Foundation Server delegates all of its data requirements to various SQL Server services. Some of these are creative in their application.

Work Items A Work Item in Foundation Server is essentially an assignment to complete a specific unit of work. When a project manager on a team needs work done, they create a Work Item in Foundation Server and assign it to the resource that is responsible for that item. These Work Items are database entries that document the work and its history.

Source Control Repository Traditionally, source control storage has been file system based, but in Team Foundation Server, all source code and all historical versions of that code, along with their labeling, are stored in SQL Server tables. This makes source control significantly more scalable and stable in other environments such as Visual Source Safe.

Methodology Data   An important part of Team Foundation Server is its support for development methodologies such as Agile. The choice of methodology affects many factors in the system, such as the types of Work Items, reports, and process guidance documentation. Methodologies are also highly customizable and an organization can create their own methodologies. The is methodology data is imported into SQL Server through Foundation Server and stored there for any future team projects to reference.

Build Data   Another feature of Foundation Server is support for Team Build processes. Repeatable builds are an important part of the application development lifecycle. They ensure that all builds are consistent and use the same configurations. To this end, historical build information must be retained so that a build administrator and/or release engineer can track what happened in each build.

Data Warehouse   All of the operational data in the Work Items database, the Build Database, and the versioning information in the Source Control Repository are used for progress and status reporting. SQL Agent Jobs are used to periodically aggregate data cubes running in SQL Server Analysis Services, thus providing reporting capabilities directly from the warehouse. You must have Analysis Services installed in order to install Foundation Server because it handles all data processing for reporting.

Report Tier   Using SQL Server Reporting Services, the report tier provides reports that interact with the data warehouse, providing information regarding schedules, budgeting, volatility, code churn, etc. Many built-in reports are available, depending on which methodology you use, but custom reports are also common, providing additional custom information regarding timelines and processes.

Looking at the Team Foundation Server architecture can teach us a very important lesson. SQL Server has the capacity to do so much if we let it do its job! Sometimes we are so focused on using SQL Server as a user data repository that we forget its role as an extremely valid cog in the overall architecture. SQL Server's ability to expose functionality through service endpoints is just one feature that makes it highly interoperable.

SQL Server Licensing

Many readers will not have to deal with licensing issues, because those choices are out of your hands, but for those of you who are small business owners or consultants, we'll say a few words on SQL Server licensing options.

WHAT DO WE KNOW?

At this writing, we do not have the specifics on SQL Server 2008 licensing. However, we have been promised that the price will not increase from SQL 2005 licensing costs. The following guidelines are based on 2005 licensing schemes and should be reviewed prior to publication.

SQL Server licensing costs and options typically depend on which edition you use. The good news is that Microsoft has stated that it does not plan to increase licensing costs for SQL Server 2008, so your costs should be similar to those for SQL Server 2005, assuming that you are planning to use comparable editions and licensing options.

The other bit of good news on licensing is that the Express edition is still free. There is, of course, a license agreement, and you cannot take advantage of free distribution of the Express edition unless you register with Microsoft and agree to its licensing terms for distributing the Express edition with your products. The Compact edition, typically used for handheld devices and embedded solutions, also falls into this category.

The Developer edition of SQL Server is a little different in terms of licensing. This edition is feature-identical to Enterprise edition, but can only be licensed to an individual developer and used for development. No production server can use Developer edition. In earlier versions of SQL Server (those before SQL Server 2000), the Developer edition was performance- and connection-throttled, which prevented its effective use in production. This was problematic because it prevented the developer from doing reasonable stress testing, performance benchmarking, etc. Fortunately, the Developer edition is no longer throttled, and now it is an outstanding option for developing enterprise-capable applications at a reasonable cost.

All other versions are licensed under one of three different options, as indicated in Table 1.1. The obvious conclusion is that the organization should choose the option that will satisfy their needs at the lowest licensing cost. The more feature-rich the edition, the higher the license fees in each category. For example, a single-processor license for the Workgroup edition would be less expensive than a single-processor license for Standard edition.

TABLE 1.1   SQL Server Licensing Options

LICENSING OPTION	DESCRIPTION	BEST SUITED FOR
Per Processor	Each available processor must be licensed. If a processor in a server is configured to be inaccessible to SQL Server, it does not have to be licensed. Licensing is done per socket, not per core/Logical CPU.	High client to server ratios and Internet accessible applications.
Server plus Device CAL	Requires a license for each server, plus a CAL for each device accessing SQL Server within your organization.	Shared devices such as shared workstations or kiosks.
Server plus User CAL	Requires a license for each server, plus a CAL for each user accessing SQL Server within your organization.	Limited number of users needing access to the server, especially if they connect with multiple devices.

Of course, licensing costs will depend on who you are. Microsoft has a variety of licensing programs as well as negotiated costs for specific customers such as large corporations, governments, and educational institutions. For more information regarding specific licensing costs, you can check Microsoft's website for current retail costs or contact your Microsoft Licensing Reseller for volume license information.

Installing SQL Server 2008

Now you should have a good feel for where SQL Server 2008 fits into the typical IT infrastructure. The next step is to look at the installation process. Like any good architecture, it all starts with a plan. When it comes to SQL Server installation, planning is key. You have a number of decisions to make when you perform an installation. It's easier to do it right the first time than to try to modify it later.

DECIDE NOW AND THEN FOREVER HOLD YOUR PEACE

In one organization that Mike Lee consulted with, some decisions regarding character sets and collations were made very early. The organization decided not to go with the default settings, which is not inherently a problem as long as a user has a defendable reason for doing so. These decisions were made early in the organization's existence. Over time, as the organization grew, it distributed databases to many customers and also used them internally.

When the organization later decided to examine and reevaluate its installation decisions because the configuration had become cumbersome, it was too late to change those decisions because many customers as well as internal systems had become dependent on the initial configuration. Ironically, no one could say why the initial decision was made. The morale of this story is to make sure you have reasons for every design choice you make and be sure that you think well into the future.

Defining an Installation Plan

Some of the choices that you must make are obvious. Which editions of SQL Server 2008 will you choose? What licensing schemes will you use? What kind of hardware should you purchase? These are some of the initial decisions. Some of your options are flexible: you can change your mind about them later if needed. For example, you can always add more memory or purchase additional Client Access Licenses (CALs).

Things get trickier when you need to decide what the database architectures will look like. How many databases should you have? Are there performance implications to your decisions? What about partitioning? Should you install multiple instances of SQL Server on a single server? You can best answer these and similar questions by looking at your enterprise data needs. Let's take a closer look at some of the major planning issues such as capacity planning, database consolidation and distribution, and archival requirements.

CAPACITY PLANNING

When planning capacity, the professional DBA must consider the projected requirements of all the major resources that SQL Server will use. More specifically, SQL Server requires resources from four major categories. Think of them as SQL Server's four basic food groups. A server must have adequate resources from each group to remain healthy.

- ◆ Disk and I/O Subsystem
- ◆ CPU
- ◆ Memory
- ◆ Network

Just as the human body needs to balance grains and proteins in its diet, SQL Server needs to have an adequate balance of each of these resources to keep operating at its maximum potential. Any one of these resources out of balance can cause a resource starvation problem in another area. Capacity planning will be covered in more detail in Chapter 3, "Managing Databases, Files, and Filegroups," so for now we will be content with a general overview. What are the important things to consider when preparing for a SQL Server installation?

Disk Resources

Databases require disk space. Although a well-normalized database will have lower disk requirements than a denormalized one, there is still a significant disk need for any production system. Data warehousing might require significant disk resources, not only to handle the volume of gathered data, but also to perform the multidimensional data modeling that is typical to data warehousing. It is also essential that the I/O subsystem be able to keep up with requests to read and write to disk, or else the overall performance of the system will suffer.

Disk storage requirements may depend on a number of factors. You have to consider the current data that the business needs to function, as well as archival requirements caused by regulatory concerns, data warehousing/mining strategies, encryption requirements, and data growth estimates. Some of these issues, specifically warehousing and archiving, may necessitate additional servers—not just more disk space.

Data growth is one of the more complex issues. You not only need to consider how much data you have now, but also how much you will have in the future. There are three basic growth models, each of which has numerous variations. You can probably evaluate your growth patterns according to one or more of these models.

Linear Growth This is the simplest growth model. It assumes that the database will grow at a constant rate over time. For example, assume 400MB database will grow at a constant rate of 50MB per month. One year from now, therefore, the database will be 1GB in size. Use the following formula to calculate linear growth:

$$FDisk = CDisk + (GAmt \times NPer)$$

In this formula, use the following:

$FDisk$ = *future disk space required*

$CDisk$ = *current disk space used*

$GAmt$ = *amount of disk growth per period*

$NPer$ = *number of periods*

Compound Growth This model assumes that the growth rate is based on a percentage growth rate rather than a fixed growth amount. As the size of the database increases, so will its future growth amount because each increment is a percentage of the current database size. A database of 100MB that grows 10 percent per year would be 110MB at the end of the first year, but 121MB at the end of the second year. Use the following formula to calculate compound growth:

$$FDisk = CDisk \times (1 + Rate)^N$$

In this formula, use the following:

$FDisk$ = *future disk space required*

CDisk = current disk space used

Rate = percentage growth rate per period

N = number of periods

Compound Growth with Compounding Growth Rate   This model assumes that as the database grows, so does the growth rate. For example, suppose that we expect the database to grow by 10 percent this year, but we expect that the growth rate itself will also increase every year by 20 percent. That means that next year, the growth rate will be 12 percent. The first year, therefore, a 100MB database will grow by 10MB. In this case, the 10MB is called the *initial increment* and the 20 percent is called the *incremental rate of growth*. Use the following formula to calculate this model:

$$FDisk = CDisk + (Init \times (1 - IncRate)^{(N+1)} + (1 - IncRate)$$

In this formula, use the following:

FDisk = future disk space required

CDisk = current disk space used

N = number of periods

Init = initial increment of growth

IncRate = incremental rate of growth per period

Of course, you must consider the I/O subsystem as well. Remember that at some point, any data that you might want to work with in your application must move from disk to memory. The speed at which this takes place will have a direct effect on the performance of your application. The specifics of monitoring and tuning resources will be covered in Chapter 10, "Monitoring SQL Server Activity," and Chapter 16, "Using Resource Governor and Policy-Based Management," respectively.

Processor Resources

When planning processor architecture, you have two primary concerns: what type of processor and how many. The decisions that you make can determine not only the amount of raw power in terms of calculations per second, but also may determine the amount of addressable memory that is available to SQL Server. Because data normally must be in current memory to be used in SQL Server, the size of the data cache may be critical for application performance.

First, for determining the number of processors, if you have an existing database that you can use to benchmark, you're way ahead in the game. Specifically, you want to look at the number of users and how much data they will be using. Most queries are not really CPU bound, especially those that focus strictly on read and write activity, but if you have a lot of procedural logic, number crunching, aggregations, or a large number of users, you will need more CPU resources.

When considering processors, you must also think about licensing costs. Remember that if you use a per-processor licensing scheme, each processor will have to be licensed. The processor affinity settings in SQL Server allow you to specify which processors SQL Server is allowed to use. When allocating processor resources to SQL Server, you must remember to allow sufficient resources for other services that might be running on the same server. You don't want to allow a situation where SQL Server could be starving other services. Of course, this brings up the question of whether the SQL Servers are dedicated machines or share responsibilities for other services. This in turn will depend on projected server activity levels and the level of resource consumption. As you make these decisions, remember that processor licensing is per socket, not per core.

THE REAL COST OF AFFINITY

Remember that the processor affinity settings in SQL Server are very tightly integrated with the licensing system. Make sure that you don't use processor affinity settings that might violate your license agreements.

When deciding on processor architecture, you must also consider your memory requirements. Chapter 2, "Understanding SQL Server Architecture," will cover the specifics of memory configuration and how memory is used, but for now, remember that the primary difference between 32-bit and 64-bit processors is the amount of memory that is addressable by the processor. The 32-bit world limits the server to 4GB addressable memory, only 2GB of which are available for SQL Server unless you use some special switches and creative manipulation. 64-bit processors significantly increase that limit. How much of an increase depends on the processor, but theoretically it could extend to 16 exabytes. This is a theoretical limit only, and all current 64-bit architectures implement limits that are a tiny fraction of this level, averaging around 32GB of addressable memory.

The real story then is not that 64-bit processors are faster. In fact, dealing with a 64-bit address can actually cause a 64-bit processor to run slower than a comparable 32-bit processor. The real issues are the amount of memory that can be addressed and the convenience with which that memory can be addressed without special configuration on the part of the administrator.

Memory Resources

In order for data to be of any use in your applications, in most cases it needs to be brought from disk into memory. The data in memory is SQL Server's real-time view of the database. Data on disk is only as current as the last flush from cache to disk. Because data must be in memory to be useful, it takes a lot of memory to drive your application, and the more data you have to work with, the more memory you need.

Just because you have large databases does not mean that you need a lot of memory. However, you should try to ensure that there is enough memory to store the commonly used data and that there is enough room to bring additional data into memory without having to constantly swap between cache and disk. Don't forget that you also need memory for other resources such as user connections, open objects, stored procedures, and locks.

ONE HAND WASHES THE OTHER

It should be obvious at this point how interdependent all of these resources are. For example, the CPU type will determine your memory architecture. The amount of memory can determine how much work the I/O subsystem will have to do. The more that you tinker with SQL Server, the more you will realize how closely related all these resources really are.

Network Resources

Because the whole idea behind SQL Server, especially from the enterprise perspective, is to make data available to a broad audience of users, it is important that the data be able to get to its ultimate destination as efficiently as possible.

A number of issues are at play. First of all, you need to make sure that your network is capable of handling the volume of data that you will need to push around. This means that you need to pay attention to things like network cards, switches, and cabling. You can only push so much data through a 10-megabit pipe.

The other thing that you need to consider is how your applications are written and whether they are using network resources appropriately. For example, are you properly restricting your result sets so that you are not returning any more data to the client than they really need? You can limit some bandwidth by doing little things like turning NOCOUNT on in all of your stored procedures.

DOCTOR, IT HURTS WHEN I DO THIS

Sometimes the easiest way to solve a performance problem is to say, "Don't do that!" For example, I had a client that was having performance problems with an application that returned a large amount of sorted data to the client. The initial concern was that it was a network problem based on the volume of data that was being returned. It became clear after testing, however, that the problem was related to the amount of extra time that it took the server to do the sorting. Because many clients were requesting sorted data, the throughput was dragging.

Because sorting does not reduce the amount of data that goes across the wire, this task could be relocated without increasing network consumption. We found that in this situation, the sorting could be offloaded to the client because there was excess capacity on the client that was not being used. Sometimes you have to be willing to accept that the server is not the best place to perform a task.

DATA CONSOLIDATION AND DISTRIBUTION

Depending on how much data you have and how your enterprise's users need to access that data, there may be varying ways to consolidate or distribute data and server resources. There can be significant advantages to each depending on your needs. Let's begin with a discussion of server consolidation.

As licensing costs and hardware costs can be high, it is very important to make sure that you get the most "bang for the buck." Are you really using all of your resources to their fullest potential? It doesn't make sense to spend extra money on servers and licenses if you are not fully utilizing what you have now.

In addition to these issues, you might also benefit from a simplification of administrative processes, auditing requirements, and security management. Fewer boxes to baby-sit means fewer things that can break.

Of course, the downside is that when things do break, it can have a much more serious impact on the organization. You might be introducing a single point of failure by performing a server consolidation. You also have to be careful not to overload your server resources. Consolidating to the point that there is no room for growth means that even small changes in the way that server resources are used can have significant effects on the overall performance of your servers.

There are many ways to consolidate. Here are a few.

Merge Databases   One approach is to create a smaller number of larger databases. Fewer databases means that there are fewer administrative tasks, but these tasks may be more cumbersome and time-consuming. There may also be problems with increased transaction activity and loss of configuration granularity.

Adding More Databases to a SQL Server Instance   Although this can solve the problems inherent in managing very large databases, it still requires that all databases running under the given instance share all server-level configurations and address space. However, for administrative reasons, it may be desirable to have many databases running in a single instance. The benefit is that you only have to configure and tune that single instance.

Installing Multiple Instances on a Single Server   The primary benefit of having multiple instances is that they can be configured and tuned individually. If databases have different server configuration needs, they do not need to run on separate servers, but instead can run in separate instances. All instances still will share the same server resources, however, and any platform tuning will affect all instances.

Using Server Virtualization   Using a tool such as VMware or Microsoft Virtual Server allows multiple virtual or emulated "servers" to coexist on the same hardware. Each one can be configured separately, although they all will still share the same actual hardware resources. This approach can be very effective when you have excess hardware capacity, but requirements that specify individual OS configuration and security.

No matter which consolidation approach you choose, remember that the ultimate goal is to make the best use of all of your hardware resources and licenses. If your consolidation scheme results in unwanted performance degradations or security compliance problems, you should rethink that strategy. Also, always remember to reserve enough capacity for reasonable growth, or you will quickly be required to start distributing some of your load.

Generally, the advantages of consolidation are also the disadvantages of distribution. The reverse is also true. While consolidation can lower licensing and hardware costs, distribution increases them. Conversely, while distribution can increase performance by providing additional resources to your applications, consolidation can result in reduced performance because too few resources are spread across too many databases or instances.

ARCHIVAL REQUIREMENTS

Another issue to consider when planning an enterprise installation strategy is archival requirements. Although your organization may have painstakingly collected mounds of data over the years, not every query that you execute has to wade through those mounds of data every single time.

Good indexing strategies can help with the performance problems that arise when you query from very large data stores, but other problems can emerge such as the maintenance costs of those indexes, the need to back up large amounts of non-changing data just to capture a small amount of live data, and so on. If you can separate those large volumes of data into other repositories, whether different tables or entire archival databases, your queries will have to trudge through much less data to complete their tasks.

> **BUT WHAT ABOUT THE WAREHOUSE?**
>
> Although this would seem a good time to bring up the subject of data warehousing, the subject is far too vast for inclusion at this point. Appendix C, "Analysis Services Overview," provides a very brief overview of SQL Server Analysis Services, which includes a general review of data warehousing concepts. However, the best place to start reading would be the work of Ralph Kimball and Bill Inmon, the true pioneers in this area. We specifically recommend the books in the Data Warehouse Toolkit series by Kimball and *Building the Data Warehouse* by Inmon, all published by Wiley.
>
> From those readings, you can decide which approach makes the most sense in your organization. Also remember that most organizations that do serious data warehousing in the real world are using a combination of theories based on the practical needs of the moment.

The first real issue when planning archival storage is to decide how to segment your data. Often, data is segmented based on date. Older data is archived while newer data is retained in the operational data store. There may be other ways in which your data should be segmented, however. Identifying the factors that differentiate current from archival data is the most important aspect of defining a successful archival strategy.

Once you have decided how to segment the data, you need to decide the best archival storage approach. In some cases, you might simply archive data into separate tables in the same database. Other cases may require you to completely separate archived data on separate servers. There are many different techniques for supporting these archives including table partitioning, partitioned views, and rowset functions. For now, the important thing is to consider what the resource load will be, based on the amount of needed archival data and what kind of server installation strategy you will need to support it.

SQL Server 2008 Installation Requirements

The official Microsoft SQL Server installation requirements are, to be polite, barely adequate. As you evaluate the true requirements for SQL Server, remember that SQL Server is a resource hog. It loves memory, can use a lot of disk space, and often requires a significant network pipe. That said, the requirements posted on Microsoft's website are barely enough to get the service running, assuming that there are no other primary services running on the same machine.

Table 1.2 lists the standard Microsoft-recommended requirements in abbreviated form. To get the complete listing, please consult the books online.

TABLE 1.2   Microsoft SQL Server Installation Requirements

COMPONENT	REQUIREMENT
Processor	64- or 32-bit (version dependent) processor at 1GHz or higher
.NET Framework	.NET 3.5 Framework SP1 (installed by the SQL Server installer)
Operating System	Windows Vista (any version)
Windows Server 2008	Windows Server 2003 SP2 Windows XP SP 2

TABLE 1.2	Microsoft SQL Server Installation Requirements *(CONTINUED)*
Visual Studio 2008	If VS 2008 is installed on the same machine as the server or client tools, it must be updated to SP1. It is not required to have VS 2008 installed in advance.
Other Software	Microsoft Internet Explorer 6 SP1 or higher Microsoft Windows Installer 3.1 or higher MDAC 2.8 SP1 or higher
Memory	1 GB or more
Hard Disk	280 MB - Complete Data Engine Core 90 MB - Complete Analysis Services 120 MB - Complete Reporting Services 120 MB - Complete Integration Services 850 MB - Complete Client Components 240 MB - Complete Books Online

Also be aware that many components will be installed by the SQL Server installer. In addition to the .NET Framework, there will be installations of MSXML support, SQL Native Client installation, and other components.

During the installation process you will be asked to identify how the SQL Server services are going to log in to Windows. You should consider this requirement before you begin installation so you can either identify or create the necessary security accounts *before* the installation process begins. This should be part of your security planning. The choice that you make can have a significant impact on the ability of the installed server to effectively communicate with other SQL Servers and resources on the local machine and in the greater enterprise environment.

The general recommendation is that you should create local or domain user accounts with the permissions necessary to perform the tasks required. Do not use the Network Service account for the Data Engine or SQL Agent services because this approach does not follow the "least privilege" principle, which states that you should only grant an account the minimum permissions necessary to perform the required task. If your SQL Server must communicate with other service to perform remote procedure calls, replication, using remote data sources, or similar tasks, you should use a domain user account rather than a local user account. If your server will access local resources only, the "local service" account may be adequate, because it has the same permissions as members of the local Users group.

The SQL Server Installation Process

The SQL Server installation process is organized into three primary phases:

1. Compatibility Check

2. Data Gathering

3. Software Installation

COMPATIBILITY CHECK

The first phase, Compatibility Check, allows the installer to verify that the hardware/software configuration of the target server meets all minimum requirements for installation. If any of these requirements are not met, the installation will be terminated and the problem must be rectified. It is best to review all of the requirements in advance and make sure that your server is properly configured before you begin. It will definitely make the installation process go more smoothly.

The installation process is wizard-driven and should not be problematic if you have installed all of the required software in advance. On the main installation screen, select Installation from the menu on the left. This dialog is pictured in Figure 1.1.

FIGURE 1.1

The SQL Server 2008 Installation Center

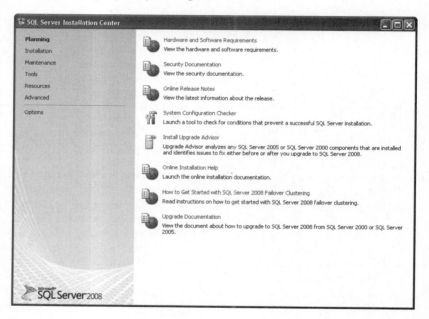

Once you launch the installer, you will be asked to accept the license agreement and install the setup support files. These steps must be completed before the formal installation process can begin.

The next screen in the installation process is the main installation control panel, pictured in Figure 1.2. From here you can perform a new installation, upgrade older servers to SQL Server 2008, or modify a SQL Server cluster.

Click the first option to perform a new standalone installation. In a moment, a new popup window will appear to begin the formal installation. It will automatically perform a compatibility check and report the results in the next screen as shown in Figure 1.3. If your system does not pass the minimum compliance check, you will not be able to continue any further until you resolve the issues. There is a button on the screen labeled Show Details. Click this button to get more information regarding the results of the configuration check. Figure 1.3 shows the detailed information. When you are ready to move on, click the OK button.

FIGURE 1.2
The SQL Server
Installation panel

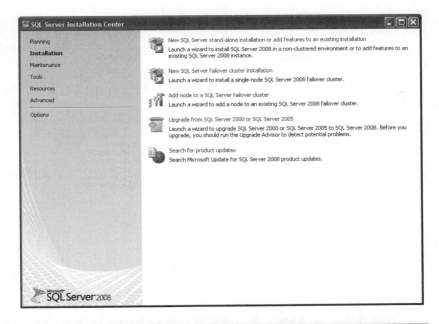

FIGURE 1.3
Viewing the com-
patibility results

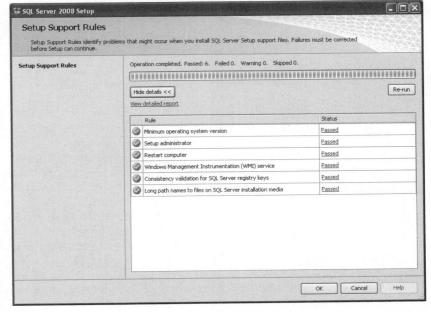

DATA GATHERING

At this point we enter the data-gathering phase of the installation. This begins with a licensing screen as pictured in Figure 1.4. You will see that you can either enter a key for a licensed version of SQL Server or select a free version such as an evaluation version. Make your selection and enter the key, if necessary. Then click Next to continue.

FIGURE 1.4
Validating
the edition

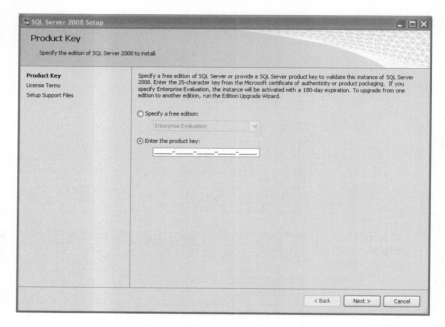

The next screen is the license terms agreement. It is not pictured here for brevity. Simply accept the license agreement and click Next to continue. The next screen will provide the installation of the setup support files. You must perform this small installation before you can continue. Again, because this is a simple dialog, it is not illustrated. Just click the Install button to advance. When complete, the installer will provide a report like the one pictured in Figure 1.5. Check for errors, and make sure that warnings, like the one in this dialog, are verified before you continue. Click Next to advance.

The next thing that the installer needs to know in this phase is which SQL Server 2008 services you want to install. SQL Server uses a unified installer, which is much more convenient than having separate installers for each service. In Figure 1.6, all options have been selected, but you can choose any combination of installed features that you like depending on your enterprise installation plan. Do not install components that you do not need because this will add additional administration requirements, could result in unnecessary resource consumption, and may be a security risk. Click Next to advance.

FIGURE 1.5
The Setup Files
Installation report

FIGURE 1.5
The Setup Files
Installation report

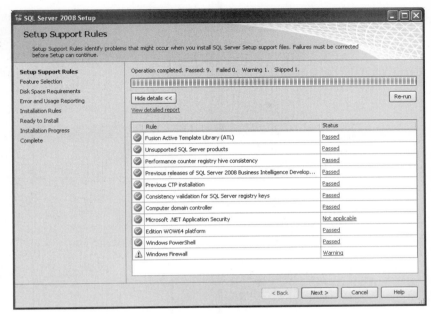

FIGURE 1.6
The Feature
Selection dialog

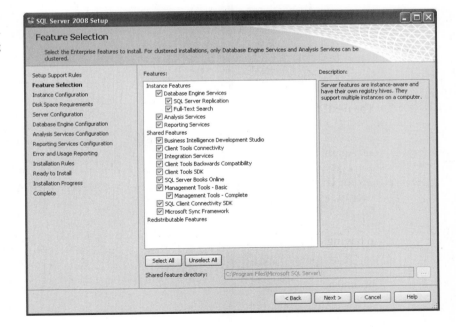

The next page in the wizard, pictured in Figure 1.7, allows you to configure the instance. Is this a named instance or the default instance? Typically, the default instance will resolve to the NetBIOS name of the computer, which is convenient, but you can have only one default instance. If you are not sure what other instances of SQL Server you have installed, this dialog will list them at the bottom. Be sure to configure the correct location for file installation and the desired instance name before you continue. Select either the default instance or provide an instance name and click Next to advance.

FIGURE 1.7
Configuring
the instance

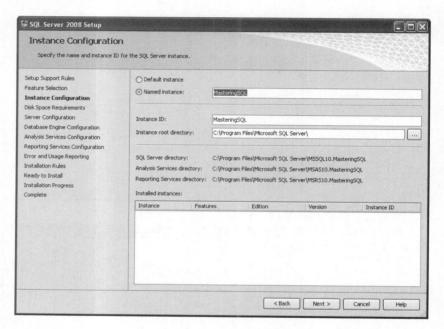

The next screen summarizes the disk space requirements. Notice that in this example, all services have been installed and it requires over 2.5GB of disk space. Figure 1.8 provides this illustration. If you do not have sufficient disk space available, you will receive an error at this point. Click Next to advance.

The next dialog, Server Configuration, allows you to configure all of the services in one location. Notice how this dialog, pictured in Figure 1.9, gives you the option of configuring service login accounts and passwords, as well as deciding the startup mode for each service. Now is the time for you to provide the login information for the accounts that you created in advance for the services. If you want, you can simplify the configuration by using a single account for all services and applying this account with one click.

Choose the account wisely. The local system account can work fine if the SQL Server does not have to communicate with other services on the network, otherwise you may want to create a domain account with appropriate permissions. This will give you more control over the service-level security architecture.

Notice also that the Collation tab allows for configuration of default collations for both the Database Engine and Analysis Services. Select your collations carefully and only depart from the defaults if there is a verifiable reason to do so. Although you can create artifacts in a database that depart from the default collations, the settings that you choose here will define a set of default rules that will be assumed to apply unless you create an exception.

If there is an error condition in any of the configurations, the tab will appear with an error symbol. At the bottom of the screen, below the grid that defines the SQL Browser and Full Text Daemon Launcher, an error bar will appear. You must resolve these errors before continuing. Click Next to continue.

FIGURE 1.8
Disk space summary

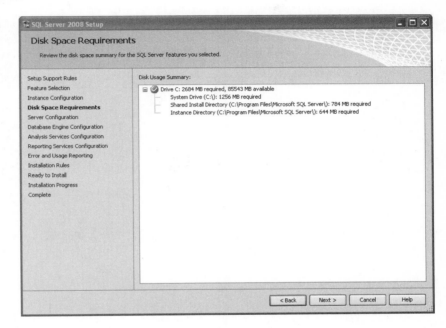

FIGURE 1.9
The Server Configuration dialog

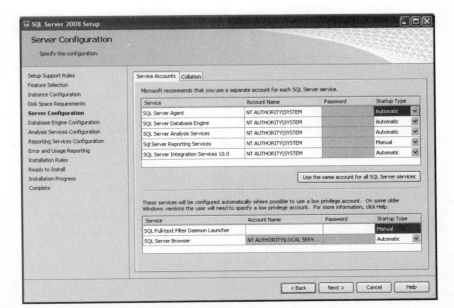

Now the installer will begin with the configuration of each individual service. First, you configure the Database Engine. This includes the security modes configuration as well as the file location and FILESTREAM configuration. On the first tab, specify the security mode. Windows Authentication mode uses the Windows identity of the logged-in user to authenticate that user to SQL Server; the Mixed mode option *also* allows SQL Server to authenticate users with its own internal authentication mechanism and login lists. We are using Windows Authentication mode. You can add yourself as an administrator by clicking the Add Current User button. Otherwise, the add button allows you to browse your accounts directory and add administrative users and groups to the server. You must add at least one administrative user before you will be allowed to continue. Figure 1.10 illustrates the Database Engine Configuration dialog.

FIGURE 1.10

The Database Engine Authentication Configuration dialog

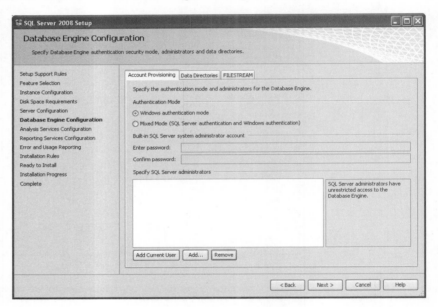

If you are unsure of which mode you need, you may want to skip ahead to the discussion in Chapter 8, "Managing User Security," and read up on the difference. This is a configuration that you can easily change after installation, however, so you are not stuck forever with the choice that you make here.

If you do choose Mixed mode, you will have to define a password for the system administrative account, which is `sa`. Otherwise, you must add appropriate Windows users or groups as administrators in the bottom part of the dialog so that an administrator will be assigned. If you try to advance beyond this dialog without providing some sort of administrative access, you will get an error message that will prevent you from continuing.

Also, don't forget to look at the other tabs in the dialog, labeled Data Directories and FILESTREAM. The Data Directories tab allows you to define the default locations for all data paths in SQL Server. Although you can override most of these when working with your data, it is a good idea to plan your default locations based on your server resources and configurations.

The FILESTREAM tab provides for the initial configuration of the FILESTREAM storage option in SQL Server. This feature allows you to define a share on the server that will store files that the data engine can stream to the user. This is an alternative to storing the file data directly in the database.

The next dialog, Analysis Services Configuration, is very similar to Database Engine Configuration and works in the same manner. This dialog allows you to specify the security and file location setting for the Analysis Server. This screen is so similar to the previous one that it is not pictured here.

The Reporting Service Configuration dialog is used to configure the deployment mode for SQL Server Reporting Services. You have a choice between Native and SharePoint modes. You can also install an unconfgured server. Make your selection in this dialog, pictured in Figure 1.11 and click Next to advance.

FIGURE 1.11
Configuring the reporting server

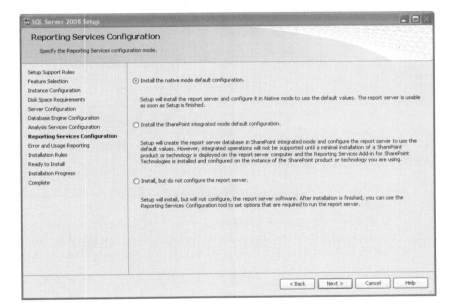

Native Mode Reporting Server   Native mode allows the reporting server to act as a standalone application server, using IIS and ASP.NET features to handle all configuration, report access, security access, etc. This is the default option and does not require any additional software installed beyond IIS and the .NET Framework.

SharePoint Mode Reporting Server   In this mode, the report server is not standalone, but rather is part of a SharePoint application deployment. Reports can be stored in SharePoint libraries and accessed by users through the SharePoint interface. This affects the ability of users to access reports through a URL, because all access must be qualified within the SharePoint hierarchy. Also, appropriate versions of Windows SharePoint Services or Microsoft Office SharePoint Server must be installed to handle the Report Server deployment before the report server can be accessed.

The next dialog, Error and Usage Reporting, gives you the option of sending experience information to Microsoft. This is very simple and is not illustrated here. After this, you get one more report dialog, validating your choices and preparing the installation. As pictured in Figure 1.12, there should be no errors on this report or you will not be able to continue.

FIGURE 1.12
Final pre-installa-
tion report

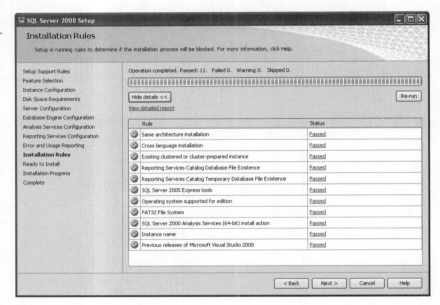

The last data-gathering dialog (not pictured) presents you with a summary of your choices for your review. Make sure that the configurations listed match your intended installation before you continue. When you are ready, click the Install button to begin the actual installation.

SOFTWARE INSTALLATION

Once you have verified your installation parameters and are ready to begin with the installation, click the Install button to begin the installation process. Installation time depends on the services that you have selected and the configuration of those services.

Once the process is complete, all of the installation options should show Success. Clicking the Next button will take you to the final dialog, which will contain a link to the installation log. Make a note of the location of the installation log files. If there are any problems with the installation, you may want to review these logs to troubleshoot your problems.

Verifying the Installation

If you did not get any errors when you ran the installation, you probably will not have any problems, but it is always a good idea to run some quick checks to make sure that everything happened the way you expected. Here is a list of some of the actions users typically take to verify an installation.

Check for the Installed Services Using the tool of your choice, ensure that the services have been correctly installed, configured, and started. Figure 1.13 illustrates the Windows Services applet. Notice that each of the services is listed, along with its login account and current state. Ensure that all services will start as configured and alter any startup options as necessary. In Figure 1.14, the SQL Server service is installed but not started. You must start a service before you can test its installation.

FIGURE 1.13
Reviewing
installed Windows
Services

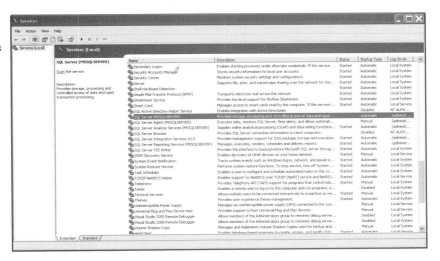

Verify Existence of Installation Folders Make sure that the configured default data folders and temp folders are present and that they contain the files that you expect, such as `.mdf` and `.ldf` files for the system databases. The location of these files will depend on the Data Directory configuration that you specified when you installed SQL Server.

Connect to the Server We will cover the SQL Server clients in more detail in a moment, but one of the verifications that you will want to do is to attempt to connect to SQL Server. The simplest way to do this is to open a console window and use the command **OSQL -E** to log into the server. This assumes that you are connecting to a default instance through Windows Authentication mode. Once you authenticate, you will see a line prompt on the screen labeled 1>. Type a simple command such as the one pictured in Figure 1.14. Press the Enter key after typing **GO** to execute the batch.

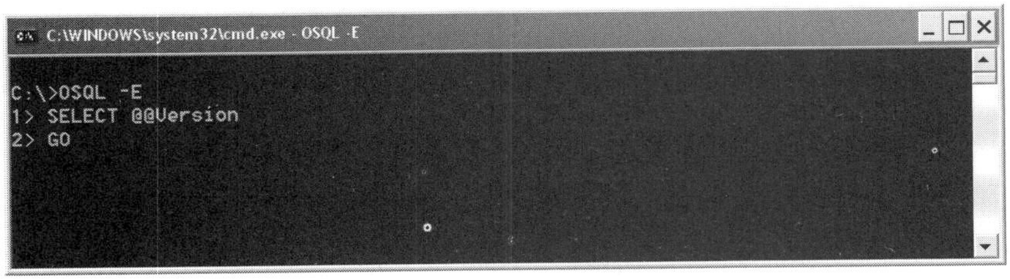

FIGURE 1.14
Connecting to SQL
Server with OSQL

```
C:\>OSQL -E
1> SELECT @@Version
2> GO
```

If all is well, the screen should return version information. If you are unable to connect or if the command returns an error, verify that your services are running, that your account has permissions to access the server, and review the installation logs as necessary for problems. Type QUIT and hit enter to end the OSQL Session. Then type **EXIT** and press Enter to close the Command Prompt window.

INSTALLING SAMPLE DATABASES

If, after installing the server, you want some sample databases to play with, you can download them from Codeplex.com. Go to the SQL Server section, where you can download installers for the various databases. Examples in this book will use the AdventureWorks sample databases, specifically the OLTP and DW databases, so you may want to have those installed for your reference.

The SQL Server Tool Set

When you installed SQL Server, you had an option to install the client utilities as well. This client tool set consists of numerous configuration clients, command-line utilities, and development tools. In addition, there is also a thriving third-party market for SQL Server client tools. You can accomplish most of your day-to-day tasks with the out-of-the-box SQL Server utilities, but some of the third-party utilities are very convenient and make up for deficiencies in the Microsoft toolkit.

The Microsoft Client Tools

Numerous utilities are installed with SQL Server. You will probably want to review the SQL Server Books Online to get a complete description of each of these and their capabilities, but the primary list is provided in the following text.

THE SQL SERVER MANAGEMENT STUDIO

This is the primary SQL Server client. Introduced in SQL Server 2005, this utility replaces the Enterprise Manager and Query Analyzer tools found in SQL Server 2000 and earlier versions. Using this one tool, you should be able to handle the majority of administrative and development tasks.

You will find the SQL Server Management Studio in the SQL Server program group in the Start menu. When you launch it, you will be prompted to log in. This is not required, but if you do log in, the tool will populate its Object Browser with catalog information and you will be able to perform tasks within SQL Server Management Studio without further authentication. How you authenticate will depend on the security setting that you chose when you installed the server. After authenticating, you will see a screen like the one pictured in Figure 1.15. If you do not see the details pane, press the F7 key on your keyboard.

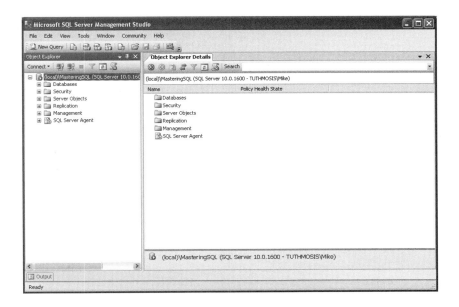

Notice the tree view on the left. This is the Object Browser. Use this part of the screen to look at and configure your resources. The dialog makes good use of your secondary mouse button, so most of the options you want should be no further than a right click away. Also notice the Connect button in the upper-left portion of the browser screen. Use this to connect to other servers or other services on the current server. For example, you can use it to connect to multiple Data Engines on different servers or instances, as well as to an Analysis Server and a Data Engine on the same instance.

To run a query, click the New Query button. A query window will open based on the current connection. This window works very much like the old Query Analyzer utility. Enter your query and click the Execute button or press the F5 key to execute the query. You will want to play around a little bit with your options in the client as you will use it often while working through this book as well as your daily work as a DBA or developer. We will address the specifics of what you can do with this client as the book progresses.

As you start working with the query editors in the SQL Server Management Studio, you will probably stumble across one of the most-requested new features for the SQL Server development clients, called Intellisense. As you type, Intellisense will prompt you with lists of valid syntax or artifacts that you can use in your queries. It will also inform you of syntax errors and other problems as you type by putting red underlines in your code. Visual Basic and .NET developers have had these tools forever, and they have finally made their way into SQL Server, to the delight of the SQL Server development community.

IN WITH THE NEW, BUT NOT OUT WITH THE OLD

One of the things that we like about the progression of SQL Server versions is that Microsoft still supports many of the old habits that you may have developed in your early days as a SQL Server developer. For example, back in the old days of SQL Server, when we used to use a tool called ISQL for query development, many of us got in the habit of using Alt+X to execute queries. That was replaced with Ctrl+E, which was ultimately replaced with F5. However, all of the old keystrokes are still functional. Author Mike Lee says, "Be it good or bad, I will probably be an Alt+X man until they play the Windows Shutdown .wav at my funeral someday."

THE SQL SERVER BUSINESS INTELLIGENCE DEVELOPMENT STUDIO

This tool is really just a set of Microsoft Visual Studio addins. It can cause confusion if you are not aware of what is happening. When you install this client, the Microsoft Visual Studio Development Environment is installed on your computer along with the specific development editors for the SQL Server Business Intelligence artifacts such as reporting, data cubes, and Integration Services packages. Remember that all of these BI artifacts are actually .NET executables, so the development environment for them is wrapped into the .NET container.

If you already have the corresponding version of Visual Studio .NET installed on your computer when you perform the SQL Server client installation, it will not need to install the development environment, but only the environments for BI development. Therefore, to see what you really have installed in Visual Studio, start the tool and select File ➤ New Project from the menu. The list of project templates will indicate what you have installed and available for use. Figure 1.16 illustrates a New Project dialog with just the BI environments available.

FIGURE 1.16
The New
Project dialog in
Visual Studio

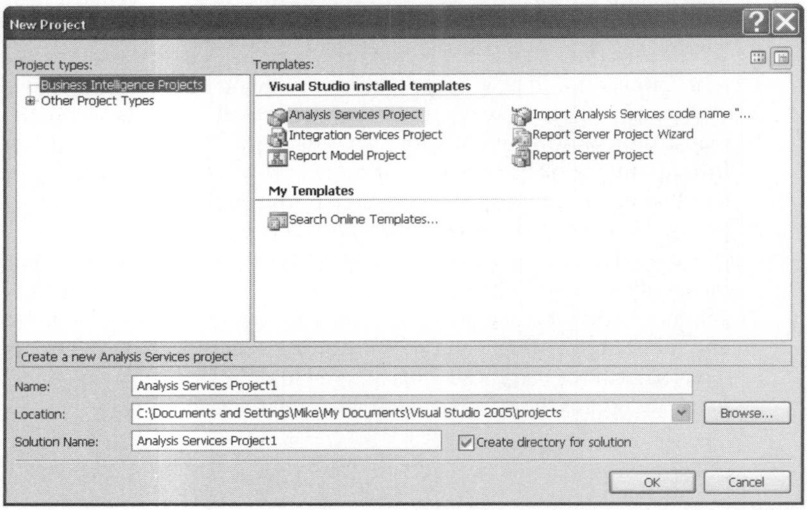

The SQL Server Configuration Manager

Another very convenient tool is the SQL Server Configuration Manager illustrated in Figure 1.17. This utility provides a central configuration tool for all SQL Server services. In addition to the actual service configuration, you can also configure .NET libraries, client connectivity, and client aliases in one location. Prior to SQL Server 2005, this was done in multiple utilities. This welcome enhancement is preserved in SQL Server 2008.

FIGURE 1.17
The SQL Server Configuration Manager

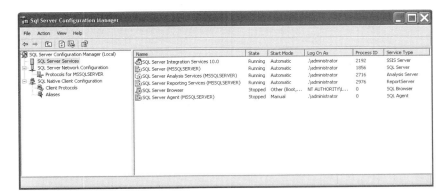

The interesting thing about the SQL Server Configuration Manger is that it is a WMI client. As you browse though this client, you may be thinking to yourself that it would be nice to be able to control these features and get this information programmatically. This is possible through WMI. With a little bit of skill in .NET, a SQL Server DBA or developer can fully exploit the capabilities of SQL Server (and simplify their life, too).

Performance Tools

If you select Start ➤ All Programs ➤ Microsoft SQL Server 2008 ➤ Performance Tools from the menu, you will see two additional tools of note, the Database Engine Tuning Advisor and the SQL Server Profiler. While each of these will be discussed in more detail in later chapters, it is worth making a quick mention now of what they bring to the toolbox.

The SQL Server Profiler is an indispensable tool for auditing SQL Server activity. In previous versions, the tool was called SQL Trace. In essence, its job is to listen for events that occur within SQL Server and log them to a file or to a table. When defining a profiler log, you can decide exactly which event you are interested in logging and what data about each event you want to log. Although the event and data lists are predefined, they are extensive. You can watch for events such as connections, procedure calls, and T SQL actions. For each of these events, you can track client information, connection information, server values, and other data.

The real value in the SQL Server Profiler, though, is that is can be used for many different purposes, such as security auditing, performance tuning, and diagnostics. One of the most useful features of the SQL Profiler is to log T SQL calls and stored procedure calls. For instance, you can use the Profiler to log calls that are made by unfamiliar client applications. This allows the SQL Server DBA to know exactly what the client is doing even if it is a shrink-wrapped client or one with no documentation. You can use this information for performance tuning client applications or debugging problems that the client may be experiencing.

The Data Engine Tuning Wizard is another tool that has been around for a while, but the average SQL Server DBA probably does not use the tool to its fullest capability. While it is certainly not perfect, if you give it proper information regarding typical workflows, the Data Engine Tuning Wizard will make very reasonable recommendations related to indexing, and other performance optimizations.

The Profiler and the Tuning Wizard work together effectively to improve performance. You can use the Profiler to capture a snapshot of typical database activity and then use this log as the input for the Tuning Wizard to make its recommendations. After altering the data structures based on the Tuning Wizard's recommendations, you can replay the trace to see if the performance metrics improve. If not, you can start the whole process over again. We will address these two tools extensively in later discussions of performance analysis and management.

Third-Party Tools and Utilities

First of all, the authors want to be perfectly clear that they are not attempting to promote, endorse, or recommend—let alone warranty—any third-party tools. There is good and bad in any tool, and just because we like a particular tool does not mean that you will, but there are a few big players in the data tools arena that you should be familiar with, if for no other reason than to give you material to captivate your audience with at the next big DBA cocktail party you attend.

Embarcadero Technologies Embarcadero makes database products that fill quite a few holes in the marketplace. Their flagship tool is called ER/Studio. This is a design utility that puts the focus on good entity design. The concept is that if you can implement a good entity design, then a good data design will certainly follow. This is also a good product to use in a team environment. All design artifacts can be easily stored in a central data repository. Team members can log into the repository through the ER/Studio client and either check out designs for alteration or view them for reference.

Another of the nice features of this tool is that it lets you export a data design structure as an HTML catalog, making it very easy to share the design with other users.

Other Embarcadero products such as Schema Examiner and Rapid SQL aid the database developer by providing a solid platform for SQL development and schema management.

Computer Associates Computer Associates (CA) makes a data modeling tool called ERWin® that is a competitor to the Embarcadero ER/Studio tool. The concepts and feature sets of the two tools are very similar, but the interfaces are different and each tends to create very loyal users who grow accustomed to the methodology behind the tool.

CA has recently been making real strides in the SQL Server user community with the ERWin tool. Although the tool itself is and has always been Window-based, CA has been enhancing the tool's image extensively within the SQL Server community, including partnering with the Professional Organization for SQL Server (PASS) to produce a series of webcasts targeted specifically to SQL Server users.

Red Gate Software Red Gate also provides a good range of utilities, but unlike Embarcadero, Red Gate specializes in tools that are specific to Microsoft SQL Server rather than tools that work with a range of databases. Their SQL Compare and SQL Data Compare Utilities are quite effective for monitoring schema and data lineage changes. However, their SQL Prompt utility, which provided an Intelisense add-in for SQL Server management Studio, is unnecessary now that this feature is native in the Microsoft toolset.

Among the most compelling Red Gate tools is the SQL Backup tool, which handles the compression and encryption of SQL Server backups. Although SQL Server 2008 now supports these features, the ease of use of the Red Gate tool and the monitoring ability that it provides are still strong selling points.

The Red Gate SQL Refactor tool is another real gem for the SQL developer because it gives you a great deal of control when formatting and refactoring code, allowing you to avoid the problems typically associated with copy-and-paste refactoring and reformatting.

Quest Software   Quest Software makes a great little development utility called TOAD. If you are an Oracle developer, you have probably heard of it, as it has become the de facto standard for Oracle development. Quest now makes a version for SQL Server.

TOAD is an easy-to-use and intuitive client. It's especially appealing at moments when the SQL Server Management Studio is a little too much to wade through—such as when all you want to do is execute some queries and write a few simple scripts. Best of all, there is a freeware version of TOAD for SQL Server, so you can try it out if you like. The full versions can be a bit expensive, but have a very loyal following.

There are many other tools out there—far too many to review here. If your favorite tool was not on this short list, we apologize; it was not a deliberate snub. The important thing is to find tools that you like and tools with which you can work. With all of the good tools on the market, you should always be able to find the right one to help you get the job done. At the same time, you owe it to yourself to evaluate additional tools when you get the opportunity. You never know what gems you might uncover if you are willing to dig a little to find them. In the end, it's all about getting the result you want as efficiently and cleanly as possible.

The Bottom Line

Utilize the Architect SQL Server services in the typical IT environment.   SQL Server provides more than just simple data services to the IT infrastructure. SQL Server is packed with so many features that it quite literally has become a data suite in a box. The key is making sure that you know what SQL Server can do and how to use the appropriate feature once you identify the need for it.

Master It   Which SQL Server feature would you use to meet each of the following business requirements?

1.   Your company has been collecting sales data for over 10 years. The director of marketing has noticed that over the last two years, sales have been dropping in North America while they have been increasing in Central and South America. You need to see if you can find a reason for the trend.

2.   Your company must comply with industry regulations that require the company to provide specific information in a specific format for regulatory inspectors. The inspectors must be able to get the information any time they choose, it must always be organized the way that they want to see it, and it must always contain current data.

3.   A significant portion of your firm's sales is handled through the Internet. The marketing department would like to have a mechanism that allows users to search for a product, and if the product is not in stock, they can log in to the system and request to receive an email when the product is available.

4.   Much of your company's data is stored as large text fields. This text data must be searchable as efficiently as possible using very fuzzy logic including word forms and proximity searches.

Install SQL Server 2008.   While the installation process itself is wizard-driven, SQL Server installation takes some planning to make sure that you have an appropriate installation with the right resources in place for the right purposes.

Master It   SQL Server needs the right balance of resources to handle the demands of the data service. What are the four primary resources that SQL Server uses and how do they interact with each other?

Use the Microsoft SQL Server toolset.   Microsoft ships a number of high-quality tools with the SQL Server product that suit many different purposes. The key is to use the right tool for the job.

Master It   Which of the SQL Server tools would you use for each of the following goals?

1.   Writing and executing a query

2.   Identifying the optimal indexing structure

3.   Performing routine security administration tasks

4.   Performing a security audit in which you try to identify failed login attempts

5.   Identifying the interaction between SQL Server and a compiled client application

6.   Configuring the network protocols that SQL Server can use

Implement other useful third-party tools.   With all the tools out there, it is important that you select the right ones. There are a lot of tools from which to choose.

Master It   What is the best third-party tool for creating entity-relationship diagrams?

Chapter 2

Understanding SQL Server Architecture

If you're going on a road trip, you better bring a map. Without that map you could end up anywhere. If you travel without a map and without clear directions, you'll probably end up far from your intended destination. The same is true with SQL Server. Unless you understand SQL Server architecture, you'll never know where you might end up on your performance-tuning and database-development journey.

This chapter strives to be your road map so that you don't have to ask for directions. Although we could never exhaustively cover SQL Server internals and architecture in one chapter, we hope that this one will at least be a good map for you to follow as you learn more about how SQL Server behaves. In this chapter, you will learn to:

- ◆ Apply your understanding of SQL Server internals to implement good logical architecture
- ◆ Utilize the SQL Server catalog to get more information about the system and your application
- ◆ Effectively implement datatypes including user-defined datatypes

Essential Internals

To begin, you need to find out what makes SQL Server tick. As you saw in Chapter 1, "Overview of Microsoft SQL Server 2008," SQL Server functionality is an interplay between many resources—primarily memory, disk space, CPU, and network. Understanding this resource balance is critical in properly maintaining a SQL Server environment, and an intimate knowledge of SQL Server internals will simplify your day-to-day administrative and development responsibilities. In this section, we will examine the SQL Server data storage process and the functionality of the data engine.

SQL Server Data Storage Architecture

SQL Server stores data durably on disk. It optimizes the format of these disk structures for performance and integrity. However, in most cases you'll need to move SQL Server data from disk into memory before a client application can use it. Try to think about SQL Server data stored on disk as a snapshot; this is the way the data appeared when it was last flushed from memory to disk. Data in memory is current. Data modifications are generally made in memory, not directly to disk. This is why it is critical to understand how and when data moves between memory and disk.

To lay the groundwork for this understanding, we will first address physical data storage structures including transaction logs. Then we will look at memory and memory configuration.

Finally, we will examine how the data engine processes the query and see how these resources work together to create a more efficient data environment.

PHYSICAL DATA STRUCTURES

Like most other applications, SQL Server data is organized into files. When you create a database, you will identify the names and locations of these files. Creating a database requires the use of two types of files: data files and transaction log files. A database can have multiple data files and transaction log files, and it is required to have at least one of each.

Data Files   Data files store all of the information in the database including data values, indexes, and even configuration data and programmatic objects such as stored procedures and functions. The data files are, therefore, the main repository in the database.

Transaction Log Files   Log files provide a durable record of all modifications to the database. SQL Server uses a write-ahead modification process that requires all changes to be written to transaction logs before they are written to the database. These logs enable a variety of data recovery and integrity features.

SQL SERVER FILENAMES

The documentation that comes with SQL Server recommends the use of specific file extensions to identify SQL Server file structures. Every SQL Server database has a data file known as the *primary data file*. The convention states that this file should use an .mdf extension. Additional data files, known as *secondary data files,* should use an .ndf extension. Transaction log files typically use an .ldf extension. Although this is the convention, SQL Server does not enforce these rules. It is a good idea, however, to comply with these conventions for clarity unless you have a specific and well-documented reason for varying from the standard.

To allow SQL Server to locate any data value quickly and efficiently, these data files must be organized in a way that gives the SQL Server data engine full control of the specific placement of any data value. SQL Server accomplishes this by organizing data file structures into 8KB blocks called *pages*. Pages are further organized into 64KB blocks called *extents*. Typically, pages in a data file are allocated specifically for only one purpose. For example, you will not see data values and index entries in the same data page. SQL Server has many kinds of pages.

Data Pages   Data pages store all data values except those typed as large value types such as text, ntext, xml, varchar(max), etc. The majority of pages in a typical database will be data pages.

Index Pages   Index pages store index entries for both clustered and nonclustered indexes. These entries typically consist of the index key values themselves plus additional information used by SQL Server to locate data entries and manage the index process.

Large Object Pages   Because SQL Server data rows cannot span multiple data pages, large data values must be stored in alternative locations in cases where the data value is too large for the data page. Datatypes such as text, ntext, xml, varchar(max), etc. will typically store a small pointer on the data page that references the large object page where the data entry begins.

Some datatypes such as `text` and `varchar(max)` will always be stored in large object pages. Others, such as `varchar` and `varbinary,` will be moved to these pages dynamically by SQL Server when the data row size exceeds 8KB. If, in the future, the variable length columns are edited and the size of the data row falls within the 8KB limit again, the data will be moved back to the data page.

Other Pages   Additionally, SQL Server stores other configuration information in special pages designed specifically for those configurations. These special page types include the Global Application Map, Index Application Map, Bulk Changed Map, and others.

Pages are organized into extents. Each extent contains exactly eight contiguous pages. Extents are the basic unit of allocation in SQL Server. When the data engine allocates disk space to an artifact such as a table or index, it will generally allocate an entire extent. This reduces the frequency of allocation and also ensures a greater degree of contiguity in the physical data structure. These extents that are allocated entirely to one artifact are referred to as *uniform extents.*

In some cases, where artifacts are very small and would not require an entire extent, it is possible for the data engine to allocate pages for multiple artifacts from a single extent. This is referred to as a *mixed extent.* Mixed extents are particularly useful when there are a large number of smaller artifacts that would not themselves fill an entire 64KB block.

Because the SQL Server data engine will need to be able to locate any data value at any time, it is important for SQL Server to keep an accurate recording of exactly which extents are allocated to which artifacts. This is also important because once an extent has been allocated to an artifact, that extent is no longer available to be allocated to another artifact.

SQL Server manages extent allocation information through the use of two allocation maps: the Global Allocation Map (GAM) and the Shared Global Allocation Map (SGAM). Each map stores allocation data for up to 64,000 extents by using bit settings to track each extent. This means that a single map page can support almost 4GB of data. The GAM uses a bit to track whether each extent is free or allocated. The SGAM specifically monitors mixed extents, using a bit to identify any mixed extent that has free pages available.

There are also special pages called *Page Free Space (PFS)* pages, which are used to track the amount of free space on each individual page and whether or not that page has been allocated. Once the data engine has allocated an extent, it uses this PFS data to determine which of the pages in the extents are being used and how much of each page is being used.

The entire allocation tracking system in SQL Server is designed to make the process of allocating new data structures as fast as possible and minimize exposure to error. Typical production databases are getting larger and a data explosion has occurred as a result of data warehousing; therefore, it should be obvious how important managing the data allocation process really is. Because a more detailed discussion of physical data structures is beyond the scope of this book, you may want to review SQL Server Books Online for more comprehensive information.

Transaction Logs

Unlike data structures, transaction logs are not organized into pages. This is because transaction logs represent a substantially different structure. Rather than being blocks of data that can be accessed on a random basis, transaction logs consist of a sequence of actions whose inherent value is in maintaining the sequence. As a result, transaction logs are stored as a sequence of operations rather than as blocks of data.

To guarantee that the sequence of actions will be preserved, every transaction log entry contains a log sequence number (LSN), which identifies the specific order in which the actions occur in the database. Multiple actions that are part of the same transaction are encoded with the same transaction ID and linked together through backward pointers, thereby ensuring that multiple operations in a transaction can be committed or rolled back atomically.

TWO DIFFERENT WORLDS

At first it seems counterintuitive that SQL Server would store data and transaction log entries in such different ways. Remember, though, that SQL Server stores data structures and transaction log structures in completely different files. This makes it easier for SQL Server to manage the different storage processes. Data files need to be organized into pages and extents. Transaction log files do not need to be organized in this way, but rather as a series of log entries. This difference in data storage process is one of the reasons that SQL Server stores data and log entries in separate files. Another important reason for the split is data recovery, which will be addressed in detail in Chapter 9, "Data Recovery."

The logical architecture of the transaction log is organized into a series of virtual logs. Because log space is freed when transaction logs are truncated, there must be a mechanism by which that free space is made available to the database engine. SQL Server accomplishes this by using a wraparound process as illustrated in Figures 2.1 through 2.3.

FIGURE 2.1
Transaction logging

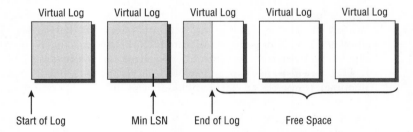

In Figure 2.1, the transaction log is organized into multiple virtual log structures. These log structures are of no predetermined size, and there is no predetermined number of virtual logs. As transaction logging begins, space is used in the virtual logs in sequence. This space comes from the one or more log files associated with the database. The MinLSN marker is the point representing the oldest log record that is required to be present in the log to perform data recovery.

Assuming that the transaction log is truncated at the point illustrated in Figure 2.1, the truncation cannot take place any further forward than the MinLSN marker. Anything before that marker is not necessary for full database recovery and can be removed. That truncated space is now free to store new transaction data. However, because that free space is located logically before the current transaction activity, SQL Server must provide some mechanism to allow that recently truncated space to be accessed.

FIGURE 2.2
Truncating the
inactive log

FIGURE 2.3
Wrapping the log

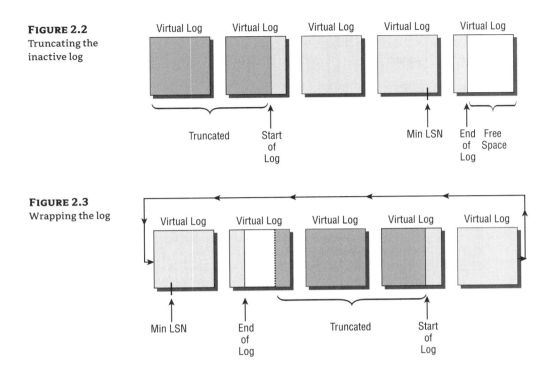

In Figure 2.3, the end of the sequence of virtual logs is reached before the transaction logging process completes. Although no more free space is available at the end of the sequence of virtual logs, there is free space back at the beginning. The log will, therefore, wrap around back to the beginning of the sequence of virtual logs and begin the process again.

VIRTUAL LOGS AND SYSTEM PERFORMANCE

Although virtual logs rarely cause performance problems, one notable exception is when incrementing transaction log size. An administrative best practice is that if files need to be increased in size, they should be increased less often and in larger increments. If an administrator chooses to take a hands-off approach by setting the transaction log file's auto increment setting, particularly if this is a small value, the result is a larger number of smaller transaction log fragments. In this case, each small fragment will be generated as its own virtual log. This can create a very large number of virtual logs and, therefore, have an adverse effect on system performance overall.

Although a few operations are not included in the transaction log, almost all data modifications are written to the transaction log before they are written to the data page. Transaction logging cannot be disabled. Although this does provide durability of data modifications, it significantly increases overhead both in memory and on disk. Exactly what values the system writes to the transaction log depends on the data modification it is performing as well as the circumstances of that modification.

When data inserts are performed, the entire inserted row is inserted into the transaction log. This allows the insert operation to be recommitted in the database if it becomes necessary to apply the transaction log due to data loss. Insert operations can be rolled back before the transaction commits by using the identifying data in the log.

The data engine also records the entire record that was deleted in the transaction log. This provides the option of rolling back the delete operation by reinserting the data recorded in the transaction log. The log also contains a marker that allows the delete to be recommitted to the database if necessary.

Update operations are more complex. Updates generally take place in one of two ways: as an update in place or as a delete/insert. These two techniques can differ significantly in the amount of overhead required to complete the update operation. Because the update-in-place technique requires significantly less overhead, the query optimizer will choose this option whenever it can. However, there are very specific requirements for executing an update in place.

Delete/Insert Updates   This is the default mode of performing a data update in SQL Server. This approach requires the greatest level of logging. After any necessary "BEGIN TRANSACTION" marker in the log, the entire row is written to the transaction log as it appeared before the updates occurred. Following the updates, the entire row is written again to the log. This provides both a "before" and "after" view of the data modification. Finally, any necessary "end transaction" markers are written to the log.

Update in Place   When certain conditions exist, it is possible to write the logical operation to the transaction log instead of performing a full delete and a full insert. Some of these conditions include:

◆   The table cannot be marked for replication.

◆   The table cannot have update triggers.

◆   The total length of the data row before and after the update must be the same.

◆   The update operation cannot modify a clustered index key.

The general rule of thumb is that an update in place is not allowed if the update operation repositions a row on the page, repositions any other row on the page, or requires a complete before and/or after view of the data due to other considerations such as replication or triggers.

In addition to data modifications, the transaction log also stores other operations (for example, extent allocations and page allocations such as creating, dropping, or truncating tables or indexes).

MEMORY ARCHITECTURE

Data is stored durably in files, but generally it must be brought into memory to be used by client applications. Having sufficient memory is vital to SQL Server performance; however, having a proper configuration to make maximum use of that memory is even more critical. In this section, we will look at the role memory plays and how to properly configure it for maximum impact.

SQL Server uses a lot of memory. Memory is required for storing process objects such as user connections and worker threads. Memory is also required to store procedure execution plans, thereby providing one of the primary benefits of the store procedure—the ability to execute the procedure from a memory-resident store. However, by far the largest allocation of memory in SQL Server is reserved for data. Data memory is dynamically managed by SQL Server, which allocates and deallocates memory as needed.

The organization of the memory reserved for data, also called *data cache* or *buffer cache*, mimics the organization of its physical disk counterpart. Just as the physical disk is organized as pages, memory is organized into a pool of 8KB buffers used to store data pages. Accessing data stored in memory is much faster than accessing data stored on disk. As long as the buffer remains intact in memory, no disk I/O is required to read or write a data value stored in the buffer.

If there is insufficient memory to store the most commonly used data, swapping must occur. This means that data must be continually moved back and forth between memory and disk. Although common in SQL Server, swapping is a time-consuming process that should be minimized to the extent possible.

So how much memory can SQL Server actually use? The answer to that question depends on a variety of factors. The primary factors are the CPU architecture of the server and the version of SQL Server that is running on that server. A 64-bit processor can address more memory than 32-bit processors; however, a 32-bit version of SQL Server running on a 64-bit architecture does not fully utilize the capacity of the hardware. When properly coerced through configuration settings, a 32-bit processor can use memory not normally accessible. Table 2.1 lists the user-addressable memory capacity of SQL Server in a variety of typical configurations. Unless otherwise specified, it is assumed that a 32-bit version of SQL Server is running on a 32-bit Windows version. The parallel assumption applies to 64-bit implementations.

TABLE 2.1   SQL Server Memory Configurations

CONFIGURATION	32-BIT	64-BIT
Conventional	2GB	Up to OS Maximum Limit
/3GB boot parameter	3GB	Option not supported
WOW64	4GB	Option not supported
AWE	OS Version Dependent	Option not supported

In a 32-bit environment, SQL Server is limited to 2GB of physical addressable memory under conventional circumstances. Due to the limitations of the Windows 32-bit memory architecture, only a total of 4GB of physical memory are addressable by the operating system. By default, 2GB of memory are reserved for operating system use only, and the remaining 2GB of memory are available for application use. Even in the most rudimentary of production scenarios, 2GB of memory is insufficient for most SQL Server applications.

Starting with Windows Server 2000 Advanced Server, the server administrator can add the /3GB switch to the boot.ini file to reallocate server memory. Using this option, the 4GB of addressable memory are redistributed such that the operating system is granted access to 1GB of memory while applications can address 3GB. This extra gigabyte of memory can make a significant difference in some applications.

Consider another situation where you may have multiple SQL Server instances running on the same physical server. Each of these instances is responsible for maintaining its own memory pool; however, with no special memory options enabled, those instances must compete for the same 2GB of available application memory. Although SQL Server will dynamically allocate memory as needed, the two instances of SQL Server will essentially starve each other's memory needs.

The solution is to use the /PAE switch in the boot.ini file. This switch controls the Physical Address Extensions that allows more than one application to use memory beyond the 4GB limit. In such cases, each SQL Server instance would get its own 2GB block of memory, assuming physical memory is available, and would not compete with the other instance of SQL Server for memory resources. If used in conjunction with the /3GB switch, each instance would have access to 3GB of physical memory.

THE PERILS OF THE /3GB SWITCH

Although it is very useful, the /3GB switch can cause problems. First, you must make sure that this switch is compatible with your version of Windows. This is an operating system option, not a SQL Server option. It is not supported on the standard Windows 2000 Server; it is supported only on Advanced Server and higher. It is fully supported on Windows Server 2003.

Another problem occurs when you use the 3/GB switch in conjunction with the /PAE option. If the /3GB switch is used when the machine has more than 16GB of physical memory, the server will not be able to access any memory over the 16GB threshold. This is because the operating system needs the full 2GB of memory to be able to address any memory over the 16GB threshold.

Another extended memory configuration option is Address Windowing Extensions (AWE). This option can significantly increase access to extended memory above the standard 2GB application limit. The amount of increase depends on which Windows version you are using. Windows 2003 Server can use up to 4GB application memory under AWE. Windows 2003 Enterprise supports up to 32GB application memory, and Windows 2003 Datacenter increases this limit to 64GB.

To configure AWE in SQL Server, set the advanced option, AWE Enabled, to 1. This option allows SQL Server to use physical memory up to the operating system limit. Before enabling this option, you should also configure the Lock Pages in Memory policy to prevent extended memory from being paged to disk. You should also consider configuring the SQL Server option Max Server Memory to an appropriate value. This is especially important if you have more than one instance of SQL Server running. In this case, each instance should have a Max Server Memory setting configured such that the total of all Max Server Memory values do not exceed the physical memory amount that will be made available to applications. You should consult SQL Server Books Online for specific details of AWE configuration.

When SQL Server is running on a 64-bit processor architecture, the rules change. If you are running a 32-bit version of SQL Server on a 64-bit platform, SQL Server can use up to 4GB of memory using WOW64 (64-bit Windows on Windows). WOW64 is nothing more than 32-bit applications running on a 64-bit platform. The platform itself, however, provides access to 4GB of memory without any special configuration.

The easiest option is to run a full 64-bit architecture. Although 64-bit architecture is capable of addressing over 18 exabytes (one quintillion bytes) of memory, this is not practical and lower limits are utilized based on processor type. X64 processors can handle up to 8TB of memory, and IA64 processors can handle up to 7TB of memory—all without any special configuration.

When choosing the optimal memory configuration for your applications, you must consider trade-offs such as the amount of memory required for your application, costs of hardware, and administrative overhead. Be advised, however, that the movement in the industry is toward a 64-bit architecture due to the ease of configuration and the extensibility of the platform for future growth.

CPU ARCHITECTURE

Although the CPU architecture does have a significant impact on memory and its configuration, the role of the processor is primarily to execute threads. Do not lose sight of this fact when you select an appropriate processor or multiprocessor architecture. Numerous options are available in the market today, including multiple sockets, multiple cores, and hyperthreading technology.

The Windows operating system uses a preemptive scheduler to assign threads to processors. This means that a single thread of execution will be able to use the processor until its time slice expires, it finishes its work, or it is interrupted by a thread of a higher priority. Although this process works well for foreground applications, it can cause significant performance problems with SQL Server because a thread may still hold locks on data resources even if it is not actively executing. For that reason, SQL Server has its own scheduler service that manages all thread activity.

Because SQL Server typically handles multiple concurrent requests from client applications, and each of these requests should hold locks for the shortest possible duration, performance can be enhanced by having multiple processors available to handle these requests. There are a number of ways this can be accomplished.

One approach is to use a mainboard with multiple processor sockets and provide SQL Server with multiple processors. Although this approach gives SQL Server the ability to process multiple threads concurrently, it does have some drawbacks, primarily cost. SQL Server is licensed per socket; therefore, a SQL Server licensed for four CPUs can use a maximum of four sockets. This is also a cost inefficient method of adding processor power.

A more common approach is to use multicore processors. Each core appears to the operating system as a separate processor, although SQL Server licenses the socket instead of the core. Four sockets with dual-core processors provide eight logical processors to SQL Server, but they require only a four-processor license. Multicore processors also have some performance advantages due to shared onboard cache.

Another option is the Intel hyperthreading technology. Hyperthreading captures the unused processor cycles from a given processor and creates from that excess capacity, a logical processor that is visible to the operating system. For each core, a "phantom" processor, which appears to be a real processor to the operating system, is created. The theory is that the phantom processor can capture all available processor cycles so that each physical processor is completely utilized. In most cases, this results in performance gains due to the full utilization of the processor resources.

In some cases when the physical processor is not already fully utilized, this can provide a performance benefit. However, in environments where the physical processor is already utilized to its maximum potential, the result is much different. Hyperthreading creates a phantom processor; but with no excess capacity from the physical processor, this phantom has no ability to efficiently handle assigned processing tasks. Because the operating system cannot tell the difference between the physical processor and the phantom processor, work cannot be effectively distributed among these resources. The result is potential performance degradation due to processor queues that cannot be handled by the phantom processors.

The Data Engine

In later chapters, we will discuss the specifics of how SQL Server executes queries and utilizes indexes. In this chapter, we will lay the groundwork and focus on the mechanics of the data engine. Specifically, we are concerned with the interaction between disk and memory and the role that this interaction plays when data extraction and manipulation takes place. Let's begin by looking at the diagram in Figure 2.4; it illustrates the interaction among these resources.

FIGURE 2.4

The SQL Server query process

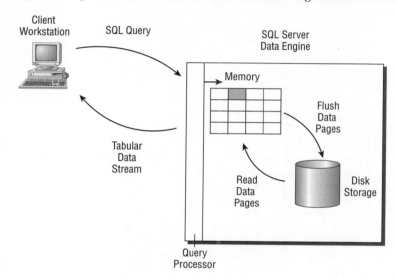

In this diagram, you can see the interaction between the client workstation and the SQL Server data engine. This diagram shows a separation between the query processor and the I/O system that is responsible for managing memory and disk behavior. Let's follow the logical flow of the query request from a client through the system.

The process begins with the client workstation submitting a SQL query to the SQL Server. Before SQL Server can determine exactly which data pages on disk or in memory must be used to return the desired results to the workstation, the query must be first parsed, optimized, and compiled into an execution plan that the data engine can follow. This execution plan will tell the data engine exactly which data pages and index pages should be used to execute the query. This indexing and optimization process will be discussed in detail in Chapter 14, "Indexing Strategies for Query Optimization."

Once the data engine has an execution plan to follow, it can retrieve the necessary data to be returned to the client. As you can see in Figure 2.4, the initial resolution of the query request is made to memory, not disk. In most cases, data reads or writes are not made directly to disk, but rather from memory.

Just as data files are organized into pages, memory is organized into buffers. Each buffer is 8KB in size and stores a single page from disk. When data is retrieved from disk into memory, an entire data page is read from disk. If a client workstation submits a query that requires data from a specific page, the initial action will be to attempt to locate that page in a memory buffer. The necessary data value can then be extracted from the buffer, packaged with the other requested values into a Tabular Data Stream (TDS), and returned to the client.

But what if the needed page is not currently stored in a memory buffer? Then the data must be read from disk. At this point, the SQL Server data engine makes an I/O request to pull a page from disk into an available memory buffer. Once in the memory buffer, the necessary data value can be extracted and returned to the user in the Tabular Data Stream. This requires additional physical I/O and will generally hurt performance.

As you can see from this scenario, if the data page has already been read into a memory buffer, no additional disk access is required to resolve the query. Because memory access is much faster than disk access, the performance of this query would be substantially better than if the query acquired data from disk. The more memory that is available to store commonly used data, the better performance will be.

This process is the same for data modifications. When executing INSERT, UPDATE, or DELETE statements, the data must be retrieved to memory before the data modification can be made. Following the data modification, the buffer will eventually be flushed back to disk.

So what happens if there is not enough memory available to store data pages that must be read from disk into memory? And what exactly constitutes available memory? To answer these questions, we must examine memory architecture a little more closely.

Each memory buffer generally exists in one of three basic states: free, available, and dirty.

Free Buffers   *Free buffers*, sometimes called *empty buffers*, are memory buffers that currently store no data. These buffers represent available space for page reads from disk to memory. Because SQL Server dynamically allocates memory based on current needs, free buffers are very fluid and they are allocated and deallocated as necessary. A consistently high number of free buffers means that memory space is not being fully utilized.

Available Buffers   *Available buffers* currently store data from disk that has not been modified since it was read from disk into memory. If the buffer has not been modified, the page on disk and the buffer in memory should look exactly the same. If this is true, the buffer can be overwritten with new data without losing any existing modifications. For this reason, SQL Server views these buffers as expendable. It will, however, use the available buffers on a "least recently used" basis. Available buffers that have not been accessed recently are more likely to be overwritten with new data.

Dirty Buffers   *Dirty buffers* are buffers that have been modified since they were read into memory. Once a page has been read into memory, it may experience data modifications requested by client applications. If the memory buffer has been modified, the buffer in memory is no longer identical to the page on disk. Remember that disk storage is simply considered a snapshot of what the data page looked like at a specific point in time. A memory buffer is considered to be the current form of the data page.

Dirty buffers must be written to disk before they can become available again to store new data. If these buffers are not written to disk, the data modifications will be lost. SQL Server uses many techniques to write dirty buffers from memory to disk, but the most common is the Checkpoint process. When a database checkpoint occurs, all dirty buffers for that database are written from memory to disk. After the checkpoint, the buffers are not cleared but rather are considered to be "available" buffers.

THE CASE OF THE DISAPPEARING DIRTY BUFFER

The Checkpoint process ensures that dirty buffers are written from memory to disk before those buffers are reused for other data. However, if the buffers did not get the opportunity to checkpoint—due to a power failure, for example—the data modifications stored in the dirty buffers are lost. Where do these data modifications go, and how can we restore them?

Author Mike Lee once had a consulting client that faced this very dilemma. This was some years ago, and the client, a small insurance agency in the Western United States, was new to SQL Server and did not have the resources to hire a full time database administrator. Not fully understanding the appropriate configuration of SQL Server, the agency had enabled an option that would truncate the transaction log with every checkpoint to ensure that the transaction log did not fill up. They did this in an effort to manage the size of the transaction log. What they did not realize was that they were exposing themselves to data loss.

As part of SQL Server's performance architecture, the data engine will allow a dirty buffer to remain in memory until the benefit of performing a checkpoint on the database is greater than the overhead of performing that operation. The longer a dirty buffer can remain in memory, the more likely it is to be modified by other client requests. By delaying the Checkpoint process, this dirty buffer may experience multiple modifications but will only have to be flushed once, thereby reducing overall I/O. To prevent exposure to data loss in the volatile memory, all transaction log records associated with a specific transaction are immediately flushed from memory to disk as soon as a transaction successfully completes. Therefore, the transaction log on disk provides the durable record of all data modifications, including those buffers that have not yet been flushed to disk.

To return to our tale, when the agency's SQL Server went down, all of the dirty buffers in memory were lost because they had not been part of a database checkpoint process. The transaction records were useless because the truncation of the transaction log with each checkpoint prevented that log from being restored back to the database. In their case, the buffers simply disappeared and could not be recovered. If they had fully understood the memory and disk architecture of SQL Server, they would have chosen different transaction log settings and could have preserved their data. The important lesson to learn from this example is that knowledge of system architecture is not just an academic exercise. In many cases, understanding the specifics of system behavior can mean the difference between a reliable data environment and a data disaster.

Data is typically flushed from memory to disk during the Checkpoint process. The frequency of the checkpoint is controlled by the server, but typically each database is evaluated for check-pointing every minute or so. If in this check, it is determined that the database has accumulated sufficient data modification to warrant a memory flush, the database checkpoint will occur.

Another technique that SQL Server uses to write pages from memory to disk is the LazyWriter. Sometimes the number of free and available buffers falls below an acceptable value before the database can checkpoint. If all buffers are dirty, the SQL Server will halt due to the inability of the server to place needed pages into available memory. The LazyWriter handles these situations. When necessary, the LazyWriter will write dirty pages from memory to disk and mark the buffers as available. This enables SQL Server to have sufficient memory for its data needs.

SQL Server and Windows

In the early days of SQL Server, the product was just for Windows. Version 4.2 of SQL Server and its Sybase predecessors also supported the Unix platform. Since the release of SQL Server 6.0, it has lived in a Windows-only world. There were a number of reasons for this transformation including:

◆ Marketing

◆ Reducing the maintenance costs of SQL Server releases

◆ Enabling tighter integration with the Windows platform

From a marketing perspective, the success of this transformation is open to debate: one substantial impact of this decision was that Microsoft's development team on SQL Server could focus their efforts on the Windows platform and exploit all the benefits that Windows provides. This has enabled Windows Server operating systems and SQL Server database systems to grow together to the point that today they are highly integrated parts of the Windows data platform. Although a discussion of Windows internals is far beyond the scope of this book, there are a few key concepts that you should understand regarding the relationship between SQL Server and the Windows platform.

SQL Server is a Windows service.   It doesn't get more basic than this. All SQL Server functionality—including the data engine, the scheduling engine, the SQL browser, etc.—runs as Windows services. Windows services have some important characteristics including:

◆ Background processing priority

◆ Service logon authority

◆ Autostart behavior

Windows performs all SQL Server I/O.   SQL Server does not perform any of its own I/O activities. It relies on Windows to perform these actions. When a data page needs to be read from disk, SQL Server sends the request to Windows, which locates the appropriate disk location and reads the data into memory. It is SQL Server's responsibility to keep track of the data on every 8KB page and provide Windows with the appropriate page address for read or write. Windows does not know or care what is on every page. Windows does not even realize that the 8KB block of data that it is reading or writing is a data page. In this way, Windows manages the physical I/O process while SQL Server manages the logical I/O process.

Windows manages all hardware.   SQL Server is not allowed to interact with any hardware, be it network cards, memory, controllers, etc. For this reason, the database administrator generally tunes hardware resources by tuning the Windows platform, not by tuning SQL Server. Although some configurations allow SQL Server to specify which hardware resources it will use, it is up to Windows to manage these resources. In other words, setting a configuration such as Processor Affinity or Max Server Memory in SQL Server will control only what SQL Server requests, not the way Windows manages that request or optimizes the resource.

To be a truly proficient database administrator, you should be comfortable with the Windows platform. Companies and data environments delegate database authority differently. Tuning and configuring the Windows platform could be the responsibility of the network administrator, or the database administrator could have no rights in this area whatsoever. Regardless, it is important for the database administrator to be knowledgeable about platform configurations so that he or she can communicate effectively with the platform professionals who are the gate-keepers of the SQL Server's operating environment.

The SQL Server System Catalog

In addition to the internals of SQL Server, the database administrator must also understand the SQL Server catalog structure. SQL Server stores information about its own configurations and all user data in a series of system tables and system databases. The proficient database administrator should be intimate with these catalog features. As SQL Server gets more complex, so does its catalog structure. Therefore, a small investment in understanding the SQL Server catalog will pay off significantly as you begin to tune and maintain your server.

The System Databases

A typical installation of SQL Server has four standard system databases. They store all the required information for SQL Server's internal configuration. These databases are

Master   The master database stores all of SQL Server's global configurations. In essence, the master database contains all of the information that SQL Server knows about itself, its own configuration, and its current status. This data is stored in system tables and is made available to the database administrator through system views and functions.

Many TSQL operations modify the master database. For example, when you create a new user database, entries are made in the master database catalog that track the file structure and the logical database structure of the database that you just created. Likewise, adding a new login to SQL Server also modifies the master database catalog.

Model   The model database is the template for every new user database created. The model database contains all of the system structures that are found in every user database. Additionally, a database administrator can add artifacts to the model database, which would include all of the artifacts in every new user database created on that server from that point forward. The model database can be extremely convenient when standardizing structure, features, or artifacts for every new user database.

Msdb   The msdb database contains all the catalog information to support the SQL Agent service, which is SQL Server's scheduling service. The SQL Agent allows the database administrator to create jobs, schedule jobs, and configure alerts for when those jobs succeed or fail. All of the scheduling information is stored in system tables in the .msdb database. This database also contains information concerning replication publication and replication schedules.

Tempdb   The tempdb database stores internal SQL Server work structures used in the process of resolving queries. This database can store worktables generated automatically by SQL Server as well as temporary tables created explicitly by the SQL developer. Tempdb is also where cursor overhead is stored, whether the cursor is generated on the server through SQL code or requested as a server-side cursor from the client. Unlike the other system databases, tempdb does not have to be backed up because it contains no permanent information. In fact, tempdb is cleared as a part of the normal shutdown process.

System Tables, Views, and Functions

In addition to the system tables that are part of the catalog of the system databases, there are also system structures that are part of every user database. In both the system databases and the user databases, the system tables are augmented with system views and functions that organize system data and make it available to the database administrator (DBA) in a consumable fashion. Using these system views and functions, the database administrator should have access to all relevant configuration information for the server as a whole or any individual database.

WHERE DID MY SYSTEM TABLES GO?

If you are familiar with SQL Server 2000 and earlier, you are used to being able to access system tables directly. Expanding the system tables node in the SQL Server Management Studio is an extremely frustrating experience if you are used to accessing any system table at any time. The list that you get is extremely empty.

Starting with SQL Server 2005, Microsoft has moved much of the information that we formerly retrieved from system tables into system views and functions. The level of system table abstraction that started with SQL Server 2005 has been extended in the 2008 release, and Microsoft plans to eliminate all direct system table access in the next release. With this in mind, you should become familiar with the system views and functions now. By using these artifacts, you can often get much better information from the system anyway.

Because the system table structure is essentially hidden from the database administrator, we will not focus on the system tables themselves; instead, we'll turn our attention to the system views and functions that make up our interactive catalog. These system views and functions are well documented in SQL Server Books Online, so rather than review them in detail here, you should consult the documentation for more detail. We will, however, take this opportunity to introduce you to some of the more critical artifacts in the catalog and walk you through the process of using them. Tables 2.2 and 2.3 list some of the SQL 2000 system tables and their corresponding system views. This is not meant to be an exhaustive list, but merely gives you a taste of the available features.

TABLE 2.2   Master Database System Views and Functions

SQL 2000 SYSTEM TABLE	CORRESPONDING SYSTEM VIEW OR FUNCTION IN SQL SERVER 2008
sysaltfiles	sys.master_files
syscacheobjects	sys.dm_exec_cached_plans
sysconfigures	sys.configurations
sysdatabases	sys.databases
syslockinfo	sys.dm_tran_locks

TABLE 2.2   Master Database System Views and Functions   *(CONTINUED)*

SQL 2000 SYSTEM TABLE	CORRESPONDING SYSTEM VIEW OR FUNCTION IN SQL SERVER 2008
syslocks	sys.dm_tran_locks
syslogins	sys.server_principals sys.sql_logins
sysmessages	sys.messages
sysoledbusers	sys.linked_logins
sysperfinfo	sys.dm_os_performance_counters
sysprocesses	sys.dm_exec.connections sys.dm_exec_sessions sys.dm_exec_requests
sysservers	sys.servers

TABLE 2.3   All Database System Views and Functions

SQL 2000 SYSTEMS TABLE	CORRESPONDING SYSTEM VIEW OR FUNCTION IN SQL SERVER 2008
syscolumns	sys.columns
syscomments	sys.sql_modules
sysconstraints	sys.check_contraints sys.default_constraints sys.key_constraints sys.foreign_keys
sysdepends	sys.sql_expression_dependencies
sysfilegroups	sys.filegroups
sysfiles	sys.database_files
sysforeignkeys	sys.foreign_key_columns
sysindexes	sys.indexes sys.partitions sys.allocation_units sys.dm_db_partition_stats
sysindexkeys	sys.index_columns

TABLE 2.3   All Database System Views and Functions   *(CONTINUED)*

SQL 2000 SYSTEMS TABLE	CORRESPONDING SYSTEM VIEW OR FUNCTION IN SQL SERVER 2008
sysmembers	sys.database_role_members
sysobjects	sys.objects
syspermissions	sys.database_permissions sys.server_permissions
sysprotects	sys.database_permissions sys.server_permissions
sysreferences	sys.foreign_keys
systypes	sys.types
sysusers	sys.database_principals

TYPES OF SYSTEM ARTIFACTS

In earlier versions of SQL Server, all system data was stored in system tables. As SQL Server matured, some system data, such as active locks and processes, was dynamically generated but still visible to the administrator via a system table structure. If you did not know which data was stored in tables and which data was dynamically generated, the structure of the catalog did not make it obvious.

This changed in SQL Server 2005 and continues in SQL Server 2008. System views and functions use naming conventions that can help us identify how the data was generated. Every system artifact begins with the prefix sys. This prefix is a system schema that is used to organize all system artifacts. (If you are not familiar with schemas, you can read about them in more detail in Chapter 8, "Managing User Security.") When you see the sys. prefix, you know that you are dealing with a system artifact. This alleviates the need for a naming convention for the actual artifacts, as was used in SQL Server 2000 and earlier.

Some artifacts use a dm_ prefix. This prefix indicates that the data returned is not being pulled exclusively from system structures, but is dynamically generated from active system state.

Knowing these conventions does not change your ability to use an artifact, but it can help you understand how the catalog is organized and how the data is being generated.

Because these system artifacts are typically views and table-valued functions, they can be used in queries in the same manner as the system tables were. In some cases, when the artifact is a table-valued function, it may be necessary to pass parameters when extracting information from the system catalog. This process can be very different from querying data directly from system tables, because the FROM clause typically does not take parameters. Let's take a closer look at each of these techniques.

First, let's look at a simple system view. One of the most common queries performed against the system tables is a check to the sysobjects table to verify an object's existence. Try executing the query in Listing 2.1 against the AdventureWorks2008 database. This query uses the sysobjects system table.

GETTING THE SAMPLE DATABASES

The following examples use the AdventureWorks sample databases for SQL Server. If you do not have these databases installed, you can get them from http://www.codeplex.com/MSFTDBProdSamples.

First, open the SQL Server Management Studio by selecting Start ➤ All Programs ➤ SQL Server 2008 ➤ SQL Server Management Studio. In the Connect To SQL Server dialog, set the Server Type to Database Engine and the Server Name to the instance to which you would like to connect. If you're using SQL Server Authentication, you must also provide a login and password. Click the Connect button. Once connected, click the New Query button on the top left of the toolbar to open a new query window. After typing the query, click the Execute button on the toolbar to run the query. You can also use the F5 key, the Ctrl+E combination or the Alt+X combination to run the query.

LISTING 2.1   Selecting from the Sysobjects System Table

```
USE AdventureWorks2008;

IF EXISTS(
        SELECT 1
        FROM sysobjects
        WHERE xtype='P'
                AND name='uspLogError'
)
        PRINT 'Proc Found';
ELSE
        PRINT 'Proc Not Found';
```

Because this procedure is located in the AdventureWorks2008 database, it should print the appropriate message to the screen. But there is a small problem. The query refers to a procedure called uspLogError, but that name does not include the schema. Because there could be multiple procedures called upsLogError, all in different schemas, this is ambiguous. Try modifying the code on the sixth line to read ***AND name='dbo.uspLogError'***. Run the query again and look at the results. This time, you should see a message telling you that the procedure was not found.

Why?

The problem is that the name of the procedure does not include its schema. So the column that stored the name in sysobjects has no reference to the schema. In fact, if you look at the sysobjects system table more closely, you will see that there are no columns in the table that reference schema information. So we will have to find another way to filter the procedure list by schema. Take a look at the query and results in Figure 2.5.

FIGURE 2.5
Querying the
sys.objects
system view

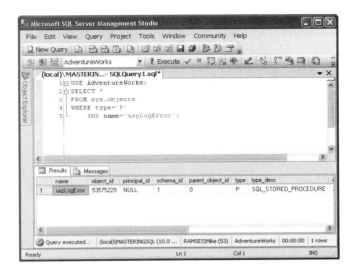

Although the name of the procedure still does not contain this schema information, a schema column contains this data. Unfortunately, the schema ID returned in this table is of limited use unless you know to which schema the ID refers. To get this information, let's evaluate another view, sys.schemas. Note that the schema ID of this procedure is 1. Look at the query execution pictured in Figure 2.6.

FIGURE 2.6
Selecting from the
sys.schemas view

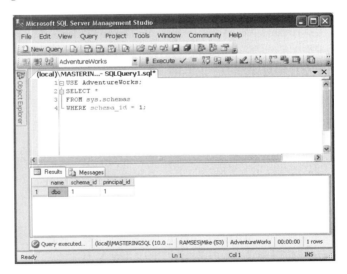

According to this query, the name of the schema having a schema_id of 1 is dbo. This means that the fully qualified name of our procedure is dbo.uspLogError. You may observe that this is a long way to get this information. There is a shorter way. By joining the views, we can create a single query that allows us to filter by schema name as well as object name. If we are performing an existence check for a procedure called dbo.uspLogError, our code should look like the example in Listing 2.2.

LISTING 2.2   Existence Checking with Catalog Views

```
USE AdventureWorks2008;

IF EXISTS (
     SELECT *
     FROM sys.objects as o
     INNER JOIN sys.schemas as s
          ON s.schema_id = o.schema_id
     WHERE s.name='dbo'
          AND o.name='uspLogError'
)
     PRINT 'Proc Found';
ELSE
     PRINT 'Proc Not Found';
```

As you can see from this example, much more information is made available to the administrator through the catalog views than was previously available through the system tables directly. You may have to change a few habits, but the benefits of using the system views as opposed to the tables can be significant. You can use other system views in much the same way as in this example. Take the time to consult the documentation and find out which views are available. Experimenting with these resources now will give you an advantage down the road.

Some of these system artifacts are not actually views, but instead are table-valued functions. Although a table-valued function can be called in the FROM clause of the query in the same way as a view, these functions sometimes accept parameters that must be provided before the function will execute correctly. These parameters are fully documented in SQL Server Books Online, but the query editor in the SQL Server Management Studio provides syntax prompts that will help you provide the needed information.

As an example, look at the code in the following snippet. This listing shows a query against the system function sys.dm_sql_referenced_entities.

```
USE AdventureWorks2008;
SELECT *
FROM sys.dm_sql_referenced_entities('dbo.uspLogError', 'OBJECT');
```

This function is similar in nature to the old sp_depends system-stored procedure, providing information about the artifacts upon which the indicated objects depends. To execute this function, we need to pass two parameters. First, we must provide the name of the referencing entity. You may optionally include the schema name if there is any chance of ambiguity. Second, we must provide a parameter called referencing_class, which indicates the type of artifact that is doing the referencing. This second parameter is a string, and it can be set to one of the following three values:

◆ OBJECT

◆ DATABASE_DDL_TRIGGER

◆ SERVER_DDL_TRIGGER

In addition to these management views and functions, SQL Server still utilizes a significant number of other functions, primarily scalar functions, as part of the Transact-SQL language. These functions and their uses should look familiar to most database developers and administrators.

Functions such as OBJECT_ID, CAST, COALESCE, etc. provide significant functionality to the SQL developer. Because most of these functions are scalar in nature, providing a single return value, they can be used in select lists, as criteria in a WHERE clause, and anywhere that a single value can be evaluated and used. Figure 2.7 shows an example of using one of the scalar functions in a query.

This query uses two scalar functions: CURRENT_USER and USER_ID. This query returns a list of all schemas that are owned by the currently logged-on user. Notice how the USER_ID function is used in the WHERE clause to provide criteria for the query. Also note how the CURRENT_USER function is used to provide a value for the user ID. Because numerous functions provide extensive functionality as part of the Transact-SQL language, you will find a wealth of convenience if you are willing to do a little bit of searching. You can also create your own scalar functions if no built-in functions satisfy your requirements. This will be discussed in Chapter 5, "Procedural Programming."

FIGURE 2.7
Using scalar
functions in
a query

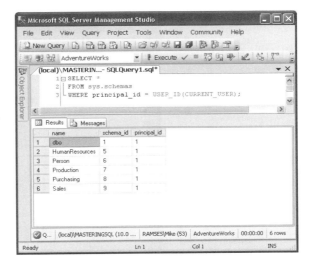

System Stored Procedures

System stored procedures are another important part of the Transact-SQL language and the server catalog. *System stored procedures* provide mechanisms by which you can alter system catalog contents without having to interact directly with the system tables. It is highly inadvisable to attempt to modify system tables. However, system stored procedures can perform these operations safely, and they should be the preferred administrative tool for performing these operations.

For example, suppose you want to modify SQL Server's configurations. Information about these configurations is stored in the system catalog. Even if you are able to locate the system tables where this information is stored, it's not really a good idea to modify those system structures directly. Instead, you should let the system stored procedures assist you in this type of task.

In this example, the appropriate system stored procedure is SP_CONFIGURE. Suppose you are interested in enabling the .NET Common Language Runtime in SQL Server. This configuration is disabled by default for security reasons. If you want to execute managed objects in SQL Server, such as stored procedures written in the C# language, you must first enable the Common Language Runtime. The following code snippet illustrates how this is done.

```
EXEC sp_configure 'clr enabled', 1;
```

This statement will modify the server configuration setting for the Common Language Runtime integration. Notice that we did not have to interact directly with any of the system table structures.

The SQL Server catalog has a lot of system stored procedures. You should review them to familiarize yourself with the capabilities that they provide. Experienced database administrators should note that a significant number of the system stored procedures are being deprecated and replaced with other Transact-SQL functionality. You should review the procedures that you commonly use before you define any new functionality in your applications or administrative scripts.

When Configuring Is Still Not Enough

The previous example illustrated the use of the `sp_configure` system stored procedure. After executing the code in the snippet, you might think that the CLR was fully enabled. Unfortunately, this is not the case. Some configurations must be *installed* before they will take effect. If you execute the `sp_configure` procedure without any parameters, it will show you currently configured and running values as illustrated in the following graphic.

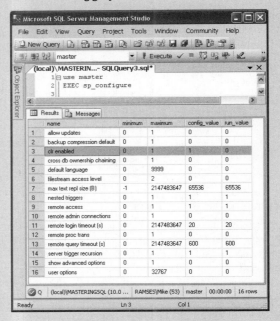

Compare the value for the `config_value` to the `run_value` for the CLR-enabled configuration. You will notice that the configuration is set for the CLR to run, but at this point the CLR has not yet launched because the run configuration value still shows the CLR as inactive. To install the configuration, you must run the **reconfigure** command. This will ensure that the SQL Server is running with all configured settings. Forgetting this extra step may result in an improperly configured server.

Datatyping

Although not part of the system architecture in the strictest sense, datatyping is included in this chapter because of its prevalence throughout the rest of the system. You cannot escape datatypes. When you define a table, you will need to specify its datatypes. Likewise, a parameter in the stored procedure or declared variable in a procedure or script will require datatypes. Additionally, you may also provide consistency in your application architecture through user-defined datatypes.

System-Defined Datatypes

The list of new datatypes seems to grow with every new release of SQL Server, and SQL Server 2008 is no exception. Table 2.4 provides a complete listing of all SQL Server 2008 datatypes along with a short description of each. You should become very familiar with this list, along with the advantages and challenges of each type.

TABLE 2.4   SQL Server 2008 Datatypes

TYPE NAME	CATEGORY	DESCRIPTION
bit	Exact Numeric	Integer storing 1, 0, "True," "False," or NULL.
tinyint	Exact Numeric	1 byte storing 0 to 255.
smallint	Exact Numeric	2 bytes storing -2^{15} to $2^{15}-1$.
int	Exact Numeric	4 bytes storing -2^{31} to $2^{31}-1$.
bigint	Exact Numeric	8 bytes storing -2^{63} to $2^{63}-1$.
decimal	Exact Numeric	Defined with precision up to 38 digits using format decimal $[(p[\ ,s])]$ where p is precision and s is scale. 17 bytes when used at maximum precision. Default precision is 18.
numeric	Exact Numeric	Functionally equivalent to decimal.
smallmoney	Exact Numeric	4-byte scaled integer (4 digits scale).
money	Exact Numeric	8-byte scaled integer (4 digits scale).
real	Approximate Numeric	4-byte floating point value.
float	Approximate Numeric	Defined using format of float$[(n)]$. 7 digits precision and 4 bytes size when n=1 to 24. 15 digits precision and 8 bytes size when n=25 to 53. Default n = 53.
smalldatetime	Date and Time	4 bytes storing date and time value from Jan 1, 1900 to June 6, 2079 with accuracy to the minute.

TABLE 2.4   SQL Server 2008 Datatypes   *(CONTINUED)*

TYPE NAME	CATEGORY	DESCRIPTION
datetime	Date and Time	8 bytes storing date and time value from Jan 1, 1753 to December 31, 9999 with accuracy to 3.33 milliseconds.
datetime2	Date and Time	8 bytes (default) storing a value from Jan 1, 1 AD to December 31, 9999AD with accuracy to 100 nanoseconds.
date	Date and Time	3 bytes storing the date only from Jan 1, 1 AD to December 31, 9999.
time	Date and Time	5 bytes storing time of day with accuracy of 100 nanoseconds without time zone awareness. User can specify scale.
datetimeoffset	Date and Time	Equivalent to datetime2 with the addition of time zone awareness.
char	Character Strings	Fixed storage of ANSI characters using 1 byte per character + 2 bytes total overhead up to 8,000 characters.
varchar	Character Strings	Variable storage of ANSI characters using 1 byte per character + 2 bytes total overhead up to 8,000 characters. Up to 2GB storage when used as varchar(max).
text	Character Strings	Variable storage of ANSI characters using 1 byte per character. Note: This datatype will not be supported in future releases.
nchar	Unicode Character Strings	Fixed storage of Unicode characters using 2 byte per character + 2 bytes total overhead up to 8,000 characters.
nvarchar	Unicode Character Strings	Variable storage of Unicode characters using 2 byte per character + 2 bytes total overhead up to 8,000 characters. Up to 2GB storage when used as nvarchar(max).
ntext	Unicode Character Strings	Variable storage of ANSI characters using 2 byte per character. Note: This datatype will not be supported in future releases.
binary	Binary Strings	Fixed storage of binary characters using 1 byte per character + 2 bytes total overhead up to 8,000 characters.
varbinary	Binary Strings	Variable storage of binary characters using 1 byte per character + 2 bytes total overhead up to 8,000 characters. Up to 2GB storage when used as varbinary(max).

TABLE 2.4   SQL Server 2008 Datatypes *(CONTINUED)*

TYPE NAME	CATEGORY	DESCRIPTION
image	Binary Strings	Variable storage of binary characters using 2 byte per character. Note: This datatype will not be supported in future releases.
cursor	Miscellaneous	Type used to store a reference to a cursor in a variable or output parameter of a stored procedure.
rowversion	Miscellaneous	Reflects the functionality of the former timestamp data-type. 8 byte value for version stamping a row that is updated whenever a value on the row changes. The old timestamp syntax will be deprecated in the next release.
hierarchyid	Miscellaneous	A variable system datatype that represents position is a hierarchy.
uniqueidentifier	Miscellaneous	A 16-byte GUID value; when used in conjunction with the NEWID function is unique on the server.
sql_variant	Miscellaneous	Can store a value of any datatype except: varchar(max) nvarchar(max) varbinary(max) xml text ntext image rowversion sql_variant any user-defined type
xml	Miscellaneous	Variable type storing up to 2GB data in a well-formed XML document or fragment format. Can enforce schemas if configured.
table	Miscellaneous	Variable type storing a table in a declared variable or stored procedure output parameter.

As you can see from this list, there have been numerous enhancements to the SQL Server datatypes. Most notably are the date and time datatypes. The addition of datetime2 increases the storage range and accuracy of date and time storage. The date type allows storage of date only without a time component, while the time type allows storage of the time only without a date component. This is an extremely useful functionality, which until the 2008 release, was missing from the SQL Server typing framework.

Also note the planned future deprecations. The text, ntext, and image datatypes will be replaced by the varchar(max), nvarchar(max), and varbinary(max) datatypes, which provide similar functionality, but are much easier and more efficient to use. Also, the timestamp datatype will be replaced by the rowversion type, which provides equivalent functionality but uses the ANSI standard name.

WHAT DO I DO WITH ALL THESE TYPES?

Because datatyping is prevalent in SQL Server, we will wait to show you the specifics of how these types are used. For now, acquaint yourself with the different types so that you become familiar with their usage and their requirements. We will expect you to be familiar with these types when we mention them in later chapters.

User-Defined Datatypes

To provide greater consistency across multiple tables and stored procedures in your database, you have the option of defining your own datatypes. When you define your own datatypes, it is always in terms of the system-supplied types that we have previously discussed. You cannot pull your own datatypes out of thin air. Each user-defined datatype is simply a specific implementation of an existing datatype for the purpose of consistent reuse within the database application. In ANSI standard terminology, user-defined datatypes are referred to as *domains*.

Why would you want to use a user-defined datatype?

Suppose you had numerous tables that store directory information. For now, assume that these tables store addresses within the United States and each address is required to include the state in which the address is located. There are many ways to store this information. You could use a character field to store the name of the state. You could also store a state abbreviation. The important consideration, however, is that you store the data in a consistent manner, ensuring that you have no stovepipe tables and all of the data can be effectively integrated.

To attain this consistency, one approach is to use a system-defined type that best reflects your desired storage. For example, if you choose to use a two-character code for every state, you could define the state column in each table using the char(2) datatype. This works fine, as long as all the developers who create tables consistently use this type. Another option is to define a custom type that can be used everywhere a state code is defined. In this case, you could define a new datatype called statecode as a char(2) datatype. From this point forward, any time a developer wants to store the two-character abbreviation for a state, she would simply use the statecode type.

The Transact-SQL statement used to create this type is the CREATE TYPE statement. The basic syntax of this statement is

```
CREATE TYPE [schema_name.]type_name
FROM base_type [NULL | NOT NULL]
```

Using the previous example, if we wanted to create a user-defined datatype called statecode as a char(2) and wanted the default table behavior to require a value to be entered for any field of this type, we would use the following syntax:

```
CREATE TYPE dbo.statecode
FROM char(2) NOT NULL;
```

At this point, you could use the `statecode` datatype like any other system-supplied type. You could use this type in the table definition, a variable declaration, a stored-procedure parameter definition, etc. For example, to declare a variable called `@stateval` using your new `statecode` datatype, you would use the following syntax:

```
DECLARE @stateval statecode;
```

A quick word of warning is called for regarding user-defined types. Unlike most artifacts in SQL Server 2008, there is no mechanism to alter any user-defined datatype. The only way to alter the type is to drop and re-create the type. You will not be allowed to drop the type if the type is currently in use in the database. For example, if you were to create a table using the `statecode` datatype and then decide later that you would prefer to use a three-character abbreviation instead of a two-character abbreviation, the resulting process would be complex. You would have to alter the table to change the `statecode` type to a different valid type before you could drop your custom type. After dropping and re-creating the `statecode` type, you could alter the table again to use the new type, but only if the data in the table was compliant with the new type definition.

The purpose of custom datatypes is to create a consistent definition that is unlikely to change over time. Do not expect that you will be able to use custom datatypes to establish a single point of change for your datatype definition. Misunderstanding this point can cause significant work by forcing you to reconstruct the database.

If you do want to drop the custom datatype, use the following syntax:

```
DROP TYPE dbo.statecode;
```

Once a custom datatype is created, you can get information about that type, as well as any system-supplied datatype, by using the `sp_help` system-stored procedure. This is an extremely useful system-stored procedure for the database administrator and the developer, as it can be used to generate information about a wide range of database artifacts. Figure 2.8 demonstrates the use of this stored procedure for the `statecode` datatype and shows its results.

FIGURE 2.8
Getting custom
datatype details

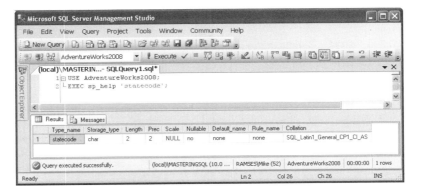

You can also get information about your datatypes by using the SQL Server Management Studio. Using the Object Explorer, expand the tree view as illustrated in Figure 2.9. Once you locate your custom type, double-click the name of the type to open the details window as illustrated in Figure 2.10. Note that in this details view you will not be able to make any changes to the structure of the type; this window is read-only.

FIGURE 2.9

Locating the custom type in the Object Explorer

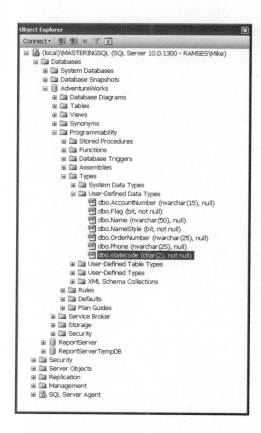

IS THERE AN EASIER WAY?

Although you should get used to using Transact-SQL code for most of your development and administrative duties, the SQL Server Management Studio does provide an interface that you can use to accomplish many of these simple tasks. You can even use this interface to script these artifacts if needed.

When you right-click on your custom datatype in the Object Explorer, the options to delete and rename the type will appear. In addition, you will see an option to create a new user-defined datatype along with the option to script an already existing type if needed. Another useful interface feature is the ability to view dependencies. Although the majority of this functionality is available through the Transact-SQL, it is convenient to be able to perform these operations in the interface as opposed to writing code.

FIGURE 2.10
Viewing the details
of the custom type

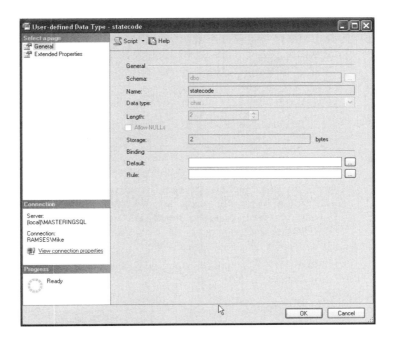

Datatypes are the building blocks of your SQL applications. Getting to know them and learning how to apply them, as well as understanding where they fit into the architectural structure of SQL Server, are critical for success as a SQL Server administrator or developer.

The Bottom Line

Apply your understanding of SQL Server internals to implement good logical architecture. It's not enough to simply understand SQL Server internals; you must also be able to apply the information to the implementation of a stable and extensible architecture. The better you understand how SQL Server works, the more likely you will be to avoid the pitfalls and design problems that often plague the novice administrator.

Master It Your SQL Server seems to be running slowly in response to some queries that process large amounts of data. As you investigate the situation more closely, you notice that there is a significant amount of disk activity. There also appears to be a significant amount of LazyWriter activity. Based on your knowledge of SQL Server internals, where should you look next to identify the problem?

You should evaluate how much memory you have in your server. If you have over 3GB of RAM, you should check your `boot.ini` file to see if the /3GB switch is set. This can give you another 1GB of RAM. If you have over 16GB of RAM but the server is not configured to use AWE, you are not getting the benefit of the extra memory. In this case, remove the /3GB switch (if it is set) because this will prevent the server from seeing memory over 16GB. Make sure that the /PAE switch is set in the `boot.ini` file, enable the Lock Pages in Memory profile setting, and enable AWE in the server configurations.

Utilize the SQL Server catalog to get more information about the system and your application. All of the information that you need about the SQL Server configurations and settings is available if you know where to go to get it. When properly mined, the SQL Server catalog can provide extensive information that can be invaluable as you diagnose, tune, and maintain your servers.

Master It What SQL query would you use to get the following information?

1. Details on the files used in the AdventureWorks database.

2. A list of all the user tables in the AdventureWorks database.

3. A list of all the user tables and their schema names for the AdventureWorks database.

Effectively implement datatypes, including user-defined datatypes. As the foundation for all SQL Server applications, datatypes define how SQL Server will store every piece of information it receives. If this storage is efficient or inefficient, fast or slow to retrieve, or large or small in its storage, you can't always blame SQL Server. Sometimes it's up to you to provide appropriate storage definitions.

Master It Which of the SQL Server datatypes would you use to store each of the following data values?

1. A United States Postal Service zip code with five digits.

2. The first name of a customer.

3. A memo field that stores freeform comments and may contain a lot of data.

4. The total cost of an order.

5. The date of an order (assuming that you process all orders daily and all orders placed on the same day are treated the same).

Chapter 3

Databases, Files, and Resource Management

Creating and managing databases, files, and their resources are required tasks for many administrators and developers working with SQL Server. Before many things can be accomplished with SQL Server, you must create a database to store database objects. In this chapter, we will focus on planning and creating new databases, understanding the options available for database creation, and maintaining databases and their resources on an ongoing basis.

In this chapter, you will learn to:

◆ Create new SQL Server databases

◆ Discover information about existing databases

◆ Manipulate database files and filegroups

◆ Take advantage of database snapshots

Planning a Database

Before we can do anything pertaining to a new application using SQL Server, you must create one or more databases.

Before you create a new database, it's important to have a plan for its implementation on the server. This plan can include many things, such as the estimated size of the database, the placement of data files, and the tolerance for data loss. In this section, we'll examine the mechanics for planning a database and the components and options available for sizing, file placement, and recovery.

Planning for Database Usage

When planning a new database, you need to have at least a basic understanding of what information the database will store and how that information will be used. This will enable you to make better decisions about structuring and sizing the database and its files. A database of constantly changing values will need more space available to keep track of modifications than a database that is mostly queried. It is also important for you to understand the server environment that will be hosting the database. You will want to use all of the resources at hand in the most efficient way possible. Understanding reliability and availability expectations is also incredibly important.

FULLY UTILIZE WHAT YOU HAVE!

It's not unusual to come across SQL Servers that are using only a small percentage of the resources they actually have. One example that comes to mind involves servers that have dedicated volumes for database and log files that aren't used, or are only partially used. When working with a new server that has separate volumes for database and log files, verify that the database files and log files are stored in the appropriate places, and not on the C: drive.

The following query displays a list of all databases, with their data and log file locations.

```
SELECT DB_NAME(database_id) As dbname,
    type_desc,
    name,
    LEFT(physical_name, 2) As DriveLetter
FROM sys.master_files;
```

DATABASE CONCEPT REVIEW

A database in SQL Server consists of one or more data files, and at least one transaction log file, and may also include one or more folders designated for FILESTREAM storage. The data files contain the objects and data within the database. The transaction log keeps track of all modifications to a database and is required for recovery in the event of a system failure.

When a new database is created, the model system database is used as a template. The database settings on the model are used as the defaults for any new databases created on that server. Any user objects that exist in the model will also exist in all new user databases created on the server.

While many databases will contain one data file and one transaction log file, some will contain many files divided into *filegroups.* Filegroups are named collections of files that allow a database developer to place database objects into specific sets of files. Filegroups can be used to improve performance, as well as aid in the back up and recovery of large databases.

DATABASE STORAGE REQUIREMENTS

The size of your database will depend on two things: what you store in it and how much that data is modified. A large amount of space is used by the data files to store all objects in the database. The transaction log is responsible for storing all modifications to data and maintaining transactional integrity. When you are creating a new database, it is important to choose the size of these files appropriately, rather than relying on SQL Server to automatically grow the files as needed.

Planning for Recovery

Every database in SQL Server has a recovery model. The recovery model determines if the transaction log will be allowed to accumulate all of the changes made to the database, or only a limited amount of changes for recovery purposes. The recovery model chosen will impact how the database is backed up and how much data loss can be prevented in the event of a failure.

UNDERSTANDING RECOVERY REQUIREMENTS

In order to choose an appropriate recovery model for a database, it is important to determine its sensitivity to data loss and the availability requirements. Several questions that need to be considered include:

◆ How much data loss is acceptable?

◆ Will the database ever need to be restored to a point in time?

◆ Can the database easily be re-created from other sources?

◆ How often does the data in the database change?

◆ How much space is available for backup storage?

The answers to these questions will impact your decisions when choosing a recovery model and backup strategy.

DATABASE RECOVERY MODELS

The database recovery model determines if the transaction log is allowed to accumulate all changes to a database, a subset of changes, or only enough changes for database recovery. The recovery model also determines if transaction log backups are required to free space for new transactions. In cases where recovery to the last full backup is acceptable, the transaction log can be set to automatically truncate every time a new checkpoint occurs, freeing up log space.

There are three database recovery models: Full, Simple, and Bulk-Logged. In the following text, we will explore the characteristics of each model.

Full Recovery   When using the full recovery model, the transaction log accumulates all changes made to the database. To keep a record of all modifications, the transaction log is periodically backed up. If the transaction log isn't backed up, the log will continue to accumulate changes until no more space is available. Therefore, a log backup strategy is very important. For most installations of SQL Server, this is the default recovery model.

Simple Recovery   When using the simple recovery model, the transaction log accumulates enough information to recover the database in the event of a system failure. Transactions are periodically truncated from the transaction log to free up disk space and shorten the recovery time. When a database is using the simple recovery model, only full and differential backups are allowed. Transaction log backups are not used. Therefore, restoring the database is only possible up to the last full or differential backup. Simple recovery is most appropriate for databases that can easily be re-created in the event of a hardware failure, and where a certain amount of data loss is acceptable.

Bulk-Logged Recovery   The bulk-logged recovery model is similar to the full recovery model, but in it less information about certain bulk operations is written to the transaction log. An advantage of this model is that less space is used for bulk operations, thereby minimizing the amount of space required for backups. Because less information is logged about these operations, only full transaction log backups can be restored; point-in-time recovery is not supported.

As we mentioned, the default recovery model for a new database on SQL Server is full. However, you can change the default recovery model for new databases by changing the recovery model of the model system database.

To view the recovery models of all user databases on a SQL Server instance, use the following query:

```
SELECT name, recovery_model_desc FROM sys.databases;
```

The recovery model may be changed by modifying the properties of the database in Management Studio, or by using the ALTER DATABASE statement. To change the recovery model using SQL Server Management Studio, right-click on the database and choose Properties. You can change the recovery model on the Options page. The syntax for changing the recovery model using the ALTER DATABASE statement is as follows:

```
ALTER DATABASE databasename
  SET RECOVERY { SIMPLE | FULL | BULK_LOGGED };
```

When changing the recovery model, be sure to perform a full database backup to begin the transaction log chain.

Capacity Planning

When you are creating a new database on SQL Server, it is important to have an idea of how much space to allocate. A good practice is to allocate as much space as possible to avoid costly Autogrowth operations as data is loaded into the database. In situations where table structures, row counts, and index structures are known ahead of time, Books Online provides good documentation on estimating the amount of space that will be taken up in the database files by each object.

DATA AND LOG FILE PLACEMENT

It is important to place your database and log files in appropriate locations to maximize performance and improve recoverability. Placing the database and log files on separate volumes improves performance by separating I/O operations.

Database files are best placed on disks with high read and write performance. Another important aspect to consider when placing database files is fault tolerance. RAID (Redundant Array of Independent Disks) is a commonly used component in SQL Server. There are several RAID levels available:

RAID 0: Disk Striping   In RAID 0, data is striped among all of the disks in a set. High performance is achieved because multiple disks are able to handle operations in parallel. Fault tolerance isn't provided by this RAID level, and RAID 0 isn't generally used by itself in database operations for this reason. RAID 0 can be combined with RAID 1 for fault tolerance and improved performance

RAID 1: Disk Mirroring/Disk Duplexing   In RAID 1, data is mirrored to two different disks simultaneously. This provides a separate, redundant copy of all data with very little performance degradation in the event of a failure. This option is a fantastic choice for transaction log storage, because data is generally written to only one area of the transaction log at a time.

RAID 5: Disk Striping with Parity   RAID 5 provides a fault-tolerant storage mechanism but does not need as much disk space as storing a completely separate copy of the data. Fault tolerance is provided using parity calculations.

RAID 1+0 (or 0+1): Disk Mirroring with Striping   RAID 1+0 (or 0+1) is excellent in terms of fault tolerance and performance. However, it is fairly expensive in terms of actual storage space used. While RAID 5 is commonly used for database file storage, keep in mind that parity calculations will impact some of the performance gained by striping the data across several disks.

PLANNING MULTIPLE FILEGROUPS

Database files can be grouped into filegroups for performance and administrative reasons. Filegroups allow an administrator to control the placement of a database object, such as a table or index, into a set of data files. Filegroups also perform the following functions:

- ◆ Allow I/O operations for heavily used tables and indexes to be focused on a specific disk or array.

- ◆ Enable individual database files to be backed up separately from the rest of the database.

- ◆ Enable piecemeal restore, which lets you bring different pieces of the database online in phases during disaster recovery. Piecemeal restore will be covered in more depth in Chapter 9, "Data Recovery."

- ◆ Separate read-only data from the rest of the database.

The primary filegroup exists in every database on SQL Server. The primary filegroup contains all data files that haven't been specifically assigned to a user-defined filegroup, and it is the default filegroup for new database objects. If the primary filegroup becomes full, no other data files can expand, because the primary filegroup contains all of the system tables. For this reason, it is recommended that a user-defined filegroup be set as the default for creating new database objects.

Here are some more hints for using filegroups:

- ◆ Most databases work well with a single data file and a single transaction log file. Make sure you have clear reasons for using additional filegroups in a database.

- ◆ When using multiple files, creating an additional filegroup and setting that filegroup to be the default will allow isolation of the system tables from the rest of the database objects. Make sure to size each file appropriately.

- ◆ Creating filegroups on as many disks and RAID arrays as possible will provide the best performance.

- ◆ Placing tables and indexes into separate filegroups on separate volumes can improve query performance.

In the next section, we will explore how to create databases with multiple filegroups.

Creating Databases

Creating a database is a fairly simple step, assuming you have gathered the appropriate information. There are several methods for creating a database including using Transact-SQL, Management Studio, or SQL Server Management Objects (SMO). Specifying appropriate file locations, sizes, and growth increments is critical to the performance of the database. Depending on the complexity of the database, you also may need to create the appropriate filegroups.

Several script templates are available in the Template Explorer within Management Studio for creating databases. You may also use the Script button at the top of the Create Database window to script out the creation statements based on what was configured in the user interface.

Creating the Database

You can create a new database using either Management Studio or Transact-SQL. When you create a new database, you must specify a name for the database, logical and physical names for each file, and size information for each file. A file may use Autogrowth to automatically grow by a percentage or number of megabytes until it reaches a maximum size. Make sure to specify large Autogrowth increments so that the database doesn't need to grow very often, because this can be an expensive process. The following example shows how to create a new database named SimpleDB with a single database file and single transaction log file.

To create a new database using Management Studio, perform the following steps:

1. Open SQL Server Management Studio and connect the Object Explorer to the database engine on SQL Server where you want to create the database.

2. Right-click the Databases folder and select New Database. The dialog shown in Figure 3.1 appears.

FIGURE 3.1
The New
Database window

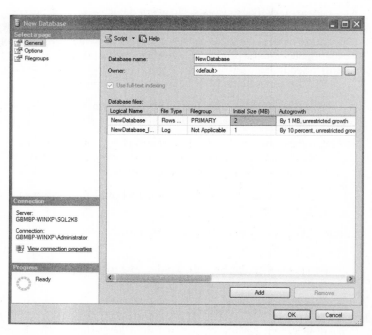

3. Enter the name for the new database in the Database Name text box.

4. If the database will contain user-defined filegroups, select the Filegroups page and add the appropriate filegroup names. Switch back to the general page.

5. Configure the properties for each data and log file by filling in the appropriate information under Database Files.

    A. Set an initial size that will accommodate the information contained in each file.

    B. Set the Autogrowth and Maximum File Size properties for each file by clicking on the ellipsis in the Autogrowth column. The dialog is shown in Figure 3.2.

FIGURE 3.2
The Change Autogrowth window

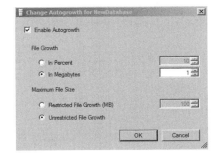

    C. Choose an appropriate path and filename for each file.

6. To add additional data files, click the Add button at the bottom of the window and fill out the appropriate options for the file.

7. Select the Database Options section, and configure the recovery model and other database options, which are covered in detail later in the chapter.

8. Click the OK button to create the new database.

Transact-SQL can also be used to perform the same operations as Management Studio. For many operations, including creating databases, a script can be generated using the Script button at the upper-left area of the Create Database window. After the script is generated, you can click the Cancel button to allow you to view, change, and execute the code.

The example in Listing 3.1 creates a database named SimpleDB with a single database file and log file. In order to run the following examples, you must create the directories C:\SQL\DataFiles and C:\SQL\LogFiles.

LISTING 3.1   Creating a New Database Using Transact-SQL

```
CREATE DATABASE SimpleDB
ON PRIMARY (
   NAME = SimpleDB,
   FILENAME = 'C:\SQL\DataFiles\SimpleDB.mdf',
   SIZE = 10MB,
   MAXSIZE = 20MB,
   FILEGROWTH = 5MB)
LOG ON (
   NAME = SimpleDB_Log,
```

```
FILENAME = 'C:\SQL\LogFiles\SimpleDB.ldf',
SIZE = 2MB,
MAXSIZE = 10MB,
FILEGROWTH = 10%);
```

Another common situation is to create a database with multiple filegroups. The example in Listing 3.2 creates a database with a user-defined filegroup named UserFG, and sets the UserFG filegroup to be the default for new objects.

LISTING 3.2　　　Creating a New Database with Multiple Filegroups Using Transact-SQL

```
CREATE DATABASE FileGroupDB
ON PRIMARY (
  NAME='FGDB_Primary',
  FILENAME='C:\SQL\DataFiles\FileGroupDB.mdf',
  SIZE=5MB,
  MAXSIZE=10MB,
  FILEGROWTH=1MB),
FILEGROUP UserFG (
  NAME='UserFG_data1',
  FILENAME='C:\SQL\DataFiles\FileGroupDB_UserFG.ndf',
  SIZE=5MB,
  MAXSIZE=10MB,
  FILEGROWTH=1MB)
LOG ON (
  NAME='FGDB_log',
  FILENAME='C:\SQL\Logfiles\FileGroupDB.ldf',
  SIZE=5MB,
  MAXSIZE=10MB,
  FILEGROWTH=1MB);
GO
ALTER DATABASE FileGroupDB
  MODIFY FILEGROUP UserFG DEFAULT;
GO
```

UNDERSTANDING FILESTREAM STORAGE

Filestream storage is a new feature of SQL Server 2008 that integrates the database engine with the NTFS file system. Data that is stored in a column that is defined as FILESTREAM can be accessed by retrieving a file handle and using that file handle with Win32 API calls. Columns using the varbinary(max) data type with the FILESTREAM column attribute can provide access to the data using traditional methods or as files on the file system. Applications may modify the files as needed, while continuing to maintain transactional consistency.

For small amounts of data, better performance may be achieved if you can access them directly through the database streaming interfaces. To determine if you should consider using FILESTREAM storage, ask the following questions:

◆ Are the files to be stored larger than one megabyte on average?

◆ Is fast, flexible read access important?

◆ Are you developing applications that use a middle tier for application logic?

To use FILESTREAM storage, you must enable FILESTREAM for the instance, create a filegroup to store FILESTREAM data, and create a table that contains a varbinary(max) column with the FILESTREAM attribute.

To enable FILESTREAM for an instance, use the SQL Server Configuration Manager tool. To access the dialog shown in Figure 3.3, you must right-click on your SQL Server instance, choose Properties, and choose the FILESTREAM tab. In order to access the files from a remote computer, you must enable FILESTREAM for file I/O streaming access and allow remote clients to have streaming access to FILESTREAM data.

FIGURE 3.3
Configuring
FILESTREAM

Once you've enabled FILESTREAM at the instance level, you can then create a new database or alter an existing database to use FILESTREAM by creating a filegroup that specifies a path for storing FILESTREAM data. Listing 3.3 uses the C:\SQL\FILESTREAMData folder for storing data. This folder must not exist when creating the filegroup.

LISTING 3.3   Creating a Database with a FILESTREAM Filegroup

```
CREATE DATABASE FileStreamDB ON PRIMARY
  ( NAME = FileStreamDB_data,
    FILENAME = 'C:\SQL\DataFiles\FileStreamDB_data.mdf',
    SIZE = 10MB,
    MAXSIZE = 50MB,
    FILEGROWTH = 15%),
```

```
FILEGROUP FileStreamData CONTAINS FILESTREAM
  ( NAME = FileStreamData,
    FILENAME = 'C:\SQL\FileStreamData')
LOG ON
  ( NAME = 'FileStreamDB_log',
    FILENAME = 'C:\SQL\LogFiles\FileStreamDB_log.ldf',
    SIZE = 5MB,
    MAXSIZE = 25MB,
    FILEGROWTH = 5MB);
GO
```

To store data using FILESTREAM, you must create a table that contains a unique ROWGUID column that doesn't allow NULL values, as well as a column using the varbinary(max) datatype with the FILESTREAM column attribute. Listing 3.4 shows an example of creating a table that contains a FILESTREAM column and inserting a row.

LISTING 3.4   Creating a Table with a FILESTREAM Column and Inserting Data

```
USE FileStreamDB;
GO
CREATE TABLE FileStreamTable
(FileStreamID UNIQUEIDENTIFIER ROWGUIDCOL NOT NULL UNIQUE,
  FileStreamData varbinary(max) FILESTREAM NOT NULL);
GO

INSERT INTO FileStreamTable
VALUES (NEWID(), CAST('FileStreamData' As VarBinary(max)))
```

To access data using the file system, you must use the PathName() function to retrieve a file path, and use the GET_FILESTREAM_TRANSACTION_CONTEXT() function to retrieve a transaction context for use in your application code. Listing 3.5 shows an example of using the PathName function to retrieve the file path.

LISTING 3.5   Retrieving the Path of FILESTREAM Data Using the PathName Function

```
SELECT FileStreamID, FileStreamData.PathName()
  FROM FileStreamData;
```

For detailed information on using the FILESTEAM feature in your applications and the Win32 API calls used, see Books Online.

Manipulating Database Options

Many database options are available (see Figure 3.4). Most of them are set soon after a database is created and aren't generally changed on a regular basis. Understanding how they affect the different areas of functionality in a database is very important.

FIGURE 3.4
The Database
Options window

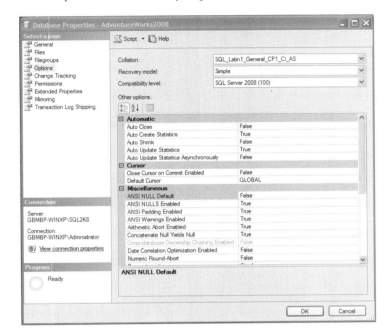

AUTOMATIC OPTIONS

Here are some of the several automatic options available for each database.

Auto Close (AUTO_CLOSE)   Controls if the database and resources are closed after the last user disconnects. The default is OFF for all editions except for SQL Server Express Edition. Turning this on can degrade performance for production databases.

Auto Shrink (AUTO_SHRINK)   This option controls if database files are automatically shrunk at 30-minute intervals and space released when more than 25 percent of the database contains unused space. By default, auto shrink is turned off. This option should be used with caution, due to its database-locking behavior and the possibility that an increase in database size will cause the database files to grow again. A better alternative to using this option is to schedule a shrink operation using the steps detailed later in this chapter.

Index statistics are used by the query optimizer to determine information about the distribution of values within a column. Index statistics and query optimization will be discussed further in Chapter 14, "Indexing Strategies for Query Optimization."

Auto Create Statistics (AUTO_CREATE_STATISTICS)   By default, this option is turned on, and any missing statistics are built during query optimization.

Auto Update Statistics (AUTO_UPDATE_STATISTICS)   When this option is on, any out-of-date statistics are rebuilt during query optimization. Any query that requires a statistics update will wait for the update operation to complete before results are returned.

Auto Update Statistics Asynchronously (AUTO_UPDATE_STATISTICS_ASYNC)   This option allows asynchronous updates to happen. When it is enabled, queries will not wait for statistics to be updated before compiling.

CURSOR OPTIONS

Cursors allow Transact-SQL statements to be executed for each row in a result set. At the database level, several cursor options are available to control their behavior.

Close Cursor On Commit Enabled (CURSOR_CLOSE_ON_COMMIT)   When this option is set to TRUE, an open cursor is closed automatically when a transaction is committed or rolled back. The ANSI SQL-92 specification expects this behavior, but the default for this option is FALSE. Cursors remain open across multiple transactions and close only when the cursor is explicitly closed, or the connection is closed.

Default Cursor (CURSOR_DEFAULT)   The possible settings for this option are GLOBAL and LOCAL. The default is to use global cursors, meaning that a cursor not explicitly declared as local may be referenced in any stored procedure, trigger, or batch that the connection executes.

MISCELLANEOUS OPTIONS

These options control ANSI-compliance behaviors and external access to the database. Two new options worth noting are Date Correlation Optimization and Parameterization options.

Date Correlation Optimization Enabled (DATE_CORRELATION_OPTIMIZATION)   When this option is set to TRUE, SQL Server maintains correlation statistics between any two tables in the database that are linked by FOREIGN KEY constraints and have datetime columns. By default, this option is set to FALSE.

Parameterization (PARAMATERIZATION)   This option determines if queries are parameterized based on behavior of previous versions of SQL Server, or if forced parameterization is used. Forced parameterization can benefit databases that execute many concurrent queries without explicit parameterization used. The default is to use SIMPLE parameterization.

Options that are carried over from prior releases include:

ANSI NULL Default (ANSI_NULL_DEFAULT)   This option determines if a column in a CREATE TABLE statement that doesn't specify nullability will be specified as NULL or NOT NULL by default. When set to TRUE, columns that don't specify nullability will allow null values.

ANSI NULLS Enabled (ANSI_NULLS)   This option determines if any value ever equals NULL. When doing comparisons for NULL values, it is best to use IS NULL. If this option is set to TRUE, comparisons to null are allowed to match values.

ANSI Padding Enabled (ANSI_PADDING)   This option determines if trailing blanks will be padded to the full length of varchar and nvarchar columns. By default, ANSI Padding Enabled is set to FALSE.

ANSI Warnings Enabled (ANSI_WARNINGS)   This option determines if additional warnings are displayed, such as divide by zero, that would otherwise not be displayed. By default, ANSI Warnings is set to FALSE.

Arithmetic Abort Enabled (ARITHABORT)   When this option is set to TRUE, any query that results in an overflow or divide-by-zero error is terminated, and an error message is displayed. The default for this option is FALSE, which will result in only a warning message for these situations.

Concatenate Null Yields Null (CONCAT_NULL_YIELDS_NULL)   When this option is set to TRUE, concatenating a NULL value to a string results in a NULL value. By default, this option is set to FALSE, and the NULL value is treated as an empty string.

Cross-Database Ownership Chaining Enabled (DB_CHAINING)   This option controls if the database can be the source or target of a cross-database ownership chain. This setting is only recognized when the Cross DB Ownership Chaining server option is set to 0 (OFF); otherwise all databases on the instance can participate in cross-database ownership chaining.

Numeric Round-Abort (NUMERIC_ROUNDABORT)   When this option is set to TRUE, any expression that results in a loss of precision generates an error. By default, this option is set to FALSE, and losses of precision do not generate error messages. The result is rounded to the precision of the column storing the result.

Quoted Identifiers Enabled (QUOTED_IDENTIFIER)   This option determines if strings surrounded by double quotes are treated as object identifiers, or as string literals. By default, this option is set to FALSE, and items surrounded by double quotes are treated as string literals. When true, items in double quotes are treated as object identifiers. Note that regardless of this setting, square brackets can always be used to delimit an object identifier.

Recursive Triggers Enabled (RECURSIVE_TRIGGERS)   This option controls if a trigger defined on a table that modifies itself can cause the same trigger to fire again. By default, this option is set to FALSE.

Trustworthy (TRUSTWORTHY)   This option determines if stored procedures and user-defined functions can use an impersonation context to access resources outside of the database. By default, stored procedures and user-defined functions executing in an impersonation context cannot access resources outside of the database.

RECOVERY OPTIONS

The two database recovery options are the database recovery model discussed earlier and the Page Verify option. The Page Verify option controls the type of verification method used when reading and writing pages to disk. There are three possible options to select for Page Verify:

CHECKSUM   When Page Verify is set to this, checksums are used to find incomplete page writes caused by disk I/O errors. The checksum is computed over the entire contents of the data page and stored in the page header when it is written to disk. When the page is subsequently read from disk, the checksum is recomputed and compared to the value stored in the page header. If there is a mismatch, error message 824 is raised. Any I/O errors detected by the operating system are logged using error message 823.

TORN_PAGE_DETECTION   When Page Verify is set to this, a bit is reversed for each 512-byte sector in a database page when the page is written to disk. If the bit is in the wrong state when the page is later read, the page was written incorrectly, and a torn page is detected.

NONE   When Page Verify is set to this, future data pages written won't use checksums or reserved bits, and pages will not be verified when read, even if checksums or reserved bits exist.

State Options

This category contains options that control aspects of the database state. These include:

Database Read-Only   This option determines if the database is considered read only. Changing this option affects the database state.

Encryption Enabled (ENCRYPTION)   This option determines if transparent data encryption is enabled. Data encryption is covered in detail in Chapter 13, "SQL Server Data Security."

Restrict Access (MULTI_USER, SINGLE_USER, RESTRICTED_USER)   The default access restriction for a database is MULTI_USER, which allows all users with appropriate permissions to access the database. When this option is set to SINGLE_USER, only the database owner can access the database. When this option is set to RESTRICTED_USER, only members of the db_owner, dbcreator, or sysadmin roles can access the database.

More detailed discussion of manipulating database and file states is covered in the next section.

Managing Databases, Files, and Filegroups

Managing a database and its files has many aspects. This section will provide the how and why of each of the operations you will likely encounter. Nearly all of these operations can be performed using Management Studio or Transact-SQL.

Altering a Database

Altering a database allows us to change many aspects of the database after it has been created. This may involve changing database-level options, expanding data or log files, or even adding additional files. Most of the changes made to the database's Properties window (Figure 3.5) in Management Studio results in an ALTER DATABASE statement being generated. Always remember that you can script the changes you have made in the Database Properties window using the Script button at the top.

Changing Database and File States

A database is always in a single state, hopefully ONLINE most of the time. Other common database states include OFFLINE, RESTORING, SUSPECT, or EMERGENCY. You can view the current state of the databases on a SQL Server by querying the state_desc column of the sys.databases catalog view.

Management Studio allows you to take a database offline or bring it back online by right-clicking on the database and viewing the Tasks submenu. You may also use the following syntax:

```
USE master;
ALTER DATABASE SimpleDB SET [ OFFLINE | ONLINE ];
```

FIGURE 3.5

The Database
Properties window
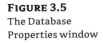

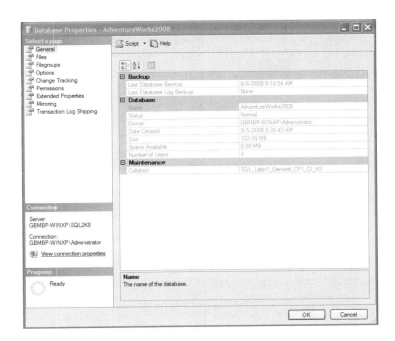

A database may be put into EMERGENCY state for troubleshooting. By setting a database to the EMERENCY state, the database is marked read only, and access is limited to members of the sysadmin server role. A database marked as SUSPECT can be changed to the EMERGENCY state to allow an administrator to further examine the data that is available.

A database can be observed in the RESTORING state when a restore is taking place, and there are more backups to be applied. Backup and Restore operations will be discussed further in Chapter 9.

Individual files also have a state tracked independently of the database. The state of individual database files may be viewed by querying the sys.database_files or sys.master_files catalog views. Use caution when setting a file to the OFFLINE state, as the file may only be set online by restoring that file from a backup.

CHANGING DATABASE FILE LOCATIONS

Sometimes, you will encounter databases that have files in inappropriate locations. As a consultant, I've seen many databases with files residing on the system drive of the SQL Server, even when better locations are available. Moving these database files involves taking the database offline until the files are moved into their new location. Keep in mind that the following procedure is intended for locations on the same server.

To move one or more files for a user database to a different location, use the following steps:

1. Take the user database offline:

   ```
   ALTER DATABASE db_name SET OFFLINE;
   ```

2. Move the files to a new location.

3. For each file that was moved, run the following code:

```
ALTER DATABASE db_name
  MODIFY FILE (
   NAME = logical_name
   FILENAME = 'X:\Path\File.Name' );
```

4. Bring the user database back online:

```
ALTER DATABASE db_name SET ONLINE;
```

The steps for moving most of the system databases are similar, with the exception of the master database. Please refer to Books Online for the process of moving system databases.

ATTACHING AND DETACHING DATABASES

The attach and detach features allow you to move or copy databases between instances and servers, as well as remove a database from an instance without deleting the associated data and log files. Detaching a database removes references to the database from the master system database, but does not delete database or log files. After a database has been detached, the associated files can be moved or copied to their new location, and attached. Attaching a database adds a reference to the database and associated files to the master database on the SQL Server instance.

Before detaching a database, verify that the following conditions have been met:

◆ No database snapshots exist for the database about to be detached. (Database snapshots are covered in more detail later in the chapter.)

◆ The database is not being mirrored.

◆ The database is not being replicated.

◆ The database is not marked as suspect. (In order to detach a suspect database, you must first put the database into EMERGENCY mode. For more information, see the "Changing Database and File States" section earlier in this chapter.)

Detaching a database may be accomplished using SQL Server Management Studio, or by using the sp_detach_db system stored procedure. To detach a database using SQL Server Management Studio, follow these steps:

1. Open SQL Server Management Studio, and in the Object Explorer view, connect to the server that contains the database you would like to detach. Expand the Databases folder, and find the database to detach.

2. Right-click on the database, and choose Tasks ➤ Detach from the context menu.

3. In the Detach Database window (shown in Figure 3.6), choose the appropriate options:

◆ The Drop Connections checkbox will drop all connections to the database before performing the drop operation.

◆ The Update Statistics checkbox is equivalent to setting the skipchecks parameter of `sp_detach_db` to TRUE. Updating statistics makes the database easier to use with read-only media, otherwise you don't need the update.

◆ The Keep Full Text Catalogs checkbox is equivalent to the KeepFulltextIndexFile parameter of the `sp_detach_db` system stored procedure. By default, full text indexes are maintained as a part of the database.

FIGURE 3.6

The Detach Database dialog

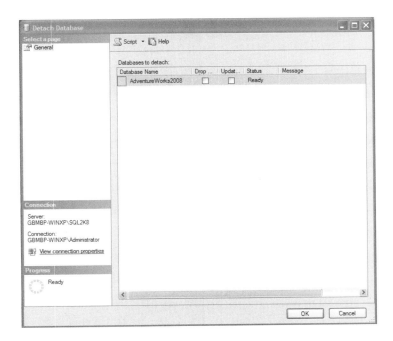

Attaching a database may be accomplished in several ways. Using the CREATE DATABASE FOR ATTACH syntax is the recommended way. The system stored procedure `sp_attach_db` is provided for backward compatibility, and it will be removed in a later version of SQL Server. To attach a database using SQL Server Management Studio, follow these steps:

1. Open SQL Server Management Studio, and in the Object Explorer view, connect to the server that you would like to attach the database to.

2. Right-click the Databases folder, and choose Attach from the context menu.

3. In the Attach Databases window (shown in Figure 3.7), click the Add button, and choose the primary data file of the database you would like to attach.

4. Verify that any secondary database files and log files are in the appropriate paths.

5. Click OK to attach the database.

FIGURE 3.7
The Attach Data-
base window

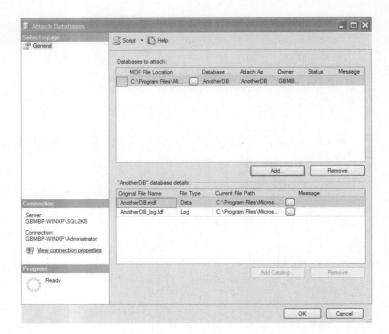

Growing and Shrinking Databases and Files

Database file size needs to be maintained over time. File size can be maintained automatically using database features such as automatic growth and auto shrink. The automatic growth and auto shrink options are covered earlier in this chapter under the section setting database options.

In many cases, greater control over database and file size is needed than the automatic options provide. In order to provide this control, database and file sizes can be managed manually. This section will examine the methods for manually managing database and file sizes by using SQL Server Management Studio and by executing Transact-SQL statements.

INCREASING THE SIZE OF A DATABASE

Manually increasing the size of a database is a simple process. You may increase the size of existing files or add new secondary data files to a database in order to increase the size. Adding additional database files allows a database to expand across several volumes.

Instead of writing all the data to the first file until it is full, SQL Server fills each file in a filegroup proportionally to the amount of free space in the file. When all database files are full, each data file in the filegroup is expanded in a round-robin manner.

To increase the size of a database using Management Studio, use the following steps:

1. Open SQL Server Management Studio, and in the Object Explorer view, connect to the server that contains the database you would like to manage. Work your way down to the Databases folder.

2. Right-click the database you would like to modify and select Properties from the short-cut menu.

3. Choose the Files page from the upper-left corner of the window.

4. Make the required changes as follows:

◆ To expand existing files, change the Initial Size (MB) to a larger number.

◆ To add a new database file, click the Add button at the bottom of the screen, and fill out the required information for the new file, including the initial size and location.

5. Click the OK button to make the change.

When changing the size of a database file using the Database Properties window, the size may only be increased beyond the current size. Inputting a value smaller than the current size will result in an error. The process for shrinking database files is covered later in this chapter.

Database files' properties may also be changed using the ALTER DATABASE Transact-SQL statement. The Transact-SQL statements in Listing 3.6 increase the size of the TestDB_Primary device to 50 megabytes, and add a secondary database file to the TestDB database:

LISTING 3.6   Manipulating Database Files

```
ALTER DATABASE SimpleDB
  MODIFY FILE (
    NAME=SimpleDB,
    SIZE=100MB )
GO
ALTER DATABASE SimpleDB
  ADD FILE (
    NAME=SimpleDB_Secondary,
    FILENAME='C:\SQL\DataFiles\SimpleDB_Secondary.ndf',
    SIZE=50MB,
    MAXSIZE=100MB,
    FILEGROWTH=25MB );
```

When modifying existing files, other attributes such as MAXSIZE and FILEGROWTH can also be modified for each file. To verify that your changes have occurred, you can query the sys.database_files catalog view.

SHRINKING DATABASES AND DATABASE FILES

As data is removed from a database, the space used remains allocated to the database files. Shrinking a database allows free space that is no longer used by a file to be released to the operating system. Leaving adequate space for growth in a database is important. If you don't expect the database to reclaim the available space in the near future, it is best not to shrink it. Excessive shrinking of a database can lead to file fragmentation, and to an increased number of automatic growth operations if the database is configured for automatic growth.

To shrink an entire database, use these steps:

1. Open SQL Server Management Studio, and connect the Object Explorer to the server that contains the database you would like to shrink. Expand the Databases folder.

2. Right-click the database you would like to shrink, and select Tasks ➤ Shrink ➤ Database from the context menu to display the Shrink Database dialog shown in Figure 3.8.

FIGURE 3.8
The Shrink Database dialog

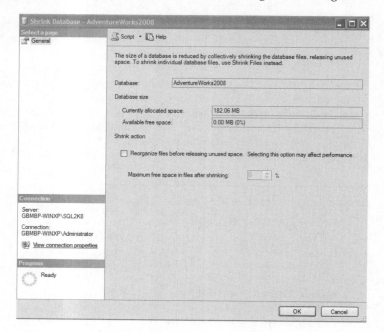

3. Examine the amount of currently allocated space and available free space to determine if you really want to shrink the database.

4. To reorganize the data pages and move them to the beginning of the file, select the Reorganize Files Before Releasing Unused Space checkbox. Leaving this checkbox cleared is equivalent to using the DBCC SHRINKDATABASE statement with the TRUNCATEONLY option, meaning the size is reduced without moving any data.

5. If the Reorganize Files Before Releasing Unused Space checkbox is selected, you may specify the maximum percent of free space remaining in the database files.

6. Click OK to begin the shrink operation.

To shrink an individual database file, use these steps:

1. Open SQL Server Management Studio, and connect the Object Explorer to the server that contains the database with the files you would like to shrink. Expand the databases folder.

2. Right-click on the database with the file you would like to shrink, and select Tasks ➢ Shrink ➢ Files from the context menu to show the Shrink File dialog shown in Figure 3.9.

FIGURE 3.9
The Shrink File dialog

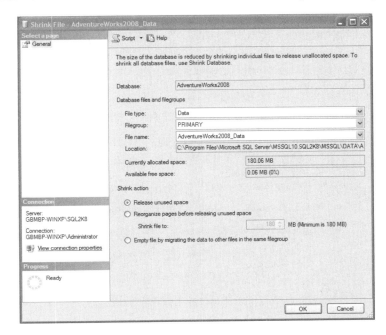

3. Select the file you would like to shrink using the File type, Filegroup, and Filename menus. Examine the amount of currently allocated space and available free space to verify the action you are taking.

4. Choose the appropriate shrink action:

Release Unused Space   Truncates free space from the end of the file without moving data pages. This is equivalent to using the DBCC SHRINKDATABASE with TRUNCATEONLY statement.

Reorganize Pages Before Releasing Unused Space   Reorganizes data pages by moving them to the beginning of the file. After selecting this option, you may select the desired file size in the Shrink File To selection area. This is equivalent to using the DBCC SHRINKFILE statement and specifying the amount of free space you would like left in the target file.

Empty File (By Migrating the Data to Other Files in the Same Filegroup)   Migrates the data contained in the data file to other files in the same filegroup. This is equivalent to using the DBCC SHRINKFILE with EMPTYFILE option. This operation prepares the file to be removed with an ALTER DATABASE statement.

5. Click the OK button to begin the Shrink File operation.

To shrink a database file using Transact-SQL, use the DBCC SHRINKFILE command.
To shrink a database using Transact-SQL, use the DBCC SHRINKDATABASE command.

Creating Database Snapshots

A database snapshot is a read-only, static view of a database. Database snapshots were introduced in the Enterprise edition of SQL Server 2005. A database snapshot can use considerably less space than a separate read-only copy of a database.

Database snapshots work by capturing changes as they are made to the source database. Only the modified page values are stored in the files used for the database snapshot. This process is accomplished using sparse files and copy-on-write technology present in the NTFS file system.

As the source database's pages are modified, SQL Server saves the original data pages in a sparse file using a copy-on-write process. This ensures that only changed database pages take up physical space on disk for the snapshot, and this can considerably reduce the amount of storage used in comparison to a separate, read-only copy of a database. The amount of storage needed can very significantly based on the age of the snapshot and the volume of changed data in the source database.

Some common scenarios for using database snapshots include:

- Maintaining historical data for reporting purposes

- Using a mirrored database created for availability purposes for reporting

- Protecting data against administrative or user error

- Managing a consistent test environment where changes can easily be rolled back

Database snapshots can introduce some important limitations on the source database as well as the snapshot itself.

- Performance is reduced due to increased I/O from the copy-on-write operation that occurs when data pages are modified.

- The source database may not be dropped unless all snapshots are also dropped.

- The database snapshot must reside on the same instance as the source database.

- Database files must be stored on an NTFS partition.

CREATING A DATABASE SNAPSHOT

In order to create a database snapshot, you must use the Transact-SQL CREATE DATABASE...AS SNAPSHOT OF statement. While you can view database snapshots in SQL Server Management Studio, you cannot create snapshots from within the user interface; you must use Transact-SQL. When creating a new snapshot, you must specify a new path and filename for the logical name of every database file of the source database.

The example shown in Listing 3.7 creates a snapshot of the AdventureWorks database. Note that because snapshots are read only, o log file is specified. All logical database files must be specified, or an error will result.

LISTING 3.7   Creating a Snapshot of the AdventureWorks Database

```
CREATE DATABASE AdventureWorks_ss0800
ON (
  NAME = AdventureWorks2008_Data,
  FILENAME = 'C:\SQL\DataFiles\AdventureWorks_data_0800.ss' )
AS SNAPSHOT OF AdventureWorks2008;
```

MANAGING DATABASE SNAPSHOTS

After creating a database snapshot, it may be queried like a normal database. When examining the properties of each snapshot file using Windows Explorer, it is important to note that the reported size and size on disk are different, as shown in Figure 3.10.

FIGURE 3.10
Windows Explorer
file properties of a
database snapshot

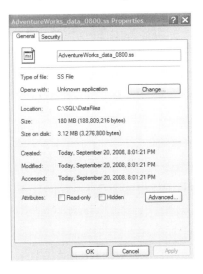

An alternative method to view the actual space used for a file in a database snapshot is to use the `fn_virtualfilestats table-valued` function, and examine the BytesOnDisk column. The maximum size of a database snapshot can be viewed by querying either the `sys.database_files` or `sys.master_files` catalog views.

Dropping a database snapshot is similar to dropping a database.

A database may be quickly reverted to the state stored in a snapshot by issuing a RESTORE DATABASE...FROM SNAPSHOT command as shown in Listing 3.8, so long as only one snapshot of the database exists.

LISTING 3.8   Reverting to a Database Snapshot

```
RESTORE DATABASE AdventureWorks2008
  FROM DATABASE_SNAPSHOT = AdventureWorks_ss0800;
```

A successful revert operation will automatically rebuild the transaction log, so it is recommended that a transaction log backup be taken before a revert operation.

The Bottom Line

Create new databases.   Creating new databases is a common and fundamental operation. Understanding what happens when a new database is created is a critical step.

> **Master It**   What system database is used as a template when creating a new database on SQL Server? How could you create an object that would exist in any new database on the SQL Server?

Plan databases.   Adequate planning for user databases is very important. From choosing the appropriate recovery model to properly placing files, these choices will prepare the database for future operations.

> **Master It**   What is the most appropriate recovery model for a mission-critical database that needs the ability to restore to a point in time?

Discover information about existing databases.   There are many ways to retrieve information about existing databases and their files. Management Studio can be an easy place to view information about individual database options; however, it's important to remember that this information can be retrieved using system catalog views.

> **Master It**   What catalog view displays information about every database and database file on the server, including sizes and file options?

Chapter 4

Tables and CRUD Operations

Now that you have seen how to create and manage databases and files, it's time to take the next step and actually put something in the database. Obviously, a database is a big container—that's all, a container just begging for something to be put inside. Generally, we put two kinds of artifacts into a database: tables and indexes. All of the other artifacts (such as stored procedures, functions, and views) are actually stored in system table structures. A table is the most fundamental component that you will work with in SQL Server.

Tables, however, are just containers, and the ultimate goal is to get data into the tables for storage and then manipulate that data at will. The table defines the structure that you will use to store the data, and the Data Manipulation Language (DML) code will give you the power to make that data do anything you like. CRUD stands for Create, Read, Update, and Delete, which is essentially the full range of what you will be able to do with your data.

In this chapter, you will learn to:

◆ Plan and implement appropriate normalization strategies

◆ Design and create tables using all of the SQL Server table features

◆ Write simple to complex SELECT statements for returning data to the client

◆ Perform data modification operations using the INSERT, UPDATE, DELETE, and MERGE SQL DML statements

Designing Data Storage

In 1970 when E. F. Codd released his famous paper, "A Relational Model of Data for Large Shared Data Banks," the database world began to slowly change forever. By the early 1980s, relational database design became more fashionable. Today, we almost take it for granted. With the host of benefits that relational design can bring to a large database management system, relational design today is the assumption rather than the exception.

Still, if you ask two database developers for their definitions of what constitutes a relational database, you will probably get two different answers—maybe even three! Relational data structure has its advantages and disadvantages, but today it is generally accepted as the preferred model for large-scale data storage and manipulation. The most fundamental advantage is that it eliminates data redundancy without sacrificing the "any data anywhere" benefit of relational storage. A larger amount of meaningful data can be packed into less space because nothing is repeated. Optimizing storage by eliminating redundancies is called *normalization*.

Although relational data structure is still considered the industry-preferred model, fully normalized data does have its drawbacks. A fully normalized data structure can suffer terribly in select performance when compared to nonrelational data storage due to its dependencies on *join operations*. When data is needed from multiple tables, the tables must be joined to access the data. The process of resolving joins can be time-consuming and can adversely affect the performance of the entire database. However, when data is updated, the data modifications are confined to a single point of change. This elimination of data redundancy increases the ability to maintain data integrity.

Implementing a Normalized Design

Normalization is the process of removing all redundancy from your data storage. When data is fully normalized, there is no repetition of data across tables with the exception of the key that is used to join the tables. The advantages of data normalization can be enormous in terms of space and cost savings, as well as the increased efficiency with which data can be updated and maintained.

In this section, you will look at the rules of normalization, otherwise known as the *normal forms*. The normal forms, or rules of normalization, define exactly what information can be placed in each table and how this information relates to the fields defined as primary keys. Entire books have been written on the subject of normalization; this section will simply hit the highlights and illustrate the first three normal forms, which are the most critical in preserving the integrity of your data.

SKIP IT IF YOU MUST

If you are a professional developer, this discussion of database design and normalization may seem a little simplistic. You may be able to design databases in your sleep. If that is the case, feel free to catch a quick nap while we review these concepts for the professional database administrators in the group who do not develop databases as part of their jobs. When the topic turns to database backup operations in a later chapter, the administrators will get a few minutes to nap while the database developers learn some new tricks.

Before we turn to the rules of normalization, let's review a few terms that we will be using.

Entity   A topic or subject that you will describe. For example, an entity can be a customer, an order, or a check. Entities are created in databases by creating tables.

Field   An attribute of an entity. If the entity is a check, its attributes would include check number, date, amount, payee, etc. Because entities are represented in databases as tables, attributes are the fields of the table.

Record   An instance of an entity. Assuming again that the entity is a check, every check you write would be an instance of the entity. When these checks are entered into a check register, each line of the register represents an individual check or in other words, an instance of the check entity.

Using the check entity as an example, the register is actually a table. It has records (or rows) that represent each check written, and it has fields (or columns) that define the individual attributes of each check.

THE FIRST NORMAL FORM

The first normal form dictates that *every instance of an entity referenced in the table will be unique and that all of the fields in the table will contain data that is nondecomposable.* Nondecomposable data is data that cannot be broken down into smaller pieces. The first normal form sounds complicated, but it can be broken down very easily into some component parts.

First, every record in the table must be unique. This means that every time you enter information about an instance of an entity, that instance will be unique to the table. The easiest way to identify a record as unique is to declare a primary key on the table. In fact, this is just what the first normal form requires.

Primary keys must comply with a number of different conditions. Any data entered into a primary key field anywhere in that table must be unique in that table and no duplications can occur. The primary key must not allow null entries. There must be a primary key entry for every record. Although not required, it is more efficient and, therefore, preferable if the primary key is a small numeric value.

The second component of the first normal form is that all data entered in the table must be nondecomposable. Consider, for example, a field in the table called Name in which we enter the first name, middle initial, and last name of every customer. Such a field would be a violation of the first normal form because it could be broken down into smaller pieces.

If you have created a field called Name, you can still sort by either first or last name all you have to do is parse the name value for every single record and pull out only the information with which you want to work. Then you can write a custom procedure to sort, search, or otherwise manipulate the data you have extracted. However, this is a high-overhead solution.

If you break the field down into pieces, you shouldn't have to go through as much effort to re-create the field in its entirety. Fortunately for us, SQL Server assumes that you will be working with nondecomposable data as a general rule, and the Transact-SQL language includes the mechanisms that can reassemble data.

This nondecomposable data rule applies to records as well as individual fields. Sometimes it is better to break a single record into multiple records to avoid decomposable data at the record level. For example, assume that in your Order table you have a field for order number, order date, customer number, and then a series of fields called product1, product2, product3, and so forth that represent all of the individual products requested in a single order. This structure is actually a violation of the first normal form because the record itself is decomposable. Figure 4.1 shows an example of the structure. Note that the Product table is aliased three times to support each of the three relationships.

FIGURE 4.1

Violation of the first normal form

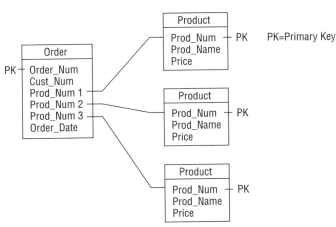

This situation can be rectified in a couple of different ways. One way is to change the primary key on the Order table to a composite key of the two fields that includes the order number and an invoice line number. The composite key will then represent a single line item in the invoice. Although this will solve the initial problem, it could be argued that this violates our entity relationship model because obviously now we are treating an order and the line item within an order as individual entities. Figure 4.2 illustrates this approach.

FIGURE 4.2
Composite key
solution

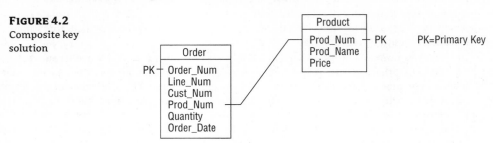

The most appropriate solution to this problem would be to create a many-to-many relationship between the Order table and the Product table. Creating this type of relationship requires another table to be created to hold the detail between the Order table and the Product table. In the example in Figure 4.3, it is called the Invoice_line table. This type of table, often called an *association table,* represents a single line item on an invoice. Note that the primary key on this table is a composite of the invoice number and the product number, a combination that will never be repeated.

FIGURE 4.3
Many-to-many
solution

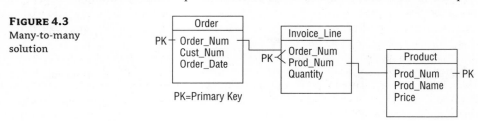

THE SECOND NORMAL FORM

The second normal form states that *every field in the table should relate to the primary key field in its entirety.* This is primarily an issue when tables have composite primary keys consisting of multiple fields. If a composite key is present, then every field in that table must relate to all fields comprising that key, not just to one or some.

In our previous example, we created a table called Invoice_line that held a many-to-many relationship between the Order table and the Product table. The entity being described by this table is a single line item on invoice. Referring back to Figure 4.3, notice that the Price field is being stored in the Product table and not in the Invoice_line table. If the Invoice_line table defines a single line item in an invoice, why isn't the Price field held in this table?

The answer relates to the second normal form. If the Price field were included in the Invoice_line table, that would be a violation of the second normal form. This is because the price of the product is really an attribute of the product itself, not an attribute of the entire order or a line item in an order. If the Price field were to be included in the Invoice_line table, then that field would relate only to one of the fields in the composite key, namely the Prod_num field. This is a textbook violation of this rule.

THAT DEPENDS ON WHAT YOU MEAN BY PRICE

Where a field is defined can often depend on how that data is used and interpreted. For example, in the previous illustration the Price field is included in the Product table because the assumption is that product price is fixed for each product. This assumption may not always be true. What if the price the customer pays for the product depends on something else, such as the number of units ordered?

In this case, there may actually be two different prices that you need to store. While the Product table stores the base price for the product, the Invoice_line table may store another price that is inclusive of discounts, customer promotions, and so forth. To avoid ambiguity, you should use a different column name in the Invoice_line table, such as Extended_price or Discounted_price, to indicate that the price paid on this order line item might be different than the base price stored in the Product table. This would not be a violation of the second normal form because the value of Extended_price would be specific to the order line item (not the product itself).

THE THIRD NORMAL FORM

The third normal form states that *any non-key field in a table must relate to the primary key of the table and not to any other field*. The primary key in this case may either be a composite or single field key. This form forces all data found in a table to relate exclusively to the entity that the table describes.

Assume that in our previous business model example, customers will only order a single product from the firm. This restriction eliminates the need for a many-to-many relationship and an Invoice_line table. In this scenario, all of the information needed to track an order is found in the Order table.

In Figure 4.4, there is a violation of the third normal form. Note that the Price field is included in the Order table. As discussed previously, the price relates to the product, not the order. Although the Prod_num field is found in the table, it acts as a foreign key field in relation to the Product table, not as a primary key field. Because every field in the table must relate to the primary key field and not any other field, the Price field violates the third normal form.

FIGURE 4.4
Violation of the
third normal form

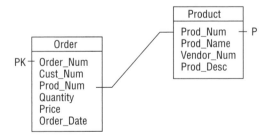

ADVANTAGES AND DISADVANTAGES OF NORMALIZATION

Although some of the advantages and disadvantages of normalization were alluded to earlier in this chapter, they are definitely worth repeating. Normalized data structures can have significant advantages over non-normalized structures as they relate to data entry and data maintenance. Yet these same structures can suffer from some prohibitive performance problems.

On the positive side of the normalization picture is that it completely removes data redundancy, therefore optimizing storage space on the data source. With redundancy virtually eliminated, you can use the space to store more data instead of restoring the same data redundantly in more than one place. The maintenance tasks also get much easier when you have a truly normalized design. Because there is no data redundancy, you'll never have to change a value in more than one place. If your data is extremely volatile, this is an advantage that usually outweighs all possible disadvantages.

Although there are a number of good things about normalized data structures, they still have some weaknesses. The primary weakness of normalization lies in its strength: the subdividing of information into single-entity tables. This separation of information requires multiple tables to be related to get all of the information that you need. These joins can be quite costly.

SQL Server has a variety of mechanisms that it can use to resolve join operations, but the most common of these is *nested looping*. Nested looping arranges the joined tables sequentially so that whenever a qualifying record is found in an outside table, an inside table is scanned to find all matching records. For example, assume that you are joining two tables together. Assume further that a total of 25 qualifying records will be extracted from the outside table. This means that for every qualifying record of the outside table, you must scan the inside table once to find all matching and qualifying records. If there are a total of 25 qualifying records in the outside table, there will be a total of 26 accesses to the set of tables: 1 on the outside and 25 on the inside.

Although indexes and join orders can make this process much more efficient, it is still a time-consuming and I/O-intensive process. If joining two tables is troublesome, imagine what will happen when you start joining three and four tables. More tables simply multiply this effect, making it nearly impossible to join large numbers of tables with any reasonable performance.

Denormalization

Even if you have taken the time to build a normalized database your old college professor would be proud of, it still may not be perfect. The performance problems caused by a normalized design might be far too substantial for you to accept. In this case, it is time to start considering various approaches to denormalization. Denormalization is the process of deliberately breaking the rules of normalization in the hope that you will gain some performance benefits. There is no magic ticket to denormalization. It is a process of cost-benefit analysis, testing and retesting, and constant reevaluation.

Of course, every denormalization will have costs to maintain. These must be considered before a normalized or denormalized design is chosen. You should consider those denormalized designs only when the benefits of denormalization outweigh the cost of maintaining the denormalization.

DUPLICATE ATTRIBUTES

There are numerous approaches to denormalization. One approach is to provide redundant attributes and tables. In the previous examples, you determined that placing the Price field in the Order table violated the third normal form. If you follow the rules exactly, you will need to do a join from the Order table to the Product table to access pricing information for the order products.

This may be a time-consuming JOIN statement if you are constantly running reports to calculate the total cost of goods sold. You might consider placing the Price field in the Order table as well as the Product table. Although this violates the rules, the benefits are obvious. You no longer have to perform a JOIN statement to access price information for ordered products.

The maintenance costs of this approach include updating duplicate attributes when the original attributes are updated. Although this can be handled very easily using procedures that will update all required fields in all tables, it may significantly slow the update process if the attributes are modified on a regular basis. It is best if duplicate attributes are nonvolatile.

DUPLICATE KEYS

As discussed earlier, every table that you add to the JOIN list multiplies exponentially the number of scans required. The fewer scans required, the less I/O will be needed to satisfy the data request. Providing redundant keys is one way to reduce the number of joins.

Take a look at another join scenario. Figure 4.5 illustrates an Employee table that is related to a Customer table. Each customer has one employee assigned to him or her. The Customer table is then related to an Order table that shows the orders made by the customer. To generate a report about the orders sold by an employee, a join would have to be made between all three tables.

The costs associated with this approach mirror those incurred with the duplicate-attribute approach. When every key value changes, the value must be updated in all tables. Once again, this approach is best when used with nonvolatile values.

FIGURE 4.5

Normalized three-table join

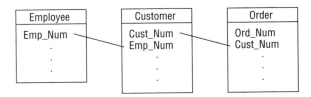

Although it will require breaking some rules, you can reduce the total number of joins required to execute this query. Including the Emp_num field in the Order table will provide a direct relationship between employees and orders. Identifying the orders placed by every employee's customers will be more efficient because you won't need to go through the Customer table if customer information is not needed.

TABLE PARTITIONING

The entity relationship model and the rules of normalization both specify that only one table per entity should exist inside a database. This is a perfectly reasonable requirement; however, this means that often tables become quite large and they may contain a significant amount of data that is not frequently used. If the data can be broken into multiple tables, a query will have to wade through much less data to find what is actually desired. These tables can be broken apart in two ways: either by row or by column partitioning.

If you regularly work with every record in the table, but you tend to use only a few fields of the table, you may consider partitioning the table by column. Using this strategy, you will create two tables, each with a different structure. Although they will both contain the primary key value for each record, the other fields will be placed in the tables based solely on their frequency of access. One table will have the fields that are accessed on a regular basis, and the other table will contain less-frequently accessed fields. Because each of these tables contains the primary key, they can be easily related to reconstruct the entire table if needed.

Perhaps you have a very large table full of both current and historical information. When these types of tables are present in a database, the current information is usually accessed quite frequently and the historical data is accessed much less often. This situation may lend itself to breaking down the table by rows.

To accomplish this, create two identical tables, each with every field being tracked. The current information will be placed in one table and the historical information will be placed in the other table. Periodically, data will be moved from the current table to the historical table as the data ages. Using a UNION statement to reconstruct the original table, you can easily reassemble the data.

PARTITIONING MADE EASY

Archiving data into multiple tables based on frequency of use is such a common and useful technique that SQL Server 2008 includes significant enhancements to make this process easier. Rather than requiring you to create multiple tables, SQL Server 2008 allows you to define multiple partitions on a single table and define segmentation logic that helps automate the process of data archival. This will be discussed in greater detail later in this chapter in the section on table partitioning.

As you proceed with your database designs, be sure to consider normalization and denormalization strategies as appropriate. Design your application for performance, but also design for extensibility and maintainability. Remember that a poorly designed data structure can have far-reaching consequences. Once bad designs are rolled into production, they can be very difficult to refactor without some pain. Always consider the future needs of your designs and your expected performance metrics before making the final decisions on your database design proposals.

Creating and Dropping SQL Server Tables

Now that we have walked through the design concepts, it's time to take a look at the mechanics of creating tables. You have two options for creating tables. You can either perform the action by using Transact-SQL code, or you can use the graphical user interface provided by the SQL Server Management Studio tool. We will show you both approaches. As you have probably already noticed, most operations in SQL Server can be accomplished in the same two ways, so from this point out, we will show you both methods unless there is a particular task that can only be completed using one approach or the other.

THIS IS ONLY A TEST

If you are going to follow along with any of the examples in this book, it is a good idea to install a separate instance of SQL Server specifically for that purpose. This way the configuration changes you make to the server will not affect any of the other work you are doing or (ouch!) your production servers. Give yourself a playground where you will not be concerned about the impact of your actions on anything else. In this chapter, we will use the database name "SandboxDB," but you can replace that with any name that reminds you that this is the database you are using for your sandbox.

The Basics of Table Creation

The simple form of the CREATE TABLE statement is this:

```
CREATE TABLE
  [ database_name . [ schema_name ] . | schema_name . ] table_name
  ( <column_definition> [ ,...n ] )
[ ; ]
```

This syntax allows the developer to identify the table by name and by schema. Following the name of the table is a list of column definitions placed in parentheses.

Within each column definition, column constraints can be provided if necessary. Also, table constraints can be defined in the CREATE TABLE statement. Constraints will be addressed in Chapter 6, "Managing Data Integrity," so we will defer our discussion of that portion of the syntax until that time. The column definition can contain the following:

Datatype   You must specify a datatype for each table column. These datatypes, discussed in Chapter 2, "Understanding SQL Server Architecture," define storage requirements for each column in the table.

Collation   You have the option of defining collations for each individual column that differ from the table collation or the server default collation.

Nullability   Every column can be explicitly specified as to whether it will allow null values. If not provided, the database option `ANSI NULL default` is used.

Identity   This auto-number property allows automatic incrementing of integer values for the indicated column, sometimes used as a contrived key or identifier.

As an illustration, suppose that you wanted to create a customer table with the following characteristics:

◆   An auto-incrementing ID value, entry required

◆   A customer name with a maximum of 25 characters, entry required

◆   A customer state code fixed to two characters, entry required

◆   A customer credit limit that can potentially accept decimals, entry optional

Given this set of characteristics, the SQL statement to create this table would be written as illustrated in Listing 4.1. Note that the formatting in this listing is not required, but we have included it for readability. You should follow your own organization's standards for code formatting. (If there is no standard, maybe it's time to create one.)

LISTING 4.1   Creating a Customer Table

```
USE SandboxDB;
GO

CREATE TABLE dbo.Customer
(
        CustomerID      int             NOT NULL    IDENTITY(1,1),
        CustomerName    varchar(25)     NOT NULL,
        StateCode       char(2)         NOT NULL,
        CreditLimit     money           NULL
);
GO
```

If you want to create the same table using the SQL Server Management Studio:

1. Begin by opening the client and connecting to your server through the Object Explorer.

2. Expand the target database in the Object Explorer and locate the Tables folder.

3. Right-click the Tables folder and choose New Table from the menu. This will open a dialog that you see in Figure 4.6.

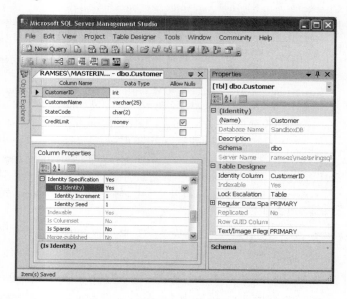

Note that in Figure 4.6, the screen is divided into three pieces. The upper-left portion of the screen defines the columns, the lower-left portion of the screen defines column properties, and the right side of the screen defines table properties. In this dialog, the CustomerID column is selected and some of its column properties are displayed in the lower-left portion of the dialog. You see here that the identity specification is defined in the column properties including the *identity seed* (the starting point) and the identity increment values.

The table properties on the right are not specific to any individual column, but rather to the table as a whole. This is where the table name is specified along with its schema identifier. Note, however, that there is some redundancy. The Identity column is also defined in the table properties. Because there is a rule that says that we can have only one identity column per table, this option is also listed in the table properties.

Computed Columns in Tables

One of your options when creating a table is to include computed columns. Although including decomposable data in the table is a violation of the first normal form, it can sometimes be convenient to include this information to avoid performing the calculations when the data is queried. As with any denormalization, there will be trade-offs.

In its basic form, the computed column simply stores the formula logic in the table definition so that extracting data from this column will automatically perform the desired calculation. Using this approach, no computed data is actually stored in the table. The primary benefit of this technique is that if you have a calculation that is frequently performed in your queries, you will no longer have to include that calculation in your query logic but instead can select from the computed column, which will perform the calculation for you.

There are some limitations to the use of a computed column. It cannot be configured with a default constraint (covered in Chapter 6) or as a foreign key, nor can it be the target of an update operation.

If you want to complete the denormalization, you can mark the computed column as persisted.

This takes the extra step of storing the value of the calculation into the table. This approach shifts the overhead of performing the calculation from the point in time that the data is selected to when the data is inserted and updated. This approach works best when the calculation is frequently needed, but the fields that make up the calculated value are nonvolatile. This action also requires a calculation to be deterministic in nature but permits the creation of an index on the computed column.

CALCULATIONS AND DETERMINISM

Numerous features of SQL Server, such as indexed views and persisted computed columns, require formulas that are deterministic. A *deterministic calculation* is one that can be repeated at any point in the future and will always return the same result as long as the inputs do not change. For example, suppose you have a CustomerOrder table with Price and Quantity columns. These columns could be used to create a computed column for the total. As long as the values entered in the price or quantity columns do not change, the total will never change. This calculation is deterministic.

However, suppose that you want to calculate the number of days that payment is past due. Assuming that you are storing the due date of the payment in your table, you would perform the calculation by comparing the current date and time with the due date and time. Because the function GetDate() returns a different value with every subsequent execution, any calculation that uses this function, such as our past-due example, would be *nondeterministic* in nature. Although you could still use this formula in a computed column, it cannot be persisted.

To include a computed column in a table, specify the column formula along with a column name in the column definition list. Optionally, you can also specify that the column should be persisted if you want to use this feature and the calculation is deterministic. Listing 4.2 illustrates the use of a computed column in a CREATE TABLE statement for a CustomerOrder table.

LISTING 4.2 Using Computed Columns in the Table

```
USE SandboxDB;
GO
CREATE TABLE dbo.CustomerOrder
(
      OrderID     int        NOT NULL    Identity(1,1),
      ProductID   int        NOT NULL,
      Price       money      NOT NULL,
      Quantity    int        NOT NULL,
      Total as Price * Quantity PERSISTED
);
GO
```

```
INSERT INTO dbo.CustomerOrder (ProductID, Price, Quantity)
VALUES (1, 10, 10);

SELECT * FROM dbo.CustomerOrder;
GO
```

In this listing, the Total column is expressed as a computation of the price value times the quantity value. Because this calculation is deterministic, it can be persisted. The use of the *PERSISTED* keyword in the column definition indicates that this value will be stored in the table data pages so that the calculation will not have to be performed with every extraction. Following the CREATE TABLE statement, the row is inserted into the table by providing ProductID, Price, and Quantity values. Notice that no values are provided for OrderID or Total. These values are determined automatically by the data engine based on the table specifications.

Dropping Tables

Dropping a table from a database is a simple process. Assuming that you are the owner of the table or you have the necessary permissions, you can drop a table by using the DROP TABLE statement. Assuming that you wanted to remove the CustomerOrder table from the database, you could use this statement.

```
USE SandboxDB;
GO
DROP TABLE dbo.CustomerOrder;
GO
```

Be careful! Once you execute this statement, it is committed. The table and its data will be removed from the database and you will have to restore from a backup if you want to recover the data.

Table Partitioning

Another common denormalization is table partitioning. In the past, you may have performed table partitioning manually by creating multiple tables and separating data into the appropriate tables. Partitioning using this approach can be very labor intensive. If data will be placed in separate tables at the time that it is inserted into the database, your procedures must be aware of the partitioning and be written to accommodate that logic. This creates a brittle architecture because if your partitioning needs ever change, it might require significant work to modify the application to implement that change.

The benefit of this denormalization, however, can be significant. For this reason, Microsoft has included table partitioning in the Transact-SQL syntax, which provides extensive support for custom table partitioning logic. This approach greatly simplifies table partitioning, particularly the process of maintaining and potentially modifying those partitions. This technique requires you to create both a *partition function*, which will define how the tables will be broken down, and a *partition scheme*, which will define how the partition function will be implemented. A table can then be created on that scheme. This makes the process of partitioning the table transparent to the procedural developer.

NOTES ABOUT PARTITIONING

Although we have not yet discussed the process of creating indexes, the concept of partitioning also applies to indexes. It is also possible to base a table partition and its associated index partitions on the same partition functions, thereby providing consistency in the partition logic. You should consider both tables and indexes when designing a partition plan because this will provide the most reliable and maintainable partition architecture.

Also, there are some enhancements to the way that table partitions are processed by the Query Optimizer and data engine that allow thread-per-partition execution on parallel plans. This can significantly speed performance and can reduce competition for "hot" resources. If you evaluated table partitioning in SQL Server 2005 and were unhappy with the performance result, you might want to reevaluate it in SQL Server 2008 if query activity is likely to be spread across multiple partitions.

Although this feature is supported only in the Enterprise and Developer editions of SQL Server 2008, it is available in the Evaluation edition if you want to test drive the benefits before committing to an Enterprise Edition license.

CREATING THE PARTITION FUNCTION

A partition function is a model that defines how data in a table or index will ultimately be broken down. The partition function consists of three elements:

◆ A function name

◆ An input datatype that represents the datatype of the column in the table or index on which the partition is based

◆ A set of partition boundaries that represents the breakpoints which will determine into which partition a data row will be placed

The basic syntax looks like this:

```
CREATE PARTITION FUNCTION partition_function_name ( input_parameter_type )
AS RANGE [ LEFT | RIGHT ]
FOR VALUES ( [ boundary_value [ ,...n ] ] )
[ ; ]
```

Assume that you have one or more tables that you want to partition by date. In this example, we will assume that anything entered in the current calendar year should be in one partition, anything in the previous calendar year should be in another partition, and anything earlier than the previous calendar year should be in a third partition. Assuming that the current calendar year is 2008, that would mean that the previous calendar year is 2007 and anything prior to 2007 would be in the third partition. Let's call this function CalendarPartition as defined in the following snippet:

```
USE SandboxDB;
CREATE PARTITION FUNCTION CalendarPartition (DATE)
AS RANGE RIGHT
FOR VALUES('01/01/2007', '01/01/2008');
```

In this example, the datatype specified in the function definition is DATE. This means that any table or index that is partitioned using this function must contain a column of type DATE; the partitioning process will be performed using this column. By providing two breakpoints, we are effectively defining three partitions. One partition will include everything before the first breakpoint, another will include the values between the two breakpoints, and the last will include all values after the final breakpoint.

Which partition will include the breakpoint values themselves? Notice the second line of the snippet: AS RANGE RIGHT. This means that the breakpoints will be included in the right partition. In this example, therefore, the first partition would contain any date up to but not including January 1, 2007. Because that date is the breakpoint, it would be included in the partition on the right. Using this same logic, a value of January 1, 2008 would belong in the third partition. Alternatively, we could have said AS RANGE LEFT, which would have included the endpoints in the first and second partitions, respectively.

CREATING AND IMPLEMENTING THE PARTITION SCHEME

Once the table partitions are created, you will have to store them somewhere. Because one of the primary benefits of partitioning a table or index is the distribution of that table or index across multiple physical locations to avoid contention, you will typically split each partition into a separate filegroup. (You can have multiple partitions—or even all partitions—in a single filegroup, however, if that architecture best meets your needs.) The basic syntax looks like this:

```
CREATE PARTITION SCHEME partition_scheme_name
AS PARTITION partition_function_name
[ ALL ] TO ( { file_group_name | [ PRIMARY ] } [ ,...n ] )
[ ; ]
```

In this syntax, you will notice that the partition scheme is tied to a partition function. Therefore, whenever the scheme is referenced, the function is implied. The filegroup list at the end of the partition scheme indicates where the partitions will be placed. You can't place partitions directly on files, only filegroups. The code statement below assumes that you have created four filegroups in the database, named FG1 to FG4. Refer to Chapter 3, "Databases, Files, and Resource Management," if necessary to get more information about filegroups.

If you specify more filegroups in the partition scheme than the number of partitions defined in the partition function, you can use the additional filegroups if new partitions are added later. The following code shows a partition scheme using the CalendarPartition function previously defined.

```
USE SandboxDB;
CREATE PARTITION SCHEME CalendarScheme
AS PARTITION CalendarPartition
TO (FG1, FG2, FG3, FG4);
```

Because the partition function only defined three partitions, but the scheme defines four filegroups, SQL Server must decide what to do with the remaining filegroup. Upon executing this code, you would get this message back from SQL Server:

```
Partition scheme 'CalendarScheme' has been created successfully. 'FG4' is marked as
the next used filegroup in partition scheme 'CalendarScheme'.
```

SQL Server is telling you that because it did not have to use the filegroup FG4 in the current scheme, it has been reserved and marked as the filegroup that will be used next if needed.

Now that you have created the partition scheme, you can use the scheme in a CREATE TABLE statement like this:

```
USE SandboxDB;
CREATE TABLE PartitionedTable
(
    Id          int   NOT NULL     Identity(1,1),
    DateValue   date  NOT NULL,
)
ON CalendarScheme(DateValue);
```

When you specify the partition scheme that the table will use, you will also have to specify the Data column in the table that it will use it to perform the partition. In this case, the value entered in the DateValue column will determine the partition location of the data row. When data is inserted into the table, the partition is completely transparent and does not affect the syntax at all. For example, each of the three insert statements below would insert data into a different partition of the table even though the code does not specify where the data will go. The partition function performs this task.

```
USE SandboxDB;
INSERT INTO PartitionedTable (DateValue) VALUES ('December 15, 2006');
INSERT INTO PartitionedTable (DateValue) VALUES ('December 15, 2007');
INSERT INTO PartitionedTable (DateValue) VALUES ('December 15, 2008');
```

To verify the existence of the partitions, you can use this query:

```
USE SandboxDB;
SELECT partition_id, partition_number, rows
FROM sys.partitions
WHERE object_id = object_id('PartitionedTable');
```

You can also verify the range breakpoints by using this query:

```
USE SandboxDB;
SELECT f.name, r.boundary_id, r.value
FROM sys.partition_functions as f
INNER JOIN sys.partition_range_values as r
    ON f.function_id = r.function_id
WHERE f.name = 'CalendarPartition';
```

After inserting the data into the table, you can also verify the partition location of each data row by using the $partition keyword. Remember that when you queried from sys.partitions you returned the partition_number value and the number of rows in each partition. Compare the results of that query with this one:

```
USE SandboxDB;
SELECT DateValue,
    $Partition.CalendarPartition(DateValue) as Partition_Number
FROM PartitionedTable;
```

These results show that the rows have been effectively distributed across filegroups with no additional work on the part of either the developer or the database administrator. A user or procedural developer would never have to know that the table was partitioned.

BUT WHAT IF YOU LIKE GUI PARTITIONS?

SQL Server 2008 frequently has artifacts that you can view or script from the Management Studio, but that you can't create directly using the GUI tools. Partition functions and schemes fall into this category. If you look at the Object Explorer in the following graphic, you will see that although you can script and drop partition artifacts from the GUI, you can't create them here.

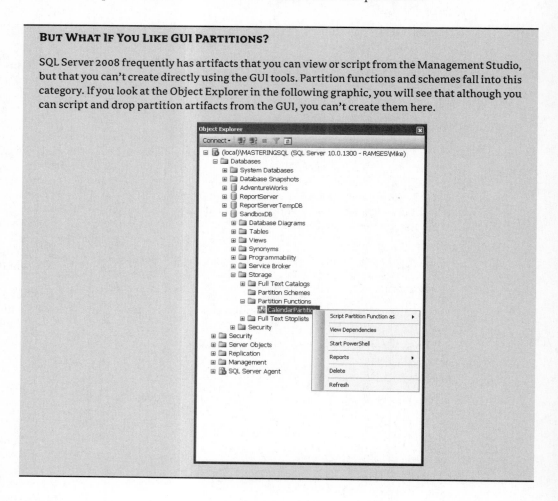

MODIFYING PARTITIONS

In the typical business, archiving and partitioning needs change over time. In the year 2008, our partitioning scheme may make perfect sense, but what do we do on January 1, 2009? Do we still want to load current data with the calendar year 2008 data? Probably not, but how do we make the change? What we need to do in this situation is add another partition to store the calendar year 2009 data and merge the 2007 data into the first partition. Let's take a closer look at how we would do this.

The first thing that we need to do is to modify the partition function to define the partition behavior of a value entered for the calendar year 2009. You can do this by executing an ALTER PARTITION FUNCTION statement like this one:

```
USE SandboxDB;
ALTER PARTITION FUNCTION CalendarPartition()
SPLIT RANGE ('01/01/2009');
```

If you re-execute the previous query that joined the sys.partition_functions view and the sys.partition_range_values view, you will notice that there is another boundary point in our function. This function now defines four partitions instead of three. The change has also been committed to the artifacts that use the function. Execute the following statements and evaluate the results:

```
USE SandboxDB;
INSERT INTO PartitionedTable (DateValue) Values ('December 15, 2009');
SELECT DateValue,
       $Partition.CalendarPartition(DateValue) as Partition_Number
FROM PartitionedTable;
```

As you will see from the results, simply adding the new partition to the function provided the information necessary for the new data to be inserted into the new partition. Because the FG4 filegroup was previously marked as the next used filegroup, it automatically becomes the host of the new partition. Note that you can use the ALTER PARTITION SCHEME statement if you want to change the next used filegroup.

This only gets us part of the way there, however. Now we have four partitions. What we really wanted was three partitions, because we wanted to merge the 2007 data into the first partition with the rest of the archived data. To do this, we need to make another alteration to partition function. Use the following code to merge the 2007 data into the archive:

```
USE SandboxDB;
ALTER PARTITION FUNCTION CalendarPartition()
MERGE RANGE ('01/01/2007');
```

This code removes the boundary for January 1, 2007. This means that the first boundary value is now January 1, 2008, so we are back to three partitions again: one for everything before 2008, one for the year 2008, and one for 2009 and later. If you have been following along with this example and entering this code, re-execute some of the previous queries and take a look at how the partitions are currently organized. You should see a total of three partitions. There will be two rows in partition 1, and one row each on partitions 2 and 3. This simple process can then be repeated as necessary without ever having to modify any portion of the actual application.

Selecting Data from a Table

If you have had any previous exposure to SQL Server, the first things you probably learned how to do were logging in to the server and executing a simple SELECT statement. In this book we assume that you are not brand new to SQL Server, so we can safely pass over much of the basic SELECT syntax. In this section, however, we will cover some more advanced query statements with which you may not have been able to spend a lot of time. For those of you who have written a lot of simple queries but have not yet taken the next step, we hope that these next few pages will be help bring it all together. Even if you are already an accomplished developer, you may want to skim through this section to see if there is anything you have missed.

WHAT ABOUT THE BASICS?

We assume that most readers of this book have already been exposed to the basic concepts of the SQL query. If that is not the case for you, you might want to do a little background reading before tackling this chapter. There are plenty of resources online that cover the basics of SQL syntax. A search should return numerous resources. You might also want to look at the book *SQL for Dummies* (John Wiley & Sons Inc., 2006), which has a great overview of basic SQL syntax.

Aggregation and Grouping

Shifting our attention back to the AdventureWorks2008 sample database, let's suppose that you want to return a list of contacts from the Person.Person table in ascending order by last name.

You could use the following query:

```
USE AdventureWorks2008;
SELECT FirstName, MiddleName, LastName
FROM Person.Person
ORDER BY LastName ASC;
```

WHAT IS A PERSON.PERSON?

A fully qualified artifact reference in SQL Server uses what is called the *four-part naming convention*. The four parts of the convention are ServerName.DatabaseName.SchemaName.ObjectName. Therefore, the fully qualified name of the table that we are selecting from in this example is <Your server name>.AdventureWorks2008.Person.Person.

Because you are executing the query on the server you are connected to, you do not have to restate the server name. It is understood. The same is true with the database name. Because you already issued a USE statement to change the database context to AdventureWorks2008, there is no need to include the database name in the query.

However, best practice in most cases is to include the last two parts of the name in every query. There is a schema in the database called Person. The best way to think of the schema is as a namespace for other artifacts. It is a way of grouping artifacts, such as tables and stored procedures, that have special relationships. Person.Person represents a Person table in the Person schema.

We will talk more about schemas later when we deal with user security. For now, just note that every artifact is in a schema and that we should include that schema name in every query.

This query will give us the list of people sorted in the way that we like. But what if you need to know the total number of people who have the same last name? For example, how many

Johnsons do we have? How many Robinsons are there? You could take the list that you just generated and manually count the entries for each last name, but that would be a very time-consuming task. For example, if you look at the results of the query that you just executed, you will notice that it returned almost 20,000 rows, far too many to start counting by hand.

Fortunately, SQL supports numerous aggregate functions that, when used in conjunction with the GROUP BY clause, can give you the breakdown you are seeking. You can use these aggregates to do everything from simple counts to more advanced calculations such as summations, averages, or even statistical standard deviations. Table 4.1 provides a list of standard aggregate functions in SQL Server 2008, along with a description of each.

TABLE 4.1   Aggregate Functions in SQL Server 2008

FUNCTION	DESCRIPTION
AVG	Returns the average value in the set. Ignores null values; can be configured to average all values (the default) or only distinct values in the set.
CHECKSUM_AGG	Returns the checksum of the values in the group, either all or distinct, ignoring null values.
COUNT	Returns the number of rows, all or distinct, based on an expression or (optionally) a simple row count.
COUNT_BIG	Executes like COUNT, except that it returns a bigint rather than an int datatype.
GROUPING	Indicates if a specified column in a GROUP BY list is aggregate. Returns 0 or 1.
MAX	Returns the maximum value in the set based on the provided column name.
MIN	Returns the minimum value in the set based on the provided column name.
SUM	Returns the sum of values in the set based on the provided column name.
STDEV	Returns the statistical standard deviation of all values based on the provided column name.
STDEVP	Returns the statistical population standard deviation of all values based on the provided column name.
VAR	Returns the statistical variance of all values based on the provided column name.
VARP	Returns the statistical population variance of all values based on the provided column name.

In this case, we are interested in a COUNT aggregate. Because the value returned for each breakpoint will not be larger than an int (a 4-byte integer), we will use the COUNT function rather than the COUNT_BIG function, which would return an 8-byte integer value.

The resulting query would look like this:

```
USE AdventureWorks2008;
SELECT LastName, COUNT(LastName) as CountOfNames
FROM Person.Person
GROUP BY LastName
ORDER BY LastName ASC;
```

This query produces a new column called CountOfNames that contains the total number of entries in the table for any specific last name. Notice how the query is grouped by last name. This is very important because the syntax rule requires that any SELECT list that contains both aggregated and nonaggregated data must be grouped by the nonaggregated content. Notice how the GROUP BY clause provides breakpoints for the aggregate. If you want to find out how many people have exactly the same first name and last name, you need to use a query like this one:

```
USE AdventureWorks2008;
SELECT FirstName,LastName, COUNT(LastName) as CountOfNames
FROM Person.Person
GROUP BY FirstName, LastName
ORDER BY LastName ASC;
```

Because the SELECT list now contains both first name and last name, both first name and last name must also be in the GROUP BY clause. Notice that the COUNT function uses only LastName as a parameter. This function, which can only take a single column name as a parameter, uses this column to know what values to count.

Try executing the same query again, but modify the COUNT function so that it reads COUNT(MiddleName) as CountOfNames. Notice what this does to your counts. Because the MiddleName column frequently contains nulls, which are not counted by the aggregate, there are numerous first name–last name combinations that return a count value of 0. You are now answering a new question: How many people in each first name–last name combination have a middle name provided?

Here is another example. Assume you wanted a count of *all* rows, including those that may contain some null values. To get this, you would use COUNT(*) as CountOfNames. This counts rows instead of counting non-null entries in a particular column. Also, You could also use a WHERE clause to filter out null values before aggregating, in which case you would not have to use the column name. As you can see from these examples, you have to decide what the real question is before you can formulate a query that will provide the correct answer.

Consider the following three queries:

```
USE AdventureWorks2008;

SELECT COUNT(*) FROM Person.Person;

SELECT COUNT(MiddleName) FROM Person.Person;

SELECT COUNT(*) FROM Person.Person Where MiddleName IS NOT NULL;
```

The first query will return a count of all rows in the table. The second and third queries will give you exactly the same information: the number of people who have a middle name provided in the database. Frequently, multiple queries will return the same value. When this is the case, you should try to use the query format that will give you the best performance or (depending on circumstances) the one that is the easiest to maintain and modify later.

SPECIAL AGGREGATE CONDITIONS

Be aware that COUNT and COUNT_BIG are the only aggregates that give you an option to include all rows by using the asterisk (*) as a parameter. This really does not make sense for other aggregates. For example, look at the MAX aggregate. This function provides the maximum value in the column provided as a parameter. This function would make no sense in the MAX(*) format because there would be no indication of which column to use to locate a maximum value.

An aggregate that returns only a single value (a scalar aggregate) can also be used anywhere a value expression can be used, such as in a WHERE clause. Be careful when using a scalar aggregate, because doing so can have some negative performance impacts.

Another useful technique when executing aggregates is to use a HAVING clause. Unlike a WHERE clause in a query, which filters out individual rows before the result set is created, a HAVING clause filters out groups that do not meet specific conditions. For example, assume you want to get a result that provides a count of all "persons" with a last name beginning with the letter "A" that have the same last name. Assume further that you only want the query to return the groups that have at least 10 last names.

Your query will actually perform two different operations. The first operation filters out the data to create the groups. Only people with a last name starting with the letter "A" will be counted. The second operation eliminates any group that does not produce a count of at least 10 "persons." Look at the following query as an example:

```
USE AdventureWorks2008;
SELECT LastName, COUNT(LastName) as CountOfNames
FROM Person.Person
WHERE LastName LIKE 'A%'
GROUP BY LastName
HAVING COUNT(LastName) >= 10;
```

One somewhat frustrating feature of this type of query is that you can't use the column alias as an identifier in the having clause. Notice that we had to use the syntax HAVING COUNT(LastName) >= 10 and not HAVING COUNT(CountOfNames) >= 10. Be aware of this quirk so you don't drive yourself nuts trying to figure out what's wrong with your query.

Joins and Table Correlation

In a relational data model, you will often have to join tables to extract relevant information. The type of JOIN statement you use, the join fields that you choose, and the order of the tables that you provide in your JOIN statement can all have an impact on both the data that the query will return and the performance of the query. In fact, the I/O cost resulting from join operations in queries is frequently the most resource-consuming and performance-affecting part of the query process.

Let's begin by considering a simple join operation. Suppose that you wanted to get a list of all of the people in your database who have a phone number in the 702 area code. You are planning a trip to Las Vegas and you want a place to stay. The problem is that the names of the people are in the Person.Person table, but their phone numbers are in the Person.PersonPhone table. This design complies with the first normal form. Because it is possible that one person could have multiple phone numbers, such as home phone, mobile phone, business phone, etc., these numbers had to go into a separate table. There is a common column between the two tables, though. That column is BusinessEntityID. To correlate the date between the two tables, we will have to write a JOIN statement that will link the tables on this field. Consider the following query:

```
USE AdventureWorks2008;
SELECT p.FirstName, p.LastName, pp.PhoneNumber
FROM Person.Person as p
INNER JOIN Person.PersonPhone as pp
    ON p.BusinessEntityID = pp.BusinessEntityID
WHERE pp.PhoneNumber LIKE '702%';
```

In this example, you will see that there are two tables listed in the FROM clause, but these two tables are correlated through a JOIN statement. A JOIN statement generally contains two pieces of information: which tables you are joining and which columns in each of the tables that you will use for the join.

You have a variety of options for the JOIN operator that you choose. Although inner joins are the most common, they are by no means the only option. The five join options in SQL Server 2008 are listed in Table 4.2. Note that the alias value listed in the table can be substituted for the formal JOIN operator if you like.

TABLE 4.2   SQL Server 2008 Join Types

JOIN TYPE	ALIAS	DESCRIPTION
INNER JOIN	JOIN	Returns requested data for every row in each table only where there is an exact match on the join field.
LEFT OUTER JOIN	LEFT JOIN	Returns requested data for all rows from the first table stated in the join operation; only returns data for rows from the second stated table where there is a matching value. This can result in null values in the result when the first stated table in the join has a row with no matching row(s) in the second stated table.
RIGHT OUTER JOIN	RIGHT JOIN	Returns requested data for all rows from the second table stated in the join operation; only returns data for rows from the first stated table where there is a matching value. This can result in null values in the result when the second stated table in the join has a row with no matching row(s) in the first stated table.
FULL OUTER JOIN	FULL JOIN	Returns requested data for all rows in both correlated tabled, but the result will contain null values for rows with no matching join value on the other side.

TABLE 4.2   SQL Server 2008 Join Types   *(CONTINUED)*

JOIN TYPE	ALIAS	DESCRIPTION
CROSS JOIN	N/A	Returns a Cartesian (Cross) product; in other words, all possible combinations of rows between the two tables.

In our previous query example, what would happen if someone listed in the Person.Person table did not have a phone number provided in the Person.PersonPhone table? Because the query is written using the INNER JOIN operator, it would return only people with at least one matching record in the PersonPhone table.

What if you were to write the query like this?

```
USE AdventureWorks2008;
SELECT p.FirstName, p.LastName, pp.PhoneNumber
FROM Person.Person as p
LEFT OUTER JOIN Person.PersonPhone as pp
     ON p.BusinessEntityID = pp.BusinessEntityID
WHERE pp.PhoneNumber LIKE '702%';
```

In this case, the JOIN operator is LEFT OUTER JOIN, meaning that all rows will be returned from the Person table, but only matching rows will be returned from the PersonPhone table. This means that some "persons" may be without a registered phone number.

A null value will appear in the PhoneNumber column for these rows, because the value is unknown for that person. Note that in the AdventureWorks 2008 database, every person in the Person.Person table has a corresponding entry on the Person.PersonPhone table, so in this case, will all Person rows having matching rows in PersonPhone, the results of the two queries will be the same.

Now suppose that you want to join three tables instead of two. For example, this query will give you the name and phone number, but you also need to know if it is a home phone, mobile phone, etc. As you look at the PersonPhone table, you will see that there is no text field that gives you this information, but there is a column named PhoneNumberTypeID. This column relates to the Person.PhoneNumberType table, which contains the data that you need. To get this information, you will have to join the previous query results to the third table, as illustrated in this query:

```
USE AdventureWorks2008;
SELECT p.FirstName, p.LastName, pp.PhoneNumber, pnt.Name
FROM Person.Person as p
INNER JOIN Person.PersonPhone as pp
     ON p.BusinessEntityID = pp.BusinessEntityID
INNER JOIN Person.PhoneNumberType as pnt
     ON pp.PhoneNumberTypeID = pnt.PhoneNumberTypeID
WHERE pp.PhoneNumber LIKE '702%';
```

As you can see from these examples, basic JOIN syntax is not difficult to use, but it does require a good understanding of the structure of your database. You have to know where all of the data is and which fields you should use to correlate all of the data. Spending time with your data schemas and learning how the data is distributed will pay off in the long run, because it gives you the tools to give your data consumers exactly what they need to answer their questions.

Real World Scenario

PREPPING FOR THE UPGRADE

If you have previously converted applications from SQL Server 2000 to SQL Server 2005, you have probably already removed the non-ANSI JOIN syntax from your code. The mainstream support for the old syntax was removed in SQL Server 2005, requiring you to run in SQL 2000 compatibility mode if you still wanted to use it. If this does not ring a bell for you, consider the following case.

As consultants, we frequently work with companies that are migrating applications from one version of SQL Server to another. Updating obsolete syntax in scripts and stored procedures is particularly problematic in a conversion. One of the syntactical statements that tends to be very problematic is the JOIN syntax.

Prior to SQL Server 6.5, the JOIN syntax was part of the WHERE clause. A typical join query looked something like this:

```
SELECT a.au_lname, ta.royaltyper
FROM authors as a, titleauthor as ta
WHERE a.au_id = ta.au_id
```

Notice that the WHERE clause, which should contain filter criteria, contains a join correlation. Left joins were performed by using an *= in the WHERE clause and right joins used an =* operator.

Version 6.5 of SQL Server introduced the ANSI JOIN syntax that we now use. Any code written in SQL Server 6.0 or earlier should have been upgraded when the move was made to SQL Server 6.5.

One client decided not to modify the code on an upgrade because they were concerned that there was too much code to modify and it would increase the cost of the upgrade. While that was true, all the client did was delay the inevitable. With the release of SQL Server 2005, Microsoft no longer supported the non-ANSI syntax unless the database compatibility option is set to SQL 2000 or earlier. This client is now in a bit of a jam, because the only way to leverage the new language features of SQL Server 2005 is to upgrade their code to ANSI JOIN statements.

As of this writing, they are still using the old syntax and running SQL Server 2005 in 2000 compatibility mode.

As of the release of SQL Server 2008, the non-ANSI JOIN syntax is on the deprecated list, meaning that in the next release it will not be supported at all because the 2000 compatibility mode will be going away. So the client now has to make the changes if they want to make the upgrade—and they only have the limited time window provided by SQL Server 2008 in which to do the modifications.

Meanwhile, because they did not want to support code that used multiple syntax approaches, they have almost doubled the amount of code that will have to be modified to make the change.

The moral of this story is that if you know that something has to be changed, do it while you can. Waiting too long to transition your code causes two serious problems. First, you will probably increase your total costs for the transition, because the longer you wait, the more disconnected your developers will probably be from the original code. Second, you will not get the full benefits of the upgrades that you *do* perform if you do not using the syntax, configurations, and other features that the new options present. If you are going to spend the money on an upgrade, you might as well get the most benefit for your money that you can.

Subqueries, Derived, and Temporary Tables

Subqueries and derived tables are nothing more than nested SELECT statements. These tools are used to dynamically pull data from the tables so that data can be used to resolve another query. By allowing the query logic to get all of its data from the database (having data-driven logic) instead of hard-coding values (which gives you brittle fixed logic), you increase your ability to maintain the code.

Subqueries can be scalar or can return a list of values. When a subquery returns both columns and rows, it is often referred to as a *derived table*. This can be a useful way to avoid using temporary tables.

SCALAR SUBQUERIES

When a subquery returns exactly one row and one column of data, it is considered a scalar subquery. A scalar subquery is typically constructed either as a query that selects a single column based on a unique key or as an aggregate value with no grouping. In either case, the result of the query is used in place of the value in the containing query. Consider the following query.

```
USE AdventureWorks2008;
SELECT SalesOrderID, OrderQty, UnitPrice
FROM Sales.SalesOrderDetail
WHERE UnitPrice > (
      SELECT AVG(UnitPrice)
      FROM Sales.SalesOrderDetail
      )
AND OrderQty > (
      SELECT AVG(OrderQty)
      FROM Sales.SalesOrderDetail
);
```

This query will return a list of sales orders that meet the conditions of having a higher than average unit price and higher than average order quantity. In other words, it returns your highest value orders.

The great thing about a query like this is that even if the data changes, this query will always return accurate results. By comparison, if you calculate the average unit price and average order quantity by hand and hard-code those values into this query, the results will be correct right now, but as soon as the data is modified, adding new orders or changing existing orders, the result set will no longer be accurate.

STRUCTURING A SUBQUERY

There are a few rules to remember about subqueries. First, if the subquery is preceded by a comparison operator such as =, <, >, etc., then the subquery must be scalar. It can only return one value.

Second, you will also notice from the syntax that every subquery is contained in a set of parentheses. You don't have to use the same format as in the previous example—because white space is ignored by the parser, you can put parentheses where you want them—but you must put them around every subquery.

SUBQUERIES THAT RETURN LISTS

When a subquery returns a list of values, it can be used after an IN operator in a query. For example, the following query returns a list of sales territory IDs that are in the North American region.

```
USE AdventureWorks2008;
SELECT TerritoryID
FROM Sales.SalesTerritory
WHERE [Group] = 'North America';
```

WHAT'S ALL THAT BRACKET OUT THERE?

Just in case you have not seen this syntax option in SQL Server before, take a moment to look at the WHERE clause and notice that the column name *Group* is enclosed in square brackets. Because the word *Group* is a SQL Server 2008 *reserved word*, it requires special treatment. You can use reserved words like this as identifiers in SQL Server, but you must mark them as identifiers so that the SQL Server parser does not treat them as keywords. If you have the option "Quoted Identifiers" turned on, you can use double quotes to mark identifiers, but the standard syntax is to enclose keywords in brackets. The best practice is to avoid using keywords as identifiers altogether.

Because this query returns more than one value, it can't be used as a scalar subquery would. Instead, this query provides a set of possible values that the outer query can use as a filter. Think of it as an advanced "OR" logic.

What if you want to return a list of customer IDs and account numbers for each of your customers in North America? One way to write this query would be like this:

```
USE AdventureWorks2008;
SELECT CustomerID, AccountNumber
FROM Sales.Customer
WHERE TerritoryID IN (
        SELECT TerritoryID
        FROM Sales.SalesTerritory
        WHERE [Group] = 'North America'
);
```

In this example, we just took the query that returned the TerritoryID and used it as a subquery to provide that information to the outer query and act as a filter. It is worth mentioning that a subquery of this nature implies distinctiveness. In other words, there is no need to use the DISTINCT keyword in the subquery. It is implied.

Of course, this is not the only way to write this query. We can often rewrite subqueries as join operations and get the same results. For example, the next query will give you exactly the same results as the previous one. Your decision to use one or the other will depend on your performance metrics and maintenance requirements.

```
USE AdventureWorks2008;
SELECT c.CustomerID, c.AccountNumber
FROM Sales.Customer as c
INNER JOIN Sales.SalesTerritory as st
    ON c.TerritoryID = st.TerritoryID
WHERE st.[Group] = 'North America';
```

DERIVED TABLES

You may want to create a temporary table structure, such as a work table, to process intermediate results in your procedure. There are a number of ways to do this. You can use temp tables, table variables, or derived tables. Each method has its own pros and cons. Listing 4.3 illustrates the use of a table variable to temporarily store data.

LISTING 4.3   Using Table Variables

```
USE AdventureWorks2008;

DECLARE @NameAndRole table
(
ContactName          nvarchar(101),
BusinessRole         nvarchar(50),
ModifiedDate         datetime
);

INSERT INTO @NameAndRole
SELECT Name, 'Vendor', ModifiedDate
FROM Purchasing.Vendor;

INSERT INTO @NameAndRole
SELECT p.FirstName + ' ' + p.LastName,e.JobTitle , p.ModifiedDate
FROM Person.Person as p
INNER JOIN HumanResources.Employee as e
    ON p.BusinessEntityID = e.BusinessEntityID;

SELECT ContactName, BusinessRole
FROM @NameAndRole
WHERE ModifiedDate > '20010101';
GO
```

In Listing 4.3, you can see how data that is very different in structure can be merged to provide a temporary set of values, which is further processed by filtering the set by ModifiedDate. In this case, we are using a table variable, but there is an alternative. You could use a temporary table to do the same thing. Look at Listing 4.4, which achieves the same result using a temporary table.

LISTING 4.4   Using Temporary Tables

```
USE AdventureWorks2008;

CREATE TABLE #NameAndRole
(
ContactName        nvarchar(101),
BusinessRole       nvarchar(50),
ModifiedDate       datetime
);

INSERT INTO #NameAndRole
SELECT Name, 'Vendor', ModifiedDate
FROM Purchasing.Vendor;

INSERT INTO #NameAndRole
SELECT p.FirstName + ' ' + p.LastName,e.JobTitle , p.ModifiedDate
FROM Person.Person as p
INNER JOIN HumanResources.Employee as e
     ON p.BusinessEntityID = e.BusinessEntityID;

SELECT ContactName, BusinessRole
FROM #NameAndRole
WHERE ModifiedDate > '20010101';
GO
```

The primary difference between these two listings is the duration of the temporary structure. Because declared variables are removed from memory after the batch that defines them is complete, the table variables are out of scope as soon as the GO statement executes. Temporary tables on the other hand will remain in scope until the connection that creates them is closed. There are also some performance differences, although it is difficult to say which is better. Depending on the situation as well as the version and service pack of SQL Server that is installed, the performance metrics of table variables versus temporary tables can change! Unless the performance metrics change significantly using one or the other, your best option is to pick the one that makes the most sense in the current situation and stick with it.

Another alternative is to use a derived table. In the case of a derived table, the scope is limited to the query itself. It is not available anywhere else in the batch or within the current connection scope. Due to this limited scope, derived tables are often the best way to resolve this type of query when the limited scope is acceptable.

Listing 4.5 provides the same results as Listings 4.3 and 4.4 using a derived table.

LISTING 4.5   Using Derived Table Subqueries

```
USE AdventureWorks2008;
SELECT ContactName, BusinessRole
FROM (
        SELECT Name as ContactName,'Vendor' as BusinessRole, ModifiedDate
        FROM Purchasing.Vendor

        UNION ALL

        SELECT p.FirstName + ' ' + p.LastName,e.JobTitle,p.ModifiedDate
        FROM Person.Person as p
        INNER JOIN HumanResources.Employee as e
            ON p.BusinessEntityID = e.BusinessEntityID
        ) as ContactList

WHERE ModifiedDate > '20010101';
GO
```

The example in Listing 4.5 is fairly simple, but a derived table can be used in much more complex scenarios. Derived tables can be used in aggregates, joins, and even as outer queries for additional subqueries or derived tables. Remember, though, that once the query has finished executing, the derived table is out of scope and can no longer be accessed.

CORRELATED SUBQUERIES

Sometimes, a subquery cannot process without information from the outer query. In these cases, table aliases are used to define the scope of the query arguments and allow the subquery to be "parameterized" from the outer query. The inner query is, therefore, *correlated* to the outer query. The net effect is a "back and forth" execution where a single row from the result of the outer query is permitted to pass parameters to the inner query for execution. The following query shows an example of a correlated subquery.

```
USE AdventureWorks2008;
SELECT    p.FirstName + ' ' + p.LastName as FullName,
            e.JobTitle,
            (SELECT Name
            FROM HumanResources.Department as d
            WHERE d.DepartmentID = edh.DepartmentID) as DepartmentName
FROM Person.Person as p
INNER JOIN HumanResources.Employee as e
    ON p.BusinessEntityID = e.BusinessEntityID
INNER JOIN HumanResources.EmployeeDepartmentHistory as edh
    ON e.BusinessEntityID = edh.BusinessEntityID
WHERE edh.EndDate IS NULL;
GO
```

Because of the way the database is normalized, returning a list of employees with their job titles and current department names is not an easy task. The name information is stored in the Person.Person table, while the job title is in the HumanResources.Employee table. This is a simple join. However getting the current department name is a little trickier. The HumanResources.Department table has the name of the department along with a DepartmentID key. However, the HumanResources.Employee table does not contain the DepartmentID foreign key. This is because it is possible that a single employee has worked in many departments in their career. To maintain this historical data, an EmployeeDepartmentHistory table is created.

This table contains one row for every department assignment that an employee has had, along with the DepartmentID and the start and end dates of service with that department. If the entry in the EmployeeDepartmentHistory table has a NULL value for end date, that means that the row represents the employees current department assignment. After filtering out for only NULL values in the end date column, we can turn out attention to getting the department name.

You will that the SELECT list contains a subquery, but this subquery uses edh.DepartmentID in its WHERE clause. This value is not defined in the subquery; it comes from the WHERE clause in the outer query. The result is that the subquery is correlated to the outer query. For each row produced by the outer query, the edh.DepartmentID value for that row is passed to the inner query and executed to return the appropriate department name for the SELECT list. This is repeated for every row produced by the outer query. Because the outer query in this example produced 290 rows, the inner query must be executed 290 times to return the appropriate data.

THE OPTIMIZER IS SOMETIMES SMARTER THAN WE ARE

If executing the inner query 290 times to get the department names seems like a lot of work, you are right. Even with only 16 departments in our database, we would be executing the same query over and over again to get the same data. That is very inefficient.

Luckily, the query optimizer is not stupid. It would look at this query, decide to create a temporary hash key list, and actually resolve this query with a hash join operation to the Department table, rather than running 290 executions of the same query. This process—whereby the optimizer rewrites the query to find a better way to solve the problem—is sometimes called *flattening*.

When this happens, take it as a hint: If you were paying attention, you probably could have written this query as a join rather than using a subquery. Perhaps that would have been a better option, given that the optimizer chose to use that approach anyway.

If you are an accomplished SQL developer, you probably looked at that query and said, "What a moron, he should have just used a join!" Guess what? You are both right and wrong. For performance, it would have been better to use a join, but if we had, then we couldn't have had this wonderful conversation about query flattening, could we?

Common Table Expressions

The Common Table Expression (CTE) was introduced in SQL Server 2005. The purpose of the CTE is to provide a syntactical option that allows the developer to work with temporary data structures logically rather than physically. Instead of having to create temporary tables or table variables to accomplish more complex tasks, the SQL developer can now use the CTE and simplify the logic significantly. The basic format of the CTE is

```
WITH expression_name [ ( column_name [,...n] ) ]
AS
( CTE_query_definition )

SELECT <column_list>
FROM expression_name;
```

The CTE structure is divided into two parts. The first part defines the expression using an expression name and the SQL code that makes up the expression. If you have had previous experience with SQL Server, you might recognize this first section as having the same basic format as a view. The difference is that a view is a procedural object that, when created, physically stores the view metadata in the database so that it can be called again. By contrast, a CTE does not store the definition; it is only valid for that execution. (You might want to think of it as a temporary view.)

The second part of the CTE structure is the execution of the CTE, which will generally be a SELECT statement. This must occur immediately after the CTE definition and can't be separated from it by a GO statement. Rewriting the previous example that we used for temporary and derived tables would give us a result that looks like Listing 4.6. Note that the results would be the same as those for the previous listings.

LISTING 4.6   Using Common Table Expressions Instead of Temporary or Derived Tables

```
USE AdventureWorks2008;
WITH Contact_CTE (ContactName, BusinessRole, ModifiedDate)
AS
(
        SELECT Name,'Vendor', ModifiedDate
        FROM Purchasing.Vendor

        UNION ALL

        SELECT p.FirstName + ' ' + p.LastName,e.JobTitle,p.ModifiedDate
        FROM Person.Person as p
        INNER JOIN HumanResources.Employee as e
            ON p.BusinessEntityID = e.BusinessEntityID
)
SELECT ContactName, BusinessRole
FROM Contact_CTE
WHERE ModifiedDate > '20010101';
GO
```

Because the CTE is considered a table within the scope of the SELECT statement that follows, you can do anything with this CTE that you can do with any other table, including join operations and aggregating and grouping. The purpose of using this syntax rather than derived tables is to provide cleaner code. It lets the developer define a derived structure in advance so that the SELECT statement that follows does not have to be cluttered with the structure of the derived table, which can be very difficult to read and maintain.

Another advantage of using the CTE is that it supports recursive queries. Recursion is one of those operations that has always been challenging in the SQL language. If often requires the use of temporary tables and is usually difficult to read and maintain. The CTE can significantly simplify this logic. This is the basic structure of a recursive query using a CTE.

```
WITH cte_name ( column_name [,...n] )
AS
(
CTE_query_definition -- Anchor member is defined.
UNION ALL
CTE_query_definition -- Recursive member is defined referencing cte_name.
)
-- Statement using the CTE
SELECT *
FROM cte_name
```

In this syntax, the CTE definition starts with what is called the *anchor member*. This represents the top-level query of the recursion (the query before any recursion is performed). After the union, the second part, also called the *recursive member,* references the expression name to specify how the upper-level values will be passed to the recursive layers.

You can select from the CTE, and it will perform any necessary recursion for you. Listing 4.7 illustrates the use of a CTE for recursion. Because you may not have the AdventureWorks database handy for testing, a partial result set is provided in Figure 4.7.

SORRY, NOT MY DATA

Please note that this code uses data in the AdventureWorks database, also available from Codeplex, rather than the AdventureWorks2008 database that we have been using. This is because the AdventureWorks database contains data that lends itself to this illustration. If you want to execute this example, you will have to install the appropriate database.

LISTING 4.7   Using Common Table Expressions for Recursive Operations

```
USE AdventureWorks;
WITH DirectReports (ManagerID, EmployeeID, EmployeeName, Title)
AS
(
-- Anchor member definition
  SELECT e.ManagerID, e.EmployeeID, c.FirstName + ' ' + c.LastName, e.Title
```

```
    FROM HumanResources.Employee AS e
    INNER JOIN Person.Contact as c
            ON e.ContactID = c.ContactID
    WHERE ManagerID IS NULL
    UNION ALL
-- Recursive member definition
    SELECT e.ManagerID, e.EmployeeID,c.FirstName + ' ' + c.LastName ,e.Title
    FROM HumanResources.Employee AS e
    INNER JOIN DirectReports AS d
      ON e.ManagerID = d.EmployeeID
    INNER JOIN Person.Contact as c
            ON e.ContactID = c.ContactID
)
-- Statement that executes the CTE
SELECT EmployeeID, EmployeeName, Title, ManagerID
FROM DirectReports
GO
```

FIGURE 4.7
Recursive query
results

	EmployeeID	EmployeeName	Title	ManagerID
1	109	Ken Sánchez	Chief Executive Officer	NULL
2	6	David Bradley	Marketing Manager	109
3	12	Terri Duffy	Vice President of Engineering	109
4	42	Jean Trenary	Information Services Manager	109
5	140	Laura Norman	Chief Financial Officer	109
6	148	James Hamilton	Vice President of Production	109
7	273	Brian Welcker	Vice President of Sales	109
8	268	Stephen Jiang	North American Sales Manager	273
9	284	Amy Alberts	European Sales Manager	273
10	288	Syed Abbas	Pacific Sales Manager	273
11	290	Lynn Tsoflias	Sales Representative	288
12	285	Jae Pak	Sales Representative	284
13	286	Ranjit Varkey Chudukatil	Sales Representative	284
14	289	Rachel Valdez	Sales Representative	284
15	275	Michael Blythe	Sales Representative	268
16	276	Linda Mitchell	Sales Representative	268
17	277	Jillian Carson	Sales Representative	268
18	278	Garrett Vargas	Sales Representative	268
19	279	Tsvi Reiter	Sales Representative	268
20	280	Pamela Ansman-Wolfe	Sales Representative	268
21	281	Shu Ito	Sales Representative	268
22	282	José Saraiva	Sales Representative	268
23	283	David Campbell	Sales Representative	268
24	287	Tete Mensa-Annan	Sales Representative	268
25	21	Peter Krebs	Production Control Manager	148

In the results of the query, you will see that employee number 109 is the chief executive officer. He has no manager, so his ManagerID value is null. The anchor member of the CTE specifically identifies the employee with no manager number. The entire organization will flow down from this record. You will also see in the recursive member how the recursive portion of the query joins to the CTE by correlating the ManagerID field of the recursive member to the EmployeeID field of the parent member in the recursion. Although this syntax can look a little intimidating at first, once you write a couple of these you will see how much easier it is to execute recursion using a CTE than through more traditional means.

Modifying Data

SQL Server 2008 supports four primary data modification keywords: INSERT, UPDATE, DELETE, and MERGE. These Transact-SQL operations are extremely flexible and will provide the tools necessary for the vast majority of data modifications your applications may require. As their names imply, each modification statement is targeted to a specific modification activity. Let's look at each of them in turn and see how to apply them.

The *INSERT* Process

The INSERT keyword is used to add data to an already existing table. The simplified syntax looks like this. Remember that square brackets in these syntax statements mean optional sections.

```
INSERT
  [ INTO ]
  { <object> }
  [ ( column_list ) ]
  { VALUES ( ( { DEFAULT | NULL | expression } [ ,...n ] ) [ ,...n ])
  | derived_table
  | execute_statement
  | DEFAULT VALUES
```

Let's turn our attention back to the SandBoxDB database that we used earlier in this chapter. We created a table called Customer in that database. If you need to flip back a few pages to reacquaint yourself with this table, go ahead and do that now, as we will be working with this table over the next few sections.

Our first step will be to add a row to this table. Because the CustomerID column supports the IDENTITY property, we will be able to ignore that column for now. To insert a row into the table, we might use a statement like this:

```
USE SandboxDB;
INSERT INTO dbo.Customer
VALUES ('The Computer Store', 'PA', 1000);
```

This is the simplest form of the INSERT statement. We do not have to specify the columns into which we are inserting the data as long as we insert them in the same order as they are listed in the table. Because the CustomerID column automatically gets its values from the IDENTITY property, we can skip that column. Although we do not have to provide column names, it would be a best practice to do so, because it makes the code more adaptable to changing schemas and also makes it easier to understand. This also allows you to omit columns if needed. For example, the credit limit column allows null values. If you did not want to provide a credit limit, your code would look like this.

```
USE SandboxDB;
INSERT INTO dbo.Customer (CustomerName, StateCode)
VALUES ('RAM Warehouse', 'OR');
```

Performing an insert operation using a VALUES list works just fine, but if you look back at the syntax statement, you will see that you also have the option of using a derived table. This format allows you to do everything that you can do with a VALUES list, and provides additional flexibility to insert data into a table based on more complex extraction rules. For example, you could rewrite this code using this syntax. Note the use of the two sequential single quotes to represent one single quote within a quoted string.

```
USE SandboxDB;
INSERT INTO dbo.Customer (CustomerName, StateCode)
SELECT 'Buffalo Bill''s Boot Shop', 'WY';
```

In this example, the SELECT statement returns two literal values in a derived table that will be inserted into the Customer table.

What if we want to insert data into this table based on data from another table in this or another database? This is where the derived table form of the INSERT statement really shines. Suppose we have an Employee table in our database. (We don't, so just pretend for a moment.) Suppose further that we want to add all of our employees as customers and give each one a $500 credit limit. If we have only two or three employees, then it will not be difficult to write two or three INSERT statements that use VALUES to perform each insert. But what if there are 2,000 employees? As long as the data that we need is in an Employee table, we can do it all with the following query:

```
USE SandboxDB;
INSERT INTO dbo.Customer (CustomerName, StateCode, CreditLimit)
SELECT FirstName + ' '+ LastName, StateCode, 500
FROM Employee;
```

Now it does not matter how many employees are in the table. They will all be inserted into the Customer table in one statement.

This technique is extremely useful for loading temporary table structures with data from the database for further processing. Because this form is inclusive of the functionality that you would get from using the VALUES statement, it is a generally accepted best practice to use this form for all INSERT operations.

A corollary of this syntax is that you can also use a stored procedure to provide the data for the insert operation, as long as the procedure returns the data in the correct order and datatype as required by the first line of the INSERT statement.

Now let's suppose that you had a stored procedure called GetEmployeeList that returned the needed data from the employee table. You could use this statement to load the data into the Customer table. You can read more about stored procedures in Chapter 5, "Procedural Programming."

```
USE SandboxDB;
INSERT INTO dbo.Customer (CustomerName, StateCode, CreditLimit)
EXEC GetEmployeeList;
```

INSERTING WITH A CTE

Previously, we saw that you can create a CTE from which you can subsequently select data. You can also insert, update, and delete data from the CTE. However, you must perform all actions on the CTE *before* executing the GO statement and ending the batch, because at that point the CTE falls out of scope and is no longer available. In this respect, the CTE acts very much like a table variable.

So far, we have been avoiding the IDENTITY column in our inserts, relying instead on the property to provide the next available value. But what if we need to insert a value into this column to maintain data integrity? For example, suppose that you want to use the EmployeeID column from the Employee table as the CustomerID in the Customer table to provide consistency between these two tables. You would not be allowed to insert the value into the CustomerID column until you told SQL Server that you were going to provide your own information for that column using the IDENTITY_INSERT statement. The syntax would look like this.

```
USE SandboxDB;
SET IDENTITY_INSERT Customer ON;
GO
INSERT INTO dbo.Customer (CustomerID, CustomerName, StateCode, CreditLimit)
SELECT EmployeeID, FirstName + ' '+ LastName, StateCode, 500
FROM Employee;
SET IDENTITY_INSERT Customer OFF;
GO
```

Note that if you want to insert a NULL value explicitly into a table, assuming that the column in question accepts NULLs, you can use the keyword NULL in the SELECT list of the derived table. If the column selected in the derived table contains a NULL, it will use that value on insert. If there is an alternative default value defined by a constraint, that value can be explicitly inserted using the DEFAULT keyword in your derived table or VALUES list.

The *DELETE* Process

Deleting data from a table is a simple process in Transact-SQL. The basic form of the syntax looks like this.

```
DELETE
   [ FROM <table_source> [ ,...n ] ]
   [ WHERE <search_condition> ][;]
```

Suppose that you want to delete all of the rows from the Customer table with which you have been working. This simple statement will do the trick.

```
USE SandboxDB;
DELETE FROM Customer;
```

That's it. It doesn't get much simpler than that, does it? But how often will you want to delete all of the entries in a table? Maybe sometimes, but there is a better way to do that and we will talk about it later in this chapter.

Usually you will only want to delete some of the data in the table. That means your DELETE query must have a WHERE clause to provide criteria. Suppose, for example, that you want to delete every customer with a credit limit below 500. You would use a query like this one.

```
USE SandboxDB;DELETE FROM Customer
WHERE CreditLimit < 500;
```

That is more realistic.

Still another scenario might be this: Assume you just added all of your employees to the customer list in the previous operation, and now you need to remove them for some reason. The criterion in this case is that you want to remove data in the Customer table based on data in the Employee table.

There are two ways to write this query. The first would be a subquery like this.

```
USE SandboxDB;
DELETE FROM Customer
WHERE CustomerID IN (
       SELECT EmployeeID
       FROM Employee
);
```

In this code, the subquery returns a list of EmployeeID values to the outer query. Because you added the employees to the Customer table using their EmployeeIDs as their CustomerIDs, you can use this to our advantage in deleting the data. As we said before, though, often subqueries can be flattened out to JOIN statements. This query uses a join to accomplish the same result.

```
USE SandboxDB;

DELETE FROM Customer
FROM Customer as c
INNER JOIN Employee as e
       on c.CustomerID = e.EmployeeID;
```

This code is a little strange at first glance. There are two FROM clauses in the query. This is a special situation that only occurs with the DELETE statement. The first FROM in the query indicates the tables from which you want to delete. This FROM is actually optional—the first line of the query could have been written simply DELETE Customer, thereby avoiding the confusion. The second FROM clause is like the one in a SELECT statement. It provides context for the operation. In essence, you are saying that you only want to delete something from the Customer table where there is a match between Customer.CustomerID and Employee.EmployeeID.

YOU SAY DELETE AND I SAY TRUNCATE

If you really want to delete all of the data from a table, you should consider using the TRUNCATE TABLE statement instead of the DELETE statement. It can be a lot faster, depending on how much data is involved. The delete process is fully logged, so every row that you delete is written to the transaction log. When it truncates a table, SQL Server deallocates the data pages in the table, thereby removing all of the data in the table. Although the page deallocation is logged, each individual row is not, so this is definitely the way to go if you need to remove a lot of data. However, truncating a table will also reset its Identity column (if any) back to its original seed value for the next insert.

If the name of the table is *Customer*, then the full syntax would be:

```
USE SandboxDB;
TRUNCATE TABLE Customer;
```

The *UPDATE* Process

Although the INSERT and DELETE processes modify entire rows at a time, the UPDATE process is used to modify one or more columns on an already existing row of data. This adds a little complexity, but it is still an easy statement to use. The simplified syntax looks like this:

```
UPDATE
       { <object> }
SET
       { column_name = { expression | DEFAULT | NULL } } [ ,...n ]
       [ FROM{ <table_source> } [ ,...n ] ]
       [ WHERE { <search_condition> ][;]
```

Consider our Customer table. One of the customers is Buffalo Bill's Boot Shop. What happens if Bill's brother Bob purchases the boot shop and decides to rename the place? Assuming that the boot shop is currently CustomerID number 3, we would have to execute a query like this one:

```
USE SandboxDB;
UPDATE Customer
SET CustomerName = 'Buffalo Bob''s Boot Shop'
WHERE CustomerID = 3;
```

Without a WHERE clause, we would have inadvertently updated every customer's name. This is not what we intend here, so the WHERE clause is critical. This is one similarity to the DELETE operation.

Sometimes the intended action is more global in nature. For example, what if you have been directed to increase every customer's credit limit by 10 percent? In this case, a query such as the following, which lacks a WHERE clause, might be appropriate.

```
USE SandboxDB;
UPDATE Customer
SET CreditLimit = CreditLimit * 1.1;
```

Like the DELETE operation, the UPDATE process lets you use data from other tables to provide context for your update operation. Suppose that when you entered your employees into the Customer table you gave each one a credit limit of 500, and now you want to increase every employee's credit limit to 1,000. Using a JOIN statement like the one in the previous DELETE example would work. Try this query:

```
USE SandboxDB;
UPDATE Customer
SET CreditLimit = 1000
FROM Customer as c
INNER JOIN Employee as e
       on c.CustomerID = e.EmployeeID
```

UPDATE lets you can modify more than one field at the same time. Suppose you want to increase each employee's credit limit, and for accounting purposes, you also want to indicate in your Customers table that every employee is located in the state of California. You might use a query similar to this one:

```
USE SandboxDB;
UPDATE Customer
```

```
SET CreditLimit = 1000,
        StateCode = 'CA'
FROM Customer as c
INNER JOIN Employee as e
        on c.CustomerID = e.EmployeeID
```

The *MERGE* Process

The MERGE keyword was introduced in SQL Server 2008. Its purpose is to perform all appropriate insert, update, and delete operations in a table based in data in joined tables. Using one command, you can execute multiple data operations. This is very useful technique for maintaining data consistency and integrity. The result is that the statement merges the changes from the target table into the source table. The basic syntax looks like this.

```
MERGE <target>
USING
(SELECT <expression> FROM <source>) as <alias>
  ON <intersection>
WHEN MATCHED
  THEN <UPDATE | DELETE>
WHEN TARGET NOT MATCHED [AND <conditions>]
  THEN <INSERT>
WHEN SOURCE NOT MATCHED [AND <conditions>]
  THEN <UPDATE | DELETE> [;]
```

The code in Listing 4.8 presents a simple scenario where two tables, identical in schema, are to be merged. Although the two tables, List1 and List2, use the same schema, their data content is different.

As you read through the code, pay special attention to the tables' aliased source and target.

LISTING 4.8   Data Modification Through the Merge Process

```
USE SandboxDB;

-- Create two new List tables
CREATE TABLE List1
(
      Id          int,
      Val         varchar(20)
);

CREATE TABLE List2
(
      Id          int,
      Val         varchar(20)
);
```

```
-- INSERT data into the new tables
INSERT INTO List1
VALUES
(1,'Apples'),
(2,'Oranges'),
(3,'Grapes');

INSERT INTO List2
VALUES
(1,'Apples'),
(4,'Pears');

-- Execute the MERGE
MERGE List1 as target
USING
(SELECT * from List2) as source
ON source.Id = target.Id
WHEN MATCHED
THEN UPDATE SET target.Val = source.Val
WHEN TARGET NOT MATCHED
THEN INSERT VALUES(source.Id, source.Val)
WHEN SOURCE NOT MATCHED
THEN DELETE;

-- View the results
SELECT * FROM List1;
SELECT * FROM List2;

-- Drop the List tables
DROP TABLE List1;
DROP TABLE List2;
```

In this example, List 1, the source, is the table that will be modified. List 2, the target, is the table that provides the context for the merge. There are three conditions that you can evaluate.

There is a match between a source and target row. If there is a key match between the source and the target, the target table can either have its matching row updated or deleted. In this case, the matching row is updated to ensure that the value of the VAL column in the source table is used to update the VAL column in the target. This ensures consistent values between the two tables in all matching rows.

There are no matching rows in the target table for rows that exist in the source (target not matched). If the source table has rows that are not matched in the target table, you can execute an INSERT to add the rows to the target. Inserting data into the target is your only option for this condition. You can also choose to not include the condition if you do not want to merge the rows into the target table.

There are no matching rows in the source table for rows that exist in the target (source not matched). If the target table has rows that are not matched in the source table, you can either delete them or update them in the target. If you delete them, then it will make them consistent with the source table. If they do not exist in the source, they should not exist in the target. You also can issue an UPDATE statement to set a flag of some kind in the target table to indicate that the row is not present in the source.

Although the statement is relatively new, the need is not. You can probably already think of recent instances when you were trying to scrub data that you wanted to ensure that table contents were consistent. The MERGE statement can do that for you easily. Now you have that feature available if you need it.

Also, be aware that the source does not have to be a table at all. Because the source is never modified, it can be a derived table based on a SQL statement. This means that you can make multiple changes to a target table in one statement as long as you can write a single query that will represent what that data should look like when you're done. This is an incredibly powerful feature that, if used correctly, can really overhaul the way that you write your Transact-SQL code.

Using the *OUTPUT* Clause

INSERT, UPDATE, DELETE, and MERGE statements all provide support for an OUTPUT clause that you can use to capture the data that has been inserted or deleted from the table so that you can take other actions with that data. An OUTPUT clause behaves somewhat like a trigger in that it lets you store the desired values in a memory-resident table, but unlike a trigger, it is not a permanent part of the table structure. OUTPUT clauses execute only when you ask them.

For example, in a previous snippet you saw how to insert data into the Customer table based on a SELECT from the Employee table. Suppose that you wanted to log or otherwise process the rows that were inserted into the table. You could add an OUTPUT clause to the query like the one in Listing 4.9.

LISTING 4.9   Using OUTPUT with INSERT

```
USE SandboxDB;
SET IDENTITY_INSERT Customer ON;
GO

DECLARE @InsertedData table
(
      CustomerName        varchar(50),
      CreditLimit         money
);

INSERT INTO Customer(CustomerID, CustomerName, StateCode, CreditLimit)
OUTPUT INSERTED.CustomerName, INSERTED.CreditLimit
      INTO @InsertedData
SELECT EmployeeID, FirstName + ' ' + LastName, 'NV', 500
FROM Employee;

SELECT * FROM @InsertedData;

SET IDENTITY_INSERT Customer OFF;
GO
```

When you use the OUTPUT statement with the query in the listing, a special memory-resident table is created into which the values just inserted into that table are placed. Once the query ends, the special tables are gone, so if you want to do something more with the data, you must cache it in the query. In this example, the data is cached into a table variable called *@InsertedData* and selected in the subsequent statement.

When using the OUTPUT clause, a table called the inserted table is created for all INSERT operations. A table called the deleted table is created for delete operations. Update and merge operations create both inserted and deleted tables as appropriate to represent before and after views of the data.

The Bottom Line

Plan and implement appropriate normalization strategies. With a little planning, a database can be designed for efficiency and future growth. Using good normalization practices now can save a lot of headaches later as you try to maintain your application.

Master It Which normal form is being enforced in each of the following situations?

1. You create a CustomerID column in the Customer table to uniquely identify the customer.

2. A row in the Product table is identified by its ProductCode field and its VendorCode field. You also include the cost that each vendor charges for the product in the same table.

3. A row in the Product table is identified by its ProductCode field and its VendorCode field. The ProductColorCode is also in this table. You need to provide special processing instructions for products that are ordered in the color red. You choose to put those instructions in a separate ProductColorCode table.

4. In the Employee table, you choose to split the employee name into a separate FirstName and LastName column.

Design and create tables using all of the SQL Server table features. Tables define the structure for all of the data that you will store in your database. With the exception of filestream data, everything will be in a table. Good table design is critical to efficient data storage.

Master It Which table design feature would you use in each of these scenarios?

1. You need to provide an auto-incrementing key for a table.

2. A deterministic value is frequently calculated when you select from a table and you would prefer to store the data in the table.

3. You want to force a specific column to have a value for every row.

4. You want to separate some data into an archive structure and facilitate the process of keeping the archive current.

Write SELECT **statements from simple to complex for returning data to the client.**   A database is useless without a mechanism to extract the data once entered. In SQL, this is done with the SELECT statement. Because these statements are very flexible, a good Transact-SQL developer should be able to use the SELECT statement to manipulate the data to tell exactly the story that is needed.

> **Master It**   In the AdventureWorks2008 database, there are tables that provide every employee's pay history. Write a SELECT statement that will return the first and last name of each employee from the Person.Person table and their current pay rate from the HumanResources.EmployeePayHistory table. Assume that the current pay is the record with the latest ModifiedDate.

Perform data modification operations using the INSERT, UPDATE, DELETE, and MERGE SQL DML **statements.**   The statements that we use to modify data are not difficult to master, but they are critical. Any time that you need to make a modification to your database, you will be using one of these statements.

> **Master It**   Write the necessary code to insert the first name, last name, and phone number of every person in our database to a temporary table called #TempPerson.

Chapter 5

Procedural Programming

In this chapter, we'll explore Transact-SQL as a procedural programming language and develop an understanding of *procedural objects*. Understanding the procedural structures available to you in Transact-SQL is an essential step in the process of creating stored procedures and user-defined functions.

SQL Server provides many procedural programming possibilities. We will first explore the statements that make up the different procedural structures. You will learn about conditional logic, control-of-flow, error handling, and more. You will also learn the syntax for the different procedural structures, as well as the reasoning behind the usage of objects in SQL Server. Get ready to program using Transact-SQL.

In this chapter, you will learn to:

◆ Use procedural structures in your Transact-SQL scripts

◆ Create stored procedures

◆ Create views

◆ Create user-defined functions

◆ Create synonyms

Procedural Structures

In this section, we will explore batches, control-of-flow language elements, error management, and basic transaction processing. All of these items are used in the creation of stored procedures, user-defined functions, and triggers.

Batches

A *batch* is a set of Transact-SQL statements that are submitted together to SQL Server for execution. Each batch is submitted to SQL Server separately to be compiled into an execution plan and executed.

From an application perspective, each set of statements executed is considered to be a separate batch. Generally, each time an application executes SQL statements, it is in a separate batch.

A Transact-SQL script can include one or more batches. When writing scripts, you can include multiple batches of statements by separating blocks of Transact-SQL with the keyword GO. GO signifies the end of a batch to whatever tool is executing the script; it itself is not submitted to SQL Server. Whenever you see a line beginning with two hyphens, it is a single-line comment marker. Consider the following example:

```
USE SandboxDB;
-- Batch 1
CREATE TABLE T1 (C1 int NOT NULL);
INSERT INTO T1 VALUES (1);
GO
-- Batch 2
CREATE TABLE T2 (C2 int NOT NULL);
INSERT INTO T2 VALUES (2);
```

SANDBOXDB

All of the examples in this chapter use an empty database named SandBoxDB. This database was used previously in Chapter 3. You can reuse the existing database if you have already created it, or you can easily create a new database by executing the following statement:

```
CREATE DATABASE SandboxDB;
```

When the preceding statement is executed, the first batch is submitted to SQL Server, compiled, and executed. After the first batch is completed, the second batch is submitted to be compiled and executed.

There are several rules that must be followed in regard to batches.

◆ Some statements need to be submitted in their own batch, including CREATE PROCEDURE, CREATE VIEW, CREATE FUNCTION, CREATE DEFAULT, CREATE RULE, CREATE SCHEMA, and CREATE TRIGGER.

◆ Any variables must be defined and used in the same batch.

◆ Multiline comments using /* and */ must begin and complete within the same batch.

◆ A table's structure cannot be changed or new columns referenced in the same batch.

A compilation error for a batch, such as a syntax error, will prevent the execution of the entire batch. In general, a runtime error will stop the statement that caused it and prevent the execution of the remaining statements in a batch. This means that a batch could be only partially executed due to a runtime error. Some runtime errors will stop only the current statement and allow the rest of the batch to execute. Constraint violations are examples of this.

Beginning in SQL Server 2005, statement-level compilation has been used. This can cause behavior differences from previous versions of SQL Server. Consider the following example:

```
USE SandboxDB;
DROP TABLE T1;
GO
CREATE TABLE T1 (C1 int NOT NULL);
INSERT INTO T1 VALUES (1);
```

```
INSERT INTO T1 VALUES (2,2);
INSERT INTO T1 VALUES (3);
GO
SELECT * FROM T1;
```

In SQL Server 2005 and later versions, the behavior is as follows. Because the table T1 does not yet exist, the CREATE TABLE statement is compiled, but the INSERT statements are not. The CREATE TABLE statement is executed, and one by one, the INSERT statements are compiled and executed. Because the second INSERT statement provides too many values, it causes a runtime error, canceling the rest of the batch. The SELECT statement returns a single row.

By comparison, in SQL Server 2000 and prior versions, the process is similar; however, all of the INSERT statements are compiled and executed as a unit. Because of the error in the second statement, the batch would fail, but no rows would be inserted. Further, the SELECT statement would return zero rows.

Variables

A *variable* is a container for a single data value of a particular type. In Transact-SQL, all variables are preceded by an @ symbol. It is possible to define up to 10,000 variables in a single batch.

Local variables are used in Transact-SQL Scripts for a variety of purposes including:

◆ Storing values to be tested by control-of-flow statements

◆ Acting as a counter in a loop

◆ Storing the results of an expression

◆ Retrieving field values for a single record using a SELECT statement

Variables are also used to pass values into parameters for stored procedures and user-defined functions.

When declaring a variable, you must specify its name, datatype, and sometimes the length and precision of the datatype. You can optionally use the word AS when declaring variables. The DECLARE statement can be used to declare multiple variables by separating them with commas.

```
DECLARE @Var1 int;
DECLARE @Var2 as int;
DECLARE @Var3 varchar(25),
  @Var3 decimal(5,2);
```

The previous code declares three variables using two DECLARE statements. The varchar datatype requires you to specify the length. The decimal datatype requires you to specify the length and precision. @Var3 will store a decimal value with five numbers total and two to the right of the decimal point.

The preferred way to set the contents of a variable is to use the SET statement. It is also possible to use the SELECT statement to set the value of one or more variables. When using the SET statement, you may only set the value of one variable at a time. To set the values of multiple variables, you must use multiple SET statements.

```
SET @Var1 = 5;
SET @Var2 = 'A varchar string';
SELECT @Var2 = 'Another varchar string',
  @Var3 = 123.45;
```

You can also set the value of a variable to the field of a single record in a SELECT statement. Be careful with this approach, because if more than a single record is returned, only the values of the last record will be placed into the variables.

```
USE SandboxDB;
DECLARE @CustName varchar(50);
SELECT @CustName = CustomerName
 FROM Customer
 WHERE CustomerID = 1;
```

Local variables are scoped from the point where they are defined until the end of the current batch. An error will result if a variable is referenced outside of its scope, as shown here:

```
DECLARE @Test int;
SET @Test = 5;
GO
-- The statement below results in an error.
PRINT @Test;
```

GLOBAL VARIABLES?

Although statements such as @@Version are sometimes referred to as global variables, they are in reality *system functions*. There is no such thing as a global variable in Transact-SQL.

Control-of-Flow Statements

In Transact-SQL, control-of flow statements control the flow of execution of statements based on the evaluation of Boolean expressions. These statements are frequently found in stored procedures and functions.

BEGIN...END

Groups of statements used with IF, WHILE, and CASE statements must be grouped together using the BEGIN and END statements. Any BEGIN must have a corresponding END in the same batch.

IF...ELSE

IF statements evaluate a Boolean expression and branch execution based on the result.

```
IF @@ERROR <> 0
BEGIN
  PRINT 'An error occured in the previous statement.';
  RETURN;
END
ELSE
  PRINT 'No error occured in the previous statement.';
```

In the preceding example, the variable @@ERROR is checked for a nonzero value. If the condition evaluates to True, the statement or block of statements directly following the if are executed. If the condition evaluates to False, and an ELSE block exists, it is executed instead.

In any situation where more than a single statement needs to be executed in response to an IF or ELSE, use the BEGIN and END constructs.

WHILE

WHILE repeatedly executes a statement for as long as an expression remains True. (If more than one statement is to be repeated, use BEGIN and END.) An example of using WHILE with a counter is shown here:

```
DECLARE @Counter int;
SET @Counter = 1;
WHILE (@Counter <= 10)
BEGIN
  PRINT @Counter;
  SET @Counter = @Counter + 1;
END
```

WHILE may also be used with the EXISTS keyword to determine if there are any results returned from a query. For example:

```
WHILE EXISTS (SELECT * FROM T1 WHERE C1 = 1)
BEGIN
  -- Do some operation to rows of T1 where C1 = 1
END
```

CASE

The CASE statement is used for replacing the values of a column in a SELECT statement based on one or more expressions. In Transact-SQL, the CASE statement processes items row by row within a SELECT statement; it is not used for statement-level evaluation, as in other languages.

The CASE statement can be used wherever a column is allowed inside of a SELECT statement. It is commonly used to replace identifiers or codes with more descriptive values, but it can be useful for many other purposes.

The following example from AdventureWorks2008 demonstrates the use of a simple CASE statement that replaces department names with a two-character identifier for each department.

```
USE AdventureWorks2008;
GO
SELECT Name,
 CASE Name
  WHEN 'Human Resources' THEN 'HR'
  WHEN 'Finance' THEN 'FI'
  WHEN 'Information Services' THEN 'IS'
  WHEN 'Executive' THEN 'EX'
  WHEN 'Facilities and Maintenance' THEN 'FM'
 END AS Abbreviation
FROM AdventureWorks2008.HumanResources.Department
WHERE GroupName = 'Executive General and Administration';
```

CASE can also be used with Boolean search expressions. The order of these expressions is very important, because once a match is found, it will be used, and none of the following expressions will be evaluated. Here is an example of using CASE with search expressions:

```
USE AdventureWorks2008;
GO
SELECT ProductNumber,
       Name,
  CASE
   WHEN ListPrice = 0 THEN 'Not For Resale'
   WHEN ListPrice < 49 THEN 'Under $50'
   WHEN ListPrice BETWEEN 50 and 499 THEN '$50 - $499'
   WHEN ListPrice BETWEEN 500 and 1000 THEN '$500 - $1000'
   ELSE 'Over $1000'
  END As PriceRange
FROM AdventureWorks2008.Production.Product
ORDER BY ProductNumber;
```

Error Management

It is inevitable that you will encounter errors in Transact-SQL statements. It is important to understand the different types of errors and the options available for error handling.

Syntax Errors Syntax errors are common occurrences, generally resulting from typing mistakes. When a syntax error is encountered, no statements in the batch are executed because the error was encountered during compilation, before any of the statements began to execute. It is important to remember that you cannot respond to a syntax error using code; you can only correct the syntax and try to resubmit the batch.

```
USE AdventureWorks2008;
PRINT 'Does not run.';
SELECT ** FROM HumanResources.Employee;
PRINT 'Also does not run.';
```

In the previous example, the PRINT statement is never executed, because the syntax error occurs while compiling the query. Only the following is reported back from SQL Server:

```
Msg 102, Level 15, State 1, Line 2
Incorrect syntax near '*'.
```

Runtime Errors Runtime errors occur for many reasons in SQL Server. These errors happen while the code is executing, after the execution plan has been compiled. Runtime errors can be handled by using error-handling logic. This logic may reside in the application running the statements, but it may also be written using Transact-SQL. The way that errors are managed in the application depends on the database API used to run the queries. In ADO.NET, the SqlException class is available to retrieve all of the details about the error that occurred. For more information about ADO.NET, refer to Chapter 17, "SQL Server and the .NET Client."

```
PRINT 'Before Error';
SELECT 1/0;
PRINT 'After Error';
```

The previous code results in division by zero, which occurs in the second statement. All three statements execute, however, as is shown in the following output:

```
Before Error
Msg 8134, Level 16, State 1, Line 2
Divide by zero error encountered.
After Error
```

ERROR MESSAGES

Error messages generated from SQL Server are stored in the `sys.messages` catalog view. When an error is raised, the following are properties of the error:

Error Number The number of the error as defined in `sys.messages`. Error numbers 50,000 and above are user-defined errors. Numbers up to 50,000 are reserved for system errors.

Severity Level A number representing the error's severity.

State A number representing where the error occurred. If the same error is raised from multiple locations in a piece of code, different states should be used.

Line Number The approximate line number where the error occurred.

Error Message The message describing the error. Parameter placeholders are used here.

The error properties retrievable from code depend on the method used to capture the error. When using the TRY...CATCH construct, all information about an error can be retrieved in the CATCH block. When using the @@ERROR system function, only the error number can be retrieved, and only in the statement directly following the one that caused the error.

HANDLING ERRORS USING *TRY...CATCH*

The TRY...CATCH construct was introduced with SQL Server 2005 for error handling using Transact-SQL. Statements to be tested for an error are enclosed in a BEGIN TRY...END TRY block. A CATCH block immediately follows the TRY block, and error-handling logic is stored here. The following example shows the basic syntax:

```
BEGIN TRY
  -- Code that may produce errors
END TRY
BEGIN CATCH
  -- Error Handling Logic
END CATCH;
```

SQL Server evaluates each statement in the TRY block sequentially. If a runtime error is encountered, control immediately jumps to the CATCH block, and error information can be retrieved, logged, and displayed to the user.

Within the CATCH block, several functions are available that retrieve information about the error that occurred (Table 5.1). It is important to note that these functions will all return NULL outside the scope of the CATCH block.

TABLE 5.1   CATCH Block Error Functions

FUNCTION NAME	DESCRIPTION
ERROR_LINE()	The line number the error occurred on
ERROR_NUMBER()	The SQL Server error number
ERROR_MESSAGE()	The error message, including any values that were passed on using parameter placeholders
ERROR_PROCEDURE()	If the error occurred in a procedure, the procedure name is returned, otherwise NULL is returned
ERROR_SEVERITY()	The severity level of the error
ERROR_STATE()	The state value of the error

These system functions can be used to log information about the error to a table, or to print the error messages to the user. The following example displays information about the error in a result set with a single row:

```
USE AdventureWorks2008;
BEGIN TRY
  SELECT 1/0;
END TRY
BEGIN CATCH
  INSERT INTO dbo.ErrorLog (Line, Number, ErrorMsg,
    [Procedure], Severity, [State])
  VALUES (ERROR_LINE(), ERROR_NUMBER(), ERROR_MESSAGE(),
    ERROR_PROCEDURE(), ERROR_SEVERITY(), ERROR_STATE());
END CATCH;
```

HANDLING ERRORS USING @@ERROR

Another way to handle runtime errors using Transact-SQL is to check the value of the @@ERROR value after every statement that could possibly generate an error. If an error occurred, the value of @@ERROR is the error number. If no error occurred, the value is 0.

Using @@ERROR results in a very different style of error-handling code and is generally much more difficult to maintain. Error-handling logic must be located after every statement that could cause an error. It is also important to store the value of @@ERROR before doing any testing, as the return value is reset after each SQL statement.

```
SELECT 1/0;
PRINT @@ERROR;
```

In the previous example, the value 8143 is printed, because a division-by-zero error occurred. However, consider the following example:

```
SELECT 1/0;
IF @@ERROR <> 0
  PRINT @@ERROR;
```

When running the preceding code, the printed result will be 0, because @@ERROR is reset after the IF statement is evaluated.

Because of this, it is common to see code that uses the following logic:

```
DECLARE @SaveError int;
SELECT 1/0;
SET @SaveError = @@ERROR;
IF @SaveError <> 0
  PRINT @SaveError;
```

Another disadvantage of @@ERROR is that only the error number—not the error message—can be retrieved using this strategy. The error message could be retrieved from the sys.messages catalog view based on this error number, but any parameter placeholder values would be lost. You may have violated a constraint, but without those parameter placeholder values, you wouldn't know which constraint you violated. The main advantage to this method is that it has been supported much longer than TRY...CATCH in Transact-SQL.

WHY SHOULD I USE @@ERROR?

You may be tempted to use the TRY...CATCH construct everywhere you can. Using @@ERROR can be cumbersome; however, it is supported in all previous versions of SQL Server. If your code must execute on versions of SQL Server prior to SQL Server 2005, you must avoid using TRY...CATCH, and use @@ERROR for error handling instead.

RAISING ERRORS

There may be situations where you would like to raise a user-defined error message. This message may be stored as a user-defined error in the sys.messages table, or it may be dynamic text. If dynamic text is used, the error number is always 50,000. User-defined errors are created at the instance level, and they can introduce conflicts if more than one application tries to use the same error number. Use the sp_addmessage system stored procedure to add user-defined error messages.

The following code adds a user-defined error with parameter placeholders:

```
EXEC sp_addmessage 50005, -- Message ID
     10, -- Severity Level
 'The current database ID is: %d, the database name is: %s.';
```

The RAISERROR statement is used to generate an error that can be handled by the calling procedure or Transact-SQL code. RAISERROR uses the following basic syntax:

```
RAISERROR ( { msg_id | msg_str | @local_variable }
 { ,severity ,state }
 [ ,argument [ ,...n ] ] )
 [ WITH option [ ,...n ] ]
```

As shown, RAISERROR can take either a numeric message ID or a message string as its first argument. The severity indicates the type of error encountered. A severity of 10 is informational (meaning not very severe). For more information on the available severity levels, refer to SQL Server Books Online.

The following is an example of using the RAISERROR function with two parameter placeholders and a user-defined error as added in a previous example:

```
DECLARE @DBID int;
DECLARE @DBNAME nvarchar(128);
SET @DBID = DB_ID();
SET @DBNAME = DB_NAME();
RAISERROR (50005,
 10, -- Severity.
 1, -- State.
 @DBID, -- First substitution argument.
 @DBNAME); -- Second substitution argument.
GO
```

RAISERROR can be used in conjunction with stored user-defined messages, or by passing a message into it. If a message is used in place of an error number, the message number is always 50,000.

```
RAISERROR ('Custom Message',
    10, -- Severity
    1); -- State
```

Basic Transaction Processing

Transactions ensure that a modification or set of modifications is processed entirely or not at all. They can be closely related to error handling within a database based on the business rules of an organization.

In this section, we'll discuss the default transaction behavior of SQL Server and learn about explicit transactions. For more detailed information on transaction processing and the process that goes on behind the scenes, refer to Chapter 15, "Transactions and Locking Strategies."

We all want our databases to be able to maintain data integrity, and transactions are a critical component of this. Transactions have the four properties shown in Table 5.2.

TABLE 5.2   Properties of Transactions

PROPERTY	DESCRIPTION
Atomicity	A transaction behaves as an atomic operation: it is either committed or rolled back as a unit.
Consistency	All database structures must be consistent. Tables and indexes must remain in sync.
Isolation	Transactions are isolated from one another with locks. The degree of isolation is determined by the transaction isolation level. Both locking and transaction isolation levels will be covered in more detail in Chapter 15.
Durability	Transactions must persist in the event of a system failure. Transaction logging in SQL Server supports this requirement.

AUTOCOMMIT TRANSACTIONS

By default, SQL Server considers each statement that makes a modification a separate transaction. Either the statement completes entirely, or not at all. For example, an UPDATE statement will either update all the records in its search criteria, or none of them. If an error is encountered in the middle of the update process, any changes that have been made must be rolled back.

It is important to understand the behavior of batches running in Autocommit mode. When runtime errors are encountered, the statement that generated the runtime error is rolled back; however, the batch will continue to execute. Consider the following batch:

```
USE SandboxDB;
CREATE TABLE T3
 (c int PRIMARY KEY NOT NULL);
INSERT INTO T3 VALUES (1);
INSERT INTO T3 VALUES (2/0);
INSERT INTO T3 VALUES (3);
SELECT * FROM T3;
```

When this batch is executed, the table is created, and the first INSERT statement executes successfully. The second INSERT statement in this batch causes a divide-by-zero runtime error. The second INSERT statement is terminated due to a runtime error, and the third INSERT statement executes. When the results of the SELECT statement are examined, the table T3 contains two rows.

If a syntax error occurs, the entire batch is prevented from executing. Consider the following batch:

```
USE SandboxDB;
CREATE TABLE T4
 (c int PRIMARY KEY NOT NULL);
INSERT INTO T4 VALUES (1);
INSERT INTO T4 VALUES (2//0);
INSERT INTO T4 VALUES (3);
SELECT * FROM T4;
```

In the preceding example, there is a syntax error in the second INSERT statement. Because of this error, the batch cannot be compiled into an execution plan, and none of the statements can run, including the CREATE TABLE statement.

EXPLICIT TRANSACTIONS

SQL Server allows you to group statements into a single transaction. BEGIN TRANSACTION indicates the beginning of a transaction. COMMIT TRANSACTION means that all changes since the BEGIN TRANSACTION statement should be committed to the database. ROLLBACK TRANSACTION allows any modifications made to be undone by the database engine.

XACT_ABORT is a session option that controls the behavior of runtime errors in transactions. XACT_ABORT can be set to ON or OFF, and its default is OFF. When XACT_ABORT is turned on, any statement that causes an error will automatically roll back the transaction and cancel execution of the rest of the batch. Consider the following:

```
USE SandboxDB;
SET XACT_ABORT ON;
CREATE TABLE T5
```

```
 (c int PRIMARY KEY NOT NULL);
BEGIN TRAN;
  INSERT INTO T5 VALUES (1);
  INSERT INTO T5 VALUES (2);
  INSERT INTO T5 VALUES (2);
  INSERT INTO T5 VALUES (3);
COMMIT TRAN;
SELECT * FROM T5;
```

A violation of the table's primary key constraint occurs in the third INSERT statement in the transaction. Because the XACT_ABORT option is turned on, this runtime error automatically rolls back the transaction and cancels the rest of the batch. The SELECT statement is never executed.

If the same script were run without turning on XACT_ABORT, the runtime error would terminate only that statement, not the entire batch. The results of the SELECT statement would contain three rows.

Because XACT_ABORT is turned off by default, critical pieces of a transaction should be wrapped in TRY...CATCH blocks, as shown here:

```
USE SandboxDB;
CREATE TABLE T6
 (c int PRIMARY KEY NOT NULL);
BEGIN TRY
  BEGIN TRAN;
    INSERT INTO T6 VALUES (1);
    INSERT INTO T6 VALUES (2);
    INSERT INTO T6 VALUES (2);
    INSERT INTO T6 VALUES (3);
  COMMIT TRAN;
END TRY
BEGIN CATCH
  PRINT 'An Error Occured';
  ROLLBACK TRAN;
END CATCH;
SELECT * FROM T6;
```

Stored Procedures

Stored procedures are sets of operations stored on the server and executed by client applications. Parameter values can be passed into a stored procedure as input. Output parameters can be used to return variable values to the calling code. Stored procedures can accept up to 2,100 parameters in total. A single-integer return value is generally used to indicate success or failure.

There are many operations that can be performed by stored procedures in a database. Modifying database structures and performing user-defined transactions are common operations. Stored procedures can be used to return the results of SELECT statements, but in general they are much less flexible with the results than a table-valued user-defined function. We will cover user-defined functions later in this chapter.

We will focus on building Transact-SQL stored procedures in this section, but it is also possible to build stored procedures using .NET integration. When building CLR-stored procedures, any .NET language may be used, including C# and VB.NET. This will be covered in Chapter 18, "Leveraging the SQL Server .NET CLR."

Using stored procedures has many benefits, including security, modular programming, and network traffic reduction.

Security   Stored procedures are granted access separately from the database objects they reference. In general, a user who is granted access to execute a stored procedure is allowed to perform all of the operations in the stored procedure. It is also possible for a stored procedure to execute as another user. For more information on permissions, and executing as another user, refer to Chapter 8, "Managing User Security."

Modular Programming   Stored procedures promote the reuse of Transact-SQL logic in an application. They also allow complicated procedures to be broken into separate modules.

Network Traffic Reduction   Using stored procedures can reduce the amount of network traffic between client and server. Sending a call to execute a stored procedure that contains 100 lines of code uses less traffic than sending the 100 lines of code every time. It can also reduce the amount of conversation back and forth to complete a multistep operation in the database.

Designing Effective Stored Procedures

In older versions of SQL Server, stored procedures may have been the only way to accomplish an operation. It is important to fully understand the options available for solving a problem rather than immediately choosing a stored procedure for every operation in your database.

Stored procedures can execute nearly any Transact-SQL statement, with a few minor exceptions. An object such as a table may be created and used in the same procedure, so long as the table is created first.

Here are the operations that are not allowed in a stored procedure:

- Creating or altering any of the following objects:

    - Aggregate

    - Default

    - Function

    - Procedure

    - Rule

    - Schema

    - Trigger

    - View

- The USE statement

- SET PARSEONLY or SHOWPLAN variants

Objects other than these listed types can be created, altered, and dropped in the current database from within a stored procedure. Database modifications and user-defined transactions are prime candidates for encapsulating as stored procedures.

A stored procedure can return one or more result sets to the calling application. A table-valued user-defined function should be considered instead of a stored procedure that returns a single result set. The results from a stored procedure cannot be used in the FROM clause of a query.

Stored procedures can use temporary tables in their operations. Any local temporary tables last only for the duration of the stored procedure execution. A nested stored procedure can access local temporary tables created inside of the calling stored procedure.

When referencing objects inside of a stored procedure, they should be qualified with a schema name. A nonqualified name would first default to searching the schema of the stored procedure. If the object isn't found, the user's default schema is searched. This could result in errors for a user who doesn't have the correct default schema set, or if the user's default schema is changed.

Two session options are saved when a stored procedure is created. They are QUOTED_ IDENTIFIERS and ANSI_NULLS. QUOTED_IDENTIFIERS determines if double quotes may be used to surround identifiers, or if they should be interpreted as string literals. ANSI_NULLS determines comparison behavior in relation to NULL values. If ANSI_NULLS is turned on, only comparisons using the IS operator with NULL values will return rows in a SELECT statement.

When it is created, a stored procedure may reference tables that don't exist. Table names are resolved when a procedure is first executed. If a table does exist when the stored procedure is created, all of the columns referenced must exist at creation time.

Creating and Executing a Simple Stored Procedure

Let's start by creating a simple stored procedure. The following stored procedure is designed to be executed from within the CATCH block of a TRY...CATCH construct:

```
USE SandboxDB;
GO
CREATE PROC dbo.uspPrintError
AS
PRINT 'Error ' + CONVERT(varchar(50), ERROR_NUMBER()) +
  ', Severity ' + CONVERT(varchar(5), ERROR_SEVERITY()) +
  ', State ' + CONVERT(varchar(5), ERROR_STATE()) +
  ', Procedure ' + ISNULL(ERROR_PROCEDURE(), '-') +
  ', Line ' + CONVERT(varchar(5), ERROR_LINE());
PRINT ERROR_MESSAGE();
GO
```

In this procedure, we print information about an error. This code can be used in any situation we want to print error information, and it promotes reuse.

Now, let's try to execute this procedure. Remember, because this procedure uses the error information functions, it needs to be called from within a CATCH block. To view any messages returned, remember to switch to the Messages tab.

```
BEGIN TRY
 SELECT 1/0;
END TRY
BEGIN CATCH
 EXEC dbo.uspPrintError;
END CATCH;
```

The output from running the preceding Transact-SQL statements is:

```
Error 8134, Severity 16, State 1, Procedure -, Line 2
Divide by zero error encountered.
```

A stored procedure's contents can be modified using the ALTER statement. Using ALTER replaces the definition of the procedure without affecting any permissions that have been applied to the procedure. The following code modifies the uspPrintError stored procedure to print a usage error message when the error number is NULL:

```
USE SandboxDB;
GO
ALTER PROC dbo.uspPrintError
AS
IF ERROR_NUMBER() IS NULL
 BEGIN
 PRINT 'This procedure must be used within a CATCH block';
 RETURN(1);
 END
ELSE
 BEGIN
 PRINT 'Error ' + CONVERT(varchar(50), ERROR_NUMBER()) +
   ', Severity ' + CONVERT(varchar(5), ERROR_SEVERITY()) +
   ', State ' + CONVERT(varchar(5), ERROR_STATE()) +
   ', Procedure ' + ISNULL(ERROR_PROCEDURE(), '-') +
   ', Line ' + CONVERT(varchar(5), ERROR_LINE());
 PRINT ERROR_MESSAGE();
 END
GO
```

When a stored procedure is no longer needed within a database, it is deleted by dropping it:

```
USE SandboxDB;
DROP PROC dbo.uspPrintError;
```

Using Parameters

Most of the stored procedures you will create use parameters. Parameters can be used to provide input values to a stored procedure, as well as output values to the caller. In this section, we'll examine several examples of using the different types of parameters.

INPUT PARAMETERS

Input parameters are variables defined in the header of a stored procedure. When the stored procedure is executed, values for these variables must be provided. The following is a stored procedure that shows our three options for defining input parameters:

```
USE SandboxDB;
GO
CREATE PROC uspInputParam
 @param1 int = 5,
 @param2 int = NULL,
```

```
  @param3 int
AS
IF @param2 IS NULL
BEGIN
 PRINT 'You must supply a value for @param2.';
 RETURN(1);
END
PRINT @param1 + @param2 + @param3;
GO
```

In the preceding procedure, three input parameters are defined in the header. @param1 and @param2 both have default values provided for them. The second parameter is checked for a NULL value before the rest of the procedure is allowed to continue. If the value is still NULL, a friendly error message is printed. The RETURN statement exits the procedure unconditionally. The third parameter has no default value, and is considered a required parameter by SQL Server. The first two parameters are both considered optional because default values have been provided.

Let's examine the different methods of executing this procedure using Transact-SQL. One option is to pass the parameters in the order they are defined in the header of the stored procedure:

```
-- Passing by Position
EXEC uspInputParam 1, 2, 3;
```

When this code is executed, the number 6 is printed, because we supplied values for all of the parameters.

```
-- Passing by Position without supplying all values
EXEC uspInputParam 1, 2;
```

If you miss any required parameters, an error message is generated by SQL Server:

```
Msg 201, Level 16, State 4, Procedure uspInputParam, Line 0
Procedure or function 'uspInputParam' expects parameter '@param3', which was not
supplied.
```

It is also possible to pass parameters by name. When passing parameters by name, you may skip parameters, as well as provide the parameters in any order.

```
-- Passing by Name, missing value for @param2
EXEC uspInputParam @param3 = 5;
```

In the preceding example, we provide a value only for the third parameter. Because of the IF statement at the beginning of the procedure, the following error message is printed:

```
You must supply a value for @param2.
```

Our last execution of this stored procedure will accept the default value for the first parameter:

```
-- Passing by Name, using default value for @param1
EXEC uspInputParam @param3 = 5,
    @param2 = 5;
```

Because all required values have been provided, the stored procedure executes, and the output of this execution is 15.

Another, more realistic example of using input parameters is shown in the following example. It is an example used in the AdventureWorks2008 database to update employee salary information, and log the changes made into the EmployeePayHistory table.

```
USE AdventureWorks2008;
GO
CREATE PROCEDURE HumanResources.uspUpdateEmployeeHireInfo
 @BusinessEntityID int,
 @JobTitle nvarchar(50),
 @HireDate datetime,
 @RateChangeDate datetime,
 @Rate money,
 @PayFrequency tinyint,
 @CurrentFlag dbo.Flag
AS
SET NOCOUNT ON;
BEGIN TRY
 BEGIN TRANSACTION;
 UPDATE HumanResources.Employee
 SET JobTitle = @JobTitle
  ,HireDate = @HireDate
  ,CurrentFlag = @CurrentFlag
 WHERE BusinessEntityID = @BusinessEntityID;
 INSERT INTO HumanResources.EmployeePayHistory
  (BusinessEntityID
  ,RateChangeDate
  ,Rate
  ,PayFrequency)
 VALUES (@BusinessEntityID, @RateChangeDate, @Rate, @PayFrequency);
 COMMIT TRANSACTION;
END TRY
BEGIN CATCH
 IF @@TRANCOUNT > 0
 BEGIN
  ROLLBACK TRANSACTION;
 END
 EXECUTE dbo.uspLogError;
END CATCH;
```

This stored procedure performs the modifications within a user-defined transaction. If any errors are encountered, the transaction is rolled back, and errors are logged using a nested stored procedure call.

OUTPUT PARAMETERS

Output parameters allow you to pass data values out of a stored procedure using variables. Specifying the OUTPUT keyword is required both when defining the parameter and when referencing the parameter during execution.

When returning a single record from a stored procedure, using several output parameters can provide less overhead than returning a result set containing a single record to the client. The following example gets the AccountNumber for a specific customer:

```
USE AdventureWorks2008;
GO
CREATE PROC Sales.uspGetCustomerAccountNumber
  @CustomerID int,
  @AccountNumber varchar(10) OUTPUT
AS
SELECT @AccountNumber = AccountNumber
 FROM Sales.Customer
 WHERE CustomerID = @CustomerID;
GO
```

In order to execute this procedure using Transact-SQL, we will need to provide a variable to store the contents of our output parameter, and use the OUTPUT keyword after the variable name. Note that the variable name storing the output and the parameter name don't need to be the same. An example of execution is listed here:

```
USE AdventureWorks2008;
DECLARE @Acct varchar(10);
EXEC Sales.uspGetCustomerAccountNumber 1, @Acct OUTPUT;
PRINT @Acct;
```

Another example of using an output parameter exists in the uspLogError stored procedure we executed earlier. Note that even though we provide an output parameter here, it doesn't have to be retrieved when executing the stored procedure.

```
USE AdventureWorks2008;
GO
ALTER PROCEDURE dbo.uspLogError
 @ErrorLogID int = 0 OUTPUT
AS
SET NOCOUNT ON;
BEGIN TRY
 -- Return if there is no error information to log
 IF ERROR_NUMBER() IS NULL
  RETURN 1;
 -- Return if inside an uncommittable transaction.
 -- Data insertion/modification is not allowed when
 -- a transaction is in an uncommittable state.
 IF XACT_STATE() = -1
 BEGIN
  PRINT 'Cannot log error since the current transaction ' +
```

```
      'is in an uncommittable state. '
   RETURN 1;
 END
 INSERT dbo.ErrorLog
  (UserName, ErrorNumber, ErrorSeverity,
  ErrorState, ErrorProcedure, ErrorLine, ErrorMessage)
 VALUES
  (CONVERT(sysname, CURRENT_USER), ERROR_NUMBER(), ERROR_SEVERITY(),
  ERROR_STATE(), ERROR_PROCEDURE(), ERROR_LINE(), ERROR_MESSAGE());
 -- Pass back the ErrorLogID of the row inserted
 SET @ErrorLogID = @@IDENTITY;
END TRY
BEGIN CATCH
 PRINT 'An error occurred in stored procedure uspLogError: ';
 EXECUTE dbo.uspPrintError;
 RETURN -1;
END CATCH
```

Managing Return Values

Stored procedure return values should be used to indicate success or failure of the stored procedure. Unless specifically documented, system stored procedures return nonzero values to represent failures.

To return any other information from the stored procedure, output parameters should be used. A stored procedure may return a single integer value, but it can return many output parameters.

When a stored procedure encounters a RETURN statement, it exits immediately to the calling code. The default return value is 0, which generally represents success. Nonzero return values usually represent failures of some sort. A NULL value will never be returned from a stored procedure; it will be converted to a 0 and a warning will be raised.

To capture the return value of a stored procedure, use the following syntax:

```
CREATE PROC uspMyProc
AS
RETURN 1;
GO
DECLARE @retval int;
EXEC @retval = uspMyProc;
PRINT @retval;
```

User-defined functions offer more flexibility in the use of their return values, and they will be covered later in this chapter.

Understanding Compilation

Now that we've had the opportunity to explore how stored procedures are created and executed, let's examine how they are compiled and executed.

When a stored procedure is first created, it is parsed for accurate syntax, and the Transact-SQL statements are stored. The statements inside a stored procedure aren't compiled into an execution plan until the first time it is executed. This allows delayed name resolution to work—a good thing, because objects may be referred to that don't yet exist.

When a query is executed the first time, an execution plan is created from the statements and parameter values used. The plan is then placed into the procedure cache.

An execution plan has two components: a query plan and an execution context. A query plan defines the physical process and order for database operations to occur. For a given Transact-SQL statement, there may be many ways to perform the physical operations. The function of the query optimizer is to build efficient query plans from the statements and values provided. The query optimizer determines the indexes that need to be used, order of operations, join strategies, and many other operations to arrive at an efficient plan for execution. The query optimizer will be discussed in more detail in Chapter 14, "Indexing Strategies for Query Optimization."

Most SQL statements can be broken into the components of execution and parameter values. The execution context consists of the parameter values for each separate execution of a stored procedure. A query plan may be reused many times with differing parameter values. The query plan and execution context together are considered an execution plan.

Eventually, execution plans need to be removed from the procedure cache. Plans that haven't been used for a period of time are aged out of the cache to make room for new execution plans. Structural changes to the database, including changes to the structure of the referenced objects or indexes being dropped, can also invalidate execution plans

If an index that an execution plan uses is dropped, the plan must be recompiled to use the available objects. This is automatically detected and accomplished by the database engine.

SQL Server 2008 provides statement-level recompilation for stored procedures. When a change occurs to a database that causes plan recompilation, only the statements that were affected by the change are recompiled.

MANAGING COMPILATION

There are several situations where you will want to manage the compilation process for execution plans.

Sometimes a stored procedure receives widely varying parameter values. The most common situation is in range searches. If a query were returning information for five records, it would likely use a different plan than if it were retrieving five million records. A stored procedure that receives widely varying range searches may benefit from being recompiled each time it's executed. This can be accomplished by creating the procedure using the WITH RECOMPILE option:

```
USE AdventureWorks2008;
GO
CREATE PROCEDURE uspOrderRange
 @BeginDate datetime,
 @EndDate datetime
WITH RECOMPILE
AS
SELECT *
 FROM Sales.SalesOrderHeader
 WHERE OrderDate BETWEEN @BeginDate AND @EndDate;
```

`WITH RECOMPILE` can also be specified when executing a stored procedure. Using this syntax will cause the stored procedure to recompile for just one execution. Subsequent executions will use the cached plan:

```
EXEC uspOrderRange '12/1/2006', '12/1/2009' WITH RECOMPILE;
```

Execution plans are automatically invalidated when required, but they aren't able to use objects that have been created since the execution plan was compiled. For example, if a procedure plan were cached, and an index is created that would be useful, SQL Server will continue to use the cached plan until it is aged out of cache. The `sp_recompile` statement can be used to flag plans for recompilation for:

◆ Individual stored procedures

◆ Individual user-defined functions

◆ Tables

◆ Views

After creating new indexes for a table, it is a good practice to run `sp_recompile` to flag any procedures using that table for recompilation.

Views

A *view* is a query that is stored on the server as an object and referenced like a table. With the exception of indexed views, the results of the query aren't stored, only the definition of the query is saved within the database.

Using a view is very similar to using a table. The results of a view can be joined with other tables in the `FROM` clause of a query. It is a good practice to use a prefix to identify a view when choosing a name, so that it can be easily differentiated from a table.

A view can reference other views. This feature can cause performance problems, as SQL Server needs to combine the components of several `SELECT` statements into a single execution plan. If possible, you should try to reference tables directly. If a view needs to reference another view, ensure that unneeded logic isn't being applied.

A view can be modified with some restrictions. `INSERT`, `UPDATE`, and `DELETE` statements are allowed, so long as they follow these rules:

◆ Modifications can affect only one table at a time.

◆ Modifications must satisfy all constraints of the underlying table.

　　◆ If a view doesn't provide all columns without default values, you can't insert into the view.

◆ Calculated columns, and views that use `GROUP BY` operations, cannot be modified.

It is possible to allow more modifications to a view by writing the logic required into an `INSTEAD OF` trigger. These will be covered later, in Chapter 6, "Managing Data Integrity."

Why Use Views?

Views can provide many benefits to a database developer. The following are some of the advantages of using views in the design of a database:

Views simplify data retrieval.   Common queries can be created as views in the database to simplify query writing. Calculations, derived columns, and grouping logic can make the process of writing queries easier.

Views focus users on specific data.   A view allows the user to focus on relevant data by filtering out unneeded or sensitive columns and rows. A view can reference system functions to further focus data.

Views provide abstraction from change.   When an application is referencing views and stored procedures, it can allow the database developer more flexibility in making later changes to the table structure. As the table structure changes, the views can be modified to compensate without requiring changes to the applications accessing the data.

Views provide performance benefits.   An indexed view can provide performance benefits by storing the result set in the database. For database operations that summarize data, this can provide a significant performance gain. Indexed views will be covered in Chapter 14.

Views separate securable objects.   A view can be granted permissions independently of a table. This means that someone can be granted access to a view without needing access to the underlying table so long as both objects are owned by the same database user.

SQL Server rechecks permissions whenever one object references another object that is owned by a different user, a condition that can result in broken ownership chains.

Standard Views

Creating a view is a simple task. The main step is writing the query that produces the result set you want. The following example retrieves the name and title of each current employee in the AdventureWorks2008 database:

```
USE AdventureWorks2008;
GO
CREATE VIEW HumanResources.vEmployeeInfo
AS
SELECT p.Firstname,
       p.LastName,
       e.JobTitle
 FROM Person.Person p
 INNER JOIN HumanResources.Employee e
 ON p.BusinessEntityID = e.BusinessEntityID
WHERE e.CurrentFlag = 1;
GO
```

After the view has been created, it can be queried as though it were a table.

```
SELECT * FROM HumanResources.vEmployeeInfo
 WHERE JobTitle LIKE '%manager%';
```

Altering a view is similar to altering a stored procedure. The view definition is overwritten, but any permission granted on the view remains in place. The following example adds a department field to our vEmployeeInfo view:

```
ALTER VIEW HumanResources.vEmployeeInfo
AS
SELECT p.Firstname,
       p.LastName,
       e.JobTitle,
       d.Name As DepartmentName
 FROM Person.Person p
 INNER JOIN HumanResources.Employee e
 ON p.BusinessEntityID = e.BusinessEntityID
 INNER JOIN HumanResources.EmployeeDepartmentHistory edh
 ON edh.BusinessEntityID = e.BusinessEntityID
 INNER JOIN HumanResources.Department d
 ON d.DepartmentID = edh.DepartmentID
WHERE e.CurrentFlag = 1 AND
   edh.EndDate IS NULL;
```

A view may be renamed using the sp_rename system stored procedure. When renaming a view, the original name stays inside of the view definition.

To drop a view, use the DROP VIEW statement as follows:

```
DROP VIEW HumanResources.vEmployeeInfo;
```

VIEW OPTIONS

When you create a view, two options can be specified: WITH SCHEMABINDING and WITH CHECK OPTION.

Creating a view WITH SCHEMABINDING will bind the view definition to the objects that are being referenced. By default, any objects that a view references may be dropped. In this event, the view will produce an error the next time it's queried. When WITH SCHEMABINDING is used, an error will be produced if any object that a view references is tried to be dropped.

When data is modified through a view definition, the modifications aren't checked against any filters in the WHERE clause of the query. This could allow modifications to records in the view that would cause them to be invisible the next time the view is queried.

User-Defined Functions

User-defined functions are routines written using Transact-SQL or the .NET Common Language Runtime. In this chapter, we'll be focusing on Transact-SQL user-defined functions. For more information on building functions using the .NET languages, refer to Chapter 18.

User-defined functions receive one or more parameters, perform calculations or other operations, and return either a scalar value or a result set. Functions that return a result set are considered to be table-valued functions, and they are used in the FROM clause of a query. Scalar functions can be used in queries, CHECK constraints, computed columns, control-of-flow statements, and many other locations.

Functions Versus Stored Procedures

User-defined functions have some similarities to stored procedures, as well as some major differences. Stored procedures have been available in SQL Server for much longer than user-defined functions, and many developers tend to gravitate toward them even when user-defined functions may be a more flexible option. User-defined functions provide many of the same advantages as stored procedures, including:

Modular Programming   User-defined functions promote the reuse of Transact-SQL logic in an application. User-defined functions can be referenced in many more locations than stored procedures.

Network Traffic Reduction   Using user-defined functions can reduce network traffic in a similar way to stored procedures. A function may contain many statements, and a function may be reused in several sections of a query.

Execution Plan Caching   Execution plans created from user-defined functions are cached in a similar way as stored procedures. This keeps the query optimizer from needing to rebuild query plans for the same pieces of code being reused in different queries.

Two major differences between stored procedures and user-defined functions are the way they are executed and the way they return data. User-defined functions usually provide more execution flexibility than stored procedures that return scalar values or a single result set. Also, using user-defined functions rather than stored procedures can offer clearer, more readable, and more maintainable code in the right situation.

Stored procedures that return a single result set can usually be rewritten as a function. When executing a stored procedure, a result set cannot be easily joined to other tables in a query without first creating a temporary table:

```
CREATE TABLE #temp (…)
INSERT INTO #temp
EXEC uspExample 1, 2;
SELECT * FROM #temp JOIN anotherTable…
```

A table-valued user-defined function that returned the same results as the preceding stored procedure could be referenced in a single SELECT statement:

```
SELECT * FROM udfExample(1, 2) JOIN anotherTable…
```

Stored procedures that return scalar values require a variable to be defined if those values are to be reused in subsequent stored procedure calls.

The following example shows the process required to execute a stored procedure with the output of another, and print the ultimate result:

```
DECLARE @proc1out int,
  @proc2out int;
EXEC proc1 @param1, @param2, @proc1out OUTPUT;
EXEC proc2 @proc1out, @proc2out OUTPUT;
PRINT @proc2out;
```

Functions can use the output of another function as an input parameter. The following example could be an equivalent way of doing a similar calculation using two functions:

```
PRINT Function1(Function2(@param1, @param2));
```

Built-In Functions Revisited

SQL Server provides many built-in system functions. These functions are available in many categories including string manipulation, mathematical, and metadata functions. User-defined functions are very similar to built-in functions in their usage. In many cases, user-defined functions will include system functions in their body.

Built-in functions can be categorized into deterministic functions and nondeterministic functions. A deterministic function will always return the same result given the same set of input values and database conditions. An example of a deterministic function would be SUBSTRING; given the same input parameters it will always produce the same output:

```
PRINT SUBSTRING('ABCDE', 2, 1);
```

The preceding code will always produce the letter B. GETDATE()is an example of a nondeterministic function. The result of the following code would always vary depending on the current date and time:

```
PRINT GETDATE() + 1;
```

Scalar Functions

Scalar functions operate on one or more parameters to produce a single value. When defining functions, parameters must be contained between parentheses. A scalar function can return any datatype except for text, ntext, cursor, and timestamp. If the function contains more than one statement, you must use BEGIN and END.

Scalar functions may be used in many locations, including:

◆ SELECT statements

   ◆ Column list

   ◆ WHERE clause

   ◆ ORDER BY

   ◆ GROUP BY

◆ SET clause of an UPDATE statement

◆ INSERT statements

◆ CHECK constraints

◆ DEFAULT constraints

◆ Computed columns

◆ Control-of-flow statements

◆ Within functions and stored procedures

Here is an example of a scalar user-defined function that returns the quarter and year for a given date:

```
USE AdventureWorks2008;
GO
```

```
CREATE FUNCTION dbo.Qtr
 (@InDate datetime)
 RETURNS char(9)
AS
BEGIN
  RETURN 'FY' + CAST(YEAR(@InDate) As varchar) +
  '-Q' + CAST(DATEPART(qq, @InDate) AS varchar);
END
GO
```

This function formats the return value in a way commonly used for reporting. Dates will be converted so that a date falling in Quarter 1 of fiscal year 2008 would be displayed as FY2008-Q1. An example of using the function in a PRINT statement is shown here:

```
PRINT dbo.Qtr('3/20/2008');
```

A scalar function can be used anywhere a scalar expression is allowed. For example, the following query will use the function to display data summarized by quarter:

```
SELECT dbo.Qtr(OrderDate) As OrderQuarter,
  SUM(TotalDue) As TotalSales
FROM Sales.SalesOrderHeader
GROUP BY dbo.Qtr(OrderDate)
ORDER BY dbo.Qtr(OrderDate);
```

Scalar user-defined functions can do much more than format dates. Any set of Transact-SQL statements that doesn't modify data can be used to compute a scalar value for return.

The following function is an example from the AdventureWorks2008 database. It is designed to calculate the total stock in inventory for a given product.

```
USE AdventureWorks2008;
GO
CREATE FUNCTION dbo.ufnGetTotalInventoryStock
 (@ProductID int)
 RETURNS int
AS
BEGIN
 DECLARE @ret int;
 SELECT @ret = SUM(p.Quantity)
 FROM Production.ProductInventory p
 WHERE p.ProductID = @ProductID;
 IF (@ret IS NULL)
  SET @ret = 0;
 RETURN @ret;
END;
```

An example of using this function is shown here:

```
SELECT ProductNumber, Name,
  dbo.ufnGetTotalInventoryStock(ProductID) As InventoryCount
FROM Production.Product
WHERE ProductNumber LIKE 'EC%'
```

The previous function is executed for every row returned by the query. This function could also be very useful combined with control-of-flow statements in a procedure, for example:

```
IF dbo.ufnGetTotalInventoryStock(@ProductID) < 500
BEGIN
 -- Perform an operation related to low product stock
END;
```

Table-Valued Functions

Table-valued functions provide powerful result-set generation capabilities. They can be used anywhere that a table or view would be allowed inside of a query. A table-valued function is more flexible in its usage than a stored procedure that returns a result set because the result set of a function can be joined to other tables in a query.

There are two types of table-valued functions in SQL Server. *Inline table-valued functions* are similar in concept to a view with parameters. A *multistatement table-valued function* allows multiple statements to build a result set in a table variable to be returned.

INLINE TABLE-VALUED FUNCTIONS

Inline table-valued functions are simple to create. The content of an inline table-valued function is a SELECT statement with parameters. The return datatype is always table, but the structure of the returned table is defined by the structure of the SELECT statement. Below is an example of an inline table-valued function that retrieves the total sales by product for a given CustomerID:

```
USE AdventureWorks2008;
GO
CREATE FUNCTION Sales.ufnSalesByCustomer (@CustomerID int)
RETURNS TABLE
AS
RETURN
(
 SELECT P.ProductID, P.Name, SUM(SD.LineTotal) AS Total
 FROM Production.Product AS P
  JOIN Sales.SalesOrderDetail AS SD
  ON SD.ProductID = P.ProductID
  JOIN Sales.SalesOrderHeader AS SH
  ON SH.SalesOrderID = SD.SalesOrderID
 WHERE SH.CustomerID = @CustomerID
 GROUP BY P.ProductID, P.Name
);
GO
```

Notice that the body of this function consists of a single RETURN statement. An example of a query using this function is shown here:

```
SELECT * FROM Sales.ufnSalesByCustomer(30052);
```

Inline table-valued functions are powerful tools worth considering for situations that require parameterized queries. They offer much greater flexibility in the way the result set may be used.

MULTISTATEMENT TABLE-VALUED FUNCTIONS

A multistatement table-valued function allows many Transact-SQL statements to build the contents of a table. Multistatement table-valued functions provide a powerful alternative to stored procedures that build result sets using multiple steps.

Multistatement table-valued functions allow a developer to dynamically populate a table in multiple steps that are similar to those of a stored procedure, but they can be referenced as tables in a SELECT statement.

When using a multistatement table-valued function, the structure of the table must be defined in the header of the function. A variable name is used for the table, and all operations that modify data can reference only the table variable.

The following example shows a function similar to ufnSalesByCustomer, which we created in the last section. We will first populate the table variable, and then update the table variable to include total product inventory using our previously created scalar function. The statements required to create the function are shown here:

```
USE AdventureWorks2008;
GO
CREATE FUNCTION Sales.ufnSalesByCustomerMS (@CustomerID int)
RETURNS @table TABLE
( ProductID int PRIMARY KEY NOT NULL,
 ProductName nvarchar(50) NOT NULL,
 TotalSales numeric(38,6) NOT NULL,
 TotalInventory int NOT NULL )
AS
BEGIN
 INSERT INTO @table
 SELECT P.ProductID, P.Name, SUM(SD.LineTotal) AS Total, 0
 FROM Production.Product AS P
 JOIN Sales.SalesOrderDetail SD ON SD.ProductID = P.ProductID
 JOIN Sales.SalesOrderHeader SH ON SH.SalesOrderID = SD.SalesOrderID
 WHERE SH.CustomerID = @CustomerID
 GROUP BY P.ProductID, P.Name;

 UPDATE @table
 SET TotalInventory = dbo.ufnGetTotalInventoryStock(ProductID);

 RETURN;
END;
```

Executing this function is exactly the same as executing our previous inline function:

```
SELECT * FROM Sales. ufnSalesByCustomerMS (30052);
```

Using Synonyms

A *synonym* allows you to create alternative names for objects inside of the database. If an object is renamed, or the schema of an object is changed, a synonym can allow existing applications to continue to use the old names.

Synonyms can also reference objects in different databases, or even different servers, by using three-part or four-part object names. A synonym must reference a database object, and not another synonym. Multiple names can be created for a single database object, so long as they all refer directly to the database object.

While synonyms provide alternative names, permissions are still maintained at the database object level. A user can be granted access to a synonym, but unless the required access to the underlying object is available, statements using that synonym will fail.

Why Use Synonyms?

You will find synonyms to be useful in many situations, including when:

- ◆ Objects are renamed.
- ◆ Objects are moved to a different schema.
- ◆ Objects are moved to a separate database.
- ◆ Objects are moved to a different server.
- ◆ Alternative names for a database object are needed.

Synonyms can reference many types of database objects, and they allow flexibility in naming and location. They make database maintenance easier, and they allow a separate layer of abstraction from applications that directly access objects.

Creating a Synonym

Creating a synonym can be accomplished using Transact-SQL statements, as well as the SQL Server Management Studio interface. To create a synonym using Transact-SQL, use the following syntax:

```
CREATE SYNONYM schema.synonymName FOR baseObject;
```

The following is an example of creating an alias in the Person schema for the HumanResources.Employee table in the AdventureWorks2008 database:

```
USE AdventureWorks2008;
GO
CREATE SYNONYM Person.Employee FOR HumanResources.Employee;
```

Synonyms can also be created for views, functions, and stored procedures, as shown here:

```
CREATE SYNONYM Person.vEmployee FOR HumanResources.vEmployee;
CREATE SYNONYM dbo.SalesByCust FOR Sales.ufnSalesByCustomer;
CREATE SYNONYM Production.getBOM FOR dbo.uspGetBillOfMaterials;
```

Synonyms can even be created for objects in other databases or on other linked servers. The following examples assume that ownership chaining has been set up and a linked server named server2 has been set up:

```
USE TempDB;
CREATE SYNONYM dbo.ExampleTbl
FOR AdventureWorks2008.HumanResources.Employees;

USE AdventureWorks2008;
CREATE SYNONYM dbo.RemoteProducts
FOR Server2.AdventureWorksRemote.Production.Product;
```

The Bottom Line

Create stored procedures.   Stored procedures provide powerful mechanisms for encapsulating database processes. Understanding how stored procedures are created and executed is an important goal for the DBA.

Master It   Can a stored procedure reference objects that don't exist? How about columns that don't exist in tables that do?

Create views.   Views are queries stored as objects and referenced as tables. Creating views allows flexibility in building and storing database queries.

Master It   What are three advantages of using views?

Create user-defined functions.   Creating user-defined functions allows flexibility, both in processing of scalar values, and in processing of result sets.

Master It   What advantage does a table-valued function have over a stored procedure that returns a result set?

Chapter 6

Managing Data Integrity

Data integrity controls help to guarantee the accuracy, validity, and correctness of data stored in a database. Data integrity controls can be thought of as rules regarding what is considered to be valid data. Data integrity can be enforced using stored procedures, or it can even be enforced outside of SQL Server in the calling application.

However, data integrity is mainly enforced by constraints and triggers. Constraints are additional rules applied to a table that determine valid data. They are automatically enforced by the database engine.

Triggers are special stored procedures that execute in response to events on the server. Data Manipulation Language (DML) triggers can respond to, or execute instead of insert, update, and delete events on a table or view.

Default and rule objects are similar to constraints, but they are created as separate objects. Both are provided for backward compatibility and should be avoided in new development.

In this chapter, you will learn to:

- ◆ Choose appropriate methods to enforce data integrity
- ◆ Create and manage constraints
- ◆ Create and manage DML triggers

Understanding Data Integrity Controls

Data integrity guarantees the correctness and consistency of data stored in a database. Data integrity is enforced by the database engine, primarily through constraints and triggers defined on a table, although other data integrity controls exist. A *constraint* is a rule that limits the allowable values for storage in a table. A DML (Data Manipulation Language) *trigger* is a special stored procedure associated with an insert, update, or delete event against a particular table.

Some of the most basic data integrity controls are the datatype associated with a column and whether the column allows null values. For example, a string can't be stored in a column defined as an integer datatype.

Stored procedures, which are covered in Chapter 5, "Procedural Programming," can be a way of enforcing data integrity so long as they are always used for modifications. This is because ad hoc modifications to tables would bypass any integrity logic contained in a stored procedure. If a rule should always be enforced against a table, triggers or constraints are usually the best choice.

Constraints and triggers are the main data integrity controls we'll focus on in this chapter. We will also discuss rule and default objects.

Enforcing Data Integrity

Data integrity isn't always enforced by the database engine. In many existing applications, it is up to the client application to enforce data integrity rules. For example, you might have a rule that allows only the values between 1 and 10 for a field. An application may enforce this rule in different ways, but it should also be enforced as part of the database, so that invalid values aren't introduced when working outside of the application. If someone were to directly insert or update records in the table, they might not be aware of the allowable values for the column. Unless the database knows that we only want to allow values between 1 and 10 in a field, it would allow any value that the column datatype allows. Therefore, data integrity controls should be placed in the database as well as in the application.

Within a database, data integrity is enforced in two ways: *declarative integrity* and *procedural integrity*.

Declarative integrity is automatically enforced by the database engine. Declarative integrity controls describe the rules that need to be enforced, but not how to enforce them. The main way of enforcing declarative integrity is by using constraints. Default and rule objects are provided for backward compatibility and are similar in function to constraints. It is best to use declarative integrity whenever possible because it requires less overhead than procedural integrity.

Procedural integrity allows more flexibility in defining data integrity rules. Procedural integrity consists of logic written in either Transact-SQL or a .NET language that is enforced by triggers and stored procedures. Although procedural integrity provides greater flexibility, it also requires greater overhead to enforce. Procedural integrity should be used only when declarative integrity controls don't meet the functional needs of the application.

Data Integrity Categories

There are three categories of data integrity: entity integrity, domain integrity, and referential integrity. Categories refer to the area of the table where a data integrity rule is enforced. *Entity integrity* refers to the uniqueness of rows. *Domain integrity* refers to the values allowed in a column, and *referential integrity* preserves the relationships between tables. Procedural or declarative integrity can be used to enforce any of the data integrity categories.

Entity integrity ensures that each row in a table can be uniquely identified by a column or set of columns. Entity integrity is enforced by using indexes to check for duplicate values. Primary key and unique constraints are both used to enforce entity integrity.

Domain integrity determines the allowable values for a column. The datatype used for the column is one way that domain integrity is enforced.

A Check constraint allows us to limit the values allowed in a column based on a logical expression. A Foreign Key constraint determines the values allowed in a column based on the contents of a primary key or unique constraint. Domain integrity can be enforced using procedural methods when constraints don't offer enough flexibility.

Referential integrity preserves and enforces relationships within a database. Foreign key and Check constraints are declarative methods of enforcing referential integrity. Check constraints can reference multiple columns in the same table using an expression. A Foreign Key constraint references a primary key or unique constraint, usually in another table, to maintain the relationship. Referential integrity can also be enforced procedurally by using triggers. Triggers are useful for relationships that are too complex to model using foreign keys.

Working with Constraints

Constraints define data integrity rules on tables that are enforced by the database engine. Constraints are used to enforce entity, domain, and referential integrity, as shown in Table 6.1. Some of the constraints can enforce multiple categories of data integrity. Because of the extra overhead required by triggers, constraints should be used to enforce data integrity whenever they meet the functional requirements of the application.

TABLE 6.1   How Data Integrity Categories Map to Constraints

Data Integrity Category	Enforced By
Entity Integrity	PRIMARY KEY UNIQUE
Domain Integrity	NULL or NOT NULL DEFAULT CHECK FOREIGN KEY
Referential Integrity	FOREIGN KEY CHECK

Primary Key and Unique Constraints

It's a good idea to have a way to uniquely identify every row in a table. Without some sort of a unique identifier, there is no way to tell the difference between duplicate records in a table. *Primary key* and *unique constraints* both ensure that duplicate values aren't allowed in a column or set of columns.

Primary key and unique constraints are very similar in several ways. Both enforce entity integrity to ensure against duplicate records in a table, and both use indexes for enforcing these rules. There are several differences, however:

◆ A table can contain only one primary key, but a table can contain many unique constraints.

◆ A primary key cannot store NULL values, but a unique constraint can be defined on a column that allows NULL values.

◆ A primary key uses a clustered index by default unless a clustered index already exists for the table. A unique constraint uses a nonclustered index by default.

An example of how to create a primary key and unique constraint is shown in Listing 6.1

LISTING 6.1   Creating a Table with a Primary Key and Unique Constraint

```
USE SandboxDB;

CREATE TABLE CategoriesPK (
  CategoryID int NOT NULL PRIMARY KEY,
  CategoryCode char(3) NOT NULL UNIQUE,
  CategoryName varchar(50) NOT NULL
);
GO
INSERT INTO CategoriesPK VALUES (1, 'AAA', 'Category 1');
INSERT INTO CategoriesPK VALUES (1, 'BBB', 'Category 2'); -- Fails
-- Any subsequent statements in the batch aren't executed
GO
INSERT INTO CategoriesPK VALUES (2, 'CCC', 'Category 3');
INSERT INTO CategoriesPK VALUES (3, 'AAA', 'Category 4'); -- Fails
```

The CategoriesPK table in Listing 6.1 will allow only unique values for the CategoryID and CategoryCode fields. If an attempt is made to insert a duplicate value into either field, an error occurs and the batch is cancelled. The second and fourth statements in Listing 6.1 each violate a constraint because they attempt to insert duplicate values.

Sometimes you may need to use more than one column to uniquely identify each row. A composite key uses a combination of two or more columns to uniquely identify each row. Because a composite key affects multiple columns, it needs to be defined separately from the column definition. Listing 6.2 shows an example of creating a composite primary key.

LISTING 6.2   Creating a Composite Primary Key

```
USE SandboxDB;
CREATE TABLE CategoriesComp (
  CategoryID int NOT NULL,
  CategoryCode char(5) NOT NULL,
  CategoryName varchar(50) NOT NULL,
  CONSTRAINT PK_Categories
      PRIMARY KEY (CategoryID, CategoryCode)
);
INSERT INTO CategoriesComp VALUES (1, 'AAA', 'Cat 1');
INSERT INTO CategoriesComp VALUES (1, 'BBB', 'Cat 2');
INSERT INTO CategoriesComp VALUES (2, 'AAA', 'Cat 3');
INSERT INTO CategoriesComp VALUES (2, 'AAA', 'Cat 4'); -- Fails
```

When creating a composite primary key, specify the columns from most unique to least unique. Doing this makes a more efficient index structure. Indexes will be discussed in further detail in Chapter 14, "Indexing Strategies for Query Optimization."

Sometimes you will need to add a primary key or a unique constraint to an existing table. It's important to understand that the data in the table is validated to make sure that it's unique by creating an index that is used to enforce the key. Listing 6.3 shows an example of using the ALTER TABLE statement to add constraints.

LISTING 6.3   Adding Constraints Using ALTER TABLE

```
USE SandboxDB;
CREATE TABLE Categories (
  CategoryID int NOT NULL,
  CategoryCode char(5) NOT NULL,
  CategoryName varchar(50) NOT NULL
);
ALTER TABLE Categories
 ADD CONSTRAINT PK_CategoryID
 PRIMARY KEY (CategoryID);
ALTER TABLE Categories
 ADD CONSTRAINT UQ_CategoryCode
 UNIQUE (CategoryCode);
```

It will take a while to create a primary key or a unique constraint on a large table because indexes need to be created, and the existing data needs to be verified.

PRIMARY KEY AND UNIQUE CONSTRAINTS IN MANAGEMENT STUDIO

Another option for manipulating the primary key and unique constraints on a table is to use the Table Designer in SQL Server Management Studio, shown in Figure 6.1. It doesn't matter if you're creating a new table or modifying an existing table, the process for manipulating constraints is the same. To create primary key and unique constraints in SQL Server Management Studio, follow these steps:

1. Open the Table Designer in SQL Server Management Studio (shown in Figure 6.1) by doing either of the following:

   A. Right-click on an existing table and choose Design.

   B. Right-click on the Tables folder, choose New Table, and create the required columns in the table.

FIGURE 6.1

The SQL Server Management Studio Table Designer

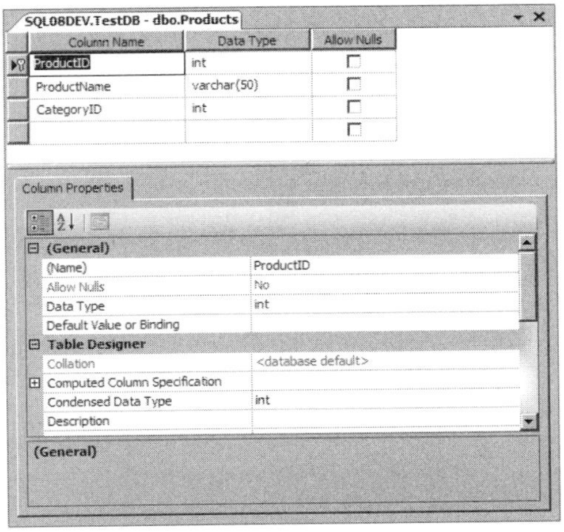

2. To specify a primary key for the table, either right-click on the column, or select the column and access the Table Designer menu, as shown in Figure 6.2, and choose Set Primary Key. To select multiple columns, hold down the Ctrl key while clicking on each one.

FIGURE 6.2
The Table Designer
menu options

3. To create a unique constraint or modify an existing constraint, choose Indexes/Keys from the Table Designer menu to bring up the Indexes/Keys dialog shown in Figure 6.3.

A. Click the Add button to add a unique constraint to the table.

B. Choose the column or columns on which to define the unique key.

C. Change the Type property to Unique Key.

D. Change other key options as required.

FIGURE 6.3
The Indexes/Keys
dialog

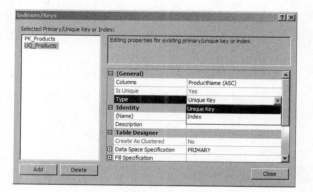

Foreign Key Constraints

Foreign keys define and enforce relationships in a database, and they are usually the primary means of enforcing referential integrity. A foreign key defined on a column determines valid values for that column by referencing a primary key or unique constraint defined on another table. For example, consider the foreign key defined on the Products table in Figure 6.4. Records in the Products table rely on records in the Categories table.

FIGURE 6.4
The Categories-
Products
relationship

The Foreign Key constraint shown in the Figure 6.4 enforces several rules:

◆ For each record in the Products table, there must be a corresponding record in the Categories table. Inserting a product record with an invalid category ID would violate the Foreign Key constraint and result in an error.

◆ Category records can't be deleted if they are referenced by a record in the Product table. This rule can be modified by turning on cascading delete operations.

◆ The primary key of a category record can't be updated if there are product records referencing it. This rule can be modified by turning on cascading update operations.

◆ Without turning on cascading updates, the following process must be used to update the primary key:

1. Insert a new category record.

2. Update product records that point to the old category so that they point to the new category.

3. Delete the original category record.

Now that we've had a chance to study the behavior of Foreign Key constraints, let's explore the syntax required to create them. The code in Listing 6.4 shows the statements used to create the categories and products tables used in the previous example.

LISTING 6.4   Creating a Foreign Key Relationship When Creating a Table

```
USE SandboxDB;
CREATE TABLE Categories (
  CategoryID int PRIMARY KEY NOT NULL,
  CategoryCode char(5) UNIQUE NOT NULL,
  CategoryName varchar(50) NOT NULL
);
CREATE TABLE Products (
  ProductID int PRIMARY KEY NOT NULL,
  ProductName varchar(50) NOT NULL,
  CategoryID int NOT NULL FOREIGN KEY
    REFERENCES Categories(CategoryID)
);
```

Foreign Key constraints can allow delete and update operations to cascade through related tables. Cascading updates can make modifying related tables easier, but they also can make it much easier to modify many records unintentionally. Cascading delete operations should be used with caution, as deleting a single record may result in many more deletions depending on the number of tables related by cascading foreign keys. Listing 6.5 shows an example of a foreign key that allows cascading updates and cascading deletes.

LISTING 6.5   Creating a Cascading Foreign Key Constraint

```
USE SandboxDB;
CREATE TABLE ProductsCascade (
  ProductID int PRIMARY KEY NOT NULL,
  ProductName varchar(50) NOT NULL,
  CategoryID int NOT NULL FOREIGN KEY
    REFERENCES Categories(CategoryID)
    ON UPDATE CASCADE
    ON DELETE CASCADE
);
```

An update to the primary key of the categories table would cause each related record in the ProductsCascade table to change. Deleting a category would cause the related products to be deleted.

There are four possible settings for cascading update and delete operations using a foreign key:

◆   NO ACTION

◆   CASCADE

◆   SET NULL

◆   SET DEFAULT

The default cascading behavior of a foreign key is NO ACTION. If the behavior is CASCADE, the operation will cascade between related tables. For example, updates to the categoryID field in the Categories table will cascade to the Products table. If a category is deleted, the corresponding products will also be deleted in the example in Listing 6.5. If SET NULL or SET DEFAULT is used, the categoryID will be set to NULL or a DEFAULT value in the ProductsCascade table, and the records will no longer be linked.

Sometimes, a foreign key may need to use more than one column to create a relationship. A Foreign Key constraint can be defined at the table level, as a separate column definition, as shown in Listing 6.6.

LISTING 6.6   Creating a Table-Level Foreign Key Constraint

```
USE SandboxDB;
CREATE TABLE CategoriesComposite (
  CategoryID int NOT NULL,
  CategoryCode char(5) NOT NULL,
```

```
    CategoryName varchar(50) NOT NULL,
    PRIMARY KEY (CategoryID, CategoryCode)
);
CREATE TABLE ProductsComposite (
    ProductID int PRIMARY KEY NOT NULL,
    ProductName varchar(50) NOT NULL,
    CategoryID int NOT NULL,
    CategoryCode char(5) NOT NULL,
    FOREIGN KEY (CategoryID, CategoryCode)
    REFERENCES CategoriesComposite(CategoryID, CategoryCode)
);
```

A foreign key can also reference a primary key or unique constraint in the same table to maintain a hierarchical relationship. This can be useful whenever a hierarchy of records needs to be modeled in a single table, such as an employee organizational chart, or a parts explosion tree. The example in Listing 6.7 defines an employee-manager relationship.

LISTING 6.7   Creating a Self-Referencing Foreign Key

```
USE SandboxDB;
CREATE TABLE Employees (
    EmployeeID int PRIMARY KEY NOT NULL,
    EmployeeName varchar(75) NOT NULL,
    ManagerID int NOT NULL
    FOREIGN KEY REFERENCES Employees(EmployeeID)
)
```

A foreign key can also be created after the table already exists by using the ALTER TABLE statement, as is shown in Listing 6.8. Existing data is verified when the Foreign Key constraint is created, unless WITH NOCHECK is specified. Using WITH NOCHECK will speed up the creation of the Foreign Key constraint because it doesn't verify existing data; however, it should be used with extreme caution, because it can result in orphaned records.

LISTING 6.8   Adding a Foreign Key to an Existing Table

```
USE SandboxDB;
CREATE TABLE Employees2 (
    EmployeeID int PRIMARY KEY NOT NULL,
    EmployeeName varchar(75) NOT NULL,
    ManagerID int NOT NULL
);
ALTER TABLE Employees2
 ADD FOREIGN KEY (ManagerID)
     REFERENCES Employees(EmployeeID);
```

FOREIGN KEY CONSTRAINTS IN MANAGEMENT STUDIO

Foreign Key constraints are managed using the Relationships dialog of the Table Designer in SQL Server Management Studio. To access the Relationships dialog, use these steps:

1. Access the Table Designer by creating a new table, or by right-clicking on an existing table in Object Explorer and choosing Design.

2. Choose the Table Designer menu, and select Relationships.

3. The Relationships dialog appears. (See Figure 6.5.)

FIGURE 6.5
The Foreign Key Relationships dialog

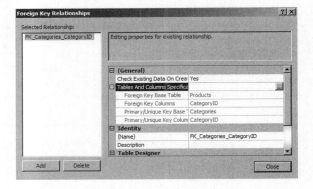

Foreign key relationships can also be viewed and modified under the Keys folder beneath a table in Object Explorer. To modify the foreign key, you can right-click the object and select Modify.

Default Definitions

A default definition provides a default value for a column. If an INSERT statement doesn't define a value for the column, the default value is used. If a column allows NULL values, but doesn't have a default defined, the default value for that column is NULL.

A default can use a static value or dynamic value built from an expression. Dynamic values can be created by referencing scalar system or user-defined functions.

A default can be created on any type of column except for the following:

◆ Identity columns

◆ Sparse columns (discussed in Chapter 4, "Tables and CRUD Operations.")

◆ Columns using the timestamp datatype

◆ Columns with a default that is already defined

Listing 6.9 shows a table that contains two default definitions. If no column values are provided for the first or second column when a new record is inserted, the default values will be used. A value must be provided for the third column because it doesn't allow NULL values, and it doesn't have a default definition.

LISTING 6.9   Table with Default Definitions

```
USE SandboxDB;
CREATE TABLE DefaultTable (
    col1 int NOT NULL
        DEFAULT (0),
    col2 datetime NOT NULL
        DEFAULT (GETDATE()),
    col3 varchar(5) NOT NULL
);
```

A default definition can be added to an existing table by using the ALTER TABLE statement. Adding a default to a table with existing data doesn't have any effect on current data in the table. Subsequent insert statements that don't provide a value will use the new default.

The only time that a default definition will have an effect on existing data inside of a table is when a new column with a default definition is added to an existing table, as shown in Listing 6.10.

LISTING 6.10   Adding Default Definitions to an Existing Table

```
USE SandboxDB;
-- Wouldn't modify existing records
ALTER TABLE DefaultTable
  ADD DEFAULT ('Test') FOR col3
-- Adds a column with a value of 5 for existing records
ALTER TABLE DefaultTable
  ADD col4 int DEFAULT (5) NOT NULL;
-- Insert several records
INSERT INTO DefaultTable (col1, col2) VALUES (1, '1/1/2008');
INSERT INTO DefaultTable (col1) VALUES (2);
INSERT INTO DefaultTable (col3) VALUES ('QWER');
INSERT INTO DefaultTable DEFAULT VALUES;
```

To obtain information about existing defaults in a database, you can query the sys.default_constraints system view.

To create or modify default definitions using the SQL Server Management Studio Table Designer, use the Default Value or Binding property for a column, shown in Figure 6.6.

FIGURE 6.6
The Column Properties tab in the Table Designer

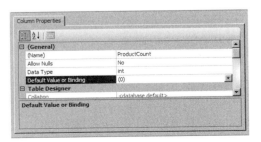

Check Constraints

A Check constraint limits the values allowed in a column. The allowed values are determined by using a logical expression. You can use any expression that is valid in a WHERE clause as the rule for a Check constraint. Check constraints are a primary enforcement mechanism of domain integrity. A Check constraint can be part of a CREATE TABLE statement, or it can be added to an existing table.

When a Check constraint is added to an existing table with data, the data is validated against the rules of the Check constraint unless the NOCHECK option has been specified. NOCHECK is useful when you are sure that existing data already conforms to the constraint definition.

Check constraints can reference one or more columns in the same table. A column-level Check constraint can be defined with the column definition. A table-level Check constraint is created as a separate column definition. A table-level Check constraint can reference multiple columns in its expression. Examples of both column-level and table-level Check constraints are shown in Listing 6.11.

LISTING 6.11   Creating a Table with Check Constraints

```
USE SandboxDB;
CREATE TABLE CheckTbl (
  CheckID int NOT NULL
    PRIMARY KEY,
  PositiveValues int NOT NULL
    CHECK (PositiveValues >= 0),
  RangeValues int NOT NULL
    CHECK (RangeValues BETWEEN 1 and 10),
  FormattedValue varchar(5) NOT NULL
    CHECK (FormattedValue LIKE '[0-9][0-9][A-Z][A-Z][A-Z]'),
  StartDate datetime NOT NULL,
  EndDate datetime NULL,
  CHECK (StartDate <= EndDate OR EndDate IS NULL)
);
```

Four constraints are defined on CheckTbl in Listing 6.1. The expressions used in the Check constraints determine the allowable values for each column. The PositiveValues column includes a Check constraint that enforces that all values must be greater than or equal to 0. The RangeValues column has a Check constraint that limits the column to values between 1 and 10. The FormattedValue column uses a LIKE comparison to ensure that the first two characters of the column are numbers and the last three characters are letters. The last Check constraint enforces that the value in the StartDate column must be less than or equal to the value in the EndDate column, or the EndDate column may be NULL.

A Check constraint can also be added to an existing table. Data is validated when the Check constraint is added, so adding a Check constraint to a large table can take a while. Listing 6.12 shows how to add a Check constraint to an existing table.

LISTING 6.12   Adding a Check Constraint to an Existing Table

```
USE SandboxDB;
ALTER TABLE CheckTbl
 ADD CHECK (CheckID Between 1 and 10000);
```

It is possible to skip data validation when adding a new Check constraint to an existing table by using the WITH NOCHECK option. However, use caution when skipping validation. If there are rows that don't conform to the expression of the Check constraint, errors will occur when modifying other columns of the same row, confusing applications.

CHECK CONSTRAINTS IN MANAGEMENT STUDIO

Check constraints can be created and modified using the Check Constraints dialog of the Table Designer in SQL Server Management Studio. To access the Check Constraints dialog, shown in Figure 6.7, use these steps:

1. Access the Table Designer by creating a new table, or by right-clicking on an existing table in Object Explorer and choosing Design.

2. Choose the Table Designer menu, and select Check Constraints.

3. To add a new Check constraint, click the Add button, and fill out the Expression property.

FIGURE 6.7
The Check
Constraints dialog

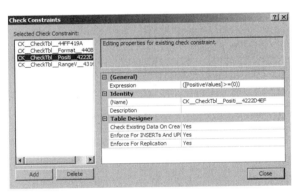

Check constraints are also displayed in the Object Explorer tree view under the Constraints folder.

An alternative way to add a constraint is to right-click on the Constraints folder and choose New Constraint.

Working with DML Triggers

DML (Data Manipulation Language) triggers allow powerful and flexible data integrity capabilities. They allow more complex integrity enforcement than declarative integrity methods, but they also require more overhead. Some business rules can't be implemented using constraints, and triggers provide the flexibility to enforce these rules within the database. In this section, we'll explore the different types of DML triggers and the guidelines for using them.

Understanding Triggers

A *trigger* is a special type of stored procedure that executes in response to events. Triggers are not executed directly, and they don't accept parameter values. They retrieve information about their execution environment by using special inserted and deleted tables in the case of DML triggers, or the EVENTDATA() function for logon triggers and DDL triggers. SQL Server 2008 supports the three different types of triggers shown in Table 6.2.

TABLE 6.2   Supported Trigger Types in SQL Server 2008

TRIGGER TYPE	DESCRIPTION
Logon triggers	Fire in response to server logon events. Logon triggers are covered in further detail in Chapter 8, Managing User Security.
Data Definition Language (DDL) triggers	Fire in response to data definition language events such as CREATE, ALTER, and DROP statements. DDL Triggers are covered in further detail in Chapter 10, "Monitoring SQL Server Activity."
Data Manipulation Language (DML) triggers	Fire in response to INSERT, UPDATE, and DELETE statements.

In this chapter, we'll focus on Data Manipulation Language events, including INSERT, UPDATE, and DELETE statements.

A DML trigger always executes as a transaction that can be rolled back within the trigger. When modifying a table that has a DML trigger defined on it within a transaction, the trigger may cause the transaction to be rolled back.

Some of the common uses for triggers include:

◆ Preventing incorrect INSERT, UPDATE, and DELETE statements that require more complex logic than constraints can provide.

◆ Comparing the state of data before and after modification.

◆ Displaying user-defined error messages.

◆ Cascading changes through related tables in a database that cannot be accommodated by a foreign key.

DML TRIGGER TYPES

Two types of DML triggers are supported: AFTER triggers and INSTEAD OF triggers.

An AFTER trigger executes after a data modification takes place, but before the transaction is committed. Constraints are checked before any data is modified; if any constraints are violated, an AFTER trigger won't execute.

AFTER triggers can only be created on tables. There can be multiple AFTER triggers for an action (INSERT, UPDATE, or DELETE). The first and last trigger to execute can be specified using the sp_settriggerorder stored procedure. This provides some degree of control over the order in which multiple triggers execute, but it is important to understand that triggers other than the first and last are executed in an undefined order.

An INSTEAD OF trigger is executed in place of the actual data modification, before constraints are checked. This allows pre-processing of data to conform to constraints. An INSTEAD OF trigger can be created on both tables and views. Because the trigger executes in place of the manipulation operation, logic can be written to redirect appropriate manipulations to any underlying tables referenced by the view. Only one INSTEAD OF trigger per action is allowed on a table.

In this chapter, we'll focus on triggers written in Transact-SQL. Triggers can also be hosted in the .NET CLR, which is covered in more detail in Chapter 18, "SQL Server and the Common Language Runtime."

COMPARING TRIGGERS AND CONSTRAINTS

Triggers support all of the functionality of constraints. However, just because they can be used to perform an operation doesn't mean that they should be used for that operation.

Data integrity should be enforced at the lowest level possible, so long as it meets the functional needs of the application. Constraints are automatically enforced by the database engine and require less overhead than do triggers. Therefore, constraints should be used if possible, unless the application needs are more complex than can be enforced by constraints.

Enforcing entity integrity should always be done using constraints. Entity integrity refers to the uniqueness of rows. Primary keys and unique constraints are nearly always the best way of enforcing entity integrity.

For domain integrity enforcement, use Check constraints if possible. Check constraints allow you to use an expression that returns a Boolean result to determine if the row should be allowed in a table. In situations where evaluation of a row takes multiple steps, or requires queries to other tables, triggers can be very useful.

Use Foreign Key constraints when possible to enforce referential integrity. A Foreign Key constraint can only create relationships based on equality comparisons, so for more complex relationships, a trigger may be required.

When evaluating the use of constraints or triggers, always use constraints if they can meet the functional needs of the application. A trigger should be considered if custom error messages are required in response to error conditions, or in situations where more complex logic is required than constraints can provide.

UNDERSTANDING INSERTED AND DELETED TABLES

When a DML trigger is executing, it has access to two memory-resident tables that allow access to the data that was modified: Inserted and Deleted. These tables are available only within the body of a trigger for read-only access, and they are automatically created and managed by SQL Server. The structures of the inserted and deleted tables are the same as the structure of the table on which the trigger is defined.

For insert operations, all inserted rows are available in the inserted table. For delete operations, all deleted rows are available in the deleted table.

An update can be thought of as a delete followed by an insert. Both the inserted and deleted tables are available within an UPDATE trigger. The deleted table stores the records before modification (old values), and the inserted table stores records after they were updated (new values).

How Triggers Execute

Triggers execute in response to data modifications. When a modification occurs, the following steps occur:

1. The statement is executed (INSERT, UPDATE, or DELETE).

2. If an INSTEAD OF trigger is defined on the table, it executes in place of the actual modification. It is possible to manipulate the data so that it conforms to constraints at this point. If a rollback transaction is encountered, the process is stopped.

3. Any constraints on the table are checked. If constraints are violated, an error is returned and the process is stopped.

4. AFTER triggers are fired. The first and last trigger to fire can be specified; the rest of the AFTER triggers execute in an undefined order. If a rollback transaction is encountered, all modifications must be rolled back.

5. The transaction is committed.

A trigger executes once per INSERT, UPDATE, or DELETE statement even if multiple rows are modified. It is common for UPDATE and DELETE statements to affect multiple rows, but this is also possible with INSERT statements. The inserted and deleted tables contain a copy of all affected rows.

It's important to design triggers so that they work properly for both single-row and multiple-row actions. The @@ROWCOUNT system function can be used to determine how many rows were modified in the body of a trigger. Avoid using cursors within a trigger body; there can be a very large performance hit.

A trigger always executes as part of a transaction. If a trigger executes a rollback statement, the batch containing the modifying statement is terminated. Listing 6.13 shows an example of this.

LISTING 6.13   Transaction Rollback Cancels the Rest of the Batch

```
UPDATE TableWithTrigger …     -- Results in rollback from trigger
INSERT INTO AnotherTable …    -- Statement Not Executed
GO
DELETE YetAnotherTable        -- Execution resumes at the next batch
```

Whenever a trigger rolls back a transaction, the rest of the batch is canceled, and execution is moved to the following batch.

It's also important to understand the behavior of a trigger rollback in a user-defined transaction. If a trigger is rolled back, the entire user-defined transaction is rolled back. An example is shown in Listing 6.14.

LISTING 6.14   Rollback Trigger Rolls Back a User-Defined Transaction

```
BEGIN TRANSACTION
    INSERT INTO AnotherTable   -- Insert is rolled back because of
                               -- the statement below.
    UPDATE TableWithTrigger    -- Update causes trigger to rollback
```

Using *AFTER* Triggers

Now that we've explored the types of triggers and the behavior, let's begin building AFTER triggers. The SQL Server engine has supported AFTER triggers for many releases. The basic syntax for creating an AFTER trigger can take on either of the forms shown in Listing 6.15:

LISTING 6.15   Different Ways to Create an AFTER trigger

```
-- Using the AFTER keyword
CREATE TRIGGER trigger_name ON table_name
AFTER action
AS
...
-- Using the FOR Keyword
CREATE TRIGGER trigger_name ON table_name
FOR action
AS
...
```

INSERT, UPDATE, or DELETE can be substituted for the action in the preceding examples. AFTER and FOR are equivalent keywords when creating AFTER triggers.

Multiple triggers can be created on a table for an action. Controlling the order of execution is somewhat limited; you can only set the first and last triggers to execute. All other triggers for that action will execute in an undefined order. To control the first and last triggers, use the system stored procedure `sp_settriggerorder`.

AFTER INSERT TRIGGERS

Now that we've had a chance to understand the behavior of AFTER triggers, let's create a few. The table structures used for the next few examples are shown in Listing 6.16

LISTING 6.16   Products and Categories Tables with TotalProductCount Field

```
USE SandboxDB;
CREATE TABLE TrigCategories (
  CategoryID int PRIMARY KEY NOT NULL,
  CategoryName varchar(50) NOT NULL,
  ProductCount int NOT NULL
);
```

```
CREATE TABLE TrigProducts (
  ProductID int PRIMARY KEY NOT NULL,
  ProductName varchar(50) NOT NULL,
  CategoryID int CONSTRAINT FK_TrigCategories_CategoryID
     FOREIGN KEY REFERENCES TrigCategories(CategoryID) NOT NULL
);
```

We'll create a trigger on the Products table that updates the ProductCount field of the Categories table every time a new product is inserted. To access the newly inserted records, we can use the inserted table.

In order for the logic to work in these examples, it's important that the ProductCount field is never manually modified. This will be accomplished later with an INSTEAD OF trigger.

The structure of the inserted table in Listing 6.17 is the same as that of the Products table, except that it only contains rows that have been inserted.

LISTING 6.17   INSERT Trigger to Maintain TotalProductCount Field

```
USE SandboxDB;
CREATE TRIGGER trg_TrigProduct_Insert ON TrigProducts
AFTER INSERT
AS
SET NOCOUNT ON
UPDATE c
 SET ProductCount = ProductCount +
                        (SELECT COUNT(*)
                          FROM Inserted
                          WHERE CategoryID = c.CategoryID)
  FROM TrigCategories c JOIN Inserted i
  ON c.CategoryID = i.CategoryID
```

AFTER DELETE Triggers

Now that we've built a trigger to increase the value of the product count when products are added, let's build one to decrease the total product count when records are deleted.

In a DELETE trigger, rows that have been deleted are stored in the deleted table for use within the trigger. The example shown in Listing 6.18 is similar to the logic used in our AFTER INSERT examples.

LISTING 6.18   DELETE Trigger to Maintain TotalProductCount Field

```
USE SandboxDB;
CREATE TRIGGER trg_TrigProduct_Delete ON TrigProducts
AFTER DELETE
AS
```

```
SET NOCOUNT ON
UPDATE c
 SET ProductCount = ProductCount -
                        (SELECT COUNT(*)
                         FROM Deleted
                         WHERE CategoryID = c.CategoryID)
 FROM TrigCategories C JOIN Deleted d
 ON c.CategoryID = d.CategoryID;
```

AFTER UPDATE TRIGGERS

An UPDATE trigger can evaluate the data values before and after modification. Both the inserted and deleted tables are available for use within our trigger body. The deleted table stores the records with an old value, and the inserted table stores records with a new value. Listing 6.19 shows an AFTER UPDATE trigger that maintains the ProductCount field in the Categories table when product records are updated. The UPDATE() function is used to determine if a specific field has been updated.

LISTING 6.19   UPDATE Trigger to Maintain TotalProductCount Field

```
USE SandboxDB;
CREATE TRIGGER trg_TrigProducts_Update ON TrigProducts
AFTER UPDATE
AS
SET NOCOUNT ON
IF UPDATE(CategoryID)
BEGIN
  -- Decrement old product numbers
  UPDATE c
   SET ProductCount = ProductCount -
                          (SELECT COUNT(*)
                           FROM Deleted
                           WHERE CategoryID = c.CategoryID)
   FROM TrigCategories C JOIN Deleted d
   ON c.CategoryID = d.CategoryID
  -- Increment new product numbers
  UPDATE c
   SET ProductCount = ProductCount +
                          (SELECT COUNT(*)
                           FROM Inserted
                           WHERE CategoryID = c.CategoryID)
   FROM TrigCategories c JOIN Inserted i
   ON c.CategoryID = i.CategoryID
END
```

AFTER TRIGGER GUIDELINES

When building AFTER triggers, it is important to follow several guidelines.

An AFTER trigger should avoid using the rollback transaction statement because all operations leading up to the trigger execution must be undone. Evaluate whether an INSTEAD OF trigger would be more appropriate to report an error message without needing to undo the modification.

As we've discussed previously in the chapter, a trigger will fire only once for modifications that affect multiple rows. It is very important to verify that logic will work for both single-row and multiple-row modifications. An example of a trigger that only works for single-row actions is shown in Listing 6.20.

LISTING 6.20   Trigger That Only Works for Single-Row Actions

```
USE AdventureWorks2008;
GO
CREATE TRIGGER trg_NewPODetail_SingleRow
ON Purchasing.PurchaseOrderDetail
AFTER INSERT
AS
UPDATE PurchaseOrderHeader
 SET SubTotal = SubTotal + LineTotal
 FROM inserted
 WHERE PurchaseOrderHeader.PurchaseOrderID = inserted.PurchaseOrderID;
```

The problem with the trigger in Listing 6.20 is that it assumes that there will be only a single record in the inserted table. If multiple records are in the inserted table with the same purchase order ID, the update statement won't execute as expected.

The @@ROWCOUNT system function can be used to determine the number of rows that are modified, and take different actions depending on the modification. A rewritten example of Listing 6.20 is shown in Listing 6.21

LISTING 6.21   Trigger That Takes Different Actions Based on @@ROWCOUNT

```
USE AdventureWorks2008;
CREATE TRIGGER NewPODetail_Multirow
ON Purchasing.PurchaseOrderDetail
FOR INSERT
AS
IF @@ROWCOUNT = 1
BEGIN
    UPDATE PurchaseOrderHeader
    SET SubTotal = SubTotal + LineTotal
    FROM inserted
    WHERE PurchaseOrderHeader.PurchaseOrderID = inserted.PurchaseOrderID
```

```
END
ELSE
BEGIN
   UPDATE PurchaseOrderHeader
   SET SubTotal = SubTotal +
      (SELECT SUM(LineTotal)
      FROM inserted
      WHERE PurchaseOrderHeader.PurchaseOrderID
       = inserted.PurchaseOrderID)
   WHERE PurchaseOrderHeader.PurchaseOrderID IN
      (SELECT PurchaseOrderID FROM inserted);
END
```

Using *INSTEAD OF* Triggers

INSTEAD OF triggers are used primary to allow more flexible updates to views. An INSTEAD OF trigger is executed instead of the modification. An INSTEAD OF trigger can ignore modifications to certain fields, ignore part or all of a batch, or take an alternative action in case of an error. INSTEAD OF triggers execute before any constraints are checked, so it is possible to modify data to conform to constraint definitions from within an INSTEAD OF trigger.

Unlike AFTER triggers, INSTEAD OF triggers can be created on views as well as tables. INSTEAD OF triggers can be very useful for allowing flexible data modification through views that normally wouldn't be allowed. An INSTEAD OF trigger can redirect modifications from a view to the appropriate base tables. It can also change the type of modification based on procedural logic.

Because only one INSTEAD OF trigger can be created per action, there is no need to set the order of INSTEAD OF triggers.

Consider the table and view definition shown in Listing 6.22. Normally, the vFullNames view won't allow changes because it is a derived field.

LISTING 6.22   Objects Used for INSTEAD OF Trigger

```
USE SandboxDB;
CREATE TABLE Names (
  NameID int NOT NULL PRIMARY KEY,
  FirstName varchar(20) NOT NULL,
  LastName varchar(20) NOT NULL
)
GO
CREATE VIEW vFullNames
AS
SELECT NameID,
       FirstName + ' ' + LastName AS FullName
FROM Names;
```

We can create INSTEAD OF triggers to allow modifications to the view by breaking apart values in the FullName field of the view in to their respective first and last names. Listing 6.23 shows an example of two INSTEAD OF triggers that will redirect insert and update operations to the Names table from the view.

LISTING 6.23   INSTEAD OF Triggers That Redirect Modifications to a Base Table

```
USE SandboxDB;
CREATE TRIGGER trg_vFullNames_Insert
ON vFullNames
INSTEAD OF INSERT
AS
INSERT INTO Names
 SELECT NameID,
        LEFT(FullName, CHARINDEX(' ', FullName) - 1),
        RIGHT(FullName, CHARINDEX(' ', FullName) - 1)
 FROM Inserted;
GO
CREATE TRIGGER trg_vFullNames_Update
ON vFullNames
INSTEAD OF UPDATE
AS
UPDATE Names
 SET NameID = i.NameID,
     FirstName = LEFT(FullName, CHARINDEX(' ', FullName) - 1),
     LastName = RIGHT(FullName, CHARINDEX(' ', FullName) - 1)
 FROM Names JOIN Inserted i
  ON Names.NameID = I.NameID;
```

INSTEAD OF triggers can also be useful for undoing unwanted changes before modifications have been made. Rolling back a transaction within an INSTEAD OF trigger is more efficient than in an AFTER trigger. Listing 6.24 shows an example of an INSTEAD OF trigger that prevents product records from being deleted. Ignoring the delete operation is more efficient than rolling back the delete operation.

LISTING 6.24   INSTEAD OF Trigger That Ignores a Delete Operation

```
USE SandboxDB;
CREATE TRIGGER trg_InsteadOfProductDelete
ON Products
INSTEAD OF DELETE
AS
RAISERROR('Products may not be deleted', 10, 1);
```

Special Considerations

Here are some special considerations in regard to triggers.

It is recommended that a trigger not return a result set. This has been a best practice in the past, but is becoming even more important because the feature will be removed in a later version of SQL Server. The Disallow Results from Triggers server option can be set to 1 to turn on this future behavior. If a trigger returns a result set, error number 524 is raised. This option is very useful for verifying compatibility with future releases of SQL Server.

NESTED TRIGGERS

When a trigger performs an action on another trigger's behalf, this is considered a *nested trigger*. Triggers can be nested up to 32 levels deep. If the 32-level nesting limit is exceeded, the entire transaction is rolled back and an error is returned. Regardless of the number of method calls inside, a trigger that is written using the .NET CLR counts as a single nesting level.

Nested triggers are useful for cascading changes through related tables using more complicated logic than a Foreign Key constraint would allow. By default, nested triggers are turned on. Listing 6.25 shows an example of a trigger that tracks changes to the ProductCount field and a table to store the changes. Inserting a new product would cause the TRG_PRODUCT_INSERT trigger to fire, which was shown previously in the chapter in Listing 6.17. The TRG_PRODUCT_INSERT trigger updates the ProductCount field in the Categories table, and by doing so causes our trigger to fire.

LISTING 6.25   Using Nested Triggers

```
USE SandboxDB;
CREATE TABLE ProductCountAudit (
   AuditID int NOT NULL PRIMARY KEY IDENTITY(1,1),
   CategoryID int NOT NULL,
   OldProductCount int NOT NULL,
   NewProductCount int NOT NULL,
   ChangeDate datetime NOT NULL
     DEFAULT (GETDATE())
);
GO
CREATE TRIGGER trg_Categories_ProductCountAudit
 ON Categories
 FOR UPDATE
AS
IF UPDATE (ProductCount)
BEGIN
  INSERT INTO ProductCountAudit
   (CategoryID, OldProductCount, NewProductCount)
  SELECT i.CategoryID,
         d.ProductCount,
         i.ProductCount
  FROM Deleted d JOIN Inserted i
   ON d.CategoryID = i.CategoryID;
END
```

RECURSIVE TRIGGERS

In the right situation, a trigger can cause itself to fire by using either direct recursion or indirect recursion.

Direct recursion happens when a table with a trigger defined on it modifies the same table, causing that trigger to fire again. It's important to use a recursion termination check to keep from exceeding the 32-level nesting limit.

Indirect recursion happens when a nested trigger causes a modification to one of the tables in the nesting sequence. If each of the tables—let's call them t1 and t2—has a trigger defined on it that modifies the other table, this can start a sequence of one table modifying the other.

Direct recursion is disabled by default, but it can be enabled by using the Recursive Triggers database option. Indirect recursion is controlled by the Nested Triggers server option. To disable indirect recursion, you must disable Nested Triggers.

Rule and Default Objects

Rule and default objects provide backward compatibility with applications that use them. They are similar to constraints in many ways, but they are SQL Server-specific and shouldn't be used in new development.

Unlike a constraint, which is defined as part of a table definition, defaults and rules are defined as separate objects that must be bound to columns before they can be used.

Default Objects

A *default object* is very similar to a default definition. It provides a user-defined default value for a column. The default object is created separately from the table and is bound to columns as required. Listing 6.26 shows the creation of a table that uses both a default constraint definition and a default object.

LISTING 6.26   Creating and Binding a Default Object

```
USE SandboxDB;
CREATE TABLE DefaultExample (
  pkcol int NOT NULL PRIMARY KEY,
  defaultdef int NOT NULL DEFAULT (0),
  defaultobj int NOT NULL
)
GO
CREATE DEFAULT example_default AS 0;
GO
EXEC sp_bindefault example_default, 'DefaultExample.defaultobj';
```

Rules

A *rule object* is very similar to a Check constraint. A rule object consists of an expression that limits the allowable values for a column. The difference between a rule object and a Check constraint is how they are bound to a table. A Check constraint is part of a table definition, where a rule object is created separately and bound to a specific column. Rule objects are less flexible than Check constraints because only a single rule object can be bound to a column. Listing 6.27 shows an example of using a rule object, as well as a Check constraint that is equivalent.

LISTING 6.27   Creating and Binding a Rule Object

```
USE SandboxDB;
CREATE TABLE RuleExample (
  pkcol int NOT NULL PRIMARY KEY,
  checkcol int NOT NULL
    CHECK (checkcol between 1 and 10),
  rulecol int NOT NULL
);
GO
CREATE RULE example_rule AS @var between 1 and 10;
GO
EXEC sp_bindrule example_rule, 'RuleExample.rulecol';
```

Defaults and rules will be removed in a later release of SQL Server, so you should avoid using them.

The Bottom Line

Choose appropriate methods to enforce data integrity.   For a given data integrity rule, there can be several options to enforce that rule. Choosing the appropriate data integrity enforcement mechanism is important for performance.

Master It   What category of data integrity is being enforced by each of the following situations?

1. A unique constraint that is defined on a combination of two columns

2. A Check constraint that only allows values between 1 and 10

3. A Check constraint that forces a Bill Date column to be between period start and period end

4. A Foreign Key constraint that references another table

Create and manage constraints.   Constraints provide declarative integrity enforcement. Creating and managing constraints is important to ensure that integrity rules are enforced by the database.

> **Master It**   When you add a Check constraint to an existing table, is the data verified by default? Can you control this verification? What problems could you encounter?

Create and manage DML triggers.   Triggers provide a more robust, procedural method of enforcing data integrity rules than constraints. Choosing the appropriate type of trigger is important to properly enforce complex integrity rules.

> **Master It**   It's important to choose the appropriate type of trigger in a given situation. Would it be more appropriate to use an AFTER trigger or an INSTEAD OF trigger if you want the trigger to:
>
> **1.** Maintain aggregate values in a separate summary table?
>
> **2.** Ignore updates for a column?
>
> **3.** Modify data to conform to constraints?
>
> **4.** Audit record modifications?

Chapter 7

SQL Server and XML

SQL Server and XML are from different data universes. SQL Server is a relational database environment, and XML is a hierarchical data structure. Getting the two to talk to each other has been a challenge. With the release of SQL Server 2000 and the SQLXML infrastructure, Microsoft began making significant strides in integrating these disparate data environments. With each subsequent release, the toolset and the feature list gets better.

Now in SQL Server 2008, we have better XML support than ever. This chapter addresses these features and demonstrates how you can effectively integrate XML and relational data through SQL Server and its client applications.

In this chapter, you will learn to:

- Implement the FOR XML Transact-SQL structure

- Implement the xml datatype

- Validate XML in SQL Server with XSD schemas

- Implement basic XQuery structures

- Implement XML indexes for performance

DOING YOUR HOMEWORK

This chapter assumes that you are familiar with XML and its associated technologies, such as XPath and XSL. We will not take the time to cover those concepts here. If you are new to XML, you may want to brush up on it before tackling this chapter. An Internet search on XML programming or on specific XML topics will return more information than you can read in a month. You should have no problem finding reference material if you need it.

Returning XML from SQL Server Using *FOR XML*

Relational data is not organized the same as hierarchical data. Although that may seem to be extremely obvious, the fact that they are very different in structure does not alleviate the need for the two formats to interact, nor does it prevent developers and administrators from trying to make them. With the release of SQL Server 2000, Microsoft introduced the capability of formatting return data streams from SQL Server as XML, as opposed to the standard tabular data stream format that is typical for SQL Server. This capability has been improved in every subsequent release, giving the database developer the ability to easily reformat relational data into XML as it is extracted and returned to the client.

SQL Server supports this capability through a Transact-SQL (TSQL) clause called FOR XML. This clause provides instructions to the data engine to output the results of the query in an XML format. Using various options, you have significant control over the format of that output, which gives you the ability to structure the data in a reasonable manner that the developer can then transform using Extensible Stylesheet Language (XSL) if desired. The basic structure of the FOR XML clause looks like this:

```
[ FOR <XML> ]
<XML> ::=
XML
    {
      { RAW [ ('ElementName') ] | AUTO }
        [
          <CommonDirectives>
          [ , { XMLSCHEMA [ ('TargetNameSpaceURI') ]} ]
          [ , ELEMENTS [ XSINIL | ABSENT ]
        ]
      | EXPLICIT
        [
          <CommonDirectives>
          [ , XMLDATA ]
        ]
      | PATH [ ('ElementName') ]
        [
          <CommonDirectives>
          [ , ELEMENTS [ XSINIL | ABSENT ] ]
        ]
    }

    <CommonDirectives> ::=
    [ , BINARY BASE64 ]
    [ , TYPE ]
    [ , ROOT [ ('RootName') ] ]
```

This syntax illustrates that you can follow the FOR XML statement with one of four options: RAW, AUTO, EXPLICIT, or PATH. Each of these options has its own arguments, but they can all use the common directives found at the bottom of the syntax statement. We will look at each of these four options in more detail and assess the scenarios for which each option will be the most beneficial.

Creating XML with RAW Mode Queries

RAW mode is the simplest XML output structure. This example shows the use of the RAW mode query in its simplest form.

```
USE AdventureWorks2008;
SELECT FirstName,MiddleName,LastName
FROM Person.Person
FOR XML RAW;
```

THE MISSING LINK

In SQL Server 2000, executing a FOR XML query was a bit frustrating because it was difficult to see the results. Starting with SQL Server 2005, this changed. If you execute the query into a grid in SQL Server Management Studio (SSMS), the XML output will appear as a link. Simply click on this link to view the entire data stream. This is a very convenient feature that also extends to XML storage. Even if you are not using the FOR XML feature, you will get this same output when you query a table that contains an xml datatype. This allows you to more closely examine the XML returned by any query executed from SSMS.

A RAW mode query returns each row of data in the result set as an element with the generic label <row>. If you look at the results, you will see that each row element represents a single row in the result set. Although the generic row element does not provide any useful information, each attribute name comes directly from the underlying catalog. Here are a few rows of results from this query:

```
<row FirstName="Syed" MiddleName="E" LastName="Abbas" />
<row FirstName="Catherine" MiddleName="R." LastName="Abel" />
<row FirstName="Kim" LastName="Abercrombie" />
```

One thing about this output that stands out is that as written, it is technically not a well-formed XML document. This example requires the addition of a root element to make it well formed. Microsoft refers to this structure as a *well-formed fragment*, meaning that if you were to wrap this entire block into a root element, it would be well-formed. To add this root element, use the ROOT condition in the query.

If you like, you can also return the list as element-based XML as opposed to the current attribute-based format. Simply add the ELEMENTS condition to the clause, and the query will return elements instead of attributes. However, because some of the person rows listed do not have last names, this can result in missing elements. Use the XSINIL condition with the ELEMENTS condition to solve this problem. Combining these techniques would modify the query to look like this:

```
USE AdventureWorks2008;
SELECT FirstName,MiddleName,LastName
FROM Person.Person
FOR XML RAW ('Person'),
   ROOT('Persons'),
   ELEMENTS XSINIL;
```

This query renders a much different XML result. A well-formed partial listing of the result would look like this:

```
<Persons xmlns:xsi="http://www.w3.org/2001/XMLSchema-instance">
  <Person>
    <FirstName>Syed</FirstName>
    <MiddleName>E</MiddleName>
    <LastName>Abbas</LastName>
  </Person>
  <Person>
```

```
    <FirstName>Catherine</FirstName>
    <MiddleName>R.</MiddleName>
    <LastName>Abel</LastName>
  </Person>
  <Person>
    <FirstName>Kim</FirstName>
    <MiddleName xsi:nil="true" />
    <LastName>Abercrombie</LastName>
  </Person>
  ...
</Persons>
```

WATCH YOUR CASE

Remember that XML is case sensitive, and SQL Server is not. This means that you will have to be careful about case. If you intend to use data results in XML streams, you might want to consider your database design as it relates to case. *CamelCasing*, the generally accepted practice in XML, requires an initial lowercase character with internal uppercase, as in the tag <firstName>. Case sensitivity is a consideration for your queries as well, because the case that you use when defining your element names or your root element will be retained in your XML output.

You can also include a generated schema in your XML. Using the XMLSCHEMA condition in the FOR XML clause will generate a schema with a defined target namespace. You can also define your own target namespace identifier by supplying the condition using the format XMLSCHEMA ('urn:sampleNamespace'). SQL Server will tag the data stream to that target namespace. This technique can be useful when returning data to utilities that require schema information for binding purposes.

Creating XML with AUTO Mode Queries

Using AUTO mode in the FOR XML clause will give you fewer options than using RAW mode, because SQL Server generates the XML structure for you. Although you can still use the ROOT, ELEMENTS, and XSINIL directives, you cannot rename the row tags. The following query uses the AUTO mode.

```
USE AdventureWorks2008;
SELECT BusinessEntityID,FirstName,MiddleName,LastName
FROM Person.Person
FOR XML AUTO,
  ROOT('Persons'),
  ELEMENTS XSINIL;
```

The syntax is virtually identical to that of the RAW mode query. The results are also similar, except that the rows are defined based on the schema.object format from the system catalog. Here is a partial listing of the results. (Note that we've added the BusinessEntityID column to this example; it was not present in the previous example.)

```
<Persons xmlns:xsi="http://www.w3.org/2001/XMLSchema-instance">
  <Person.Person>
    <BusinessEntityID>285</BusinessEntityID>
    <FirstName>Syed</FirstName>
    <MiddleName>E</MiddleName>
    <LastName>Abbas</LastName>
  </Person.Person>
  <Person.Person>
    <BusinessEntityID>293</BusinessEntityID>
    <FirstName>Catherine</FirstName>
    <MiddleName>R.</MiddleName>
    <LastName>Abel</LastName>
  </Person.Person>
  <Person.Person>
    <BusinessEntityID>295</BusinessEntityID>
    <FirstName>Kim</FirstName>
    <MiddleName xsi:nil="true" />
    <LastName>Abercrombie</LastName>
  </Person.Person>
  ...
</Persons>
```

Neither the AUTO mode nor the RAW mode will let you rename columns in the query; however, you can use standard SQL syntax to accomplish the same thing. For example, suppose you want to use a standard CamelCase for your XML output stream, but the underlying data is not cased in that manner. Assume that you are using AUTO mode, which does not directly support the renaming of row elements. All you have to do is go back to the basics.

Consider this query:

```
USE AdventureWorks2008;
SELECT
  BusinessEntityID as id,
  FirstName as firstName,
  MiddleName as middleName,
  LastName as lastName
FROM Person.Person as person
FOR XML AUTO,
  ROOT('persons'),
  ELEMENTS XSINIL;
```

Remember that in the body of the query, you have full control over the output. Formatting the results as XML does not require you to throw all of your other skills out the window. You can rename tables and columns, perform calulations and aggregations, joins, and all of the other techniques in your standard toolbox.

The previous query generates the following partial result. This looks more like the XML output you would be interested in generating.

```
<persons xmlns:xsi="http://www.w3.org/2001/XMLSchema-instance">
  <person>
    <id>285</id>
    <firstName>Syed</firstName>
    <middleName>E</middleName>
    <lastName>Abbas</lastName>
  </person>
  <person>
    <id>293</id>
    <firstName>Catherine</firstName>
    <middleName>R.</middleName>
    <lastName>Abel</lastName>
  </person>
  <person>
    <id>295</id>
    <firstName>Kim</firstName>
    <middleName xsi:nil="true" />
    <lastName>Abercrombie</lastName>
  </person>
</persons>
```

What we see from this example is that when combined with appropriate query techniques, there is little difference between AUTO mode and RAW mode. You control all of the output in terms of the naming, schemas, and nullability. What you cannot substantively control with either of these techniques is the structure of the XML output. You end up with a structure that is defined by the mode. RAW mode will always return a flat-row structure, and AUTO mode will nest elements as necessary based on join logic.

Let's look at another RAW mode query.

```
USE AdventureWorks2008;
SELECT
  person.BusinessEntityID as id,
  person.FirstName as firstName,
  person.MiddleName as middleName,
  person.LastName as lastName,
  email.EmailAddress as emailAddress
FROM Person.Person as person
INNER JOIN Person.EmailAddress as email
  ON person.BusinessEntityID = email.BusinessEntityID
FOR XML RAW,
  ROOT('persons'),
  ELEMENTS XSINIL;
```

This RAW mode query returns the following partial output. Notice the flat structure that still returns one row element for each row in the output.

```
<persons xmlns:xsi="http://www.w3.org/2001/XMLSchema-instance">
  <row>
    <id>285</id>
```

```
        <firstName>Syed</firstName>
        <middleName>E</middleName>
        <lastName>Abbas</lastName>
        <emailAddress>syed0@adventure-works.com</emailAddress>
      </row>
      ...
    </persons>
```

If you change the mode from RAW to AUTO, and change nothing else in the query, you should notice a difference in the structure of the XML. The nested structure is caused by the presence of the join in the query.

```
    <persons xmlns:xsi="http://www.w3.org/2001/XMLSchema-instance">
      <person>
        <id>285</id>
        <firstName>Syed</firstName>
        <middleName>E</middleName>
        <lastName>Abbas</lastName>
        <email>
          <emailAddress>syed0@adventure-works.com</emailAddress>
        </email>
      </person>
      ...
    </persons>
```

In some cases, this new shape makes sense. If the relationship between the Person table and the EmailAddress table is a one-to-many relationship where a single person could have many email addresses, a nested set of email addresses might be preferable to a repeating list of email addresses in a flat structure.

The important point here is that in neither case do you have any significant control over the structure of the output. The mode of the query will determine the structure. If you want to control the structure of the output, you must either use EXPLICIT or PATH mode for your query.

Creating XML with EXPLICIT Mode Queries

By allowing you to determine the specific placement of data in an XML structure using hierarchical identifiers, EXPLICIT mode gives you complete control over the structure of the XML document. For EXPLICIT mode to work correctly, you have to write your query in a very specific way. The format of the output of your query must follow a structure called a universal table structure.

This structure marks every row in the output with a tag indicating its level in the XML document hierarchy and a parent identifier, which indicates the tag of its parent element. You rename each column based on its position within the hierarchy. For example, to produce flat attribute-oriented XML output, similar to that produced by default by RAW mode, you could use the following query.

```
    USE AdventureWorks2008;
    SELECT
      1 as tag,
      null as parent,
```

```
      person.BusinessEntityID  as [person!1!id],
      person.FirstName         as [person!1!firstName],
      person.MiddleName        as [person!1!middleName],
      person.LastName          as [person!1!lastName],
      email.EmailAddress       as [person!1!emailAddress]
   FROM Person.Person as person
   INNER JOIN Person.EmailAddress as email
     ON person.BusinessEntityID = email.BusinessEntityID
   FOR XML Explicit,
     ROOT('persons');
```

Every row in this output is tagged at level 1 with a parent of null. This will produce a flat result. In your query, you will need to name each column based on its position in the hierarchy. BusinessEntityID, for example, is located at level 1 in an element called person.

Note that the column alias identifies the name of the element, not the table alias in the FROM clause. Every column that defines itself at the same level in the document must use the same element name.

For example, using [personElement!1!firstName] for the name of the firstName column after the ID column had already been declared within the context of an element called "person" would result in an error because they both claim to be at level 1. Element names must be consistent throughout.

The preceding query would produce the following partial result.

```
<persons>
  <person id="285" firstName="Syed" middleName="E" lastName="Abbas"
emailAddress="syed0@adventure-works.com" />
  <person id="293" firstName="Catherine" middleName="R." lastName="Abel"
emailAddress="catherine0@adventure-works.com" />
  <person id="295" firstName="Kim" lastName="Abercrombie" emailAddress="kim2@
adventure-works.com" />
  ...
</persons>
```

By adding the optional ELEMENT condition to the column aliases, you can push some of the data to the nested-element level instead of the attribute level. This is something you cannot do with either RAW or AUTO mode queries, because they are always element-based or attribute-based in their entirety. EXPLICIT mode allows you to mix the two to create a more realistic output. Consider the following query. Pay special attention to the difference in the column aliases.

```
USE AdventureWorks2008;
SELECT
   1 as tag,
   null as parent,
   person.BusinessEntityID  as [person!1!id],
   person.FirstName         as [person!1!firstName!ELEMENT],
   person.MiddleName        as [person!1!middleName!ELEMENT],
   person.LastName          as [person!1!lastName!ELEMENT],
   email.EmailAddress       as [person!1!emailAddress!ELEMENT]
FROM Person.Person as person
```

```
INNER JOIN Person.EmailAddress as email
  ON person.BusinessEntityID = email.BusinessEntityID
FOR XML Explicit,
  ROOT('persons');
```

Because the ID column does not use the ELEMENT condition but the rest of the column names do, the ID column remains an attribute at level 1, while the rest of the columns become elements nested immediately under level 1. Here is a partial result from this query.

```
<persons>
  <person id="285">
    <firstName>Syed</firstName>
    <middleName>E</middleName>
    <lastName>Abbas</lastName>
    <emailAddress>syed0@adventure-works.com</emailAddress>
  </person>
  ...
</persons>
```

This is a simple example; in the real world, XML data can be much more deeply nested into significantly more elaborate hierarchies. EXPLICIT mode queries support even the most complex hierarchies through relatively simple syntax. If you want your query to support a more elaborate hierarchy, you will have to go through a two-step process when you define it.

1. Create a query that will act as a template. This query will define all of the column aliases that map to the levels of the data you want to extract. Using the preceding syntax, you can define columns in the alias at any level of depth.

2. Use the UNION statement to append additional queries to the template to fill in the details for the levels below level 1. Be sure to add the ORDER BY clause at the end of the last query in the union so that the levels will process from top down. Otherwise, the lower levels will be orphaned.

Look at this query as an example.

```
USE AdventureWorks2008;
SELECT
  1                          as Tag,
  NULL                       as Parent,
  employee.NationalIDNumber  as [employee!1!id],
  employee.JobTitle          as [employee!1!title!ELEMENT],
  NULL                       as [name!2!firstName!ELEMENT],
  NULL                       as [name!2!lastName!ELEMENT]
FROM HumanResources.Employee as employee
UNION ALL
SELECT
  2                          as Tag,
  1                          as Parent,
  employee.NationalIDNumber,
  NULL,
```

```
    person.FirstName,
    person.LastName
FROM Person.Person as person
INNER JOIN HumanResources.Employee as employee
  ON person.BusinessEntityID = employee.BusinessEntityID
ORDER BY [employee!1!id],[name!2!lastName!ELEMENT]
FOR XML EXPLICIT,
  ROOT('employees');
```

In this example, the first query in the union defines the structure of the document. In this case, employee is at level 1 and name is at level 2. The ID column maps to an attribute of level 1. The firstName and lastName columns map to elements nested under level 2. The second query in the union shows the relationship between levels 1 and 2. The second query is tagged as level 2, and its parent is identified as level 1.

Note that each query in the union only needs to select the data it uses at its level and the values that are needed to correlate it to its parent level. In this case, the second query in the union does not need to return a job title. SQL Server will ignore this information because it is not used at this level. It must, however, return the ID number because this is the data that correlates the name information to the employee data at level 1.

The following partial result shows the output of this query.

```
<employees>
  <employee id="10708100">
    <title>Production Technician - WC50</title>
    <name>
      <firstName>Frank</firstName>
      <lastName>Miller</lastName>
    </name>
  </employee>
  <employee id="109272464">
    <title>Production Technician - WC10</title>
    <name>
      <firstName>Bonnie</firstName>
      <lastName>Kearney</lastName>
    </name>
  </employee>
  ...
</employees>
```

Creating XML with PATH Mode Queries

Similarly to EXPLICIT mode, PATH mode gives you complete control over the structure of the resulting XML. However, instead of performing the operation by using a universal table structure, PATH mode uses XPath patterns to define the hierarchy.

If you are familiar with XPath, you know that it is very simple. If you have any exposure to using PATH names in DOS, the concept is the same. You define the hierarchy of the document by using fully or partially qualified PATH identifiers. The result is a much simpler syntax than that used by EXPLICIT mode, but it offers the same amount of control. The following query will produce exactly the same results as the last EXPLICIT mode query we reviewed. Note how much simpler the syntax is.

```
USE AdventureWorks2008;
SELECT
  employee.NationalIDNumber  as "employee/@id",
  employee.JobTitle          as "employee/jobTitle",
  person.FirstName           as "employee/name/firstName",
  person.LastName            as "employee/name/lastName"
FROM Person.Person as person
INNER JOIN HumanResources.Employee as employee
  ON person.BusinessEntityID = employee.BusinessEntityID
ORDER BY employee.NationalIDNumber
FOR XML PATH ('employee'),
  ROOT('employees');
```

In this query, the PATH condition at the bottom defines the name for the row which will reside immediately under the root in the hierarchy. This is much like the RAW mode syntax we saw earlier. All of the other columns use this position as their base point of reference. The @ symbol signifies that the column is an attribute rather than a nested element. Using this syntax, you can create very complex XML structures with a fraction of the code and frustration that EXPLICIT mode requires.

INTEGRATING WITH THE CLIENT

When used with the ADO.NET data-access model, the FOR XML technique provides an alternative method of extracting data that might be useful in some applications. By using a method of the SqlCommand class, the ADO.NET data provider for SQL Server has the ability to generate an XML-based cursor called an XmlReader object. When the command executes a query that uses the FOR XML clause and the command captures the result in an XmlReader object, the XML data stream becomes a very versatile data structure that you can easily stream to any application anywhere without passing additional heavy objects or performing formal serialization. This is just another way that Microsoft's development platform takes advantage of all of the resources and capabilities available.

Although we could certainly dive deeper into the use of the FOR XML clause, this should give you a good feel for how the process is used. When you need to return XML to a client application, these techniques can be invaluable; you can use them to either prepare the data for more elaborate transformations or circumvent the need for additional transformation.

Real World Scenario

ONE SIZE DOES NOT FIT ALL

With the implementation ease of features such as XML output, it might be tempting to use them as an architectural cure-all. Every technology comes with its trade-offs, though, and XML is no exception. Although XML is very versatile and it promotes the interoperability of data between heterogeneous platforms, it is not the all-powerful fix that some would like to believe.

The XML features of SQL Server made their debut in version 2000, and the technology began to stabilize in the 2005 version. In version 2005, companies started to give this option a much more serious look. In one consulting project, a client that did significant data interaction with multiple platforms and data environments made the architectural decision to use the XML output capabilities of SQL Server to promote this interoperability requirement. The results were mixed.

While the interoperability results were positive from a data management perspective, performance was disappointing. This was due primarily to the large amount of data with which they were working and the weight of the XML data stream. The standard mechanism for returning data from SQL Server to the calling application is called the Tabular Data Stream (TDS), which is optimized for bandwidth conservation using the SQL Server network libraries.

In some cases, outputting XML directly to the target service resulted in better performance than shipping the TDS to a mid-tier component that converted the data to XML and sent the stream to the service. In other cases, they were better off using a service endpoint to request data directly from SQL Server through a service interface, although Microsoft has deprecated this technique in SQL Server 2008.

The important point to remember is that there is no magic bullet. There's a reason why there are so many alternatives. When designing your enterprise, you must consider all architectural factors, including performance, security, maintainability, and extensibility. A single architectural option is rarely going to be the best for all situations. The best enterprise data architects are familiar with all of their architectural options and their trade-offs, and they know how to implement the right option for a given situation.

The *xml* Datatype

The ability to store XML in a database is nothing new. After all, XML is simply text. Any text datatype of sufficient size can store XML data. What is special about the xml datatype in SQL Server is that it is implicitly connected to an XML parser and, optionally, a validation engine. You are not simply storing text when you use an xml datatype, but rather you are parsing and potentially validating the XML content whenever you use it. In this section, we will look at the xml datatype and its implementation in tables and procedures. Then we will see how to effectively use it in applications for storage and extraction.

Implementing the *xml* Datatype

As with any other datatype, you can use the xml datatype to provide a foundation for XML storage in tables and queries. Because the xml type is simply character-based storage, it has a lot in common with the other text-based datatypes. You identify XML literals with single quotes just as with other nvarchar types.

The storage of XML implies the use the MAX keyword, meaning that it can potentially store about 2GB of text as a Binary Large Object (BLOB).

IT'S ALL ABOUT SIZE

The default encoding for the xml datatype is UTF-16. If you want to use alternative encoding for the XML storage, you must specify it. Encoding is one of the characteristics of an XML document that is typically located in the XML declaration-processing instruction. Make sure that the encoding of your XML document and the treatment of that document in SQL Server is consistent.

Defining a table, variable, or procedural parameter as XML is no different from using any other datatype. In a CREATE TABLE statement, you would use the xml datatype in place of an nvarchar(max) to enforce well-formed XML structures. For example, the following code creates a table using an xml datatype. You can create this in any test database you like.

```
USE TestDB;
CREATE TABLE OrderData
(
  OrderID     int NOT NULL IDENTITY(1,1) PRIMARY KEY,
  OrderDetail xml
);
```

In this snippet, the xml datatype is used just like any other type. This statement created the table with a BLOB storage structure to store up to 2GB of XML data for every data row. SQL Server will parse the XML on insert to ensure that it is well-formed as you insert it into the database. The following example also shows the definition of an XML-typed variable called @xmlOrderData.

```
DECLARE @xmlOrderData xml;
SET @xmlOrderData =
N'<item id="12">
  <description>250 GB Hard Drive</description>
  <price>120</price>
</item>';

INSERT INTO OrderData (OrderDetail)
VALUES (@xmlOrderData);

SELECT * FROM OrderData;
```

This code inserts a well-formed XML document into the xml datatype in the OrderDetail table. Note that the string for the XML variable has been marked as a Unicode literal by using the "N" prefix. The last line of the code that performs the select will return a result set containing that data.

VIEWING XML OUTPUT

If you use SQL Server Management Studio to execute your query in a grid, the xml datatype returns as a hyperlink. Click on this hyperlink to view the complete XML data structure.

If the XML document had not been well-formed, the result would have been different. This is one of the important differences between the nvarchar(max) datatype and the xml datatype. If you remove the close tag for price in the preceding snippet, the assignment of the data to the variable will error, as in this slightly modified example.

```
DECLARE @xmlOrderData xml;
SET @xmlOrderData =
N'<item id="12">
  <description>250 GB Hard Drive</description>
  <price>120
</item>';
```

In this case, the insert operation will give the error shown in the following snippet. If you had defined the storage of the data as an nvarchar(max) instead of an xml datatype, you would not have received this error. However, you want this error to occur if the XML is not well-formed.

```
Msg 9436, Level 16, State 1, Line 8
XML parsing: line 4, character 7, end tag does not match start tag
```

An interesting property of the xml datatype in SQL Server is its tolerance for the violation of the single-root rule of well-formed XML. Normally, you would be required to have a single root element for all XML streams. SQL Server, however, does not enforce this by default. The rationale for this is that the data rows may need to contain XML fragments that are rolled into other XML data structures later. For example, look at this snippet:

```
DECLARE @xmlOrderData xml;
SET @xmlOrderData =
N'<item id="12">
  <description>250 GB Hard Drive</description>
  <price>120</price>
</item>
<item id="25">
  <description>USB Mouse</description>
  <price>25</price>
</item>';
```

You might expect this statement to fail because there is no root element. However, because SQL Server allows this structure, which Microsoft calls a well-formed fragment, the statement proceeds without error. You can change this behavior, but only if you use schema-typed XML, which we will discuss later in this chapter.

Shredding XML Data to Relational Output

In our discussion of the FOR XML clause, you saw how to convert relational data to XML output. It is also possible to go the other way. Data that you store in the database or in a variable in XML format can return to the client in a TDS as opposed to an XML stream. You perform this operation by using the OPENXML function built into SQL Server 2008.

This process requires multiple steps.

1. Create a memory-resident data tree from the XML data.

2. Generate a rowset from the XML tree by using XPath to identify positions within the tree.

3. Process the data. You might want to return it to the client as a rowset or insert the data into other tables in your database.

4. To reclaim the memory, remove the data tree from memory.

EVERY EXCEPTION HAS AN EXCEPTION

Although the ability to store fragments in an xml datatype is an exception to the general XML rule, there is one situation when SQL Server will not allow fragments. This is when you are shredding XML with the OPENXML statement. In this situation, you must ensure that there is a single root node to the XML that you are processing; otherwise, the XPath statements you use to identify the data you want to extract will not function correctly, resulting in an error. If you are working with fragments, you can easily wrap them in a root element by using XQuery INSERT statements, which we will discuss later in this chapter.

You can see each of these steps in the following snippet. This code begins by assigning XML data to a variable. (You could just as easily pass the XML data to a procedure through a parameter or select it from a table.) Two stored procedures are used to prepare the XML document into a memory tree and destroy the tree when finished. The variable @ptrDoc is declared as an integer and points to this memory tree that the OPENXML function uses to walk through the memory tree.

```
DECLARE @xmlOrderData xml;
SET @xmlOrderData =
N'<items>
  <item id="12">
    <description>250 GB Hard Drive</description>
    <price>120</price>
  </item>
  <item id="25">
    <description>USB Mouse</description>
    <price>25</price>
```

```
    </item>
</items>';

DECLARE @ptrDoc int;

EXEC sp_xml_preparedocument @ptrDoc OUTPUT, @xmlOrderData;

SELECT *
FROM OPENXML(
  @ptrDoc,
  '/items/item',
  3
)
WITH (
  id int,
  description varchar(30),
  price money
);

EXEC sp_xml_removedocument @ptrDoc;
```

The OPENXML function is divided into two pieces. The first section defines the context for the extraction. You must provide two parameters for this first section: the pointer to the prepared document and an XPath statement indicating the starting point for the extraction. Remember that XML can be deeply nested, so you have to tell the function where the extraction begins.

This function contains a third argument, into which we are passing the value 3. This is a *flag* that specifies which parts of the XML document the function will try to pull. You can choose to extract only attributes, only elements, or both. The values of the flags are listed in Table 7.1.

TABLE 7.1   OPENXML Flags

VALUE	DESCRIPTION
0	Default mappings (attributes)
1	Retrieve only attributes with names that match the WITH list
2	Retrieve only elements with names that match the WITH list
3	Retrieve both elements and attributes with names that match the WITH list

In the preceding example, the mapping flag is set to 3, which means that the WITH list, which is the second part of the function, can contain references to both elements and attributes. Any item in the WITH list that does not map to a specific mapped element or attribute in the XML tree will return NULL.

The results of this statement look like this:

```
id          description                     price
----------- ------------------------------- --------------------
12          250 GB Hard Drive                   120.00
25          USB Mouse                            25.00
```

(2 row(s) affected)

You can also do explicit mapping in the WITH list by using an XPath statement to qualify the location in the XML document. This option also gives you the ability to rename the data elements as you return them. The OPENXML statement in the following example uses this alternative approach. The flags parameter is absent because the explicit mappings in the WITH list would override this setting anyway, rendering the flags functionally useless.

```
SELECT *
FROM OPENXML(
  @ptrDoc,
  '/items/item'
)
WITH (
  ItemID int './@id',
  ItemDescription varchar(30) './description',
  ItemPrice money './price'
);
```

This code returns the same data as the previous snippet, but with different column names. This alternative approach also gives you a great deal of flexibility because the data that you pull does not have to be confined to a single tier in the XML document. Between the OPENXML and the FOR XML functionalities, you have a tremendous degree of flexibility to move data from relational to XML formats and back.

Validating XML with Schemas

Well-formed XML data does not require any specific tagging as long as the tagging structure is consistent with the rules and requirements of XML. There are times, however, when you may need to dictate the content of an XML document including, but not limited to, the tags that you can use, the order of those tags, and the datatypes of the contents. XML supports this structural validation with a document called a *schema*. Specifically, Microsoft supports the W3C standard XML Schema Definition (XSD) structure in SQL Server 2008.

GETTING THE DETAILS

The World Wide Web Consortium (W3C) is the standards body for XML and other web-based technologies and protocols. If you are not familiar with them or the XML schema specification, you may want to consult their website at http://www.w3.org. All of their supported technologies are listed on the left side of the main page. We will not cover any schema specifics in this chapter. However, if you need more information about XML or schemas, this is a good place to start.

Using the XML Schema Collection

Before you can use an XML schema to validate an XML document or data stream, you must first import that schema into SQL Server by adding it in an XML schema collection. Each schema collection is a named artifact and contains one or more schemas that you use to validate your XML documents and streams. You can create an XML schema collection using the CREATE XML SCHEMA COLLECTION TSQL command, as in this example.

```
CREATE XML SCHEMA COLLECTION ItemCollection
AS
N'<?xml version="1.0" encoding="utf-16"?>
<xs:schema
  elementFormDefault="qualified"
  attributeFormDefault="unqualified"
  xmlns:xs="http://www.w3.org/2001/XMLSchema">
  <xs:element name="items">
    <xs:complexType>
      <xs:sequence>
        <xs:element maxOccurs="unbounded" name="item">
          <xs:complexType>
            <xs:sequence>
              <xs:element name="description" type="xs:string" />
              <xs:element name="price" type="xs:decimal" />
            </xs:sequence>
            <xs:attribute name="id" type="xs:integer" use="required" />
          </xs:complexType>
        </xs:element>
      </xs:sequence>
    </xs:complexType>
  </xs:element>
</xs:schema>';
```

This creates an XML schema collection object called ItemCollection. To use this collection, simply include the collection name in the XML type declaration. You can use this technique for both variables and tables. If you wanted to enforce validation of an XML data structure using this schema, you could use code like this:

```
DECLARE @xmlOrderData xml(DOCUMENT ItemCollection);
SET @xmlOrderData =
N'<items>
  <item id="12">
    <description>250 GB Hard Drive</description>
    <price>120</price>
  </item>
  <item id="25">
    <description>USB Mouse</description>
    <price>25</price>
  </item>
</items>';
```

In the preceding example, the `xml` datatyped variable requires that any XML data inserted adheres to the rules specified in the ItemCollection schema collection object. Using the DOCUMENT keyword additionally specifies that well-formed fragments do not pass validation. Only full documents that include a root node and also adhere to the structural requirements of the schema will pass validation. To test this, you can modify the XML document by removing a section, such as the price section, from one of the tags. Although still well-formed, it will no longer pass validation because the schema requires that a price element is located in every item below the description element.

Using Namespaces in Schemas

Another common characteristic of a schema is the inclusion of a namespace. In XML, a namespace is an identifier for an XML type. If you think of an XML schema as the rules for a particular document structure, another way to look at that is as a document type. Every type should have a name. The XML schema collection object can have multiple schema definitions within the collection, so each schema has to have a unique identifier to provide the ability to uniquely identify them.

In addition, you can think of each XML document as an instance of a schema. The schema defines the type, and the actual XML document is the implementation of that type. To identify an XML document or section of a document as being an instance of a particular schema type, you include the type or namespace name in the XML tags in your document.

Because namespaces must be unique identifiers, the standard for namespace identifiers is to use a URL format. This can be a bit misleading at first. Although the URL format can contain a protocol header like `http://`, this does not mean that the namespace is a navigable place on the Web, nor does it require web access to resolve. XML is simply using this format to help you ensure that all namespaces are universally unique.

Assume that you wanted to create a unique namespace name for the Items schema that you just created in the XML schema collection. This is a simple addition to the schema opening tag to include references to the target namespace that you are defining. Change the opening schema tag to look something like the following code snippet. (If you have already created the XML schema collection, you can either drop and re-create the collection or use the `alter` statement to modify it.)

```
<xs:schema
  targetNamespace="http://schemas.sybexdemos.com/masteringsql/items"
  xmlns="http://schemas.sybexdemos.com/masteringsql/items"
  elementFormDefault="qualified"
  attributeFormDefault="unqualified"
  xmlns:xs="http://www.w3.org/2001/XMLSchema">
  ...
</schema>
```

The address referenced by the namespace is not a navigable location on the Web, but that does not matter. What matters is that you are providing a name that will not clash with any other name that could possibly be used in the same environment, thereby guaranteeing that you have in fact uniquely identified the type by name.

If you attempt to load the XML document into the schema-typed variable after making this change to the schema, it will fail. This is because you have now named the schema, meaning that only documents that are tagged to use that schema will pass validation. To tag the XML to use the schema, change the opening tag for the <items> node to include the schema namespace. It should look like this:

```
DECLARE @xmlOrderData xml(DOCUMENT ItemCollection);
SET @xmlOrderData =
N'<items xmlns="http://schemas.sybexdemos.com/masteringsql/items" >
...
</items>';
```

Of course, it is up to you whether you use schemas at all, and if so, how specific you will want to be with regard to namespaces and type identification. On the downside, XML validation with schemas is a time-consuming activity with significant overhead, but it also can mean the difference between preserving data integrity and just throwing garbage into your database.

Implementing XQuery

XQuery is a W3C standard; the W3C accorded it "recommended" status in early 2007. As such, compared with more mature XML technologies such as XPath and Extensible Stylesheet Language Transformations (XSLT), the XQuery standard is the newcomer to the party. The purpose of XQuery overlaps slightly with XSLT, as both perform transformations of document structures. The general intent of XQuery, however, is to present a SQL-like syntax for querying XML data structures. With the extensive support that SQL Server now provides for XML, this is a natural fit.

In SQL Server, the XQuery functionality is implemented through the query() method of the xml datatype. This is a bit of a departure from other SQL programming techniques, which do not generally make heavy use of methods associated with types, but it works very well in this context. The query method takes parameters that define the XQuery structure and the namespaces if necessary, returning XML from the expression that represents the results of the XQuery request.

Simple XQuery Expressions

In its simplest form, an XQuery expression is merely an XPath statement. After loading the XML data into an xml-typed object, such as a table column or variable, you can use the XPath to retrieve the selected data from the XML structure, as in the following example. This query will return only the section of XML data that relates to item 25. Because the XML data is untyped, there is no need to resolve a namespace reference.

```
DECLARE @xmlOrderData xml;
SET @xmlOrderData =
N'<items>
  <item id="12">
    <description>250 GB Hard Drive</description>
    <price>120</price>
  </item>
  <item id="25">
    <description>USB Mouse</description>
    <price>25</price>
```

```
  </item>
</items>';

SELECT @xmlOrderData.query(
  '/items/item[@id="25"]'
);
```

KEEPING IT CONSTANT

All of the queries in this section assume that the query executes on the same XML data structure listed in the previous example. Because there is no need to include this structure and variable assignment again, we will assume that the xml-typed variable has already been assigned and is ready for use.

Structuring Complex XQuery Syntax

The query we just looked at is a simple example. However, XQuery syntax can be significantly more complex. The structure of a complex XQuery expression is similar to a SQL statement in that it is divided into clauses. Just as a SQL query has a SELECT, FROM, and WHERE clause, XQuery also has distinct sections that do specific tasks. The W3C has defined the following structure for XQuery expressions using the abbreviation FLWOR (pronounced "flower"). It stands for:

for: sets the context

let: sets the variables

where: sets the conditions

order by: sets the sort

return: sets the response

THE DATA WILL COME TO ORDER

SQL Server 2008 does not support the order by functionality as defined in the XQuery specification. If you want to order your XML data, you will have to do it either at the SQL Level before extract to an XML format or you can send the XML data resulting from an XQuery expression to a middle-tier component where you can easily order it using XSLT techniques.

As in SQL, you do not need to have all the clauses in a FLWOR statement for it to be valid. You only need to have a for clause and a return clause. For example, to execute the same statement as the preceding XPath query using the FLWOR syntax, you could use this code, which only uses the `for` and `return` clauses. Note that this XQuery statement uses the XPath filter syntax to include only the item in the XML data having an `id` attribute equal to 25.

```
SELECT @xmlOrderData.query(
  'for $item in /items/item[@id="25"]
  return ($item)'
);
```

Another way to accomplish this would be to use the `where` clause of the XQuery statement. The following code does the same thing as the previous snippet, but it does so using the `where` clause.

```
SELECT @xmlOrderData.query(
  'for $item in /items/item
  where $item/@id = "25"
  return ($item)'
);
```

You can also use functions in your XQuery statements. Although XQuery is technically an expression-based environment, a significant number of functions are built in to XQuery and XPath, and you can use them to your advantage. For example, if you want to get a list of all items having a price that is greater than the average price of all items in the XML data structure, you could use this code.

```
SELECT @xmlOrderData.query(
  'for $item in /items/item
  where avg(/items//price) < $item/price
  return ($item)'
);
```

In the preceding example, the list of prices is passed as a parameter to the `avg` function. Since the context of this price list descends from the root, it includes all prices in the document. Therefore, the calculation of the average is the average price for all the items in the data structure.

For readability, you can define this price list as a variable and reuse it later in your XQuery structure. You do this through the `let` statement, like this:

```
SELECT @xmlOrderData.query(
  'for $item in /items/item
  let $prices := /items/item/price
  where avg($prices) < $item/price
  return ($item)'
);
```

Notice how the code defines the price list using a variable called `$prices`. From that point on, anywhere in your query that you want to refer to the entire set of prices, you can substitute this variable instead. This is extremely convenient when you are using values or value sets that resolve to different points in the XML data hierarchy.

Let's change the data structure a little bit. Assume that there are now three items in the item list. The new item has a higher price point; therefore, return data would require the return of two items instead of one, since both items have a price point that is above the average price. Assume the source data structure looks like this:

```
DECLARE @xmlOrderData xml;
SET @xmlOrderData =
N'<items>
  <item id="12">
    <description>250 GB Hard Drive</description>
    <price>120</price>
  </item>
  <item id="25">
    <description>USB Mouse</description>
    <price>25</price>
  </item>
  <item id="21">
    <description>USB Wireless Network Adapter</description>
    <price>135</price>
  </item>
</items>';
```

If you reuse the query that returns the list of items having an average price that is greater than the average price, you will get the following response.

```
<item id="12">
  <description>250 GB Hard Drive</description>
  <price>120</price>
</item>
<item id="21">
  <description>USB Wireless Network Adapter</description>
  <price>135</price>
</item>
```

Creating an XML Structure with XQuery

The problem with this response stream is that it is not well-formed. It is a fragment. Although you could store this fragment in an untyped XML variable or column, you could not store this as type xml, nor would it parse by XML parsers that require a well-formed document. Fortunately, XQuery solves this problem by letting you enclose the return data in an alternative structure, giving you the ability to inject literal data or wrap responses. Look at the following query as an illustration.

```
SELECT @xmlOrderData.query(
  '<items> {
    for $item in /items/item
    let $prices := /items/item/price
    where avg($prices) < $item/price
    return $item
  } </items>'
);
```

Wrapping the <items> node around the entire XQuery structure ensures that this is now compliant with well-formed rules. It should also give you a couple of other clues about XQuery. You can nest query elements within literals, or if needed, place literals inside your query output. You can also nest multiple XQuery statements within each other, which is very useful when one query uses the context of another for its content and point of reference.

The preceding query would produce this result:

```
<items>
  <item id="12">
    <description>250 GB Hard Drive</description>
    <price>120</price>
  </item>
  <item id="21">
    <description>USB Wireless Network Adapter</description>
    <price>135</price>
  </item>
</items>
```

In this case, the items are in no particular order. They are simply in the order in which they were retrieved in the document. This is the standard behavior in SQL Server 2008, as it does not support the order by syntax in the XQuery specification. If you need to order your results, you can still use XSLT in a middle-tier component to easily accomplish that task.

XQuery and Namespaces

Namespaces are very important parts of XML because they identify the unique types and data patterns that the XML data can take. If the XML data is typed in SQL Server 2008 through an XML schema collection, you must identify that namespace to your XQuery expressions so that the parser can successfully find the data. Assume you are working with the following XML data structure.

```
DECLARE @xmlOrderData xml (DOCUMENT ItemCollection);
SET @xmlOrderData =
N'<items  xmlns="http://schemas.sybexdemos.com/masteringsql/items" >
  <item id="12">
    <description>250 GB Hard Drive</description>
    <price>120</price>
  </item>
  <item id="25">
    <description>USB Mouse</description>
    <price>25</price>
  </item>
  <item id="21">
    <description>USB Wireless Network Adapter</description>
    <price>135</price>
  </item>
</items>';
```

If you attempt to execute one of your XQuery statements from the previous examples on this xml variable now, you will get errors telling you that it cannot find the tags in your document. The error is a little misleading, because it is not that it cannot find the tag at all, but it is looking for the tag by that name that is not in the context of a namespace. If the XML document is defined as an instance of a namespace, XQuery needs to know what that namespace is so that it can locate the tags in that context.

Namespaces in XML can either be default or aliased. Every XML data structure is allowed one default namespace, which represents the namespace context of all tags that are not preceded with an alias. However, because it is possible that tags in a document might come from multiple namespaces, you also have the option of defining the namespace with an alias. Whenever the tag is preceded by the alias, you know that it should be considered within the context of that namespace. This prevents the name clashing that can occur when tags from different namespaces are used in the same document.

DECLARING THE DEFAULT NAMESPACE

If you have an XML data structure like the one in our example that uses a default namespace, you must declare that namespace in your XQuery expression before it will understand how to process your data and be able to find your tags. The declaration of the namespace is part of the XQuery structure itself, as illustrated in this code snippet.

```
SELECT @xmlOrderData.query(
  'declare default element namespace
    "http://schemas.sybexdemos.com/masteringsql/items";
  <items> {
    for $item in /items/item
    let $prices := /items/item/price
    where avg($prices) < $item/price
    return $item
  } </items>'
);
```

In this example, the namespace is declared as the default element namespace, which means that all of the tags in the XML document that do not have a namespace prefix are assumed to be part of this default namespace. It also means that this same namespace defines the resulting structure as well. The results of this query look like this:

```
<items xmlns="http://schemas.sybexdemos.com/masteringsql/items">
  <item id="12">
    <description>250 GB Hard Drive</description>
    <price>120</price>
  </item>
  <item id="21">
    <description>USB Wireless Network Adapter</description>
    <price>135</price>
  </item>
</items>
```

Using Aliased Namespaces

If there are tags from multiple namespaces in your documents, they will have to be aliased. This is often a common practice even when you could use default namespaces because it makes it easier to organize your documents and identify the tags. This will require a slight change to the XML document, as depicted in this example.

```
DECLARE @xmlOrderData xml (DOCUMENT ItemCollection);
SET @xmlOrderData =
N'<it:items  xmlns:it="http://schemas.sybexdemos.com/masteringsql/items" >
  <it:item id="12">
    <it:description>250 GB Hard Drive</it:description>
    <it:price>120</it:price>
  </it:item>
  <it:item id="25">
    <it:description>USB Mouse</it:description>
    <it:price>25</it:price>
  </it:item>
  <it:item id="21">
    <it:description>USB Wireless Network Adapter</it:description>
    <it:price>135</it:price>
  </it:item>
</it:items>';
```

In the preceding example, the namespace was prefixed with it, and this same prefix now precedes all tags in the document. Using the XQuery statement without the prefixes would fail, because this statement assumes that the namespace in question is the default namespace. To make it work, you must change your XQuery statement to use the it prefix with code, as in this example:

```
SELECT @xmlOrderData.query(
'declare namespace it="http://schemas.sybexdemos.com/masteringsql/items";
  <it:items> {
    for $item in /it:items/it:item
    let $prices := /it:items/it:item/it:price
    where avg($prices) < $item/it:price
    return $item
  } </it:items>'
);
```

Notice that in addition to adding the it prefix to the namespace declaration, you must also add that prefix to any reference in your XQuery statement that uses tags defined in that namespace.

The result of the preceding query would look like this:

```
<it:items xmlns:it="http://schemas.sybexdemos.com/masteringsql/items">
  <it:item id="12">
    <it:description>250 GB Hard Drive</it:description>
    <it:price>120</it:price>
  </it:item>
  <it:item id="21">
```

```
      <it:description>USB Wireless Network Adapter</it:description>
      <it:price>135</it:price>
    </it:item>
  </it:items>
```

Other XML Datatype Methods

In addition to the query() method and the xml datatype, there are other methods that you can use to explore and manipulate XML data. These methods are

value()   Returns a scalar value from an XML document

exist()   Returns a value indicating if the PATH node exists in a document

modify()   Provides for modification of an XML document through the XQuery modification
extensions

nodes()   Provides a mechanism for shredding an XML document to a relational structure

To help you better understand what these statements do, we will look at some samples of each. They are all very straightforward, and a few code illustrations should get the point across. To keep these examples simple, we will go back to the chapter's first XML data structure. As a reminder, here is the data that we will use:

```
DECLARE @xmlOrderData xml;
SET @xmlOrderData =
N'<items>
  <item id="12">
    <description>250 GB Hard Drive</description>
    <price>120</price>
  </item>
  <item id="25">
    <description>USB Mouse</description>
    <price>25</price>
  </item>
</items>';
```

RETRIEVING SCALAR VALUES FROM XML

The value() method uses an XPath statement to return the value of a particular point in the XML structure. As its name implies, it returns a single scalar value. If you want to extract multiple values, you can use a more comprehensive XQuery statement or make multiple calls. In this example, suppose you wanted to retrieve the value of the price field for the first items in the document. Using the value() method, the code would look like this:

```
SELECT @xmlOrderData.value(
  '(/items/item/price)[1]', 'decimal'
);
```

In this example, the XPath statement must guarantee that it returns on a single value. The purpose of the [1] in the code is to ensure that this takes place. Notice that there are two parameters. The first parameter describes the target node (here, the price node). The second parameter indicates the datatype that the value statement returns to the calling expression.

PERFORMING AN EXISTENCE CHECK

Another useful technique in SQLXML is to use the `exist()` method to check for the presence or absence of a single node in the data structure. Remember that sometimes the absence of data can be as meaningful as the data itself.

   This method also takes an XPath statement as a parameter, but it returns a 1 if the referenced element exists and a 0 if it does not. If you are checking for the existence of an item with an `id` of 25, you could use code like this:

```
SELECT @xmlOrderData.exist(
  '/items/item[@id="25"]'
);
```

This syntax, which is very simple, is often used in the context of much more complex operations as a nested structure.

MODIFYING XML THROUGH XQUERY EXTENSIONS

The XQuery specification is certainly not complete, and while XQuery 1.0 currently enjoys recommended status, work is ongoing to continue improving the functionality of XQuery. One element of this progress is the XML DML extensions for XQuery. These extensions are currently works in progress, but they are supported in SQL Server 2008 through the `modify()` method of the `xml` datatype. The XQuery DML extensions have three supported operations:

- ◆ `insert`
- ◆ `delete`
- ◆ `replace value of`

The approach is similar for each. Set a base point of reference by storing the starting XML in an `xml` variable or column, and then use the method to make a modification to that XML.

   Suppose that you wanted to add another item to your items list. This would be an `insert` operation and could be done dynamically by using this code:

```
SET @xmlOrderData.modify('
insert
  <item id="21">
    <description>USB Wireless Network Adapter</description>
    <price>135</price>
  </item>
as last
into (/items)[1]
');
SELECT @xmlOrderData;
```

This code snippet contains two statements. The first statement makes the change to the XML data structure stored in the variable by adding another item as the last item in the list. You could also specify where to add the new data: first, before, or after the referenced node. The second statement is a simple SELECT that will give you the results of the modification. When you run this code, you should see three items in the list instead of two, like this:

```
<items>
  <item id="12">
    <description>250 GB Hard Drive</description>
    <price>120</price>
  </item>
  <item id="25">
    <description>USB Mouse</description>
    <price>25</price>
  </item>
  <item id="21">
    <description>USB Wireless Network Adapter</description>
    <price>135</price>
  </item>
</items>
```

Deleting data is very similar. You identify the node to be deleted, which makes the change to the stored XML data structure. Assume that you wanted to remove the first item from the list. You would need to reference the item uniquely using an approach similar to the scalar query. This code provides an example.

```
SET @xmlOrderData.modify(
'delete (//items/item)[1]'
)
SELECT @xmlOrderData;
```

The last modification process uses the replace value of syntax. This syntax identifies the node value to be changed and then allows you to provide a replacement value. Because you can replace the value of an individual node or an entire branch of the tree, this is a very versatile operation. Here is an example where the price of the second product in the list is modified.

```
DECLARE @xmlOrderData xml(DOCUMENT ItemCollection);
SET @xmlOrderData =
N'<items xmlns="http://schemas.sybexdemos.com/masteringsql/items" >
  <item id="12">
    <description>250 GB Hard Drive</description>
    <price>120</price>
  </item>
  <item id="25">
    <description>USB Mouse</description>
    <price>25</price>
  </item>
</items>';


SET @xmlOrderData.modify(
```

```
'declare default element namespace "http://schemas.sybexdemos.com/masteringsql/
items";
replace value of (/items/item[2]/price)[1]
with (160)'
)
SELECT @xmlOrderData;
```

One of the requirements of the `replace value of` syntax is that the data must be typed if you want to make modifications to individual data elements. Therefore, in this example you will see that the variable is once again typed with the XML schema collection reference, and the query declares the namespace as in the other XQuery patterns that you have already seen.

SHREDDING XML WITH XQUERY

Although you can use the OPENXML statement that we discussed earlier in this chapter to convert XML data to a tabular structure, you can accomplish the same thing with the `nodes()` method of the xml datatype. This method exposes all of the elements at a particular level of depth in an XML document as a set of nodes. You can then treat these nodes as if they were rows in a table, mapping elements in the node structure to columns in a result set. Suppose you wanted to return a standard result set from the data in the XML structure. You could use the nodes method as follows.

```
DECLARE @xmlOrderData xml;
SET @xmlOrderData =
N'<items >
  <item id="12">
    <description>250 GB Hard Drive</description>
    <price>120</price>
  </item>
  <item id="25">
    <description>USB Mouse</description>
    <price>25</price>
  </item>
</items>';

SELECT
  item.value('./@id[1]', 'int') as ID,
  item.value('./description[1]', 'varchar(30)') as Description,
  item.value('./price[1]', 'money') as Price
FROM @xmlOrderData.nodes('/items/item') as ItemList(item);
```

XML Indexes

Like any other data, access is faster if you have the right index. XML data is a little different. Traditional indexes do not make any sense on an XML data structure. If you place a nonclustered index on an xml-typed column in a database, the impact would be disastrous. So much so, in fact, that SQL Server does not even allow it. However, if there were a way to create an index on the actual XML contents of a table column, this could prove to be a substantial benefit. SQL Server 2008 supports two different categories of XML indexes.

Primary XML Indexes The primary XML index shreds the entire XML data structure into a set of index rows. All tags, values, and paths in the XML data structure are part of the index. You can only create an XML index on a column in a table if the table has a clustered index on the primary key. Every index row stores the tag name, value, and path, and correlates this information with the primary key value for that data row for searching purposes.

Secondary XML Indexes Although primary XML indexes provide basic XML searching support, to improve the performance of certain XML search operations, you can also create secondary XML indexes. You must first create a primary XML index before you can create secondary XML indexes. These secondary indexes come in three types:

PATH **Index** PATH indexes support XQuery statements that search based on path expressions. Simple XQuery statements using only an XPath address or a full XQuery statement that looks up data based on a path can benefit from this index type.

VALUE **Index** VALUE indexes support queries where a specific value is referenced in the path, like in a filter statement. A statement such as /items/item[@id="25"] is an example of a value-based query as the filter expression is tied to a value that the index will search.

PROPERTY **Index** PROPERTY Indexes support scalar queries. When the XQuery statement uses the value() method of the xml datatype, a PROPERTY index might provide a performance benefit as all values are indexed.

CREATING XML INDEXES

Creating an XML index is very similar to creating a standard index. The requirements and behavior, however, are quite different. Prior to creating an XML index, you should evaluate the following considerations:

◆ The table containing the XML column that you want to index must have a clustered index on the primary key.

◆ You must create a primary XML index before creating any secondary XML indexes.

◆ If you have an XML index on a table, you cannot alter or drop the clustered primary key on that table.

◆ You cannot create an XML index on an xml-typed column in a view, table-valued variable, or an xml-typed variable.

The syntax for creating an XML index is very similar to the standard DDL for indexes. We cover this syntax in more depth in Chapter 14, "Data Availability and Distribution." For now, all you need to know is the basic structure. To begin, assume that you have created the following table and inserted an xml value, as in the following code.

```
USE TestDB;
CREATE TABLE OrderData
(
  OrderID     int NOT NULL IDENTITY(1,1) PRIMARY KEY,
```

```
  OrderDetail  xml(DOCUMENT ItemCollection)
);

DECLARE @xmlOrderData xml(DOCUMENT ItemCollection);
SET @xmlOrderData =
N'<items xmlns="http://schemas.sybexdemos.com/masteringsql/Items" >
  <item id="12">
    <description>250 GB Hard Drive</description>
    <price>120</price>
  </item>
  <item id="25">
    <description>USB Mouse</description>
    <price>25</price>
  </item>
</items>';

Insert Into OrderData (OrderDetail)
Values (@xmlOrderData);
```

To create a primary XML index on this table, you would use the following statement.

```
CREATE PRIMARY XML INDEX idxPrimaryXML ON OrderData (OrderDetail);
```

The secondary indexes all follow the same basic form as well. If you wanted to create a PATH index, you would use the following code. Notice how the secondary index makes reference to the primary index. For any other secondary index, simply substitute the appropriate keyword (VALUE or PROPERTY) in place of PATH in the following example.

```
CREATE XML INDEX idxPath ON OrderData(OrderDetail)
USING XML INDEX idxPrimaryXML
FOR PATH;
```

If you decide that you do not need the XML index any more, you can easily drop it. You must drop all secondary indexes before you can drop the primary. The syntax is exactly the same as with standard indexes. To drop the previous secondary index, you would use this statement.

```
DROP INDEX idxPath ON OrderData;
```

NEED WHAT YOU USE

Make sure that you really need the XML indexes you create. They can take up a lot of space, and if you use the indexes to simply store XML data, there is little benefit. They are designed specifically to aid in XQuery and XSLT environments. When you do nothing but insert an entire XML document and retrieve the entire document, there is no benefit to having the index. Why waste the space?

The Bottom Line

Implement the FOR XML **Transact-SQL structure.** Even if you store data relationally in a database, that doesn't mean you cannot retrieve it as XML. In some cases, it makes sense to do just that. Using the FOR XML clause in the Transact-SQL, you can retrieve data in a variety of XML formats and structures.

Master It Explain the difference between the following types of FOR XML statements.

1. RAW

2. AUTO

3. EXPLICIT

4. PATH

Implement the xml **datatype.** In SQL Server 2008, the xml datatype is a full datatype at peer with other character datatypes such as nchar and nvarchar. SQL Server implements the type as an nvarchar(max), but it also associates an xml parser with the datatype to ensure that all data stored in an xml datatyped container is well-formed.

Master It List the steps and the code structures that you would use to shred a relational data structure from data stored in an xml datatype.

Validate XML in SQL Server with XSD schemas. Because the XML specification does not define the tags you can use in your documents, there must be a mechanism for ensuring that XML data has the right tags and in the right order. You can use schemas to do this. You can create a schema by using an XML schema collection object in SQL Server.

Master It Write statements that will do the following:

1. Declare a variable called @xmlData as untyped xml.

2. Declare a variable called @xmlData as typed xml using the SampleCollection XmlSchemaCollection that can store fragments.

3. Declare a variable called @xmlData as typed xml using the SampleCollection XmlSchemaCollection that can store only well-formed documents.

Implement basic XQuery structures. The XQuery standard, which is defined by the W3C, is supported in SQL Server through the xml datatype. The SQL developer can use the xml datatype to query data in a variety of ways, and even modify XML data if necessary.

Master It For each of the listed scenarios, specify the xml datatype method you would use to address the issue.

1. You want to return a single scalar value from an XML document.

2. You want to return a subset of XML from the document.

3. You want to make a change to an existing XML document.

4. You want to see if a particular note is present in an XML document.

Implement XML indexes for performance.   Data stored as XML is not stagnant. You don't have to return the entire XML document structure in your query. Using XQuery, you can return individual subsets or values from an XML document. This versatility makes it much more reasonable to store data as XML because you know that you can actually get to it and use it after it is stored.

Master It   You want to create a PATH index on an XML column called OrderXML in a table called Orders. What do you have to do to create the index? Include any actions that are prerequisites to creating the index.

Chapter 8

Managing User Security

When someone knocks on the front door of your house, you want to know who is there before you open the door and let him or her inside. It is a matter of security. Before you let someone into your house, you must first verify their identity. But you can't stop there! Not only do you have to know who is at the door, but based on that information you also have to determine what you will allow that person to do in your home once inside. What permissions will you give them? Will you allow them to eat your food or sleep in your bed, or will they never even be allowed past the front entry?

You should have the same concerns for your databases. They must be secure. You must be able to lock out those individuals you do not want inside your databases. Even those you give admission to may need to have some restrictions placed on them; it may not be reasonable for them to be able to do anything they want in the database. In this chapter, we will teach you about managing user security.

In this chapter, you will learn to:

◆ Describe the components of the SQL Server security infrastructure

◆ Implement authentication and principals

◆ Manage permissions

The SQL Server Security Infrastructure

The security infrastructure in SQL Server 2008 is very similar to the security model used in other Microsoft platforms and products. The good news, then, is that if you are accustomed to the Microsoft way of managing security, you are halfway there. To get the rest of the way, you are required to apply the security model to the specific nuances of working in a database environment.

To design a good security model, you must understand how the model is organized and be able to identify its architectural characteristics. Then you can use this information to define and implement a security model that will provide the correct balance of convenience and protection, which is the hallmark of any flexible security model. In this section, we will look at the elements of the SQL Server security infrastructure and explain the role these elements play in a security model.

THE ASSUMPTION OF NETWORK SECURITY

Any secure SQL Server environment requires that the network administrator be able to keep unauthorized users out of the network. Because this book is not intended to provide an in-depth discussion of platform security, we will not address those issues here. For more information on platform security, consult *Mastering Windows Server 2003* (Sybex, 2003).

SQL Server 2008 Security Architecture

There are many aspects to the SQL Server security architecture, including authentication, validation, and rights management. The functional architecture is based on three basic artifacts:

- Principals: Security accounts

- Securables: Objects to be protected

- Permissions: Rights provided on securables to principals

These artifacts provide the foundation for all SQL Server authentication and permissions structures. The interaction among these security entities provides the framework for controlling all SQL Server access. We will first look at the authentication process, and then we will explore the various artifacts that SQL Server uses to manage identities and rights.

SQL SERVER AUTHENTICATION

SQL Server uses two mechanisms to authenticate users. SQL Server can authenticate logins using its own internal mechanisms, or it can rely on Windows to authenticate logins. Each of these approaches has its advantages and disadvantages.

SQL Server Authentication   This was the standard mechanism for authenticating logins in early versions of SQL Server. With this technique, SQL Server stores a login and encrypted password in the SQL Server master catalog. Regardless of how the user has authenticated to the operating system, the user is required to provide credentials to SQL Server before that user is allowed to access server resources.

The primary advantage of using this authentication scheme is that SQL Server can authenticate any login no matter how they may have authenticated to the Windows network. This is the preferred method when pass-through authentication is not an option, such as with non-Windows clients. This option is typically less secure, however, because it gives access to anyone who has the SQL Server password, without regard to his or her Windows identity.

Windows Authentication   This authentication method relies on Windows to do all of the work. Windows performs the authentication and SQL Server trusts that authentication and provides access to the Windows accounts as configured. Windows user and group accounts can be mapped to SQL Server, allowing all authentication to be managed at the Windows level. This technique is also called *Integrated Security* or *Trusted Security*.

We would generally consider this technique more secure than SQL Server authentication because the database administrator (DBA) can configure SQL Server not to recognize any user that has not previously authenticated with Windows under a mapped account.

Therefore, the level of SQL Server access is inseparable from the Windows identity of the login. It also provides single sign on (SSO) support and integrates with all Windows authentication schemes, including Kerberos authentication through Active Directory.

PASSWORDS AND CASE

One of the changes in SQL Server security from SQL 2000 to SQL 2005 is the case sensitivity and optional complexity requirements of SQL Server-authenticated passwords. This trouble spot caused some headaches in the transition from 2000 to 2005, as passwords are case sensitive in SQL Server 2005 and later. If you are transitioning directly from SQL Server 2000 to 2008, be sure to consider this as part of your migration strategy. This is especially true if you rely on a client application to provide credentials directly to SQL Server.

The DBA can configure these authentication schemes in two ways:

◆ Mixed Security: The login can make either a SQL Server or a Windows Integrated connection.

◆ Windows Only: The SQL Server does not permit non-Windows authentication.

You can configure the authentication setting by using the SQL Server Management Studio (SSMS). You can access this setting in SSMS by taking the following steps.

1. Open SQL Server Management Studio and connect to the server that you want to configure.

2. Right-click on the server name in the Object Explorer window and select Properties from the shortcut menu.

3. Select the Security tab on the left side of the Properties window.

4. In the Server Authentication section of the dialog, you can select either Windows Authentication mode or "SQL Server and Windows Authentication mode."

5. Click OK to accept your change. You will have to restart your SQL Server data engine before this change will take effect.

UNDERSTANDING SCHEMAS

A SQL Server *schema* is a logical namespace within a database. A DBA can use schemas to organize the large number of objects that a database stores, as well as the permissions granted to those objects. A schema both acts as a collection of securable objects and *is* a securable object itself.

When a database developer creates an object such as a table or a procedure, that object is associated with a database schema. By default, every database contains a schema called "dbo." The DBA can create additional schemas as necessary. Schemas provide three basic features in a database application.

Organization   Schemas provide a context of organization so that it is easier to understand larger sets of objects. For example, multiple artifacts that provide support for a specific application or department could be grouped into a single schema. Organizing objects into schemas does not change the behavior of the objects themselves, but it can provide a needed logical layer that makes large server applications understandable.

Resolution   Schemas provide a context for the user accounts in a database. Each user is associated with a default schema. SQL Server will use the dbo schema for the default if the DBA does not provide an alternative. The data engine uses this schema to resolve object references.

For example, suppose that a database contains two schemas called "production" and "sales." Also, assume that each schema contains a table called "contracts." These two different tables, although named the same, represent very different entities. The sales.contracts table could represent contracts that our sales force has in place with customers, while the production. contracts table could represent contract that we have with vendors to provide materials for production.

If a user were to execute the query SELECT * FROM contracts, which contracts table will SQL Server query? The answer depends on the schema with which the user is associated. If the user's default schema is sales, the query will return data from sales.contracts. The same is true for the production schema. If the user's default schema is dbo, then they would get an error stating that the table named "contracts" could not be found because there is no contracts table in the dbo schema.

Object resolution will, therefore, execute hierarchically. The data engine checks the user's default schema for the referenced object first, and then defers to the dbo schema if the object does not exist in the user's schema. If the object does not exist in the dbo schema either, an error will occur. Of course, you always have the option of fully qualifying the object using a two-part name, which eliminates the potential ambiguity. For example, if you were to write the query as SELECT * FROM sales.contracts, there is no doubt as to where the data will come from and the user's default schema assignment would be irrelevant in this case.

Please note that associating a user with a default schema does not provide any explicit permission to that user. Even if a user has been associated with the sales schema by default, for example, you would still have to grant them permissions to interact with the objects as needed. The schema association is strictly for resolution purposes, not for security purposes.

Permission Hierarchy   You can also use schemas to define permissions hierarchically. For example, if you wanted to grant permissions to a user to select from every table in a schema, one option would be to grant individual permissions for each table to the user. If there were ten tables in the schema, this would require ten separate grants.

To consolidate this action, you could simply grant the user permission on the entire schema. The result is one grant statement instead of ten. In addition, if you add more tables to the schema later, you would not need to apply any additional grants. Adding the new tables to schema will automatically grant the permission to the user, as the he or she already had permissions defined at the schema level.

You must first create the schemas in the database before you can assign users or objects to those schemas. You can do this in two different ways, either through SSMS or through Transact-SQL. To create a schema in SSMS, use these steps:

1. Open SSMS and connect to the desired server instance.

2. Open the Databases folder and then open the folder representing the database into which you want to create the new schema.

3. Open the Security folder and the Schemas subfolder to display a list of schemas. You should see schemas such as dbo and sys in the list.

4. Right-click the Schemas folder and select New Schema from the shortcut menu. The resulting dialog provides you with a textbox that you can use to name the schema as well as to provide for a schema owner. We will discuss the effects of schema ownership later in the "Permissions" section of this chapter.

5. Click OK to create the schema.

You can also create a schema with Transact-SQL code. Assuming that you wanted to create a schema called demo that is owned by the dbo user, you could use the following statement.

```
CREATE SCHEMA demo AUTHORIZATION dbo;
```

SECURITY PRINCIPALS

A *principal* is a SQL Server representation of an entity that has the authority to perform some action. You can configure a variety of different entities as principals. Principals exist hierarchically, and the hierarchical level of the principal affects the securables that are visible to that principal.

Principals can exist as either individual entities or collections. For example, you can configure a Windows login account as a principal that is an individual entity, but you can also configure a Windows group, which is a collection, as a principal as well. Here is a list of the primary principals that you will encounter:

Windows-Level Principals   The highest level in the principal hierarchy is the Windows principal. The entities at this level exist as Windows entities as opposed to SQL Server entities. This level consists of:

- ◆ Windows domain logins/groups
- ◆ Windows local logins/groups

For example, configuring a Windows local group as a SQL Server principal provides SQL Server access to any Windows account in the group, including Windows logins, Windows domain groups and other Windows local groups.

SQL Server-Level Principals   These are not Windows entities, but rather SQL Server logins that are defined and authenticated by SQL Server. They do not map to any specific Windows account, and the identity of the Windows user does not impact the ability of that user to access the server using a SQL Server login.

The most common use of SQL Server logins is to provide non-Windows client applications with a connection option to SQL Server when Windows principals are not an option. They are also commonly used for backward compatibility for older systems that relied on SQL Server logins.

Database-Level Principals   Once authenticated to the server, an entity gains access to an individual database through a database principal. These entities exist on individual databases and represent mappings of Windows or SQL Server login accounts to those individual databases. Database-level principals include the following.

Database User   The *database user* is a mapping of an individual Windows login or group, or a SQL Server login account, to the database. Because the user can represent an authenticated collection, such as a Windows group, the database user can provide a consolidated behavior for the entire collection as well as an individual login. Database users are primarily intended as vehicles for granting database access to login accounts.

Database Role   A *database role* represents a functionality or task set in the database that requires specific permissions. The database administrator aggregates permissions to the role and then associates database users with the role. Although you can assign permissions directly to users, roles provide a significantly cleaner approach for managing the permission process.

Application Role   Like a database role, the *application role* aggregates permissions. Users cannot be assigned to an application role. The application invokes the role programmatically, which provides a set of permissions specific to the application. They override all user permissions to all users except administrative users.

Special Principals   Some principals in each category have some unique characteristics. It is worth mentioning these special cases, as you will certainly run into them later in your security designs.

The "sa" Login   This special SQL Server principal, whose name stands for "system administrator," has full administrative permissions on the server instance. It is automatically created when you perform a new installation of SQL Server. The sa login is usable only when you configure the server to allow SQL Server standard authentication. A new feature of SQL Server 2008 lets you rename the sa account during installation in addition to providing a password. This solves a security problem with the administrative account in prior editions of SQL Server, wherein a known account name existed that a hacker could potentially compromise.

The "public" Role   Every database has a role called "public." Every database user is automatically a member of this role including any guest user you might provide. You can use this role to define a base level of permissions that will apply to all users on the server. This database role is fixed and you cannot remove it.

SQL SERVER SECURABLES

A *securable* is a SQL Server artifact that provides some functionality to an authenticated user. Securables can exist at different levels called *scopes*, specifically server, database, and schema. Remember that because securables are also organized into a hierarchy, both the database and schema scopes are securables themselves.

Server Scope Securables   Some securables exist at the *server scope*. As such, permissions to these securables can be granted only to server-level principals. This securable scope contains the following objects.

◆   Endpoint

◆   Login

◆   Database

Database Scope Securables   Securables at the *database scope* are objects that apply to database security overall. This scope includes the following objects.

◆ User

◆ Role

◆ Application Role

◆ Schema

◆ Certificate

There are additional artifacts in this scope that are not listed here. They deal primarily with Service Broker behavior, which we will discuss in detail in Chapter 20, "Service Oriented Architecture and the Service Broker."

Schema Scope Securables   This list will look the most familiar. *Schema scope securables* represent the basic building blocks of a server application. Some of these objects are listed here. Again, this is not a complete list, but it gives you a flavor of the types of artifacts at the schema level.

◆ Function

◆ Table

◆ Procedure

◆ View

◆ Constraint

◆ Queue

PERMISSIONS

Permissions represent the nexus between a principal and a securable. To provide the ability for a principal to interact with a securable, the principal must have permission for the desired action on the securable. Some securables support a variety of permissions, so each permission granted represents a single action that the principal is authorized to perform on the securable. Table 8.1 provides a list of common permissions assignable to schema scope securables.

A SEA OF PERMISSIONS

With every new release of SQL Server, Microsoft seems to add additional securables and, therefore, additional permission options. The best way to stay current is to consult the SQL Server Books Online. If you search for the topic called "Permissions (Database Engine)," you will get a complete list of securables and their associated permissions. Rather than reprint those here, we suggest that you refer to this article for the complete list. Table 8.1 is an abbreviated list.

TABLE 8.1   SQL Server Schema Object Permissions List

PERMISSION	DESCRIPTION	APPLICABLE SECURABLES
SELECT	Execute a SELECT query against the securable	Synonyms Tables Views Table-valued functions
INSERT	Execute an INSERT query against the securable	Synonyms Tables Views
UPDATE	Execute an UPDATE query against the securable	Synonyms Tables Views
DELETE	Execute a DELETE query against the securable	Synonyms Tables Views
EXECUTE	Execute a procedural object	Procedures Scalar and aggregate functions Synonyms
CONTROL	Provides all permissions available on the object	Procedures All functions Tables Views Synonyms
TAKE OWNERSHIP	Take ownership of the object if needed	Procedures All functions Tables Views Synonyms
CREATE	Create an object	Procedures All functions Tables Views Synonyms
ALTER	Modify an object	Procedures All functions Tables Views Synonyms

Implementing SQL Server Principals and Authentication

Now that you have a feel for the general security architecture, the next step is to implement your desired security model through SQL Server. The majority of SQL Server security features can be implemented through either SQL Server Management Studio (SSMS) or through Transact-SQL (TSQL) code. In this section, we will examine the specific techniques that you will use to implement your desired infrastructure.

SSMS VERSUS SCRIPTING

Although it is often easier to accomplish a task through SSMS than by writing a script, we strongly encourage you to become familiar with the scripting process. Not only will you find that you have more flexibility with scripting, but there are some tasks that you cannot perform through SSMS and will require scripting. You might want to use the Scripting button in SSMS's dialogs at first to get a feel for the commands you will need to learn. Do not rely entirely on your ability to script objects from SSMS, though. Like most script generators, they tend to be very verbose and include elements you may not need or want in your scripts.

The other advantage of scripting is portability and version control. You can easily pick up a script and execute it on any server needed. This makes your artifacts and configurations much more portable. Additionally, using a source control utility such as Team Foundation Version Control, Visual Source Safe, or even Subversion, you can save history and version information about your scripts. This can be very beneficial when you go back to work with your objects again later.

Implementing Logins

The first step in implementing a security infrastructure is to define logins. Because logins can be either SQL Server authenticated or Windows authenticated you must first determine which authentication scheme you will use and plan accordingly.

If you plan to implement a Windows authentication scheme of any kind, you must first create or identify the Windows accounts you will map to SQL Server. They can be either Windows user or group accounts, and they can include domain and Active Directory accounts. We recommend that you use Windows groups. This gives you the ability to add Windows users to SQL Server by adding them to the Windows group.

OK, WE LIED

There are actually four types of logins. We just don't talk about the other two types here. In addition to Windows logins and SQL Server authenticated logins, SQL Server 2008 also supports authentication through asymmetric keys and certificates. You can map these keys to SQL Server logins and database users just like any other login. This option is increasingly popular when the user is not a member of the Windows domain, but you want a stronger security option than a simple username and password. Because the last two options require the use of certificates and keys, we will address them in Chapter 13, "SQL Server Data Security," at the same time that we examine the entire SQL Server key infrastructure.

CREATING WINDOWS AND SQL SERVER LOGINS

Once you have planned how the login will authenticate, you can create the principal account in SQL Server. To create the account in SSMS, use the following steps.

1. Open SSMS and connect to the server instance in which you want to create the login principal account.

2. Expand the Security folder and locate the Logins subfolder. Open this folder to view all of the current logins. You should see both the sa and the Builtin\Administrators login in this list.

3. Right-click the Logins folder and select New Login from the shortcut menu. This will open the New Login window pictured in Figure 8.1.

At this point, you will fill out this form in one of two slightly different ways, depending on whether you are creating a SQL Server login or a Windows login. We will look at the Windows login first.

1. In the Login Name text box, enter the full name of the Windows account to which you want to provide SQL Server access. You must enter the full name in the format of *Domain\User_or_Group*. If you prefer to search for the name, click the Search button.

2. At the bottom of the screen, you will be able to specify the default database and default language of the login. The default will be the database to which the login is mapped when initially connected.

If you plan to use a SQL Server login instead of a Windows account, you will need to take these steps instead.

1. Click the Option button for SQL Server Authentication. This will enable the text boxes for Password and enable checkboxes to provide Password Policies.

FIGURE 8.1
The New
Login window

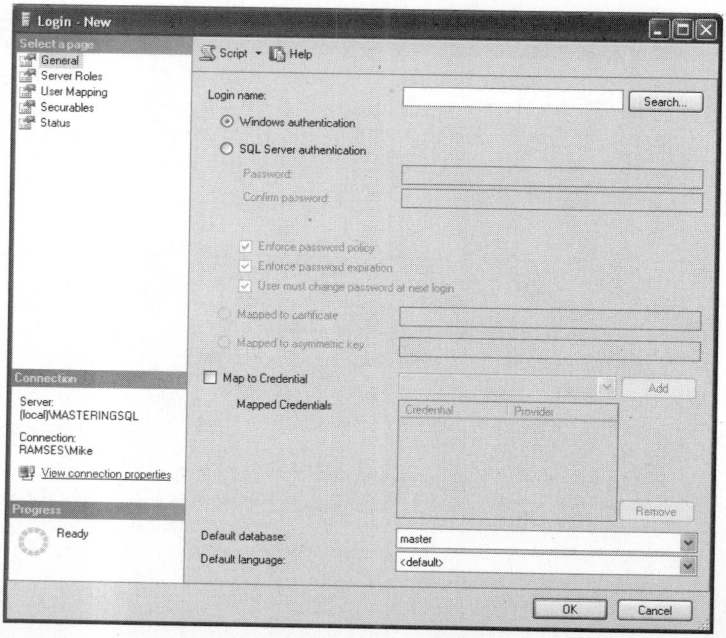

2. Enter a login name of your choosing in the Login Name text box. Remember that this name does not map to a Windows account.

3. Enter a password and confirm that password. The checkboxes below the Password text boxes will provide password policy enforcement if desired.

Starting with SQL Server 2005, the data engine has been capable of enforcing password policy as defined in Windows. This feature is supported only when running on Windows 2003 or later. Checking the Enforce Password Policy checkbox will require SQL Server logins to comply with the setting specified for password policy in the Windows group policy. If you want to also enforce password expiration or require the user to change the password at next login, you must have the enforce Password Policy checkbox selected.

Configuring Logins

In the New Login dialog, notice the other options for customizing the behavior of logins. As you will see, you can control much of the login configuration process from this single dialog.

Credentials   In the General tab of the dialog, you will see an option to map the login to Windows credentials. A *credential* is nothing more than a cached Windows identity that the SQL Server login is allowed to impersonate when attempting to access resources outside SQL Server.

This is most commonly an issue with SQL Server logins. Because there is no mapping between a SQL Server login and a Windows account, problems occur if the SQL Server login needs to access resources that are not contained within the SQL Server securables list such as a file system. This is where credentials take over.

You create credentials in SSMS by locating the Credentials folder under Security. Right-click on the folder and select New Credential from the menu. Provide the Windows account and password information along with the name of the credential. Figure 8.2 illustrates the New Credential window.

FIGURE 8.2
Creating a
credential

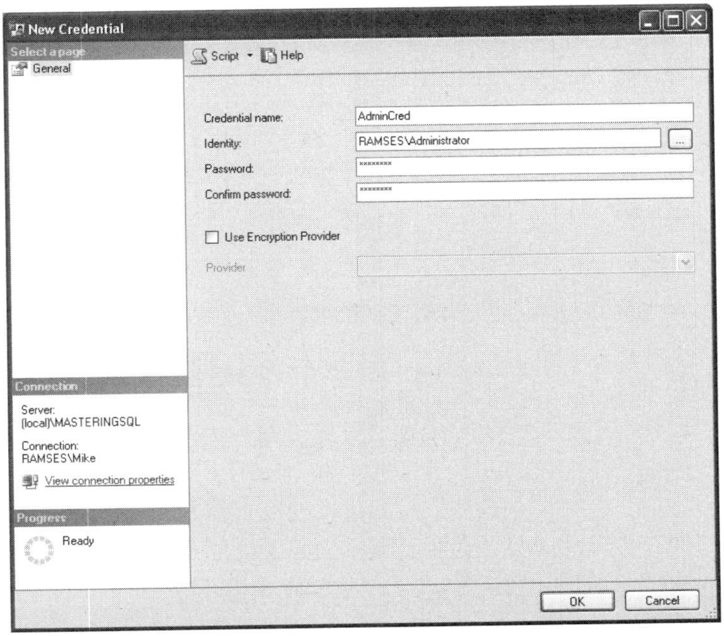

Once you have created the credential on the server, you can associate the login with the credential in the New Login dialog. This will allow that login to access Windows resources with the credential level of access.

ADMINISTRATIVE CAUTION

In Figure 8.2, we created a credential based on the local Administrator account. You should be very careful about using Windows credentials. Best practice dictates that you should use the least-permissions principle when creating credentials and associating them with SQL Server Logins. Remember that whoever can gain access to the SQL Server through this logic can potentially access server resources using this Windows credential. In other words, don't use the Administrator account. Be more judicious in your choice of Windows authority.

Server Roles   Selecting the Server Roles tab on the left of the dialog will present you with a set of checkboxes. Each item in the set is a server role, which provides a specific set of permissions. This is not new, and seasoned users of SQL Server will recognize the items in this list. These roles are fully documented in the SQL Server Books Online, so we will not repeat that information here. You should make sure that the logins are not associated with server roles that will provide them with any more authority than needed.

User Mapping   Just because SQL Server authenticates or trusts the login does not mean that the authenticated user will have access to any of the databases in the in the server instance. You must configure this access by providing user mapping. If you select the User Mapping tab, you will see a dialog like the one in Figure 8.3.

FIGURE 8.3
User mapping

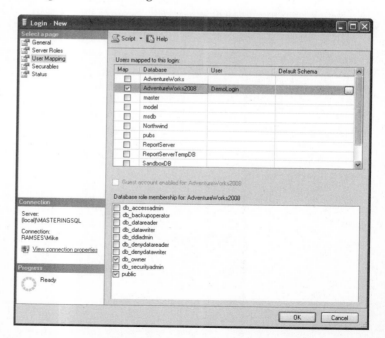

In this figure, a SQL Server login called DemoLogin is being configured for database access. To permit the login to access the AdventureWorks2008 database, you would place a check next to the database in the top pane and specify a username is the User column. If you wanted to configure a default schema for the user, you would specify that schema in the Default Schema column. In this example, the username is the same as the login, which is convenient, but not a requirement.

This action does two things. First, it grants access to the database for the authenticated login. Second, it creates a database user principal in the database that maps to the login. The database user is then assignable to fixed database roles as listed in the lower pane of the dialog. In this case, the user is a member of the public role. You cannot remove a user from this role. Additionally, the user is associated with the db_owner role, which gives the user fill administrative authority in the database.

The other fixed database roles should be familiar to existing SQL Server developers. They are fully documented in the SQL Server Books Online.

Server Scope Permissions   On the Securables tab, you can configure permissions to any of the three server-scoped securables. Figure 8.4 shows the tab in the process of configuring permissions on the Builtin\Administrators login for the DemoLogin account. In this figure, we see that the login named Ramses\Mike is granting Alter permission on the Builtin\Administrators login account to the DemoLogin account. This would enable the DemoLogin account to modify the configuration of the Builtin\Administrators login. Selecting the With Grant checkbox would also give DemoLogin the authority to grant that same right to other logins. Deny is a negation of permission. If a nonadministrative principal is ever denied permission to perform an action, that action is never allowed, even if the principal has permissions acquired through other means.

FIGURE 8.4
Server scope
securables

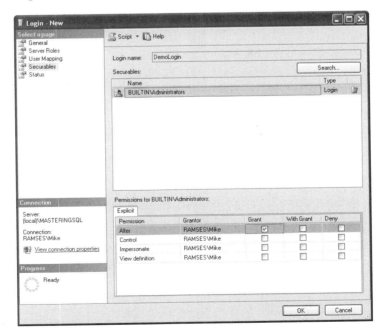

Setting Login Status The final tab on the dialog is the Status tab. This dialog, pictured in Figure 8.5, is very simple. It allows the DBA to enable and disable the login, grant or deny permission to access the server, and remove a lockout from a SQL Server login that was imposed due to too many authentication attempts.

FIGURE 8.5
Setting the
login status

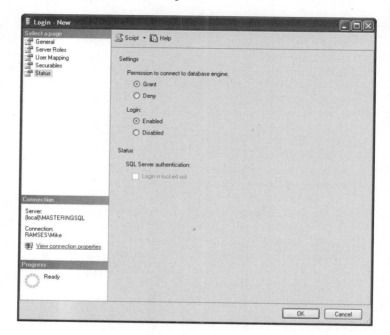

SCRIPTING LOGIN CREATION

All of the options provided in SSMS are also available through TSQL code. The dialog does not map to a single TSQL statement, though. There are many TSQL commands that correlate to the functionality of this one tabbed dialog. Again, for a full description of all the options, consult the SQL Server Books Online

The most important is the CREATE LOGIN statement. The basic syntax of the statement looks like this:

```
CREATE LOGIN loginName { WITH <options> | FROM <sources> }
```

In a nutshell, what this statement does is create a login as specified in the statement and provides for other options, such as a password for SQL Server logins, password policy enforcement keywords, and mapped credentials. You would use the <sources> section for any non-SQL Server authenticated logins. This includes Windows, certificates, and asymmetric keys.

As an example, creating a SQL Server-specific login called DemoLogin that used a password of "Pa$$w0rd" and maps to a credential called AdminCred would look like this:

```
CREATE LOGIN DemoLogin
WITH PASSWORD='Pa$$w0rd',
DEFAULT_DATABASE=AdventureWorks2008,
CREDENTIAL=AdminCred;
```

Alternatively, a Windows login that maps to the Windows local group called DemoUsers on a computer named Testing with the same default database would look like this:

```
CREATE LOGIN [Testing\DemoUsers]
FROM Windows
WITH DEFAULT_DATABASE=AdventureWorks2008;
```

Notice that the login name is enclosed in brackets. This format is required. In addition, there is no password because the login is trusted from Windows. There is no need for a credential because the account already represents an authenticated Windows user.

These statements create only the logins. They do not create any of the user mappings or configure any permissions. We will discuss the SQL statements that perform those actions later in this chapter, when we address creating users and assigning permissions.

You can also associate a login with a fixed server role using TSQL code. The fixed server roles, such as sysadmin and serveradmin, provide sets of permissions for many common server-based tasks. Associating a login with a server roles requires the sp_addsrvrolemember system stored procedure. To associate the DemoLogin principal with the sysadmin server role, you would use the following statement.

```
EXEC sp_addsrvrolemember DemoLogin, sysadmin;
```

Implementing Users

Remember that users are database principals. Users are mapped to logins, and as a result, the login executes all operations in a database under the identity of its mapped user account. Just as you did with logins, you can create users either with SSMS or through TSQL code.

CREATING USERS WITH SSMS

We have already shown you how to create users with the New Login dialog in SSMS. After you have created the login, you can go back to that dialog at any time by right-clicking the login in the server logins list and selecting Properties from the shortcut menu. This will bring up the Login Properties window. Clicking on the User Mapping tab will take you back to the screen illustrated in Figure 8.3, and you can set the user mapping exactly as before.

Another approach is to use the User folder within each database. In SSMS, expand the Security folder of the database to which you would like to grant the login access. There you will see the Users folder. Expand this folder to see the list of current users. If you look in the User folder of any database, you will see a user called dbo that maps to the sa login on the server instance. To add another user mapping to the database, right-click the Users folder and select New User from the menu. This will bring up a dialog like the one pictured in Figure 8.6.

In this figure, we see a new user called DemoUser that maps to the DemoLogin server login account. The dialog sets the default schema for this user to dbo. Additionally, you will see two panes underneath the user configuration section. The top pane is for configuring schema ownership. Database users can own database schemas. The owner of the schema automatically owns all of the objects in that schema. This will be an important fact later as we discuss ownership chaining and its effect on permissions.

The bottom pane permits the association of the user with a database role. While server roles are fixed, database roles are not. In addition to the fixed database roles that SQL Server defines, you can also create your own database roles and assign permissions to these roles. This example shows that the DemoUser in the database is a member if the db_owner role, which provides administrative permission in the database to that user.

The Securables tab of the dialog works the same way as the Securables tab on the Login dialog except that we would use this tab to define permissions for objects at the Database and Schema scope instead of the Server scope.

The last tab, entitled Extended Properties, is a common tab found in many SQL Server dialogs. You can use this tab to provide extended properties for an object. Extended properties are generally considered metadata, but you can use them programmatically to affect the treatment and implementation of SQL Server artifacts.

FIGURE 8.6
Creating a new user in Adventure-Works2008

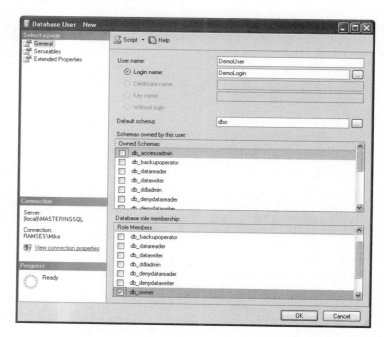

SCRIPTING USER CREATION

To create users with TSQL, we use the CREATE USER statement. The same action illustrated in Figure 8.6 could also be coded with the following statements.

```
USE AdventureWorks2008;
CREATE USER DemoUser FOR LOGIN DemoLogin WITH DEFAULT_SCHEMA=dbo;
```

Associating the user with the database role requires the use of another system stored procedure. In this case, it is the sp_addrolemember procedure. This is very similar to the other procedure that we used to add a login to a server role. The difference with this one is that we use it to associate a database user with a database role instead. The syntax to add the DemoUser to the db_owner role would look like this:

```
USE AdventureWorks2008;
EXEC sp_addrolemember 'db_owner', 'DemoUser';
```

Once you have associated the user with a database role, the user will inherit all the permissions associated with that role. This mechanism allows a high level of flexibility in managing permissions, as we will note in our examination of database roles.

THE GUEST USER

If you look at the list of users in a default build of the model database, you will see a user called "guest." Because this user is in the model database by default, it is also in every user database by default. The guest user is special because it does not map to any specific login account. Rather, the guest user is intended as a failsafe user account. If a login has no mapping to a database, that login will authenticate as the guest user. Any permissions granted to the guest user, either directly or through its role membership, will be granted to any unmapped login.

Although this can be a very convenient feature, be cautious with permissions to the guest account and ensure that any permissions assigned to guest are required for an application to function as desired. This can be a serious security hole that a knowledgeable hacker will exploit if you give them the opportunity.

OPEN TO THE PUBLIC

Don't forget that the guest account is also a member of the public role and you can't change that behavior. That means that at a bare minimum, any login that does not have a direct mapping into a database will have all the permissions assigned to the guest user, but also the public role. Remember that the public role is truly public. Using the guest account, it can also contain unexamined users that came in through the back door.

Implementing Roles

Roles are all about permissions; specifically permissions that we don't want to assign specifically to users. With the ability to assign all needed permissions to the roles and simply associate users with roles, you can easily add and drop users from defined functionality through manipulations of role association. Configurable roles come in two flavors, database roles and application roles.

CREATING DATABASE ROLES

The database roles are listed in SSMS under the Security folder. To view the database roles for the AdventureWorks2008 database, use the following folder path in SSMS: Server\Databases\ AdventureWorks2008\Security\Roles\Database Roles. To add a new custom role, use the following procedure.

1. Right-click the Database Roles folder in SSMS and select New Database Role from the menu. This will display the dialog pictured in Figure 8.7.

2. Enter the Role Name and Owner of the role. The owner can be any database user or other role. The owner is the principal with authority to drop and modify the role. This example uses dbo as the owner.

3. The rest of the dialog should look familiar. You can specify schemas that the role owns and add database users or other roles to the membership of this role. This dialog assigns the DemoUser to the new role.

4. The Securable tab allows the assignment of permissions at the Database and Schema scopes as in other dialogs. The Extended Properties tab also behaves identically to other dialogs.

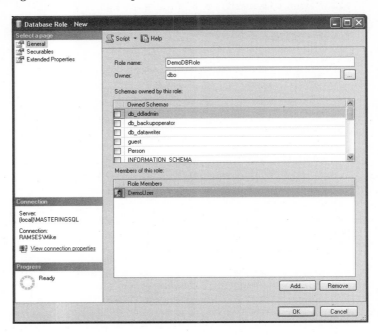

FIGURE 8.7
Creating a database role

You can also create a database role using TSQL code. Use the CREATE ROLE statement to do this. The syntax is very simple. Just define the role name, and optionally an owner. We could duplicate the dialog in Figure 8.7 by using the following code statements.

```
USE AdventureWorks2008;
CREATE ROLE DemoDBRole AUTHORIZATION dbo;
EXEC sp_addrolemember DemoDBRole, DemoUser;
```

The CREATE ROLE statement generates a new role called DemoDBRole with ownership assigned to the dbo user. The subsequent system stored procedure call associates the DemoUser with the new role. Now, any permissions assigned to the role will affect the user's ability to interact with objects in the database.

CREATING APPLICATION ROLES

Application roles differ from database roles in that you cannot assign users to application roles. In fact, rather than provide user permissions, SQL Server uses application roles to replace user permissions with the permissions assigned to the application role. The idea is that if you have an application that has specific requirements, but you do not want to assign the rights needed by the application to specific users or database roles, you can use the application role instead.

The client application or middle tier component is responsible for activating the application role and its associate permissions. As such, the permissions belong to the application, rather than the user. A user with no permissions whatsoever could still access the database through the application role. A user that has been assigned permissions that are more generous than the application role will lose those permissions when accessing through the application. Only administrative users remain unaffected.

There are three steps to using an application role. First, you must create the role. Second, you should assign permissions to the role. Finally, the application must activate the role to enable the permissions assigned to the role.

Creating the Application Role   An application role is little more than an identity with a password assigned to it. To create the application role, you will provide the name of the role along with a default schema and a password that the application will use to activate the role.

In SSMS, you can add a new application role by right-clicking the Application Roles folder under Security\Roles in the target database and selecting New Application Role from the shortcut menu. The dialog looks like the one pictured in Figure 8.8. This example creates a new role called DemoAppRole and defines the dbo schema as its default. The dialog also provides the password and confirmation. The other sections of the dialog are similar to those previously discussed.

FIGURE 8.8
Creating the
application role

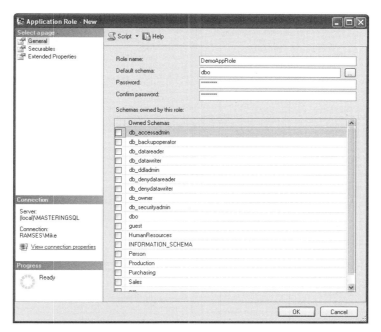

You can also create the role using the CREATE APPLICATION ROLE **TSQL** statement. This statement requires a role name and a password. Optionally, you can also define a default schema to the role. The statement to create the role pictured in Figure 8.8 looks like this:

```
USE AdventureWorks2008;
CREATE APPLICATION ROLE DemoAppRole
WITH PASSWORD = 'Pa$$w0rd',
DEFAULT_SCHEMA=dbo;
```

Assigning Role Permissions   You must assign permissions to the role before it is useful. The process of assigning permissions to an application role is identical to permission assignments for any other principal. We will discuss this process in detail later in this chapter.

Activating the Role   You must activate the role before the permissions associated with the role become active. To activate the application role, the client must execute the `sp_setapprole` system stored procedure. This call requires the name of the role and the password like this:

```
EXEC sp_setapprole DemoAppRole, 'Pa$$w0rd';
```

Optionally, the caller can choose to encrypt the password in transit. The default mechanism is to send the password in clear text, so it is a best practice to encrypt the password. Some conditions must be met before you can encrypt the password.

1. The client must connect through ODBC. If connecting through ADO.NET, you cannot use the SQLClient. You must use ODBC or the OLE DB provider for SQL Server.

2. You must send the password as Unicode. To marshal the password as Unicode, preface the password in the call with the uppercase N character.

The following example shows the same call with an encrypted password transmission.

```
EXEC sp_setapprole @rolename = DemoAppRole, @password = N'Pa$$w0rd', @encrypt = odbc;
```

The application role remains active until the user either closes the connection or executes the `sp_unsetapprole` stored procedure.

ENCRYPTION, BUT NOT REALLY

The ODBC encrypt function does not provide encryption across networks, only on the local machine. Do not rely on this function to protect passwords that are transmitted over a network. If this information will be transmitted across a network, use SSL or IPSec. With these restrictions, although it is a best practice to encrypt the password, you may choose to perform the encryption by alternative means, such as a wire protocol such as SSL or through the .NET cryptography API.

Implementing Permissions in SQL Server

It does not do you much good to go through the bother of authenticating someone if you are not going to use that information to restrict or permit their activities. In SQL Server, permissions granted to principals on securables are the basis for all access restrictions. SQL Server manages all permissions at every scope through three TSQL statements:

◆ Grant

◆ Deny

◆ Revoke

In this section, we will explore how permissions work in SQL Server and how to grant permissions at varying levels. We will also discuss the effect of object ownership on permission management.

Understanding Permission Behavior

Whether you are using SSMS or TSQL to set permissions, the concepts are all the same. Permissions management is tied to the concepts of grant, deny, and revoke. Before we apply these concepts, we will examine them more closely and make sure that we fully understand their behavior.

Remember that the functional permissions that are assigned to a principal are the aggregate permissions that principal has based on their association with multiple roles, or permissions that may be assigned directly to the account. For example, suppose that Paulette, a database user, is associated with both the salesperson role and the manufacturing role. If we grant the salesperson role permissions to select from the sales.contract table and we grant the manufacturing role permissions to select from the production.contract table, then Paulette would be able to select from both tables.

THE GRANT STATEMENT

The default condition for any principal is that unless it has been initially configured as an administrative principal, it has no rights to perform any action. The rights must be granted before the actions are allowed. Granting permissions is an affirmative process that provides authorization to perform an action. To perform a *grant*, you need to know three things.

- The principal

- The securable

- The permission

The principal is the security account. As we have seen in great detail in this chapter, the principal can be in a server- or database-level principal. The securable is the artifact for which we are setting access rights. Finally, the permission is the specific access right, such as SELECT or EXECUTE.

When you grant a permission, you are explicitly giving the principal the authority to perform an action dictated by the permission. That permission remains in effect unless it is later revoked or the permission is denied by some other means. Therefore, granting a SELECT permission on the sales. contract table to Paulette would be a permanent action that would affect her rights until the permission was later revoked or denied.

THE DENY STATEMENT

If a grant is an affirmative process, a *deny* is the polar opposite. It explicitly prevents the principal from acquiring the authority to perform an action, even if that authority is defined somewhere else.

For example, suppose that Paulette from the previous example is also associated with the denyproduction role. Assuming that the DBA has denied SELECT rights on the production.contract table to the role, Paulette's association with that role denies her the right even though that right is explicitly granted through her association with the manufacturing role.

The deny is, therefore, used as a negation flag. In other words, all permissions must be unanimous in the affirmative before SQL Server will allow the action. Even one deny will prevent the action. Note how this is very different from having no permission at all. If Paulette has no explicit permissions on an object, she cannot execute the action. As soon as permission is granted, SQL Server permits the action. If, however, Paulette had a deny on the action already registered, granting the permission through some other means would have no effect.

> **YOU CAN'T DENY THE ADMINISTRATOR**
>
> If your account is administrative in nature, such as the sa login or the dbo user, a deny permission has no effect. For example, suppose that you denied the public role the SELECT permissions on the sales.contract table. This would prevent everyone from accessing that table since everyone is a member of the public role. However, the dbo user would still be able to select from the table. Even though it is also a member of the public role, you cannot deny permission to dbo.

THE REVOKE STATEMENT

The REVOKE statement removes all permissions including grant and deny and returns the principal to its original state of having no permissions at all. Think of the REVOKE as a permission eraser. No matter what you have done with permissions, the revoke will take you back to square one.

For example, assume that we revoke the right to select data in the sales.contract table from the salesperson role. Because Paulette's right to perform the select were acquired through the role, she would no longer be able to perform the read operation.

In other cases, a revoke can actually give an account more rights. Because the revoke will remove both grant and deny actions, It is possible to remove a deny with a revoke and leave the user with more rights as a result. Again, assume that we revoke the deny that we placed on the denyproduction role that prevented Paulette from selecting data from the production.contract table. Because the revoke removed the deny flag, Paulette is left with her former permissions. She had already been granted permissions to do the select through the manufacturing role, so as long as she is sill associated with the manufacturing role after executing the revoke, she will have the ability to select data from the production.contract table again.

Setting Permissions

Once again, you are faced with two roads. You can either set permissions using SSMS, or you can script permissions using TSQL code. We have already seen the Securables tab in the Principal Configurations dialog that you can use to configure permissions, but you can also configure the permission through the actual securable. We will first examine the techniques for setting permission in SSMS and then look at using TSQL to perform the same actions.

SETTING PERMISSIONS THROUGH SSMS

Because permissions represent many-to-many relationships between principals and securables, you can come at this problem from two different directions. You could start with the principal and configure the access that you want that principal to have on all available securables. Alternatively, you can start with the securable and decide which permissions you want to assign to for each principal. It doesn't matter from which direction you come at it. You will get exactly the same result either way, so it is a matter of preference or convenience.

We have already seen that you can configure permissions on a securable as you create the principal. If you want to go back and modify these permissions later, you will use the same dialog. For example, assume that you wanted to grant to the role DemoDBRole in the AdventureWorks2008 database the right to select from the Person.Person table. You would take the following steps.

1. Locate the role in the Database Roles list under the `Security\Roles` path in SSMS. Right-click on the role to open the Role Properties dialog.

2. Click the Securables tab on the left of the screen to open the securables configuration.

3. To locate the Person.Person table, click the Search button. The dialog allows you to browse all objects, only objects of a specific type, or only objects belonging to a specific schema. You could locate the table using any of these techniques. Select "All Objects of the Types ..." and click OK.

4. This dialog allows you to select the type of object you want to secure. Note that this list will be different depending on the scope of the principal. Select the Table checkbox and click OK. This will populate the securables list with tables.

5. Locate the Person.Person table in the list and select it. This will activate the bottom pane with permissions for that table. Click the box to grant a SELECT permission, as pictured in Figure 8.9.

6. Click OK to close the dialog. The permission is now set.

YOU CAN GET TOO DETAILED IF YOU ARE NOT CAREFUL

In Figure 8.9, you will see a button labeled "Column Permissions." This button opens a Column Permission editor. Although you can set column-level permissions, we do not recommend going to this level of granularity. If you want to control permissions at the column level, you should consider using views to define the columns that are available, and then assign permissions to the view rather than the table. In a well-designed model, you should never have to grant table-level permissions anyway. We will explain why later in this chapter.

You can take a similar approach when configuring permissions through the securable. To perform exactly the same operation through the securable, use these steps instead.

1. Locate the Person.Person table in the tables list in SSMS. Right-click on the tale and choose properties. This will open the Table Properties dialog.

2. Click the Permissions tab on the left of the screen to open the Permissions Configuration. You will need to find the role in the top pane by clicking the Search button.

3. Click Browse to open a list of applicable principals at this level of scope and locate the DemoDBRole. Click the checkbox next to the role and click OK.

4. Click OK in the Select Users or Roles dialog, and this will add the DemoDBRole to the top pane of the dialog.

5. Select the DemoDBRole in the top pane to activate the permissions for that role in the bottom pane. Click the checkbox to grant SELECT permissions, as pictured in Figure 8.10.

6. Click OK on the Table Properties dialog to close the window. The permissions are now set.

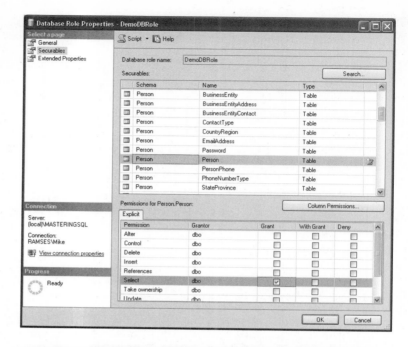

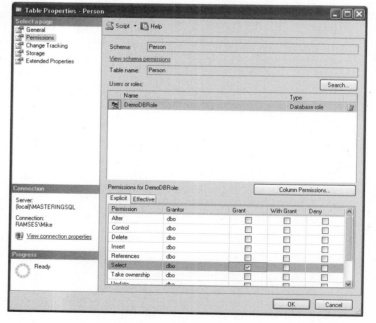

Also, note that at the database scope, there are numerous permissions that we call "statement permissions." These are not permissions to access objects, but rather to do things such as creating and altering objects. If you look at the Permissions tab of the Database Properties window, you will see numerous statement permissions for the database. These are also important permissions if you want to control who can execute Data Definition Language (DDL) statements.

SETTING PERMISSIONS THROUGH TSQL

The whole permissions functionality is primarily provided with three TSQL statements, GRANT, DENY, and REVOKE. All of these statements follow the same general pattern.

```
{GRANT|REVOKE|DENY} <permission> ON <Securable> {TO|FROM} <principal>
```

As an example, if you wanted to grant SELECT permissions on the Person.Person table to the DemoDBRole, the code would look like this:

```
GRANT SELECT ON Person.Person TO DemoDBRole;
```

You also have some special options that you can include. If necessary, you can give the grantee the right to grant the same permission to others. This is called a *grant option*. The code is the same, simply reference the grant option at the end of the statement, like this:

```
GRANT SELECT ON Person.Person TO DemoDBRole WITH GRANT OPTION;
```

To explicitly deny SELECT permission on that table to the DemoDBRole principal, the code would be very similar. We just use the command for deny instead of grant, like this:

```
DENY SELECT ON Person.Person TO DemoDBRole;
```

Logically, whatever you grant or deny, you must be able to revoke. If you had either granted or denied SELECT permission on the Person.Person table to the DemoDBRole, you could remove those permissions with the following statement.

```
REVOKE SELECT On Person.Person FROM DemoDBRole;
```

If you have granted the permission with a grant option, you must also decide what to do with the permissions that the principal from whom you are revoking permissions has granted. For example, if you granted Paulette select permissions on Person.Person with a GRANT option through the DemoDBRole, and then she grants the SELECT permission to Bob, what happens when we revoke the permission from the DemoDBRole? Is it still safe for Bob to have those permissions? SQL Server says no, and you must use the CASCADE keyword in the revoke to revoke the permission from Bob as well. The statement looks like this:

```
REVOKE SELECT On Person.Person FROM DemoDBRole CASCADE;
```

You can also revoke just the GRANT option without actually revoking the permission entirely. If you want to revoke the GRANT option only from the DemoDBRole but do not want to revoke the actual SELECT permission, you would use this code.

```
REVOKE GRANT OPTION FOR SELECT ON Person.Person FROM DemoDBRole Cascade;
```

Real World Scenario

Maybe That Was Not Such a Great Idea After All

Be very careful about using the GRANT option. As one client found out the hard way, trying to simplify permission management through GRANT options can come back to bite you later if you are not careful.

It started out innocently enough. The DBAs, who are generally notorious control freaks and very conservative by nature, went against their better judgment and agreed to grant a few select individuals GRANT options on selected permissions. The goal was to make the organization more responsive by giving certain trusted individuals the right to grant a particular permission so that they would not have to wait for a DBA to do it. It looked great on paper, but in practice it was another thing altogether.

The chief DBA was not willing to give the identified users full administrative authority in the database, but GRANT options are fairly limited in scope, so that was accepted as an alternative. The individuals and the permissions were identified, and the GRANT option was given. Everything went fine for quite a while, until one of the grantors got caught giving permissions that he should not have been granting.

Of course, the DBA's reaction was to immediately pull the GRANT option from that user with cascade to ensure that there were no unauthorized permissions outstanding. This is when we got the call to step in and determine why principals who were supposed to have been explicitly denied permissions were now suddenly able to perform the denied actions. After correcting the problem and doing a little digging, we determined that this is what happened.

When you revoke a GRANT option with cascade, you revoke all permissions that have been assigned by that user—but remember, those permissions come in two flavors: grant and deny. When the DBA pulled the GRANT option, he also inadvertently pulled all of the deny perms that had been assigned by that user as well as the grants. In many cases, this left the users with more rights than they had previously, because the deny bit was removed and they were free to access the resources that they had not been able to access previously.

The moral of the story is twofold. First, be very careful about the GRANT option. It may sound like a great idea, and it may start out well; but when you pull the GRANT option, cleaning up after it can be a real pain. The other lesson learned is more important. The more complex SQL Server becomes as a product, the more likely you are to miss something. Nobody, even the authors, can possibly know everything. You are bound to miss something once in a while, so be sure to do your research before you pull the trigger. A little time spent reading and researching an issue can pay off a lot on the back end.

Statement permissions work a little differently because there is no securable. The permission itself is the securable. If you want to grant the DemoDBRole permissions to create stored procedures, for example, you do not have a target securable. You just want to grant permission to use the statement. The syntax would look like this:

```
GRANT CREATE PROCEDURE TO DemoDBRole;
```

To find the names of the statement permissions that you can use, either look them up in the SQL Server Books Online or go to SSMS. The names of the permissions in SSMS dialogs are the same names that you would use in your code.

Ownership Chains

In Chapter 5, "Procedural Programming," we discussed procedural objects, such as stored procedures and views. One of the benefits of using procedural objects is that you can require your applications to reference the procedural objects instead of the underlying table itself. This can make things more secure because you may not have to grant any explicit permissions to the underlying table as long as there is no break in ownership between the procedural object and the table. This is called an *ownership chain.*

As an illustration, suppose that you wanted to limit access to certain columns in the Person.Person table for the DemoDBRole. Assuming that you only wanted the members of DemoDBRole to be able to select the FirstName and LastName from the table, one approach would be to create column-level permissions. You could grant SELECT on just those two columns in the table and no others. You can imagine how difficult this scenario would be to maintain over time.

Another option would be to create a view or a stored procedure that returned only those columns from the table. You could give DemoDBRole the authority to select from the view or execute the procedure without having to grant any permission on the table. This provides two benefits:

◆ It is easier to maintain permissions because you only need to make sure that the view or procedure returns the desired data.

◆ The user is not able to connect to the table and query ad-hoc, thereby preventing the user from going around your business rules. The can interact only with the views or procedures, not the table directly.

It sounds like a great plan, but there is a catch. For this to work, there can be no ownership breaks between the objects. That means that whoever owns the stored procedure must also own the table. The logic is sound if you think about it. If I am the dbo user and I own both the Person.Person table and the stored procedure that selected the data from that table, I would have implied authority on the table. If I grant DemoDBRole execute permissions on the procedure, I am implicitly giving the role the ability to interact with the table through the procedure. I can do that because I own the table and have all rights to the table.

If I own the stored procedure and Paulette owns the table, I would no longer have the implicit right to grant other people the right to select the table through my procedure. I can grant EXECUTE permission on the stored procedure, but Paulette would also have to grant the appropriate rights at the table level before the DemoDBRole members could execute the procedure. This is because there is a break in ownership.

It logically follows, then, that procedural objects such as views and stored procedures are most useful when the same user owns them all as well as the table upon which they depend. We would argue that the user that should own all objects is the dbo user.

If you recall, SQL Server bases object ownership on schema ownership. Whoever owns the schema owns all of the objects that are contained within that schema. This simplifies object ownership significantly, because you do not have to track ownership of individual objects. This whole discussion boils down to the following best practices.

◆ Do not allow users to select directly from tables. It is a security best practice to require all user access to go through a procedural interface of some kind, such as a view or stored procedure.

◆ To exploit the advantage of unbroken ownership chains, the dbo user should be the owner of all schemas in the database and, therefore, all objects in the database. This will ensure unbroken ownership chains and facilitate database access through procedural interfaces.

The Bottom Line

Describe the components of the SQL Server security infrastructure.   The SQL Server security model is typical of other Windows-based security infrastructures. Principals, securables, and permissions provide a complete environment for protecting your assets and allowing flexible database interactions for authenticated parties.

Master It   In the following list, identify whether the entity is a principal, securable, permission, or scope. In some cases, an entity can exist in multiple categories.

1. Database

2. Select

3. User

4. Application Role

5. Schema

6. Table

Implement authentication and principals.   There are different forms of authentication that you can choose based on your infrastructure and requirements. Once authenticated, principals represent these authenticated parties and are the basis for all access control in SQL Server.

Master It   For each of the following scenarios, specify which authentication mode would be the best fit for the facts.

1. You want to provide a single sign-on environment for your Active Directory-based Windows Infrastructure.

2. Most of your clients are Windows workstations that are members of a domain, but you do have a few Linux workstations.

3. All of your clients are external to your organization. You do not know what operating systems that they use, and they have no accounts in your network.

Manage permissions. A permission is the right to perform an action or to interact with an object in a specified way. Permissions are the connecting points between principals and securables in a SQL Server security model, which you will use to control access to all of your database assets.

Master It Write a statement that will perform the desired permissions action based on each of the following requirements.

1. Database-user Pam requires the right to add new rows to the sales.stores table.

2. The MonitorApp Application role should be explicitly prevented from executing the banking.deposit stored procedure.

3. Database-user Bill needs the right to create new tables in the database.

4. The DemoLogin principal requires permissions to make alterations to the SampleLogin principal.

Data Recovery

Databases are mission-critical components of many organizations. Everything from financial records and important customer information, to basic information that an organization requires to operate is stored in databases. More and more organizations rely on their databases to be able to do business. Entire companies have gone bankrupt, closed shop, or had to lay off employees due to database failures that could have been prevented with an appropriately implemented data recovery plan. A database can be negatively impacted by everything from hardware failures to natural disasters that leave your office in ruins, to accidental or even malicious deletions and modifications. Database corruption happens when you least expect it.

Having a documented and tested backup and restore strategy may very well be the thing that can save your job as a database administrator when the worst happens. Having an appropriate data recovery strategy can be thought of as an insurance policy against the unexpected. A big part of a database administrator's job description is to make sure that the databases in an organization are properly backed up and that recovery can be done in a timely manner when problems occur.

To protect your organization's data and ensure the availability and recoverability of its databases, you will need a solid and well thought-out data recovery plan.

In this chapter, you will learn to:

- ◆ Understand SQL Server's transaction architecture

- ◆ Understand the impact that a database recovery model has on backup and restore strategies

- ◆ Choose an appropriate backup and data recovery plan for the databases in an organization

- ◆ Perform regular database backups to prevent against data loss

- ◆ Perform database restores using a variety of recovery strategies

Transaction Architecture

Understanding the transaction architecture of SQL Server is important because it's so closely tied to data recovery. Knowing the process behind how transaction logging works will allow you to make more intelligent decisions about sizing, locating, backing up, and restoring your databases and transaction logs.

Let's quickly review some important facts. Every SQL Server database has a transaction log. The transaction log stores records for all of the changes that are made to a database. Modifications are first recorded in the transaction log before they are committed to the database files. Records are written sequentially to the transaction log, and every transaction is given an identifier. Periodically, a checkpoint process occurs, which is marked in the transaction log. When a checkpoint occurs, all changes since the last checkpoint are written to the database files.

Nearly every modification to a SQL Server database is transactional. A transaction will commit entirely, or not at all. Individual INSERT, UPDATE, and DELETE statements that are executed outside of a user-defined transaction are implicitly part of a transaction because they are modifying data within the database. Implicit transactions automatically commit their changes after they are finished executing. Explicit or user-defined transactions use BEGIN TRANSACTION and COMMIT TRANSACTION statements to group related changes together. A user-defined transaction can be rolled back if an error is encountered or if an explicit ROLLBACK TRANSACTION statement is encountered.

One of the main reasons that the transaction log always receives modifications first is for database recovery. If a SQL Server were to suddenly lose power, the transaction log is available to show exactly where SQL Server was when power was lost. The recovery process automatically runs for each database on the server when the SQL Server service starts. This process examines the transaction log from the last checkpoint, rolls forward any completed transactions, and rolls back any transactions that were incomplete at the time of failure. The recovery process is something that you will learn to control when restoring a series of database backups.

Database Recovery Models

The recovery model that you choose for a database determines how the transaction log is truncated, and if the transaction log can be backed up. For a database using the Simple recovery model, the transaction log is truncated after every checkpoint. Backing up the transaction log isn't possible when using the Simple recovery model because the transaction log won't contain a complete record of the modifications made to the database. In Simple recovery, the log is mainly used to recover the database during service start-up. There is much less work loss exposure when a database uses the full or Bulk-logged recovery models.

When using the Full or Bulk-logged recovery models, the transaction log should be regularly backed up. Both recovery models allow transactions to accumulate in the log beyond the checkpoint process, assuming that the database has had a full backup. A full backup is required so that there is something to which the backed up transactions can be applied. Both recovery models keep modifications within the transaction log until it is backed up. Most production databases will use the Full recovery model because it provides the least amount of work-loss exposure. The Bulk-logged recovery model uses less space for bulk operations, such as creating an index, or executing a SELECT..INTO statement. The main downside to using the Bulk-logged recovery model is that we can restore only an entire transaction log backup, so restoring to a point in time isn't possible. We'll discuss recovery models in more depth later in this chapter.

The Internals of Transaction Logging

We won't be having an exhaustive discussion of all the internals of transaction logging, but there are several important items to understand.

Think of the transaction log as a sequence of records that represents all of the modifications that are made to a database. Each record is assigned a sequential Log Sequence Number (LSN), as well as a transaction ID that links it to other records in the same transaction. Backups contain metadata about the range of Log Sequence Numbers contained inside of them. This metadata can be used to determine the sequence of restore operations required to recover a database. Related log records are linked in a chain to speed up the rollback of a transaction if required. Any rollback operations are written to the transaction log as well, whether they were caused by an explicit ROLLBACK statement or an error.

Modifications in the transaction log can be recorded in two different ways, depending on the type of modification. Some modifications will simply record a record of the logical operation itself. To roll back a logical operation, the opposite operation is executed. Some modifications may be tracked with a before and after snapshot of the changed record. To undo these modifications, the before snapshot of the data can be used.

The transaction log is stored as one or more physical files on disk. Most databases have a single transaction log file. It's best to think of the transaction log logically as a continuous sequence of records. Log records are truncated either by backing up the transaction log when using the Full or Bulk-logged recovery model, or by a checkpoint occurring when a database is using the Simple recovery model. Once records have been truncated from the transaction log, the space is available for reuse.

The transaction log is considered to be a "wrap-around" file, because when we reach the end of the physical file, records can continue to be written at the beginning of the file assuming that there is available space that has been freed by truncating the log. When log truncation occurs, the space that is truncated is available for reuse within the file. A database can use more than one transaction log file, but only one is ever used at a time. When multiple transaction log files are used, each file is reused before starting at the beginning of the first log file.

If the transaction log becomes full, and the log is configured to automatically grow, then the transaction log will automatically expand using the configured autogrowth increments up to the maximum size specified for the file. If the transaction logs can't be expanded any further, error 9002 is returned, indicating that the transaction log is full, and must be backed up. When the transaction log is full, no modifications may be made to the database until space is freed. Backing up the transaction log is the most common way to free up space in the log.

The physical log files are divided into virtual logs that are automatically managed and dynamically sized by the database engine. Using small autogrowth increments can increase the number of virtual log files when the database is expanded. Having too many small virtual logs can slow down database recovery, as well as backup and restore processes. The default autogrowth increment of 10 percent is generally sufficient.

How Transaction Logging Is Used

The transaction log is used for many operations in a database. Only modifications are recorded in the transaction log. (SELECT statements don't get recorded, and so they don't take up any space.) The following operations are recorded as records in the transaction log:

- The start and end of each transaction

- All data modifications, including INSERT, UPDATE, and DELETE statements

- Creation, alteration, and dropping of tables and indexes

- Allocation and deallocation of pages and extents in the database

Figure 9.1 shows a simplified example of a sequence of operations in the transaction log, and what would happen in the event of a power failure. Transactions are written sequentially to the log, and periodically a checkpoint process occurs, which applies committed transactions to the database files.

FIGURE 9.1

Example of check-point operations and recovery after a power failure

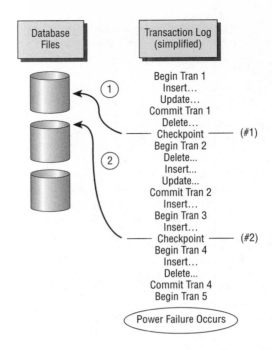

When the first checkpoint occurs, Transaction 1 and the implicit DELETE statement are applied to the database files. When the second checkpoint occurs, Transaction 2 and the INSERT statement are committed to the database. Transaction 3 hasn't yet committed when the checkpoint occurs, so its operations aren't applied to the database files. When the power failure occurs, and SQL Server restarts, it goes through a recovery process starting at the last checkpoint. Transaction 3 and Transaction 5 are rolled back because they never committed before the power failure occurred. Transaction 4 is rolled forward during the recovery process.

The transaction log is used by SQL Server for the following operations:

Recovering Individual Transactions   If the database detects an error during a transaction, or if an explicit ROLLBACK statement is encountered, the log records are used to undo the modifications that had been made in the transaction up to that point.

Recovering Incomplete Transactions During Startup   When SQL Server starts, it scans the transaction log to recover the database to a consistent state. When SQL Server is stopped normally, there generally isn't much recovery required. If the SQL Server stops unexpectedly due to something like a power failure, the log is used to roll forward any committed transactions that haven't been written to the database, and to roll back any incomplete transactions.

The recovery process occurs for every database on the server when SQL Server starts, and it is done automatically. Messages are written to the Windows event log and SQL Server error log indicating the number of transactions rolled back and rolled forward.

Recovering a Database to the Point of Failure   The transaction log is used to apply changes to a restored database, allowing recovery up to the point of failure, so long as the transaction log is still available for a tail-log backup. The recovery process during a restore is similar to the recovery process during database startup. Recovery should be delayed until the last log backup in the sequence is restored. We will examine the recovery process in more detail later in the chapter.

Supporting Database Mirroring and Log Shipping   Database mirroring allows every update on the primary database to be applied to a mirror database. Transaction log records are immediately sent to the mirror server to apply the required changes when using database mirroring.

Log shipping allows a primary database to periodically send log backups to a standby server to be restored on a schedule.

Both database mirroring and log shipping are covered in Chapter 12, "Data Availability and Distribution."

Supporting Transactional Replication   Transactional replication allows changes to be applied to subscribers for objects that are marked for replication. The log reader agent is responsible for reading records from the transaction log and forwarding them to the server in the distributor role. Replication, including transactional replication, is covered in Chapter 12.

Backup and Restore Strategies

It's important to have a documented and well-understood strategy for both the backup and recovery of your databases. It's not enough to only back up your user databases; system databases need to be backed up as well. We will discuss the methods used to recover system and user databases later in this chapter.

In order to determine your backup and restore strategy, several questions need to be asked.

How important is the data you're backing up?   A mission-critical accounting or manufacturing system will certainly have higher recoverability requirements than a read-only database that is used infrequently. Understanding the type of information and its value to the organization can help you calculate the amount of work-loss exposure that is acceptable.

What type of databases are you backing up?   It's also important to make sure you're backing up the system databases in addition to your user databases to ensure that the configuration of your SQL Server can be recovered. While you won't need to back up the master database every hour, the master database should be backed up whenever new databases are added, logins are created, or any system-wide configuration change is made. The msdb database stores the SQL Server Agent configuration, backup history tables, DTS and SSIS package definitions, and more. Your use of the features that the msdb database supports will determine the frequency of backups. The model database is simply a template for new databases on your SQL Server and should be backed up when changes are made. Make sure you don't forget to back up your system databases as well as your user databases!

What are the database use patterns?   Some databases will need to be available 24 hours a day, while others may be accessed only during business hours. Knowing the usage patterns of a database will help you schedule the backup process so that the least impact is made on user performance.

How frequently does the data change?   It's a fact that some databases change more than others. Databases with a large amount of change should be backed up more frequently. A read-only database doesn't need to be continuously backed up, unless the data changes. A database that is loaded nightly should be backed up after the changes are made.

How much work loss is acceptable?   Your initial answer may be none, but some databases, such as test or development databases, can afford a much greater work loss than others.

How quickly do you need to recover the data?   Some backup strategies will take much longer to restore than others. The amount of time required to restore a mission-critical database may cause you to change the backup strategy.

Will a large amount of data change regularly, or will changes be isolated to certain parts? When a small part of a database changes frequently, it may be beneficial to separate the changing data into a separate filegroup that is backed up more often than the rest of the database, if possible. Restoring an individual file or filegroup can take significantly less time than restoring an entire copy of a very large database.

How much storage space is available for backups?   Different types of backups will have different space requirements. Your backup strategy can't require more space than you have. It's also important to understand how long you'll be keeping the backups, as this will have a major impact on the amount of backup storage required.

Backing up databases is different than backing up workstations and servers because you will need to use a combination of backup techniques to ensure maximum recoverability. Many databases will use a combination of full, differential, and transaction log backups so that data loss potential is minimized.

A recovery plan should include the type and frequency of backups, where backups are stored, who is responsible for recovery operations, and a process for testing the recovery plan. It's very important to test the recovery plan to ensure that it will work in the event of a database failure. The recovery plan should be documented in an operations manual.

Recovery Models and Backup Strategy

Choosing an appropriate recovery model is critical to planning and executing an appropriate backup strategy. The two main options are Full recovery and Simple recovery. Bulk-logged recovery can be used in combination with the Full recovery model to optimize the performance of bulk operations and minimize the amount of log space taken up by the transactions. Most production databases use the Full recovery model, and regularly back up the transaction log to minimize the potential for data loss.

THE SIMPLE RECOVERY MODEL

Using the Simple recovery model for a database requires the least amount of maintenance, but also has the most potential for data loss in the event of a system failure. When using the Simple recovery model, only full and differential backups are allowed. The transaction log is used for recovery purposes, but it doesn't keep a running set of all changes. At every checkpoint, the inactive portion of the log that has already been committed to the database is truncated.

Simple recovery is appropriate in the following situations:

♦   It is acceptable to lose information since the last full backup in case of system failure.

♦   The maintenance requirements of backing up the transaction log outweigh the benefits.

♦   The database is a test or is read-only, and it can be re-created easily.

THE FULL RECOVERY MODEL

When a database is using the Full recovery model, all modifications made to the database are kept in the transaction log after the first full database backup has been made. Until the first full database backup is made, the log automatically truncates on checkpoint. This is because there must be something to which the modifications in the transaction can be applied. After the first full backup, log backups are used to free space in the transaction log so that new transactions can occur.

When using the Full recovery model, the size of a transaction log depends heavily on the amount and types of modification, and how frequently the transaction log is backed up. Databases with a large amount of modification activity will need more available space in their transaction log. Backing up the log frees space, and more frequent backups would result in a smaller transaction log size.

Using the Full recovery model in combination with a series of backups can allow you to restore the database to any point in time within the series. The Full recovery model can also allow you to recover to the point of a database failure, assuming that the tail of the transaction log is available. This is one of the reasons that it's important to keep transaction logs on separate fault-tolerant storage from the database files.

The Full recovery model is appropriate in the following situations:

◆ You need to keep data loss to a minimum in the event of a system failure.

◆ You want to be able to recover the database to the point of failure.

◆ You want the ability to restore the database to a point in time.

◆ You want the ability to restore individual database pages.

◆ You are willing to incur the administrative overhead of doing regular transaction log backups.

When using the Full recovery model, all transactions are fully logged, including bulk operations such as SELECT..INTO and CREATE INDEX. Logging the complete details of bulk operations can slow down the performance of the bulk operations, and requires considerable log space, but it does allow recovery to a point in time.

THE BULK-LOGGED RECOVERY MODEL

The Bulk-logged recovery model allows less information to be written to the transaction log when bulk operations occur, thus speeding up the bulk operations at the expense of point-in-time recoverability. Only the changed extents affected by the bulk operation, rather than the entire operation, are written to the log backup. This can allow less storage space to be used for bulk operations. Because only the changed extents are logged, you must restore the entire log backup. Point-in-time recovery isn't supported on log backups that contain Bulk-logged operations. Operations that can be minimally logged when using the Bulk-logged recovery model include:

◆ SELECT..INTO operations

◆ INSERT..SELECT operations

◆ Bulk Imports (using bcp or the BULK INSERT statement)

◆ Index DDL Operations including creating new indexes, rebuilding or reindexing an existing index, or dropping a clustered index, causing a heap rebuild.

The Bulk-logged recovery model should be used intermittently in combination with the Full recovery model. The database can be switched to Bulk-logged recovery prior to bulk operations occurring, and then can be switched back to Full recovery once the bulk operations are completed. Because changed extents are copied directly to the log backup, the database files containing the bulk changes must be available for the log backup to succeed.

Backup Types

SQL Server supports two main types of data backups: Full and Differential, as well as transaction log backups. A full backup takes a complete copy of the data and writes it to the backup file, as well as portions of the transaction log to capture changes that happened while the full backup was occurring. A differential backup stores changed data since the last full backup. The size of a differential backup depends on the amount of data that has changed since the last full backup. Full and differential backups may be taken for an entire database, a filegroup, or for individual database files.

A differential backup requires a previous full backup to track changes against. This full backup is known as the base of the differential. In order to restore a differential backup, the base must be restored first. A differential backup can take considerably less time to restore than a series of transaction logs, depending on the amount of modification that's taken place. A differential backup only stores the final data values, not intermediate changes.

Transaction log backups are supported for databases using the Full or Bulk-logged recovery models. A transaction log backup only makes sense when a full backup has been made that the transactions could be applied to. Before the transaction log can be backed up, a full database backup must be completed.

Partial backups were introduced in SQL Server 2005, and allow backups to be taken of all read-write filegroups. A partial backup isn't supported by the database maintenance plan wizard, or by management studio. To create a partial backup, you must use the READ_WRITE_ FILEGROUPS option with the BACKUP Transact-SQL statement.

Copy-Only Backups allow a backup to be taken without interrupting the normal chain of backup processes. Taking a normal full backup to make a copy of a database

Performing Backups

Backups can be performed using Transact-SQL statements or by using SQL Server Management Studio. In this chapter, we will focus mainly on using Transact-SQL for backing up and restoring databases. Understanding the Transact-SQL syntax will help you to gain a better understanding of what is going on behind the scenes with the Management Studio dialog boxes.

TestDB

The examples contained in this chapter assume that a database named TestDB has been created and that the directory C:\Backups exists. The following code is the simplest way to create the TestDB database:

```
CREATE DATABASE TestDB;
```

You may find it helpful to use the Script button at the top of the Backup Database dialog in Management Studio to generate the corresponding Transact-SQL statements for the backup operation.

Full Backups

Performing a full backup is a simple process. A full database backup contains all of the data in the database. Individual filegroups and files can also be backed up for a database that has been split into multiple files. The advantage of backing up a filegroup or a file separately from a full database backup is that in the event of a failure, only the affected files or filegroups need to be restored. This can take considerably less time than restoring a full database backup, especially for large databases.

For databases using the Simple recovery model, only full and differential backups are supported. If a failure were to occur, all transactions since the last backup would be lost. You cannot restore a database using the Simple recovery model to the point of failure. Schedule full and differential database backups based on the amount of data loss you can tolerate. For databases that require more recoverability, use the Full recovery model in combination with differential and transaction log backups.

A full database backup can be created using Transact-SQL statements, SQL Server Management Studio, or by using Database Maintenance Plans. We'll begin by using Transact-SQL statements that perform backups. Listing 9.1 backs up the TestDB database to a temporary disk-based backup device. If the file doesn't exist, it will be created. A backup device can store more than one backup. If the file already exists, by default, the data will be appended to it.

LISTING 9.1   Creating a Full Database Backup

```
BACKUP DATABASE TestDB
   TO DISK = 'C:\Backups\TestDBFullBackup.bak';
```

Backup Devices, Media Sets, and Media Families

When performing a backup, you need to specify where the backup is stored. Backups are stored on physical backup devices in SQL Server. A physical backup device may be a file on disk or a tape device. In most cases, disk devices are used for database backups, because the speed of a disk is generally much faster than a tape device.

A physical backup device can be given a logical name by adding a dump device to SQL Server. Using logical backup devices can allow the location of backup storage to be changed without modifying the scripts that use the device. Listing 9.2 uses the sp_addumpdevice system stored procedure to create a new logical backup device. Two full backups are then written to the backup device. A backup device can store more than one backup. By default, backups are appended to a backup device.

LISTING 9.2   Adding a Dump Device and Performing Two Full Backups to the Device

```
EXEC sp_addumpdevice 'disk', 'TestDB_Full',
                     'C:\Backups\TestDB_Full.bak';
GO
BACKUP DATABASE TestDB TO TestDB_Full;
BACKUP DATABASE TestDB TO TestDB_Full;
```

To overwrite all of the backups instead of appending to the backup devices, the WITH INIT option can be used, as shown below.

```
BACKUP DATABASE TestDB TO TestDB_Full WITH INIT;
```

When a backup is written to a backup device, a backup set is created. A backup set can be thought of as an individual backup written to one or more files, known as the *media set*. A media set is an ordered collection of one or more backup devices that is used together to store backups. (Even a single backup device is considered a media set.) It is possible to use more than one backup device to store a backup. When using more than one device, the devices are related together and are considered to be part of the same media set. The example shown in Listing 9.3 shows a backup that is striped across two devices.

LISTING 9.3   Striping a Backup Across Two Dump Devices

```
EXEC sp_addumpdevice 'disk', 'TestDB_Stripe1',
                     'C:\Backups\TestDBStripe1.bak';
EXEC sp_addumpdevice 'disk', 'TestDB_Stripe2',
                     'C:\Backups\TestDBStripe2.bak';
GO
BACKUP DATABASE TestDB TO TestDB_Stripe1, TestDB_Stripe2;
```

Backups may be spanned across multiple physical backup devices, so long as they are the same type of device (disk or tape). A media set that uses more than one device stripes the backups across all of the devices in the media set. By using several physical backup devices, you can speed up the backup operation. The example in Listing 9.3 uses a single disk device (the C: drive) to store both striped backups to allow the example to run in most environments. In practice, you would need to use separate disk devices to see the performance improvement.

Devices in a media set cannot be reused separately without first reformatting the device.

Backups can also be mirrored to multiple devices. Mirroring a backup creates duplicate backup devices for redundancy. When creating a set of mirrored backups, the WITH FORMAT option must be used, as shown in Listing 9.4. Backup mirroring is only an option when using Transact-SQL statements to perform the backup. The SQL Server Management Studio user interface cannot be used to perform mirrored backups.

LISTING 9.4   Mirroring a Backup to Separate Backup Devices

```
EXEC sp_addumpdevice 'disk', 'TestDB_Mirror1',
                     'C:\Backups\TestDB_Mirror1.bak';
EXEC sp_addumpdevice 'disk', 'TestDB_Mirror2',
                     'C:\Backups\TestDB_Mirror2.bak';
GO
BACKUP DATABASE TestDB
 TO TestDB_Mirror1
 MIRROR TO TestDB_Mirror2
 WITH FORMAT;
```

The example in Listing 9.4 uses a single disk device to store both mirrored backups to allow the example to run in most environments. In practice, you would use separate devices to provide additional recoverability.

Backup devices that are used together in a media set for striping or mirroring are considered to be part of the same *media family*. The number of devices used in a media set determines the number of family members. Later in this chapter, we'll examine how to retrieve metadata about the backup sets, media sets, and media families.

A common pattern is to make backups to files on disk, and then archive those files to tape for storage off-site. This allows quick access to the backup files in case a restore is needed. If at all possible, store your backups on a separate disk—not the one where the information you're backing up is stored.

Differential Backups

Performing differential backups has similar syntax to performing a full backup, except that the WITH DIFFERENTIAL option must be specified in the BACKUP statement. In order to perform a differential backup, a previous full backup must be created. A differential backup stores all changes since the previous full backup. The full backup is known as the differential's *base*. Differential backups can speed up both the backup and restore processes. The size of a differential backup depends heavily on the amount of data that has changed since the base of the differential was created.

An example of performing a differential backup using Transact-SQL is shown in listing 9.5.

LISTING 9.5   Performing a Differential Backup Using Transact-SQL

```
BACKUP DATABASE TestDB
 TO DISK = 'C:\Backups\TestDB_Diff.bak'
 WITH DIFFERENTIAL;
```

It is also possible to do differential backups when using file or filegroup backups. Differential backups of an individual file or filegroup can have more than a single differential base. Multibase differential backups are complex to manage and restore. It is recommended that you use single-base differential backups to simplify the restore process when possible. For more information on multi-base differential backups, refer to SQL Server Books Online.

Transaction Log Backups

Creating transaction log backups using Transact-SQL has a very similar syntax to creating other backup types. Transaction log backups may only be taken on databases that use the Full or Bulk-logged recovery models. Listing 9.6 shows an example of creating a transaction log backup using Transact-SQL.

LISTING 9.6   Performing a Transaction Log Backup Using Transact-SQL

```
BACKUP LOG TestDB
  TO DISK = 'C:\Backups\TestDB_Log.bak';
```

After backing up the transaction log, the backed up portion is truncated to free up space for further transactions. All of the log backups should be kept until the next full backup is created to allow for maximum recoverability.

If the database is damaged, you may need to back up the tail of the log before beginning a restore process. When backing up the log tail, use the WITH NORECOVERY option, as shown in Listing 9.7 if the database is still online to avoid an error. If the database is offline and doesn't start, use the NO_TRUNCATE option. You should only use NO_TRUNCATE if the database is damaged.

LISTING 9.7   Performing a Tail-Log Backup Using Transact-SQL

```
BACKUP LOG TestDB
  TO DISK = 'C:\Backups\TestDB_TailLog.bak'
  WITH NORECOVERY;
```

Partial Backups

A partial backup is useful for databases that contain one or more read-only filegroups. Partial backups were designed for use with large databases in using the Simple recovery model, although they are supported using all of the recovery models. A partial backup is similar to a full database backup, except that read-only filegroups are excluded. Listing 9.8 shows an example of creating a partial backup.

LISTING 9.8   Creating a Partial Database Backup

```
BACKUP DATABASE TestDB READ_WRITE_FILEGROUPS
  TO DISK = 'C:\Backups\TestDB_PartialBackup.bak';
```

Creating Backups Using Management Studio

SQL Server Management Studio's user interface can be used to create backups. The management studio interface is capable of generating a script of the configured options using the Script button at the top of the window. Using scripting can be very helpful for users who are new to the Transact-SQL syntax.

To perform backups using SQL Server Management Studio, follow these steps:

1. Open SQL Server Management Studio, and connect the Object Explorer to the SQL Server instance that contains the database you would like to back up.

2. Expand the Databases folder, and optionally the System Databases folder depending on which database you would like to back up.

3. Right-click on the database that you would like to back up, choose Tasks, and then choose Back Up.

4. The Backup Database dialog appears, as shown in Figure 9.2. Verify that the correct database is selected in the Database dropdown list.

FIGURE 9.2

The Backup Database dialog

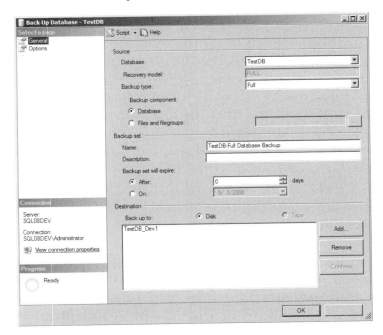

5. Choose the appropriate backup type (Full, Differential, or Transaction Log).

6. Choose the appropriate backup component. For transaction log backups, you may skip this step.

7. Optionally, give the backup set a name, description, and expiration date.

8. Add the devices that you will use to store the backup by clicking on the Add button. The Select Backup Destination dialog box appears, as shown in Figure 9.3. You may use either a file name, or a logical backup device.

FIGURE 9.3
The Select
Backup Device
Destination dialog

9. Select the Options page in the upper-left corner. The options page is shown in Figure 9.4

FIGURE 9.4
The Options Page
of the Backup
Database dialog

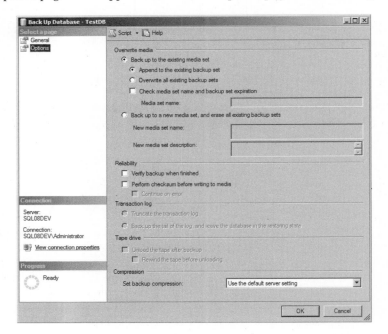

10. By default, a backup is appended to an existing media set. To overwrite all existing backup sets in a media set, choose the Overwrite All Existing Backup Sets option. This is the equivalent of using the WITH INIT Transact-SQL option. The Back Up to a New Media Set, and Erase All Existing Backup Sets option is the equivalent of using the WITH FORMAT Transact-SQL option.

11. If you would like to verify the backup when finished, or perform checksums before writing to media, select the appropriate options under Reliability.

12. If a transaction log backup is being performed, the default is to truncate the log when backing it up. This is appropriate, unless you are backing up the tail of the transaction log prior to recovering a damaged database. Tail-log backups will be discussed in greater depth in the Restoring Databases section of this chapter.

13. If using tape devices, you may choose to unload and rewind the tape.

14. When using the Enterprise Edition of SQL Server, backup compression is supported. Choose whether you would like to use compression or accept the default server setting.

15. To view the Transact-SQL statements used to create the backup, you may use the Script button at the top of the Back Up Database dialog. If you prefer to run the Transact-SQL scripts, make sure to click Cancel to exit the Back Up Database dialog.

16. Click OK to begin the backup.

Partial backups aren't supported by the SQL Server Management Studio user interface. To perform a partial backup, you must use Transact-SQL statements.

Performing Restores

The process of performing a database restore depends on the backups that are available. Before you restore a database, you should know which backups are available, and back up the tail of the transaction log if possible. This section reviews several backup and restore scenarios.

Retrieving Backup Metadata

Before you begin to perform a restore operation, it's important to understand the backups that are available for the database. SQL Server writes records to several tables in the msdb system database when backup operations are performed. These tables are used by SQL Server Management Studio to determine the available backups for a database when performing a restore operation using the user interface. Restoring a database using the SQL Server Management Studio user interface is covered later in this chapter. You can query the tables yourself to understand the backups available for a given database. Table 9.1 shows the tables available in msdb that store information about backups.

TABLE 9.1 Tables That Store Backup Metadata in the msdb Database

TABLE NAME	DESCRIPTION
Backupset	Contains one record for each backup set created for a database. A backup set represents a single, successful backup operation.
Backupfilegroup	Contains one row for each filegroup in the database when it was backed up. This table relates to the Backupset table using the backup_set_id column.
Backupmediafamily	Contains one row for each media family. If a mirrored media set was used, this table will contain a row for each mirror in the media set.
Backupmediaset	Contains one row for each media set used in backup operations.
Backupfile	Contains one row for each file within a database. This includes data and log files. The row describes the configuration of the file when the backup was taken.

When performing a restore operation, it's critical to plan the steps used before starting. For damaged databases that use the Full recovery model, a tail-log backup can allow recovery up to the point of failure. When you encounter a failed database, always make sure to perform a tail-log backup if possible so that you have maximum recoverability options.

Performing a Complete Restore

When performing a complete database restore, the process will differ depending on the recovery model chosen for a database. In this section, we'll explore different restore scenarios when you want to completely restore a database and all files.

RESTORING WITH THE SIMPLE RECOVERY MODEL

When you are working with a database using the Simple recovery model, you have fewer restore options than with a database that uses the Full or Bulk-logged recovery models. Full and Differential backups may be restored, but all changes since the last backup will be lost. If you were to perform a full backup at noon, and encountered a failure at 3 P.M., you would lose the last three hours of data.

For situations where the data is less critical, read only, or could easily be re-created, the Simple recovery model can work well. Listing 9.9 shows an example of backing up and restoring a database from a full database backup.

LISTING 9.9   Performing a Full Database Restore Using the Simple Recovery Model

```
USE Master;
GO
ALTER DATABASE TestDB SET RECOVERY SIMPLE;
GO
BACKUP DATABASE TestDB
 TO DISK = 'C:\Backups\TestDB_Full_Example.bak';
GO
RESTORE DATABASE TestDB
 FROM DISK = 'C:\Backups\TestDB_Full_Example.bak'
 WITH RECOVERY;
```

The code in Listing 9.9 sets the recovery model of the TestDB database to Simple, performs a full backup, and restores the full backup. Because we are only restoring a single full backup, the database is recovered after restoring.

It's common to use differential backups to speed up the backup and restore process when using the Simple recovery model. Listing 9.10 shows an example of restoring differential backups. Because there are other backups to restore after the full database backup, we specify the NORECOVERY option.

LISTING 9.10   Performing a Differential Restore Using the Simple Recovery Model

```
USE Master;
GO

ALTER DATABASE TestDB SET RECOVERY SIMPLE;
GO
BACKUP DATABASE TestDB
  TO DISK = 'C:\Backups\TestDB_Diff_Example.bak'
  WITH INIT;
GO
BACKUP DATABASE TestDB
  TO DISK = 'C:\Backups\TestDB_Diff_Example.bak'
  WITH DIFFERENTIAL;
GO
RESTORE DATABASE TestDB
  FROM DISK = 'C:\Backups\TestDB_Diff_Example.bak'
  WITH FILE=1, NORECOVERY;
GO
RESTORE DATABASE TestDB
  FROM DISK = 'C:\Backups\TestDB_Diff_Example.bak'
  WITH FILE=2, RECOVERY;
```

RESTORING WITH THE FULL RECOVERY MODEL

Databases that use the Full recovery model will require that the transaction log be backed up. When restoring a series of transaction logs, the order in which you restore them is very important. It's also critical to retrieve the tail of the transaction log, if possible, to capture any transactions that have occurred since the last transaction log backup. The example shown in Listing 9.11 shows a scenario where only Full and Transaction Log backups are used.

LISTING 9.11   Performing a Database and Log Restore Using the Full Recovery Model

```
USE Master;
GO

ALTER DATABASE TestDB SET RECOVERY FULL;
GO
BACKUP DATABASE TestDB
  TO DISK = 'C:\Backups\TestDB_Full_Demo1.bak';
GO
BACKUP LOG TestDB
  TO DISK = 'C:\Backups\TestDB_Full_Demo1.bak';
```

```
-- Database Failure Occurs
-- Capture the Tail of the transaction log
BACKUP LOG TestDB
 TO DISK = 'C:\Backups\TestDB_Full_Demo1.bak'
 WITH NORECOVERY;
GO
-- Begin the restore process
RESTORE DATABASE TestDB
 FROM DISK = 'C:\Backups\TestDB_Full_Demo1.bak'
 WITH FILE=1, NORECOVERY;

RESTORE LOG TestDB
 FROM DISK = 'C:\Backups\TestDB_Full_Demo1.bak'
 WITH FILE=2, NORECOVERY;

RESTORE LOG TestDB
 FROM DISK = 'C:\Backups\TestDB_Full_Demo1.bak'
 WITH FILE=3, RECOVERY;
```

Using differential backups can decrease the number of restore operations required to bring a database current. Restoring a differential backup allows you to skip over log backups that occurred prior to the differential backup. Listing 9.12 shows an example of a backup strategy that uses Full, Differential, and Transaction log backups.

LISTING 9.12   Using Differential Backups with the Full Recovery Model

```
USE Master;
GO

ALTER DATABASE TestDB SET RECOVERY FULL;
BACKUP DATABASE TestDB
 TO DISK = 'C:\Backups\TestDB_Full_Demo2.bak'
 WITH INIT;
GO
BACKUP LOG TestDB
 TO DISK = 'C:\Backups\TestDB_Full_Demo2.bak';
GO
BACKUP LOG TestDB
 TO DISK = 'C:\Backups\TestDB_Full_Demo2.bak';
GO
BACKUP DATABASE TestDB
 TO DISK = 'C:\Backups\TestDB_Full_Demo2.bak'
 WITH DIFFERENTIAL;

-- Database Failure Occurs --
```

```
-- Capture the Tail of the transaction log
BACKUP LOG TestDB
 TO DISK = 'C:\Backups\TestDB_Full_Demo2.bak'
 WITH NORECOVERY;
GO
-- Restore the full backup
RESTORE DATABASE TestDB
 FROM DISK = 'C:\Backups\TestDB_Full_Demo2.bak'
 WITH FILE=1, NORECOVERY;
-- Restore the Differential Backup, Skipping both log backups
RESTORE DATABASE TestDB
 FROM DISK = 'C:\Backups\TestDB_Full_Demo2.bak'
 WITH FILE=4, NORECOVERY;
-- Restore the tail log backup
RESTORE LOG TestDB
 FROM DISK = 'C:\Backups\TestDB_Full_Demo2.bak'
 WITH FILE=5, RECOVERY;
```

Performing Point in Time Recovery

A database using the Full recovery model can be recovered to a specific log marker or a point in time. This is accomplished by restoring only part of a transaction log backup. Any modifications after the point of restore are lost. Assuming the appropriate log backups exist, a database may be restored to the following recovery points:

◆ A specific point in time within the transaction log backup

◆ Before a log marker

◆ At a log marker

Transaction log backups containing Bulk-logged modifications cannot be partially restored because of the way bulk modifications are tracked in transaction log backups.

RESTORING TO A POINT IN TIME

Restoring to a point in time is accomplished using the following syntax:

```
RESTORE LOG <database_name>
 FROM <backup_device>
 WITH STOPAT = <datetime>, RECOVERY;
```

To ensure that you don't need to restart the restore process, it's a good idea to specify the STOPAT option for each transaction log backup being restored. If the time specified is before the time range in the log backup, the restore operation fails, because we've already restored past the stop time. If the time specified is after the time range in the log backup, the roll forward succeeds, but the database isn't recovered because the specified time hasn't yet been reached. If the time specified is within the interval of the transaction log backup, transactions are rolled forward up to that point, and the database is recovered.

RESTORING BEFORE OR AT A LOG MARKER

You can also restore a database to the point before or at a log marker. A log marker is created by beginning a named transaction using the WITH MARK option and specifying a description for the mark.

```
BEGIN TRANSACTION logMarkName WITH MARK 'Description of log mark'
...
COMMIT TRANSACTION
```

Log marks are tracked in the logmarkhistory table in the msdb database. You can query this table to see the different log marks that have been made for databases on the server.

When restoring the transaction log that contains the log marker, you can use either the STOPATMARK or STOPBEFOREMARK options. The STOPATMARK option will use the marked transaction as the last transaction that is applied to the database during the restore operation. The STOPBEFOREMARK option will stop immediately before the marked transaction.

Any transactions that occurred after the log mark or point in time to which you are restoring will be lost.

The example in Listing 9.13 creates three tables in the TestDB database. The second table is created as part of a transaction with a log marker. After the restore sequence finishes, tbl1 exists in the database, because it existed before the log marker we stopped at. If STOPATMARK is used instead of STOPBEFOREMARK, both tbl1 and tbl2 will exist in the restored database. In either case, tbl3 will be lost.

LISTING 9.13   Restoring a Database Using a Log Marker

```
EXEC sp_addumpdevice 'disk', 'TestDB_PointInTime',
                    'C:\Backups\TestDB_PointInTime.bak';

BACKUP DATABASE TestDB
 TO TestDB_PointInTime
 WITH INIT;

USE TestDB;
GO

CREATE TABLE tbl1 (c1 int);

BEGIN TRAN DemoTran WITH MARK 'Demo Description'
  CREATE TABLE tbl2 (c1 int);
COMMIT TRAN

CREATE TABLE tbl3 (c1 int);
GO

-- Backup the transactions that just occured
USE Master;
BACKUP LOG TestDB
 TO TestDB_PointInTime;
```

```
-- Restore the full database backup
RESTORE DATABASE TestDB
 FROM TestDB_PointInTime
 WITH NORECOVERY;

-- Restore the log stopping before DemoTran
RESTORE LOG TestDB
 FROM TestDB_PointInTime
 WITH FILE=2, STOPBEFOREMARK='DemoTran', RECOVERY;
```

If duplicate log markers exist in a transaction log backup, you should specify a time using the AFTER keyword as shown here.

```
RESTORE LOG <database_name>
 FROM <backup_device>
 WITH STOPBEFOREMARK='<mark_name>' AFTER <datetime>, RECOVERY;
```

Performing a File or Filegroup Restore

Some databases are divided into multiple files or filegroups. If only specific files fail, it is possible to restore only the damaged files. This can significantly speed recovery because it is much faster than restoring the entire database. When using the Simple recovery model, only read-only filegroups can be restored individually.

The examples in this section assume that the database is using the Full recovery model.

If you're using the Enterprise Edition of SQL Server, you can restore a damaged file while the rest of the database remains online, so long as the damaged file isn't part of the primary filegroup. Any attempts to access the damaged filegroup will result in an error until it is recovered.

All of the other editions of SQL Server support file and filegroup restores while the database is offline. In order to restore a damaged filegroup, you must first perform a tail-log backup to capture the active portion of the transaction log, so that the damaged file can be recovered. If the transaction log is damaged, and you cannot perform a tail-log backup, you must restore the whole database, so that all files are in a consistent state.

Listing 9.14 shows an example of backing up and restoring an individual file. An entire filegroup may also be specified by replacing the FILE keyword with the FILEGROUP keyword in the backup and restore statements.

LISTING 9.14   Performing File Backup and Restore Operations

```
CREATE DATABASE FileGroupDemo
 ON PRIMARY
  (NAME='FileGroupDemo_PrimaryData',
   FILENAME='C:\FileGroupDemo_PrimaryData.mdf',
   SIZE=3MB),
 FILEGROUP FG1
  (NAME='FileGroupDemo_FG1Data',
   FILENAME='C:\FileGroupDemo_FG1Data.ndf',
   SIZE=1MB)
```

```
        LOG ON
          (NAME='FileGroupDemo_Log',
           FILENAME='C:\FileGroupDemo_Log.ldf',
           SIZE=1MB);
GO

USE Master;
GO

BACKUP DATABASE FileGroupDemo
 TO DISK = 'C:\Backups\FileGroupDemo_Full.bak'
 WITH INIT;

BACKUP DATABASE FileGroupDemo FILE='FileGroupDemo_FG1Data'
 TO DISK = 'C:\Backups\FileGroupDemo_FG1.bak'
 WITH INIT;

BACKUP LOG FileGroupDemo
 TO DISK = 'C:\Backups\FileGroupDemo_Log.bak'
 WITH INIT;

-- Damage occurs to FG1

-- Take the damaged file offline
ALTER DATABASE FileGroupDemo MODIFY FILE (NAME='FileGroupDemo_FG1Data', OFFLINE);
GO
-- Take a Tail-Log Backup
BACKUP LOG FileGroupDemo
 TO DISK = 'C:\Backups\FileGroupDemo_TailLog.bak'
 WITH INIT, NORECOVERY;

RESTORE DATABASE FileGroupDemo FILE='FileGroupDemo_FG1Data'
 FROM DISK = 'C:\Backups\FileGroupDemo_FG1.bak'
 WITH NORECOVERY;

RESTORE LOG FileGroupDemo
 FROM DISK = 'C:\Backups\FileGroupDemo_Log.bak'
 WITH NORECOVERY;

RESTORE LOG FileGroupDemo
 FROM DISK = 'C:\Backups\FileGroupDemo_TailLog.bak'
 WITH RECOVERY;
```

Performing Page Restore Operations

Performing page restore operations allows recovery of the damaged pages without requiring a full restore of the database. Restoring a few pages might be faster than a file restoration because of the amount of data that needs to be restored. If you need to restore more than a few pages in a file, it might be quicker to restore the entire file. It is usually better to restore a file with many damaged pages to a different location if possible, because many suspect pages might indicate a pending device failure.

When a disk begins to fail, you may begin to encounter errors on specific pages. Page errors are reported to a client application when they occur, as well as when they are being written to the SQL Server error log. Pages that have encountered errors are marked as suspect and logged to the suspect_pages table in the msdb database. In order to restore specific pages, you must determine the page IDs of the suspect pages.

Page restore operations are only supported on databases that use the Full or Bulk-logged recovery models.

Using SQL Server Management Studio to Restore a Database

SQL Server Management Studio provides a powerful interface for restoring databases, filegroups, and transaction logs. The restore database dialog allows individual restore operations from backup devices, much as we did using Transact-SQL. It also provides an interface that helps to discover previous backups of existing databases. You can choose the backup sets that you would like to restore, and Management Studio will execute the appropriate Transact-SQL to restore the backups you choose. SQL Server Management Studio uses several tables in the msdb database to retrieve information about the backups available.

To restore a database using SQL Server Management Studio, follow these steps:

1. Back up the tail of the transaction log if possible, before beginning the restore process. If you don't perform a tail-log backup, you will receive the error message shown in Figure 9.5, indicating that a tail-log backup should be performed.

FIGURE 9.5
The error dialog received if you forget to perform a tail-log backup before restoring a database

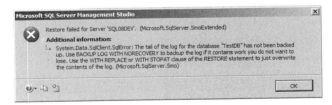

2. Open SQL Server Management Studio and connect to the SQL Server instance where you would like to restore the database.

3. Right-click on the Databases folder and choose Restore Database. The Restore Database dialog appears.

4. Choose an existing database, or type a new database to restore.

5. If you would like to restore the database based on previously taken backups on the server, choose the database from the dropdown list. The list box at the bottom of the screen displays the existing backup sets that can be restored, as shown in Figure 9.6

FIGURE 9.6

The Restore Database dialog with backup sets available to restore

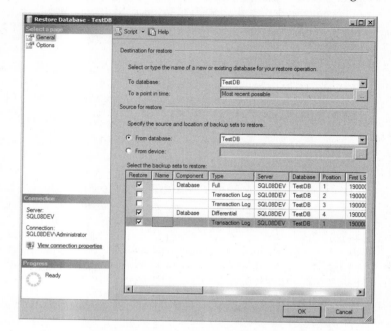

6. If you would like to restore from a specific backup device, click the ellipsis next to From Device. Browse for the backup device from which you would like to restore.

7. Choose the backups you would like to have restored by selecting the checkboxes next to each backup at the bottom of the dialog.

8. If you would like to specify a point in time for the restore, click the ellipsis next to the "To a Point in Time" label, and choose the date and time to which you would like to restore. To restore using log markers, you must use Transact-SQL statements.

9. Choose the Options page to verify that the restore options are correct. Select the appropriate restore options, database file locations, and recovery state as shown in Figure 9.7.

10. If you would like to review the script used to restore the databases, use the Script button at the top of the page, and then click the Cancel button. Otherwise, click OK to begin the restore process.

FIGURE 9.7

The Restore
Database dialog
Options page

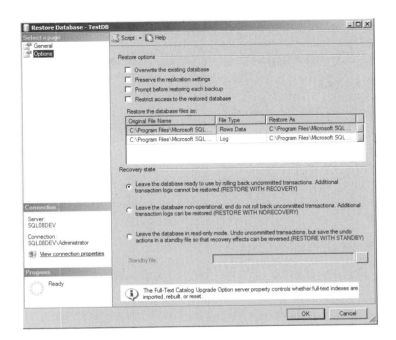

The process for restoring files and filegroups is very similar to the process just described, except that you will choose Restore Files and Filegroups instead of Restore Database in step 3.

When you use the Restore Database dialog, SQL Server Management Studio does quite a bit behind the scenes. Many experienced users prefer to verify the Transact-SQL statements used during the restore to double-check such an important process.

Other Issues

We've covered a majority of the backup and restore process so far in this chapter, but there are several other areas we need to cover. System databases need to be backed up on a regular basis, and the recovery process for each should be understood. Backup security should also be a concern, and we will cover the associated best practices. Finally, we will examine the options for optimizing the performance of backup and restore processes.

System Database Recovery

SQL Server contains several critical system databases that should be backed up regularly. Table 9.2 shows the system databases and their recommended backup strategies.

TABLE 9.2   Description of SQL Server System Databases

DATABASE NAME	BACK UP?	DESCRIPTION
master	Yes	The master database stores all system-level configuration settings for a SQL Server. This includes logins and other server-level objects. master should be backed up regularly.
model	Yes (If Changed)	The model database is used as a template for new databases. If you add objects to the model database, or otherwise modify its options, it should be backed up.
msdb	Yes	msdb contains history tables, SQL Server Agent Jobs, Alerts, and Operators, as well as Integration Services packages stored on SQL Server. Full database backups are generally used for the msdb database.
resource	No	The resource database is a read-only database that contains definitions of all of the system objects. The resource database isn't displayed as a system database, and it is stored in the Mssqlsystemresource.mdf file. It is possible to back up this file, but not as a database.
tempdb	No	tempdb is cleared and re-created every time SQL Server starts. You cannot back up tempdb.

CONSIDERATIONS FOR THE *master* DATABASE

It is critical to back up the master database regularly. It contains all system-level information including login accounts, system configuration settings, and links to user databases. Make sure to back up the master database when any of the following operations occur:

◆ Adding or modifying logins

◆ Changing server-wide configuration settings

◆ Creating or deleting a user database

◆ Creating or removing logical backup devices

The master database uses the Simple recovery model, and only full database backups of master are supported.

If the master database is damaged, the SQL Server service cannot start. In order to get the SQL Server service to start, you must first rebuild the master database, and then restore from a backup if one exists. If you don't have a backup of the master database, you must reattach all user databases, re-create all server-level objects, and reconfigure any server-wide settings. It is critical to keep a current copy of the master database available.

Rebuilding the master database also involves rebuilding the msdb and model databases. You must rebuild all three system databases as a unit; you cannot currently rebuild one without rebuilding the others. To recover from a failed copy of master, follow these steps:

1. Ensure that you have access to backups of the master, model, and msdb databases for restore. If you don't, you'll lose most of your configuration.

2. Insert the original SQL Server Installation disc, and open a Command Prompt window. Change to the drive that contains the installation disc.

3. Launch the following command:

   ```
   Setup /QUIET /ACTION=REBUILDDATABASE /INSTANCENAME=<instancename> /
   SQLSYSADMINACCOUNTS=<list of accounts to be granted sysadmin rights>
   ```

4. After the command executes, it will return without printing any messages. Setup log files are located in C:\Program Files\Microsoft SQL Server\100\Setup Bootstrap\Log by default.

5. If you are restoring a copy of master, you must start SQL Server in Single User mode using the -m switch. You must ensure you start the service using the same user account that the service is normally started with or you will encounter permission problems.

6. Connect to your instance using SQLCMD and restore your copy of the master database. The service will automatically stop after the master database is restored.

7. Start the SQL Server Service and restore copies of the msdb and model databases if needed.

Backup Security

SQL Server automatically sets permissions on database files and backup files so that the SQL Service account and the local administrators group have the appropriate permissions. If the service account doesn't have permissions to access a backup file, it will attempt to impersonate the windows user executing the backup or restore operation. It is recommended that you set restrictive access control list permissions on any folders that are used to store backup files.

SQL Server supports password protection for backup media and backup sets, but the password protection is weak. The main intention of the password is to prevent an incorrect restore, rather than prevent reading of backup data. The password feature will be removed in the next version of SQL Server and should be avoided in new development. For more information on securing specific data in the database using encryption, refer to Chapter 13, "SQL Server Data Security."

Make sure to physically protect any SQL Servers and backup tapes by storing them in a secure location. Backups should be stored in an offsite, secure location if possible.

It's important to make sure that any backups restored to your SQL Server are from trusted sources. Before you use a database from an unknown source, it should be checked and examined on a nonproduction server. Make sure to examine any user-defined code before executing it to confirm that there aren't any malicious operations.

Backup Performance and Optimization

There are two strategies for optimizing the performance of backup and restore operations in SQL Server:

- ◆ Optimizing the speed of the backup operations
- ◆ Minimizing the recovery time required in the event of a failure

When performing backups, one thread is used per backup device to write information out to the backup files from the database or transaction log. The speed of a backup operation is dependant on how fast we can read from the thing we're backing up, and how fast we can write the data out to the backup medium. In most cases, you will find that writing data to the backup medium is the bottleneck, especially in the case of tape devices. The main method used to increase the performance of a backup operation is to increase the number of backup devices used in that operation. This allows SQL Server to use parallel I/O operations to increase the speed of backup and restore operations. Earlier in the chapter, we saw that a backup can be striped to more than one backup device. In order to see a performance improvement, the backup devices should be located on separate disks.

Restore operations also need to be optimized. Using a combination of full, differential, and transaction log backups allows maximum flexibility in restoring the database. The speed of the backup media greatly impacts the time it takes to restore a database. It is usually faster to restore a database from a disk device rather than from a tape device. Having disk-based backups that are also backed up to tape ensures speedy recoverability while also ensuring against a natural disaster, assuming the tapes are stored off-site. Databases that are divided into multiple files or filegroups allow restoration of failed files without requiring the entire database to be restored. Restoring a damaged file or filegroup can be much quicker than restoring a full backup of a very large database.

Backup Compression

SQL Server 2008 Enterprise Edition supports the compression of backup files. Compressed backups can only be created using the Enterprise Edition, but can be accessed using other editions of SQL Server.

Backup compression can decrease the amount of I/O and storage space required for storing backups, but it can increase the amount of CPU usage because of the overhead of doing the compression. Different data sets will give different levels of compression. You can examine the compressed size of a backup by examining the compressed_backup_size column of the backupset table in the msdb system database.

To enable compression for a backup, you can add the WITH COMPRESSION option to a BACKUP statement. You can also change the default for compression on new backups by changing the "backup compression default" server option. This can be accomplished by modifying the properties of a server in Management Studio, or by using the following Transact-SQL statements:

```
-- Turn on Backup Compression by defaut
EXEC sp_configure 'backup compression default', '1';
RECONFIGURE WITH OVERRIDE;
```

The Bottom Line

Understand SQL Server's transaction architecture.   It's important to study the transaction architecture of SQL Server in order to understand what is going on during backup and restore operations.

> **Master It**   What would happen to each of the following transactions during database recovery?

1. A transaction that began and committed prior to the last checkpoint.

2. A transaction that began before the last checkpoint and committed after the last checkpoint but prior to system failure.

3. A transaction that began after the last checkpoint and never committed prior to system failure.

Understand the impact that a database recovery model has on backup and restore strategies.   The recovery model that you choose for a database impacts the options available for backup and recovery. Choosing an appropriate recovery model is critical to ensure proper recoverability of your databases.

> **Master It**   What recovery model would be most appropriate for the following situations?

1. A development database that only requires full database backups.

2. A production database that must minimize its work loss exposure, and must be able to be recovered to a point in time.

3. A production database that has bulk operations performed on a schedule.

Choose an appropriate backup and data recovery plan for the databases in an organization. Choosing the appropriate backup strategy for a database is an important step in creating a disaster recovery plan for any database.

> **Master It**   What kind of backups should be performed on the following databases?

1. A read-only database.

2. A mission-critical database that is constantly changing, and must be restored with a minimal amount of data loss and recovery time.

3. A development database that can tolerate some data loss.

Perform regular database backups to prevent data loss.   Performing the appropriate backups is critical to ensuring database recoverability in the event of a failure.

> **Master It**   Write a Transact-SQL statement to perform the following operations:

1. Full database backup of a database named DB1 to a backup device named DB1_Backup. Overwrite any backups that already exist on the DB_1 backup device.

2. A differential backup of a database named DB1 to a disk-based backup device stored in the E:\Backups folder. Overwrite any backups that exist in the file.

3. A transaction log backup of the tail of the transaction log on a database named DB1 to a backup device named DB1_Log. Append the backup to any existing backups on the device. Assume that the database files are unavailable.

Perform database restores using a variety of recovery strategies. When you're confronted with a situation that requires the recovery of a database, it's important to know the proper procedure to restore the database with a minimal loss of data.

Master It The disk containing the data files for a database named CriticalDB has failed. The disk containing the transaction log is still available. CriticalDB uses the Full recovery model, and a backup device named CriticalDB_Backup contains the five backups listed here:

1. Full backup of CriticalDB

2. Transaction log backup of CriticalDB

3. Transaction log backup of CriticalDB

4. Differential backup of CriticalDB

5. Transaction log backup of CriticalDB

After replacing the disk that housed the data files, what procedure would you use to restore the database? Provide the appropriate Transact-SQL statements to recover to the point of failure.

Chapter 10

Monitoring SQL Server Activity

As a database administrator, you need to understand the options available for monitoring your SQL Servers. Knowing where to look will help you isolate performance issues. This chapter focuses on the tools available for monitoring different aspects of a SQL Server. We'll begin by monitoring system performance as a whole, and then we'll move into more specific methods of watching activity and patterns in SQL Server. In this chapter, you will learn to:

- ◆ Use System Monitor to identify performance bottlenecks
- ◆ Use Profiler and design appropriate traces to monitor events on SQL Server
- ◆ Build DDL (Data Definition Language) triggers
- ◆ Use event notifications to asynchronously capture events occurring on your SQL Server

Using System Monitor

Monitoring SQL Servers can be a tough job that requires understanding the performance of many areas. Although many organizations try to solve their performance problems by throwing more hardware at them, that isn't usually the most effective way to solve them. You need to monitor at several levels to determine if increasing hardware is going to help the particular problem you're facing. The levels of monitoring and some of the available tools are shown here:

Server Level	SQL Server Level	Database Level	Application Level
System Monitor	Current activity	DDL (Data Definition Language) triggers	Index and query tuning
Performance logs and alerts	SQL Server Profiler	Event notifications	Normalization strategies
	Dynamic management views		Efficient stored procedure design
	System stored procedures		Efficient application design
			Index and query tuning

It's important to understand your options for monitoring the system, both in times of trouble and times of triumph. Knowing how the various levels are performing in good times is almost as important as knowing where to look when things slow down. Having a baseline of performance is important so that you have something to compare.

We'll begin working at the highest level: monitoring the physical server with System Monitor and Performance Logs and Alerts. There are many factors that can impact performance at a server level.

TIP

Whenever possible, SQL Server should be installed on a dedicated server because it minimizes the effects that other services or applications could have. In practice, however, you will probably encounter shared servers—maybe a SQL Server that also runs a web server or file server services. If the other services on the machine receive a high level of activity, this can degrade the performance of the SQL Server applications.

Basic Monitoring Concepts

System Monitor is a Microsoft Management Console (MMC) snap-in that is part of the Performance console that you'll find in the Administrative Tools program group. System Monitor comes bundled as a part of the operating system. Many people still call this tool Performance Monitor because of its similarity to the Performance Monitor tool that was included with Windows NT 4.0. System Monitor and is very similar to the old Performance Monitor tool in many ways, but there are some major differences in how performance data is logged. Performance Monitor forced you to log the data for an entire performance object, giving you many measurements that were not useful and increased the size of the log.

Some of the main uses for System Monitor include:

◆ Monitoring real-time performance both locally and remotely

◆ Analyzing performance data collected from logs

◆ Displaying performance data in graph, histogram, and report formats

◆ Saving and loading sets of performance counters for monitoring

When working with System Monitor and its associated tools, you'll be looking at performance objects, counters, and instances. Figure 10.1 shows the Add Counters dialog box from System Monitor. For a more detailed explanation of what is being measured by a counter, click the Explain button.

A *performance object* is a group of counters and instances that relate to some area of the system component or application being monitored. Some performance objects relate to specific pieces of hardware such as Memory, Processor, or PhysicalDisk. Some performance objects relate to operating system components, such as Process or LogicalDisk. Other performance objects map to software components installed on the server. SQL Server provides many performance objects, such as SQL Server: Databases, for analyzing different areas of performance.

FIGURE 10.1
The Add Counters
dialog box

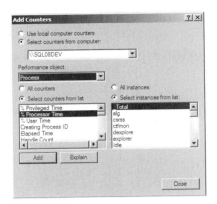

Some of the performance objects contain multiple instances. The performance object selected determines the instances available. In Figure 10.1, the process object is selected, so all of the processes currently running on the machine are available as instances. If the SQL Server: Databases object is selected, all of the databases available on the local server would be available.

A *performance counter* represents a metric that you want to measure. Performance counters return numeric values that can be analyzed in real time or logged for later analysis. Some common performance objects, instances, and counters are shown in Table 10.1.

TABLE 10.1 Common Performance Objects, Instances, and Counters

OBJECT	INSTANCES	COUNTERS
Processor	0, 1, 2, etc. depending on the number of processors and cores	% Processor Time % User Time % Privileged Time
Memory	None	Pages/sec Available Bytes/KBytes/Mbytes Page Faults/sec
PhysicalDisk	0 C:, 1 D:, etc. representing each physical disk seen by the operating system	% Disk Time Avg. Disk Queue Length Disk Reads/sec Disk Writes/sec
SQL Server: Databases	Each database on the targeted SQL Server Instance	Data File(s) Size (KB) Log File(s) Size (KB) Percent Log Used Transactions/sec

Graphs, Logs, and Alerts

System Monitor is used to display performance counter data. The data can be analyzed in real time, or you can analyze previously created performance logs. Figure 10.2 shows System Monitor charting several performance counters.

FIGURE 10.2

System Monitor charting performance counters

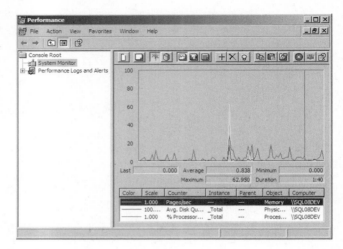

System Monitor can use three display modes: Chart, Histogram, or Report. The Chart display mode shows the values of Performance Monitor counters charted over time. The Histogram display mode shows the values of Performance Monitor counters using colored vertical bars. The Report display mode shows the actual values of Performance Monitor counters in a text-based report format.

By default, System Monitor displays performance data in real time. This is useful for short-term performance monitoring when you want to view performance data in real time.

To add performance counters, use the toolbar button with the plus (+) symbol. The Add Counters dialog box that appears is shown in Figure 10.1.

To modify System Monitor properties, you can use the Properties button on the toolbar. You can change various properties including the sampling interval and the way that data is represented in the Report and Histogram views.

If you want to log performance data over a period of time, you'll want to use Performance Logs and Alerts. Performance Logs and Alerts is implemented as a Windows service with an MMC snap-in for administration, so the console doesn't need to be running in order to collect performance data.

The Performance Logs and Alerts snap-in provides three services for background performance monitoring: Counter logs, Trace logs, and Alerts.

Counter logs are used to write counter data to various log file formats at a defined interval. Performance data can also be logged to a database via ODBC. Depending on the format chosen, log data may be analyzed by many different applications, including Microsoft Excel. Counter logs may be loaded into the System Monitor application to view the data as a chart, histogram, or report.

Trace logs can be used to monitor detailed system events including disk I/O operations and page faults. SQL Server provides its own tracing engine that is separate from Trace Logs in the Performance Logs and Alerts console. We'll cover SQL Server tracing later in this chapter.

Alerts are used to monitor the values of counters and perform actions when they move above or below a certain level. The alerts defined in the Performance Logs and Alerts console are different from SQL Server Agent alerts. SQL Server Agent alerts will be covered in detail in Chapter 11, "Using the SQL Server Agent Service."

Selecting Resources and Counters

When monitoring system performance, you usually need to focus on three main areas: disk, memory, and processor usage. Each of these areas should be examined to determine potential bottlenecks. It's important to get a good general view of system performance before focusing on more specific measurements because problems in one area can affect the others. For example, a high amount of disk I/O activity doesn't always mean that applications are heavily using the disk. If a system is running low on memory, the operating system will use the disk to compensate by paging areas of memory out to the disk. Having limited amounts of memory will also increase the amount of CPU utilization because of the paging process.

When monitoring system performance, it's also important to consider the importance of good application design. A poorly designed application can easily consume all of the available resources of a SQL Server. Throwing more hardware at the problem doesn't always result in performance improvements, especially if the problem is due to application behavior.

MONITORING DISK PERFORMANCE

It should come as no surprise that SQL Server generally uses the disks in a system heavily. Disk I/O is a frequent cause of system bottlenecks.

When monitoring the performance of your disk subsystem, you will want to watch the overall amount of disk I/O so that you can compare it to the disk I/O caused by SQL Server. Disk activity can also be caused by other applications running on the same server, or by excess paging due to memory constraints. Be sure to examine the overall I/O picture before focusing too deeply on SQL Server-specific I/O.

The following three counters monitor overall disk activity:

- PhysicalDisk: % Disk Time
- PhysicalDisk: Avg. Disk Queue Length
- PhysicalDisk: Current Disk Queue Length

The % Disk Time counter monitors the percentage of time a disk is busy with I/O activity. This counter should generally stay below 90 percent, although spikes will certainly occur. For systems with hardware RAID, % Disk Time may report over 100 percent.

The *Disk Queue Length* is another important measurement that determines how many operations are waiting for the disk. The Disk Queue Length shouldn't be sustained at more than two times the number of spindles that make up the disk. Most disks are considered to be single spindle, although RAID arrays usually have more than one spindle. The Current Disk Queue Length represents the I/O occurring on the system when the sample is taken, where Average Disk Queue Length is an average based on the sampling interval. The Average Disk Queue Length will usually give a better picture of the disk queue, especially when longer intervals are used between samplings.

When the % Disk Time and Disk Queue counters are high, several options are available for improving performance, including:

- Moving some files to a different disk or array

- Adding disks to an existing RAID array

- Replacing the disk or array with a faster one

The counters we've monitored so far show an overall picture of disk I/O on the system. You will want to isolate the source of disk activity once you've gotten an overall picture.

High amounts of I/O can be caused by memory page fault operations. To determine if page faults are causing excessive I/O, you can monitor the Memory: Page Faults/sec counter. If you see a large number of page fault operations, you can dig further by looking at the Process: Page Faults/sec counter. Each process on the machine is represented by an instance in the process object. Monitor the `sqlservr` instance to determine if the SQL Server process is causing the page faults to occur. A high number of page faults can indicate that you need to tune the memory.

To determine if the disk I/O is being caused by SQL Server activity, you can monitor these two counters:

- SQL Server: Buffer Manager: Page Reads/sec

- SQL Server: Buffer Manager: Page Writes/sec

If the values of these counters are approaching the limits of the I/O hardware, try to reduce the values by reducing the number of I/O operations. You have several options to help reduce the amount of I/O:

- You can tune the database by:

  - Improving index coverage and creating better indexes

  - Evaluating normalization strategies

  - Evaluating filegroup usage and file placement

  - Utilizing advanced features, such as indexed views or partitioned tables

- You can increase the amount of available memory, thereby enabling more data to be cached.

- You can increase the I/O capacity of the hardware.

MONITORING MEMORY USAGE

Memory is a critical resource for SQL Server. SQL Server heavily uses memory for caching data and executing plans. SQL Server will dynamically change its memory requirements based on the available system resources wherever possible.

Use these counters to evaluate general memory availability and paging activity:

- Memory: Available Bytes/KBytes/Mbytes

- Memory: Pages/sec

- Memory: Page Faults/sec

The Memory: Available Bytes counter shows the amount of physical memory available to processes running on the computer. A low amount of available physical memory may be a sign that further investigation is needed.

There are two types of page faults: hard and soft. *Hard page faults* require access to the disk, and *soft page faults* mean that the page is located in a different location in physical memory. Most processors can handle a large number of soft page faults without significant consequences. Hard page faults will affect disk I/O performance.

Pages/sec reports the rate at which pages are read from or written to disk in order to resolve hard page faults. Page Faults/sec reports the total number of both hard and soft page faults. Both counters should be monitored to determine if paging operations are causing excessive disk I/O.

The process object lets you look at the memory statistics for each process running on the server. SQL Server runs under the `sqlservr` process, so you can use these counters to determine how much memory SQL Server is consuming and if page faults are being caused by SQL Server or another process. The Process: Page Faults/sec and Process: Working set counters are two important counters.

To dig even further into memory usage within SQL Server, the SQL Server: Buffer Manager and SQL Server: Memory Manager performance objects can be useful. Two specific counters worth monitoring are SQL Server: Buffer Manager: Buffer Cache Hit Ratio and SQL Server: Memory Manager: Total Server Memory (KB).

The *buffer cache hit ratio* indicates how often SQL Server is able to use buffers in memory instead of going to the hard disk to retrieve data. For most On-Line Transaction Processing (OLTP) applications, this value should exceed 90 percent when possible. The lower your buffer cache hit ratio is, the more often SQL Server needs to use the disk to retrieve data. Increasing the amount of memory available will usually help the buffer cache hit ratio.

It's also important to monitor the Total Server Memory counter. If this counter is consistently close to the amount of physical memory in the machine, you may consider increasing the amount of memory. A system with fully utilized memory may be prone to bottlenecks when competition for resources increases.

Monitoring CPU Utilization

It's important to ensure that CPU utilization is within normal ranges on a SQL Server. Continuously high CPU usage can indicate that you are approaching the performance limits of your processor. It can also indicate a poorly tuned or designed application. You should expect spikes in CPU utilization based on server load, but if CPU utilization is constantly above 80 percent usage, your processor may be a bottleneck.

There are several counters that provide detail about CPU utilization:

- Processor: % Processor Time
- Processor: % Privileged Time
- Processor: % User Time
- System: % Total Processor Time
- System: Processor Queue Length

The processor object contains an instance for each processor in the system. Multicore processors will show up as multiple processor instances depending on the number of cores. The % Processor Time counter shows the total usage percentage of both kernel and user-mode processes. The % Privileged Time counter shows the percentage of time spent performing kernel-mode requests. A large amount of privileged time combined with high disk utilization can sometimes point to an inefficient disk subsystem. Different disk controllers and drivers will use different amounts of kernel processing time. The % User Time counter corresponds to the percentage of execution dedicated to user processes such as SQL Server.

When monitoring the % Processor Time counter, remember that it is based off of a specific processor instance. For multiprocessor machines, monitor the System: % Total Processor Time counter to get an average for all processors.

The System: Processor Queue Length counter refers to the number of threads waiting for processor time. A high system processor queue length means that many threads are waiting for processor time, resulting in a bottleneck. Installing faster processors or installing additional processors will generally improve performance because more processor cycles are available for waiting threads.

When monitoring the processor utilization on a SQL Server, ensure that CPU usage isn't being caused by other processes on the system, such as antivirus tools. The process object is very useful for isolating activity to a specific process.

Using SQL Profiler & Trace

SQL Server provides an incredibly powerful tracing engine. A trace captures detailed information about various events that occur on your SQL Server. There are many reasons you might want to run a trace, including:

◆ Viewing Transact-SQL statements being executed by an application including query plans

◆ Watching for long running queries

◆ Troubleshooting locking issues including deadlocks

◆ Tracing stored procedure executions down to the statement level

◆ Auditing security

◆ Analyzing activity on a user connection

◆ Correlating performance data with activity occurring on the SQL Server at the time

A trace can be created using several system stored procedures, or by using the graphical SQL Server Profiler tool. Most administrators prefer to use the SQL Server Profiler tool because of its extended capabilities and ease of use. Using stored procedures to create a trace can be useful for automating traces, or when you would like the trace controlled by a custom application. We will focus on using the SQL Server Profiler tool in this chapter.

Designing a Good Trace

A Profiler trace is used to capture information about events occurring on the server. Events can be anything from server login and logout events, to SQL batches starting and completing, to execution of stored procedures. Be careful about the number and types of events that you choose to monitor because we want to minimize the overhead produced by the trace. Events can be viewed in real time, as well as logged to trace files or trace tables for later analysis.

Each event has data columns that provide information about the event. The data columns available depend on the event being monitored. Some of the common data columns include TextData, ApplicationName, NTUserName, LoginName, CPU, Reads, Writes, and Duration. Make sure to choose only the data columns that are relevant to your analysis. Keeping track of excess information only adds to the amount of overhead that the trace will take.

Filtering the trace is important so that only relevant events and data columns are captured. Filtering is one of the most important aspects of designing a good trace, both because it reduces overhead and because it reduces the amount of data to analyze. For example, if you are looking for long-running queries, you would filter the trace so that only events are returned that ran for duration of greater than 30 seconds.

To create a trace, follow these basic steps:

1. Name your trace and choose where the trace output should be stored.

2. Choose the events you want to monitor.

3. Choose the data columns that contain the information about the events that interest you.

4. Filter your trace so that it only returns relevant information.

5. Start the trace and analyze the output.

We will examine these steps in more detail in the next section.

Selecting Data Columns and Events

As we mentioned in the last section, choosing the appropriate events and data columns and filtering those events are critical to reducing the amount of overhead that a trace requires on the server. Make sure that you're clear about what you're looking for. Some of the more common Profiler event classes are shown in Table 10.2.

TABLE 10.2   Commonly Used Profiler Event Classes

CATEGORY	EVENT	DESCRIPTION
Security Audit	Audit Login Audit Logout	Tracks when a new connection is logged in and logged out since the trace started. Audit logout has more available data columns that give information about resource usage by the connection.
Sessions	ExistingConnection	Used to show any connections that existed when the trace was started. Login events aren't generated for existing connections.

TABLE 10.2   Commonly Used Profiler Event Classes   *(CONTINUED)*

CATEGORY	EVENT	DESCRIPTION
TSQL	SQL:BatchStarting SQL:BatchCompleted	Tracks when new batches start and complete. A batch can contain multiple SQL statements, and statistics are tracked for the group of statements.
	SQL:StmtStarting SQL:StmtCompleted	Tracks when individual SQL statements start and complete. More granular than the BatchStarting and BatchCompleted events.
Stored Procedures	RPC:Starting RPC:Completed	Tracks when a stored procedure starts, and completes when executed from a remote procedure call. These events occur when an application calls a stored procedure, but not when a stored procedure calls another stored procedure. These events don't fire if the stored procedure is executed from a batch.
	SP:Starting SP:Completed	Tracks when a stored procedure starts and completes regardless of how it was called. This includes nested stored procedures.
	SP:StmtStarting SP:StmtCompleted	Tracks when individual statements within a stored procedure start and complete. Useful for tracking down performance issues within stored procedures.
Locks	Deadlock graph	Provides an XML description of a deadlock situation, and produces a graphical rendition showing the resources, connections, and queries that caused the deadlock. A deadlock graph diagram is shown later in this chapter.

TABLE 10.2   Commonly Used Profiler Event Classes   *(CONTINUED)*

CATEGORY	EVENT	DESCRIPTION
	Lock:Timeout	Tracks situations where a lock timeout was exceeded. Timeout is determined by the @@LOCK_TIMEOUT system function and is set using the SET LOCK_TIMEOUT statement.
Performance	Showplan XML	Provides an XML description of a query plan. This event fires every time a SQL statement is executed, and can cause significant overhead. A graphical rendition of the query plan is shown when using SQL Server Profiler.
Scans	Scan:Started Scan:Stopped	Tracks when table and index scans start and stop. Scan operations should be avoided where possible by creating appropriate indexes or tuning the query that's causing the scan.

Table 10.2 only shows a small sampling of the available events that can be monitored. Many more are available, as you'll see when you begin digging into the Profiler interface. For detailed information about any event class, see the topic "SQL Server Event Class Reference" in SQL Server Books Online.

CREATING A NEW TRACE

To create a new trace using SQL Server Profiler, use the following steps:

1. Open SQL Server Profiler by navigating to Start ➤ All Programs ➤ Microsoft SQL Server 2008 ➤ Performance Tools ➤ SQL Server Profiler.

2. Create a new trace by choosing File ➤ New Trace. You can also start a new trace by using the New Trace button in the toolbar. The Connect to Server dialog box appears.

3. In the Server Name dropdown list, type the server name to which you would like to connect. Choose the appropriate authentication method, and fill out a user name and password if required. Click the Connect button.

4. The Trace Properties dialog box appears, as shown in Figure 10.3. Fill out the general trace properties, including the name of the trace.

FIGURE 10.3
The General Trace
Properties dialog

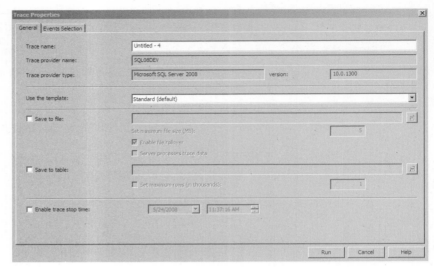

5. Choose a trace template. The trace templates packaged with SQL Server Profiler are described in Table 10.3.

TABLE 10.3   Profiler Trace Templates

TEMPLATE NAME	DESCRIPTION
Blank	A blank trace template with no events or data columns selected.
SP_Counts	A template for tracing stored procedure execution. The SP:Starting event is traced, and output is grouped by EventClass, ServerName, DatabaseID, and ObjectID.
Standard (Default)	The default template is used to monitor general database activity. All stored procedure executions, Transact-SQL batches, and connection-related events are tracked. Many data columns are included to provide statistical information about the tracked activity.
TSQL	A template for reviewing Transact-SQL sent from client applications. This template is similar to the Standard template, but with much fewer data columns logged.
TSQL_Duration	A template that's used for identifying slow queries and stored procedures. The RPC:Completed and SQL:BatchCompleted events are tracked, and grouped by the execution duration.
TSQL_Grouped	A template that captures connection-related classes and Transact-SQL statement execution. The data is grouped by ApplicationName, NTUserName, LoginName, and ClientProcessID.

TABLE 10.3   Profiler Trace Templates   *(CONTINUED)*

TEMPLATE NAME	DESCRIPTION
TSQL_Locks	A template that captures all Transact-SQL statements including those used in stored procedures, along with exceptional lock events. This template is useful for troubleshooting lock timeouts, blocked processes, and deadlocks.
TSQL_Replay	A template that captures all of the events and data columns required for replaying a trace. Replaying a trace is useful in performance tuning, and will be covered in detail later in this chapter.
TSQL_SPs	A template for capturing detailed information about stored procedure execution. Tracks connection, stored procedure, stored procedure statement execution, and batch submissions.
Tuning	A template for capturing information about running SQL statements that can be fed into the Database Engine Tuning Advisor. The database tuning wizard gives index recommendations based on a given workload, and is covered in more detail in Chapter 14, "Indexing Strategies for Query Optimization."

6. If you'd like to save the trace output to a file, choose the Save to File checkbox and choose the file to which you would like to log.

    ◆   *Set Maximum File Size (MB)* allows you to set a maximum file size. If Enable File Rollover isn't selected, this is the maximum size of the trace data being logged.

    ◆   *Enable File Rollover* allows new trace files to be created when the maximum file size is reached.

    ◆   *Server Processes Trace Data* determines whether SQL Server Profiler or the server processes trace data. When this checkbox is selected, no events will be skipped, even under stress conditions. When allowing SQL Server Profiler to process trace data, events may be skipped if the server is experiencing a heavy load.

7. If you'd like to save the trace output to a table, choose the Save to Table checkbox. You're given the opportunity to connect to a SQL Server and choose the database where the table will be created. The default name for the new table is the name of the trace. The structure of the table depends on the data columns chosen for the trace.

8. Choose the Events Selection tab. The dialog shown in Figure 10.4 appears. The events and data columns displayed are based on the trace template chosen in the previous screen.

    ◆   Use the Show All Events and Show All Columns checkboxes to display all the events and columns if you want to modify the trace from the template.

    ◆   Hovering over the event names or data column checkboxes shows the description at the bottom of the dialog.

◆ Reducing the number of events and data columns will reduce the amount of overhead required by the trace. Only choose the information you'll need for later analysis. The checkboxes next to the event names will show all possible data columns for the event. Make sure to deselect any data columns you don't need to analyze.

FIGURE 10.4
The Events Selection tab of the Trace Properties dialog.

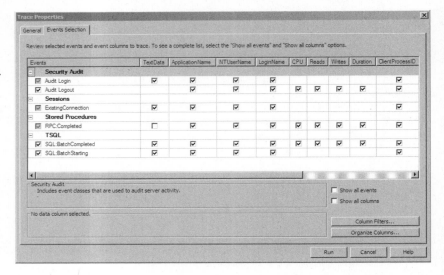

9. Click the Column Filters button. The dialog shown in Figure 10.5 appears. To get to the filters for a specific data column, click the column header. Click the OK button when you are finished.

FIGURE 10.5
The Edit Filter dialog

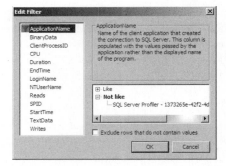

◆ The options available for filtering depend on the datatype of the column.

◆ For columns with character data, the options are Like and Not Like.

◆ For columns with numeric data, the options are Equals, Not Equal To, Greater Than or Equal, or Less Than or Equal.

◆ For columns that contain date data, the options are Greater Than and Less Than.

◆ All datatypes can use the Exclude Rows That Do Not Contain Values checkbox.

10. Click the Organize Columns button to display the dialog shown in Figure 10.6. You can reordered or regroup the columns by using the Up and Down buttons. Click the OK button when you are finished.

11. Click the Run button to start the trace.

FIGURE 10.6

The Organize
Columns dialog

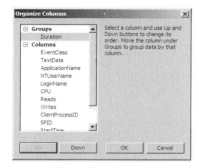

WORKING WITH TRACE TEMPLATES

Getting a trace to contain exactly the events, columns, grouping, and filtering that you want can be quite a lot of work. Trace templates can save you from having to redo the same trace configuration over and over again. A template stores the events, data columns, and filters for reuse.

Once you've configured a trace, saving it as a template is easy. Simply use the File ➤ Save As ➤ Trace Template menu. You will need to provide a name for the template, but after you do that, the template will be available whenever you need to create a new trace.

Rather than running a trace and saving its template as a definition, you can also create a trace template from scratch. To create a new trace template, select File ➤ Templates ➤ New Template. You can also edit existing templates by choosing File ➤ Templates ➤ Edit Template. In the Edit Template dialog box, you can also make a template the default.

Templates can also be imported and exported from SQL Server Profiler after they've been created. When exporting a template, you need to choose the server type that you will be replaying against. This is because of differences between event classes available in each version of SQL Server. After you've chosen a template and server type, you will be prompted to save the template to the location of your choice. Template files have the extension .tdf.

Evaluating Trace Output

Once you've started a trace, you're going to want to analyze the captured events. Some analysis can be accomplished by scrolling through the events of a running trace, as shown in Figure 10.7, but much more is possible.

For most analyses, you want to save the trace output to a trace file or a trace table. Both of these options are available when you create the trace, but you can also save the output of a trace by using the File ➤ Save As menu.

FIGURE 10.7

Running a trace in
SQL Server Profiler

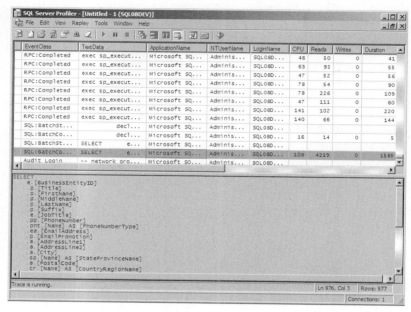

ANALYZING TRACE OUTPUT WITH TRANSACT-SQL

Saving trace output to a table allows you to write Transact-SQL queries to analyze the trace output. When querying trace tables, you'll find that the columns are similar to what you would see in SQL Server Profiler's user interface, with two differences. First, a rownumber column is available in the trace table so that you can order the events the same way they were ordered in the Profiler interface. The second difference is that the EventClass column contains an integer value instead of the friendly event class names used in SQL Server Profiler. You can retrieve the event class names by using the sys.trace_events system view. The following query retrieves all SQL batches that took longer than 1 second to execute:

```
SELECT  te.name As EventName,
        s.TextData,
        s.CPU,
        s.Reads,
        s.Writes,
        s.Duration,
        s.ApplicationName
FROM StandardTraceTable s
 INNER JOIN sys.trace_events te
 ON s.EventClass = te.trace_event_id
WHERE s.Duration > 1000000
 AND te.Name = 'SQL:BatchCompleted'
ORDER BY s.RowNumber;
```

WATCH OUT FOR THE DURATION DATA COLUMN

In SQL Server 2005 and later, the SQL Server Profiler GUI displays duration values in milliseconds (one thousandth of a second) by default. When saving the output of a trace to a file or trace table, the Duration field is written in microseconds (one millionth of a second).

You can display duration in microseconds in the Profiler GUI if you modify the options. You can do this by going to the Tools ➢ Options menu.

The amount of analysis you can perform on trace data stored in a table is limited only by your imagination and your Transact-SQL knowledge. The following example retrieves the 10 longest running batches in the trace:

```
SELECT TOP 10 TextData,
            Duration,
            NTUserName,
            ApplicationName
FROM StandardTraceTable
WHERE EventClass = 12 -- RPC:BatchCompleted
ORDER BY Duration DESC;
```

ANALYZING TRACE OUTPUT USING SQL SERVER PROFILER

To analyze data in SQL Server Profiler, you should save the output of your trace and then reopen it. If you try to modify the properties of a trace after it's stopped, you'll find that any changes will result in you rerunning the trace. However, if you close and reopen the trace file, you can do quite a bit of analysis in the Profiler interface including:

◆ Choose which events and data columns to display.

◆ Change the order of columns and group columns that weren't originally grouped.

◆ Add filters to the data that didn't originally exist in the trace.

◆ Summarize information based on a data column.

You can always save the output of a trace, even if that wasn't what you specified when you created the trace. To save a trace, use File ➢ Save As ➢ Trace File or File ➢ Save As ➢ Trace Table. After you've saved the trace output, close the current trace window and then reopen the trace file.

Almost all filtering, grouping, and aggregating is accessed through the Properties dialog. Figure 10.8 shows the Properties window of a trace that's been closed and reopened. (If you compare this to the Figure 10.3 earlier in the chapter, you will notice that there is an OK button instead of a Run button.)

FIGURE 10.8
The Trace File
Properties dialog

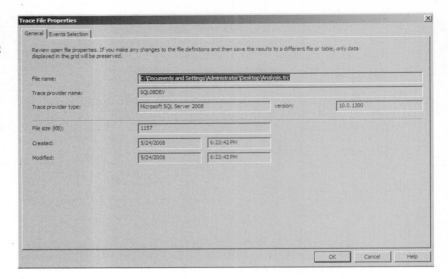

Modifying the properties of a saved trace file only changes how the data is displayed. You can focus on specific events and data columns by working in the Events Selection tab. Uncheck anything that you don't want to see right now. You can also modify the order of columns, change column groupings, and even add additional filters to the trace. Figure 10.9 shows a trace that's been grouped by EventClass in aggregated view. Aggregated view is accessible only when grouping by a single column, and it displays a count of events. To switch between grouped and aggregated view, right-click within the trace.

FIGURE 10.9
The trace file in
aggregated view

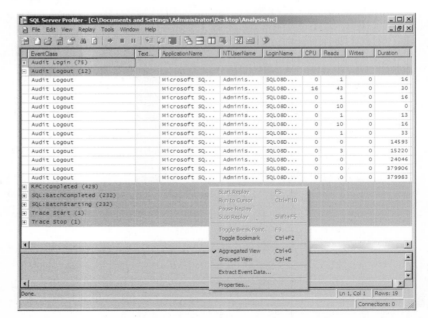

CORRELATING PERFORMANCE COUNTERS WITH TRACE EVENTS

Earlier in the chapter, we covered how to create a Performance counter log by using Performance Logs and Alerts. SQL Server Profiler can import this performance data to allow you to correlate spikes in Performance counters with events occurring in SQL Server. (See Figure 10.10.)

FIGURE 10.10

The SQL Server Profiler displays a chart of Performance counter data.

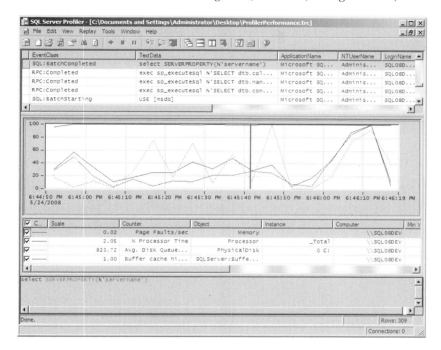

In order to import performance data, you must be working with data stored in a trace file or a table that has been opened for analysis. You must also have logged performance data that contains information that corresponds to the time the trace was taken.

To import performance data into SQL Server Profiler, follow these steps:

1. Open an existing trace file or table. If you're working with a stopped trace, the Import Performance Data menu item will be grayed out.

2. Choose File ➤ Import Performance Data. Select the performance log file that contains the data you want to analyze.

3. Select a point in time by clicking on the graph area or by selecting an event. A red line appears, and events that were occurring at that time are displayed.

Replaying Traces for Performance Analysis

So far you have been learning about the activity on our SQL Server. Profiler allows us to replay a saved trace table or file against a SQL Server instance. It includes breakpoint and run-to-cursor features that allow debugging, as well as a multithreaded playback engine to simulate the many connections that make up a trace. There are a number of reasons why you would want to replay trace activity, including:

- Simulating a load on an application for stress testing

- Testing the result of index modifications to verify a performance improvement of a set of queries

- Reproducing a problem in an application, and verifying that the fix will work again given the same workload

- Replaying a load against a test version of an application with data that was captured from production

- Isolating where a problem is occurring in an application by stepping through a workload and setting breakpoints

You can't replay all trace files because there needs to be an adequate amount of information in the trace file. Profiler will return an error when you try to replay if pieces of information are missing from the trace file. The TSQL_Replay Trace template includes all of the events and data columns required to replay a trace. Make sure that you restrict activity to include the only events you want to replay. Depending on your situation, certain event classes (Table 10.4) and data columns (Table 10.5) will need to be included in order to replay a trace file.

TABLE 10.4 Event Classes Required to Replay a Trace

SITUATION	EVENT CLASSES
These event classes must always exist in a trace to be replayed.	Audit Login Audit Logout ExistingConnection RPC:Starting RPC:Completed RPC Output Parameter SQL:BatchStarting SQL:BatchCompleted
Only need to be included when replaying server-side cursors.	CursorOpen CursorClose CursorPrepare CursorUnprepare CursorExecute
Only need to be included when replaying server-side prepared SQL statements.	Prepare SQL Exec Prepared SQL

TABLE 10.5   Data Columns Required to Replay a Trace

DATA COLUMNS		
EventClass	Database ID	StartTime
EventSequence	ClientProcessID	EndTime
TextData	HostName	IsSystem
ApplicationName	ServerName	NTDomainName
LoginName	Binary Data	NTUserName
DatabaseName	SPID	Error

If you are replaying a trace against a different server, errors may occur unless the following things are true:

◆ The logins and users are the same as the source server, including permissions and passwords.

◆ There is a match between the database IDs. If this is not possible, the database name can be used for the match.

Replaying traces that include modifications against a database that has already had the same activity can result in various errors including primary key violations and duplicate records. Always back up the database before replaying a trace that includes any modification activity.

Use these steps to replay a trace:

1. Create a new trace with the required events and columns. Filter the activity so that you are capturing only the events you want to replay.

2. Save the output of the trace to a file.

3. Close the open trace.

4. Open the saved trace file.

5. Set any breakpoints that you want to use by right-clicking on the row and choosing Toggle Breakpoint. You can also use the F9 shortcut key.

6. Use one of the following to begin the replay process:

   ◆ Use Replay ➢ Step to begin stepping through the trace line by line.

   ◆ Use Replay ➢ Start to run the replay in its entirety.

   ◆ Use Replay ➢ Run to Cursor to run the replay to the selected row.

7. The Connect to Server dialog appears. Choose the server name you would like to replay against and enter the authentication information.

8. The Replay Configuration dialog appears, as shown in Figure 10.11.

FIGURE 10.11
The Basic Replay
Options tab

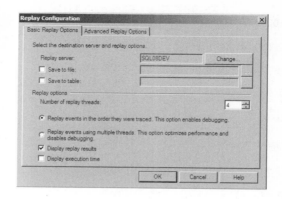

9. Configure the following options:

◆ If you want to save the replay output, choose the location to which you would like to save it.

◆ Configure the number of replay threads. Using more threads can simulate a more realistic load, but don't use too many or you will overwhelm the machine using Profiler.

◆ Decide if you want to replay the events in the order they were traced. You must use this option if you want to use any of the debugging options such as breakpoints. If you are trying to simulate a realistic load, choose the option to Replay Events Using Multiple Threads.

◆ Decide if you want to display trace results. For large traces, you will see better performance if you uncheck this box.

10. Click the Advanced Replay Options tab, as shown in Figure 10.12.

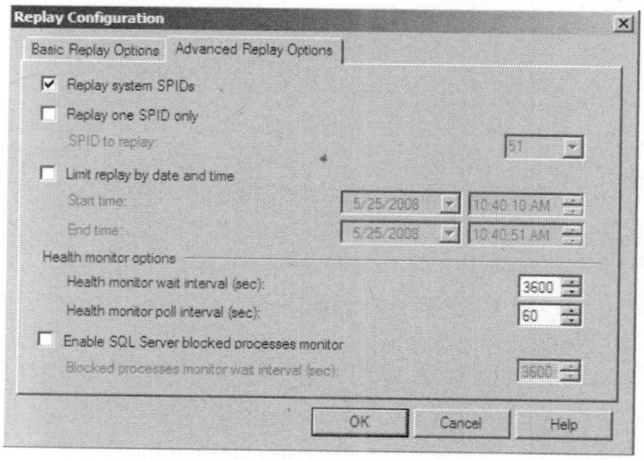

FIGURE 10.12
The Advanced
Replay Options tab

11. Configure the following options:

◆ Decide if you want to replay system SPIDs.

◆ Decide if you want to replay only one SPID or all of them.

◆ Decide if you want to limit the replay by date and time.

◆ Configure the Health Monitor poll and wait intervals.

◆ Decide if you want to use the Blocked Process Monitor. The Blocked Process Monitor is an application thread that monitors for blocking processes from the simulated trace and terminates them after a configurable interval.

12. Click the OK button. The trace begins replaying as shown in Figure 10.13. You can use the F10 key to step statement-by-statement if enabled, and you can use Ctrl+F10 to run to the currently selected row.

FIGURE 10.13
A SQL Server Profiler trace is replayed.

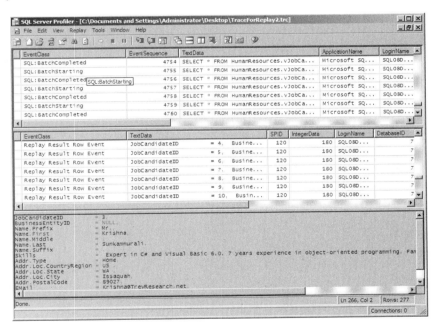

DDL Triggers

SQL Server Profiler allowed us to view and replay events. DDL triggers allow us to run Transact-SQL statements in response to DDL actions at the server and database level. *DDL* stands for *Data Definition Language*, which most people think of as CREATE, ALTER, and DROP statements. DDL triggers can respond to these all of these statements, as well as security actions (GRANT, DENY, REVOKE).

DDL triggers have many uses, including:

◆ Saving a log of schema modifications for a database

◆ Saving a log of permission changes for a database

◆ Disallowing certain actions such as DROP statements for production databases

◆ Building an index modification log

◆ Auditing server-wide activity such as creating databases or linked servers

DDL triggers can respond to actions on a particular database or actions performed against the server instance. A DDL trigger could respond to CREATE_TABLE events on a particular database; it could also be written to respond to CREATE_TABLE events in all databases on a server instance. Some events, such as CREATE_DATABASE or CREATE_LOGIN events, can occur only at the server scope.

There are many different types of DDL events, as well as event groups, to which a trigger can respond. Event groups allow you to monitor for a set of events using a single keyword, such as DDL_TABLE_EVENTS, which would monitor for all CREATE TABLE, ALTER TABLE, and DROP TABLE statements.

Retrieving metadata about DDL triggers depends on the scope of the trigger. Triggers scoped at the server level can be viewed by querying the sys.server_triggers view or by expanding Server Objects ➢ Triggers using Object Explorer in SQL Server Management Studio. Triggers that are scoped at the database level can be viewed by querying the sys.triggers view, or by expanding Database ➢ Programmability ➢ Database Triggers in Object Explorer.

DDL Triggers Versus DML Triggers

In some ways, DDL triggers are similar to DML triggers, but there are some significant differences. Both types of triggers are executed in response to events, but the types of events are different. DML triggers execute in response to INSERT, UPDATE, and DELETE statements, where DDL triggers execute in response to DDL operations. DML triggers are scoped at the table level, where DDL triggers can be scoped at the database or server-instance level. Other similarities between DDL and DML triggers include:

◆ Both types of triggers execute as part of a transaction.

◆ Both types of triggers have code similar to a stored procedure.

◆ Both types of triggers can be defined on multiple actions.

◆ Both types of triggers can be written using Transact-SQL or .Net languages through CLR integration.

◆ Both types allow multiple triggers to be created for an action.

Although DDL and DML triggers are similar in these ways, there are some significant differences, as shown in Table 10.6.

TABLE 10.6   Differences Between DDL Triggers and DML Triggers

DML TRIGGERS	DDL TRIGGERS
Respond to INSERT, UPDATE, and DELETE statements	Respond to CREATE, ALTER, and DROP statements
Scoped per table	Scoped at database or server instance
Create inserted and deleted tables to give information about the event that occurred	Don't create any tables. Information about the DDL operation is retrieved using the EVENTDATA() function
Can create INSTEAD OF and AFTER triggers	DDL triggers always execute after a DDL operation has occurred. You cannot create INSTEAD OF DDL triggers.

Trigger Events

Looking at the syntax for creating a DDL trigger can help you understand the scope and event types. The following is a simplified syntax for creating DDL triggers:

```
CREATE TRIGGER trigger_name
ON { ALL SERVER | DATABASE }
{ FOR | AFTER }
{ event_type | event_group } [ ,...n ]
AS { sql_statement [ ; ] [ ,...n ]
| EXTERNAL NAME < method specifier >}
```

All events can be created at the ALL SERVER scope. Some events, such as CREATE_LOGIN, can be created only at the ALL SERVER scope, because logins are managed per instance. Even database-specific operations, such as CREATE_TABLE, can be scoped at the ALL SERVER level.

Event names are usually created by replacing spaces with underscores for the event. For example, DROP INDEX would use DROP_INDEX as an event name for DDL triggers. Table 10.7 shows events that can be created at both the server and database level, and Table 10.8 shows all of the server-level-only events.

TABLE 10.7   Server- and Database-Level Events

CREATE_, ALTER_, AND DROP_ MAY BE USED	
APPLICATION_ROLE	PROCEDURE
ASSEMBLY	QUEUE
ASYMMETRIC_KEY	REMOTE_SERVICE_BINDING
CERTIFICATE	ROLE
CREDENTIAL	ROUTE

TABLE 10.7   Server- and Database-Level Events   *(CONTINUED)*

CREATE_, ALTER_, AND DROP_ **MAY BE USED**		
EXTENDED_PROPERTY	SCHEMA	
FULLTEXT_CATALOG	SERVICE	
FULLTEXT_INDEX	STATISTICS (UPDATE_STATISTICS instead of ALTER)	
FUNCTION	SYMMETRIC_KEY	
INDEX	TABLE	
MASTER_KEY	TRIGGER	
MESSAGE_TYPE	USER	
PARTITION_FUNCTION	VIEW	
PARTITION_SCHEME	XML_INDEX	
PLAN_GUIDE	XML_SCHEMA_COLLECTION	
CREATE_ AND DROP_ MAY BE USED		
CONTRACT	EVENT_NOTIFICATION	SYNONYM
COUNTER_SIGNATURE	RULE	TYPE
DEFAULT	SIGNATURE	
Other Events		
ALTER_AUTHORIZATION	UNBIND_DEFAULT	
ALTER_AUTHORIZATION_DATABASE	RENAME	
ADD_COUNTER_SIGNATURE	ADD_ROLE_MEMBER	
DROP_COUNTER_SIGNATURE	DROP_ROLE_MEMBER	
GRANT_DATABASE	BIND_RULE	
DENY_DATABASE	UNBIND_RULE	
REVOKE_DATABASE	ADD_SIGNATURE	
BIND_DEFAULT	DROP_SIGNATURE	

TABLE 10.8   DDL Events That Have Server Scope Only

CREATE_, ALTER_, AND DROP_ **MAY BE USED.**		
DATABASE	LINKED_SERVER	MESSAGE
ENDPOINT	LOGIN	REMOTE_SERVER
CREATE_ AND DROP_ MAY BE USED		
EXTENDED_PROCEDURE	LINKED_SERVER_LOGIN	
Other Events		
ALTER_AUTHORIZATION_SERVER	REVOKE_SERVER	
ALTER_INSTANCE	ADD_SERVER_ROLE_MEMBER	
GRANT_SERVER	DROP_SERVER_ROLE_MEMBER	
DENY_SERVER		

NOTE

Some DDL triggers respond to certain system stored procedures as well as DDL events; for example, both the sp_addtype system stored procedure and CREATE TYPE statement will cause the CREATE_TYPE event to occur.

As you can see, DDL triggers can respond to quite a few events. The example in Listing 10.1 would execute for CREATE TABLE events in all databases on the server.

LISTING 10.1   Server-Level CREATE_TABLE Trigger

```
CREATE TRIGGER Trg_CreatedATable
ON ALL SERVER
FOR CREATE_TABLE
AS
PRINT 'You Created a Table';
```

You could rewrite the trigger in Listing 10.1 so that it executed only in a particular database. To do that, specify ON DATABASE instead of ON ALL SERVER.

A trigger can respond to multiple events if you separate the event names with commas. There is also another shortcut to capturing multiple events, called *event groups*. Listing 10.2 shows an example of two triggers that do the same thing, but one uses an event group to simplify the syntax.

LISTING 10.2   Using Event Groups

```
-- Created using multiple events
CREATE TRIGGER Trg_TableEvent
ON DATABASE
FOR CREATE_TABLE, ALTER_TABLE, DROP_TABLE
AS
PRINT 'You Performed a Table Operation';
GO

-- Created by using an event group
CREATE TRIGGER Trg_TableEvent_Group
ON DATABASE
FOR DDL_TABLE_EVENTS
AS
PRINT 'You Performed a Table Operation';
```

Event groups are also hierarchical. Figure 10.14 and Figure 10.15 show the DDL event groups in their hierarchy for the server-level and database-level events, respectively. All database-level groups may also be monitored at the server level.

FIGURE 10.14
Server-level
event groups

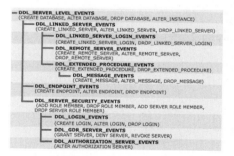

As you look at the previous figures, you may notice that some event groups are below others in the hierarchy. Event groups encompass all the events of their children, so DDL_TABLE_VIEW_ EVENTS encompasses all of the events in DDL_TABLE_EVENTS, DDL_VIEW_EVENTS, DDL_INDEX_ EVENTS, and DDL_STATISTICS_EVENTS. Event groups can allow you to monitor many different types of events with the same trigger without needing to name each event individually.

Listing 10.3 shows an example of a trigger that would fire for all database-level events.

LISTING 10.3   Trigger That Fires for All Database-Level Events

```
CREATE TRIGGER Trg_DatabaseEvents_Group
ON DATABASE
FOR DDL_DATABASE_LEVEL_EVENTS
AS
PRINT 'You Performed a Database Level Operation';
```

FIGURE 10.15
Database-level
event groups

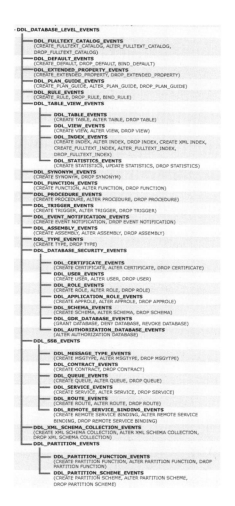

EVENTDATA and Its Schema

Now that we've had a chance to learn about available scopes, events, and event groups, it's time to see how we can extract information about the event that occurred by using the EVENTDATA() function. EVENTDATA() returns an xml datatype. The structure of the XML document returned depends on the event that occurred. You can find the schema for the XML document by viewing the following file:

```
C:\Program Files\Microsoft SQL Server\100\Tools\Binn\schemas\sqlserver\2006\11\
events\events.xsd
```

One easy way to begin understanding the XML returned by the EVENTDATA() function is to return it in a result set from within your trigger, as shown in Listing 10.4

> **NOTE**
>
> You should never return result sets from triggers in production applications. This feature will be removed from a future version of SQL Server.

LISTING 10.4   Trigger That Returns EVENTDATA() as a Result Set

```
CREATE TRIGGER Trg_CreateTable_ReturnsResult
ON DATABASE
FOR CREATE_TABLE
AS
SELECT EVENTDATA();
GO

CREATE TABLE t1 (c1 int);
```

When you execute the statements in Listing 10.4 in SQL Server Management Studio, you receive a result set that contains the XML result. You can click on the XML to open it as a document, which looks like the following:

```
<EVENT_INSTANCE>
  <EventType>CREATE_TABLE</EventType>
  <PostTime>2008-05-26T10:16:36.733</PostTime>
  <SPID>55</SPID>
  <ServerName>SQL08DEV</ServerName>
  <LoginName>SQL08DEV\Administrator</LoginName>
  <UserName>dbo</UserName>
  <DatabaseName>DataCollection</DatabaseName>
  <SchemaName>dbo</SchemaName>
  <ObjectName>t1</ObjectName>
  <ObjectType>TABLE</ObjectType>
  <TSQLCommand>
    <SetOptions ANSI_NULLS="ON" ANSI_NULL_DEFAULT="ON"
             ANSI_PADDING="ON" QUOTED_IDENTIFIER="ON"
             ENCRYPTED="FALSE" />
    <CommandText>
      CREATE TABLE t1 (c1 int)
    </CommandText>
  </TSQLCommand>
</EVENT_INSTANCE>
```

We can use XQuery to retrieve specific element or attribute values from the XML data returned by the EventData() function. For more information on using XQuery, refer to Chapter 7, "SQL Server and XML."

The example in Listing 10.5 will log index operations to a table. Various events are extracted using the XQuery value method.

LISTING 10.5   Extracting Data from EventData() Using XQuery

```
CREATE TABLE IndexLog (
  LogID int identity(1,1) primary key not null,
  EventType nvarchar(100) NOT NULL,
  LoginName nvarchar(100) NOT NULL,
  CommandText nvarchar(max) NOT NULL,
  EvtData xml NOT NULL
);
GO

CREATE TRIGGER Trg_IndexLog
ON DATABASE
FOR DDL_INDEX_EVENTS
AS
DECLARE @edata xml;
SET @edata = EVENTDATA();

INSERT INTO IndexLog
  (EventType, LoginName, CommandText, EvtData)
VALUES (
@edata.value('(/EVENT_INSTANCE/EventType)[1]', 'nvarchar(100)'),
@edata.value('(/EVENT_INSTANCE/LoginName)[1]', 'nvarchar(100)'),
@edata.value('(/EVENT_INSTANCE/TSQLCommand/CommandText)[1]',
              'nvarchar(max)'),
@edata);
GO

-- Test our index logging trigger
CREATE INDEX idx_EventType ON IndexLog(EventType);
DROP INDEX IndexLog.idx_EventType;
```

Another example of using DDL triggers is shown in Listing 10.6. This trigger won't allow modifications to tables in the production schema.

LISTING 10.6   Rolling Back a DDL Trigger

```
CREATE TRIGGER Trg_NoProductionChanges
ON DATABASE
FOR DDL_TABLE_EVENTS
AS
```

```
DECLARE @schema sysname;
SET @schema = EVENTDATA().value('(/EVENT_INSTANCE/SchemaName)[1]',
                                'sysname');

IF @schema = 'production'
BEGIN
   PRINT 'To modify tables in the production schema,';
   PRINT 'disable the trigger Trg_NoProductionChanges';
   ROLLBACK TRAN;
END
GO
-- Test our NoProductionChanges Trigger
-- The following statement will fail.

CREATE TABLE production.test (c1 int);
```

Event Notifications

Event notifications allow you to respond to DDL events and certain SQL Trace events asynchronously by using Service Broker messaging. An event notification allows you to log information about the event outside the scope of the transaction that caused the event. Event Notifications can produce less overhead in transactions than a DDL trigger would.

Service Broker is a platform for building reliable messaging and queuing applications, and is covered in detail in Chapter 20, "Service Oriented Architecture and the Service Broker."

A Service Broker application usually consists of several components working together to accomplish a business task. These components can be divided across many servers.

An event notification works by sending messages to a Service Broker service when an event occurs. The message is passed in an XML format that uses the same schema as the XML returned from the EVENTDATA() function covered in the last section. The service will store the message into a queue, which can be processed in several ways:

◆ Activate a stored procedure to process the message.

◆ Send an external application a notification to start another queue reader.

◆ Have a continuously running application process messages as they arrive.

◆ Start a job on a schedule to process messages.

The examples in this chapter use a stored procedure that is activated whenever new messages are received in the queue. That stored procedure will receive the messages and insert them into a table.

One advantage of using event notifications is that the messages can be sent to a remote server for processing. Many servers could send event notifications to a centralized service.

Event Notifications Versus DDL Triggers

Event notifications and DDL triggers are similar in several ways, but there are also some important differences. An event notification can respond to all of the events and event groups that DDL triggers can respond to, but they can also respond to certain SQL Trace events as well.

DDL triggers execute as part of a transaction, and are able to take action and roll back that transaction. An event notification only sends a message that the action occurred; no rollback is possible. No code is directly executed in response to an event notification; a message is sent to a Service Broker service for processing in an asynchronous manner.

DDL triggers are always processed on the local server, and they are tightly coupled to the transaction. Event notifications can be processed on a remote server.

Event Classes

An event notification supports all of the DDL events and event groups covered earlier in the chapter, in Tables 10.7 and 10.8. In addition, event notifications support a subset of the SQL Trace events.

You can retrieve a full list of event classes that can be used for event notifications by querying the sys.event_notification_event_types system view. There are over 300 events that can be monitored.

Implementing Event Notifications

In order to implement event notifications, several things need to be prepared ahead of time. To create an event notification, we need the following components:

◆ A contract that specifies message types (already exists)

◆ A queue

◆ A Service Broker service

◆ An application to process the queue (which for our example will be a stored procedure to log information and a table to store information)

In this example, we'll do the following:

1. Create a new database called NotificationDemo and enable Service Broker on that database. NotificationDemo will contain the Service Broker objects and store the results of our event notifications:

```
USE master;
CREATE DATABASE NotificationDemo;
GO

-- Enable service broker on the database
ALTER DATABASE NotificationDemo SET ENABLE_BROKER;
```

2. Create a table to hold the result of our event notifications.

```
USE NotificationDemo;
GO

CREATE TABLE DatabaseLog
( LogID int PRIMARY KEY identity(1,1) NOT NULL,
  DatabaseName varchar(100) NOT NULL,
  Operation varchar(50) NOT NULL,
  OperationDate datetime NOT NULL,
  XmlMessage xml NOT NULL );
```

3. Create a stored procedure to process items from the Service Broker queue.

```
CREATE PROC s_ReceiveDatabaseMessage
AS
DECLARE @message_body xml;

-- Receive a message from our queue (created in step 4)
RECEIVE TOP(1) @message_body = message_body
 FROM DatabaseLogQueue;

INSERT INTO DatabaseLog
 (DatabaseName, Operation, OperationDate, XmlMessage)
SELECT @message_body.value('(/EVENT_INSTANCE/DatabaseName)[1]',
                    'varchar(100)'),
    @message_body.value('(/EVENT_INSTANCE/EventType)[1]',
                    'varchar(50)'),
    @message_body.value('(/EVENT_INSTANCE/PostTime)[1]',
                    'datetime'),
    @message_body;
GO
```

4. Create a queue that activates the stored procedure when new items arrive.

```
CREATE QUEUE DatabaseLogQueue
  WITH STATUS = ON,
  ACTIVATION (
    STATUS = ON,
    PROCEDURE_NAME = s_ReceiveDatabaseMessage,
    MAX_QUEUE_READERS = 4,
    EXECUTE AS 'dbo' );
```

5. Create a Service Broker service on the queue using the PostEventNotification contract. This contract is one of the system objects created in Service Broker databases.

```
CREATE SERVICE DatabaseLogService
ON QUEUE DatabaseLogQueue
(
[http://schemas.microsoft.com/SQL/Notifications/PostEventNotification]
);
```

6. Create an event notification that sends messages to the Service Broker service.

```
CREATE EVENT NOTIFICATION NotifyDatabaseEvents
  ON SERVER
  FOR CREATE_DATABASE, DROP_DATABASE
  TO SERVICE 'DatabaseLogService', 'current database';
```

If the service where the event notification is being sent isn't a part of the same database where it's being created, you must specify the Service Broker guid of the database instead of "current database." You can retrieve the Service Broker guid of a database by running the following query:

```
SELECT service_broker_guid FROM sys.databases
  WHERE name = 'Database_Name';
```

Now that we've created the event notification and the required components to support it, you can test the notification by creating and dropping a sample database. Each of these actions will result in the event notification firing, which causes a message to be delivered to the DatabaseLogService service, which is stored in the DatabaseLogQueue and activates the s_ReceiveDatabaseMessage stored procedure. This stored procedure then logs the event and associated information into the DatabaseLog table.

```
-- Both statements cause event notifications to fire
CREATE DATABASE TestEventNotifications;
DROP DATABASE TestEventNotifications;

-- View the messages
SELECT * FROM DatabaseLog;
```

The Bottom Line

Use System Monitor to identify performance bottlenecks. System Monitor allows you to evaluate the performance of Windows and SQL Server components in order to identify bottlenecks.

Master It What three main resources are commonly monitored by System Monitor counters?

Design appropriate traces to monitor events on SQL Server. SQL Server Profiler allows you to monitor many different types of events occurring on a SQL Server instance.

> **Master It** What guidelines should be followed in order to ensure that a trace has a minimal impact on the server being monitored?

Build DDL triggers. Data Definition Language (DDL) triggers make it possible to execute Transact-SQL statements and control transactions.

> **Master It** What function is used to retrieve information about the event that caused a DDL trigger to fire?

Use event notifications to asynchronously capture events occurring on your SQL Server. Event notifications allow Service Broker messages to be sent in response to DDL and trace events.

> **Master It** Can an event notification cause a transaction to be rolled back?.

Chapter 11

Using the SQL Server Agent Service

Keeping everything running smoothly is a goal of every database administrator. It's important to know that backups and other automated tasks are running properly and as scheduled. It's also important to be alerted when things aren't running smoothly. SQL Server Agent is a service that allows us to accomplish both of these tasks and more. Whether you're administering a single server or hundreds of servers, SQL Server Agent will enable you to schedule and automate various tasks across those servers, and be notified when problematic situations occur. In this chapter, you'll learn to:

- ◆ Configure Database Mail for email notification
- ◆ Create Jobs to automate routine tasks
- ◆ Create Alerts to detect and respond to various situations

SQL Agent and Automation

There are many tasks that must be routinely executed in the course of administering a SQL Server. Some of the tasks might include:

- ◆ Backing up databases
- ◆ Reorganizing and rebuilding indexes
- ◆ Checking database consistency
- ◆ Performing data transfers that must run on a schedule
- ◆ Monitoring for and responding to errors
- ◆ Monitoring for and responding to performance issues

SQL Server Agent allows you to accomplish these tasks and more by creating jobs, alerts, and operators to automate administrative tasks. In this section, we'll explore how SQL Server Agent can help to reduce administrative overhead, how the components of SQL Server agent fit together, and the configuration tasks required prior to using.

Reducing Administration Overhead

SQL Server Agent allows you to reduce administrative overhead by giving you a job scheduling and alerting system that is tightly integrated into the database engine.

Jobs allow you to automate various tasks. Jobs can be created with multiple steps, and the order of step execution can be controlled. Nearly any operation can be scheduled to execute on a

SQL Server using a job. An operator can be notified on the success, failure, or completion of any job. The results of a job's execution are automatically logged.

Alerts monitor for error messages, performance conditions, or Windows Management Instrumentation (WMI) query responses from the SQL Server WMI provider. WMI queries can monitor for DDL and trace events similar to event notifications. An alert can notify operators, as well as execute a job to respond to the condition that caused it.

The SQL Server Agent Architecture

SQL Server Agent is implemented as a Windows Service that is installed with SQL Server. If the person installing SQL Server configures the SQL Server Agent service to start automatically, several extended stored procedures are enabled. Otherwise, the extended stored procedures are enabled when SQL Server Agent is first started.

There are several components that make up the majority of the SQL Server Agent service shown in Figure 11.1. We will begin by understanding what each component does, and how it interacts with the other components.

FIGURE 11.1
SQL Server Agent
architecture

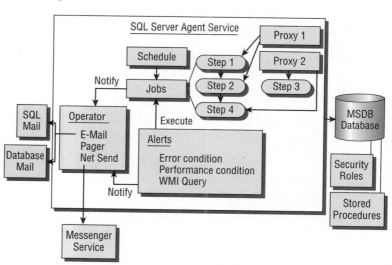

Jobs A *job* is a set of steps that perform administrative operations. Most jobs run on a schedule, but they can be started manually, either when the SQL Server is idle or when SQL Server Agent starts. A job can notify operators on success, on failure, or on completion. Job execution is logged in the msdb database every time the job is executed.

Job Steps A *job* usually has one or more steps to accomplish a particular task. You can control the flow of execution between steps based on success or failure. Several subsystems can be used to create job steps, including:

- Transact-SQL scripts

- Operating system commands

- Integration Services Package execution

- PowerShell scripts

- ActiveX scripts

- Replication operations

- Analysis Services commands and queries

Proxies A job usually executes as the SQL Server Agent Service Account. Proxies allow job steps to execute with an alternative set of credentials. Proxies can be specified per subsystem, and users are given permission to use a particular proxy. A proxy is based on a stored credential in SQL Server.

Schedules A job can be associated with one or more schedules. A schedule can be shared between multiple jobs. Schedules allow jobs to execute on a recurring basis, but they also allow execution:

- Once, at a specific date and time

- When SQL Server Agent starts

- When the CPU is considered idle

Operators An operator is a person or group of people to be notified. An operator can be notified on success, on failure, or on completion of a job. Operators can be contacted via email, pager email, or net send messages. Pager email addresses can be given a schedule when they are considered to be on duty. An operator uses the messenger service for net send messages.

Database Mail and SQL Mail Database Mail and SQL Mail are both mail subsystems that SQL Server Agent can use. Database Mail allows mail profiles to be configured without installing additional software on the SQL Server. Database Mail uses SMTP servers to send email messages to recipients. Database mail can also be used to send email using Transact-SQL.

> **NOTE**
>
> SQL Mail is a deprecated mail subsystem provided for backward compatibility. SQL Mail uses MAPI to send email messages. In order to use SQL Mail, a MAPI client, such as Outlook, must be installed and configured on the SQL Server.

Alerts An *alert* notifies operators about an event that occurs on SQL Server. An alert may also execute a job to respond to the situation. Alerts may be defined on:

- Errors written to the application log

- Performance conditions using SQL Server performance objects

- WMI query results

msdb Database The msdb database stores the SQL Server Agent's configuration, including job, alert, and operator definitions. Several database roles exist to control access to SQL Server Agent. SQL Server Agent stored procedures and views reside in the msdb database. Job execution history is also stored here.

MULTISERVER ADMINISTRATION ARCHITECTURE

SQL Server Agent can allow you to centrally define jobs on a master server, which are periodically downloaded and executed on target servers. After execution, history information is sent back to the master server from the target servers. A target server can have only one master server. In order to change to a different server, the target must be defected from the master server.

Target servers can also be configured to forward errors to the master server, so that centralized alerts can be defined. Event forwarding can be configured for all errors, unhandled errors, and errors above a certain severity level. Figure 11.2 shows the relationship between master and target servers.

FIGURE 11.2
Multiserver
Administration
architecture

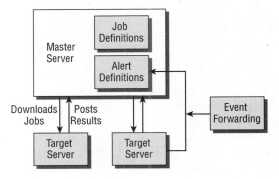

SQL SERVER AGENT SECURITY

In order to use SQL Server Agent, you must have appropriate permissions. Members of the sysadmin fixed server role are given full administrative control over the SQL Server Agent service. There are also several database roles in the msdb database that allow you to grant lesser permissions, as shown in Table 11.1.

TABLE 11.1   msdb Database Roles for SQL Server Agent

ROLE NAME	DESCRIPTION
SQLAgentUserRole	The least privileged role. Can only view jobs and schedules that they have created. Can only edit jobs that they own. Cannot delete job history, create operators or alerts.
SQLAgentReaderRole	Has all the permissions of SQLAgentUserRole, but can view all jobs, including multiserver jobs.
SQLAgentOperatorRole	Has all the permissions of SQLAgentReaderRole, but can view all jobs, alerts, and operators. Can view and delete job history. Can modify only jobs that they own.
sysadmin Server Role	Has full administrative access to SQL Server. In order to create an alert, multiserver job, or view error logs, you must be a member of this server role.

The SQL Agent roles easily allow permissions to be granted to create and work with jobs. With the exception of the sysadmin role, all of the above roles can only modify jobs that they own. To create alerts, operators, or multiserver jobs, you must be a member of the sysadmin fixed server role.

Configuring the SQL Agent Service

Several configuration tasks need to be completed before you use SQL Server Agent. You will want to determine an appropriate service account to run SQL Server Agent, configure mail, and configure the SQL Server Agent properties.

CONFIGURING THE SERVICE ACCOUNT

SQL Server Agent needs a service account to run. You can select a service account by using SQL Server Configuration Manager. There are several options available:

Local System account The local system account has unrestricted access to all local resources. While it has a large number of permissions on the local system, it cannot be used to access network resources. It is recommended that you avoid using the local system account to run SQL Server Agent.

Network Service account The network service account is authenticated to network resources as the computer account. Several services on the same machine may use this account, making it hard to control the rights for each individual service.

This Account The This Account option allows you to specify a domain or local user account to run the service. It is recommended that you use a domain user account so that access to network resources can be tightly controlled. It is recommended that the account chosen not be a member of the local administrators group, although this can be difficult if you want to configure multiserver administration. If the account is not a member of the local administrators group, the following operating system permissions need to be granted:

- Adjust memory quotas for a process
- Act as part of the operating system
- Bypass traverse checking
- Log on as a batch job
- Log on as a service
- Replace a process-level token

> **DON'T USE LOCALSERVICE!**
>
> The NT AUTHORITY\LocalService account is available for selection when choosing a service account, but it isn't supported to use with SQL Server Agent. LocalService uses a null login to access network resources.

The SQL Server Agent account requires sysadmin fixed server role membership regardless of the account type used. To use multiserver processing, the account also must be a member of the TargetServers database role in the msdb database. For more information on creating logins and managing permissions, see Chapter 8, "Managing User Security."

CONFIGURING MAIL

There are two subsystems that can be used to send email messages from SQL Server Agent: Database Mail and SQL Mail. Database Mail was introduced with SQL Server 2005 as a new way of sending email using standard SMTP servers. The alternative, SQL Mail, has been around for quite a bit longer than Database Mail, but it uses extended MAPI calls to send email messages. In order to use SQL Mail, you must have a MAPI client, such as Outlook installed on the SQL Server. Although SQL Mail is still supported in SQL Server 2008, it will be removed in a future version.

It is recommended that you use Database Mail for email functionality, because it offers greater flexibility, and several advantages over SQL Mail, including:

- No external software to install, or MAPI profiles to configure.

- Database Mail allows multiple SMTP Servers to be specified for redundancy.

- Database Mail runs as a separate process outside of SQL Server, providing better isolation.

- Database Mail supports multiple mail profiles, and accounts.

- Database Mail logs email activity to the msdb database, and keeps copies of messages and attachments so that you can easily audit usage.

- Database Mail delivers messages asynchronously using Service Broker technologies.

Before you can send email using SQL Server Agent, you must configure a database mail profile. A mail profile contains one or more accounts, in order of priority. If an email can't be sent using the first account, the second is tried, and so on. Mail profiles can be used by SQL Server Agent, or by database users with the appropriate permissions. A database user can send email using the sp_send_dbmail system stored procedure. A diagram showing the relationship between mail profiles and accounts is shown in Figure 11.3.

FIGURE 11.3
Database Mail architecture

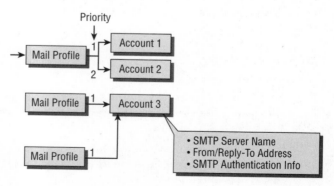

You can use the Database Mail Configuration Wizard in Management Studio to enable database mail and create a profile for use with SQL Server Agent. To configure Database Mail, follow these steps:

1. In SQL Server Management Studio, connect the Object Explorer to the server you want to administer.

2. Expand Management, right-click on Database Mail, and choose Configure Database Mail. An introductory screen appears.

3. Click Next to bypass the introductory screen. You are presented with the following options:

   ◆ Set up Database Mail by performing the following tasks:

      1. Create a new email profile and specify its SMTP accounts

      2. Specify profile security

      3. Configure system Parameters

   ◆ Manage Database Mail accounts and profiles

   ◆ Manage profile security

   ◆ View or change system parameters

4. Choose the first option, and click Next to set up Database Mail. You may see a dialog box stating that the database mail feature isn't enabled. To enable the feature, click Yes on the dialog box. The dialog shown in Figure 11.4 appears.

5. Fill in a Profile Name, and click the Add button to add a new account to the mail profile. The dialog shown in Figure 11.5 appears.

FIGURE 11.4
The New Profile dialog in the Database Mail Configuration Wizard

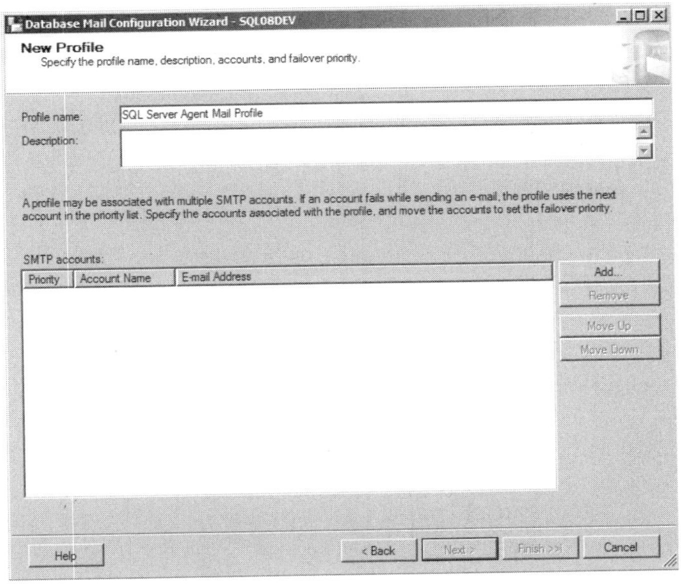

FIGURE 11.5
The New
Database Mail
Account dialog

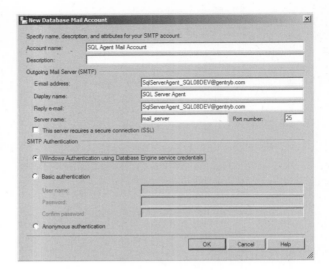

6. Fill out an Account Name, E-mail Address, Display Name, Reply E-mail, and Mail Server Name. Choose an authentication method for connecting to the mail server. Click OK.

7. If you would like to configure more mail accounts, repeat steps 5 and 6 for each one. When you're finished adding mail accounts, click Next. The Manage Profile Security dialog appears.

8. Configure access to the profile. A public or private profile can be used by SQL Server Agent. It is recommended that you create a private profile that only allows access to the SQL Agent Service Account, as shown in Figure 11.6.

FIGURE 11.6
The Configure Pro-
file Security dialog

9. Click Next. The Configure System Parameters dialog appears. Configure the following settings:

  ◆ Account Retry Attempts

  ◆ Account Retry Delay (seconds)

  ◆ Maximum File Size (Bytes)

  ◆ Prohibited Attachment File Extensions

  ◆ Database Mail Executable Minimum Lifetime (seconds)

  ◆ Logging Level

10. Click Finish to complete the wizard.

11. Right-click on the Database Mail icon and choose Send Test E-Mail. Choose a profile, input an email address, and click the Send button. If you don't receive the email, query the sysmail_event_log table in the msdb database for more information about the error.

Now that we've enabled database mail, and configured a mail profile, we need to configure SQL Server Agent to use this mail profile. This is accomplished by modifying the SQL Server Agent Properties. Follow these steps:

1. In Management Studio, right-click on the SQL Server Agent icon and select Properties.

2. Choose the Alert System page. The dialog shown in Figure 11.7 appears.

3. Check the Enable Mail Profile checkbox, and choose the mail profile you created in the previous exercise. Click OK.

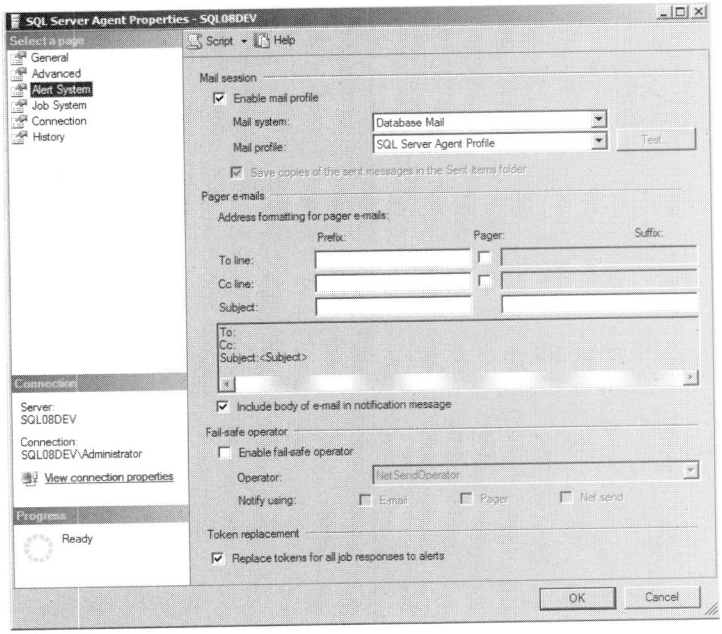

FIGURE 11.7
The SQL Server
Agent Alert System
Properties dialog

Creating Jobs

There are many situations where creating a job to perform a task is useful. Sometimes it's a recurring process that needs to run. Sometimes there might be a task that you need to perform, but not right now. SQL Server Agent jobs are versatile components that allow the automation of nearly any task. Jobs can have one or more steps that use a wide variety of job subsystems to perform operations. Each job step can execute as a different user, thanks to proxies. Each job can have one or more schedules that determine when it will execute.

You might have noticed a button at the top of many SQL Server Management Studio dialogs that looks like Figure 11.8.

FIGURE 11.8

The Script button in SQL Server Management dialogs

This button will generate a job with a single step that includes a Transact-SQL script to perform whatever operation that dialog would have done. For example, you might need to change a database recovery model, but you want to wait until after 5:00 P.M. You could do the modification using SQL Server Management Studio, but instead of clicking OK to perform the operation, you can use the Script button at the top of the screen to generate a job. If you do this, make sure to click Cancel to close the dialog, otherwise you will end up performing the operation now, as well as creating a job to perform the operation.

You can also script database objects to a job. For example, you might need to drop a login, but not until 5:00 P.M. today, when the day is over. In Management Studio, you could right-click the object and use the scripting options shown in Figure 11.9.

As you can see, embedded tightly within the Management Studio interface there are several ways of creating jobs.

FIGURE 11.9

The Script menu in Object Browser

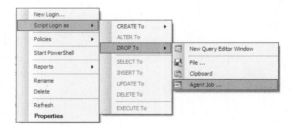

Creating Jobs

The most common way to create a job is to use SQL Server Management Studio. You will find existing jobs in the Object Explorer in a folder under the SQL Server Agent icon. The overall process of creating a job usually consists of 4 steps:

1. Create the job itself and give it a name and description.

2. Create one or more job steps to perform operations within the job.

3. Create or use an existing job schedule to specify when the job should execute.

4. Define which, if any, operator should be notified when the job succeeds, fails, or completes.

Jobs can be organized using categories. To manage job categories, right-click on the Jobs folder in Object Explorer, and choose Manage Job Categories. The dialog shown in Figure 11.10 allows you to create new categories, and modify existing job categories.

FIGURE 11.10
The Manage Job
Categories dialog

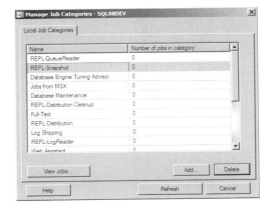

Creating a new job is a simple operation. To create a new job, follow these steps:

1. Expand the SQL Server Agent icon in Object Explorer. Right-click on the Jobs folder, and choose New Job. The dialog shown in Figure 11.11 appears.

2. Fill out the fields on the general page. A job name is required.

Technically, those are the only steps required to create a job; however, the created job doesn't do anything. Every job has one or more job steps, which are covered next.

FIGURE 11.11
The New Job dialog

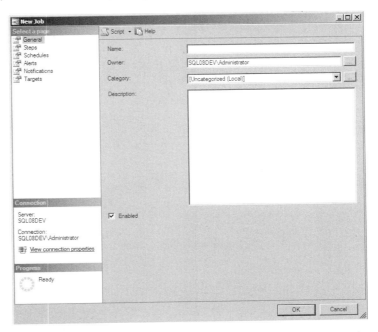

Creating Job Steps

There are many types of job steps that can be created. Different types of operations are made possible using step subsystems. Each subsystem allows different types of operations to occur. The following types of job steps can be created:

◆ Transact-SQL script

◆ Operating system commands

◆ Integration Services Package execution

◆ PowerShell script

◆ ActiveX script

◆ Analysis Services commands and queries

◆ Replication operations

Many of the jobs that you create will have a single step. Creating a job step is a simple process. The configuration necessarily depends on the subsystem that is used. You have different configuration options for a Transact-SQL script than an operating system command or an ActiveX script.

To create a new job step, follow this process:

1. Choose the Steps page on a new job, or the properties of an existing job.

2. Click the New button. The dialog shown in Figure 11.12 appears.

3. Enter a Name for the Job Step, choose the type of step, and fill out the required fields depending on the step type.

FIGURE 11.12
The New Job
Step dialog

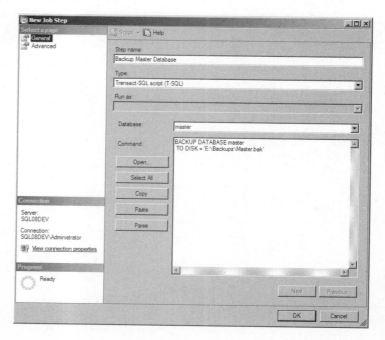

4. Select the Advanced page. A dialog similar to the dialog shown in Figure 11.13 appears. The exact layout will depend on the step type chosen.

FIGURE 11.13

The Job Step Advanced properties

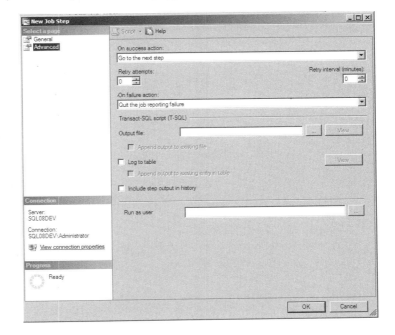

5. Configure the success and failure actions, output file options, and step history options as needed.

6. Click OK to create the job step.

Each job can have one or more steps, and each step can use any available subsystem. You can control a step's flow of execution based on success or failure of the step, as shown in Figure 11.13. A flowchart of a multistep job is shown in Figure 11.14.

FIGURE 11.14

Multistep job-flow chart

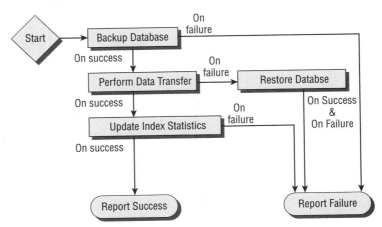

The configuration of the multistep job is shown in Figure 11.15. This was accomplished by modifying the success and failure action for each job step.

FIGURE 11.15
The Multistep
Job Configuration
dialog

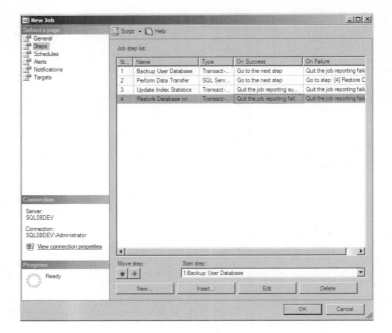

USING PROXIES

Each job step can be executed using different credentials. This is accomplished by using proxies. A *proxy* is associated with a credential that is created at the server level. The credential stores the username, password, and domain. A proxy is based on a single credential and can be used for one or more step subsystems. Figure 11.16 shows the relationship between job steps, proxies, and credentials.

FIGURE 11.16
Proxy architecture

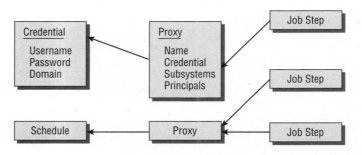

You can control who is allowed to use a proxy by changing the principals page. The following can be granted access to use a proxy.

◆ SQL Server login

◆ msdb database role

◆ Server role

All of the job subsystems except Transact-SQL script can use proxy accounts for execution. To designate one to do so, select the proxy in the Run As section of the Job Step properties. Transact-SQL scripts may choose a user to "run as" in the Advanced properties of the job step. If a proxy account isn't selected, a job step executes as the SQL Server Agent Service Account.

USING REPLACEMENT TOKENS IN JOB STEPS

You can use various replacement tokens in a job step. *Replacement tokens* allow substitution of various values within the body of a job step.

When you use a replacement token, you must use an escape macro to ensure that the output is allowed. A list of escape macros is shown in Table 11.2.

TABLE 11.2   Escape Macros for Job Step Tokens

MACRO NAME	DESCRIPTION
ESCAPE_NONE	Passes token value without escaping any characters
ESCAPE_SQUOTE	Replaces any ' characters with ''
ESCAPE_DQUOTE	Replaces any " characters with ""
ESCAPE_RBRACKET	Replaces any] characters with]]

Several replacement tokens are available to be used with these macros. The replacement tokens available are shown in Table 11.3.

TABLE 11.3   Job Step Tokens

TOKEN NAME	DESCRIPTION
(DATE)	Current Date (in YYYYMMDD format)
(INST)	Instance Name. For a default instance, this token is empty.
(JOBID)	SQL Server Agent Job ID
(MACH)	Computer Name

TABLE 11.3 Job Step Tokens *(CONTINUED)*

TOKEN NAME	DESCRIPTION
(MSSA)	SQL Server Agent Service Account Name.
(OSCMD)	Prefix for the program used to run CmdExec tasks.
(SQLDIR)	The SQL Server Installation Directory.
(STEPCT)	The number of times this step has been executed including retries..
(STEPID)	Job Step ID.
(SRVR)	Computer Name running SQL Server including instance name.
(TIME)	Current Time (in HHMMSS format).
(STRTTM)	The Time (in HHMMSS format) that the job began executing.
(STRTDT)	The Date (in YYYYMMDD format) that the job began executing.
(A-DBN)	Database Name when the job is run from an alert and token replacement for alerts is on.
(A-SVR)	Server Name when the job is run from an alert and token replacement for alerts is on.
(A-ERR)	Error Number when the job is run from an alert and token replacement for alerts is on.
(A-SEV)	Error severity when the job is run from an alert and token replacement for alerts is on.
(A-MSG)	Error Message Text when the job is run from an alert and token replacement for alerts is on.
(WMI(property))	WMI property value for when jobs are run in response to a WMI alert. WMI alerts are covered later in this chapter.

The syntax for using a job replacement token is

```
$(MACRO_NAME(TOKEN))
```

The macro/token syntax can be used for any of the job steps. If you attempt to use a token without a macro, you will receive an error.

> **NOTE**
>
> This behavior changed in SQL Server 2005 SP1, so you may encounter jobs that use tokens without macros that were created in SQL Server 2005 versions prior to SP1.

A script is available online in Microsoft Knowledge Base Article 915845 that can automatically update old jobs to contain replacement macros as required.

In order for token replacement to occur when alerts cause a job to execute, the "Replace tokens for all job responses to alerts" option needs to be turned on. You can find the option in SQL Server Agent properties on the Alert System page. For more information on using escape macros, refer to the topic "Using Tokens in Job Steps" in SQL Server Books Online.

Creating Schedules

Most jobs execute on a recurring schedule, but you can also create jobs that run:

◆ When SQL Server Agent starts

◆ When the CPU is considered idle

◆ Once, at a specific date and time

Schedules can be shared between multiple jobs, and they can be managed by right-clicking on the Jobs folder and choosing Manage Schedules. New schedules can be created, and existing schedules can be added from the Schedules page of the job. The New Job Schedule dialog is shown in Figure 11.17.

FIGURE 11.17
The New Job
Schedule dialog

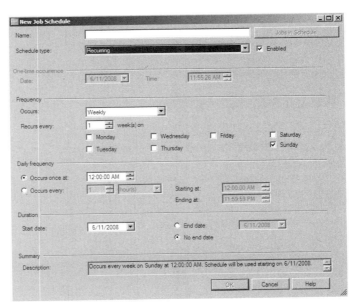

You can schedule a job to run when the CPU is considered idle, but you must define what an idle condition is before you use this type of schedule. You can define an idle CPU condition in the SQL Server Agent Properties, on the Advanced page, as shown in Figure 11.18.

FIGURE 11.18
The SQL Server
Agent Properties—
Advanced page

FIGURE 11.18
The SQL Server
Agent Properties—
Advanced page

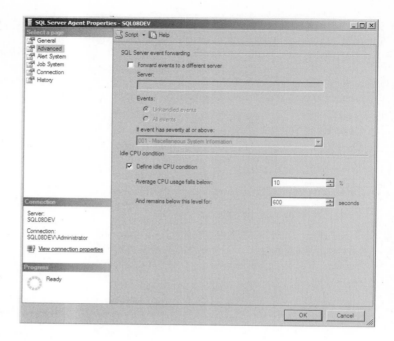

Executing Jobs

Jobs are generally executed according to schedules, although jobs can also be started manually, using SQL Server Management Studio, or the `sp_start_job` system stored procedure.

To start a job in Management Studio, right-click on the job, and choose Start Job at Step. If the job has more than one step, you will be prompted to choose the starting step, as shown in Figure 11.19.

FIGURE 11.19
The Start Job at
Step dialog

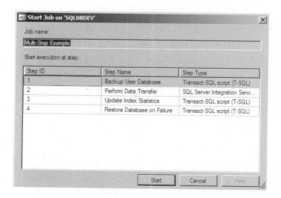

To start a job using Transact-SQL, use the `sp_start_job` system stored procedure, located in the `master` database. The syntax for `sp_start_job` is shown here:

```
sp_start_job
    {   [@job_name =] 'job_name'
      | [@job_id =] job_id }
    [ , [@server_name =] 'server_name']
    [ , [@step_name =] 'step_name']
```

Viewing Job History

Jobs store execution history in the msdb database. You can control the amount of history stored using the History page in the SQL Server Agent Properties dialog. To view the job execution history, right-click on the job, and choose View History. A dialog similar to the one shown in Figure 11.20 appears.

FIGURE 11.20

The Log
File Viewer

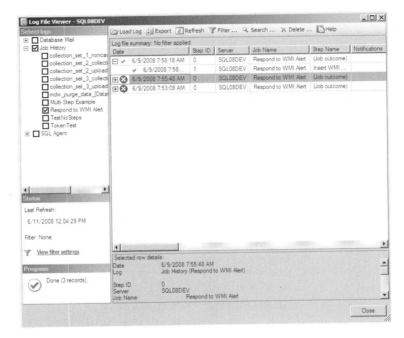

Each job execution is represented with a row in the Log History Viewer. Expand each row to view the step execution details.

Creating Alerts

Alerts are automated responses to events that occur on SQL Server. An alert can notify operators, as well as execute a job to respond to an event. An alert can be defined on:

◆ Error messages that are written to the event log

◆ SQL Server performance counter conditions

◆ WMI query results from DDL or trace events

Alerts that are defined on error messages can be filtered for an error number, error severity level, message text, and database. In order for an alert to be defined on an error message, the message must be written to the Windows application log.

An alert can also be defined based on the value of a SQL Server performance counter. Only the SQL Server performance counters are available. If you want to monitor the value of Windows performance counters, you must use the performance logs and alerts MMC snap-in. You can monitor for counter values rising above, becoming equal to, or falling below a certain value.

Alerts that are defined on a WMI query can only query for DDL operations and certain trace event classes. An alert that is defined on a WMI query is similar to an event notification. The alert will fire based on the event or event group queried. WMI property values may be retrieved by using job replacement tokens when enabled.

Monitoring the Event Log

SQL Server Agent constantly monitors the Windows application log for events on which an alert is defined. Many different error messages are written to the event log, but the following will always be written:

◆ Errors with a severity level of 19 or higher

◆ Any RAISERROR statement invoked using WITH LOG

◆ Any other error message that is marked as "always logged"

You can retrieve a list of error messages that are written to the event log by executing the following query:

```
SELECT * FROM sys.messages
 WHERE is_event_logged = 1;
```

You can also modify an existing error message so that it is always written to the event log by using the sp_altermessage system stored procedure.

To create an alert that monitors the Windows application log, follow these steps:

1. Expand SQL Server Agent in Object Explorer.

2. Right-click on the Alerts folder and select New Alert. The dialog shown in Figure 11.21 appears.

FIGURE 11.21
The New
Alert dialog

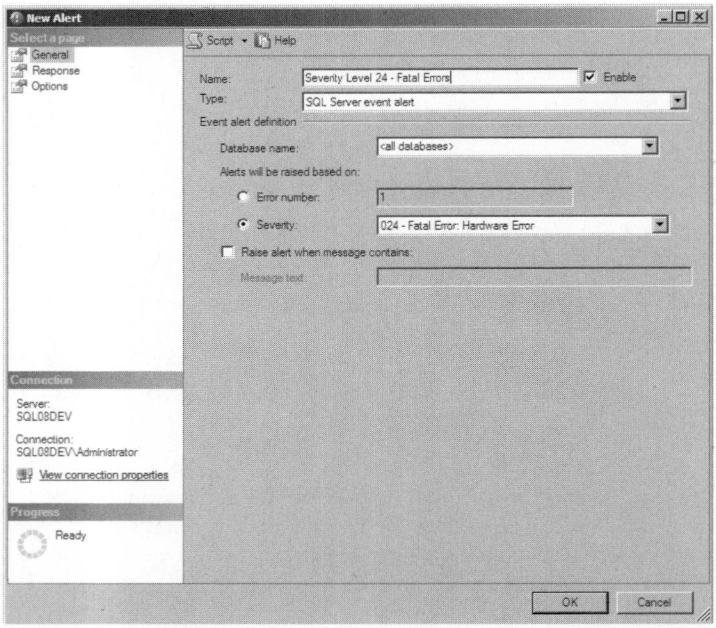

3. Choose the Response page. The dialog shown in Figure 11.22 appears.

FIGURE 11.22

The Alert
Response page

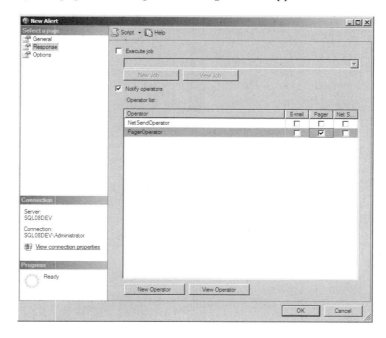

4. Select a job to execute in response to the alert, and select the operators to be notified when the alert is fired.

5. Choose the Options page. The dialog shown in Figure 11.23 appears.

FIGURE 11.23

The Alert
Options page

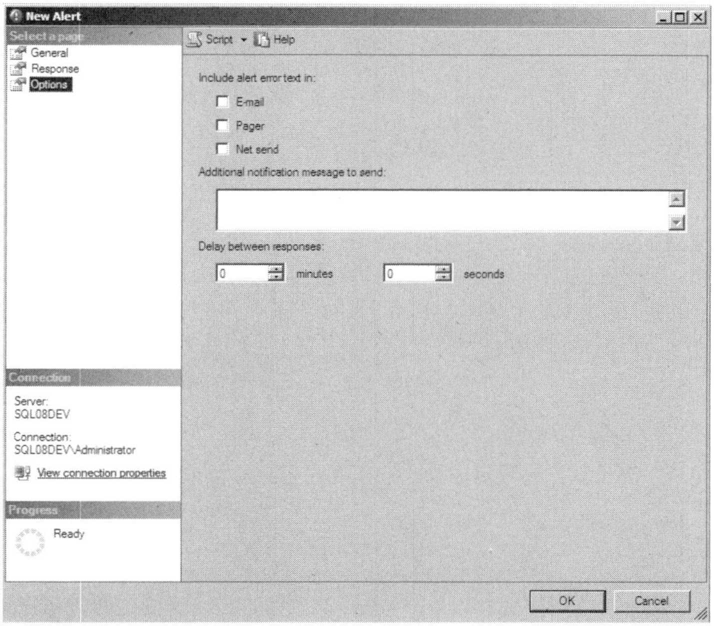

6. If the error message text should be included in different types of notifications, select the appropriate checkboxes. Type any additional message text to send with the alert, and configure the delay between responses.

7. Click OK to create the alert.

Responding to Performance Alerts

An alert can also be defined on performance conditions. You can monitor all of the SQL Server performance objects and counters. Windows performance counters aren't supported using SQL Server Agent, but they can be monitored using the Performance Logs & Alerts console.

Configuring a performance alert is similar to configuring an alert defined on an error condition. An alert defined on a performance condition is shown in Figure 11.24.

FIGURE 11.24
An alert defined on a performance condition

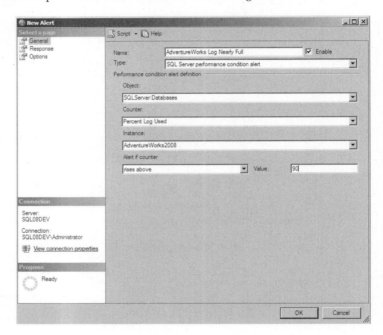

Understanding WMI Alerts

Alerts can be based on the results of a WMI query, although the classes available for query are limited to those exposed by the WMI Provider for Server Events. DDL and trace event and event groups can be queried using WMI query syntax, similar to SQL:

```
SELECT event_property, ...n | *
  FROM event_class
  WHERE filter_clause
```

An alert created using WMI queries is similar to an event notification. You use the same class names as when creating event notifications. The available properties depend on the event queried. For information about available event classes, and available properties, refer to `C:\Program Files\Microsoft SQL Server\100\Tools\Binn\schemas\sqlserver\2006\11\events\events.xsd`. This is an XML schema file that defines the different events and properties that can be retrieved. Many of the complex types defined in this file can be queried, and the elements of that type can be used as columns and filters in the WMI queries.

Most WMI alerts will execute a job in response to the alert. The WMI token can be used inside of job steps along with appropriate escape macros to retrieve information about the event. In order for the event information to be available, you must enable token replacement for job responses to alerts. You can access this setting using the SQL Server Agent properties dialog, as shown previously in the chapter, in Figure 11.7.

An example of using a WMI event query is to create an alert that executes a job in response to all events that work with logins on a server. This job can use any of the tokens within job steps to retrieve information about the event that occurred. The WMI query would be

```
SELECT * FROM DDL_LOGIN_EVENTS
```

The information about the login event could then be used within a job step. For a login event, properties such as LoginName, ServerName, and CommandText could be replaced in the alert text. For example, a macro such as the following could be used in a job to retrieve the command text used to perform the login event:

```
$(ESCAPE_NONE(WMI(CommandText)))
```

Replacement tokens can be used in any of the job step types. Again, remember to enable token replacement for all job responses to alerts in SQL Server Agent properties.

Creating Operators

An operator is notified in response to a job or alert. A single operator can be notified for each response type for a job. For an alert, multiple operators can be notified.

Operator Types

An operator can contact you using any of three ways:

- Email
- Pager
- Net Send

In order to use email or pager messages, you must configure and specify a database mail profile. For more information on how to do this, refer to the Configuring Database Mail section earlier in the chapter.

Pager messages are actually emails that should be sent to an email to pager gateway. The main difference between pager messages and email messages is that an operator can be given a pager duty schedule. SQL Server Agent will look to see who is on duty before sending out a response to an alert via pager.

SQL Server Agent can also send network messages using the net send command and the messenger service. In order to send and receive network messages, the messenger service must be started on the server, as well as any clients that want to receive notifications through network messages.

Configuring Operators

Configuring an operator is a simple task. To create a new operator using SQL Server Agent, follow these steps:

1. Expand SQL Server Agent in Object Explorer.

2. Right-click on the Operators folder and choose New Operator. The dialog shown in Figure 11.25 appears.

FIGURE 11.25
The New Operator dialog

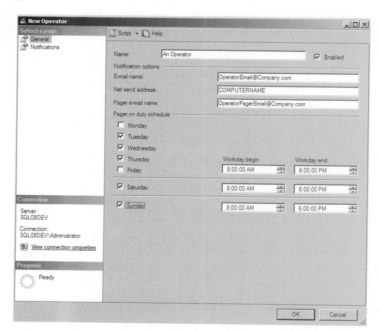

3. Enter contact information for the operator, and set a pager schedule if required.

4. Click OK to create the operator.

When configuring SQL Server Agent to use operators, it's important to specify a fail-safe operator. A fail-safe operator is contacted when an error occurs during other responses, or when nobody is on duty to be contacted. In order to specify a fail-safe operator, you must first create an operator. Once you've configured an operator, you can access the SQL Server Agent Properties, on the Alert System page, as shown in Figure 11.26, to specify which operator should be used for fail-safe operations.

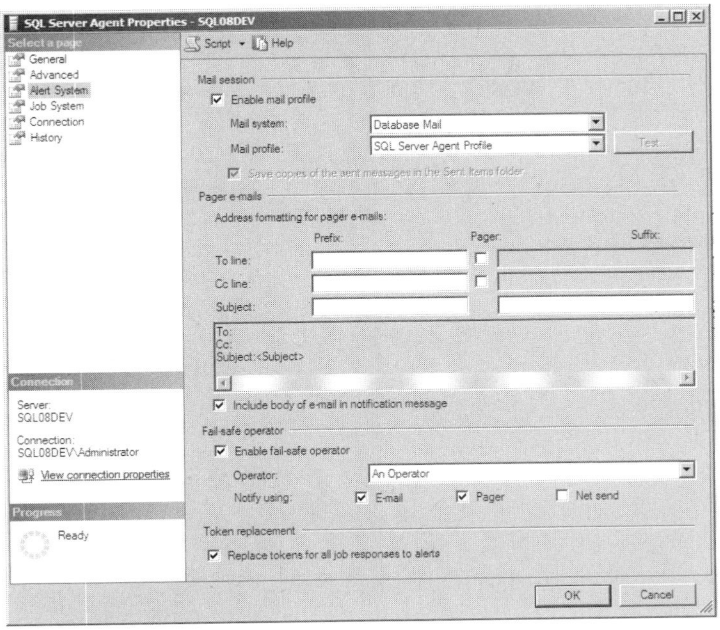

FIGURE 11.26
The SQL Server
Agent fail-safe
operator

Associating Operators with Jobs and Alerts

An operator is notified in response to an alert, or in response to a job succeeding, failing, or completing. You can easily configure operator response to alerts by modifying the properties of the operator and using the Responses page, as shown in Figure 11.27.

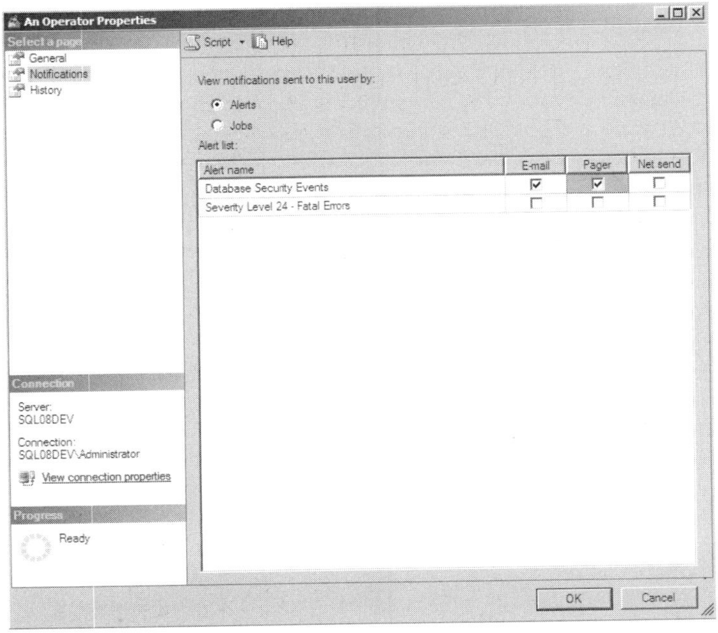

FIGURE 11.27
Configuring
the operator
notifications

If you choose the Jobs button in Figure 11.27, you can view which jobs will notify the operator, but you can't modify job notifications. In order to change who is notified by a job, you must modify the job properties. Only one operator can be notified per notification method on a job, as shown in Figure 11.28.

FIGURE 11.28
Configuring the operator notifications for jobs

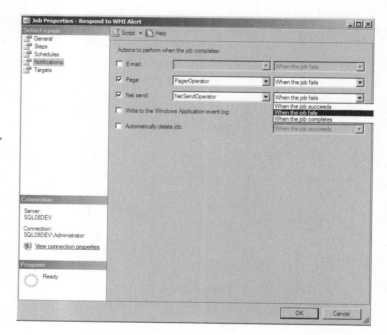

Scripting the SQL Agent

SQL Server Agent can be controlled by using several system stored procedures in the msdb database. These stored procedures are used by SQL Server Management Studio to create and manipulate jobs, alerts, and operators.

Understanding the SQL Agent System Stored Procedures

There are several stored procedures that must be used to create a job, alert, or operator via Transact-SQL. Table 11.4 shows some of the stored procedures that can be used.

TABLE 11.4   SQL Server Agent Stored Procedures

STORED PROCEDURE	DESCRIPTION
sp_add_job	Creates a new job. Configures job notification options.
sp_add_job_step	Creates a new job step using any of the available subsystems.
sp_update_job	Updates various properties of a job. Should be called after a step is created to specify a starting step for the job.

TABLE 11.4 SQL Server Agent Stored Procedure *(CONTINUED)*

STORED PROCEDURE	DESCRIPTION
sp_add_job_server	Used to specify which servers the job will run on. In multiserver administration environments, a job may run on multiple servers.
sp_add_category	Adds a job category.
sp_add_alert	Adds an alert for any of the alert types.
sp_add_operator	Adds an operator for any of the operator types.

Scripting Existing Jobs

You can script an existing job, alert, or operator by right-clicking on the object and using the script options. An example of a scripted job is shown in Listing 11.1.

LISTING 11.1 Script to Create a Job to Back Up the master Database

```
USE [msdb];
GO

BEGIN TRANSACTION
DECLARE @ReturnCode INT;
SELECT @ReturnCode = 0;

IF NOT EXISTS (SELECT name FROM msdb.dbo.syscategories WHERE name=N'[Uncategorized
(Local)]' AND category_class=1)
BEGIN
  EXEC @ReturnCode = msdb.dbo.sp_add_category @class=N'JOB',      @type=N'LOCAL', @
name=N'[Uncategorized (Local)]';
  IF (@@ERROR <> 0 OR @ReturnCode <> 0) GOTO QuitWithRollback
END

DECLARE @jobId BINARY(16)
EXEC @ReturnCode =  msdb.dbo.sp_add_job
            @job_name=N'Backup Master Database',
            @enabled=1,
            @notify_level_eventlog=0,
            @notify_level_email=0,
            @notify_level_netsend=0,
            @notify_level_page=0,
            @delete_level=0,
            @description=N'No description available.',
            @category_name=N'[Uncategorized (Local)]',
            @owner_login_name=N'SQL08DEV\Administrator',
            @job_id = @jobId OUTPUT;
```

```
    IF (@@ERROR <> 0 OR @ReturnCode <> 0) GOTO QuitWithRollback

    EXEC @ReturnCode = msdb.dbo.sp_add_jobstep @job_id=@jobId, @step_name=N'Backup
Master',
                @step_id=1,
                @cmdexec_success_code=0,
                @on_success_action=1,
                @on_success_step_id=0,
                @on_fail_action=2,
                @on_fail_step_id=0,
                @retry_attempts=0,
                @retry_interval=0,
                @os_run_priority=0, @subsystem=N'TSQL',
                @command=N'BACKUP DATABASE Master
  TO DISK = ''E:\Backups\Master.bak''',
                @database_name=N'master',
                @flags=0;
IF (@@ERROR <> 0 OR @ReturnCode <> 0) GOTO QuitWithRollback
 EXEC @ReturnCode = msdb.dbo.sp_update_job @job_id = @jobId, @start_step_id = 1;
IF (@@ERROR <> 0 OR @ReturnCode <> 0) GOTO QuitWithRollback
EXEC @ReturnCode = msdb.dbo.sp_add_jobschedule @job_id=@jobId,
                @name=N'EveryWeek',
                @enabled=0,
                @freq_type=8,
                @freq_interval=1,
                @freq_subday_type=1,
                @freq_subday_interval=0,
                @freq_relative_interval=0,
                @freq_recurrence_factor=1,
                @active_start_date=20080612,
                @active_end_date=99991231,
                @active_start_time=0,
                @active_end_time=235959,
                @schedule_uid=N'c14c209d-47df-4316-9cfe-1cef9e4e4697';
IF (@@ERROR <> 0 OR @ReturnCode <> 0) GOTO QuitWithRollback
EXEC @ReturnCode = msdb.dbo.sp_add_jobserver @job_id = @jobId, @server_name =
N'(local)';
IF (@@ERROR <> 0 OR @ReturnCode <> 0) GOTO QuitWithRollback
COMMIT TRANSACTION
GOTO EndSave
QuitWithRollback:
    IF (@@TRANCOUNT > 0) ROLLBACK TRANSACTION
EndSave:

    GO
```

> ## WHY CAN'T I RUN THIS CODE?
>
> If you try to execute the SQL code, you will probably get the following error message:
>
> ```
> Msg 515, Level 16, State 2, Procedure sp_add_job, Line 137
> Cannot insert the value NULL into column 'owner_sid', table 'msdb.dbo.
> sysjobs'; column does not allow nulls. INSERT fails.
> The statement has been terminated.
> This message appears because the scripted output includes a machine name in
> the @owner_login_name parameter. When you script the steps, you will replace
> the machine name with a valid owner.
> ```

The Bottom Line

Configure Database Mail for email notification.　Database Mail allows us to send email from SQL Server Agent and stored procedures. Database Mail uses SMTP servers, where SQL Mail uses extended MAPI calls.

Master It　If you're having problems sending email messages using SQL Server Agent, which table can you query to retrieve detailed information about the error messages?

Create jobs to automate routine tasks.　Jobs allow us to automate routine tasks using the many available step subsystems.

Master It　Imagine you've created a job, and you've tested its execution. The job executes periodically, until one day it stops executing. This occurs right after a reboot of the server? What's the most likely problem?

Create Alerts to detect and respond to various situations.　Alerts can respond to performance conditions, error messages, and WMI events, by executing jobs and notifying operators.

Master It　If you're executing a job in response to an alert that uses replacement tokens, and the replacement tokens aren't being populated properly, what's the first thing you should check?

Chapter 12

Data Availability and Distribution

What's the use of having a database if you can't access your data when you need it? In today's world of mission-critical database applications and 24/7 businesses requiring minimum downtime, the job of DBA is more challenging than ever before. You not only have to create a great database application, you also have to make sure that it is up and available when anyone needs it.

The cousin to availability is data distribution. Sometimes the issue is not as much about having constant uptime as it is the distribution of data to the consumer who needs it. In some cases, the same solutions as those used for availability are appropriate. In others, you will need new solutions to solve the data-distribution problem. Some solutions are software-based and others are hardware-based. Some require constant babysitting while others are self-managing. There is no single solution that is best for every scenario. If there were, all of the others would disappear. Your job as a database professional is to know what options are available and be able to target the best option for any situation. Therefore, in this chapter you will learn about the primary solutions available to you.

In this chapter, you'll learn to:

- ◆ Identify the elements and benefits of RAID and clustering
- ◆ Implement transaction log shipping
- ◆ Implement database mirroring
- ◆ Implement SQL Server replication

Overview of SQL Server Availability and Distribution Options

We should begin by defining some terms. What exactly are availability and distribution? Why are these concepts important in a production database environment? The answers to these questions will set the stage for the remainder of our discussion on these topics.

Availability   *Availability* is the characteristic of a database that relates to its uptime. Losing access to a database can cause significant business problems. Without the database, many business processes cannot continue. An availability solution focuses on the steps necessary to minimize downtime. This might include providing for necessary hardware redundancy as well as data redundancy to guarantee that data systems are available when client applications need them.

Distribution   *Data distribution* is the process of placing data geographically based on the data needs of the client applications or the performance requirements of the applications. Distributing data is one way to offload activity from transactional data stores or reduce bandwidth requirements when many applications are interacting with data in a central location.

Data distribution is similar to availability in one respect. Like availability, distribution can also involve data redundancy and, therefore, requires some mechanism to maintain data synchronization.

Hardware Considerations

Any availability solution must provide for both hardware availability and data availability. One is not a replacement for the other any more than a database backup is a replacement for an effective availability strategy. A complete discussion of hardware strategies is beyond the scope of this book, but you should consider hardware-based availability as an important component of any availability architecture. Here are a few of the things you should consider.

REDUNDANT ARRAY OF INDEPENDENT DISKS (RAID)

Also called Redundant Array of Inexpensive Disks (the original term for the technology), RAID is a technique where an operating system or hardware I/O system uses multiple hard drives to distribute data across multiple disks in an effort to provide fault tolerance and/or performance benefits. An administrator can employ various RAID strategies. The following are the most common.

RAID 0: Stripe Set without Parity   This option is primarily intended to optimize performance. In this scenario, the RAID controller spreads that data stream across two or more physical disks. The objective is to improve performance by placing data on multiple disks simultaneously, thereby eliminating the potential I/O bottleneck of writing to a single physical disk. This option provides no fault tolerance because a single disk failure destroys the entire array and there is no parity information stored on the other disks that you can use to regenerate the lost drive.

RAID 1: Mirrored Set   Level 1 provides fault tolerance by duplicating all data writes to a mirror disk. If the data device is lost, the mirror provides a copy of the lost data and thereby minimizes downtime. A good RAID controller will use both disks for read operations, therefore increasing the performance for read operations; however, doing this adversely affects write operations due to the increased write activity.

RAID 5: Striped Set with Parity   This solution stripes data access across three or more physical disks, similar to the RAID 0 solution. Unlike RAID 0, however, the controller also writes distributed parity data across the stripe set so that the loss of a drive would not result in the loss of the database. The controller can use the parity information to respond to requests until an administrator is able to regenerate a new disk based on the parity data. In this configuration, the array is still vulnerable to the loss of a second drive. This solution also can adversely affect write performance because of the extra I/O required to calculate and write the parity data, although this can be offset somewhat by the distribution of data across multiple physical disks.

You can also combine these levels to provide options that are more complex.

- RAID 01 (0 + 1): Mirror of Striped Sets

- RAID 10 (1 + 0): Striped Mirror Sets

- RAID 50 (5 + 0): Parity Striped Mirror Sets

There are other RAID options, but these are the most common. Always remember that the goal is to ensure adequate availability without compromising performance beyond acceptable levels. Any fault tolerance always comes at a cost. The administrator's job is to find the right balance.

ALL PARITY IS NOT CREATED EQUAL

Although the Windows operating system supports various software-based RAID solutions, they are not reasonable performance alternatives to a hardware-based solution. A variety of vendors support RAID at the hardware level. Do your research and find the vendor that offers a solution that provides the balance of cost, features, and manageability that makes sense for your environment.

CLUSTERING

While RAID provides fault tolerance from disk failure, it provides no protection against other faults such as memory, CPU, or I/O controller failures. By contrast, clustering can provide effective protection from hardware failures other than disk failures. As with RAID, many different configuration options are available for clustering. The features and benefits of a particular implementation become selling points for the hardware or software vendor that provides the solution.

An in-depth discussion of clustering technology is beyond our scope, but you should be aware of the clustering options that Windows supports as well as how SQL Server behaves on those clusters.

In SQL Server terminology, the term "cluster" refers to a failover cluster only. This means that SQL Server cannot use the cluster for load-balancing-only redundancy. The general approach to setting this up is creating a two-node active/passive cluster. This requires two servers connected to a single array of disks. Clients direct activity to a "virtual" address, which represents the cluster rather than any individual server in the cluster. Only one of the servers will actively respond to requests. The other server, which is the passive node, monitors the "heartbeat" of the active node so that it can detect if the active node fails to respond. This would trigger an automatic failover, redirecting activity to the second node. The benefits of failover clustering include the following.

- Automatic detection and failover

- Ability to perform manual failover

- Transparency to the client of failover redirection

There are constraints when using clustering, however. You must license at least the Standard edition of SQL Server, which supports two-node clusters. The Enterprise edition allows additional nodes as configured by the operating system. Additionally, you must work within the following limitations.

- Clustering operates at the server level of scope. You cannot failover an individual database.

- There is no protection against disk failure. You should continue to use RAID for disk fault tolerance.

- The cluster performs no load balancing. Only the active node can be queried.

- The cluster requires signed hardware capable of working with the Windows version that you are targeting.

When clustering in Windows Server 2008, there are a few new features that can benefit SQL Server. If using the Enterprise versions of Windows and SQL Server, you can support up to 16 nodes in your cluster. In addition, Windows Server 2008 removes the requirement that all cluster nodes reside in the same subnet, thereby opening the door to increased geographical distribution of cluster nodes. In a fully geographically dispersed architecture, nodes complete with arrays can be configured in different geographical locations, thereby creating full server redundancy including array redundancy.

SQL Server Features

In addition to the hardware-based feature options previously described, there are a variety of SQL Server-specific availability/distribution features that a database administrator can include in an enterprise architecture. We will introduce these concepts here, and then spend the remainder of this chapter describing their use in detail.

DATABASE LOG SHIPPING

The goal of *database log shipping* is to create a warm standby server that you can promote to a primary server upon server failure. As a warm standby, it is not completely current, but rather is only current to the last transaction log that you have shipped and restored to the server. You can use the warm standby for reporting purposes, but you cannot make any data modification to the server. It is read-only.

Configuring a log shipping model requires you to perform initial synchronization of the two servers by taking a full database backup on the master server and restoring it on the target server. Following the synchronization, you can set up a schedule that will take periodic transaction log backups on the master server and restore them using the STANDBY switch on the target server. Failing over to the standby server requires restoring an orphaned log and then executing some stored procedures to switch server roles for the standby server.

One advantage of the log shipping model is that you can configure multiple target servers. Because each server can be used for reporting purposes, this can be an effective technique for both availability and distribution of data. This is also an easy solution to configure and maintain.

The primary disadvantage is the latency between the time that the transaction commits on the master server and the time when the master ships and restores the log to the target server(s). There is also the potential of some data loss. This potential increases when the latency increases. When the log shipping model is used as an availability solution, the manual process of failing over the target to a master server can also cause problems with the uptime of the server functionality, meaning that the server may be unavailable to users until it is manually failed over.

DATABASE MIRRORING

Unlike database log shipping, the *database mirroring* model applies transactions to the mirror server as soon as they are committed on the principal server. Database mirroring can provide an automatic failover feature like clustering does, but operates at the database level, so individual databases can be mirrored to separate servers for scalability purposes. Database mirroring also differs from clustering in that no special hardware is required.

The process of configuring database mirroring begins like log shipping. You take a backup of the principal server and restore it to the mirror target. However, instead of configuring the auto-restore of transaction log backups, database mirroring requires you to configure communication endpoints, which the service will use to commit transactions on the mirror after committing the transaction on the client.

Database mirroring can operate either synchronously or asynchronously. High-safety mode supports *synchronous* operations. The system minimizes the possibility of lost data by using a two-phase commit process. The transaction does not commit fully until the transaction commits on both servers. This approach favors data protection at the cost of performance.

Alternatively, database mirroring also supports a high-performance mode, which uses *asynchronous* commits. Transactions commit on the principal server first, and then are committed asynchronously on the mirror. The principal server does not have to wait for the mirror server to commit before committing the transaction, therefore improving the response of the principal server. This approach enables better performance but can result in some data loss.

If you want to support automatic failover, you must use a high-security mode and include a witness server in the model. A *witness server* is responsible for monitoring the activity between the partner servers in the mirror model and performing the automatic failover in the case of a fault on the principal server. If the client makes the connection using the SQL Native client, this scenario also supports transparent client redirection, which allows the client to be ignorant of the actual server that responds to its request.

There are numerous advantages to using database mirroring. When running in a high-safety mode, you can take advantage of automatic failover. You can also configure transport security and sever authentication. When using the Enterprise edition of SQL Server 2008, you get page-level fault protection: if a single database corrupts on either the principal or the mirror, the partner server can copy the page to the other server to eliminate the corruption.

The primary disadvantage of database mirroring is the overhead of running in a high-safety mode. There is also an increased hardware requirement to support witnessing, which is necessary for automatic failover. Because you can only configure one mirror for each database and the mirror database cannot be queried, this is not an effective distribution strategy, although you can combine database mirroring with log shipping or replication to provide that capability if necessary.

REPLICATION

Replication is the oldest of these techniques. The purpose of replication is to copy data or transactions from one server to another. While this can be a very effective distribution technique, there is no support for failover or transparent client redirection, so it is a marginal availability solution in most cases. SQL Server 2008 supports three major varieties of replication.

Snapshot Replication   This approach focuses on copying data from one database to another. Entire data pages are copied from the publisher to the subscriber, meaning that the data is aging from the time of the initial copy to that of each subsequent copy. While you can configure the frequency of replication, this approach works best when you have small volumes of data that are either nonvolatile or tolerate data latency.

Transactional Replication   This is the standard replication model. In this approach, the publishing server stores transactions in its transaction log for replication. Periodically, a log reader service gathers the transactions and sends them to a distribution server that then executes the transactions on each of the subscribing databases. This process can be scheduled to occur at regular intervals or can be configured to execute whenever transactions commit on the publishing server.

Merge Replication   This model values data independence over consistency. Unlike snapshot and transactional models that require the subscribing databases to be treated as read-only, the merge replication model permits changes to the subscribing servers with the ability to merge the changes made in the subscriber with the data on the publishing server. Although this increases the independence of the servers in the replication model, it also increases the probability of data synchronization problems between the publisher and subscriber databases.

There are variations on each of these techniques, including the use of a two-phase commit on the subscriber and numerous topologies such as the central publisher or central subscriber. We will discuss all of these in more detail later in this chapter.

SQL SERVER INTEGRATION SERVICES

As data-distribution techniques go, nothing in SQL Server quite approaches the usefulness of SQL Server Integration Services (SSIS). This successor to the Data Transformation Services (DTS) introduced in SQL Server 7.0 provides programmatic distribution and transformation of data through .NET executables. These executables are extremely portable and versatile and provide an excellent solution for both one-off and recurring data-distribution requirements.

We could write a book about nothing but SSIS (maybe someday we will), as it is much more expansive a topic than we have room to include in this discussion. Because SSIS is not core to the SQL 2008 Data Engine, we have not included it in this book, but it is definitely worth your time to look closer at this remarkable tool.

Now that you have a feel for the different approaches to distribution and availability supported in SQL Server, it is time to look more closely at each option and see how you configure and support each solution. We will begin the discussion with database log shipping.

Real World Scenario

TIME FOR A FIRE DRILL

Testing your availability strategy from time to time is critical. It is not uncommon to talk to an IT professional who will explain with great pride the many layers of protection and availability they have in place, but if you ask them when they last tested their strategy, they suddenly go silent.

This issue really hit home recently for one client who had made significant investments in their availability strategy, which included a sophisticated RAID solution. They had also invested in an offsite backup service to ensure that their data would never be compromised. However, they had obviously not tested their recovery strategy recently.

They lost a drive. This should not have been a significant problem because they were protected with a RAID array. However, there was a problem regenerating the drive from the parity bits, and as a result the entire array was lost. Because they did not have the hardware on hand to recover immediately, they had downtime trying to get the hardware in place.

Then it was time to restore from a backup. This is when they realized there were no onsite backups. The backups were all being sent offsite to a vault, and it would cost the client money to retrieve them. Eventually, they were able to get up and running, but in the meantime they had an entire team that could do no work at all, adding to the cost of the event.

Did they do anything wrong? Not really. These are things that could happen to any company. What went wrong was they had spent plenty of time and resources planning for the failure, but little effort planning for the recovery. Availability and uptime are critical to any business. If you don't have a fire drill once in a while, you will never know if the plan is effective. The same is true for an availability strategy. You don't want to find out that the strategy is flawed when it is too late.

Database Log Shipping

The concept of log shipping is very simple. After performing an initial synchronization between a master server and a target server, you can regularly schedule transaction log backups on the master server and ship them directly to the target server for restoration. This allows for a warm standby server. If there is a failure on the target server, you need only restore the final orphaned log from the master to the target and you can be up and running quickly. Log shipping lets you work with multiple target servers and also allows the target standby server to act in a read-only reporting role for scaling out the database solution. Still another good thing about log shipping is its wide support in all server editions of SQL Server, including the Workgroup, Standard, and Enterprise editions.

On the downside, log shipping has no manual failover process. It also requires an entire set of hardware for the target, therefore potentially increasing costs and maintenance time. Any log shipping solution would have to consider these issues.

You can configure log shipping either through the SQL Server Management Studio (SSMS) graphical interface or through Transact-SQL (TSQL) code. Either approach can give you the same result. You can also configure log shipping through SSMS and have the interface gener-ate a script for you that will repeat the functionality if you ever need to go through the process again. We will first look at the process of setting up log shipping through SSMS and then look at the TSQL code that would perform the same operation.

Configuring Log Shipping

Configuring log shipping is a simple process. You can easily manage the process through SSMS. The basic steps are as follows:

1. Configure the primary and target servers to support transaction log backups.

2. Take a full database backup on the primary server.

3. Restore the full database backup on the target server with NORECOVERY or STANDBY options selected.

4. Configure the log shipping scenario in SSMS, which will schedule the backups and log shipping through jobs.

5. Optionally configure a monitor server to record log shipping events and errors.

In this section, we will look at each of these steps in more detail. We will begin by perform-ing the server and database configuration.

CONFIGURING THE SERVERS AND DATABASES

The master or primary database is your production environment. You will do the initial con-figuration of each server individually on that server, but you will perform all configurations for the actual log shipping behavior from SSMS on the primary server. Initially, you must configure the primary database to support transaction log backups by setting the recovery interval to Full or Bulk-Logged. (Simple recovery performs a truncation of the transaction log with each check-point and prevents the transaction log backups from taking place.) You will configure the target database using this same setting.

BACKUP CONFIGURATION

We assume that you have already read Chapter 9, "Data Recovery." That chapter covers the backup and recovery process in detail, including recovery models, so we will not review that information here. If you do not have experience performing backup and restore operations, we recommend that you refer to Chapter 9 as you read this section on log shipping.

After setting the recovery model on the primary database as described, the next step is to perform a full database backup of the primary database. You must then restore this backup on the secondary server to prepare that server for the log shipping configuration. Before restor-ing the database, you will need to determine if you want the target database to be queryable. You have two choices.

Using the NORECOVERY Option   Restoring the database with this option allows you to restore additional transaction logs to the database but does not allow client applications to query the database. This is the most efficient approach to log shipping because the database does not have to roll back any uncommitted transactions after loading the database backup or any additional transaction log backups. Using the NORECOVERY option means you cannot use the server for any reporting, and it will play no role in a data-distribution model. It is strictly for availability only.

Using the STANDBY Option   When you restore the database with this option, the server rolls back any uncommitted transactions and places them into an "undo" file. These are then saved so that they can be recommitted to the database before restoring any additional transaction log backups. Because all transactions are in a consistent state after rolling back the uncommitted transactions, the database is available for reporting and querying purposes, making it a potential player in a data-distribution strategy. This higher-overhead approach requires additional resources when the log restoration process takes place.

As an additional option, you can also configure a monitor server. If you want to use a separate monitor server, you must configure it when you set up log shipping, as you will not be able to go back and add it later without dropping the entire log shipping configuration and starting over. The monitor server tracks all log shipping activities through SQL jobs and alerts. If you plan to have multiple log shipping implementations that you must maintain, a monitor server conveniently provides centralized access to all log shipping data.

While either the primary or target server can act as the monitor, we recommend that you use a separate server for monitoring so that any hardware failure of the other two servers will not affect your ability to get information.

DOWNLOADING THE PUBS DATABASE

To reduce complexity, the examples that we will use of log shipping and database mirroring will use the pubs sample database provided by Microsoft. You should be able to find this download at http://www.microsoft.com/downloads. Search for "Northwind and Pubs Sample Databases for SQL Server 2000." Even though the databases are intended for SQL Server 2000, they will install just fine in SQL Server 2008. You will be downloading an .MSI file. Executing the .MSI will create a folder with the installation scripts at C:\ SQL Server 2000 Sample Databases. Run the instpubs. sql script on your SQL 2008 instance to create the pubs database.

SETTING UP LOG SHIPPING

Once you have set the recovery model and designed your log shipping solution, you are ready to begin setting up the configuration. If you have not yet taken the database backup and restored that backup on the secondary server, you can have SSMS perform that task for you as you configure the log shipping scenario. You should also create two file shares in advance, one to place the backups from the primary database in and one to store the copied backups on the secondary server.

1. Begin by opening SSMS and connecting the Object Explorer to the primary server. If the database you want to ship has not already been marked with a full or bulk logged recovery model, do that first. In this example, we have created the pubs database on the primary server and set its recovery model to Full. Figure 12.1 illustrates the Object Explorer connected to the three instances that will be part of this scenario. The MasteringSQL default instance will act as the monitor. MasteringSQL\PrimaryServer will be the production server holding the pubs database that we want to ship and the MasteringSQL\SecondaryServer instance will be the target server.

FIGURE 12.1
Server connections
for log shipping

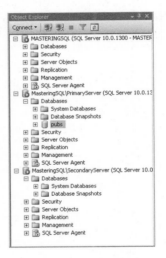

2. To configure the log shipping scenario, right-click the pubs database in the primary server and select Properties from the menu.

3. Select the Transaction Log Shipping page in the menu on the left. This will display the dialog pictured in Figure 12.2.

4. Click the check box at the top of the dialog to begin the configuration process and enable the Backup Settings button on the page.

5. Click the Backup Settings button to open the dialog pictured in Figure 12.3. This dialog will provide the information needed to perform the transaction log backups, including the location of the backups and the retention time.

6. Click the Schedule button at the bottom of this dialog to open a standard SQL Agent scheduling dialog to specify how often the system will perform the backups. If you want to rename the job, you can do that here. This job will run on the primary server. When you are finished, click OK.

FIGURE 12.2
The Log Shipping
dialog

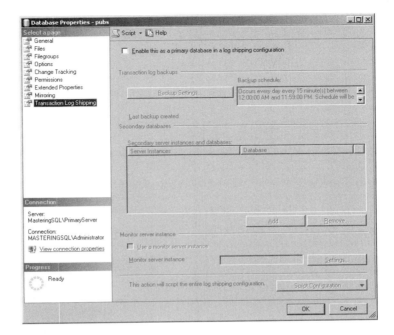

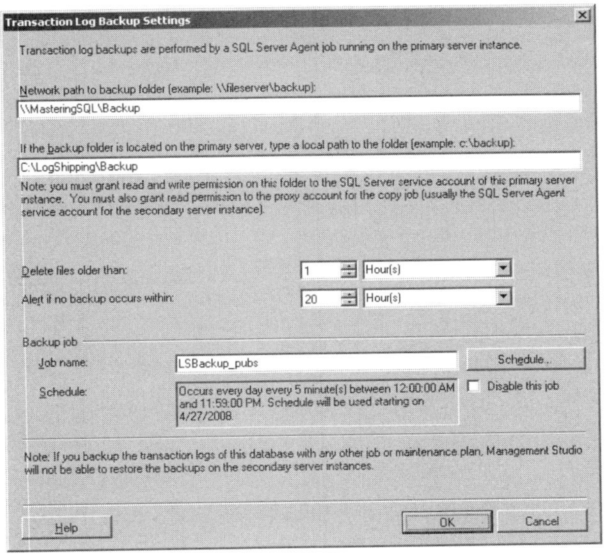

FIGURE 12.3
Configuring
backup settings

7. Now that you have configured your backup settings, the Add button under the Secondary Databases section should be enabled. Use this button to add and configure all of the target servers to which you will ship and restore the logs. Click this button to present the dialog pictured in Figure 12.4, which defaults to the first of three tabs.

FIGURE 12.4
Initializing the target server

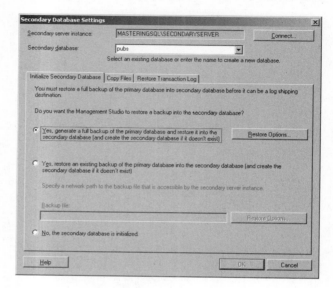

One advantage to using log shipping is that you can ship the logs to multiple servers, either creating multiple elements of redundancy or providing additional distribution of the data.

8. Before you will be able to access any of the tables, you must connect to the target server. Click the Connect button to set the server instance and database that will be the target. The first tab will then allow you to specify how to do the initial synchronization. You have three options:

◆ Have the system perform a database backup and restore that backup to the target server.

◆ Restore an already existing database backup to the target server.

◆ Do nothing (if you have already synchronized the two servers with a backup).

Because we did not synchronize the target server before we started the log shipping configuration process, we will choose the first option to perform the synchronization for us. Whether this will be done with the Standby or Norecovery option will be determined in a later step.

9. Click the Restore Options button to display a dialog, shown in Figure 12.5, that allows you to specify the locations for the data files and log files of the newly restored database.

10. The Copy Files tab of the dialog, pictured in Figure 12.5, requires a URL for the location to where the log files will be copied. Configure the Copy Files job here. This job will run on the target server. (Make sure you specify a reasonable amount of time for deletion of log files.)

11. On the Restore tab, pictured in Figure 12.6, decide which type of recovery you will use for the log restores. This example shows a Standby configuration that creates a queryable server.

Note that when you choose the standby option, you will also have the option of disconnecting users when the restore job executes. This is important if you want to make sure that the database is as current as possible. If there are users connected, the restore job will fail and will have to be repeated later.

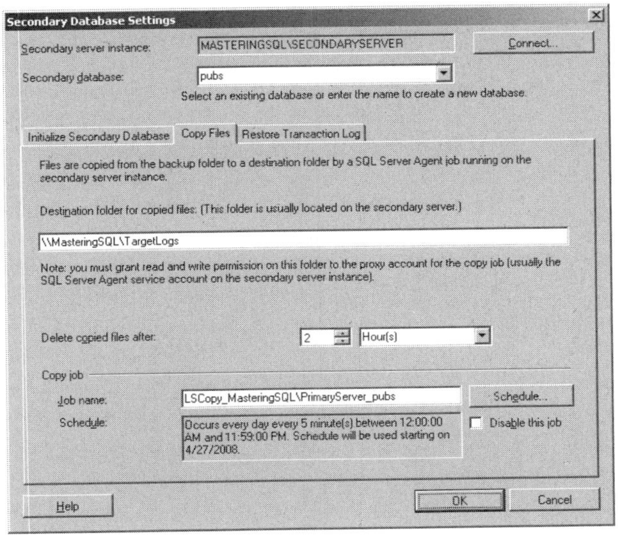

FIGURE 12.5
Configuring the
Copy Files tab

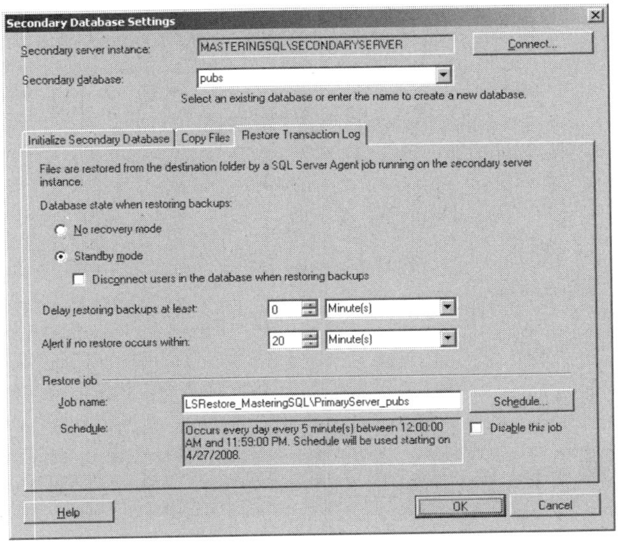

FIGURE 12.6
Configuring file
restore

12. Configure a restore delay here, if any, as well as a job name and schedule. This job will execute on the target server.

13. When you are done, click OK on the dialog and it will return you to the Log Shipping configuration screen. From here you can repeat the process if you want to add additional target servers.

14. If you want to use a monitor server to watch the log shipping activity and raise a centralized alert, do it now. You won't be able to add it later. Click the check box to add the monitor and then click the Settings button. This will open the dialog pictured in Figure 12.7. This dialog allows you to connect to the server that will act as monitor and configure the connection properties and schedule. This job will run on the monitor server.

FIGURE 12.7
Configuring the monitor

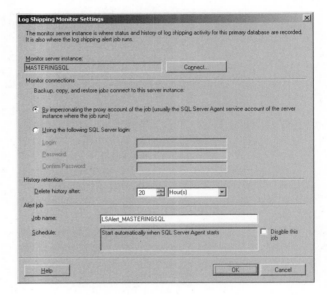

15. Click OK to close the dialog.

16. You are now ready to start the log shipping scenario that you have just configured. Click the OK button on the Database Properties window and SSMS will perform the actions that you have requested. A pop-up dialog will indicate if the process was successful. Figure 12.8 illustrates the resulting artifacts in the Object Explorer. Notice the new pubs database on the secondary server is marked as Standby/Read Only. You will also see the four jobs that we have configured in each of the SQL Agent service instances.

At this point, you can experiment with log shipping by executing queries on the primary and secondary servers. Consider the simple query and results pictured in Figure 12.9. The first name of Mr. White in our database is Johnson.

FIGURE 12.8
A successful
configuration

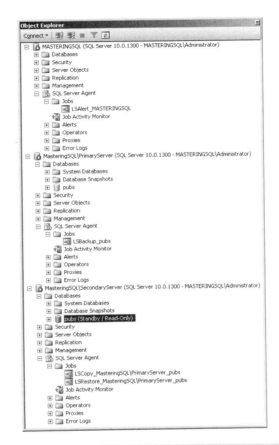

FIGURE 12.9
Returning
data from the pri-
mary server

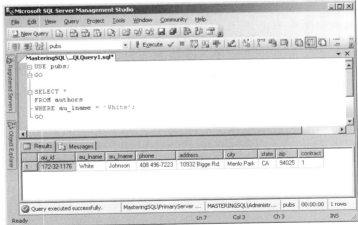

If you have executed an update statement on the primary database to change Mr. White's first name to John, executing the same query again on the primary server will return the new data. On the secondary server, however, this will not be the case. Because the transaction log has not yet had the opportunity to ship to the secondary server, the query in Figure 12.10 still returns the old data.

FIGURE 12.10
Querying the standby server

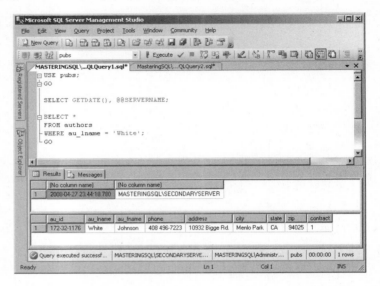

After the sequence of log shipping jobs executes, the new data will be available for querying as illustrated in Figure 12.11. Notice the difference in time in the query results. Also, remember that if you do not configure the standby server to disconnect the clients, the jobs will fail, so if you use that configuration, you will not see the new data until you disconnect long enough for the restore job to run.

FIGURE 12.11
Viewing the restored data

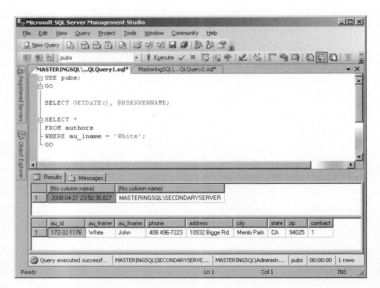

CONFIGURING LOG SHIPPING WITH TSQL

Although you will most commonly configure log shipping using SSMS because it is not a frequently performed task, you can script the process as well. If you want to save a script of the process so that you can re-create the model if necessary, you should use the Script Configuration button located at the bottom of the Transaction Log Shipping page in the Database Properties window. This button will allow you to script the configuration to a new window, to the clipboard, or to a file. Rather than print the content of the script here, we recommend that you set up a log shipping model in SSMS, script it, and then review it.

Failing Over in a Log Shipping Scenario

In case of failure of the primary server, the target server can be brought to a current state. If you like, you can then switch the roles of the primary and secondary servers. Because the secondary server is only a warm standby, you will usually have to restore all remaining log backups to the server to bring it current. Follow these steps to get to that point.

1. If possible, take a manual transaction log backup of the primary database with NORECOVERY to capture the trailing log and put the primary database in a recovering state. This will be the last log that you restore on the server.

2. Copy all remaining logs from the primary to the secondary server and apply them in order with NORECOVERY, applying the training log last.

3. After applying the last log, recover the secondary database by using this statement:

   ```
   RESTORE DATABASE <dbname> WITH RECOVERY;
   ```

Your secondary server is now recovered and current. Client applications will be able to use this server instead of the primary server for all database access requirements. If you wish, you can now switch the roles of the server so that the current server (formerly the secondary server) is the new primary. Take the following steps.

1. Remove any existing log shipping configuration. You will replace it with a new one.

2. If you were able to back up the primary database with recovery, you should be able to restore any transaction log backups taken on the secondary server since recovery back to the original primary server. If not, you will have to resynchronize the databases.

3. Reconfigure the log shipping model using the current server as the primary and the recovered server as the secondary. You will have effectively swapped roles at that point.

One disadvantage of the log shipping solution is that this must all be done manually. Having a warm standby server available can be extremely convenient and log shipping is an easy way to maintain that server without having to perform a significant amount of configuration and maintenance.

Database Mirroring

In the first release of SQL Server 2005, before any service packs were released, database mirroring was not fully supported. You had to use a trace flag to enable the feature, and the reliability of the model was questionable. Database mirroring in SQL Server 2008 is significantly improved, both in reliability and performance. If you have not looked at database mirroring since that first implementation, you owe yourself another peek.

Database mirroring provides for either a high-performance asynchronous mirror or a high-safety synchronous mirror. It is different from log shipping in a number of very important ways.

Transaction-Based   Log shipping synchronizes databases by loading log backups on the target server, which means that the target is only a warm standby. The target is only as current as the last log restore. Any transactions that have occurred on the primary server since the last log restore will not be reflected on the target server. Mirroring is different: transactions commit on the two servers at roughly the same time, with the timing dependent on whether you use a high-safety or high-performance implementation. This means that the mirror target is a true hot standby server.

Auto-Failover   While the administrator can fail over a log shipping target to the primary role, this is a manual process. In the database mirroring model, it can be an automatic process. A third server called a *witness* monitors the status of each partner server; upon failure of the primary server, the witness forces a failover to the secondary server. This makes this is a much better solution in terms of downtime.

Connections   Log shipping uses simple SQL Agent jobs to execute the backup, copy, and restore process. Database mirroring uses *endpoints*, connection points that allow the partners and the witness to be in constant contact with each other. Part of the process of configuring database mirroring is defining these connection endpoints, which must be active for the database mirroring behavior to function.

IT TAKES A QUORUM

The combination of the primary, mirror, and witness servers in a database mirroring configuration is called a *quorum*. In the following discussion, any reference to the quorum should be assumed to refer to the entire set of servers in the configuration. Any issues that deal specifically with a server role will refer to that server by role.

Configuring Database Mirroring

You must observe a number or requirements before you will be able to initialize a successful database mirroring configuration. These requirements are all fully documented in the SQL Server Books Online. The most important requirements are as follows:

◆   All servers in the quorum must be running the same version of SQL Server. For example, a primary server running SQL 2005 Standard cannot be in the same quorum as a mirror running SQL Server 2008 Enterprise.

◆ Asynchronous (High-Performance) mirroring requires an Enterprise edition of SQL Server.

◆ The primary server and the mirror server must have the same logins so that if failover occurs, client users will be able to authenticate as necessary.

◆ System databases such as `master`, `model`, and `msdb` cannot be mirrored.

◆ Although this is not a hard requirement, Microsoft recommends that both the primary and the mirror server use the same collations and sorts.

PREPARING THE SERVERS AND DATABASES

You must ensure the correct recovery model for the databases before you will be able to configure database mirroring. (This is another similarity to log shipping.) While log shipping allows either a bulk-logged or full recovery model, database mirroring uses only a full recovery model. This ensures that the mirror will fully execute all bulk operations.

You must prepare the mirror server by restoring a full database backup of the primary database to the mirror server along with at least one transaction log backup up to and including the last log. Unlike log shipping, the database mirror configuration will not create the target database for you. It must have the same name as the primary database, which means that the mirrored database must be on a separate SQL Server instance (either on the same server or a different one).

It is critical that no transactions occur on the primary database between the time you take the transaction log backup and the time you restore it to the mirror server. If any transactions do occur, you must back up the log again and restore it to the mirror server. You must also restore the database and log backups using the NORECOVERY option, enabling additional transaction logs to be restored as necessary. Don't forget to back up and restore at least one transaction log, otherwise you will get an error message that states that there is not sufficient log information to configure mirroring.

DON'T TALK TO ME, I'M RESTORING

Because the mirror database must be restored using the NORECOVERY option, it is not available for querying or reporting. This means that a mirroring configuration is not a good option for data distribution. Also, make sure that you have adequate backups of the primary server for recoverability. Because the state of a mirror server must always be "restoring" for the mirroring to work, you cannot back up the mirror server.

USING THE DATABASE MIRRORING WIZARD

Once the database and transaction logs have been restored on the mirror instance, you are ready to use the Database Mirroring Wizard to configure the mirroring scenario. Before we begin working with the wizard, let's quickly review a few terms to make sure that we have definitions clear.

Principal Database   This is the production database that we will mirror. All transactions take place on this server and are copied to the mirror database for execution. Clients interact exclusively with the principal database.

Mirror Database   This is the database copy. It must be on a different SQL Server instance than the principal database, although it can be on the same server. The mirror database is always in a state of recovery and you cannot query or report from it. Clients never interact directly with the mirror unless failover occurs.

Witness   The witness is a server that is responsible for monitoring the state of the two partner databases. If it loses contact with the primary database, it can initiate a failover. The witness is only used in a synchronous (high-safety) mode when the model requires automatic failover.

Synchronous Mirroring   Also called High-Safety mirroring, transactions are not fully committed on either the principal or mirror database unless they are guaranteed that they both can commit. This may come at a performance cost as the transactions will only be able to commit as quickly as the slowest server allows. This does, however, provide a reasonable guarantee against data loss.

Synchronous mirroring can be configured with or without a witness, depending on if you want to support auto-failover. Even without a witness, you can still failover manually at any time if needed.

Asynchronous Mirroring   Also called High-Performance mirroring, transactions are committed to the principal server immediately and then copied to the mirror for execution. There may be a time delay between the commit on the principal and the mirror. There is a possibility of some data loss if a transaction is unable to commit on the mirror after committing on the principal. Asynchronous mirroring does not support auto-failover and, therefore, never uses a witness.

Mirroring Endpoints   An *endpoint* is a communications port in SQL Server that allows services to interact with each other. SQL Server 2008 supports numerous endpoint types including TSQL, Service Broker, SOAP, and Database Mirroring. Mirroring endpoints communicate via TCP using a port number specific to the endpoint. The wizard with configure the endpoints including the grant of permissions to a service account to communicate using the endpoint. Note that if the principal, mirror, or witness ever exist on the same server, they will need to use different port numbers on their endpoints.

In the following example, we prepared the server by creating a full database backup followed by a transaction log backup on the principal instance and then restoring those backups in order to the mirror instance with NORECOVERY. Remember that before taking the full database backup in the principal server, you must first set the Recover model to Full. You should double-check the mirror database to ensure that it is in a "restoring" state. You should also create the necessary Windows accounts that SQL Server will use to communicate through the endpoints. You will configure security for these accounts in the wizard.

1. To start the wizard, connect to the principal instance in the Object Explorer and open the databases folder.

2. Right-click on the pubs database and select Properties from the menu.

3. Click the Mirroring page on the left of the dialog. This will display the dialog that you see in Figure 12.12.

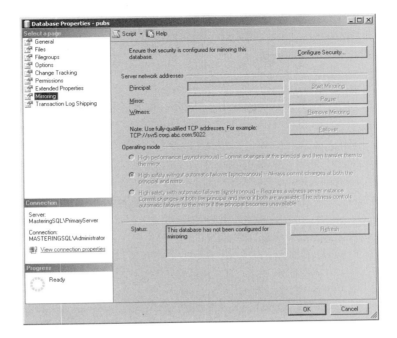

FIGURE 12.12
Configuring database mirroring

4. You will begin by creating the endpoints and configuring security. Click the Configure Security button in the dialog to start the Security Wizard.

5. Click Next on the first page of the wizard.

6. The next page will ask you if you want to configure a witness. You only need a witness if you plan to configure synchronous mirroring with automatic failover. For purposes of this exercise, select Yes on this dialog and click Next.

7. The following page will ask you to confirm the configuration locations. All three checkboxes should now be selected. Click Next again to move the first configuration page pictured in Figure 12.13.

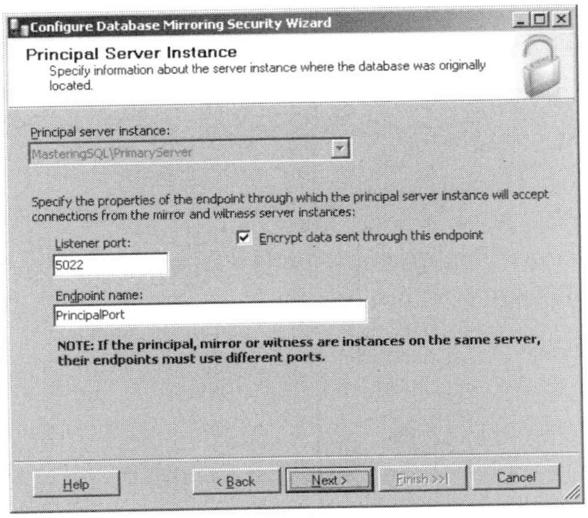

FIGURE 12.13
Configuring the principal endpoint

8. The endpoint configuration requires a port number and an endpoint name. In this case, the endpoint name is PrincipalPort and the port number is 5022, which is the default port number for database mirroring endpoints. If you want all transaction traffic to be encrypted when sent through the port, enable that option here using the checkbox.

9. Click the Next button to advance to the next page.

When advancing to the Mirror Endpoint configuration page, the dialog may prompt you to connect to the instance as pictured in Figure 12.14. You will not be able to provide endpoint names or port numbers until you click the Connect button and provide authentication credentials for the mirror server. In our example, the endpoint name will be set to MirrorPort and it will use port number 5023. Note that whenever you have more than one mirroring endpoint on the same server, you must use a unique port number for each.

FIGURE 12.14
Configuring the mirror endpoint

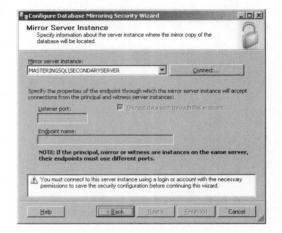

10. Click the Next button to advance to the Witness configuration page, which is the same as the previous two pages. You must first connect to the witness instance and then configure the endpoint information. In this example, the endpoint name will be WitnessPort using a port number of 5024.

11. Click Next to advance to the Service Account configuration page pictured in Figure 12.15.

If you leave this dialog blank, the wizard will use the existing service accounts. This will work fine if all the instances use the same domain account for their service account. Otherwise, you will need to enter the full domain\account name for the service accounts that the servers use so that they can be granted permission to connect to the endpoints. The wizard will configure this permission for you.

FIGURE 12.15

Configuring the service accounts

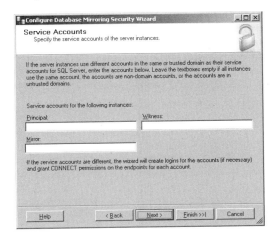

12. Because all of our server instances use the same account, leave this dialog blank and click Next, which will bring up the Summary page in the dialog.

13. Review the summery for accuracy and click Finish to complete the wizard.

14. After executing the requested configuration, you should get a success message for the three configuration tasks in the next dialog. If there are any errors, review the messages and correct any problems.

15. Close this dialog. You will bring up a message box like the one pictured in Figure 12.16 asking you if you want to start mirroring now using the default configuration. (If you select No, you will still be able to start mirroring later in the Database Properties window.)

16. You will see a completed Configuration dialog. The wizard has configured each of the endpoints, and you now have the option to start mirroring by clicking the Start Mirroring button. The dialog shows two mirroring options. You can use high-performance mode or high-safety mode with auto-failover.

The option to start high-safety mode without auto-failover is not selectable because you configured a witness. If you did not want to have the option of auto-failover, you would not have configured a witness.

17. Click the Start Mirroring button to begin the mirror process and close the dialog when finished. Now if you look back at the Object Explorer, pictured in Figure 12.17, you will see the pubs databases in the two servers, marked with their current states.

FIGURE 12.16
Starting
the default
configuration

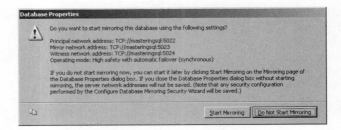

FIGURE 12.17
Viewing the results

WHAT'S MY ADDRESS?

When you click the Start Mirroring button, you may get a message box like the one pictured in the following dialog.

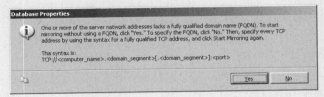

Because all of the endpoints are running on the same domain on the same server, you will not need to fully qualify the endpoint address. However, if you need to resolve domains in your model, you will have to be more specific. In that case, select No in this message box and edit the endpoint addresses in the Database Properties window before you continue.

Exploring the Mirroring Solution

If you look at the Object Explorer now, you will see several new artifacts. You may need to refresh the nodes in the Explorer to see them. Look again at the illustration in Figure 12.17. You will see that the databases are now marked as Synchronized. You will also see the endpoints along with new SQL Agent jobs that do the monitoring. At this point, any transaction executed against the principal will be synchronously executed against the mirror as well. Feel free to try it out, making some modifications to data on the principal. You will not be able to query the mirror to test for the changes, but you will be able to see the changes after failover occurs.

There are now two ways that this scenario can fail over, manually or automatically. If you want to force a manual failover, go back to the Mirroring page of the database properties dialog on the pubs database in the primary server. Clicking the Failover button on the dialog will reverse the roles of the two databases. If you go back to the Object Explorer, after refreshing the nodes, you will see that the mirror database is not online and marked as the principal. This is your only failover option if you do not have a witness. You can also manually failover by using this TSQL statement:

```
ALTER DATABASE pubs SET PARTNER FAILOVER;
```

This will break the mirror and set the status of the mirror database as the principal. The former principal will now be marked as disconnected and in recovery. After recovering the former principal server, manually failing over again on the mirror will swap the roles back so that the model is as it was before.

The other approach is an automatic failover. For example, if you stop the MSSQL Server service on the primary server, the witness will force an automatic failover. That status of the mirror will switch to Principal/Disconnected and that database will now become the principal. After the former principal database comes online again, executing a manual failover will resync the databases and swap the roles back.

As you can tell from this illustration, database mirroring is very easy to configure and use. You should experiment with different mirroring options, as there can be significant performance implications. Microsoft recommends that you implement an asynchronous mirroring scenario first, and once you can validate that approach, switch over to synchronous mirroring if desired for additional performance testing. Don't configure features that you don't need, and remember that every new and exciting feature usually comes at a performance cost.

Replication

Replication is the oldest of the Microsoft data-distribution models and has been tuned and stabilized with every release. The replication model is based in a publisher/subscriber metaphor with three distinct database roles, namely the publisher, subscriber, and distributor. These roles work together to copy transaction activity or database snapshots from one server to another to provide for a greater degree of data distribution.

We will begin this section by providing an overview of replication terminology and topology models and then look at the process of implementing these models using Microsoft replication.

Replication Overview

In the introduction to replication earlier in this chapter, we introduced you to the three standard replication types: transactional, snapshot, and merge. All three of these models use the database servers participating in the model in slightly different ways.

Publisher   In most replication scenarios, the publisher is the production server that accepts all transaction activity and makes that activity available for replication to other servers. The publisher will generally store transactions to be replicated in its transaction log until the distributor picks them up for delivery.

Distributor   This is the service that is responsible for delivery of replicated data. In a typical mode, the distributor will retrieve data from the log of the publisher and store that data in its own log until it can distribute the data to the subscriber. It is essentially a store-and-forward service.

Subscriber   The subscriber receives the replicated data from the distributor. In most cases this database must be treated as read only because the transaction activity should occur on the publisher. There are exceptions to this rule, however, including Merge replication models and updating subscribers.

Additionally, there are some replication-specific terms with which you should be familiar. We will assume that these terms are understood for the remainder of this chapter.

Push Subscription   This is a subscription model where the distributor services push data to the subscriber. SQL Agent jobs running on the distributor will periodically connect to the subscriber and execute transactions necessary to bring the subscriber current.

Pull Subscription   This is a subscription model where the subscriber services retrieve transactions from the distributor for execution to keep the subscriber current. Pull subscriptions allow some of the overhead of replication to move from the distributor to the subscriber, which may load balance the model better.

Article   An individual collection of replicated data usually associated with a table. Creating an article from a table allows the administrator to filter out columns or rows that they want to exclude from the replication scenario.

Publication   A collection of articles usually associated with a database. A subscriber can either subscribe to an individual article or to the entire publication.

In addition to these server roles and the replication types previously discussed, it is also possible to combine these components in different ways to create various replication topologies. A topology is a collection of replication services that combine in a specific way to accomplish a desired goal. Some of the more prominent topology patterns are as follows.

Central Subscriber   It is possible to have multiple publishers replicate data to a single subscriber. The data for each publisher article may even be published to the same table in the subscriber as long as each publisher's data is distinct. This pattern, illustrated in Figure 12.18, is most common where there is a centralized data need for reporting or decision making.

FIGURE 12.18
The Central
subscriber

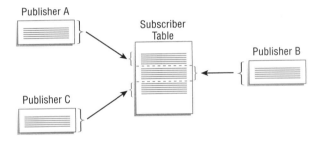

Central Publisher   You can also configure a single publisher that can partition data to various subscribers. Assuming that each subscriber only needs a subset of the data, the administrator can creates multiple articles, each one filtering out data for a particular subscriber. Each subscriber can then receive the relevant data for them. This approach, pictured in Figure 12.19, is useful when data is centrally collected but must be distributed locally for decentralized processing.

FIGURE 12.19
The Central
publisher

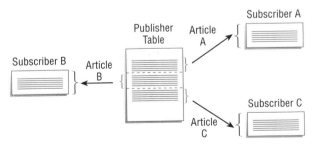

Regional Publishers/Subscribers   It is also possible that each server needs to maintain its own distinct data, but also send and receive replicated data from other servers. This approach, pictured in Figure 12.20, supports a highly decentralized environment. One of the problems with this model, however, is its ability to scale. Adding additional nodes to the model will exponentially increase the overhead for each added node.

FIGURE 12.20

The Regional publishers/subscribers

Distributed Subscriber/Republisher   Designers often use this model when data must replicate to more than one subscriber, but those subscribers are geographically located where it is either expensive or impractical to perform a direct replication. All data will replicate to a single subscriber that has more convenient access to the ultimate subscribers. The subscriber then republishes that data to the subscribers that need the data. In this model, pictured in Figure 12.21, the central server is responsible for both subscription and publication services.

FIGURE 12.21

The Distributed subscriber/republisher

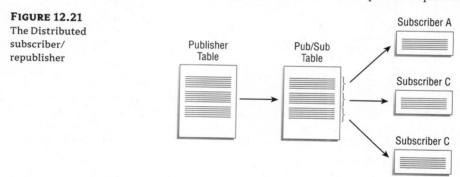

Of course, there are other patterns you can use, and almost limitless combinations of these patterns, so be creative. Just be sure to do production-level performance and reliability testing on your models before taking them live. What looks good on paper will not always work so well in the real world.

Configuring Replication

Before you can configure replication, you must first install it into the servers that will participate in your replication topology. If you have not already installed replication on all participating servers, go back to the SQL Server Installation Center and add the replication feature to your servers. It will also make the process of configuring replication easier if you connect your Object Explorer in SSMS to all the Data Engine services that will participate in your replication model.

ALL ROADS LEAD TO ROME

One of the great things, or perhaps frustrating things depending on your perspective, about replication configuration is that there are many different ways to accomplish the same things as you set up your replication model. Don't be afraid to experiment. Just because we walk you through one particular approach doesn't mean that ours is the only way to do something. You go your way and I'll go mine.

CONFIGURING THE DISTRIBUTOR

In this example, the PrimaryServer instance will act as publisher, the SecondaryServer instance will act as subscriber, and the MasteringSQL default instance will act as the distributor. Remember that it is possible for a single server to play any combination of roles.

1. Start the replication process by connecting to the distribution server.

2. Right-click the Replication node in the Object Explorer for the target distribution server and select Configure Distribution from the menu. (This Replication node will not be present if you have not installed replication.)

3. Advance past the first page of the wizard and you will see a page that asks you to either configure the selected server as a distributor or to point this server's publications to another distributor. Because this server will act only as a distributor, you will select the first option, as pictured in Figure 12.22.

FIGURE 12.22
Setting the
distributor

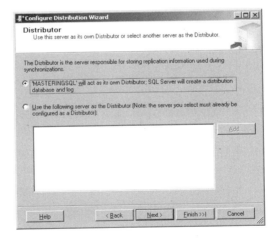

4. Click Next to advance through the wizard.

5. On the next page of the wizard, configure the location of the Snapshot folder. Whenever the distributor needs to perform a synchronization between the publisher and subscriber, it will use an article snapshot. In cases where the subscriber will use its own distribution

agents (i.e., pull subscriptions), those agents will need access to this folder. You will need to use a network location such as a UNC name before you will be able to support pull subscriptions. The SQL Agent service account on the subscriber will also need permissions to access this share. In Figure 12.23, this dialog shows the user of a share called ReplSnap. Click Next to continue.

FIGURE 12.23
The Distribution
Snapshot folder

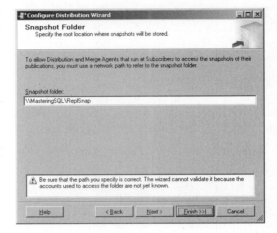

6. The screen that now appears will provides the configuration of this database, specifically the database name and file locations. The default name is "distribution," which we will retain for this example, as pictured in Figure 12.24. Note that when you configure distribution, you are creating a database that the distribution agents will use for storing and forward transaction activity. The log is heavily used in this database and should be physically positioned accordingly.

FIGURE 12.24
The Distribution
database

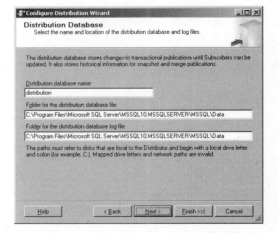

7. Click Next to advance.

8. The distribution server must authorize publishers before they will be able to use its distribution services. This next page authorizes publishers to use this distributor. By default, the distribution server can always publish to itself. You must add any other publishers here before they can use this distributor. Click the Add button at the bottom of the dialog to add a publisher. You will see that you can add either a SQL Server or an Oracle publisher. Select SQL Server and connect to the server that you plan to use as the publisher.

9. You should see a configure dialog like that shown in Figure 12.25. Click Next to continue.

FIGURE 12.25
Configuring the publishers

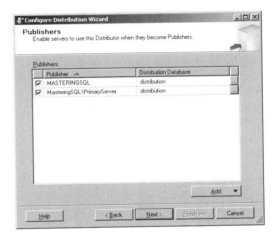

10. Enter a strong password and click Next. (This simple dialog is not pictured here.)

Publishing servers may occasionally need to connect to the distributor to perform administrative tasks on the distributor configuration. To do this, they will have to provide a distribution password. This is not the password of any existing account, but rather an administrative password that the publisher must give to be allowed to access distribution configuration.

11. The final page in the wizard allows you to immediately configure the distributor or generate a script that you can execute later or on a different server. (You can also do both if you wish.) Select the option to configure the distributor now and click Next, which navigates to the Summary page.

12. Review the page for accuracy and click Finish when ready to execute the configuration. When complete, click Close.

CONFIGURING THE PUBLISHER

Now that you have successfully configured the distributor, it is time to create publications. We will publish articles from the pubs database on the PrimaryServer instance. If you have not set the recovery model of this database to Full or Bulk Logged, you must do that now before you can configure publishing.

1. To begin, expand the Replication node of the server from which you wish to publish. Right-click on the Local Publications node and select New Publication from the menu. This will start the New Publication Wizard. Click Next to advance past the first page.

2. The next page allows you to set the distributor. This dialog is like the one illustrated in Figure 12.22. If this publisher will act as its own distributor, you can configure the distributor now. In this example, however, you will point to the distributor that we configured in the previous step. Click the second option in the dialog to enable the Add button.

3. Click the Add button and connect to the server previously configured as distributor. Then click Next to advance.

4. Provide the distributor password that you specified when you configured the distributor. (You will not be able to make an administrative link to the distributor without this resource password.) After providing the password, click Next to advance. (This simple page contains only the password prompt and is not pictured here.)

5. Select the database that you want to publish from the list of databases that are eligible for publication. In this case, only the pubs database is on the list. Data from multiple databases will be published as multiple publications. Click Next to continue.

6. You will now see the page illustrated in Figure 12.26, which lists all publication types previously discussed. Select a publication type. Refer to the introductory section of this chapter if you need a refresher on replication types.

FIGURE 12.26
Selecting a replication model

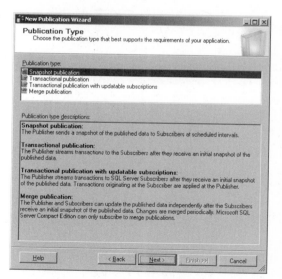

You will see one additional option; that is Transactional Replication with Updating Subscribers. This option allows data modifications at the subscriber by using a two-phase commit to persist the same change immediately to the publisher to ensure data integrity. Use this option with caution, as it can often result in significant performance degradation.

7. Select the Transactional publication option and click Next to advance. In this example, we will use a standard transactional replication. There are advantages and disadvantages to each approach, but the transactional method was the first replication model supported and it is still the most common approach due to its lower resource consumption and greatest flexibility.

TIME TO DO YOUR HOMEWORK

We wish we had the time and space to cover all of the replication models more exhaustively, but that is unfortunately not possible. The good news, though, is that this information should be enough to get you going. The replication process is very well documented in the SQL Server Books Online when you are ready to dive deeper. Again, don't be afraid to experiment with the options and be sure to do some testing before you pull the trigger in production.

Now it is finally time to decide what you are going to publish. You can publish tables, views, and stored procedures as articles. If you publish a table, it must have a primary key.

1. On the right-hand side of the dialog pictured in Figure 12.27, you will see a button with two options: one to set properties for the selected article and one for all articles. Review these properties carefully on your own. You will control much of the replication behavior here including copying related artifacts, doing type conversions, and other useful options. In our example, we will only replicate a limited number of columns in the authors table. Click Next to advance.

FIGURE 12.27
Selecting articles

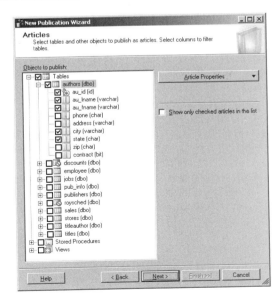

2. Select articles to filter. The previous dialog allowed you to filter out any columns that you did not need. The next dialog provides the ability to do row filtering based on criteria that you provide. Figure 12.28 illustrates a completed dialog.

FIGURE 12.28
Selecting Articles
to filter

3. To add filtering for an article, click the Add button on the right, which will be enabled if there are any articles remaining that do not have filters. This will open the dialog pictured in Figure 12.29, where you will provide a WHERE clause for the Filter Statement to indicate which data you want to include in the article. In our example, we are only publishing authors that live in the state of California. Click Next on the dialog to advance.

FIGURE 12.29
Configuring the
Article filter

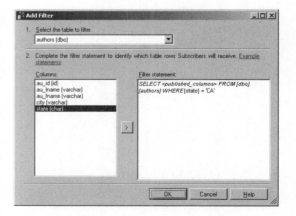

The initial synchronization of the articles requires a snapshot distribution to the subscriber. If you would like to generate the initial snapshot immediately upon a new subscriber coming online, select the checkbox on this next dialog. (This dialog has only these two options and is not pictured.) Otherwise the snapshot will be generated on a schedule and the subscription will not be available until after the snapshot generates and syncs with the subscriber.

4. Select immediate generation of the snapshot and click Next.

5. The following dialog will request security account information for two agents, the snapshot agent and the log reader agent. The snapshot agent is responsible for doing snapshot syncs and must execute under an account that has permissions to execute the snapshot on the subscriber. The log reader agent is responsible for retrieving transactions from the publishing log. You should use domain accounts with necessary permissions for these agents. This is pictured in Figure 12.30. Click Next to advance.

FIGURE 12.30
Configuring the Agent Security dialog

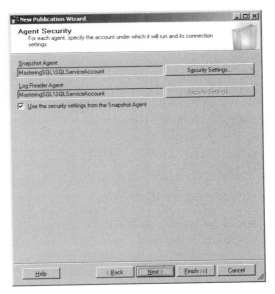

6. Decide if you want to commit the configuration at this time or generate a script to commit the configuration at a later time or place. (This is similar to the distribution configuration.) Click Next and advance to the Summary screen.

7. Don't forget to enter the name of the publication at the top of the summary screen. It's easy to miss but the Finish button will not enable without it. We will call out publication "pubs." Click Finish when you are ready to commit your configuration.

8. After the wizard reports successful creation of your publication, go back to the Object Explorer. You should now see the pubs publication in the Local Publications folder in the PrimaryServer instance.

CONFIGURING THE SUBSCRIBER

The last step is to configure the subscriber. We will use the SecondaryServer instance as the subscriber in our example.

1. Connect to that server in the Object Explorer and locate the Local Subscriptions folder.

2. Right-click the folder and select New Subscriptions from the menu. Click Next to advance past the first page of the wizard.

3. Point to the publisher. Open the publisher dropdown list at the top of the dialog and choose the option to connect to a SQL Server publisher.

4. Connect to the server that you configured as the publisher. This will list the available publications in the dialog, as illustrated in Figure 12.31. Select the pubs publication and click Next to continue.

FIGURE 12.31
Selecting a publication

5. Choose either a push or a pull subscription and click Next. (This page has only these two options and is not illustrated.) Remember that push subscriptions run the agents on the distributor and pull subscriptions use the resources of the subscriber. You must have configured the distributor to handle pull subscriptions by using a network path for the Snapshot folder before this option will execute without error.

6. The next page, pictured in Figure 12.32, has two functions. First, it allows you to specify the target database for each subscription. If you click in the cell for the subscription database, you can either select a database from a list or create a new database. If you have not already created the database that will host the subscriptions, this is your opportunity to do so. Second, this dialog also allows you to add subscriptions through the Add Subscriber button at the bottom of the page. Click Next to continue.

FIGURE 12.32
Selecting subscribers
and databases

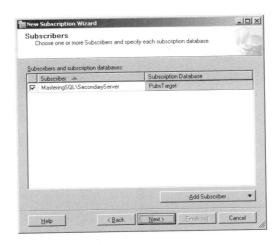

7. Similar to configuring publishing, the next dialog allows you to specify how the agents will authenticate to the servers on which they will run. Click the ellipses on each subscriber row to open the security configuration. These dialogs are similar to those previously shown and are not illustrated here. Click Next to advance.

8. The next dialog provides configuration for the synchronization schedule. You have three options.

   ◆ Run Continuously, which will run the agents whenever there is work to do. This will provide the best concurrency, but at a higher resource cost.

   ◆ Run On Demand, which will delay execution until manually triggered.

   ◆ Run On a Schedule. If you select the option to set a schedule, you will see a standard SQL Agent scheduling screen where you will be able to configure the schedule.

   Figure 12.33 shows these options. Select Continuous for this example. Click Next to continue.

FIGURE 12.33
Setting the
Synchronization
properties

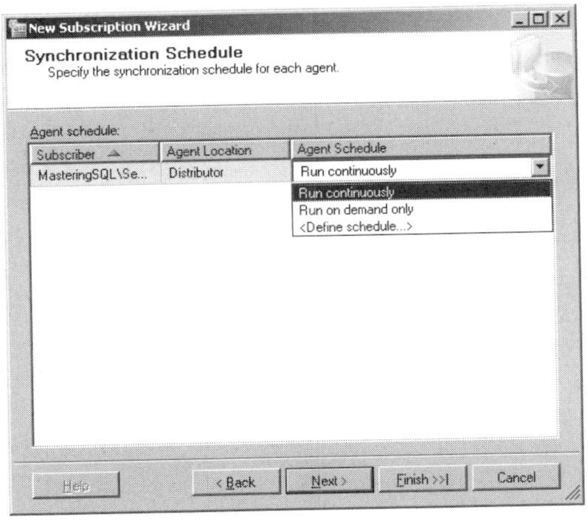

9. The next dialog is similar, except that it allows you to specify how the subscription will be initialized, either immediately or on the first sync task. If you choose to wait for the first sync task, you will not see any data in the article until a database modification occurs on the publisher and that transaction replicates to the subscriber. Choose to initialize immediately. This is a simple dialog and is not pictured here.

10. You are almost done. Click Next and choose the option to create the subscription immediately or generate a script.

11. Click Next to review the Summary page, and then click Finish to complete the wizard.

Once the wizard reports that you have successfully created the subscription, you can go back to the Object Explorer. You will see a table in the target database with the same name as the article you created, in this case "authors." Because we configured this to initialize immediately, you should be able to select from the table and see the initial snapshot of data.

Additionally, if you make a modification to the published data on the publishing server, you will be able to select from the subscription table and see the change. Do a couple of experiments with your databases and see how long it takes for the subscriptions to update.

OTHER REPLICATION ISSUES

Although we do not have the time to dig into them here, you might want to experiment with some of the other replication scenarios, such as merge replication and updating subscribers. Be cautious with these other models. Updating subscribers suffers from performance problems, and merge replication can complicate data integrity because you increase the potential of clashes between updates at various locations.

You should also consider the general overhead of replication. Any form of replication will require additional internal server metadata. In the case of merge replication especially, this overhead can be significant as the server must track the lineage of every data row so that it can adequately resolve conflicts.

Replication also increases the transaction logging overhead of a database. The server writes more data to the log and the data will usually stay in the log longer because it cannot be truncated until it is fully replicated. This is especially true of the distribution database, which must keep transactions until they have been replicated to all subscribers.

With all its faults, however, replication in SQL Server is a solid tool for data distribution that effectively automates the process of making data available to the servers and ultimately the client applications that need that data for better decision-making and reporting purposes.

The Bottom Line

Identify the elements and benefits of RAID and clustering. RAID and clustering are fault-tolerance techniques that provide an increased uptime when properly implemented. The objective is to ensure that disk or other nondisk failures will not prevent clients from access needed data.

Master It For each of the following items, specify whether RAID or clustering would be the best solution for the described situation.

1. You are concerned about your I/O system having the ability to scale to additional traffic.

2. You want to protect against possible exposure to disk failure.

3. You are concerned that if the network card in your server fails, you will have too much down time.

Implement transaction log shipping. Log shipping provides an easily maintainable solution to both availability and distribution. With minimal effort, the warm standby server can be brought online and, when properly configured, provide reporting capabilities at the same time.

Master It Describe each of the following log shipping roles.

1. Primary server

2. Target (Secondary) server

3. Monitor server

Implement database mirroring. With the hallmark of database scope automatic failover, database mirroring is an availability solution that addresses many critical recovery problems. Although not effective for a data distribution strategy, database mirroring can provide the needed protection again individual database failure.

Master It Which database mirroring mode would you use for each of the following situations?

1. You want the principal server to be able to commit its transactions as quickly as possible, even if that means a slight delay in committing the changes to the mirror.

2. You want to provide an auto-failover capability.

3. You want a high degree of synchronization between the principal and the mirror, but you do not want the overhead of using auto-failover.

Implement SQL Server replication. With very flexible implementation architecture, replication can address most data-distribution requirements with minimal maintenance. Replication is not suited for availability solutions because there is no guarantee of timely and consistent data delivery at the level required for an availability solution, but it is a very affective approach for distributing selected pieces of data where they are needed.

Master It Which replication role provides each of the following services in a transactional replication model?

1. Distribution in a push subscription

2. Distribution in a pull subscription

3. Executes initial transactions

4. Stores replication transactions ready for delivery

5. Final store of replication transactions

Chapter 13

SQL Server Data Security

Encrypting data can provide an extra layer of security against unauthorized disclosure of confidential data. In this chapter we will discuss several enhancements to data security features found in SQL Server. Encryption of an entire database is now possible without requiring applications using the database to be modified by using Transparent Data Encryption. Data and log files are automatically encrypted when written to disk and decrypted when read from disk. SQL Server also offers management of encryption keys and functions for encrypting and decrypting data. In this chapter, we will discuss these features, and we will also look at the use of encryption keys to sign code modules, such as stored procedures.

Certificates are another important way to ensure data security in SQL Server 2008. You can give a procedure elevated privileges by signing it with a certificate and mapping that certificate to a database user. Using certificates to sign a code module allows more granular permission management than ownership chaining offers, and it also offers protection against code modifications. In this chapter, you will learn to:

◆ Create and manage encryption keys

◆ Transparently encrypt a database

◆ Encrypt data using SQL Server functions

◆ Sign code modules to elevate permissions and prevent modifications

Understanding the SQL Server Key Infrastructure

Encryption is the process of scrambling data using an algorithm so that it is unreadable without access to a key to decrypt the data. Plaintext can be converted to ciphertext using several different algorithms with varying levels of strength and key size. Protecting the keys used to encrypt sensitive data is critical, and SQL Server provides an extensive key management infrastructure.

There are many ways that encryption is used in a SQL Server environment, including:

◆ To provide an additional layer of security for sensitive data

◆ To comply with regulations, standards, or laws protecting data

◆ To protect server objects, such as credentials and linked server login passwords

◆ To provide a controlled way to elevate privileges for code modules

There are two categories of encryption algorithms supported by SQL Server: symmetric key algorithms and asymmetric key algorithms.

Symmetric key algorithms use a single key to encrypt and decrypt data. The same key that is used to encrypt data is also used to decrypt the data. Symmetric key encryption offers good performance for encrypting large amounts of data.

Asymmetric key algorithms use a pair of related keys, generally called a *public key* and a *private key*, to encrypt and decrypt data. Data that is encrypted by the public key can only be decrypted by the private key. Asymmetric keys allow for more flexible key exchange than symmetric keys, but they are generally much slower and aren't appropriate for large volumes of encrypted data.

In many cases, you will find that symmetric keys are protected by asymmetric key algorithms. The symmetric key can be encrypted by the public key. Only the private key can be used to decrypt the symmetric key.

The SQL Server Keys

SQL Server uses a hierarchy of encryption keys to provide key management and automatic decryption capabilities. In the SQL Server encryption hierarchy, one key encrypts another key, and so on.

SQL Server uses the following objects in its encryption hierarchy:

◆ Service master key

◆ Database master key

◆ Symmetric keys

◆ Asymmetric keys

◆ Certificates

◆ Database encryption keys

Figure 13.1 shows the relationships between the different types of keys used by SQL Server. In this section we'll explore the creation and management of each type of key.

FIGURE 13.1
The SQL Server encryption hierarchy

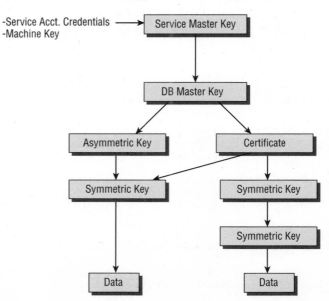

SERVICE MASTER KEY

The service master key is the root of the SQL Server encryption hierarchy. It is encrypted using the SQL Server service account credentials and local machine key, and it is stored using the Windows Data Protection API.

The service master key is automatically generated the first time it's needed to protect any of the following:

◆ Credentials

◆ Linked server passwords

◆ Database master keys

The service master key can only be opened by the windows service account that created it, or someone possessing the service account credentials. Because of this, it's important to use the ALTER SERVICE MASTER KEY statement when changing the SQL Server service account. This statement can be executed either before or after the change, but it only needs to be executed once. Listing 13.1 shows the syntax changing the account with access to the service master key.

LISTING 13.1   Changing the Account with Permissions to the Service Master Key

```
-- Use only one of the following statements:
-- Used before changing the service account
ALTER SERVICE MASTER KEY
 WITH NEW_ACCOUNT = 'DOMAIN\NewSvcAccount',
      NEW_PASSWORD = 'NewSvcPassword';

-- Used after changing the service account
ALTER SERVICE MASTER KEY
 WITH OLD_ACCOUNT = 'DOMAIN\OldSvcAccount',
      OLD_PASSWORD = 'OldSvcPassword';
```

If the service account is compromised, you may need to regenerate the service master key. Regenerating the key requires decrypting all of the items encrypted with the old key, and re-encrypting them with the newly generated key. This operation can be resource-intensive. To regenerate the service master key, you would use the following statement:

```
ALTER SERVICE MASTER KEY REGENERATE;
```

Backing up the service master key is a critical operation if any of the encryption features of SQL Server are used. Backing up keys is covered later in the chapter.

DATABASE MASTER KEY

The database master key is used to protect certificates and asymmetric keys within a database. The key exists in two places: the user database and the master database. The copy stored in master is automatically updated when changes are made.

The code shown in Listing 13.2 creates a new database named `EncryptionDB`, and creates a database master key in the database.

LISTING 13.2   Creating a Database Master Key

```
CREATE DATABASE EncryptionDB
GO
USE EncryptionDB

CREATE MASTER KEY
 ENCRYPTION BY PASSWORD = '<password>'
```

By default, the database master key is encrypted twice: once with the service master key and once with a password. The database master key is encrypted by the service master key to allow automatic decryption of certificates and asymmetric keys, which are covered later in the chapter. If the database master key has been moved to a different server, the password can be used to open it.

You can manage the encryption as well as regenerate the database master key by using the ALTER MASTER KEY statement. The syntax is shown here:

```
ALTER MASTER KEY <regenerate_option> | <encryption_option>

<regenerate_option> ::=
   [ FORCE ] REGENERATE WITH ENCRYPTION BY PASSWORD = 'password'

<encryption_option> ::=
   ADD ENCRYPTION BY [ SERVICE MASTER KEY | PASSWORD = 'password' ]
   |
   DROP ENCRYPTION BY [ SERVICE MASTER KEY | PASSWORD = 'password' ]
```

If the database master key is encrypted by the service master key, it is automatically opened when needed. If the database master key is encrypted only by a password, you must use the OPEN MASTER KEY statement before using any certificates or asymmetric keys in the database.

If you've attached the database to a new server, and want to enable automatic decryption of the database master key, use the ALTER MASTER KEY statement as shown here:

```
ALTER MASTER KEY
   ADD ENCRYPTION BY SERVICE MASTER KEY
```

Database master keys can be backed up using the BACKUP MASTER KEY statement, which is covered later in the chapter.

ASYMMETRIC KEYS

Asymmetric encryption uses a related pair of keys for encrypting and decrypting data. The public key is used for encrypting data, and the private key is used to decrypt data. Most asymmetric keys have both a public and private key stored, but you can include only a public key for verifying module signatures. Asymmetric keys in SQL Server use the RSA algorithm, and they can use a bit length of 512, 1,024, or 2,048. The longer the key, the more secure the encryption.

Asymmetric encryption is usually much more resource intensive than symmetric encryption, but it can provide a higher level of security. Because of the performance, you will probably use asymmetric keys to encrypt symmetric keys, rather than encrypting data with the asymmetric key directly. Asymmetric keys can also be used for signing code modules, which is covered later in the chapter.

An asymmetric key pair can be generated by the SQL Server engine, or it can be imported from any of the following:

◆ Strong name file generated by sn.exe (included with .NET framework SDK)

◆ Signed executable file

◆ Signed assembly

◆ EKM (Extensible Key Management) provider

Asymmetric keys can be encrypted using either the database master key or a password. Asymmetric keys that are encrypted with the database master key can be automatically decrypted without needing to specify a password. Database access controls are used to limit access to the asymmetric key to only authorized users. If an asymmetric key is encrypted with a password, the password must be provided whenever the key is used. Listing 13.3 shows several examples of creating asymmetric keys.

LISTING 13.3   Creating Asymmetric Keys

```
-- Encrypted by Database Master Key
-- Fails if the Database Master Key doesn't exist
CREATE ASYMMETRIC KEY akey_example1
  WITH ALGORITHM = RSA_2048;


-- Encrypted by Password
-- Doesn't require a Database Master Key
CREATE ASYMMETRIC KEY akey_example2
  WITH ALGORITHM = RSA_2048
  ENCRYPTION BY PASSWORD = 'StrongPassw0rd';


-- Imported from a strong name file encrypted with DB master key
-- Strong name file generated with: sn -k 2048 C:\test.snk
CREATE ASYMMETRIC KEY akey_example3
  FROM FILE = 'C:\test.snk';


-- Imported from a strong name file encrypted with a password
-- Strong name file generated with: sn -k 2048 C:\test2.snk
CREATE ASYMMETRIC KEY akey_example4
  FROM FILE = 'C:\test2.snk'
  ENCRYPTION BY PASSWORD = 'StrongPassw0rd';
```

STRONG NAME TOOL

The example in Listing 13.3 uses keys generated by the Strong Name tool (sn.exe) which is a part of the .Net framework. This tool is installed with Visual Studio .NET and can also be installed as part of the Windows SDK.

While most asymmetric keys will contain both a public and private key, the private key can be dropped. This can be useful for verifying signed code without having the ability to sign more code. The example in Listing 13.4 changes the password akey_example2 and drops the private key akey_example4.

LISTING 13.4   Modifying Asymmetric Keys

```
ALTER ASYMMETRIC KEY akey_example2
  WITH PRIVATE KEY (
    DECRYPTION BY PASSWORD = 'StrongPassw0rd',
    ENCRYPTION BY PASSWORD = 'newPassw0rd' );

ALTER ASYMMETRIC KEY akey_example4
  REMOVE PRIVATE KEY;
```

You can retrieve information about the asymmetric keys in a database by querying the sys.asymmetric_keys system view.

Asymmetric keys cannot be backed up individually, although they are included as part of a full database backup. More information about backing up keys is covered later in the chapter.

CERTIFICATES

SQL Server can also use X.509 certificates for asymmetric encryption. Certificates are similar to asymmetric keys in that they both use public and private keys for encryption. Both are resource intensive for encrypting and decrypting large amounts of data. A certificate also includes other information that is signed that ties the keys to information contained within the certificate.

Certificates can be used in SQL Server for the following:

◆ Protecting symmetric keys

◆ Protecting database encryption keys

◆ Signing code modules

◆ Protecting service broker conversations

Certificates are usually issued by a certificate authority (CA) after verifying a principal's identity. A certificate authority generates a public and private key pair and then signs the contents of the certificate. The signature of a certificate authority is used to bind the public key to the information within the certificate. A full discussion on certificate authorities and trust hierarchies is beyond the scope of this chapter.

Certificates that are generated by SQL Server are self-signed—that is, they aren't signed by a certificate authority. When SQL Server generates a self-signed certificate, it uses a 1,024-bit key length. The only available fields for a SQL Server-generated certificate are the subject, start date, and expiry date.

SQL Server can also import a certificate and associated private key from a file. Keys that are imported into SQL Server can be between 384 and 3,456 bits long in increments of 64 bits.

By default, SQL Server will encrypt a certificate's private key with the database master key if it exists. This allows automatic decryption of the certificate's private key. Access to the certificate is controlled by database access control mechanisms.

Alternatively, you can specify a password to protect the private key. If you use a password to protect the private key, you must provide the password whenever you want to use the certificate. Listing 13.5 shows several examples of creating and importing certificates.

LISTING 13.5   Creating and Importing Certificates

```
-- Encrypted by the database master key
CREATE CERTIFICATE cert_example1
 WITH SUBJECT = 'First Example Certificate';

-- Encrypted by a password
CREATE CERTIFICATE cert_example2
 ENCRYPTION BY PASSWORD = 'StrongPassw0rd'
 WITH SUBJECT = 'Second Example Certificate';

-- Imports certificate and private key from external file
-- protected by database master key
-- Generated with: makecert -sv C:\testcert.pvk C:\testcert.cer
CREATE CERTIFICATE cert_example3
 FROM FILE = 'C:\TestCert.cer'
 WITH PRIVATE KEY
    (FILE = 'C:\TestCert.pvk',
     DECRYPTION BY PASSWORD = 'StrongPassw0rd');

-- Imports certificate and private key from external file
-- protected by password
-- Generated with: makecert -sv C:\testcert2.pvk C:\testcert2.cer
CREATE CERTIFICATE cert_example4
 FROM FILE = 'C:\TestCert2.cer'
 WITH PRIVATE KEY
    (FILE = 'C:\TestCert2.pvk',
     DECRYPTION BY PASSWORD = 'StrongPassw0rd',
     ENCRYPTION BY PASSWORD = 'serverPassword');
```

Certificates can be backed up separately from the database, unlike asymmetric keys. Certificates and asymmetric keys have nearly the same functionality from an encryption perspective in SQL Server. Certificates offer greater flexibility from a key management perspective.

You can retrieve metadata about certificates within a database by querying the sys .certificates system view.

SYMMETRIC KEYS

Symmetric keys are useful for encrypting and decrypting large amounts of data because they are very efficient in comparison to asymmetric key encryption. It is recommended that you use symmetric keys to encrypt data and use the other key types to protect your symmetric keys.

When using symmetric key encryption, a single key is used for encrypting and decrypting data. The length of this key depends on the algorithm used. SQL Server automatically generates a strong key based on a password, or key source. The symmetric key is then protected by one or more of the following methods:

◆ A password

◆ A certificate

◆ An asymmetric key

◆ Another symmetric key

◆ An EKM provider

The key may be encrypted multiple times. For example, a symmetric key may be encrypted by a certificate and also by a password. This means that either the certificate or the password is required to access the symmetric key, not both.

SQL Server supports several different symmetric encryption algorithms, which are described in Table 13.1.

TABLE 13.1   Symmetric Encryption Algorithms

ALGORITHM NAME	DESCRIPTION
DES	Data Encryption Standard developed in 1976. Uses a small 56-bit key to do encryption.
TRIPLE_DES	Uses Triple DES Encryption with a 128-bit key.
TRIPLE_DES_3KEY	Uses Triple DES Encryption with a 192-bit key.
DESX	Incorrectly named. Really uses Triple DES with a 192-bit key.
RC2, RC4, RC4_128	Widely used encryption protocol used in protocols such as SSL and WEP. Designed by Ron Rivest of RSA in 1987.
AES_128, AES_192, AES_256	Advanced Encryption Standard also known as Rijndael.

Listing 13.6 shows examples of creating symmetric keys that are each protected by a different method. The actual keys used to do the encryption are generated by SQL Server. A Globally Unique Identifier (GUID) is also generated for each key so that data encrypted by it can be identified and associated with the appropriate key.

LISTING 13.6   Creating Symmetric Keys

```
-- Protected by a password
CREATE SYMMETRIC KEY sk_example1
  WITH ALGORITHM = TRIPLE_DES
  ENCRYPTION BY PASSWORD = 'StrongPassw0rd';

-- Protected by a certificate encrypted with the
-- database master key
CREATE SYMMETRIC KEY sk_example2
  WITH ALGORITHM = AES_256
  ENCRYPTION BY CERTIFICATE cert_example1;

-- Protected by an asymmetric key encrypted with the
-- database master key
CREATE SYMMETRIC KEY sk_example3
  WITH ALGORITHM = TRIPLE_DES_3KEY
  ENCRYPTION BY ASYMMETRIC KEY akey_example1;
```

If the statements in Listing 13.6 were run on two different servers, the keys generated would be different, even in the case of encrypting by password. When you specify a password, a triple DES key is derived from the password to secure the actual key.

You can be more verbose in key generation if you want to be able to create the same key on more than one server by using the IDENTITY_VALUE and KEY_SOURCE parameters when creating a symmetric key. IDENTITY_VALUE is used to generate the same GUID on each server, and KEY_SOURCE is used to derive the actual key.

Listing 13.7 shows an example of creating a symmetric key that would generate the same GUID and use the same key no matter what server it is created on.

LISTING 13.7   Creating a Symmetric Key with a Static GUID and Key

```
CREATE SYMMETRIC KEY sk_ReusableKey
  WITH ALGORITHM = AES_256,
       KEY_SOURCE = 'ComplexPassPhraseToGenerateTheKeyFrom',
       IDENTITY_VALUE = 'ComplexPassPhraseToGenerateTheGuidFrom'
  ENCRYPTION BY CERTIFICATE cert_example1;
```

Symmetric encryption keys cannot be backed up separately from the database. When you create a key using a static GUID and key, you can re-create the symmetric key from the script. Make sure to adequately protect the SQL scripts used to create symmetric keys when using a KEY_SOURCE.

You can encrypt a symmetric key more than once by adding encryption by another mechanism. For example, a symmetric key may be encrypted by a password, as well as a certificate. The certificate can be used with automatic decryption using the database master key, where the password could be used as an alternative method for accessing data encrypted by the symmetric key. Listing 13.8 shows an example of a symmetric key protected by both a password and a certificate.

LISTING 13.8   Creating a Symmetric Key Protected by a Password and Certificate

```
CREATE SYMMETRIC KEY sk_PasswordCert
  WITH ALGORITHM = AES_256
  ENCRYPTION BY PASSWORD = 'StrongPassw0rd';

CREATE CERTIFICATE cert_PasswordCert
  WITH SUBJECT = 'Certificate for protecting the sk_PasswordCert key';

-- Open the symmetric key so that we can protect it by the certificate
OPEN SYMMETRIC KEY sk_PasswordCert
  DECRYPTION BY PASSWORD = 'StrongPassw0rd';

ALTER SYMMETRIC KEY sk_PasswordCert
  ADD ENCRYPTION BY CERTIFICATE cert_PasswordCert;

CLOSE SYMMETRIC KEY sk_PasswordCert;
```

You can view the ways that a symmetric key is encrypted by querying the sys.key _encryptions system view. For more information on symmetric keys in a database, query the sys.symmetric_keys system view.

DATABASE ENCRYPTION KEY

A database encryption key is used for Transparent Data Encryption (TDE), a new feature of SQL Server 2008. TDE uses the database encryption key to transparently encrypt database and log files as they are written to disk, and transparently decrypt them as they are read.

A database encryption key is stored in the header of the database, and it is encrypted by either a certificate or asymmetric key stored in the master database. It is suggested that you use a certificate for protecting database encryption keys, because a certificate can be backed up where an asymmetric key can't be backed up individually.

More information about creating and using the database encryption key is covered in the "Using Transparent Data Encryption" section later in the chapter.

Extensible Key Management

So far, we've looked at encryption keys that are generated and managed by SQL Server. Extensible Key Management (EKM) enables SQL Server to use external providers to manage encryption keys. External providers allow the use of Hardware Security Modules (HSM). HSM devices store encryption keys in hardware specifically designed for their protection.

SQL Server uses the Microsoft CryptoAPI to interface with HSM devices for key storage. In order to use an HSM device, you must enable EKM, and register an EKM provider, as shown in Listing 13.9.

LISTING 13.9   Enabling EKM and Adding a Provider

```
EXEC sp_configure 'show advanced options', 1;
GO
RECONFIGURE;
GO
EXEC sp_configure 'EKM provider enabled', 1;
GO
RECONFIGURE;
GO
CREATE CRYPTOGRAPHIC PROVIDER Sample_EKM
FROM FILE = 'C:\EKM\SampleEKM.dll';
```

Once you've registered a cryptographic provider, you must create a credential with access to the EKM provider and add that credential to any logins needed to create keys from the provider, as shown in Listing 13.10.

LISTING 13.10   Creating a Credential to Access an EKM Provider

```
CREATE CREDENTIAL EKM_Credential
WITH IDENTITY = 'UserNameToAccessProvider',
     SECRET = 'PasswordToAccessProvider'
FOR CRYPTOGRAPHIC PROVIDER Sample_EKM;

ALTER LOGIN [DOMAIN\UserToGiveAccessTo]
   ADD CREDENTIAL EKM_Credential;
```

SQL Server can access existing keys using the EKM provider, or it can create new keys. EKM providers can be used to create symmetric and asymmetric keys. Listing 13.11 shows an example of creating several keys from a registered EKM provider.

LISTING 13.11   Creating Keys Using an EKM Provider

```
CREATE ASYMMETRIC KEY akey_EKM_ExistingKey
  FROM PROVIDER Sample_EKM
  WITH CREATION_DISPOSITION = OPEN_EXISTING,
     PROVIDER_KEY_NAME = 'ExistingKeyInProvider';

CREATE ASYMMETRIC KEY akey_EKM_NewKey
  FROM PROVIDER Sample_EKM
  WITH CREATION_DISPOSITION = CREATE_NEW,
     PROVIDER_KEY_NAME = 'NewKey';

CREATE SYMMETRIC KEY sKey_EKM_ExistingKey
  FROM PROVIDER Sample_EKM
  WITH CREATION_DISPOSITION = OPEN_EXISTING,
     PROVIDER_KEY_NAME = 'ExistingSymmetricKey';
```

Backing Up the Keys

Having backups of your encryption keys is critical. Not all of the keys can be backed up individually, but all of the encrypted keys for a database are included in a backup of the database. The following keys can be backed up individually:

◆ Service master key

◆ Database master key

◆ Certificates

A symmetric key can't be backed up as an individual object, but you can generate a symmetric key from a key source using a script, and save that script.

Asymmetric keys can't be backed up individually either, but they can be imported from strong name files. If you've imported an asymmetric key from a strong name file, you can use the strong name file as a backup.

Keys protected using EKM aren't backed up by SQL Server, because the EKM provider is responsible for managing the keys separately from the data. For more information on backing up keys, refer to vendor documentation for your HSM device.

Listing 13.12 shows an example of backing up the different types of keys. In order for the example to execute successfully, you will need to create the directory C:\KeyBackups.

LISTING 13.12   Backing Up Encryption Keys

```
BACKUP SERVICE MASTER KEY
  TO FILE = 'C:\KeyBackups\MasterKey.bak'
  ENCRYPTION BY PASSWORD = 'BackupPassw0rd';

BACKUP MASTER KEY
  TO FILE = 'C:\KeyBackups\EncryptionDB_MasterKey.bak'
  ENCRYPTION BY PASSWORD = 'BackupPassw0rd';
```

```
-- Certificate protected with Database Master Key
BACKUP CERTIFICATE cert_example1
  TO FILE = 'C:\KeyBackups\cert_example1.cer'
  WITH PRIVATE KEY (
    FILE = 'C:\KeyBackups\cert_example1.pvk',
    ENCRYPTION BY PASSWORD = 'BackupPassw0rd');

-- Certificate protected with a password
BACKUP CERTIFICATE cert_example2
  TO FILE = 'C:\KeyBackups\cert_example2.cer'
  WITH PRIVATE KEY (
    FILE = 'C:\KeyBackups\cert_example2.pvk',
    ENCRYPTION BY PASSWORD = 'BackupPassw0rd',
    DECRYPTION BY PASSWORD = 'StrongPassw0rd');
```

Using Transparent Data Encryption

Transparent Data Encryption (TDE) is a new feature of SQL Server 2008. It allows encryption of all of the data in a database by encrypting the pages of the database files and transaction log. Encryption can be enabled without requiring any changes to existing applications that use the database, and it doesn't affect the size of the database. There is an increased amount of overhead when encrypting a database because of the added encryption and decryption of pages. TDE uses a database encryption key to perform encryption and decryption. It's important not to confuse a database encryption key with a database master key. A database encryption key is used only for TDE, and it is protected by a certificate or an asymmetric key stored in the master database as seen in Figure 13.2. A database master key is used for protecting certificates and asymmetric keys within a database, and isn't directly used for TDE except in the master database.

FIGURE 13.2
Transparent Data Encryption architecture

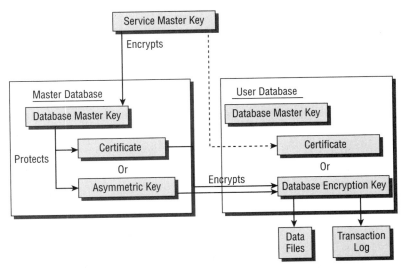

Backups of a database using TDE are encrypted using the database encryption key. In order to restore a backup, you must have access to the certificate or asymmetric key used to protect the database encryption key.

When a database is encrypted using TDE, the tempdb system database is also encrypted. This can add overhead to other databases on the same server that use tempdb.

In order to use TDE, the following must be true:

◆ The database isn't marked read-only.

◆ No filegroups are marked read-only.

◆ No backup or snapshot can be in progress.

◆ No ALTER DATABASE statements are currently executing.

Creating Keys and Certificates

In order to enable TDE, you must first create several keys:

◆ A database master key for the master database

◆ A certificate or asymmetric key in the master database

◆ A database encryption key

A database encryption key is protected either by a certificate or by an asymmetric key. Certificates are recommended unless you are using an EKM provider for asymmetric keys, because certificates can be backed up separately. The certificate or asymmetric key must exist in the master database and be encrypted by the database master key to enable automatic decryption by the SQL Server service.

The following example assumes that a database named TDEDemo has already been created. To enable Transparent Data Encryption, follow these steps:

1. Create a Master Key in the master database if one doesn't already exist. You can verify the existence of a master key by querying the sys.symmetric_keys system view.

```
USE Master
GO
CREATE MASTER KEY
  ENCRYPTION BY PASSWORD = 'StrongPassw0rd';
```

2. Create a certificate or asymmetric key in the master database that will encrypt the database encryption key. To use TDE, this certificate or asymmetric key must be encrypted by the database master key, and not a password.

```
CREATE CERTIFICATE cert_TDEDemoEncryption
WITH SUBJECT = 'Certificate to encrypt the TDEDemo database';
```

3. Create a database encryption key that is encrypted by the certificate or asymmetric key created in the previous step.

```
USE TDEDemo;
GO
CREATE DATABASE ENCRYPTION KEY
  WITH ALGORITHM = AES_256
  ENCRYPTION BY SERVER CERTIFICATE cert_TDEDemoEncryption;
```

4. Enable Transparent Data Encryption on the database option.

```
ALTER DATABASE TDEDemo SET ENCRYPTION ON;
```

5. Query the sys.dm_database_encryption_keys dynamic management view to see the status of encryption. The encryption_state column indicates the encryption status of the database. Valid values for the encryption_state column are shown in Table 13.2.

TABLE 13.2   encryption_state Column Values

VALUE	DESCRIPTION
0	No database encryption key present, no encryption
1	Unencrypted
2	Encryption in progress
3	Encrypted
4	Key Change in progress
5	Decryption in progress

Always ensure that you have a backup of the certificate or asymmetric key used to protect the database encryption key. In order to restore the database, you will need to have the certificate available.

Encrypting Data Using SQL Server

SQL Server provides Transact-SQL functions for encrypting and decrypting data using the different types of encryption keys. These functions work with encryption keys and/or passphrases to convert plaintext (unencrypted data) into ciphertext (encrypted data) and vice versa.

Encryption keys can be protected in a variety of ways, as we've seen so far. When symmetric keys are protected by certificates or asymmetric keys that are encrypted by the database master key, automatic decryption is possible without needing to specify a passphrase. Access to the encryption keys is controlled by SQL Server access control mechanisms, and SQL Server is responsible for managing the key and controlling access to it.

Encryption keys that are protected by passphrases require that the passphrase be embedded in the application that must encrypt or decrypt data. It is more secure to use automatic decryption of keys than to have the password embedded in several places.

Understanding Authenticators

When encrypting data in a table, the data is made unreadable by an encryption algorithm. This encrypted data isn't readable, but it can be manipulated by users with permissions to modify the table data.

Imagine a scenario where we have a table that stores salary data for employees. If we encrypt the Salary field, users without access to the encryption key can't read the data. A malicious user could update the table, and use the encrypted Salary value for the CEO to replace any other salary value in the table, if the data is encrypted without an authenticator.

An authenticator is a piece of unique data combined with the encrypted data to invalidate row movements. If the EmployeeID is included as an authenticator with the encrypted salary value, the value is only valid for that particular employee. This would prevent a scenario of replacing one row's encrypted data with another.

You must use caution when updating a field used as an authenticator for encryption, because it is needed to decrypt the data. If an authenticator field needs to change, the data must be decrypted with the old authenticator and re-encrypted with the new authenticator value.

Encryption with Passphrases

SQL Server can encrypt and decrypt data using only a passphrase. This option doesn't require that any keys be created prior to using the encryption functions, and the passphrase must be managed by the application doing the encryption. The TRIPLE_DES algorithm is used for encryption and decryption by passphrase. Two functions are provided for passphrase encryption:

◆ EncryptByPassPhrase

◆ DecryptByPassPhrase

Both of these functions return the **varbinary** datatype with a maximum size of 8,000 bytes, and they need to be converted to an appropriate datatype before being displayed.

The example shown in Listing 13.13 inserts two encrypted rows into a new table using EncryptByPassPhrase, and then decrypts the rows when selecting from the table. The first row is inserted without using an authenticator. If a decryption operation fails, a NULL value is returned.

LISTING 13.13   Encrypting Data with EncryptByPassPhrase

```
USE EncryptionDB;

CREATE TABLE EncryptByPP
(rowid int PRIMARY KEY NOT NULL,
 encrypted_data varbinary(128));

-- Insert an encrypted row without an authenticator
```

```
INSERT INTO EncryptByPP
   (rowid, encrypted_data)
 VALUES (1,
    ENCRYPTBYPASSPHRASE('password',          -- Passphrase
                    'MyEncryptedData'));  -- Cleartext to encrypt

-- Insert an encrypted value using rowid as an authenticator
INSERT INTO EncryptByPP
   (rowid, encrypted_data)
 VALUES (2,
    ENCRYPTBYPASSPHRASE('password',
             'MyEncryptedData',
             1,                       -- Add Authenticator = 1
             CAST(2 as SysName)));  -- Authenticator value as SysName

-- Decrypts first row without authenticator
SELECT CAST(DECRYPTBYPASSPHRASE('password',
                                 encrypted_data)
            as varchar)
 FROM EncryptByPP
 WHERE rowid = 1;

-- Decrypt Second row with Authenticator
SELECT CAST(DECRYPTBYPASSPHRASE('password',
                                 encrypted_data,
                                 1,
                                 CAST(rowid as Sysname))
          AS VarChar)
 FROM EncryptByPP
 WHERE rowid = 2;
```

Encryption with Symmetric Keys

Symmetric keys provide a stronger key for encryption than encrypting by passphrase, and they support a variety of algorithms. Symmetric keys are very efficient for working with large amounts of data. In order to do most encryption or decryption operations with a symmetric key, you must open it first.

Each symmetric key on the server has a GUID to uniquely identify the key and data encrypted by the key. The data encrypted by a symmetric key contains the GUID with each encrypted value. This GUID is used to identify the key needed to decrypt the value. For this reason, when performing decryption operations, you don't need to specify the key to decrypt a value, although the key must be open.

Listing 13.14 shows an example of encrypting and decrypting data using symmetric keys.

LISTING 13.14   Encrypting and Decrypting Data with Symmetric Keys

```
CREATE SYMMETRIC KEY skey_demo
  WITH ALGORITHM = AES_256
  ENCRYPTION BY PASSWORD = 'StrongPassw0rd';

  -- Open the symmetric key for encryption and decryption operations
OPEN SYMMETRIC KEY skey_demo
  DECRYPTION BY PASSWORD = 'StrongPassw0rd';

DECLARE @ClearText varchar(100);
DECLARE @CipherText varbinary(150);
DECLARE @DecryptedText varchar(100);

SET @ClearText = 'Text to encrypt';

SET @CipherText = ENCRYPTBYKEY(KEY_GUID('skey_demo'),
                                  @cleartext);

PRINT @CipherText;

-- Don't need to specify key GUID because ciphertext contains it.
SET @DecryptedText = CAST(DECRYPTBYKEY(@CipherText) As Varchar(100));

PRINT @DecryptedText;

CLOSE SYMMETRIC KEY skey_demo;
```

An authenticator can also be used with these functions, similar to the way they were used with EncryptByPassPhrase.

Encryption with Asymmetric Keys

Asymmetric keys are most often used to encrypt a symmetric key, rather than encrypting data itself. This is because symmetric algorithms are more efficient for encryption and decryption. The following functions are provided for working with asymmetric keys:

◆ EncryptByAsymKey

◆ DecryptByAsymKey

◆ DecryptByKeyAutoAsmKey

An asymmetric key is protected either by a password or by the database master key. Using the database master key to protect an asymmetric key enables automatic decryption without needing to use a password, and it provides stronger protection than a password alone.

Listing 13.15 shows an example of using an asymmetric key to protect a symmetric key, which is used to encrypt data. As we mentioned earlier, in order to use the symmetric key to encrypt data, you must first open the symmetric key.

LISTING 13.15   Protecting a Symmetric Key with an Asymmetric Key

```
USE EncryptionDB;

CREATE TABLE akey_encrypt
 (rowid int PRIMARY KEY NOT NULL,
  encrypteddata varbinary(150) );

CREATE ASYMMETRIC KEY akey_demo
   WITH ALGORITHM = RSA_2048;

CREATE SYMMETRIC KEY skey_protectedByAKey
   WITH ALGORITHM = AES_256
   ENCRYPTION BY ASYMMETRIC KEY akey_demo;

-- Must open the key before we can use it to encrypt data
OPEN SYMMETRIC KEY skey_protectedByAKey
   DECRYPTION BY ASYMMETRIC KEY akey_demo;

INSERT INTO akey_encrypt (rowid, encrypteddata)
   VALUES (1, ENCRYPTBYKEY(KEY_GUID('skey_protectedByAKey'), 'TextToEncrypt'));

CLOSE SYMMETRIC KEY skey_protectedByAKey;
```

To decrypt the data protected by the symmetric key that is protected by the asymmetric key, you have two options. You can open the symmetric key and decrypt as you normally would with a symmetric key, or you can use the DecryptByKeyAutoAsmKey function to automatically open and decrypt the symmetric key, given the ID of the asymmetric key that protects it. Listing 13.16 shows both methods of decrypting the data.

LISTING 13.16   Decrypting Data Using a Symmetric Key Protected by an Asymmetric Key

```
USE EncryptionDB;

-- Decrypts by opening the symmetric key
OPEN SYMMETRIC KEY skey_protectedByAKey
   DECRYPTION BY ASYMMETRIC KEY akey_demo;

SELECT CAST(DECRYPTBYKEY(encrypteddata) As Varchar(100))
   FROM akey_encrypt;

CLOSE SYMMETRIC KEY skey_protectedByAKey;

-- Automatically opens and decrypts symmetric key and closes when
-- finished.
SELECT CAST(
```

```
              DECRYPTBYKEYAUTOASYMKEY(ASymKey_ID('akey_demo'),
                                    NULL,  -- Password is NULL
                                           -- if protected by master key
                                    encrypteddata)
              As VarChar(100))
       FROM akey_encrypt;
```

It is possible to encrypt and decrypt data directly with asymmetric keys, although it isn't as efficient as using symmetric keys. It is recommended that you don't use asymmetric keys to directly encrypt data within a table.

Listing 13.17 shows an example of encrypting and decrypting data directly with an asymmetric key.

LISTING 13.17   Encrypting and Decrypting Data Using an Asymmetric Key

```
DECLARE @ClearText varchar(100);
DECLARE @CipherText varbinary(150);
DECLARE @DecryptedText varchar(100);

SET @ClearText = 'Data to Encrypt';

SET @CipherText = ENCRYPTBYASYMKEY(ASymKey_ID('akey_demo'),
                                  @ClearText);

PRINT @CipherText;

SET @DecryptedText = CAST(
                    DECRYPTBYASYMKEY(ASymKey_ID('akey_demo'),
                                                @CipherText)
                    As VarChar(100));

PRINT @DecryptedText;
```

Encryption with Certificates

Certificates are very similar to asymmetric keys from a SQL Server perspective. Both use asymmetric key encryption, with a public key and a private key; however, a certificate stores information about the person it was issued to, who issued it, and validity dates.

As we saw earlier in the chapter, a certificate can be backed up separately from the database, where an asymmetric key must be included as part of a full database backup instead.

The following functions are provided for encrypting and decrypting data using a certificate:

◆   EncryptByCert

◆   DecryptByCert

◆   DecryptByKeyAutoCert

You can encrypt and decrypt data directly using a certificate, but you will have much slower performance than if you use a symmetric key to encrypt data, and then use the certificate to encrypt the symmetric key. Listing 13.18 shows an example of encrypting data with a certificate directly:

LISTING 13.18   Encrypting and Decrypting Data with a Certificate

```
DECLARE @ClearText varchar(100);
DECLARE @CipherText varbinary(150);
DECLARE @DecryptedText varchar(100);

SET @ClearText = 'Text to encrypt';

SET @CipherText = ENCRYPTBYCERT(CERT_ID('cert_example1'),
                                @cleartext);

PRINT @CipherText;

SET @DecryptedText = CAST(
    DECRYPTBYCERT(CERT_ID('cert_example1'), @CipherText)
    As Varchar(100));

PRINT @DecryptedText;
```

If you are encrypting data within a table, using a symmetric key protected by a certificate is more efficient for encryption and decryption than using the certificate itself.

Listing 13.19 shows an example of using a symmetric key protected by a certificate to encrypt data in a table.

LISTING 13.19   Encrypting Data with a Symmetric Key Protected by a Certificate

```
USE EncryptionDB;

CREATE TABLE cert_encrypt
 (rowid int PRIMARY KEY NOT NULL,
  encrypteddata varbinary(150) NOT NULL);

CREATE CERTIFICATE demo_cert
 WITH SUBJECT = 'Demo Certificate';

CREATE SYMMETRIC KEY skey_protectedByCert
 WITH ALGORITHM = AES_256
 ENCRYPTION BY CERTIFICATE demo_cert;
```

```
-- Open the symmetric key before we use it to encrypt data.
OPEN SYMMETRIC KEY skey_protectedByCert
 DECRYPTION BY CERTIFICATE demo_cert;

INSERT INTO cert_encrypt (rowid, encrypteddata)
 VALUES (1, ENCRYPTBYKEY(KEY_GUID('skey_ProtectedByCert'), 'TextToEncrypt'));

CLOSE SYMMETRIC KEY skey_protectedByCert;
```

When decrypting data protected by a certificate, you can either open the symmetric key by using the certificate, or you can use the DecryptByKeyAutoCert function. This function automatically decrypts data with the appropriate symmetric key given a certificate. One advantage of using DecryptByKeyAutoCert is that you don't need to remember to open and close the symmetric key when using it.

Listing 13.20 shows the two methods for decrypting data that is encrypted by a symmetric key protected by a certificate.

LISTING 13.20   Decrypting Data with a Symmetric Key Protected by a Certificate

```
USE EncryptionDB;

-- Decrypt the data by using DecryptByKeyAutoCert
SELECT CAST(
          DECRYPTBYKEYAUTOCERT(Cert_ID('demo_cert'),
                               NULL, -- Certificate Password
                               EncryptedData)
             As Varchar)
FROM cert_encrypt;

-- Alternative is to open the symmetric key using the certificate
OPEN SYMMETRIC KEY skey_protectedByCert
  DECRYPTION BY CERTIFICATE demo_cert;

SELECT CAST(
          DECRYPTBYKEY(EncryptedData)
            As VarChar)
 FROM cert_encrypt;

CLOSE SYMMETRIC KEY skey_protectedByCert;
```

SQL Server provides a robust encryption hierarchy for encrypting and decrypting data, as well as protecting symmetric keys, asymmetric keys, or certificates.

Module Signing

SQL Server allows you to sign code modules, such as stored procedures or functions, with a certificate or asymmetric key. Signing a module allows you to grant additional permissions to the module by mapping the certificate or asymmetric key to a database user. This is a more flexible and granular approach than using ownership chaining to grant permissions.

To view information about signed modules, query the `sys.crypt_properties` system view. If you alter a signed module, it will invalidate the signature and won't be visible in this view.

Signing a module also prevents modifications to that module without invalidating the digital signature, thus removing the extra permissions granted. To grant the extra permissions, you must re-sign the module using the appropriate certificate or asymmetric key.

In order to use signatures with a certificate, or asymmetric key, it must be protected with the database master key rather than a password to allow SQL Server to automatically check the signature.

The process for signing a module is as follows:

1. If one doesn't already exist, create a master key in the database.

2. Create a certificate or asymmetric key for signing the procedure that is protected by the database master key.

3. Create a database user that is mapped to the certificate.

4. Grant the user the appropriate permissions.

5. Add a signature to the stored procedure to give the stored procedure the permissions of the user that is mapped to the certificate or asymmetric key.

A diagram of the module signing process is shown in Figure 13.3.

FIGURE 13.3
SQL Server
Module Signing
architecture

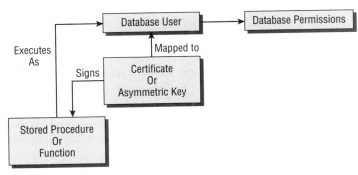

For our example of using module signing, we need to create several objects that will be used in the example. First, we'll create a user that will own a schema (to prevent ownership chaining from automatically granting permissions), and then we'll create a schema and a table.

```
USE EncryptionDB;

CREATE USER schemaowner WITHOUT LOGIN;
GO
CREATE SCHEMA s AUTHORIZATION schemaowner;
GO
CREATE TABLE s.t1 (c1 int);
```

Next, we'll create a stored procedure that queries our table, and create a low privileged database user that will be granted access to execute the procedure.

```
CREATE USER LowPriv WITHOUT LOGIN;
GO
-- Create a stored procedure in the dbo schema
CREATE PROC dbo.usp_testsigning
AS
SELECT * FROM s.t1;
GO
GRANT EXEC on dbo.usp_testsigning TO LowPriv;
```

Because the table exists in a different schema with a different owner than the stored procedure, ownership chaining doesn't apply. For example, if we were to execute the following, we would receive a permission error:

```
-- LowPriv can't select from the table without permissions
EXECUTE AS USER = 'LowPriv';
EXEC dbo.usp_testsigning;
REVERT;
```

To give this stored procedure access to the table, we will create a certificate and map the certificate to a database user. Anything that is signed with this certificate is going to execute with the permissions of that database user.

```
CREATE CERTIFICATE test_signing
 WITH SUBJECT = 'Test Cert for Signing';

CREATE USER cert_user FROM CERTIFICATE test_signing;

GRANT SELECT ON s.t1 TO cert_user;
```

Now that we have a user with the appropriate permissions, we just need to sign the stored procedure with the certificate, by using the ADD SIGNATURE statement. Adding a signature will insert a row into the sys.crypt_properties system view with the appropriate signature.

```
-- Add a signature to the stored procedure
ADD SIGNATURE TO usp_testsigning BY CERTIFICATE test_signing;

-- Now succeeds, because we have given the procedure additional permissions with
the certificate
EXECUTE AS USER = 'LowPriv';
EXEC dbo.usp_testsigning;
REVERT;
```

When we execute the usp_testsigning procedure, an additional level of access is given based on the digital signature that is mapped to a database user.

If the procedure is altered after it is signed, the signature is invalidated, and the procedure must be re-signed in order to execute properly.

```
ALTER PROC usp_testsigning
AS
```

```
SELECT c1 FROM s.t1;
GO

-- Fails because the signature was invalidated by altering the procedure
EXECUTE AS USER = 'LowPriv';
EXEC dbo.usp_testsigning;
REVERT;
```

Digital signatures can also be used to grant more granular permissions across databases than using cross-database ownership chaining. You can create a login mapped to a certificate to accomplish this.

The Bottom Line

Create and manage encryption keys.   There are many possibilities when it comes to encryption in SQL Server. Before encrypting data, you should create an appropriate key structure.

> **Master It**   What is used to protect each of the following keys?

1. Database master keys

2. Certificates

3. Asymmetric keys

4. Symmetric keys

Transparently encrypt a database.   Transparent Data Encryption allows us to automatically encrypt a SQL Server database and log files without needing to modify applications that use the database.

> **Master It**   Before enabling Transparent Data Encryption, what objects need to be created first?

Encrypt data using SQL Server functions.   SQL Server provides several functions for encrypting and decrypting data using the encryption keys. Knowing the appropriate use for each function is critical.

> **Master It**   What functions are available for encrypting and decrypting data using a symmetric key?

Sign code modules to elevate permissions and prevent modifications.   SQL Server allows us to sign modules to grant permissions, rather than relying on ownership chaining. Knowing how this process works will allow you to design and implement more secure database structures that are resistant to modification.

> **Master It**   Where can you view information about signed code modules?

Chapter 14

Indexing Strategies for Query Optimization

SQL Server applications are all about executing queries, so you need to do everything you can to make sure that those queries execute as quickly and efficiently as possible. Because SQL Server is a shared service with multiple users, tuning an application from the perspective of one user is not enough. You must also consider the impact that many users accessing data concurrently will have on performance.

Tuning a SQL Server application is a cost-based approach where you will have to evaluate the aggregate costs of the resources consumed and attempt to mitigate those costs by using optimization techniques including indexing, archiving, and load balancing to name a few. While there are many resources that you must tune in a SQL Server application, the most prominent of these is I/O, and one of the best ways to tune I/O is through indexing.

In this chapter, you will learn to:

◆ Explain the different indexing architectures and the best uses for each

◆ Create indexes

◆ Use special optimizer behaviors to boost performance

Index Architecture

The purpose of a database index, just as with the index at the back of this book, is to help you find information faster. Indexes do not provide any benefit in terms of functionality, but rather they provide a usability benefit. Your database application may work without indexes and you can *eventually* get the information you need without an index; however, finding that information may be so time-consuming that the functionality does not provide any substantial benefit for the user.

The first step in designing an indexing structure that will provide the needed usability for your application is to understand some of the index internals. In this section, we will look at the basic storage architecture of indexes and then examine the specific index structures in greater detail.

BACK TO BASICS

This discussion assumes that you are familiar with SQL Server storage architecture and terminology. If you need to brush up on terms such as *page*, *extent*, and *allocation unit*, you will find them defined in Chapter 2, "Understanding SQL Server Architecture," along with many other concepts that will help you get the most out of this chapter. We will not take the time to redefine or discuss them here.

SQL Server 2008 now supports four kinds of indexes, namely relational, XML, full-text, and spatial. This chapter covers only relational indexes, which are the traditional indexes with which you are probably most familiar. We discuss XML indexes in Chapter 7, "SQL Server and XML." We discuss full-text indexes in Chapter 22, "Full-Text Search Services." Spatial indexes are addressed in Chapter 19, "Using Spatial Data."

Index Basics

You may have heard it said that the natural state of the world is chaos. If that is true about the world in general, it must be doubly so for a database. Without any effort at maintaining structure and order, data engines tend to dump data into piles and expect you to sort through it later. This chaotic state of the database world is called a *heap*.

Think of a heap as an unordered collection of data pages. In its natural state with no indexes, every table is organized in a heap. When the table requires more data, it allocates another extent to the heap, adding to the number of pages in the pile. This is an efficient way to store data if you are concerned with the overhead of data storage. One data page is as good as any other, so the database can store the data wherever it finds room rather than having to store it in a particular place.

HOW TO GET THE DATA

The examples in this section use the AdventureWorksDW2008 database. This is the data warehouse version. This database has better data structures for the queries that you will be using to evaluate the effects of indexes. If you do not already have this database installed, you can download it from `http://www.codeplex.com`. You will download the AdventureWorksDW2008.msi file from this site. When you run the installation, it will extract a backup of the database that you will need to restore on your server before you can work with the database.

Unlike the standard AdventureWorks2008 database, the data warehouse version is denormalized and lacks some of the complexity of the standard version. It also does not use FILESTREAM storage, so you will not have to enable this feature on your server to use this database.

Tables that are organized in a heap have no specific sort or order for the data. To demonstrate, you will create a table with a heap by using a SQL query to copy data from one of the tables in the AdventureWorks2008DW database to a new table using a SELECT INTO statement as follows.

```
USE AdventureWorksDW2008;

SELECT
    p.EnglishProductName,
    p.Size,
    p.Color,
    rs.OrderQuantity,
```

```
    rs.UnitPrice,
    rs.ExtendedAmount
INTO DemoSales
FROM FactResellerSales as rs
INNER JOIN DimProduct as p
  ON rs.ProductKey = p.ProductKey;
GO
```

The resulting DemoSales table is organized into a heap by default. To verify this, you can retrieve index information from the `sys.indexes` system view using the following statement.

```
USE AdventureWorksDW2008;

SELECT o.name, i.type_desc
FROM sys.indexes as i
INNER JOIN sys.objects as o
  ON i.object_id = o.object_id
WHERE i.type = 0;
GO
```

In this query, an index type of "0" indicates that you are looking for only heaps. Every table that is currently organized as a heap will have an entry in the system catalog with an index type ID of 0, so you can always use this query to find out what heaps currently exist in your database.

When you query data from a table that is organized in a heap, the query engine does not have many choices as to how it will execute the query. With the data in no particular order, the data engine must examine every page in the heap to find the data to satisfy the query. This process of reading every page in the table is called a *table scan*. For most tables, resolving a query by using a table scan is very costly. The alternative is to use an index.

MIXING INDEXES AND HEAPS

For those of you who have more experience with SQL Server indexing, you are aware of the fact that it is possible for an indexing structure to be built on top of a data heap. We will address the various combinations of indexes and their appropriate uses later in this chapter. For now, be aware that having data in a heap does not necessary preclude you from having an index on that data.

Indexes in SQL Server use a *balance tree,* sometimes called a *b-tree,* structure. Balanced tree indexes form a tree structure where the data that you are indexing is on a group of pages called the leaf level. A narrowing structure builds on the leaf level until there is a single page called the root. The structure is called a "balanced" tree because every leaf page is exactly the same distance from the root as any other leaf page, creating a perfectly balanced structure. Figure 14.1 illustrates the general form of a balanced-tree architecture.

FIGURE 14.1
The B-Tree
Index structure

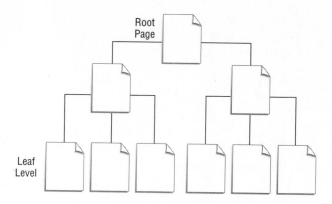

In a balanced tree, the root page contains rows that store the first index value and a page pointer for each of the index pages in the level below the root. Each level will do likewise until you reach the leaf level, which might contain actual data or it might contain a key used to retrieve the actual data from a data page. This structure will work only if the leaf-level pages are arranged in a sorted order based on the index key.

To resolve a query with an index traversal, the query processor would begin at the root page and work its way down the levels, comparing the target value with the index keys in an attempt to narrow down the possible pages upon which the data could exist. The goal is to minimize I/O by eliminating pages from consideration without having to actually read them.

Of course, in the real world, indexing options are a bit more complex than this, but the general goal is quite simple; you should filter out pages that you don't need to read to reduce your total I/O cost. Now that you have a general idea of what indexes are all about, we will explore each type of storage architecture in more detail and explain the architecture, benefits, and drawbacks of each. We will start with heaps and then move to clustered and nonclustered indexes.

Data Heaps

Remember that the norm for accessing data in a heap is to perform a table scan. Tables are stored on data pages, so a table scan is the process of reading every data page allocated to a table and extracting only qualifying data from those pages. This means that the amount of I/O needed to resolve the query will generally be equivalent to the number of data pages in the table.

For example, if we wanted to know the number of rows and the number of data pages for the DemoSales table that we created previously, we could use the following Database Console Command (DBCC) statement:

```
USE AdventureWorksDW2008;
DBCC CHECKTABLE('DemoSales');
GO
```

Although your results will vary, you should get something like this:

```
DBCC results for 'DemoSales'.
There are 60855 rows in 788 pages for object "DemoSales".
```

This tells us that the 60,855 rows in the DemoSales table currently exist on 788 data pages. One would assume, therefore, that the I/O required to execute any query that pulls data from this table, using no joins to other tables, would be 788.

GETTING I/O STATISTICS

Remember that each page read or written is considered one I/O. If we want to test our assumption, we can use the Statistics IO output to tell us exactly what our I/O was. To test this, use the following query.

```
USE AdventureWorksDW2008;
SET STATISTICS IO ON;
GO
SELECT COUNT(*) FROM DemoSales;
GO
SET STATISTICS IO OFF;
GO
```

This query will give you output that looks like the following snippet. Remember that if you are executing your results into a grid in the SQL Server Management Studio (SSMS), you will have to click on the Messages tab in the Results pane to see this information. Note that we are presenting just the first part of the message here.

```
Table 'DemoSales'. Scan count 1, logical reads 788, physical reads 0 …
```

Now you have to decode the message. *Scan count* is the number of times that the query processor had to scan the table, either as a full table scan or as an index traversal. *Logical reads* is the total number of data pages that the query processor had to read from memory to resolve the query. *Physical reads* is the number of pages that had to be read from disk into memory to make them available for the query processor. *Physical reads* of 0 in this case means that all of the required data pages were already in memory and there was no disk I/O necessary to resolve the query, in other words, there was a 100 percent cache hit for this query.

With this output, you can assume that the query was resolved by using a table scan. This is a good assumption for two reasons. First, the amount of logical I/O equals the number of pages in the table. Second, we have not created any indexes yet, so a table scan will generally be the best option; however, in some cases the query optimizer might instruct the query processor to create temporary indexes to make the query more efficient. If you suspect that the optimizer is choosing a table scan, you can verify this by using a showplan.

USING SHOWPLANS

Showplans come in many different forms. You can generate showplans graphically or you can generate them as text. You can generate the text-based showplan either as simple text or as XML. In SQL Server 2008, you can also view the estimated showplan (what the query optimizer thinks will happen) or the actual showplan (what actually happened).

You control the output of the text-based showplan through a connection SET statement. For example, to see the showplan for our previous query, you could use the following code. This output will be easier to read if you execute the query into text instead of into a grid.

```
USE AdventureWorksDW2008;
GO
```

```
SET SHOWPLAN_TEXT ON;
GO
SELECT COUNT(*) FROM DemoSales;
GO
SET SHOWPLAN_TEXT OFF;
GO
```

After displaying the code for which you are generating the showplan, the results will then give you output that looks something like the following. Again, your output may look a little different, but it will be similar.

```
|--Compute Scalar(DEFINE:([Expr1004]=CONVERT_IMPLICIT(int,[Expr1005],0)))
  |--Stream Aggregate(DEFINE:([Expr1005]=Count(*)))
     |--Table Scan(OBJECT:([AdventureWorksDW2008].[dbo].[DemoSales]))
```

The best way to read this output is from the bottom up. This output tells you that before doing any other processing, it had to do a table scan on the DemoSales table. In the context of that scan, it counted up the rows and then output the results. This output confirms that the processor did, in fact, execute the query using a table scan as we anticipated.

You can also get this information graphically. Sometimes a graph is easier to read than a text-based presentation. You can either display the estimated execution plan without actually executing the query or you can include the actual execution plan with the query output. Figure 14.2 illustrates the process of displaying an estimated execution plan. Click the highlighted button to generate the plan. Notice the tooltip on the button specifies an *estimated* execution, not an actual execution. Clicking this button will not actually execute the query.

FIGURE 14.2
Generating the estimated execution plan

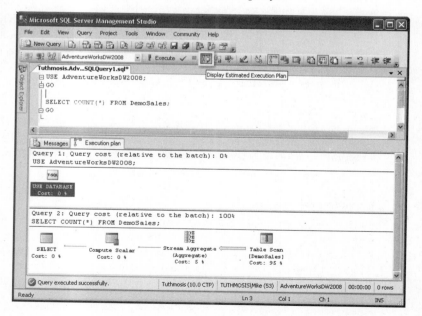

Because there are two queries in this batch, you see the execution plan for each query. Notice that the output provides a relative cost measure for each query in the batch. In this case, the cost of the USE statement is insignificant compared with the aggregate query. Each of the pictures in the output is a different operator in the query execution process. Each operator identifies the actual task that the query processor is executing. In this case, there are four operators.

Table Scan A Table Scan operator retrieves all rows from the table indicated below the icon. If the query contains a WHERE clause, it will return only the rows that satisfy the clause.

Stream Aggregate The Stream Aggregate operator groups rows by one or more columns and then calculates one or more aggregate expressions returned by the query. Subsequent operators in the query can reference the output of this operator, or the results can be returned to the client.

Computer Scalar The Computer Scalar operator calculates the scalar aggregate of an expression—in this case, the results of the Stream Aggregate operator. Subsequent operators in the query can reference the output of this operator or the results can be returned to the client.

Select The Select operator returns the output of an expression to the client. In this case, the Select operator returns the results of the Compute Scalar operator. This is generally a terminal point in the query process.

A PICTURE IS WORTH A THOUSAND WORDS

These are only a few of the icons that you will see in the graphical showplan output. Your ability to properly interpret that output will depend on your familiarity with the icons and their meanings. To get a complete list of those icons, look up "Graphical Execution Plan Icons" in the SQL Server Books Online. There you can find a set of pictures of all the icons, along with links to more detailed descriptions of their meanings. We will not take the time to fully define every icon in this chapter, so we suggest that you become familiar with them in the documentation and refer to it as needed.

After you have generated the estimated execution plan, you can hover your mouse over the icons to display more detailed costing information. For example, if you hover your mouse over the Table Scan shape in the Results pane, you will get a popup window that looks like the one in Figure 14.3. This detail tells you what the query optimizer is assuming will happen when you execute this query.

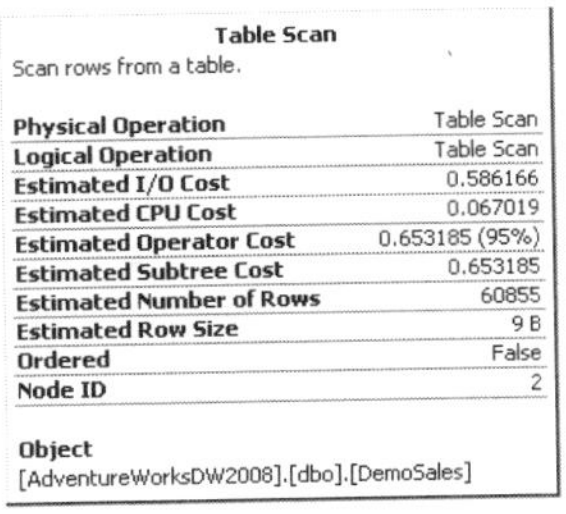

FIGURE 14.3
Costing detail for the table scan

Table Scan	
Scan rows from a table.	
Physical Operation	Table Scan
Logical Operation	Table Scan
Estimated I/O Cost	0.586166
Estimated CPU Cost	0.067019
Estimated Operator Cost	0.653185 (95%)
Estimated Subtree Cost	0.653185
Estimated Number of Rows	60855
Estimated Row Size	9 B
Ordered	False
Node ID	2

Object
[AdventureWorksDW2008].[dbo].[DemoSales]

Look at the percentage associated with the operator cost. This is the percentage cost estimated to be attributed to this single operator in the set. You will also notice an estimated number of rows as well as a row size. The optimizer uses this information to determine what the I/O cost of the operator will be.

You can also view the actual execution metrics if you like. Before you execute the query, select Query ➤ Include Actual Execution Plan from the menu to toggle the option to include actual plan output. Then execute the query as normal. You will get both a Results tab and an Execution Plan tab in the output, and if you hover over the Table Scan shape, you will also see actual row counts in addition to the estimated counts.

When the data is organized as a heap and there are no indexes present, filter criteria will generally have no impact of the execution plan that the optimizer chooses. For example, if you were to include a WHERE clause in your query, would that affect the overall I/O? Consider this query.

```
USE AdventureWorksDW2008;
GO


SELECT COUNT(*) FROM DemoSales
WHERE UnitPrice > 1000;
GO
```

Although the WHERE clause filters the resulting data and logically should require less I/O to return the count, that is not the case. Executing the query will still result in a table scan because there are no indexes to locate the data more efficiently.

Clustered Indexes

One approach to making the I/O more efficient is to use a clustered index. Creating a clustered index requires that the data engine physically sort the data at the data page level in order, based on the clustered index key. The balanced tree is then built on top of the ordered data pages. For example, suppose that you frequently select data from the DemoSales table using UnitPrice in the WHERE clause. Physically sorting the data by UnitPrice and creating an index tree on that structure could facilitate the selection of data. For example, what would the I/O for this query look like if the data was in a heap?

```
USE AdventureWorksDW2008;

SELECT EnglishProductName, UnitPrice FROM DemoSales
WHERE UnitPrice BETWEEN 1000 and 1100;
GO
```

In our sample database, this query returns less than 1,000 rows. However, if the data is in a heap, we would still need to use a table scan, which would result in 788 pages of I/O, according to our last count of pages.

How would building an index on UnitPrice affect this I/O score? We will show you the details of how you will create indexes later in this chapter, for now, just look at the results. With a clustered index on the UnitPrice column, the showplan now looks like the image in Figure 14.4.

FIGURE 14.4

Showplan with a
clustered index

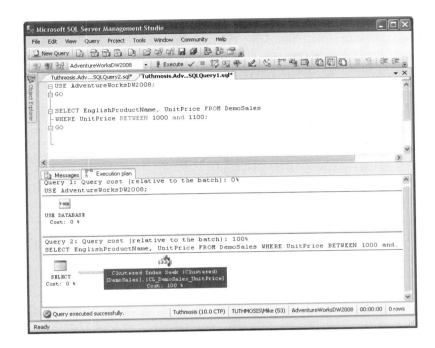

In the showplan, you will see that the operator is now an Index Seek as opposed to a Table Scan. This means that the query was resolved by traversing the index from the root page to the data leaf pages where all of the data having a UnitPrice between 1,000 and 1,100 clusters together. When the data clusters together, it takes less I/O to resolve the query. That is the primary benefit of the clustered index.

So how much was the I/O actually reduced? The showplan tells us that the query optimizer chose to resolve this query using a clustered index, but it does not give us the actual page I/O. The following code will give you that information.

```
USE AdventureWorksDW2008;
SET STATISTICS IO ON;
GO

SELECT EnglishProductName, UnitPrice FROM DemoSales
WHERE UnitPrice BETWEEN 1000 and 1100;
GO

SET STATISTICS IO OFF;
GO
```

The results of the statistic output should show a significant reduction in I/O. Our results for this experiment were as follows. Notice the reduction from 788 to 15 logical reads. That less than 1/50th of the I/O just by adding the index.

```
Table 'DemoSales'. Scan count 1, logical reads 15, physical reads 0
```

In some cases, even with the clustered index, the query optimizer may choose to perform a table scan. For example, if the query has no search arguments (SARGS) in the WHERE clause or if the clustered index key is not included in one of the SARGS, the optimizer might still have no choice but to perform a table scan. Don't assume that just because you have a clustered index, the optimizer will always be able to use it intelligently.

Regarding table scans, also be aware that the execution plan output can be a little confusing when it scans a table with a clustered index. Instead of reporting a table scan, it will report a clustered index scan. Don't be confused, because this is essentially the same thing as a table scan. The only difference is that technically you can only execute a table scan on a heap. Once a clustered index is present, it executes a clustered index scan. The end result is the same. It reads every data page in the entire table.

> ### AUTO-GENERATED CLUSTERED INDEXES
>
> In the discussion of data integrity in Chapter 6, "Managing Data Integrity," we mentioned that you get a unique clustered index by default when you create a primary key constraint. This happens automatically, so keep track of what you are doing. There is overhead associated with indexes, so it is a good idea to always know what you have.

Every index comes with a cost. Because you build an index based on a sort key, whenever the data sort changes, it can cause the data and index pages to be rearranged. This cost is generally referred to as "maintenance" cost, or in other words the cost of keeping the index up to date when the underlying data changes. For this reason, it is generally advisable to create indexes on columns that are less volatile. Frequently changing index values will significantly increase the maintenance costs associated with those indexes.

Also, because the clustered index represents the physical sort order of the data page, there can be only one clustered index per table. This index can provide a significant I/O benefit to certain kinds of queries, so choose this index well as it is a very rare commodity.

Although you are not required to create a clustered index on a table, most tables can benefit from the presence of a clustered index. One exception is a very small table where the cost of a scan is insignificant in comparison to the cost of maintaining the index. Another is a table, such as a logging table, that is almost exclusively the target of INSERT statements as opposed to any selects or updates.

Nonclustered Indexes

The structure of a nonclustered index is very similar to a clustered index. They are both based on a balanced-tree architecture consisting of leaf, nonleaf and root levels. The primary difference is that while the leaf level of the clustered index is the actual data page structure, nonclustered indexes build their own sorted leaf levels that reference the data pages. This makes for a larger index, and in the case of a large index key, can be very large.

Because creating a nonclustered index does not directly modify the data page in any way, it is possible for you to create a nonclustered index on a heap or on a table with a clustered index. The behavior differs a little between the two options, so this is worth discussing in greater detail.

CREATING NONCLUSTERED INDEXES ON A HEAP

When the data is organized in a heap, a nonclustered index leaf level contains an index row for each data row that contains the entire index key and an 8-byte RID (Row ID) that points to the data row on the underlying data page. Figure 14.5 illustrates this relationship. You can see in this diagram that the data in the heap is in no particular order. The index leaf level sorts the keys for accessibility, and each index leaf row contains the key and a pointer to the underlying data row.

FIGURE 14.5
Nonclustered
index on a heap

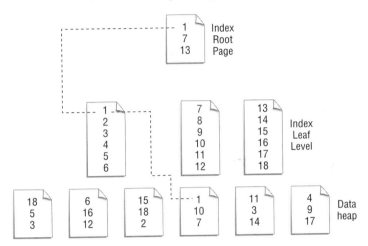

Because most situations will call for you to create a clustered index, you should consider this approach only when it makes sense. Again, small tables or logging tables may be exceptions to the clustered index rule and may be organized in a heap; however, small tables will be unlikely to require nonclustered indexes for performance and logging tables are rarely used for restrictive select operations, so they may not be good candidates. Use this approach only after validating its usefulness with appropriate testing.

CREATING NONCLUSTERED INDEXES ON CLUSTERED DATA

This is going to be the more common situation. Assume that you already have a clustered index on the data page, but now you also want to index on another key to provide additional search efficiency. In this situation, it is possible to create a nonclustered index on top of already clustered data.

Architecturally, the organization of the nonclustered index in this situation is not significantly different from that of a heap. The index is still structured in a balanced tree with a sorted leaf level. The difference is that instead of storing a RID with the key at the leaf level, the index will store a clustered search key and will use the clustered index to locate the required data.

Because there is no requirement in SQL Server that clustered indexes must be unique, this could be problematic when the nonclustered leaf level uses the clustered key to find the row. For example, suppose that you have a clustered index on an employee table that orders by the lastName field in the table. Assuming that this is not unique, what would happen if the clustered key associated with a nonclustered leaf key is a common name such as Smith? How would you know to which Smith in the table the nonclustered key should point?

To solve this problem, SQL Server takes an extra step whenever you create a clustered index using a non-unique key. In addition to the index key value, SQL Server will also generate a special row number that will be part of the clustered key. This row number is not used when searching by the data field value, but it is used when you need to locate a specific instance of a data filed value, as in the case of a nonclustered index.

Planning Clustered and Nonclustered Indexes

You have already seen how an index can provide much more efficient access to data than is possible with a heap. In most cases, you will want to have at least a clustered index on a table if not multiple nonclustered indexes as well. The big questions then become how we should determine the best indexes to create, upon which field or fields we should create them, and how to effectively balance the costs and benefits of these indexes.

> **CHECK THIS OUT**
>
> One of our favorite websites devoted to SQL Server performance tuning is http://www.sql-server-performance.com. This little gem contains a wealth of tips and, thanks to a very active online community, is always current. Subscribe to the free online newsletter and get a tip or interesting tidbit of information delivered to your Inbox every day. You'll find extensive information about index tuning if you need some direction on what to do next.

EVALUATING QUERIES AND SEARCH ARGUMENTS

There are certain parts of a query that are going to provide the bulk of the information to the query optimizer. The WHERE clause and to a lesser degree the GROUP BY and ORDER BY clauses are particularly useful to the optimizer. The JOIN statements, specifically the correlated fields, are also useful. These parts of the query provide significant opportunity for the optimizer to reduce I/O by using an index and eliminating unnecessary page reads that might occur when performing a table scan.

The WHERE clause is where most of the data filtering takes place, and correctly structuring this clause is critical. This is where the optimizer will find the Search Arguments (SARGS), which are filter statements that you write in the very specific format of:

```
Field <operator> expression
```

For example, assume that you wanted to filter an employee table based on a monthly salary greater than $1,000; however, the salary value stored in the employees table is expressed in annual terms. The following WHERE clause would be a valid SARG:

```
WHERE salary > 1000 * 12
```

Notice how the field is isolated on one side of the operator. If there is an index on the Salary field, SQL Server can evaluate that index as an option to improve the I/O score of the query. If you were to write the WHERE clause this way, it would be different.

```
WHERE salary/12 > 1000
```

In this case, the Salary field is not isolated. While there may be an index on `salary`, there is no index on `salary/12`, so SQL Server has no index that it can evaluate. If you take care to ensure that you write all filter criteria as SARGS, it will increase the probability that the optimizer will be able to use the indexes that you create on the filtered fields.

This also applies to join operations as well. For example, suppose that in the Employee table you express all salaries in annual terms, but in the Contractor table, they are monthly values. You want to find the employees that you pay the same as the contractors in a matching list. If you write the JOIN clause like this, how will this affect the optimizer's options?

```
Employee as e INNER JOIN contractor as c
   ON e.salary = c.salary * 12
```

While this is a valid JOIN statement, the optimizer has no option to use any index on the Salary field of the Contractor table. It can still use an index on the Employee Salary field, however, because you have not manipulated this field in the JOIN clause.

WHAT SHOULD YOU DO IN THE QUERY?

The best solution to the preceding problem is not to try to rewrite the query, but rather to evaluate the way you store data. Why are you storing the contractor data monthly and the employee data annually? Rather than trying to fix the query, you should try to fix the data storage to make it as consistent as possible. If you have reports or screens that need the contractor data expressed monthly, then calculate that when you select it. Maybe you can change the way you store the employee salaries if that makes for a better solution. Making data consistent is an important part of designing a good, operational database, and it becomes even more important when you design a data warehouse.

WHICH INDEXES SHOULD YOU CREATE?

Which indexes should you create? That's simple: you should create the indexes that the query optimizer will actually use. You can usually determine this through trial and error, with a little bit of planning thrown in for good measure. To effectively plan your indexes, you must learn to look at your queries the way that the optimizer will look at them. The optimizer is concerned with one thing only, resource consumption, primarily I/O.

To understand how the optimizer behaves, you have to know a few things about its design. When planning for index strategy, consider the following.

The optimizer favors throughput over response time. There are two ways to think about performance. One way is response time: How long does it take for the query to return results to the user? The other is throughput: How do we push as much activity as possible through the server given a fixed amount of resources? The answers to these two questions are often at odds with each other, but the optimizer will take an action that improves throughput before taking an action that improves response time.

The optimizer uses static statistics. To make its I/O estimates, the optimizer uses distribution statistics. These statistics store information about the distribution of key values through the index and are critical to the accuracy of the optimizer. SQL Server stores these statistics, one per index, on pages that the optimizer consults when scoring an index. These pages are generally static. Although there are database options that you can enable to automatically update statistics during server idle time, you should get in the habit of regularly updating statistics yourself as a part of your regular maintenance process. Use the UPDATE STATISTICS statement to refresh the needed statistics pages.

The optimizer depends on a well-organized query.   Don't forget to review your queries to ensure that there are valid SARGS where needed. Also provide as much information as possible with regard to possible join relationships, as they can give the optimizer more options for join orders. Because the optimizer can't optimize SARGS based on user-defined functions, be careful when using them in joins or as SARGS. Be careful with the use of temp tables and table variables because queries against them are often not able to be optimized due to late binding. This is where the trial-and-error concept comes in really handy.

SQL Server uses one index per table.   In most situations, SQL Server will use only one index per table to resolve the query. Although there are a few exceptions to this rule, such as the optimizers strategy for resolving OR operators, if you plan on one index per table, it will help you design the best indexes to meet the best aggregation of application needs. Try to get the most benefit from the fewest number of indexes.

To determine if the query optimizer is actually using an index for a query, consult the showplan output. Remember that if there is an index in the execution plan, you will see an icon in the plan that mentions the index. You may want to experiment with multiple index combinations to try to find the best aggregate collection of indexes. Remember that sometimes a *composite index*, one with more than one column in the key, can provide benefits for multiple queries. Although there are no hard and fast rules, here are some considerations for the best index selections. Start here and work your way out.

- Total I/O should never be more than a table scan. If using an index results in more I/O than a table scan, there is a problem.

- Clustered indexes generally work best for queries that select data based on range-based or non-unique searches.

- The maintenance cost of clustered indexes is very high. You should select nonvolatile columns for these indexes.

- Nonclustered indexes are generally best for very selective queries where you select a very small percentage of the data.

- Composite (multicolumn) indexes can often provide benefits for a broader range of queries, but have a higher maintenance and storage cost.

- Consider indexes for fields frequently used in SARGS.

- Consider indexes for foreign key fields in join operations.

This is definitely just a starting point. Every database is different and will require different indexing tactics. We cannot underestimate the importance of experimenting with the showplan and I/O metrics to determine the best possible indexing strategies.

🌐 Real World Scenario

THE GREAT DEBATE: PRIMARY KEYS AND CLUSTERED INDEXES

One of the continual battles we seem to have as SQL Server consultants is the conflict about the best placement of clustered indexes. It never fails; in every organization we work with, this debate comes up. The problem is that once the battle lines are drawn and entrenched, it is hard to get movement by either side. First, let's look at a little background.

The general rule of database design is that every table should have a primary key. We do not disagree with this statement at all. For both integrity and tracking reasons, we do in fact think that all tables should have a primary key.

We just discussed that most tables should have a clustered index, with very few exceptions. If you remember the discussion about primary keys in Chapter 6, you will recall that when you create a Primary Key constraint, a clustered index is also created as its default index type. Add to that the fact that there can be only one primary key per table and only one clustered index per table. When you consider all this, it stands to reason that the clustered index should always be based on the primary key fields, right? Not so fast…

As is usually the case with SQL Server performance tuning, the best answer to this question is "it depends." The best thing we can do is perform a cost-benefit analysis where we balance the costs of an index against its performance gains.

One of the arguments we always hear is that clustered indexes always give you the absolute best performance when doing a unique match. This is true. If your search argument uniquely selects a value from the table such that the query will only return one row, a clustered index will always give you the best performance. The number of pages of I/O will always be equal to the number of levels in the index. Primary keys are often the target of unique selections, so this seems like a good fit.

On the other hand, nonclustered indexes can do the same thing with just a few extra pages of I/O when performing a unique selection. A couple of pages here and there are probably insignificant, so why not use the nonclustered index here and save the clustered index for another field that might get more benefit? That sounds reasonable, but where do you put the clustered index?

One of the greatest benefits of the clustered index is that the data is clustered tightly together on the data page so that you can get ranges of data values with minimal I/O. A field that is used in range-based SARGS or perhaps a foreign key field that is commonly used in a join might be a better choice. The down-side here is the cost of maintenance. Remember that because the clustered index uses the data page as its leaf level, the maintenance cost of the clustered index is very high. Changes to a clustered index value would require a row to be physically moved, often to another page.

This is especially problematic when you are dealing with data inserts. SQL Server must position every row that you insert into the database on the appropriate data page based on the key. While you can deliberately leave empty space on a data page to accommodate these inserts, this tends to be a very high-cost process. On the other hand, if the clustered index is based in the primary key, it is much more likely that the key will be monotonic, or auto-incrementing. Monotonic keys always insert the new row at the end of the index, thus eliminating the insert overhead. SQL Server's current locking architecture also prevents a hot-page/row problem from occurring at the end of the table.

At the end of the day, the great debate is a classic case of the performance versus overhead conflict. While there is little argument that the aggregate performance of the database would be better with a clustered index placed on a non-unique or range-selected field, the overhead of maintaining that cost is often far too high to allow this as an option.

As with all cost-benefit equations, we have learned that the best thing database professionals can do is let go of the battle lines and deal with this and all performance issues on a case-by-case basis. Evaluate both sides of the argument and make judgments as impartially as possible—even if it means that you have to admit that you are wrong once in a while.

Creating and Managing Indexes

Although planning indexes can be a very complex process, creating them is very simple. You have two options. You can either create the index using the SQL Server Management Studio (SSMS) interface, or you can use the Transact-SQL (TSQL) code.

Creating Indexes with SSMS

To begin, you must connect the Object Explorer in SSMS to the server you want to target. In this example, assume that you want to create an index on the DemoSales table in the AdventureWorksDW2008 database.

1. Locate the appropriate table in the Tables folder of the AdventureWorksDW2008 database.

2. Expand the folder. You should see another folder inside labeled Indexes.

3. Right-click this folder and select New Index from the menu. This will present a New Index dialog like the one pictured in Figure 14.6.

This is the General page of the dialog. In this page, you will see that we are creating a clustered index.

4. Name your index. Although there are no index-naming rules other than the standard SQL Server naming requirements, you should use something that is indicative of the type of index key structure. Here, the name CL_DemoSales_UnitPrice indicates that this is a clustered index on the DemoSales table using the UnitPrice field as a key. As you look over the dialog, you will also see the checkbox that allows you to mark the index as unique. This will prevent the index from accepting duplicate values for the key field(s).

5. To add a field to the index, click the Add button and select the field(s) from the popup window that appears.

6. Click on the Options page to display the dialog pictured in Figure 14.7. This page shows standard options such as locking, statistics recomputation, and fill factors. Many of these options, such as fill factors, can be modified after you build the index.

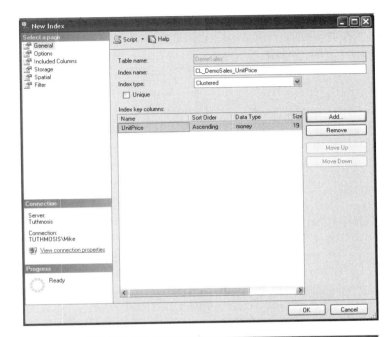

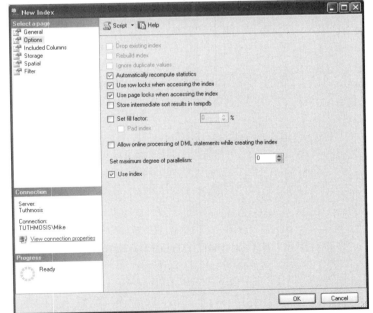

7. Look at the Storage page, which provides an interface where you can configure the physical filegroup or partition storage for the index. Most of the other pages deal only with nonclustered indexes.

8. To create the index, click the OK button on the dialog. The new index will appear in the Indexes folder of the Object Explorer.

THE USE INDEX OPTION

Also notice the option on the bottom of the page labeled Use Index. This is a convenient option that you can use in diagnostics to disable an index from consideration by the optimizer. This option allows you to easily switch between various indexes to compare and contrast their behaviors without having to completely remove and re-create the index. Be aware, though, that when you re-enable the index, SQL Server will actually execute a create operation as there is technically no "enable" option for the index.

> ### FILL FACTORS
>
> A *fill factor* is a setting that specifies how much free space SQL Server should leave on an index page when it creates the index. Although a fill factor lower than 100 percent (meaning a completely full page) will require more disk space, administrators often use this option to leave extra room so that inserts or updates into a page will not cause page splitting and shifting. It is a tradeoff between disk space and insert/update performance.

NONCLUSTERED INDEXES

Nonclustered indexes provide you with a few additional options. You can choose to include additional nonindexed columns for the purpose of covering the query. We will describe this technique in greater detail later in this chapter.

You also have the option to include a filter in a nonclustered index. Filtering is a useful feature that allows you to create a partial index. For example, assume that you have a large sales table and you frequently select from that table, but only in the UnitPrice range from 1,000 to 2,000. Rather than creating a nonclustered index on the entire table, you can filter the index to target only the portion of the data you want to access. Figure 14.8 illustrates the use of the Filter page for this purpose.

Managing Indexes and Fragmentation with SSMS

After you have created an index with the New Index dialog, it will appear in the Indexes folder of the table object in the Object Explorer. If you want to make modifications to this index, you can do it through the Index Properties dialog. To open this dialog, double-click on the index in the list, or right-click and choose Properties from the menu.

This dialog is almost identical to the New Index dialog; however, a few options are enabled that were not available before and other options might be disabled that are no longer relevant. For example, on the Options page, the option to rebuild the index is enabled, but the option to allow inline index creation is not.

You will also see a new page in the Index Properties dialog, the Fragmentation page. This page, pictured in Figure 14.9, displays general fragmentation metrics and other index information.

FIGURE 14.8
Filtering a non-clustered index

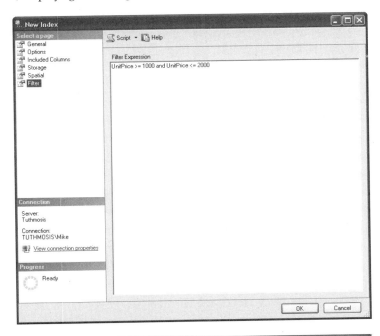

FIGURE 14.9
Index fragmentation

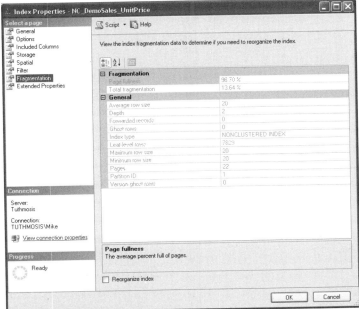

Understanding the information in this dialog is critical to your ability to properly tune your index structure. There are two types of fragmentation that you will contend with, internal and external fragmentation. Each has its own performance impact and, depending on your overall application structure, perhaps no impact at all. The Page Fullness value on the Fragmentation page is a measure of internal fragmentation, while the Total Fragmentation value is a measure of external fragmentation.

INTERNAL FRAGMENTATION

This type of fragmentation relates to the fill of the index page. If an index page in not completely full, in other words if there is free space on the page, the index takes up more space than it needs and is said to be *internally fragmented.* The negative impact of internal fragmentation relates to not only the amount of disk space that the index needs, but also the amount of I/O needed to use the index. Logically, if you spread the index across more pages, a query will require more I/O to use the index than if it had no internal fragmentation. This is especially true for a clustered index where the leaf level is the data page. This affects every operation that reads data from the data pages, even if they do not use the index directly. It even affects table scans (clustered index scans) because the data pages are spread across more pages.

Internal fragmentation can occur in a variety of ways. Deleting or updating data on a page can cause empty space on a page that formerly held data. It is also possible to design internal fragmentation into an index by using a fill factor. Internal fragmentation is not always a bad thing. Leaving free space on a page, as with a fill factor, will allow inserts and updates to occur without requiring major page reorganization and page splitting. Read-only data or monotonically inserted data should have no internal fragmentation. Volatile data or non-monotonically inserted data might benefit from some free page space.

EXTERNAL FRAGMENTATION

This type of fragmentation relates to the order in which the query thread reads data pages. This is generally an issue with full or partial scanning operations such as clustered or nonclustered index scans and many DBCC commands. External fragmentation occurs when a query thread has to skip around from extent to extent to resolve a scan operation. The cause of this fragmentation tends to be volatile data that causes page splitting and noncontiguous allocation.

To get a picture of what causes external fragmentation, you must start with the data page allocation process. When a table or index needs more space to store data, SQL Server allocates an extent to that table or index. Remember than an extent is a 64KB-block of space that consists of eight data pages. In the perfect world, SQL Server would fill each page in turn and then move on to the next page. That way when an index scan read the rows in indexed order, the query thread would read one extent in full and then switch to the next and continue until all pages had been read. Figure 14.10 illustrates this scenario.

FIGURE 14.10
Index scan with no
fragmentation

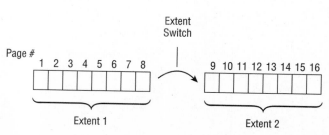

The problem arises when the query thread must switch to another extent prematurely, which can occur if the pages are out of order in the extent, which is the definition of external fragmentation. For example, what if page 5 in Figure 14.10 is completely full, but upon executing an insert into the table, the new row must go into the middle of that page based on the index key. In this situation, SQL Server must perform a page split, which consists of allocating a new extent if necessary, moving half of the data from page 5 to the new page, inserting the data into the appropriate page, and resetting the page pointers to include the new page in the proper sequence in the index. Figure 14.11 illustrates the result of this page split.

FIGURE 14.11
An index after a
page split

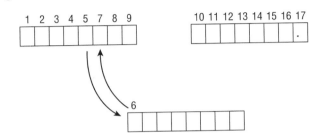

You will notice in the diagram that the page split has caused two extent switches, one to switch out to the new page and one to switch back. Because extent switching is time-consuming when performing scan operations, you should try to avoid this situation as much as possible. Deliberately planning a little bit of internal fragmentation in an index using a fill factor to accommodate these inserts and updates will delay the occurrence of external fragmentation.

External fragmentation is only an issue, however, when performing scan operations. If the query is resolved by doing index traversals, especially in the case of highly selective queries which do minimal partial leaf scanning, the level of external fragmentation will have little if any impact on the performance of the query.

MANAGING FRAGMENTATION

The best way to address fragmentation that you might have in your database is to rebuild the fragmented indexes. You have two primary options for index management, reorganize or rebuild.

Reorganize   Reorganizing an index will rearrange the index leaf pages so that they are in contiguous order. It also does some index compaction, removing empty pages by realigning the index back to the original fill factor. This operation does not hold long-term locks, and you can execute this process with online clients. If a table is spread across multiple files, reorganization cannot move data between files. For this you need a full index rebuild. Reorganize is generally sufficient for most index maintenance requirements.

Rebuild   This operation is a full-index rebuild. It is equivalent to dropping and re-creating an index; therefore, this is an offline operation. This process requires an exclusive lock on the index, and in the case of a clustered index, this will be an exclusive lock on the table. This operation will provide the most complete fragmentation reduction, and you should consider this option if the reorganization approach fails to produce the desired results or if there is significant fragmentation across multiple files.

SSMS provides options for both rebuilding and reorganizing indexes. The Options page of the Index Properties dialog contains a checkbox that allows you to specify an index rebuild. Simply open the dialog, check this option, and click OK on the dialog. The result is a complete index rebuild.

If you want to reorganize only the index, use the Fragmentation page of the dialog. At the bottom of the dialog, you will see a checkbox labeled Reorganize Index. Check this box and click OK on the dialog to commit the reorganization operation.

Creating and Managing Indexes with TSQL

Index manipulation in TSQL falls into the general category of Data Definition Language (DDL) operations. There are three primary DDL statements that are applicable to index management. Everything that you can do with SSMS, you can also do with these three statements:

◆ CREATE INDEX

◆ ALTER INDEX

◆ DROP INDEX

CREATING INDEXES WITH TSQL

To create an index or to completely rebuild an index by using an actual drop and re-create process as opposed to a rebuild, you will use the CREATE INDEX statement. The essential syntax of this statement is as follows:

```
CREATE [ UNIQUE ] [ CLUSTERED | NONCLUSTERED ] INDEX index_name
  ON <object> ( column [ ASC | DESC ] [ ,...n ] )
  [ INCLUDE ( column_name [ ,...n ] ) ]
  [ WHERE <filter_predicate> ]
  [ WITH ( <relational_index_option> [ ,...n ] ) ]
  [ ON { partition_scheme_name ( column_name )
    | filegroup_name
    | default
    }
  ]
```

In this syntax, your relation index options (the section after the WITH clause) are as follows:

```
PAD_INDEX = { ON | OFF }
| FILLFACTOR = fillfactor
| SORT_IN_TEMPDB = { ON | OFF }
| IGNORE_DUP_KEY = { ON | OFF }
| STATISTICS_NORECOMPUTE = { ON | OFF }
| DROP_EXISTING = { ON | OFF }
| ONLINE = { ON | OFF }
| ALLOW_ROW_LOCKS = { ON | OFF }
| ALLOW_PAGE_LOCKS = { ON | OFF }
| MAXDOP = max_degree_of_parallelism
| DATA_COMPRESSION = { NONE | ROW | PAGE}
```

Most of these options should already look familiar as they correspond directly to the index dialogs that we saw in the previous discussion. The Options page contains most of the relational index options in this syntax, and the General page defines most of the basic settings such as the index name and column list. The ON clause, which allows you to specify a filegroup or partition as the target of the index, is addressed in the Storage page of the dialog. The INCLUDE clause and the WHERE clause, which are valid for nonclustered indexes only, can be graphically configured in the Included columns and Filter pages, respectively.

This is very simple and precise syntax, and it allows you to create exactly the index you want and need. For example, to create a clustered index on UnitPrice in the DemoSales table, you would use this statement.

```
USE AdventureWorksDW2008;

CREATE CLUSTERED INDEX CL_DemoSales_UnitPrice
ON dbo.DemoSales(UnitPrice);
GO
```

If the index already existed on the table and you wanted to drop the index in order to re-create it, you could use this statement. Note that you accomplish the same thing here with a rebuild, which is addressed in the ALTER INDEX syntax. The usual logic behind a drop_existing option is to change the column list or locations that cannot be addressed with a rebuild.

```
USE AdventureWorksDW2008;

CREATE CLUSTERED INDEX CL_DemoSales_UnitPrice
ON dbo.DemoSales(UnitPrice)
WITH DROP_EXISTING;
GO
```

Suppose you had an employee table that contained a social security number field called SSN. Although the employee_id field would be the primary key, the SSN field might still benefit from an index and should be enforced as unique. One way to do this would be to create a unique index on the field, as in the following statement.

```
CREATE NONCLUSTERED INDEX NC_employee_ssn
ON dbo.employee(ssn DESC)
WHERE employee_id > 1000
WITH (
  ONLINE = ON,
  MAXDOP = 1
)
```

This hypothetical statement provides the following characteristics:

Descending Sort Order   It creates the nonclustered index on the SSN column, but sorts the index in descending order instead of the default ascending order. This can be useful in cases where you want to do similar sorts in your queries and you want index support for the sorts.

Partial Index   It creates just a partial index. Only employees with ID values greater than 1,000 are in the index. The goal is to conserve maintenance overhead by including only the rows you will actually query in the index.

Online Operation   This statement is marked as an online operation, which means that although the process may be more time-consuming, you can execute this query while there are still users in the database. The Max Degrees of Parallelism switch specifies how many parallel execution plans you will use to optimize the process. If you have multiple processors, each processor can execute a part of the parallel plan. Setting this value to 1 indicates that you do not want parallel plans created. This can be useful in online operations where parallel plans can occasionally cause deadlocks with other parallel branches or with users interacting with the database.

WHY CAN'T I RUN IT?

Please note that this statement is for illustrative purposes only. It does not reference data in the AdventureWorksDW2008 database and will fail if you execute it. It is intended only to provide an example of some of the index options available and a syntax pattern for those options.

DROPPING AND ALTERING INDEXES WITH TSQL

The DROP INDEX statement has limited options. While you can use the ONLINE and MAXDOP options with the CREATE statement, the general form of this statement is simply this:

```
DROP INDEX <index_name> ON <object_name>
WITH (<relational_index_options>)
```

Using this syntax, if you wanted to drop the CL_DemoSales_UnitPrice from the DemoSales table, the statement would look like this:

```
DROP INDEX CL_DemoSales_UnitPrice ON dbo.DemoSales;
GO
```

The ALTER INDEX syntax is a bit more involved because there are many options that you can modify when altering an index. The basic syntax of this statement is as follows:

```
ALTER INDEX { index_name | ALL }
      ON <object> {
      REBUILD | DISABLE | REORGANIZE
      | SET ( <set_index_option> [ ,...n ] )
  }
```

The main body of this syntax allows you to do three things. You can rebuild the index, reorganize the index, or disable the index. You will address any other index options though the SET clause. These options are the same as those in the CREATE INDEX statement, so you can control things such as fill factors, statistics recomputation, and all the other options in the previous list.

DISABLE IS A ONE-WAY STREET

Although you can disable an index, meaning that it will not be evaluated by the query optimizer, you cannot enable it again through the alter process. There is no enable option. If you want to enable the index again, you can execute a CREATE INDEX statement with a DROP_EXISTING option or use the ALTER INDEX with the REBUILD option.

Special Index Considerations

As always, there are some exceptions to the rules. While most indexing strategies provide support for standard optimizer behavior, there are always special cases and they can have both positive and negative impacts on performance. Being aware of these special cases allows you to take advantage of performance opportunities and avoid potential pitfalls.

In this section, we will discuss a few of these special issues. We will first address the concept of index covering and then look at logical operator processing.

Covering a Query

Covering is the process of retrieving all necessary data from an index instead of going to the data page. This behavior is specifically related to nonclustered indexes. The concept is simple. Nonclustered index leaf pages contain more rows per page than the data page does. Because your performance objective is to reduce page I/O, reading pages with more rows means that overall you will read fewer pages. Therefore, if all the data you need is on the index page, why read the data page at all?

Assume for a moment that you have an employee table with an average row size of 100 bytes. This means that you can store about 80 rows on a data page. If you have 100,000 rows in the table, you need about 1,250 pages to store the data with no fill factor. If you ever do a table or clustered index scan on the table, you would execute 1,250 pages of I/O.

Now assume that you have a query that selects the employee first name and last name for each employee. If there is no WHERE clause in the query, this would require a data page scan. But what if you created an index on the firstname and lastname columns in the table? You might initially assume that because the query had no SARGS, the index would not be useful, as it would provide no ability to filter the data. However, it might actually be of value to you.

Remember that all indexes at the leaf level will store the entire index key. If you create an index on the firstname and lastname columns, this entire key will exist in the nonclustered index leaf level for every row. Because the query only requires the firstname and the lastname data, why read the table when the query can get what it needs from the index? In this case the index is said to "cover" the query. This situation is automatically detected and scored by the query optimizer as an option for query execution.

The I/O that you save may be significant. Assume that each index key uses 40 bytes of space for the index key and any other row overhead. This is a 60 percent savings on a per row basis. Do the math and you will find that using the index would reduce the overall I/O to 500 pages.

If you create indexes with covering in mind, you could significantly reduce I/O by adding a few well-placed columns here and there in your indexes to ensure that you will get the benefit of covering. In the early days of SQL Server, you had to create composite indexes to get this advantage, meaning that all of the index fields had to be sorted and maintained when values changed. Now, however, you have the option of including nonindexed values in the index. They basically get to tag along for free, included with the index key but no additional sort overhead.

To accomplish this, you can either use the Included Columns page in the Index Properties dialog, or you can use the INCLUDE clause in the CREATE INDEX statement. Be careful not to include too many columns. There comes a point where too many columns create an index leaf level that is so large you lose the advantage of covering. When strategically placed, however, this can be an incredible advantage over standard data page scanning.

Logical Operator Processing

Logical operators such as AND, OR, and NOT pose particular challenges to the query optimizer. Remember that generally, SQL Server can use only one index per table when resolving a query. Logical operators can either provide more information to the optimizer or doom you to a leaf-level scan if the operator precludes the use of any specific index.

NOT   **The NOT** operator usually has catastrophic effects on query optimization because it provides no argument containment. Unless there is another SARG that the optimizer can use to provide effective filtering, you will end up with a scan of some kind. Although this operator is sometimes a requirement, you should attempt to recode the query to avoid it whenever possible.

AND   **The AND** operator is the optimizer's best friend. This operator provides a collection of conditions that must all be true. If each of the conditions is a valid SARG, the optimizer suddenly has a choice of which index to use and will likely choose the index that provides the most selective filtering, thereby eliminating more I/O.

For example, if a query has two **SARGS** related with an AND operator, the optimizer will score each one. If the first **SARG** selects a fewer number of rows than the second and scores with less I/O, it will use that index to resolve the query and then apply the other condition to results of the index-based extraction.

OR   **The OR** operator can be problematic. If the filter criteria are not based on the same column, this operator provides no guarantee that a single index could access all qualifying data. For example, consider the following WHERE clause:

```
WHERE salary > 50000 OR department = 'Engineering'
```

Both of these criteria are valid SARGS, but using an index on one to filter the data would preclude some of the values that the other might need to capture.

BE CAREFUL OR ELSE

Assume that the optimizer chose to use an index on salary. It could traverse the index to start searching for salary values greater than 50,000 and then pull all of those rows that are in the engineering department, but this would miss all of the engineering rows with a salary less than or equal to 50,000. No, the query must evaluate each of these criteria separately for each row of data.

Traditionally, this would result in a table scan. One trick to get around this problem was popular many years ago: if you have a query that requires an OR operator, break the query into two separate SELECT statements and then perform a union operation to merge the results again. Because you are executing two separate SELECTs, each SELECT can use its own index. Then the union can aggregate the individual results into a single result set.

The SQL Server optimizer is smarter than this now, however. In this situation, it will perform the split and union for you. Each SARG related with an OR operator executes as its own query. The optimizer scores each section separately, so you no longer need to split them up.

The catch to this is that if the optimizer detects that even one of the SARGS cannot be resolved using an index that would improve performance over a scan, it scraps the entire process and uses a scan instead. This makes sense because it has to perform a scan to address one argument. Why bother going through all of the extra I/O to use indexes for the other arguments?

The end result is that you must be cautious about how you match indexes to SARGS with OR operations. Unlike an AND operation, where the optimizer benefits from having any index on any SARG with which to resolve the query, the OR operation requires all SARGS to have a usable index or there is no benefit whatsoever. Keep very close watch on your OR operations, or you are sure to feel the negative performance effects that they can cause.

The Bottom Line

Explain the different indexing architectures and the best uses for each.   SQL Server supports a variety of indexing options and a very flexible index implementation model that you can use to optimize query performance. It is critical that you, as a database professional, understand these architectures so that you can create the best indexing strategy to meet your performance goals.

Master It   For each of the following query scenarios, identify which indexing architecture you think would be the best suited. For now, disregard maintenance costs and evaluate the indexes only on their merits. There are no definitively right answers. Explain your reasoning.

1. Uniquely selective query (one row returned)

2. Very selective query (few rows returned)

3. Range-based filter

4. Query with no SARGS

Create and manage indexes. The CREATE INDEX is simple but very comprehensive. You have many options to make sure that the index implementation is optimal for your performance scenario.

> **Master It** Identify which clause of the CREATE INDEX statement you would use to implement each of the following features.
>
> 1. Set the maximum degrees of parallelism to create two parallel query plans.
>
> 2. Allow indexes to be created while users are using the table.
>
> 3. Configure the index to leave 20 percent of the leaf-level pages free.
>
> 4. Drop and rebuild the index in one statement.
>
> 5. Add the lastname column to the index leaf level as a nonindexed field.

Use special optimizer behaviors to boost performance. The query optimizer is very flexible, but to get the most out of it, you must play by its rules. Understanding how the optimizer will react to special situations gives you a greater ability to capitalize on advantages or avoid pitfalls.

> **Master It** Write a CREATE INDEX statement that will give you the best index performance for the following query. Assume that @param is an input parameter in a stored procedure that could differ in value with each execution.
>
> ```
> SELECT ProductName, Price
> FROM Orders
> WHERE Price > @param
> ORDER BY Price DESC;
> ```

Chapter 15

Transactions and Locking

Business systems are complex. Frequently, data modifications that take place in one area of the database must occur concurrently with modifications made somewhere else. These processes must occur transactionally to ensure that you maintain data integrity. Transactional operations follow the ACID formula, which states that all transactions should be atomic, consistent, isolated, and durable. The "I" in ACID stands for isolated, which means that the data impacts of one transaction will influence no other transaction until the isolated transaction completes, either by committing or rolling back. SQL Server enforces isolation through its locking architecture. Locks on resources prevent operations in this shared data environment from interfering with each other, which is critical for data integrity.

Data integrity is critical for your business, and maintaining this integrity is complicated by the activities of multiple users in the same data space. Although SQL Server will handle the locking process for you, these locks can have significant performance impacts on your server activity. Understanding and manipulating transactional behavior and locks is, therefore, critical to your ability to tune database and server performance. In this chapter, you will learn to:

◆ Understand and utilize the SQL Server locking architecture

◆ Implement an effective transaction management strategy

◆ Implement an effective distributed transaction strategy

◆ Get transaction and locking information

The SQL Server Locking Architecture

There is a reason that almost every book or class on database administration or development deals with these two topics together. They are almost impossible to separate. Transaction activity has a direct relationship with locking. The types of actions in the transaction plus the duration of the transaction will determine which locks it holds and the level of contention for resources that those locks create. Conversely, the current status of the locks determines transaction performance, deadlocking, and other characteristics that can restrict overall database throughput.

We will begin this chapter by looking at the locking architecture. In later sections of this chapter, we will see how that architecture impacts transactional behavior.

There are a variety of different resources that SQL Server can lock and a number of different kinds of locks that it can hold. Each locked object and lock type plays a distinct role in the system. In this section, we will learn how the locking system works, then learn how to apply this knowledge to manage these resources and their concurrency effectively.

> **THE CHICKEN OR THE EGG**
>
> Discussing transactions and locks can be a bit difficult because you need to understand one concept to understand the other. The whole discussion is conceptually recursive. We have to start somewhere, so we will start with locking. We will assume that you already understand the basic concepts of transactions.
>
> If you need a refresher, look back to Chapter 5, "Procedural Programming," where we introduced transactional concepts. Feel free to skip back and forth in this chapter between the concepts of transactions and locking. At the conclusion of the entire discussion, the dust will settle and you should be able to see the whole picture more clearly.

What Gets Locked

SQL Server is a collection of resources. Most of these resources are shared, meaning that many users could be trying to access the same resources at the same time. To complicate matters further, many shared resources are hierarchical. For example, a database is a resource that a user may need. If that user is using a database, you do not want another user to attempt a database-level action, such as a drop or restore of the database. However, databases contain tables. If another user works with a table, they are also implicitly working with the database.

To extend this concept, a user reading a single row of data is also using the data page on which the row resides. The table contains the page, and the database contains the table. Therefore, SQL Server not only has to manage the locking for the actual consumed resource, but also the locking or potential locking for all of the other objects in the entire hierarchy. This set of locks is often called the *lock chain*, which refers to all of the locks necessary to ensure isolation of any specific resource at a particular level of hierarchy in the database.

Table 15.1 provides a list of resources that the data engine is able to lock. You can find this list in the SQL Server Books Online under the topic of Lock Granularity, which organizes the resources from the most local and granular (RID) to the most global and least granular (database).

TABLE 15.1   Lockable Objects

OBJECT	DESCRIPTION
RID	A row identifier used to lock a single row within a heap
Key	A row lock within an index
Page	An 8KB data or index page in a database
Range	A set of resources locked to prevent new inserts within the set
Extent	A set of eight contiguous pages
HoBT	A heap or a B-Tree used to protect data heap structures or index structures
Table	An entire table including all data and index pages
File	A database file used to allocate physical storage to a database

TABLE 15.1   Lockable Objects   *(CONTINUED)*

OBJECT	DESCRIPTION
Allocation Unit	Sets of extents usually devoted to storing either in-row data or large object (lob) resources
Database	The entire database

PHYSICAL VERSUS LOGICAL

The artifacts in Table 15.1 can be broken down into two categories: physical structures and logical structures. *Physical structures* are those associated with the physical allocation of space for database objects. Examples include allocation units, extents, and files. *Logical structures* deal with the logical organization of data in a database. These structures include the RID, key, and table. Physical structures generally lock for different reasons than logical structures, so it is important to make the distinction.

*Physical structure*s lock when SQL Server modifies the physical data structure or the allocation of that data structure. For example, if the database administrator (DBA) enlarges a database by increasing the size of a data file, the file will lock before the process begins and will release when the process completes. Likewise, if an allocation unit is allocated to a database when the database enlarges or if SQL Server allocates an extent to a table or index, those resources will lock as well. This prevents the allocation and configuration problems that can occur if two processes attempt to concurrently allocate or modify the same artifact.

Logical structures lock when data modifications require the lock for protecting data integrity. The action taken will determine the level in the hierarchy at which the lock will occur. For example, a data modification to an individual row will usually activate a RID lock, while a build of a clustered index will lock the entire table with a single table lock.

Pages are interesting artifacts in that they seem to have characteristics of both physical and logical structures. While pages are physical in that a page represents a physical block of 8KB of disk space or memory, SQL Server uses them like logical structures. Once SQL Server allocates an extent to a table or index, that table or index effectively owns all of the pages on the extent. The table or index uses the pages as needed and can lock them when data modifications that affect that page take place.

OVERHEAD VERSUS CONCURRENCY

To manage resource consumption, sometimes called overhead, SQL Server can lock objects at different levels of granularity. Every SQL Server lock uses roughly the same overhead, whether that lock manages a row or the entire database. It is possible that instead of using different levels of locks, SQL Server could use only low-level locks, but that would dramatically increase overhead.

For example, if a table has 100,000 rows and you want to build a clustered index on that table, SQL Server could use 100,000 row locks to manage concurrency and resource contention. Alternatively, SQL Server could use one table lock, which would employ less overhead by a factor of 100,000. The data engine must evaluate the trade-offs and make the best choice. The goal is to reduce overhead, while increasing concurrency. The more granular the lock, the more total overhead will be needed to manage those locks, but the more concurrency the server will support. Imagine that you designed a database engine that used byte locks. Every byte of data in the database is potentially lockable. If two users modify the same row, even the same field in a row, they would not interfere with each other as long as they did not modify the same actual byes of data. Is this solution possible? Perhaps, but it is not reasonable. While concurrency in this system would be phenomenal, the overhead would be outrageous.

By contrast, you could also design a system that had a single database lock. Any time a user wanted to perform any action in the database, the system would require them to acquire the database lock first and release it when completed. This would significantly reduce locking overhead; in fact, it would be virtually nonexistent. However, this is also an impractical solution in a multi-user database environment because it does not allow for any user concurrency.

MANAGING THE TRADE-OFF

To help better manage the trade-off between overhead and concurrency, SQL Server uses a process of *dynamic lock escalation*. Once the server grants a certain proportion of finer grain locks, it can escalate the request to a coarser grain lock to benefit overhead at a potential concurrency cost. The logic is that as the quantity of fine grain locks that the server grants goes up, the probability of causing a contention problem due to lock escalation goes down. We will discuss this process in greater detail later in this section.

Types of Locks

In addition to supporting different granularities of locks, the SQL Server locking architecture also supports numerous types of locks for different situations. Some locks are stricter than others. For example, two transactions attempting to read the same data at the same time does not cause the same level of exposure to corruption as two transactions writing to the same data structure at the same time. This distinction is reflected in the type of lock that SQL Server activates in any given situation.

Not all objects can use all kinds of locks. Some locks are specific to physical structures, while others are specific to logical structures. Still others might only be relevant to a certain type or class of object. Table 15.2 lists the most common types of locks. This is not a complete list, but it shows the lock types that you will need to understand to effectively manage the locking infrastructure in SQL Server. For a more complete listing, consult the Lock Modes topic in the SQL Server Books Online.

TABLE 15.2   Lock Types

LOCK TYPE	DESCRIPTION
Shared	Set when executing a statement that will not modify data, such as a select operation
Exclusive	Set when executing a data modification statement
Update	Set during update operations; that allows shared locking in the read phases of an update with an exclusive escalation for modifications
Intent	Set on coarser grain artifacts in a lock hierarchy to prevent integrity problems at different grains and to allow escalation if needed

Each lock type is used in specific situations and has certain levels of compatibility with other locks. Understanding lock behavior and compatibility is essential to managing lock contention and throughput. Let's look at each of these types and their compatibility in greater detail.

Shared Locks   Shared locks are essentially "read" locks. Whenever an operation reads, but does not modify, data, it assigns a shared lock. Shared locks are markers that signify that a transaction is reading the resource, so no one can make changes until the transaction releases the lock. Shared locks are compatible with other shared locks, allowing more than one transaction to read a given block of data concurrently. SQL Server commonly places shared locks on the RID, page, or table artifacts as needed based on the operation and the level of escalation.

Exclusive Locks   Exclusive locks are "write" locks. Whenever a data modification occurs, SQL Server places exclusive locks on the resources that it modifies. Exclusive locks are not compatible with any other lock type. A shared lock can prevent the placement of an exclusive lock, as can another exclusive lock. If the resource is already locked, the transaction will wait for the lock to be released so that it can continue. This is called *blocking*. Because shared locks are more compatible than exclusive locks, they are less likely to cause blocking.

Update Locks   These locks are acquired in situations when an update operation requires multiple passes through the data to manage the update process. For example, depending on the complexity of the UPDATE statement or the modified columns, it might be necessary for the database engine to make a read pass through the data to identify the rows that must update prior to performing any actual updates. This is where the update lock is convenient.

The update lock is a hybrid. It starts its life as a shared lock during the initial read process. During this read operation, before the updates occur, there is no reason to prevent other transactions from also performing data reads. After identifying the rows that it must modify, the data engine will escalate to an exclusive lock to execute the actual modifications. Hence the update lock is compatible with shared locks or other update locks in the read stage, but incompatible with any other locks in the write stage.

Intent Locks   Technically, the intent lock is not really a lock at all, but a lock marker. It plays two roles. First, it acts as a marker to tell a transaction that other resources at a finer granularity are locked and that it must wait accordingly. For example, if you have locked a RID exclusively pending an update, it will also set an intent lock at the page level and the table level. This will prevent another transaction from performing a table-level operation, such as dropping the table or building a clustered index on the table. The lock indicates that this would affect a finer-grain resource below and the table operation must wait until the initial transaction releases the intent lock.

Second, it also marks a potential intent to escalate the lock in the future. Any lock on a RID may be escalated to the page level or the table level. Without an intent lock marking its intention, it might not be possible to escalate this lock when needed. To control this behavior, intent locks support subtypes including intent shared and intent exclusive. These subtypes indicate the type of down-chain lock the intent lock supports. Table 15.3 shows a compatibility matrix for the most common types of locks.

TABLE 15.3   Lock Compatibility Matrix

	IS	S	U	IX	X
Intent Shared (IS)	Yes	Yes	Yes	Yes	No
Shared (S)	Yes	Yes	Yes	No	No
Update (U)	Yes	Yes	No	No	No
Intent Exclusive (IX)	Yes	No	No	Yes	No
Exclusive (X)	No	No	No	No	No

Controlling Locks

Although you cannot turn off locking entirely, there are many things that you can do to control lock behavior. In most cases, you will want to let SQL Server manage locks for you. The data engine optimizes locking to provide the optimal balance among three competing factors: data integrity, overhead, and concurrency. Whenever you try to manipulate any of these factors, it will likely come at the cost of something else.

You can control locking through three different mechanisms. These are *database configurations*, *locking hints*, and *transaction isolation settings*.

Database Configurations that Affect Locking

Locking may not be appropriate in all situations, but there is actually a database option that you can use to essentially turn off locking. Although there is no miracle switch labeled "Disable Locking" anywhere in SQL Server, the Database Read-Only option will have this effect if you can live with the consequences. Figure 15.1 illustrates the database properties dialog where you can configure this option. Notice the section labeled "State" in the bottom right of the dialog.

If you cannot modify the data in a database in any way, there is no need to hold any locks on logical data structures. Rather than set shared locks, the Database Read-Only option disables the logical data structure locking chain altogether. Yes indeed; this option will do just what it says; it will mark your entire database as read-only. Of course, the side effect of this action is that you will not be able to modify the data.

Although this sounds like an unreasonable restriction, there may be times that it makes sense. For example, suppose that you have a warehouse or a reporting system that you update periodically. Perhaps you use batch updates every evening to update the database using SQL Server Integration Services packages or Bulk Insert operations. In these cases, the database might be truly read-only most of the time, especially during operating hours when disabling the lock could really help performance. You could switch this option off before your update and back on when the update completes. This is a specialized case, but it shows that there are times when the options are valid.

FIGURE 15.1
Configuring the
database options

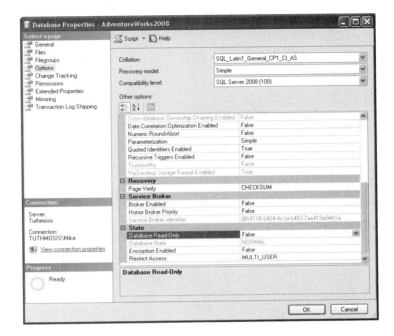

Transact-SQL Locking Hints

When you write your Transact-SQL (TSQL) code, you can include hints that provide specific instruction to the data engine about how to manage locks. Although they are called hints, they are really more like commands. Using hints, you can do things like:

- Request a particular lock type
- Request that no locks be held
- Request a specific lock granularity
- Request other specific locking behaviors

The syntax for most locking hints is the same. In the body of your TSQL statement, you can indicate the type of lock you want to request or the lock behavior that you want by using the WITH (*Hint*) statement, as in this snippet:

```
USE AdventureWorks2008;
SELECT *
FROM Person.Person WITH (TABLOCK)
WHERE LastName LIKE 'K%';
```

This hint requests that SQL Server use a table lock rather than following the default, which would be to use RID locks unless the optimizer determines an escalated lock would be a better option. This is just one of many hints that you can use to fine-tune the locking behavior in SQL Server.

Table 15.4 provides a list of additional useful hints. This list is not complete. For additional options, look up the topic Table Hints in the SQL Server Books Online.

TABLE 15.4   Locking Hints

HINT	DESCRIPTION
HOLDLOCK	Requests that the lock will be held for the duration of the entire transaction. Identical to SERIALIZABLE.
NOWAIT	Indicates that the query should return immediately if blocked and return an error.
NOLOCK	Requests that no locks be requested or honored.
PAGLOCK	Requests that page locks be held where RID or table locks would normally be held.
READPAST	Instructs the query to ignore any locked pages or rows instead of blocking and waiting for locks.
ROWLOCK	Requests that RID locks be held and does not permit lock escalation.
SERIALIZABLE	Requests that the lock will be held for the duration of the entire transaction. Identical to HOLDLOCK.
TABLOCK	Requests that a table lock be held instead of escalating through RID and page locks.
TABLOCKX	Works just like TABLOCK except that it creates an exclusive table lock.
UPDLOCK	Requests that an update lock be held until the transaction completes.
XLOCK	Requests an exclusive lock where shared or update locks would normally be held.

You can use hints in combinations by placing the hints in a comma-separated list. For example, if you wanted to request a table lock and you also wanted to force the query to return immediately upon encountering a locked table, you could use this syntax:

```
USE AdventureWorks2008;
SELECT *
FROM Person.Person WITH (TABLOCK, NOWAIT)
WHERE LastName LIKE 'K%';
```

If your query requires a join between multiple tables, you can use different hints for each by placing the hint after the table reference in your query. If you use a table alias in your query, you should put the hint after the alias. This syntax shows an example:

```
USE AdventureWorks2008;
SELECT FirstName, LastName, EmailAddress
FROM Person.Person as p WITH (NOLOCK)
INNER JOIN Person.EmailAddress AS e WITH (TABLOCK, READPAST)
  ON p.BusinessEntityID = e.BusinessEntityID
WHERE p.LastName LIKE 'K%';
```

DANGER AHEAD

In theory it sounds like a great idea. You can control concurrency and even other optimizer behavior, such as index selection and join order, simply by using some little hints in your code. In practice, it quickly becomes a wasp's nest of maintenance problems. Not only are you exposing yourself to potential data integrity issues, but you are also taking away the data engine and query optimizer's ability to tune and manage concurrency in the database. Once you start hinting, it is no longer "hands off" because when you insist that the data engine do one thing in a certain way, it loses the ability to manage the big picture effectively.

Be especially careful of hints like the NOLOCK. It can cause integrity problems because it allows the data engine to read locked rows and pages. The bigger problem is that it is often a symptom of a poor database design. If you have to use NOLOCK statements to keep the database accessible, it may be a red flag that there are more substantial problems.

TRANSACTION ISOLATION LEVELS

Remember that the "I" in ACID stands for *isolated*. One of the four standard characteristics of a transaction is that it is isolated from other transactions. One transaction should never interfere with or be aware of the work of another transaction. Locks enforce this isolation. Transaction isolation is something that you can control. By using database connection statements, you can specify how isolated a transaction will be.

The ANSI standard defines four levels of transaction isolation.

Read Uncommitted   The data engine allows a transaction to read resources that another transaction is modifying but has not yet committed. This is sometimes called a "dirty read." SQL Server provides for this behavior in a transaction by requesting no shared locks and honoring no exclusive locks. The behavior is the same as using a NOLOCK hint on every table at this level of isolation.

Read Committed   This is the default level of isolation. At this level, the transaction cannot read resources on which another transaction currently holds incompatible locks. Additionally, the transaction will place appropriate locks on all resources that it uses. The transaction typically holds shared locks only while the transaction reads the resource, while exclusive locks persist through the duration of the transaction.

Repeatable Read   This isolation level states that any read operation performed by a transaction should be repeatable later in the transaction. In other words, if you read a data row at the beginning of the transaction and again at the end of the transaction, as long as you do not modify the row in the transaction, those reads should yield the same result. To accomplish this, the transaction holds shared locks for the duration of the transaction instead of releasing them after reading the resource. This prevents the resources from being modified by operations outside of the current transaction.

Serializable   This level states that the transaction is completely isolated. It acts the same as repeatable read with regard to shared locks, but it also acquires range locks on read operations to prevent phantom reads, which are inserts that can occur within a range of resources that that the transaction is reading. Phantom reads result in the row counts of two serial reads being different because another transaction has inserted resources into the range read by the first transaction.

In addition to these ANSI isolation levels, SQL Server 2008 also supports a non-ANSI option called *snapshot isolation*. In this option, data modifications made by other transactions after the start of the current transaction are not visible to statements executing in the current transaction. The effect is to give the statements in a transaction a "snapshot" of the committed data as it existed at the start of the transaction. Except when a database is being recovered:

◆ SNAPSHOT transactions do not request locks when reading data.

◆ SNAPSHOT transactions reading data do not block other transactions from writing data.

◆ Transactions writing data do not block SNAPSHOT transactions from reading data.

Before you can use snapshot isolation, you must enable the ALLOW_SNAPSHOT_ISOLATION option at the database level. Due to the overhead in maintaining a snapshot record of all modified data, this option is disabled by default. To enable this option, use this statement.

```
ALTER DATABASE AdventureWorks2008
SET ALLOW_SNAPSHOT_ISOLATION ON;
```

Like most other SET statements in TSQL, the transaction isolation statements are session-level in scope. Once you set the option, it will be valid for the remainder of that session (user connection) until you close the connection or reset the setting to a different value. For example, to execute a series of queries allowing dirty reading, you could use a script like this one:

```
USE AdventureWorks2008;
SET TRANSACTION ISOLATION LEVEL READ UNCOMMITTED;
GO
SELECT FirstName, LastName FROM Person.Person;
SELECT City, StateProvinceID FROM Person.Address;
GO
```

In the previous snippet, you may have noticed that you must execute the isolation-level change with a GO statement before the change will take affect. The resulting behavior of these two select statements is identical to the result of placing the WITH (NOLOCK) statement in each query.

Altering the transaction isolation level or using lock hints will give you more control over the concurrency of the application. However, every alteration of isolation has its price. Increasing concurrency generally reduces data integrity protection and the reverse is also true. You will need to find that delicate balance between the two extremes. Generally speaking, as a best practice, do not override these settings unless there is a verifiable reason to do so.

Managing Deadlocks

Deadlocks are the bane of every database professional, but they are difficult to avoid altogether. When you are working in a multi-user environment, you will eventually run into a situation where the users will block each other. Knowing how to handle this is an important part of keeping your database up and responsive to user requests.

Deadlocks occur when two or more users need to use resources that are locked by other users before they can continue with their process. What separates this from simple blocking is its reciprocity. For example, assume that User A has row 1 locked and now needs to read row 2. However, User B has row 2 locked. This would be a simple blocking scenario. User A waits for User B to release the lock, and then it can continue.

What can cause a deadlock is when User B needs to get access to row 1 before it can complete and release its lock. Think about this. The only way that User A can continue is if User B completes or rolls back. User B is in exactly the same situation. At this point, neither of them can continue and one of them must cancel their transaction.

SQL Server deals with deadlocks in a very heavy-handed manner. It kills whichever connection has done the least amount of work up to that point. This is based on the overhead of undoing the work of the connection. SQL Server does not attempt to predict which connection is closest to completing, only which one can be cancelled the fastest and with the least overhead. Once identified, it will kill this connection immediately.

There are two ways that you can deal with deadlocking. The simplest way is to be disciplined in your code to ensure that all resources are accessed in the same order all the time. For example, if our two users both started by locking row 1 and then requested the lock for row 2, subsequently, this would merely be a blocking situation rather than a deadlock. One user would never deadlock another because it would never hold a resource lock out of order.

The other approach is a little more drastic. You can allow a connection to volunteer to be the victim of a deadlock. If you have a very low-priority connection that is deadlocking and causing the cancellation of other high-priority connections, you can configure the low-priority connection to be killed no matter how much work it has done to that point. You would accomplish this by using a session statement as follows.

```
SET DEADLOCK_PRIORITY LOW;
```

This indicates that the connection has a very low priority to continue when it deadlocks with another connection, essentially volunteering it to be the victim.

Please note that the query timeout option has no affect on deadlocking because SQL Server does not wait for a timeout to complete before killing the necessary connection. Once SQL Server detects a deadlock situation, it will kill that connection immediately.

Transaction Management

Although you can use techniques such as hinting and changing isolation levels to tune locking, the most important consideration is how you manage your transactions. The duration of a lock is generally associated with the transaction in which the data interaction takes place. Not managing your transactions effectively can cause significant performance degradation and misunderstanding transaction behaviors will lead to data integrity problems. In this section, we will look at basic transaction concepts and then see how we can code to optimize transaction behavior.

SQL Server Transaction Concepts

You will remember from the discussion in Chapter 5, "Procedural Programming," that transactions are SQL statements, usually resulting in data modifications of some sort, that are aggregated into the smallest possible unit of data integrity. The statement or set of statements must complete in its entirety or not at all. It must not interfere with or rely on the work of other executing transactions, and the results of the transaction must be durably recorded. SQL Server supports two general types of transactions: implicit and explicit.

Implicit Transactions   These are transactions that are automatically started when certain operations take place, such as an INSERT, UPDATE, or DELETE statements. Implicit transactions do not need any transaction identifiers to be supplied by the query. They begin automatically due to the type of command that the query executes.

Implicit transactions generally work in an auto-commit mode, meaning that as soon as the transaction operation completes, it will commit without any user intervention. For example, if a user executes a DELETE statement against the database that may affect multiple rows, the entire operation will occur as a transaction even though only one statement executed. If one of the deletes fails, the entire set will fail.

Explicit Transactions These are the transactions that you request using a BEGIN TRANSACTION marker in your TSQL code or by using a transactional API call from your client application. Following the command to begin a transaction, all TSQL statements that are valid inside the context of a transaction will be considered elements of the transaction until it is either committed or rolled back by the caller, or the connection terminates, which results in a rollback of any open transactions.

CONTROLLING AUTO-COMMIT BEHAVIOR

SQL Server's auto-commit behavior is not the standard in the industry. It is common for a relational database management system to use a system of implied transaction markers rather than an auto-commit behavior. For example, instead of performing the previously mentioned delete operation in an auto-commit mode, the DELETE statement would cause an explicit transaction to begin that would have to either be committed or rolled back at the conclusion of this and/or other subsequent operations. Database professionals who are transitioning to SQL Server from other systems may be more accustomed to this alternative behavior.

If you want SQL Server to assume this behavior, you can control it through the session statement SET IMPLICIT TRANSACTIONS ON. This session-scoped statement will cause any use of the following statements to begin a transaction that must be explicitly committed or rolled back:

- ALTER TABLE
- CREATE
- DELETE
- DROP
- FETCH
- GRANT
- INSERT
- OPEN
- REVOKE
- SELECT
- TRUNCATE TABLE
- UPDATE

Implementing Explicit Transactions

Explicit transactions begin when a BEGIN TRANSACTION statement executes in a SQL statement. When this occurs, SQL Server places a transaction marker in the transaction log so that it can locate the recovery point if necessary. Once the transaction is formally committed, all of the transaction log records will immediately flush from the data cache to disk, thus rendering the transaction permanent.

There are a number of different forms that this process can take. You can use a simple transaction statement like this one:

```
BEGIN TRANSACTION;
DELETE FROM table1;
DELETE FROM table2;
COMMIT TRANSACTION;
```

If you like, you can abbreviate the word "transaction" like this.

```
BEGIN TRAN;
```

You can also name a transaction if you wish. Named transactions can make it easier to understand your code and in some cases can also make it easier to recover from a backup. To use a named transaction, use this code:

```
BEGIN TRAN DemoTran;
-- statements
COMMIT TRAN DemoTran;
-- or ROLLBACK TRAN DemoTran
```

You can also place a mark in the transaction log with a named transaction that will make it simple to recover to that point again using the STOPAT option when restoring a log. The name of the transaction will be the stop at point. To add the mark, use this syntax.

```
BEGIN TRAN DemoTran WITH MARK;
```

It is possible to nest named transactions, but this really buys you nothing because only the outermost transaction is registered with the system for rollback. For example, consider the following code snippet.

```
USE AdventureWorks2008;
BEGIN TRAN T1;
SELECT COUNT(*) FROM Person.Person;
BEGIN TRAN T2;
SELECT COUNT(*) FROM Person.Person;
ROLLBACK TRAN T2;
```

Conceptually, T2 is nested within T1, so a rollback to T2 should only roll back the work that was done from the beginning of T2 to the rollback point. However, if you execute this query, you get an interesting error message that reads like this.

```
Msg 6401, Level 16, State 1, Line 6
Cannot roll back T2. No transaction or savepoint of that name was found.
```

This is a curious message, because we explicitly created a transaction named T2. However, because that transaction was nested inside T1 and only the outer transactions were registered with the system, it is literally as if the transaction point never existed. If you commit or roll back a transaction, it will commit or roll back all the way to the outermost transaction.

This does not mean that nested transactions are not recognized at all. They certainly are. It is just that you cannot roll back or commit to any point other than the outermost transaction point. For example, try rewriting the previous query just a little and see what you get.

Now execute the following statement in a new connection, ensuring that there are no open transactions before the process begins. You should get interesting results.

```
USE AdventureWorks2008;
BEGIN TRAN T1;
SELECT @@TRANCOUNT;
BEGIN TRAN T2;
SELECT @@TRANCOUNT;
ROLLBACK TRAN T2;
```

The @@TRANCOUNT global variable tells us how deeply nested the current transaction is. If you execute this snippet in a fresh connection, the first counter should return 1 and the second should return 2. This means that SQL Server has, in fact, recognized the beginning of the nested transaction, but it did not allow rollback or commit to that point in the hierarchy.

What good are nested transactions if you cannot commit or roll back to those points? The real answer is that explicit transaction statements were never meant to be nested within a single script, and this is a misuse (and often a dangerous misunderstanding) of transactional behavior.

Most nested transactions end up that way due to modular procedure structure. For example, if one stored procedure begins a transaction and then calls another procedure that also begins a transaction, you now have a nested transaction.

As you can imagine, this can be dangerous. If the called procedure were to roll back its transaction for some reason internal to the procedure, it would have an impact that extended beyond its control. The transaction that called the procedure would also be rolled back, and any executing statements that followed would then be in a nontransactional state. In this case, the called procedure should consult the value @@TRANCOUNT before rolling back its transaction to ensure that it would not affect anything out of its control.

Using Savepoints

Because nested transactions do not give you the ability to partially commit a transaction, there is another option. You can use a savepoint. *Savepoints* are markers in a transaction that represent points of integrity. Using a savepoint marks that the transaction is potentially safe to commit to that point, even if additional work is pending. Figure 15.2 illustrates the use of savepoints.

FIGURE 15.2
Using savepoints

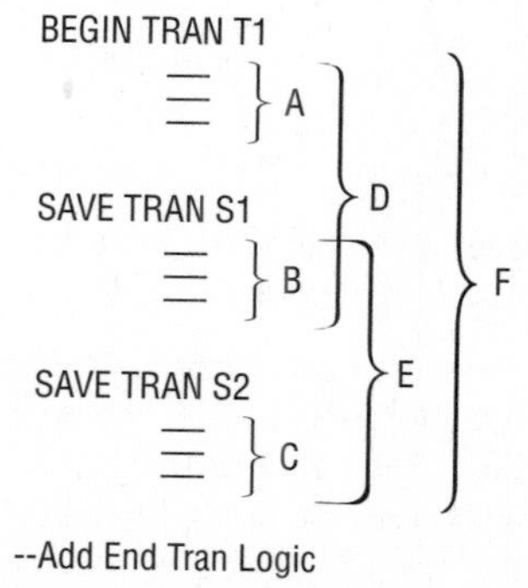

In this diagram, you will see one BEGIN marker with two SAVE markers. At the end of the transaction, the statements that you use will determine what SQL Server will commit or roll back. For example, if you were to use the statement COMMIT TRAN T1, it would commit all of the work indicated by bracket F in the diagram.

But what if halfway down the transaction you realize that you cannot commit the whole transaction? Perhaps the first part of the transaction would be safe to commit, but the last part is not. You can use a savepoint if you can identify the cutoff point for the commit in advance. In this example, we defined a savepoint called S1. Suppose that after executing additional statements, you determine that you cannot commit anything after the savepoint. You might use this logic at the end of the transaction:

```
ROLLBACK TRAN S1;
COMMIT TRAN T1;
```

These statements would roll back all of the work executed in bracket E in the diagram, and then subsequently commit the work in bracket A. Likewise, if you were to roll back to S2 instead of S1, you could undo the work in bracket C, followed by a commit of the work in bracket D.

Now consider the previous situation where one stored procedure calls another. If the called stored procedure might need to roll back any of the work that it is doing, it could use a savepoint instead of a nested transaction statement. Then if needed, it could roll back to the savepoint instead of rolling back the entire transaction. Because the called procedure rolls back only its own work, the calling procedure is never even aware that SQL Server had extended and then reversed the transaction. It can continue as if nothing had happened.

 **Real World Scenario**

TRANSACTIONS FROM OUTER SPACE

Everyone has a good transaction story. This one comes from the consulting diary of Michael Lee.

Transaction management in SQL Server is not difficult from a TSQL code perspective. Beginning a transaction and testing for errors is a simple process. However, in a highly modularized data environment, it can be a bit of a challenge.

It was just this situation that I ran into once when consulting for an entertainment retailer in the western United States. They had painstakingly crafted a procedural model intended for heavy reuse. In most cases, code reuse is a good thing. I'm all for it generally, but because their model relied on significant procedural chaining—where procedures frequently called other procedures—they ran into some significant transaction problems.

They had done an excellent job in most of their procedures to ensure that problems resulting in transactions being rolled back and error codes being raised to the client. The problem was that when a rollback occurred in a procedure that was nested three or four layers down from the initial call, the rollback operations had impacts that went far beyond the aborted transaction. We experimented with numerous transactional approaches including savepoints, but nothing seemed to work just right for the situation at hand. As a DBA consultant, I felt it was time to take extreme measures.

In a meeting with the senior DBA staff, I made what I thought was a reasonable suggestion. I suggested that they take out all of the transaction management from the stored procedures, leave the error management, which was working fine, and push the entire transactional process from the procedures to the Data Access Layer (DAL), which was written in C# with ADO.NET. From the reaction that I got, you would think that I had suggested that we all go bear hunting with sticks. In other words, my client responded with complete disbelief.

Now I realize that most DBAs love to have complete control over the database. It is up to us to protect and ensure the integrity of the database, but transaction management to me is a little different. I have always felt that transactions are really nothing more than advanced business rules. And where do all of the business rules go? They go in the object tier, in this case, on the business side of the Data Access Layer (DAL). SQL Server has a perfectly good transactional API that can be fully leveraged from OLEDB or .NET. Taking advantage of it to solve this problem seemed like a natural solution.

Even so, I will never forget a comment made by one of the DBAs at the time. He said that allowing developers to manage transactions is taking orders from creatures from outer space. Of course, my argument was that developers are responsible for a significant amount of the data integrity anyway by enforcing business logic at the component level. How is this any different?

At the end of the day, we did a limited pilot of this concept and it worked beautifully. Developers don't want data messed up any more than DBAs do. It is just that we DBAs tend to take it a little more personally.

The moral of the story is that that there are many facets to SQL Server, although we do not always have to use them all. Consider all of the tools at your disposal, not just the ones that you are comfortable with. You will have many more options for making the best application possible.

Transactions and Errors

Transactions are usually closely related to errors, because in most cases, unless a transaction component can complete without error, you should not commit that transaction. We discussed the specifics of dealing with errors in Chapter 5, so we will not repeat those here, but it is very important to consider the topic of errors concurrently with the topic of transaction management.

You have already read about TRY and CATCH statements. These statements can be very useful when managing transactions because they give you the opportunity to roll back transactions if they do not successfully complete in their entirety. Consider the following transaction.

```
DELETE FROM table1;
DELETE FROM table2;
```

As it exists right now, this represents two independent implicit transactions. To ensure that they commit or roll back together, you must add transaction markers like this:

```
BEGIN TRAN;
DEELTE FROM table1;
DELETE FROM table2;
COMMIT TRAN;
```

This code would enable both transactions to be committed if possible, but there is still a possibility that the first DELETE statement could fail and yet the second would commit. Because there is no error handling, if the first statement fails, SQL Server would simply continue to the second statement, committing it if possible. To prevent this, you must tell SQL Server to detour around the second statement if the first statement cannot commit. Consider this revision to the code.

```
BEGIN TRY
BEGIN TRAN;
   DELETE FROM table1;
   DELETE FROM table2;
   COMMIT TRAN;
END TRY
BEGIN CATCH
   ROLLBACK TRAN;
END CATCH
```

THERE'S MORE TO THE CATCH

This example is admittedly a bit simplistic. In addition to simply rolling back the transaction, you may want to raise an error to the client or capture other information—such as the error number or error description—to a log. Feel free to pad this out as necessary so that all information is communicated as necessary. Don't forget the three "R's" of transactional processing: RaiseError, Rollback, and Return.

You may also want to check the value of XACT_STATE(), which is a system function that will tell you if the transaction can be safely committed. This function returns -1 if it cannot be safely committed and should be rolled back. A return of 0 indicates that you are not in the context of a transaction and either a commit or rollback would result in an error. If it returns 1, the transaction can be safely committed. This is a useful function to use if you are unsure about the state of the transaction and what you can do with it.

Concurrency and Performance

For all the problems that transactions can solve with regard to data integrity, they can create just as many problems relating to concurrency and performance. It is critical that you consider these issues when planning your transactional strategies as well as your lock isolation and hinting structure. Being aware of the problems is half the battle, though. Here are a few things that you might want to consider as you are designing your transactional infrastructure.

Keep transactions short.   The longer the transactions are, the longer you will hold locks, and (usually) the more data you will lock. Make sure that you do any processing before you start the transaction. Do not start the transaction until you are prepared to execute the operations required by the transaction and then get out as quickly as possible. It is up to you to make sure that your locking does not become blocking.

Assume transactions will commit.   The performance assumption in SQL Server is that transactions will commit. Once the transaction begins, you are executing work that SQL Server assumes you will want to commit. Before you begin the transaction, do all you can to give the transaction the best chance possible of committing. Then you will not have to deal with rolling back the work that could not commit, which is a very high overhead process.

Use more concurrent isolation levels.   Don't be afraid of a dirty read. You should assume that transactions will commit; therefore, you should also be able to safely assume that the data that you are reading will ultimately be committed. Although you may run into a few consistency issues from time to time, dealing with those issues often uses less overhead than holding locks and blocking out or deadlocking other users.

Access only necessary data.   Try not to access more data than you really need. This is primarily an issue when selecting data. Use effective WHERE clauses and try to filter out as much of the data as possible. Not only will you improve the select performance and reduce disk and network I/O, but you will also be reducing the resources that you have to lock, which will increase concurrency on the server side. This is an easy thing to do that is usually underestimated by most developers. Keep it short and simple.

No user interaction.   This is a holdover from the old xBase days, but you might be surprised at how much the authors see this issue when tuning applications. Do not begin a transaction and then enter a user interactive mode. You never know what the user is going to do or how long they will take. You lose complete control of transaction duration when the transaction does not commit until the user hits that Save button. Instead, don't even begin the transaction until you have all of the information you need to perform the task at hand.

Use implicit transaction mode with caution.   If you come from another database system that used implicitly started transactions, you might be used to that pattern. If yours is primarily a SQL Server background, be careful. You can get very used to working with auto-commit behaviors and sometimes you don't remember that when the implicit transaction mode is enabled, once you commit or roll back a transaction, the very next statement probably starts another one. If you do not manage this process, transactions tend to get very long and brittle.

Distributed Transactions

The way that SQL Server manages transactions places a limitation on standard transactions. SQL Server can only enforce standard transactions on a single server. For example, a transaction that uses multiple tables in a single database or even across multiple databases on the same server is no problem for a standard transaction. However, if you want to include resources on a different server, then you can no longer use a standard transaction. In this case, you must use a distributed transaction.

SQL Server's standard data engine installation includes a tool called the Distributed Transaction Coordinator (DTC). This utility is responsible for maintaining the integrity of distributed transactions in a SQL Server environment. You can think of the DTC as a "traffic cop," responsible for managing the interaction among the various data engine instances that participate in the transaction. The mechanism that the DTC uses to do this is called a *two-phase commit protocol*. As its name implies, it breaks each distributed transaction into two separate phases called *prepare* and *commit*.

The Prepare Phase   The initial phase of the two-phase commit requires each service that participates in the transaction to enlist in the transaction and complete the work assigned to it. The DTC will contact every participating instance, enlist them in the transaction and verify their ability to participate. Then the DTC will give each instance the work that it must complete. The instance executes the work of the transaction but does not commit the work yet. Each service reports its ability to commit back to the DTC and awaits the second phase.

The Commit Phase   After enlisting the services in the transaction, the DTC waits for each service to report back its ability to commit. Each service must report back in a timely manner and must indicate that it is able to commit its work. Reporting must be unanimous. If any server does not respond or returns a condition that would prevent the transaction from committing, the DTC sends an abort message to all participants and they all roll back their work. If all participants indicate an ability to commit, the DTC sends a commit message and all services commit together.

WATCH YOUR OVERHEAD

Although distributed transactions sound great in concept, you really need to watch the overhead. There is a significant amount of communication that must take place to keep all of the participants in sync. There is also a lot of data that will be moving back and forth among the participants. Consider this as part of your overall distribution strategy.

Another issue to consider is the fact that for each service you enlist, you will be creating a point of failure. Even one service failure will cause all distributed transactions that use that service to fail as well, which may interfere with the work of other servers in your enterprise data infrastructure. If you are using distributed transactions to synchronize distributed data, you may want to consider other options that do not have this point-of-failure weakness, such as replication or log shipping. Those techniques can often provide the features that you need without the potential costs. Chapter 12, "Data Availability and Distribution," addresses these features in detail.

Understanding Distributed Queries

Up to this point, our examples have shown queries that execute on a single server and usually in a single database. It is possible, however, to distribute query behavior across multiple database and even multiple servers. Before we can turn our attention to distributed transactions, however, we must discuss the process of performing server-to-server communications using distributed queries. There are two ways that you can execute distributed queries across servers. One approach is to use the OpenRowset() function and the other is to use linked servers.

USING THE *OpenRowset()* FUNCTION

The OpenRowset() function is primarily a method for performing queries against a target server on an ad hoc basis. Each call using OpenRowset() is self-contained and includes everything that the query needs to know to make the connection and execute the query. The function makes all connectivity through OLEDB and, therefore, this option is available to all OLEDB-

compliant data sources. You are not limited to SQL Server data sources. The basic syntax of the
OpenRowset() function looks like this.

```
OPENROWSET
(
{'provider_name',
{'datasource';'user_id';'password'|'provider_string'},
{[ catalog.][schema.]object|'query'}}
)
```

You will note that there are three parameters for the function. The first is the name of the
OLEDB provider that you will use to connect to the remote service. If you are connecting to
another SQL Server 2008 service, use SQLNCLI as the provider name. This indicates that you will
be using the SQL Native Client. Other services have OLEDB providers as well, so you will need
to look into the documentation for those services and determine the appropriate name to use.

The second parameter is a connection string that is provider specific. This contains the information about the target service and database as well as authentication information.

The final parameter is the object that you wish to access. This could be a stored procedure that
you want to execute or a pass-through query that you want to send to the service for execution.

Before you will be able to use the OpenRowset() function, you must first configure the target
server to allow ad hoc distributed queries. You can do this by executing the following configuration code on the target server. Note that because the Ad Hoc Distributed Queries option is an
advanced Boolean option, you must execute the first statement before you will be able to make
the required change. You should then set the option back when complete.

```
EXEC sp_configure 'Show Advanced Options', 1;
RECONFIGURE;
EXEC sp_configure 'Ad Hoc Distributed Queries', 1;
RECONFIGURE;
EXEC sp_configure 'Show Advanced Options', 0;
RECONFIGURE;
```

Now that you have permitted the use of the distributed query on the target server, you are
free to execute the query. This example executes a query against an AdventureWorks2008 database on a distributed server instance. Note that you would be executing this query from the context of the server instance called "Tuthmosis," but the pass-through query will actually execute
on the service instance called "Tuthmosis\DTCTarget."

```
SELECT DISTINCT dtc.FirstName, dtc.LastName
FROM OpenRowset(
         SQLNCLI',
         'server=tuthmosis\DTCTarget;database=AdventureWorks2008;
         trusted_connection=yes',
         'SELECT FirstName, LastName FROM Person.Person'
) AS dtc
WHERE dtc.LastName LIKE 'K%';
```

This example is very selective with regard to the columns that it returns from the target
server, but not the rows. There are no filter criteria executing on the target server. What you see
here is actually two separate queries. One query is the pass-through that executes on the target
server, and the other filters out the data on the local server in the outer query. Keep in mind that

you are running multiple queries because you will want to tune each one to make sure that you are conserving bandwidth and I/O as much as possible.

This example also uses integrated security. The assumption is that the user is logged into the primary server using a Windows account that also has access to the target server. If this is not the case, you may get a login error when attempting to execute the query.

CONFIGURING LINKED SERVERS

The other option for executing a distributed query is to configure a linked server. While an ad hoc query provides authentication information every time a call to OpenRowset() executes, the linked server model will store all authentication and resolution information in the server's configuration data. This facilitates the use of the linked server by allowing a four-part name for the resources that you want to access instead of having to use an ad hoc function with each execution.

You can add a linked server to your configuration by using either a TSQL statement or the studio interface. The visual interface displays all required and available options, so we will use that approach. You can script the results of the visual configuration, however, if you need to create the same linked server reference on multiple servers in the enterprise.

To begin, open the SQL Server Management Studio (SSMS) and expand the node for the server that will be the primary server. This server will host the query that will call the other services. Locate the Server Objects node inside your server list and expand this to find the linked servers list. You will also see a Providers list containing the different providers that SQL Server installs by default. You can create a linked server to any of the databases for which there is a provider.

To create a linked server, right-click the Linked Servers node in the list on your primary server and select New Linked Server from the menu. This will display a dialog like the one illustrated in Figures 15.3 through 15.5. This dialog has three pages. The first page does the basic configuration, as shown in Figure 15.3.

FIGURE 15.3
Configuring
Linked Server
Connectivity

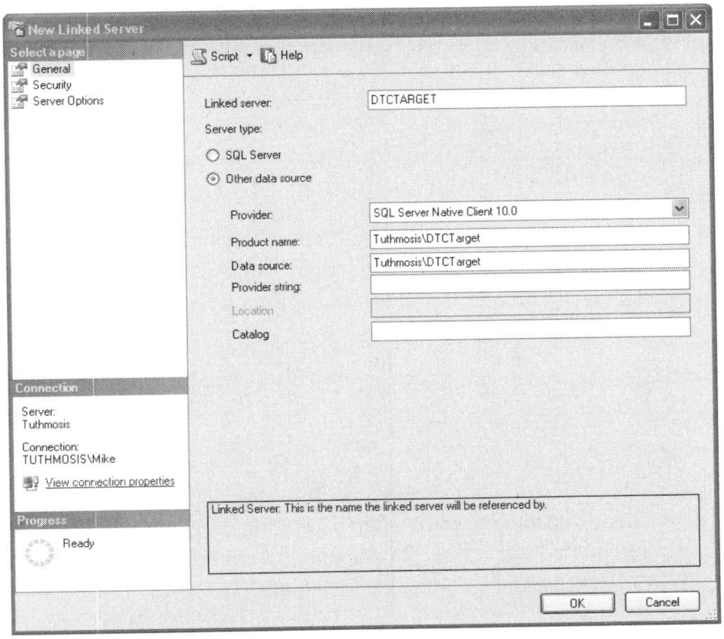

In this dialog, the name of the linked server is DTCTARGET. This is an alias that points to the actual server instance, which is Tuthmosis\DTCTarget. This linked server uses the SQL Native Client interface.

The next page in the dialog, pictured in Figure 15.4, configures linked server security.

FIGURE 15.4

Configuring linked server security

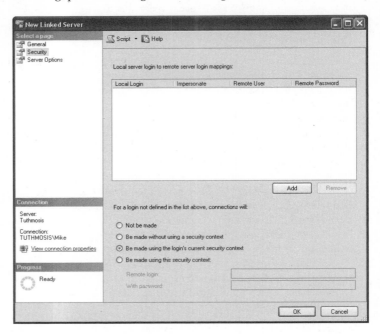

You have many options when configuring security. This dialog shows a standard integrated connection. SQL Server will use the same user account that you use to log into the primary server to log into the target server. This interface allows a very flexible security configuration. You can start by doing specific login mapping in the top section. This will allow you to map a local login to another specific remote login. Then for all local logins that are not in the top list, you can select one of the four options visible at the bottom of Figure 15.4. These options will (in order)

- Deny access

- Permit access under guest authority

- Permit access under trusted authority

- Permit access using a specific general account

The final page in the dialog, pictured in Figure 15.5, provides the linked server options. You can change these options at any time, along with the security options in the previous dialog, by accessing the linked server properties after the link has been created. If you want detailed information for each option, click the Help button at the top of the dialog for a full discussion. For now, just verify that the Data Access option is set to True. This option must be enabled before you will be allowed to use the linked server in a distributed query. When you are finished with this page, click the OK button to create the linked server.

FIGURE 15.5
Linked server
options

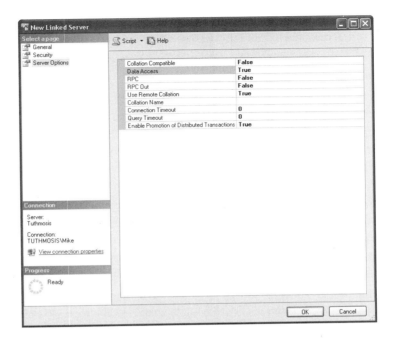

Now that you have created the linked server, you can use that link in a distributed query. There are two ways to do this. The first is to use a standard four-part name in the FROM clause of the query. This will force the target server to return the entire data structure from the target server where the primary server can continue to filter and process the data. For example, consider the following query.

```
SELECT * FROM DTCTarget.AdventureWorks2008.Person.EmailAddress
WHERE ModifiedDate >= '01/01/2000 00:00:00.000';
```

This query returns the entire content of the Person.EmailAddress table from the target server to the primary server, which applies the filter criterion and returns the results to the requesting user. This is a very convenient syntax, but if the target table is quite large, or if there are data that cannot be returned to the primary server, such as an XML column, you will need to find an alternative approach. For example, take a look at this query.

```
SELECT FirstName, LastName
FROM DTCTarget.AdventureWorks2008.Person.Person
WHERE LastName LIKE 'K%';
```

If you execute this query, you will get an error message stating that xml data types are not supported in distributed queries. Looking at the query, this seems a little odd, because you are returning only FirstName and LastName, and neither of these columns is configured as an xml data type. Remember, though, that when you use the four-part name in a query, the target server will return the entire data structure to the primary server for processing.

You can solve this problem in two different ways. One is to use stored procedures or views on the target server instead of accessing the table directly. This will force some execution on the server. Simply use the four-part name of the desired procedural target to access it through the linked server. Use the view name in the FROM clause in place of the table names. Stored procedures will execute as normal with an EXECUTE statement using a four-part name for the procedure.

The other option is to use the OpenQuery() function. This function provides for a pass-through query to be sent to the target server, much like OpenRowset(), but through the linked server rather than on an ad hoc basis as with the OpenRowset() function. To use the OpenQuery() function, try this syntax.

```
SELECT dtc.FirstName, dtc.LastName
FROM OpenQuery(
  DTCTarget,
  'SELECT FirstName, LastName
  FROM AdventureWorks2008.Person.Person'
) AS dtc
WHERE dtc.LastName LIKE 'K%';
```

Although it is a little more work, you can optimize your linked server queries using this method rather than using a simple four-part name. The performance and security prize still goes to stored procedures in most cases, though, so you should definitely consider that as an option before you default to using OpenQuery().

MAKING DISTRIBUTED MODIFICATIONS

You can use OpenQuery() to make data modifications as well. By using the OpenQuery() function in place of a table name in an INSERT UPDATE and DELETE statement, the data modification will be targeted to the data subset as defined in the OpenQuery() syntax. You can also use this syntax as part of a distributed transaction, making this a very flexible option when needed.

Defining Distributed Transactions

Once you have created the linked servers, you have completed the real work of configuring distributed transactions. SQL Server handles most of the nuts and bolts of making a distributed transaction work. By defining the linked servers, you have created all the necessary target configurations and set up the required security. Now all you have to do is request the distributed transaction.

There is one configuration option that you might want to check. If you open the Database Properties dialog and go to the Connections page, you will see a dialog like the one pictured in Figure 15.6. Toward the bottom of this dialog is an option that allows you to specify that any server-to-server communication is required to execute using distributed transactions. This is a safety mechanism that you can enable to ensure that multiple servers will stay in sync so one cannot inadvertently execute a remote operation outside the context of a distributed transaction. Be careful of the overhead, though. This option can be a real stinger. We will leave this unchecked for now.

FIGURE 15.6
Database configuration for distributed transactions

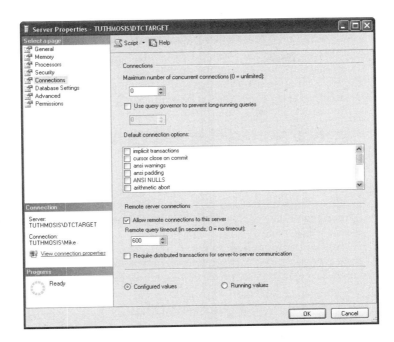

Requesting a distributed transaction rather than a standard transaction is a very simple process. Just use the statement BEGIN DISTRIBUTED TRAN to begin the transaction. Everything else will behave normally. Consider the following snippet as an illustration.

```
USE AdventureWorks2008;
BEGIN TRY
BEGIN DISTRIBUTED TRANSACTION;
UPDATE OpenQuery(
        DTCTarget,
        'SELECT BusinessEntityID, FirstName
             FROM AdventureWorks2008.Person.Person
             WHERE BusinessEntityID = 1'
   )
SET FirstName = 'Kenny'
WHERE BusinessEntityID = 1;
UPDATE Person.Person
SET FirstName = 'Kenny'
WHERE BusinessEntityID = 1;
COMMIT TRANSACTION;
END TRY
BEGIN CATCH
        ROLLBACK TRANSACTION;
END CATCH
```

This code executes a distributed transaction on the Adventureworks2008 database on both servers. The goal of this distributed transaction is to keep the two databases in sync by ensuring that any modification made to one database will also be made automatically to the other database. This, of course, requires that the DTC be installed and running, because it will act as the transaction manager in this situation, enlisting the DTCTarget server in the transaction and ensuring that the modification commits to both servers or not at all.

Getting Transaction and Locking Information

Fortunately for the DBA, the lock chain is not invisible. You can get valuable information from SQL Server about processes and locks when you need it. This information will not only help you understand SQL Server's behaviors, but will also let you use these techniques for tuning queries, managing blocking and deadlocking activity, and managing user processes. You can get access to much of this information by using either the SQL Server Management Studio or Transact-SQL code.

This will be an important part of your role as a SQL Server database administrator. You must always be aware of the current server activity, watching for problems so that you can be proactive before they occur. In this section, we will cover some of the more common tools in your arsenal.

Using the Activity Monitor Utility

The Activity Monitor utility is accessible through the Management Studio interface. To locate it, connect to the server you want to monitor using the Object Browser and expand the server node. You will see a Management node that contains other nodes and some items. One of the items is the Activity Monitor. If you double-click on the Activity Monitor icon, a dialog like the one pictured in Figure 15.7 will appear. The Activity Monitor utility allows you to look at current activity in three ways: Process Information, Locks by Process, and Locks by Object.

FIGURE 15.7
The Activity Monitor

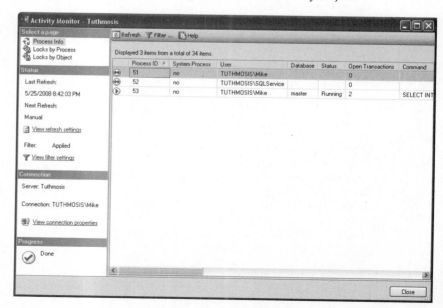

The dialog currently shows the Process Info page, where you can see all of the server processes (SPIDs) and their current statistics. This window will tell you who your users are, where they are connecting from, and how they are connecting, as well as the current transactional status. This dialog can be forced to refresh periodically, or you can filter out the content of the window as desired. The links in the Status box on the left of the dialog support these behaviors.

The other pages in the dialog display locking information, which you can view on a process or object basis depending on your needs. For example, suppose that you execute the following statement inside a transaction.

```
DELETE FROM pubs..TempAuth;
```

If the transaction has not yet committed, there will be an Intent Exclusive lock on the table TempAuth. If you were to look at the Locks by Object page of the Activity Monitor, it would look like figure 15.8. Note the type of lock listed in the Request Mode column is marked as IX, meaning an intent exclusive lock.

FIGURE 15.8
The Locks by
Object page

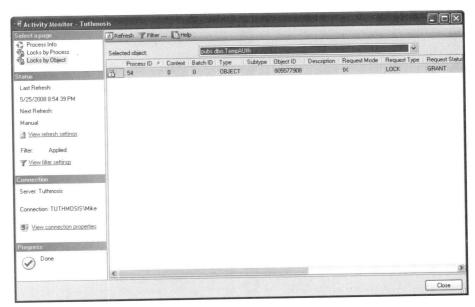

Using Transact-SQL to Monitor Activity

You can also use TSQL code to get similar information. In particular, the system stored procedures sp_lock and sp_who provide very useful information regarding locking and blocking. Figure 15.9 illustrates the sp_who stored procedure, which returns process information. Note that SPID 54 is the process from the previous example. It is currently active but not performing any work, rather, it is simply awaiting a command.

FIGURE 15.9
Using sp_who

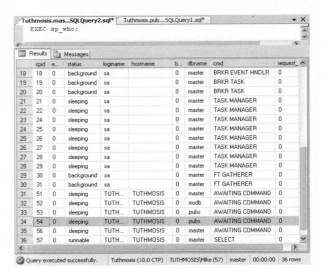

You can also get locking information like that available from the Activity Monitor by using the sp_lock procedure. Figure 15.10 illustrates the use of this procedure. Notice the locks held for SPID 54. There is a shared lock on the database. In addition, because we are deleting numerous rows from the table, we have exclusive locks on each row. Note that there are intent exclusive locks at the page level as well as the table level. The entire set of locks makes up the lock chain for this particular SPID.

FIGURE 15.10
Using sp_lock

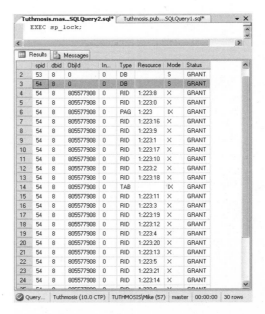

There are also some system views that provide similar information but organize it in different ways. To monitor locking, user activity, and optimizer activity, you should utilize these specific views:

◆ sys.dm_exec_connections

◆ sys.dm_exec_query_optimizer_info

◆ sys.dm_tran_current_transaction

◆ sys.dm_tran_locks

Other views are available, but this list is a good place to start. You may want to explore the list of system views and look for names that are interesting and pertinent to your current task. Doing so is a great way to become more familiar with your options.

The Bottom Line

Understand and utilize server locking architecture.   Understanding locks and their relationships to transactions is a critical part of managing a SQL Server data environment. Although SQL Server handles all locking automatically for you, you can also get information about locks and transactions through the visual interface and through Transact-SQL code. Knowing why certain locks are held at certain times and being familiar with their compatibility with other locks will also help you manage concurrency.

Master It   For each scenario, identify the lock type that will most likely be used to satisfy the scenario.

1. Select a few rows from a table.

2. Restore a database backup.

3. Rebuild a clustered index.

4. Rebuild a nonclustered index.

5. Delete all rows in a table.

6. Select a range of rows in a table using serializable isolation.

Implement an effective transaction management strategy.   Effective transactions make the difference between a consistent database and a heap of junk. The SQL language supports a strict transactional construct and through the SQL Server transaction log, complete ACID transactions are a reality.

Master It   Describe the SQL Server auto-commit behavior and explain why it is important in designing a transactional solution.

Implement an effective distributed transaction strategy.   In the larger enterprise, data will be distributed and so, therefore, transactions must also be distributed. Ensuring the integrity of distributed transactions is an important part of any enterprise data architecture.

Master It Explain the difference between the following approaches for querying a remote server:

1. `OpenRowset()`

2. `OpenQuery()`

3. Linked server query with four-part name reference

Get transaction and locking information. Even though SQL Server manages the locking infrastructure for you, it is still frequently necessary to extract information about current transaction and locking status to troubleshoot transaction or locking problems. There are numerous tools available for accessing this information.

Master It What are some of the tools that you can use to extract transaction and locking information from SQL Server?

Chapter 16

Using the Resource Governor and Policy-Based Management

SQL Server 2008 is quite a bit more robust in its management than previous versions of SQL Server. The Resource Governor allows an administrator to allocate different amounts of server resources to different applications. This can allow you to better balance varying workloads on a large SQL Server installation. In addition, policy-based management makes it much easier to verify and configure SQL Server settings according to policies. A policy can be evaluated against many servers at once, and many violations can be reconfigured directly from the policy interface.

In this chapter, you will learn to:

◆ Use the Resource Governor to manage and balance varying workloads

◆ Use policy-based management to define, evaluate, and enforce a desired configuration

The Resource Governor

Have you ever had an application that liked to hog system resources? How about an employee who occasionally produced long-running queries that had a major effect on other applications running on the server? Both of these problems can make it difficult to ensure adequate performance for all users of a SQL Server instance. With consolidation becoming the norm, it is becoming more common to see many databases with varying performance requirements being run on the same server.

The Resource Governor is a new feature of SQL Server 2008 that can help you more granularly allocate server resources to different types of connections. It works by classifying incoming connections into different workload groups, which can each be individually monitored and tuned. A workload group is contained inside of a resource pool that allows division of overall memory and CPU resources for an instance.

There are several benefits to enabling and using the Resource Governor on a SQL Server 2008 instance, including:

◆ It allows monitoring of individual workload groups and resource pools using performance counters to better understand resource usage by application.

◆ It makes it possible to prioritize one workload over another.

◆ It allows you to provide a guaranteed minimum percentage of memory and CPU resources for a resource pool.

◆ It lets you set a limit on the maximum percentage of memory and CPU usage for a resource pool.

◆ It makes it easier to run many applications with differing resource and performance requirements on the same SQL Server instance without allowing one to have an adverse impact on the others.

Figure 16.1 shows the different types of related objects involved in using the Resource Governor. The three main components are workload groups, resource pools, and a classification function.

FIGURE 16.1
The Resource Governor architecture

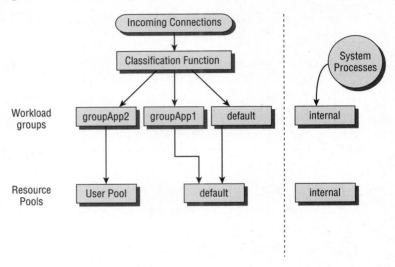

When connections are made to a SQL Server that has the Resource Governor enabled, a classification function is called to determine in which workload group the session should be placed. The classification function is a user-defined scalar function in the `master` system database. It contains logic to return the name of the workload group based on information about the connecting session. It can use several system functions to retrieve information about the connecting session, including:

◆ `APP_NAME()`

◆ `HOST_NAME()`

◆ `IS_MEMBER()`

◆ `SUSER_NAME(), SUSER_SNAME()`

◆ `LOGINPROPERTY()`

◆ `ORIGINAL_DB_NAME()`

◆ `CONNECTIONPROPERTY()`

Because the classification function is called in each new session, it is critical that it performs well. A poorly designed classification function can cause connections to time out. You can diagnose classification problems by using the Dedicated Administrator Connection, or by starting SQL Server in single-user mode.

Workload groups are useful for monitoring the activity, CPU, and memory consumption of a given set of sessions. Workload groups can be used to categorize sessions by application, or by purpose, such as reporting sessions. A workload group can be individually monitored, tuned for CPU and memory usage, and can also be given a relative importance to other workload groups in the same resource pool.

Initially, there are two workload groups: default and internal. The default workload group is used for all incoming sessions that don't have a specific, valid workload group name returned from the classification function. The internal workload group is used for all internal sessions and processes that connect to SQL Server, and it can't be used for user sessions. The internal workload group cannot be modified, but it can be monitored.

Resource pools are used to divide server resources for consumption by different workload groups. This is accomplished by providing ranges of memory and CPU resources that can be consumed by workloads in the resource pool. This can allow you to limit the maximum percentage of memory or CPU consumed by the workload groups. It can also allow you to guarantee that a minimum percentage of CPU and memory is available for workload groups in the pool.

Two resource pools initially exist: internal and default. A workload group is always part of a single resource pool. If a resource pool isn't specified when a workload group is created, the default resource pool is used.

The overall process for using the Resource Governor usually looks something like this:

1. Create workload groups for each application or area you would like to evaluate.

2. Create a classification function to classify each session into a workload group.

3. Configure the Resource Governor to use the classification function, and enable the Resource Governor.

4. Monitor the Resource Governor performance counters to better understand the workloads on the SQL Server.

5. Create resource pools to allocate specific server resources to workloads if required.

6. Tune workload group performance by specifying a relative importance, CPU, and memory limits.

7. Continue to monitor the workload group and resource pool performance counters to ensure that tuning is working as expected.

Workload Groups

The first step in utilizing the Resource Governor is deciding which workload groups to create. Workload groups are usually created by application, but they might be created by purpose or by a group of users. So long as you are able to differentiate the connections using Transact-SQL, you can separate them into a workload group.

You might have a SQL Server that is heavily used for several applications, including an accounting application, a CRM application, and a reporting application. You may want to give priority to one application over another one, or you might want to set limits on the amount of resources one of these applications can consume. Before you set limits, you will want to understand the characteristics of the workloads.

It's a simple process to create workload groups. The code shown in Listing 16.1 creates three workload groups that we will use for our examples. All of these workload groups will be initially contained in the default resource pool.

LISTING 16.1   Creating Workload Groups

```
CREATE WORKLOAD GROUP groupAccounting;
CREATE WORKLOAD GROUP groupCRM;
CREATE WORKLOAD GROUP groupReports;
```

In order to use the workload groups we've created, we will need to create a classification function and configure the Resource Governor to use it. The classification function will return the name of the workload group in which the session should be placed. Listing 16.2 shows the classification function we'll be using for our example.

LISTING 16.2   Creating a Classification Function

```
USE master;
GO
CREATE FUNCTION dbo.fn_RGClassify()
 RETURNS SYSNAME WITH SCHEMABINDING
AS
BEGIN
  DECLARE @ResourceGroupName sysname;
  IF (APP_NAME() LIKE '%Accounting%')
    SET @ResourceGroupName = 'groupAccounting';

  IF (APP_NAME() LIKE '%CRM%')
    SET @ResourceGroupName = 'groupCRM';

  IF (SUSER_SNAME() = 'DOMAIN\ReportingGroup')
    SET @ResourceGroupName = 'groupReports';

  RETURN @ResourceGroupName;
END
```

Once a classification function has been created, we need to configure the Resource Governor to use the classification function. This is accomplished using the statements shown in Listing 16.3.

LISTING 16.3   Specifying a Classifier Function and Enabling the Resource Governor

```
ALTER RESOURCE GOVERNOR
WITH (CLASSIFIER_FUNCTION=dbo.fn_RGClassify
ALTER RESOURCE GOVERNOR RECONFIGURE;
```

At this point, the Resource Governor is configured and ready to monitor. It's important that we monitor our workload before tuning so that we can better understand its characteristics. The SQL Server: Workload Group Statistics performance object provides counters for monitoring information about each workload group. Each workload group is shown as an instance of the

Workload Group Statistics performance object. Table 16.1 shows the counters available for monitoring workload groups.

TABLE 16.1   SQL Server: Workload Group Statistics Performance Counters

COUNTER NAME	DESCRIPTION
Queued Requests	The number of requests waiting to be picked up from the queue. This will be nonzero if the GROUP_MAX_REQUESTS limit is reached and throttling occurs.
Active Requests	The current number of running requests. You can also retrieve this value by counting the rows in sys.dm_exec_requests and filtering by group ID.
Requests Completed/sec	Cumulative number of requests completed/sec in this workload group.
CPU Usage %	CPU bandwidth usage for all requests in this workload group relative to the computer and normalized to all CPUs. This value changes as the amount of CPU available to the SQL Server Process changes. It isn't normalized to what the SQL Server process receives.
Max Request CPU Time (ms)	Maximum CPU time by a request currently running in the workload group.
Blocked Requests	Number of blocked requests in a workload group.
Reduced Memory Grants/sec	Number of queries that are getting less than the ideal amount of memory grants per second. Useful for determining workload characteristics.
Max Request Memory Grant (KB)	Maximum value of a memory grant for a query. Useful for determining workload characteristics.
Query Optimizations/sec	Number of optimizations in this workload group per second. Useful for determining workload characteristics.
Suboptimal Plans/sec	Number of plans per second generated in this workload group that are suboptimal.
Active Parallel Threads	Current number of parallel threads executing in the workload group.

For more information on using performance counters and system monitor, see Chapter 10, "Monitoring SQL Server Activity."

Once you've had a chance to monitor your workload, you can then use several workload group options to tune performance. The syntax for altering a workload group is shown here.

```
ALTER WORKLOAD GROUP { group_name | "default" }
[ WITH
    ([ IMPORTANCE = { LOW | MEDIUM | HIGH } ]
      [ [ , ] REQUEST_MAX_MEMORY_GRANT_PERCENT = value ]
      [ [ , ] REQUEST_MAX_CPU_TIME_SEC = value ]
      [ [ , ] REQUEST_MEMORY_GRANT_TIMEOUT_SEC = value ]
      [ [ , ] MAX_DOP = value ]
```

```
        [ [ , ] GROUP_MAX_REQUESTS = value ] )
    ]
    [ USING { pool_name | "default" } ]
```

Table 16.2 describes each of the WITH options that can be specified when creating or altering a workload group.

TABLE 16.2   Workload Group WITH Options

OPTION NAME	DESCRIPTION
IMPORTANCE	Relative importance of the workload group in relation to other workload groups in the same resource pool. Workload groups in other resource pools aren't affected by this setting. Allowable values are HIGH, MEDIUM, and LOW. The default is MEDIUM.
REQUEST_MAX_MEMORY_GRANT_PERCENT	Maximum percentage of memory that a single request can take from the pool. The default value is 25 percent. A value over 50% can result in only one query being able to execute at a time.
REQUEST_MAX_CPU_TIME_SEC	Maximum amount of CPU time in seconds that can be used by a request. This won't prevent a request from executing, but it will generate a trace event when the time is exceeded.
REQUEST_MEMORY_GRANT_TIMEOUT_SEC	Maximum time in seconds that a query will wait for a memory grant to become available. If this time is exceeded, a minimum memory grant will be used, which could result in less than optimum performance.
MAX_DOP	The maximum degree of parallelism for parallel requests.
GROUP_MAX_REQUESTS	The maximum simultaneous requests allowed to execute in the group. If the number of requests exceeds this amount, the requests are queued.

Resource Pools

Resource pools make it possible to allocate different amounts of server resources to a workload group. They make it possible to divide the CPU and memory resources of a SQL Server instance. This can be accomplished by specifying a minimum and maximum percentage of memory and CPU that will be allocated to the resource pool.

By default, there are two resource pools: default and internal. The default resource pool cannot be dropped, and any workload groups that don't explicitly specify a resource pool use the default resource pool. You can alter the ranges specified in the default pool if needed.

The syntax for creating a new resource pool is shown here:

```
CREATE RESOURCE POOL pool_name
[ WITH
```

```
        ( [ MIN_CPU_PERCENT = value ]
    [ [ , ] MAX_CPU_PERCENT = value ]
    [ [ , ] MIN_MEMORY_PERCENT = value ]
    [ [ , ] MAX_MEMORY_PERCENT = value ] )
]
```

Specifying a minimum percentage guarantees resource availability, but it also keeps other resource pools from using the reserved amount. If you had two resource pools, and one specified that it had a minimum of 25 percent CPU time, the other resource pool would have a true maximum amount of 75 percent of CPU time available for use, assuming that sessions are executing in both resource pools. This is because SQL Server always reserves 25 percent of the CPU time for workloads in the first pool, even if it could be used by the second resource pool.

The totals of all minimum percentage values for all resource pools must add up to 100 percent or less. For example, you couldn't have two resource pools that each are allocated a minimum of 60 percent of the resources.

Specifying a maximum percentage allows you to keep sessions from consuming more than a certain percentage of memory or CPU resources. For example, you may want to ensure that reporting queries take up no more than 25 percent of the server memory. This could be accomplished by specifying a minimum of 0 percent and a maximum of 25 percent.

Before tuning resource pool allocations, it is important to monitor the actual usage of resources. This can be accomplished by monitoring the SQL Server: Resource Pool Statistics performance object. The counters for this performance object are shown in Table 16.3. Each resource pool is an instance of this object. For more information on using system monitor and performance counters, refer to Chapter 10.

TABLE 16.3   SQL Server: Resource Pool Statistics Performance Counters

COUNTER NAME	DESCRIPTION
CPU Usage %	CPU bandwidth usage for all requests in this resource pool relative to the computer and normalized to all CPUs. This value changes as the amount of CPU available to the SQL Server Process changes. It isn't normalized to what the SQL Server process receives.
CPU Usage Target %	CPU usage target based on the current system load and resource pool configuration settings.
CPU Control Effect %	How much of an effect the Resource Governor is having on the resource pool. Calculated by dividing the CPU usage percentage to what the CPU usage percentage would be without using Resource Governor.
Compile Memory Target (KB)	Current memory broker target in KB for query compilations.
Cache Memory Target (KB)	Current memory broker target in KB for cache.
Query Exec Memory Target (KB)	Current memory broker target in KB for query execution memory grant.

TABLE 16.3 SQL Server: Resource Pool Statistics Performance Counters *(CONTINUED)*

COUNTER NAME	DESCRIPTION
Memory Grants/sec	Number of memory grants occurring per second in the resource pool.
Active Memory Grant Count	Total count of current memory grants.
Memory Grant Timeouts/sec	Number of memory grant timeouts/sec.
Active Memory Grant Amount (KB)	Total amount in KB of granted memory for the resource pool.
Pending Memory Grant Count	The number of requests for memory grants marked as pending in the queues.
Max Memory (KB)	Maximum amount of memory that the resource pool can have based on settings and server state.
Used Memory (KB)	The current amount of memory used for the resource pool.
Target Memory (KB)	The target amount of memory that the resource pool is trying to obtain based on server state and resource pool settings.

The diagram shown in Figure 16.2 describes our desired configuration for workload group and resource pool usage. We want to guarantee that at least 20 percent of CPU and memory resources are available for workload groups in the OLTP pool. For reporting, we want to make sure that the sessions never take up more than 50 percent of the memory and CPU resources on the server. Any other sessions will be in the default workload group which is a part of default resource pool.

FIGURE 16.2
A Resource Governor configuration

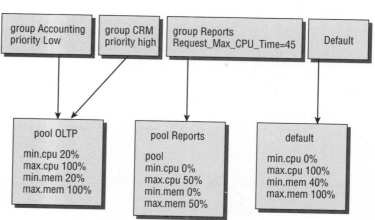

The range of available resource usage for our example is shown in Figure 16.3. The OLTP pool can take up as much as 100 percent of the total server resources, while the default pool can only take up to 80 percent of the resources because we specified a minimum of 20 percent for the OLTP pool.

FIGURE 16.3

Available resource ranges for our resource pools

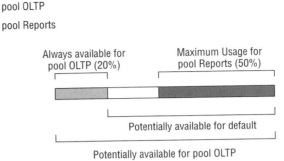

The code shown in Listing 16.4 creates the resource pools that we'll be using for our example.

LISTING 16.4   Creating Resource Pools

```
CREATE RESOURCE POOL poolOLTP
  WITH (MIN_CPU_PERCENT = 20, MAX_CPU_PERCENT = 100,
        MIN_MEMORY_PERCENT = 20, MAX_MEMORY_PERCENT = 100);


CREATE RESOURCE POOL poolReports
  WITH (MIN_CPU_PERCENT = 0, MAX_CPU_PERCENT = 50,
        MIN_MEMORY_PERCENT = 0, MAX_MEMORY_PERCENT = 50);
```

Once we've created our resource pools, we need to alter the workload groups so that they are contained in the appropriate resource pool. Listing 16.5 shows the SQL statements required to perform this operation. This also sets workload importance so that sessions in the groupCRM workload group are a higher priority than sessions in groupAccounting. In addition, a SQL trace event (CPU Threshold Exceeded) will be generated whenever a session in the groupReports workload group exceeds 15 seconds of CPU usage.

LISTING 16.5   Configuring Workload Groups to Use the Resource Pools

```
ALTER WORKLOAD GROUP groupAccounting
  WITH (IMPORTANCE = LOW)
  USING poolOLTP;
ALTER WORKLOAD GROUP groupCRM
  WITH (IMPORTANCE = HIGH)
  USING poolOLTP
ALTER WORKLOAD GROUP groupReports
  WITH (REQUEST_MAX_CPU_TIME_SEC = 15)
USING poolReports;
ALTER RESOURCE GOVERNOR RECONFIGURE;
```

Once the Resource Governor has been configured, it is important to monitor the performance objects to ensure that performance is working as expected. Any configuration changes must use the ALTER RESOURCE GOVERNOR RECONFIGURE statement before the changes will take effect.

Understanding Policy-Based Management

It's important to have your SQL Servers configured according to best practices. Microsoft published a tool for previous SQL Server versions called the SQL Server Best Practices Analyzer. It could scan one or more SQL Servers and evaluate their configuration according to predefined best practices, and produce a report of violations. It was a very useful tool for identifying any configuration-related problems without requiring a DBA to manually verify the settings on each of the servers they needed to administer.

Microsoft has extended the concept of the Best Practices Analyzer to be a core component of SQL Server 2008 called policy-based management. The technology was previously called Declarative Management Framework during some of the beta editions of SQL Server 2008.

Policy-based management makes it possible to define a policy that says how a particular area of SQL Server should be configured. This policy can be evaluated against one or more SQL Servers to produce a report of policy violations. Many of the settings that can be evaluated can also be configured directly from the report of policy violations.

For example, suppose you define a policy that the AutoShrink Database option should be false for all databases. This policy can be evaluated against the databases on one or more SQL Servers to see which databases have the AutoShrink Database option enabled. From the violation report, you can apply the policy to selected databases to automatically turn off the AutoShrink Database option.

There are also areas that can be evaluated that don't directly map to a configuration setting. For example, you might want to ensure that all databases store their database and log files on separate disks. One of the properties that can be evaluated for a database is called DataAndLogFilesOnSeperateLogicalVolumes. The policy can highlight areas where the data and log files aren't on separate logical volumes, but it can't automatically configure SQL server to conform to the policy, because it doesn't know on which logical volumes the data and log files should reside.

Another example of a policy that can't be automatically applied is one that verifies that a database has been backed up in the last seven days. We can identify databases that haven't been backed up, but we can't apply the policy to automatically back them up—more information is required in order to configure the backup job, backup storage locations, etc.

All of the policies discussed so far need to be evaluated in order to be effective. These policies are usually evaluated on demand or on a schedule. Another possibility for some policies is to have the policy enforced by the SQL Server database engine.

For example, you might want to ensure that all stored procedures in a database are named with the prefix of usp_. You can define a policy that specifies this rule, but you can also have it enforced by SQL Server whenever changes are made. Policies that are evaluated on change use either DDL triggers or event notifications to prevent or log any changes that violate policy. In order to create a policy that executes on change, it must be possible to capture the event using a DDL trigger or event notification.

One last example involves needing to configure many SQL servers in the same way. Policy-based management makes it possible to export the configuration of a component as a policy, which can then be evaluated against other SQL Servers, to see where violations have occurred, and to automatically apply the appropriate configuration changes.

Policy-based management can be useful to a database administrator in many ways, including:

◆ The ability to evaluate the configuration of one or more SQL Servers against a policy

◆ Being able to verify that a server is configured according to Microsoft best practices

◆ Being able to configure many components directly from a policy violation report

◆ The ability to export the current configuration of a component as a policy that can be used to evaluate and configure other servers

◆ Being able to enforce that certain types of additions and changes shouldn't be made to certain databases, such as enforcing an object-naming scheme for a database

Policy-Based Management Components

Policy-based management consists of several related components that work together. Figure 16.4 shows a diagram of the Policy-Based Management architecture.

Policy-based management can be used to evaluate and configure nearly every aspect of a SQL Server. There are three main components to policy-based management: policies, conditions, and facets. These three components are used together to define the desired configuration of an area of SQL Server.

A *facet* is a set of properties that model the characteristics of a managed target. For example, a database could be considered a managed target, and it has properties that map to things like the database recovery model, and other database configuration options, such as automatically creating statistics. The properties of a facet are used to create conditions that define how a property should be configured.

FIGURE 16.4
The Policy-Based Management architecture

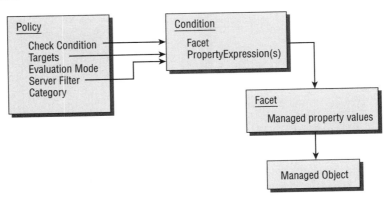

A policy must contain a check condition that uses the properties of a facet to define how an area should be configured. For example, you might create a condition that says the Recovery Model property of the database facet should be Full. The check condition is the main criteria that the policy is using for evaluation.

While a policy can be created with a single check condition, you can also use other conditions to filter which areas the policy should apply to. For example, you might not want to have the policy apply to every database, or on every server. You can filter the managed targets that a policy applies to by using target filter conditions. You can also filter which servers the policy will apply to by creating a server filter condition.

A policy can be evaluated in several different ways. You can evaluate a policy on demand, on a schedule, or for some policies, you can have them enforced when changes occur. We will cover policy evaluation modes in greater detail later in the chapter.

A policy can be a part of a category. Not every policy will apply to every database on a SQL Server. Policy categories allow administrators of individual databases to determine the optional policies to which their databases should subscribe. A category can also mandate database subscriptions, so that it will apply to all databases on a SQL Server instance.

Facets

Facets are one of the core components of policy-based management. A facet maps to one or more managed targets, and it contains properties that relate to the target's configuration. Seventy-four facets are included with SQL Server 2008.

One of the first steps in understanding policy-based management is to see which facets and properties are available. You can view a full list of facets by expanding Management ➤ Policy Based Management ➤ Facets in the Object Explorer window. The Properties window of the database facet is shown in Figure 16.5.

FIGURE 16.5
The Database Facet
Properties window

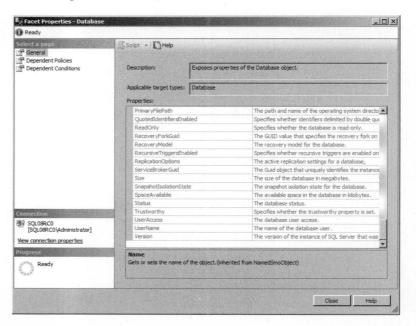

Many properties are available for the database facet. Each property is listed with a name and description. Some properties map directly to configuration settings that can be changed, and some are read-only and can only be used to evaluate configuration, rather than change it. For example, the Recovery Model can change for a database, but you can only read the Space Available property.

To view the actual values of facet properties, you can right-click on an object (for example, a database) in the Object Explorer and choose Facets. A screen similar to the one in Figure 16.6 is displayed.

Many of the properties can be configured directly from this screen if they aren't grayed out. If a property is grayed out, it is only available to read from a policy, rather than change.

A single, managed object may have many facets that apply to it. For example, the Database managed object has several facets, including Database, Database Options, Database Performance, and Database Maintenance. You can choose which facet to view by using the dropdown list shown at the top of the screen in Figure 16.6.

Most facets map to a single managed target; however, some facets can apply to multiple types of managed targets. For example, the Multipart Name facet can be applied to a table, stored procedure, view, or other object that uses a multipart name. Later in the chapter, we'll create a naming-convention policy that uses the Multipart Name facet. Figure 16.7 shows a diagram of some of the relationships between facets and managed targets.

FIGURE 16.6

The Database Facet property values

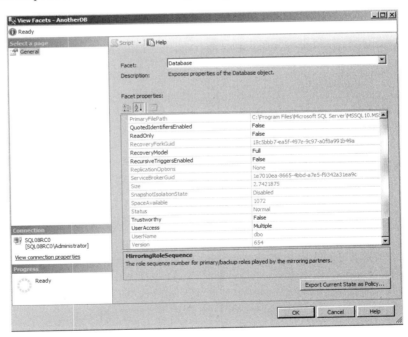

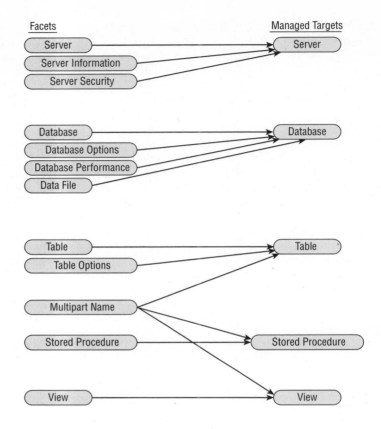

FIGURE 16.7
The relationships between facets and managed targets

CONDITIONS

A *condition* is one or more expressions that use the property values of a facet. In order to create a condition, you must choose a facet for it to use, and then define expressions that express a desired state. For example, you might create a condition that specifies that the AutoShrink property of a database should be False. Figure 16.8 shows an example of such a condition.

Conditions can be reused in more than one policy, so make sure to name them descriptively to promote reuse.

A condition can contain one or more expressions that can be combined using the AND or OR operators. You can also create more complex expressions using the Advanced Condition Editor.

Several functions are available when you use the Advanced Condition Editor, including ExecuteSql() and ExecuteWql() functions to execute SQL Statements and WQL (WMI Query Language) queries, respectively. An example of using the Advanced Condition Editor is shown in Figure 16.9.

If you use the ExecuteSql() or ExecuteWql() functions in a condition, a warning is generated when the policy is evaluated telling the administrator that there is a script that could be potentially harmful. Make sure to review and verify that any script is legitimate, especially if using a policy received from a third party.

FIGURE 16.8

Creating a
new condition

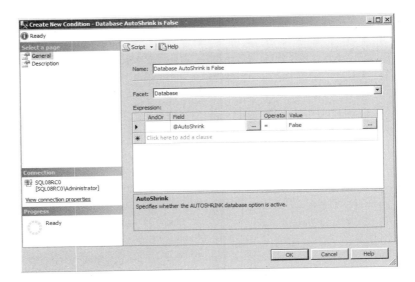

FIGURE 16.9

Using the
Advanced
Condition Editor

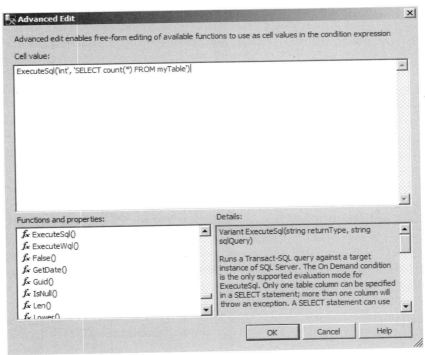

POLICIES

A *policy* consists of a check condition to be evaluated against a set of targets. The targets available depend on the check condition. A condition that uses the database facet will have databases as the target. Other conditions can use multiple types of targets (for example, a condition using Multipart Name could apply to any targets that contain a multipart name). Figure 16.10 shows an example of a policy with multiple targets.

Other conditions can be used to filter the targets to which the policy applies. By default, a condition that matches every managed target is used.

You can also use a server-restriction condition to filter the servers to which the policy will apply. A server restriction can use any of the server-based facets to define a condition that must be met to evaluate the policy on a server.

There are four possible policy-evaluation modes, depending on the type of conditions and targets selected:

- On Demand

- On Schedule

- On Change: Log Only

- On Change: Prevent

FIGURE 16.10
A policy that can
have multiple
targets

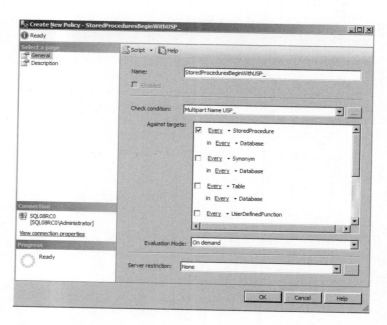

All policies can be evaluated on demand. Because the policy is evaluated using the SQL Server Management tools, an on-demand policy can be evaluated against SQL Server 2005 or SQL Server 2000 servers.

Policies that are evaluated on a schedule use SQL Server Agent jobs to automate policy evaluation. You must be using SQL Server 2008 to use any of the evaluation modes other than On Demand, because the policy must be stored on the server. When automating policy evaluation, the results are stored in the `msdb` system database. You can then use the Policy Health State button in Object Explorer to identify areas that don't conform to policy. We will be covering policy health state later in the chapter.

Some policies can be evaluated as changes occur. In order to create a policy that is evaluated on change, it must be possible to capture the event that causes the change by using either DDL triggers, or by using event notifications. The DDL triggers or event notifications used to enforce the policy are automatically maintained by the policy-based management framework. We will be creating policies that execute on change later in this chapter.

CATEGORIES

Policies can be grouped into categories. Categories can help to organize policies on a server so that individual databases can subscribe to all of the policies in a category. A policy category can also be used to mandate database subscriptions, forcing all databases on the server to subscribe to all policies in a category. Figure 16.11 shows an example of using policy categories.

FIGURE 16.11
Understanding
policy categories

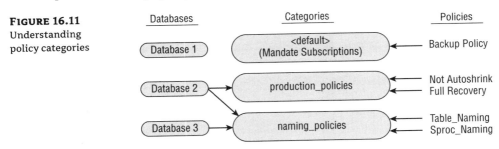

In our example, three categories contain all the policies. The only category that mandates database subscriptions is the default category. This means that all of the databases on the server will have the backup policy applied. Database 1 doesn't subscribe to any other policy categories, so the backup policy is the only one that applies to it. Database 2 uses both the production_policies category and the naming_policies category. All five policies will apply to Database 2. Database 3 uses only the naming_policies category, so three policies will apply to it: the backup policy and the two naming policies.

When creating a policy, you specify the category it belongs to on the Description page of the Create Policy window. A policy can belong to only a single category.

To manage the available policy categories, right-click on Policy Management in Object Explorer and choose Manage Categories. The dialog box shown in Figure 16.12 appears.

To change which policy categories apply to a database, you can right-click on the database in Object Explorer, and choose Policies ➤ Categories. The dialog shown in Figure 16.13 appears, allowing you to choose which categories the database should use.

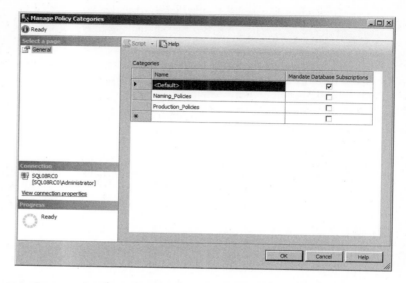

FIGURE 16.12
The Manage Policy Categories dialog

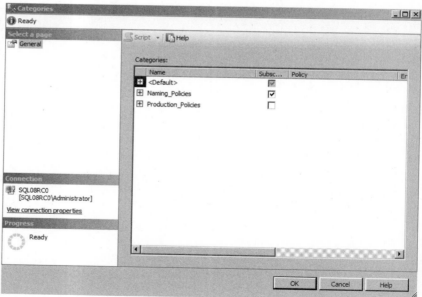

FIGURE 16.13
The Database Policy Categories dialog

Creating and Evaluating Policies

Now that you understand the components of policy-based management, we'll start to use it in practice. We'll start by examining some of the policies that are packaged with SQL Server. We'll see the different methods of evaluating policies, against one or more servers, and we'll create policies with each of the evaluation modes.

Importing Microsoft Best Practices

Microsoft has included many of the best practices that were available with the SQL Server Best Practices Analyzer from previous versions of SQL Server. The best practices have been turned into policies that can easily be imported and evaluated against one or more servers.

To use the Best Practices policies, you must first import them. You can find the policy XML files in the directory `C:\Program Files\Microsoft SQL Server\100\Tools\Policies\DatabaseEngine\1033`. All of the best practices will execute on demand, by default.

To import a policy, follow these steps:

1. Connect the Object Explorer to the SQL Server to which you would like to import the policies.

2. Expand Management ➤ Policy Management.

3. Right-click on the Policies folder and choose Import Policy. The dialog shown in Figure 16.14 appears.

4. Click on the ellipsis to choose which policy files to import. You can choose more than one policy by using the Ctrl key. Microsoft Best Practices are located in `C:\Program Files\Microsoft SQL Server\100\Tools\Policies\DatabaseEngine\1033`.

FIGURE 16.14
The Policy
Import dialog

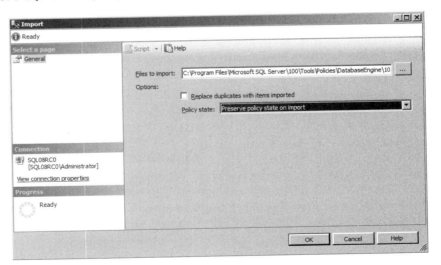

5. Choose a state (enabled or disabled) that imported policies should be placed in. The options are

◆ Preserve policy state on import

◆ Enable all policies on import

◆ Disable all policies on import

6. Click OK to import the policies. Any policies and conditions contained in the XML file(s) will be imported.

Many useful policies are included with SQL Server that you can use as is or modify to fit your requirements. All of the sample policies are evaluated on demand by default.

EVALUATING A POLICY

Policies can be evaluated in several ways. In this section, we'll look at evaluating policies on demand using SQL Server Management Studio. You can evaluate policies against SQL Server 2008, 2005, and 2000 servers when using evaluating policies on demand. Some properties are valid only for a specific version of SQL Server.

We'll begin by using the Database Auto Shrink policy that's included with the Best Practice policies. This policy says that every online user database should have the AutoShrink property set to False. Evaluating the policy will compare the configuration of each database on the SQL Server to the policy. If there are policy violations, we can make configuration changes directly from the Policy Evaluation window.

To evaluate a policy, follow these steps:

1. Expand the Object Explorer to Management ➢ Policy Management ➢ Policies.

2. Right-click on the Policies folder and choose Evaluate. A dialog similar to the one shown in Figure 16.15 appears.

FIGURE 16.15
The Evaluate
Policies dialog

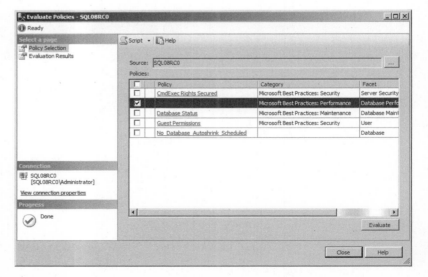

3. Choose the policies you want to evaluate and click the Evaluate button. In Figure 16.16, the Database Auto Shrink policy was evaluated. This policy was applied to four databases on the server, and one of them was in violation of the EncryptionDB policy.

FIGURE 16.16

The Evaluation Results dialog

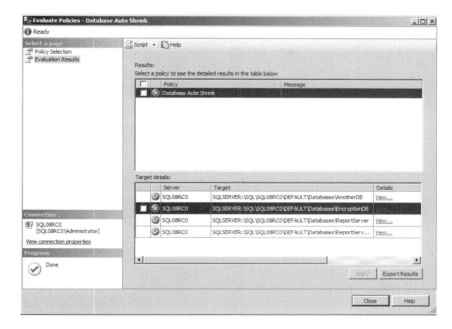

4. To view the details of a policy violation, click the Details hyperlink for the record you would like to view. A dialog similar to the one shown in Figure 16.17 appears.

5. If you can configure the settings to conform to the policy, a checkbox will appear next to each row. If you choose the checkboxes, and click the Apply button, any settings that were violating the policy are configured to conform to it. In our situation, this would set the AutoShrink option to False for the EncryptionDB database.

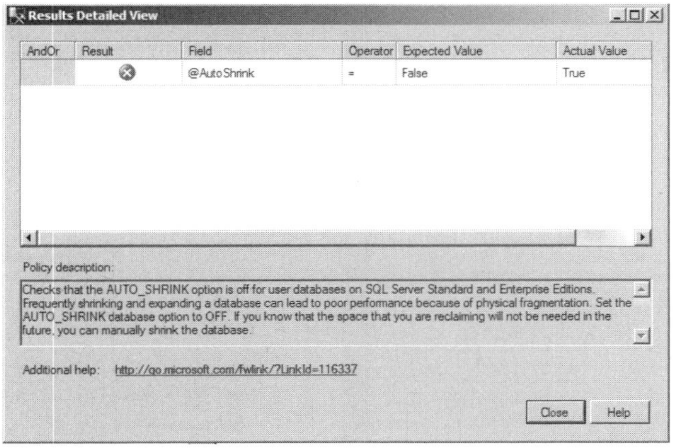

FIGURE 16.17

The Policy Result details

AndOr	Result	Field	Operator	Expected Value	Actual Value
	⊗	@AutoShrink	=	False	True

Policy description:

Checks that the AUTO_SHRINK option is off for user databases on SQL Server Standard and Enterprise Editions. Frequently shrinking and expanding a database can lead to poor performance because of physical fragmentation. Set the AUTO_SHRINK database option to OFF. If you know that the space that you are reclaiming will not be needed in the future, you can manually shrink the database.

Additional help: http://go.microsoft.com/fwlink/?LinkId=116337

EVALUATING POLICIES AGAINST MULTIPLE SERVERS

You can evaluate a policy across many servers by using a Central Management Server. A Central Management Server stores connection information for multiple SQL Servers. Think of this as a centralized list of registered servers. All connections must use trusted authentication, so there aren't any passwords stored in clear text.

To use a Central Management Server, you will use the Registered Servers window in Management Studio. A Central Management Server stores connection information about SQL Servers in the msdb database of the Central Management Server. Figure 16.18 shows the Registered Servers window with a Central Management Server defined. If the Registered Servers window isn't visible, you can turn it on by choosing View ➢ Registered Servers.

FIGURE 16.18
Central Management Servers

You can create server groups using a Central Management Server and then evaluate a policy against an entire server group. The process for evaluating a policy against multiple servers is exactly the same as evaluating the policy against a single server. If a connection can't be made to one of the servers in the group, the rest of the policy evaluation will continue on the available servers.

You can also execute queries across all servers in a group by right-clicking on the group and choosing Query.

CREATING A NEW POLICY

Creating a new policy is a fairly simple process. There are several ways that a policy can be created:

◆ Online, with a connection to a server

◆ Offline, without a connection to a server

◆ Exporting the current state of a facet as policy

The processes for creating a policy online or offline are very similar. A policy that is developed offline is saved to an XML file and can later be imported into one or more SQL Servers for evaluation. To create a new policy in offline mode, choose File ➢ New ➢ Policy in SQL Server Management Studio.

To create a new policy on a SQL Server, follow these steps:

1. Expand the Object Explorer to Management ➢ Policy Management ➢ Policies.

2. Right-click on the Policies folder and choose New Policy. The dialog shown in Figure 16.19 appears.

FIGURE 16.19

The Create New Policy dialog

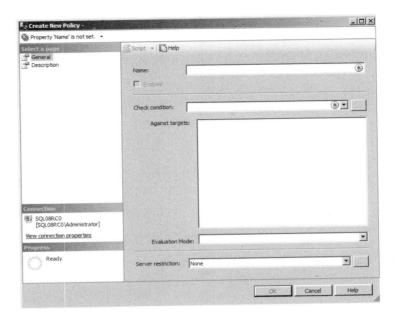

3. Type a descriptive name for your policy.

4. Use the Check Condition dropdown list to create a new condition. The dialog shown in Figure 16.20 appears.

If you're choosing an existing condition, skip to step 8.

FIGURE 16.20

The New Condition dialog

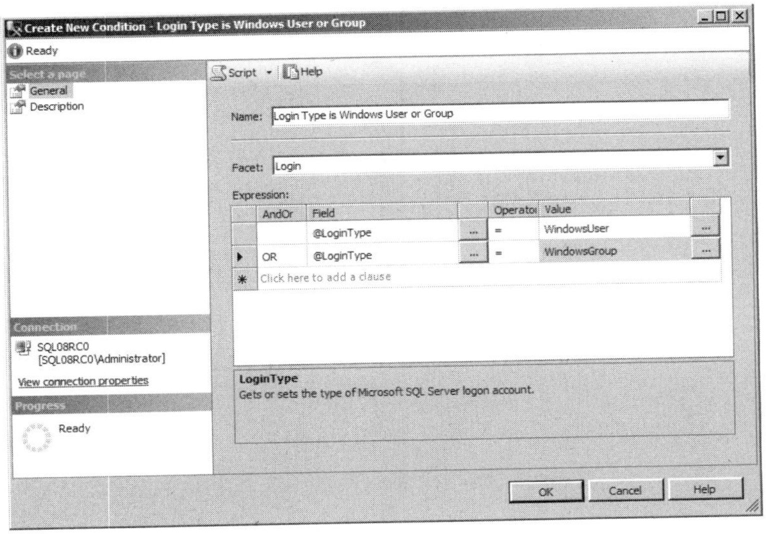

5. Type a name for the check condition, and choose the appropriate facet for your policy.

6. Use the dropdown lists in the Expression Editor to create an expression that states the way a component should be configured. Our example says that each login should be a windows user or a windows group.

7. Choose the Description pane and enter a description for your condition. Click OK.

8. Choose the targets to which the policy should apply. You can create another condition to filter the targets to which any policy applies.

9. Choose your evaluation mode. Depending on the type of condition used, you may be given different options. This is because only certain facets and properties can be captured using triggers and event notifications.

10. Optionally, choose or create a server restriction. A server restriction is a condition that uses one of the server facets to limit where this policy should apply. For example, some settings only apply to a specific SQL Server version or edition.

11. Choose the Description page of the policy, select a category, type a description, and additional help text to display.

12. Click OK to create the policy.

If you already have a component configured the way you would like to have used in a policy, you can export the current state of a facet as a policy. This is accomplished by viewing the appropriate facet of the object you would like to export, and clicking the Export Current State as Policy button. There are many objects that you can right-click on in the Object Explorer to view facets. The image in Figure 16.21 shows an example of a database configuration facet.

FIGURE 16.21
A database configuration facet

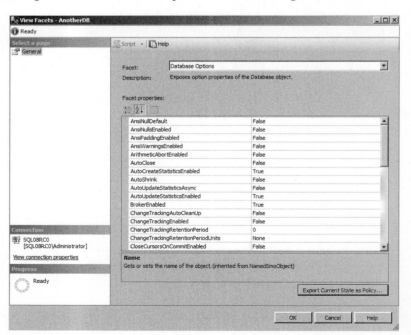

When you click on the Export Current State as Policy button, you are prompted to enter a name for the new policy and condition that will be created, as shown in Figure 16.22. You can also choose to store the policy on the local server or to an XML file.

FIGURE 16.22

The Export as Policy dialog

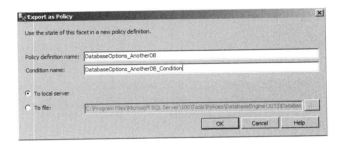

EVALUATING POLICIES ON A SCHEDULE

All of the policies we've worked with so far have used the On Demand evaluation mode. This means that in order for the policy to be evaluated or applied, it must be manually evaluated by the database administrator.

You can also evaluate a policy on a schedule. This is accomplished with a SQL Server Agent Job that uses a PowerShell script to evaluate the policy on a routine basis. The output of policy evaluation is stored in the msdb system database and can be displayed by SQL Server Management Studio.

Using scheduled policy evaluations will allow you to view Policy Health States in the Object Explorer, so you can easily identify areas that aren't configured according to policy. Figure 16.23 shows the Object Explorer with Policy Health States enabled. This can be toggled by the button at the top of Object Explorer.

FIGURE 16.23

Policy Health States enabled

The icons that contain red X's next to the Object Explorer nodes represent a policy violation in either that component or some children of that component. In the example in Figure 16.23, the icon is displayed on the server Databases folder, and EncryptionDB database. You can right-click on any of these nodes, and choose Policies ➢ View to view the policies that apply to the node and any violations, as shown in Figure 16.24.

FIGURE 16.24
The View
Policies dialog

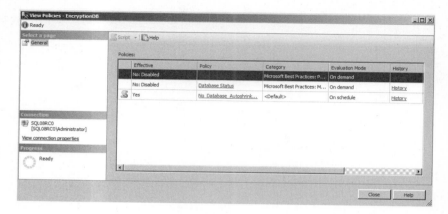

All policies can be executed on a schedule so long as their target is SQL Server 2008. A policy can be converted to execute on a schedule by changing its execution mode and specifying a schedule. If you change to a scheduled execution mode, you must remember to enable the policy in order for it to execute and be applied.

ENFORCING POLICIES—ON CHANGE, LOG

Some policies can be enforced by either logging or preventing a change that would violate the policy. In order to use either of the On Change modes for policy evaluation, you must be working with a facet that is transactional, and one on which activity can be captured using either event notifications or DDL triggers. The event notifications or DDL triggers are automatically created and maintained by the policy-based management infrastructure.

Policies that use the On Change: Log Only option won't prevent changes that would violate policy, but it will log the policy violation, and it can be immediately viewed using the Policy Health State in Object Explorer, which was discussed in the last section.

An example of a policy that uses On Change, Log Only could be a naming policy that requires all views be prefixed with V_. This policy can be created using the Multipart Name facet, and it uses the condition displayed in Figure 16.25.

When the policy is violated, the changes are logged and displayed using the Policy Health State in Object Explorer, as shown in Figure 16.26.

FIGURE 16.25
The Views Prefixed
with V_ condition

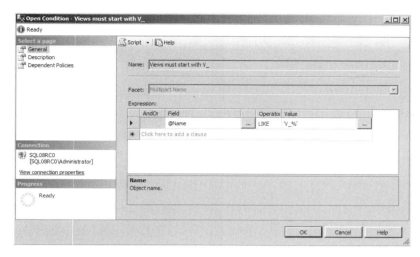

FIGURE 16.26
The Object
Explorer Policy
Health for Views

ENFORCING POLICIES—ON CHANGE, PREVENT

Policies can use an evaluation mode that will prevent changes that don't comply with the policy. This mode can be used with a limited number of facets, because events must be able to be prevented and rolled back using DDL triggers.

Because these types of policies can disrupt database operations, most of the time they should be placed into a separate category that doesn't mandate database subscriptions. This will allow individual databases to subscribe to the appropriate policies.

An example of using the On Change: Prevent evaluation mode is similar to the last example. We will require that all new stored procedures have names that are prefixed with usp_. The only difference between this example and the last one is that we will prevent changes that violate the policy when logging them.

It's important to fill out description and help information for a policy that prevents changes. Any error messages that are shown will display the description of the policy, and any help text and URL. The dialog for configuring a policy's category, description, and help text is shown in Figure 16.27.

FIGURE 16.27
The Policy
Description page

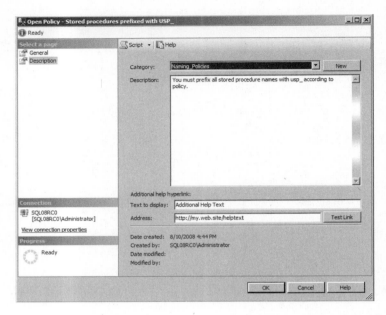

If a stored procedure is created that doesn't conform to the policy, the trigger will roll back the transaction and produce a message similar to the one shown here.

```
Policy 'Stored procedures prefixed with USP_' has been violated by 'SQLSERVER:\SQL\
SQL08RC0\DEFAULT\Databases\AnotherDB\StoredProcedures\dbo.badProcName'.
This transaction will be rolled back.
Policy condition: '@Name LIKE 'usp_%''
Policy description: 'You must prefix all stored procedure names with usp_ according
to policy.'
Additional help: 'Additional Help Text' : 'http://my.web.site/helptext'
Statement: 'CREATE PROC badProcName
AS
SELECT @@VERSION
'.
Msg 3609, Level 16, State 1, Procedure sp_syspolicy_dispatch_event, Line 65
The transaction ended in the trigger. The batch has been aborted.
```

The Bottom Line

Use the Resource Governor to manage and balance varying workloads. The Resource Governor provides powerful capabilities for monitoring and tuning varying workloads on a SQL Server. Utilizing the Resource Governor can help you better understand and balance workloads across your SQL Server.

Master It What steps must you follow to configure and use the Resource Governor?

Tune the resource pool and workload group settings as required. Use policy-based management to define, evaluate, and enforce a desired configuration. Using policy-based management makes it much easier to configure a server according to best practices and defined policies.

Master It In order to evaluate a policy against a previous version of SQL Server, how must the policy be configured?

Chapter 17

SQL Server and the .NET Client

As a SQL Server administrator or developer, you do not care about the details of how to program data access to SQL Server. Unless you are also wearing the client developer hat, it just is not relevant. However, we think that it is very important for the SQL Server professional to be aware of what is happening on the client side. How is your SQL Server database accessed by client applications or a data access layer in a multi-tier application? An inquisitive database professional should know these things, because they might affect data security, integrity, or performance.

Understand that our goal is not to provide complete coverage of data access technology. This book is about SQL Server, not data access programming. Therefore, you should not expect a great amount of detail about data access programming in this chapter. Our goal is to provide the SQL Server professional with the essential information necessary to talk effectively with .NET developers and to help you understand the impacts of the data access technology on the data server tier. As a database administrator or developer, you should read this chapter with that goal in mind. We want you to understand the effects data access technology will have on your world, but we are not trying to offer a complete discussion of client data access programming.

In this chapter, you will learn to:

◆ Connect and query a SQL Server database using ADO.NET connected and disconnected techniques

◆ Use prominent special features of ADO.NET and the SQL Native Client

◆ Understand and implement simple examples using the new Language Integrated Query (LINQ) environment

◆ Understand and implement simple examples using the ADO.NET Entity Framework

Understanding ADO.NET

Data access technology has been through a significant evolution over the last 15 years. In your early days of programming, you may have worked primarily with flat file databases or pseudo-relational engines such as Clipper, Fox Pro, Dbase, or Access. Back in those days, cursor-based data access models were the norm and processing that data typically followed this sequence:

1. Open file.

2. Query data to generate cursor.

3. Process data through cursor.

4. Close file.

As database technology evolved and relational databases came to be more commonplace in the business world, data access technology should have evolved with it. Unfortunately, this was not the case. Mainstream data access technology continued to be cursor-based rather than set-based even though the data engines in common use were capable of greater efficiencies. In the Microsoft microcosm, this was especially apparent in the evolution of data access technologies such as the Microsoft Data Access Objects, Remote Data Objects, ODBC Direct, and Active Data Objects. None of these technologies effectively leveraged the set-based nature of the relational data engine that SQL Server provided.

A CURSOR IN A SET-BASED WORLD

A *database cursor* is an artificial structure that represents underlying data through a set of pointers. Cursors allow data processing at the "row" level. By following each individual pointer to the underlying data, the client assesses and processes data values one at a time. This may seem a natural way to process data, but it is very inefficient in a relational data model. Instead, the client should process data in sets whenever possible.

Set Theory is a branch of mathematics that describes objects as collections based on common factors. Dr. E. F. Codd, the pioneer in relational database theory, was heavily grounded in set-based mathematics. He, therefore, designed his relational database theory to work with sets. The theory is that defining the parameters of a set of data values, and then manipulating that set consistently, is much more efficient than manipulating values individually. Unfortunately, far too much database code ignores this inherent superiority of set-based techniques.

When Microsoft introduced the ADO.NET model, they significantly departed from their traditional cursor-based data access technologies of the past. For the first time in Microsoft history, users had the capability of working with sets. Although much of the processing on the client application was still row-based, at least we were able to utilize the set-based nature of the SQL Server data engine while still having the option of limited cursor support when necessary.

ADO.NET supports two primary strategies for data access.

◆ Connected access through cursors

◆ Disconnected access through sets

Both of these techniques rely on some common elements, such as connections and commands, although they differ significantly in how the database returns data to the client. We will begin this discussion by looking at those common elements before discussing how those elements are used in each of our scenarios.

Figure 17.1 provides a simplified illustration of the ADO.NET 3.5 object model. The figure is not complete; it only defines key elements of the model.

FIGURE 17.1
The ADO.NET
object model

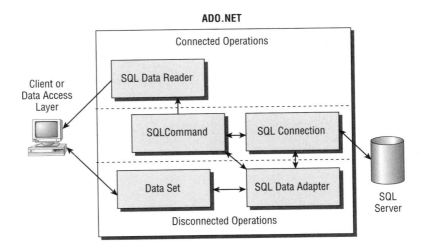

Making the Connection

Figure 17.1 shows that all communication to SQL Server happens through a SqlConnection object. Regardless of whether you are using a connected or disconnected strategy, you will need a connection to interact with the server. To make this connection, you will have to provide a connection string. Table 17.1 lists some of the common values included in a SQL Server connection string. Again, this is not an inclusive list, but rather is meant to be indicative of typical settings in common use.

TABLE 17.1   Connection String Values

VALUE	DEFAULT	DESCRIPTION
Connection Timeout	15	The time in seconds to wait for a successful connection before the attempt is terminated.
Data Source Server Address	N/A	The server name or network address of the target server of the connection.
Encrypt	'false'	When set to true and a certificate is installed, this value indicates that all data should be transmitted using SSL encryption.
Initial Catalog Database	N/A	The name of the database.
Integrated Security Trusted_Connection	'false'	When true, Windows authentication is used. When false, SQL Server Authentication is performed. Valid values are 'true', 'false', 'yes', 'no', and 'sspi' (equivalent to true).
MultipleActiveResultSets	'false'	When true, multiple result sets can be maintained for a single connection. Supported since ADO.NET 2.0.

TABLE 17.1 Connection String Values *(CONTINUED)*

VALUE	DEFAULT	DESCRIPTION
Packet Size	8192	Size of the network packet used to communicate with SQL Server.
Password Pwd	N/A	Authentication password. Only used when Integrated Security is set to false.
User ID	N/A	Authentication ID used when Integrated Security is set to false.

READING THE FINE PRINT

Because we want this chapter to offer a high-level discussion of data access technology, we need to make some significant assumptions before we can proceed. Please take a moment to read these assumptions and disclaimers.

You must speak the language. This is not the time to discuss .NET or object-oriented programming concepts. In the interest of brevity, we will be using many of these terms without defining them first. In addition, because you can develop .NET applications in many languages, we had to standardize on one for illustration purposes. We chose to use the C# language.

Do your homework. If you want to code and execute any of our examples, you may have to include additional code that we do not provide. For example, the SqlConnection class is in a .NET namespace called `System.Data.SqlClient`. If you coded the connection examples shown in the following text, you would have to either fully qualify the SqlConnection class using the namespace or provide a `using` statement in your code, removing the need to fully qualify the class name. We omitted these details from our code so that we can focus on our core issues. You will have to do your own research if you want to implement these techniques.

Know the data access model. ADO.NET is the universal data access model for .NET applications. These applications can use a variety of data sources; SQL Server is one option but not the only option. Other data sources such as Oracle, ODBC, and OLE DB easily fit into the ADO.NET framework. However, this book focuses strictly on SQL Server 2008, so we will not address any of these other implementations. We will show you only models and code relating to SQL Server implementations.

The general format of the connection string is `"keyword=value;[n…]"`. In other words, name/value pairs for each of the settings are separated with a semicolon. When you create a connection, the connection string is generally provided like this:

```
SqlConnection cn = new SqlConnection(ConnectionString);
```

Alternatively, you can also assign a value to the ConnectionString property of the SqlConnection object subsequent to that object's instantiation, as in this example:

```
SqlConnection cn = new SqlConnection();
cn.ConnectionString = ConnectionString;
```

Using the former pattern, connecting to the default instance of a SQL Server on a machine named TestServer, using a database named TestDB, and connecting using integrated security would result in the following code:

```
String sCon = "Data Source=TestServer;Database=TestDB;Integrated Security=true";
SqlConnection cn = new SqlConnection(sCon);
cn.Open();
```

Once the connection is open, you can use that connection to interact with the SQL Server. Note that in our example, we have explicitly opened the connection to the server by using the Open method of the SqlConnection object. This is not always required. In some cases, other objects, such as a SqlDataAdapter, can open the connection for you. However, any time that you want to interact with SQL Server, there must be an open connection, whether you opened it explicitly in your code or implicitly by another object in the model.

Remember that if you open something, you have to close it. When you open a connection explicitly, another object in the model will generally not implicitly close it. The notable exception to this rule is when you create an object and include an auto-close behavior in the initialization parameters.

Defining the Command

The SqlCommand class represents the statement that the client submits to SQL Server for execution. In SQL Server, this command can represent a table name, a stored procedure call, or an ad hoc SQL statement. The client issues a command through an open connection, thereby providing instructions to SQL Server as to the results that it should return.

The pattern for using SqlCommand is similar to the one used for SqlConnection. The most important parameter that you will provide is the CommandText. One option is to provide this value as a parameter in its constructor when you create the object, as with this example:

```
String sSQL = "SELECT au_fname, au_lname from dbo.authors;";
SqlCommand cmd = new SqlCommand(sSQL);
```

You can also assign the value of the CommandText property after you create the object, as in this example.

```
String sSQL = "SELECT au_fname, au_lname from dbo.authors;";
SqlCommand cmd = new SqlCommand();
cmd.CommandText = sSQL;
```

Commonly, you will also provide the connection information for your command at the same time, so that the command is aware of the connection to which it has been associated and through which it will execute. You can provide this connection information to the constructor as the object is instantiated, or alternatively by assigning a value to the Connection property of the SqlCommand object as illustrated in this example. (Please note that to compile the following code, you can use only one of the two options indicated, so comment one out if you are running the examples.)

```
String sCon = "Data Source=TestServer;Database=TestDB;Integrated Security=true";
String sSQL = "SELECT au_fname, au_lname from dbo.authors;";
```

```
SqlConnection cn = new SqlConnection(sCon);

// Option 1
SqlCommand cmd = new SqlCommand(sSQL, cn);

// Option 2
SqlCommand cmd = new SqlCommand();
cmd.CommandText = sSQL;
cmd.Connection = cn;
```

You can also use a stored procedure for your command text value. Suppose that you have a stored procedure called GetOrdersByQuantity that accepts an integer value as a parameter—called @Quantity—that represents the total number of units ordered. The procedure will return the order data based on this parameter. Assuming that you have provided a parameter value of 10, you would use code like the following to configure this command.

```
SqlCommand cmd = new SqlCommand();
cmd.CommandText = "GetOrdersByQuantity";
cmd.Parameters.AddWithValue("@Quantity", 10);
```

 Real World Scenario

THE DATABASE EFFECTS OF INAPPROPRIATE CLIENT CODE

For the SQL Server DBA or developer, this syntax should pose some interesting questions. If the client developer can provide their own SQL code when querying the database, what are the effects of this practice? What other issues arise when developers take advantage of the freedoms that the ADO.NET syntax allows?

The authors have had to deal with one or more of the following issues in virtually every SQL Server/ .NET implementation that we have addressed. Therefore, rather than presenting a single case study, we have chosen to aggregate aspects of many cases regarding this subject.

A command can be an ad hoc SQL statement, a table name, or a stored procedure name. All these options have performance and security ramifications that we must address.

Command Object Performance Issues   The SqlCommand object allows the developer to provide a table name as CommandText. This is a bad practice because it will typically return much more data to the client than is necessary. Ad hoc SQL statements can also lead to performance problems because SQL Server does not provide the same degree of caching for ad hoc SQL as it does for stored procedures. Although SQL Server does have some ad hoc caching capabilities, this cache is generally short-lived. In most cases, you will get much better performance from your SQL Server by using stored procedures exclusively for all data access.

Command Object Security Issues   Allowing ad hoc SQL to access your applications has two general security problems: unnecessary permission exposure and SQL injection.

To execute ad hoc SQL code, a user must log in with an account that has the necessary permissions to perform the desired actions. This exposes the underlying database by permitting a user with valid permissions to access the database using alternative means, thereby circumventing the business rules of the application. Although you can avoid this somewhat by using application identities with secure passwords, this approach still poses a potential security threat.

Another serious issue is the possibility of SQL injection. This occurs when an application takes string inputs directly from an end user and passes them to the SQL Server without first evaluating and verifying the inputs. Using this approach, an end user with some SQL knowledge can inject malicious code into the data engine through these inputs. Because the application treats all inputs as ad hoc SQL and executes them accordingly, this can be a very serious situation.

You can solve both of these problems with stored procedures. The database administrator can assign permission to the users to execute the procedures without having to grant any permissions relating to the underlying schema objects. When properly parameterized, procedures are also much less susceptible to SQL injections because the inputs are not raw strings.

The Solution   In the real world, we see these situations all the time. The best practice is to use stored procedures exclusively. As a SQL Server DBA, you should not allow applications to use ad hoc SQL to access your databases. You should never grant table access permissions to nonadministrative accounts. While there may be times when you need to violate these rules to accomplish certain goals, you should consider stored procedures to be your standard and enforce that standard for all data access. Trust us on this one. Down the road, you will be glad you did.

Connected Operations

Now that we have seen the basic implementation of the SqlConnection and SqlCommand objects, we are ready to apply this to data operations. We will begin with a discussion of connected operations. When we use the term "connected operations," we refer to actions that require the client to maintain a connection to the server for the entire duration of the operation. A developer can use connected operations either to retrieve data from a database or to make modifications to the database.

Retrieving data in a connected mode typically involves using the SqlDataReader object in conjunction with a SqlCommand object. Making data modifications in a connected mode does not require, or even allow, a SqlDataReader and SqlCommand object to perform the action directly.

CONNECTED RETRIEVAL USING THE SQLDATAREADER

The SqlDataReader class is the last remaining ADO.NET holdover from the cursor-based data access models in Microsoft's past. The SqlDataReader represents a read-only, forward-only cursor to SQL Server that a developer can use to retrieve and process data from SQL Server on a row-by-row basis. Because it is read only, you cannot use a data reader to make any data modifications. In addition, because it is forward only, you are only allowed to execute movement in the cursor to the next row of data. There is no random access to the data, nor is there an ability to move backward or to the end of a set without advancing through the entire set one row at a time.

To generate the SqlDataReader instance, you must use the ExecuteReader method of the SqlCommand object. This method executes the CommandText of the command through the configured connection associated with the command and generates a server-side cursor as a result. The SqlDataReader instance represents a reference to that cursor, allowing the developer to move through the data using the data reader's Read method.

Listing 17.1 provides an example of using a data reader. The purpose of this code is to execute a stored procedure that provides a list of orders to the client, which the client then displays in a console window.

LISTING 17.1   Implementing a SQLDataReader

```
using System.Data.SqlClient;
using System.Data;

public void ProcessSampleReader()
{
    // Declare all variables
    SqlConnection cn;
    SqlCommand cmd;
    SqlDataReader rd;

    // Connect and generate reader
    cn = new SqlConnection
     ("Data Source=TestServer;Database=TestDB;Integrated Security=true");
    cmd = new SqlCommand("GetOrdersByQuantity", cn);
    cmd.Parameters.AddWithValue("@Quantity", 10);
    cn.Open();
    rd = cmd.ExecuteReader(CommandBehavior.CloseConnection);

    // Process and close the reader
    while (rd.Read())
    {
        Console.WriteLine(rd["OrderNumber"].ToString());
    }
    rd.Close();
}
```

A few elements of this code listing warrant additional explanation. First, please notice that we deliberately open our connection to SQL Server before executing the ExecuteReader method of cmd. This is required. You cannot execute a reader unless the associated connection is open. However, you may have noticed that we never explicitly close that connection. The connection is implicitly closed when we close the reader object on the last line. This is because of the argument that we provided to the ExecuteReader method, called CommandBehavior.CloseConnection. This argument tells the reader to close the connection when the reader is closed.

As a database administrator, you need to ensure that your client developers are closing their connections when they are finished with them. This should be a best practice enforced throughout the organization. Without this close behavior, the application will not promptly release the connection back to the connection pool. This may cause the pool size to grow over time to its maximum allowable size. Eventually, performance will start to drag because of the insufficient number of available connections in the pool.

You should also note that the value of the parameter uses an int data type. Inside the stored procedure, the procedure uses the integer in its SQL queries for comparison purposes. The procedure expects an integer (int), not a string. Because the parameter is not a string that SQL Server can parse and execute, we have limited our exposure to SQL injection. You should enforce this practice whenever possible.

One problem area that you might run into when client developers use data readers is the overhead of creating and maintaining the cursor. If the client uses the data just once, such as to load a list box, using a data reader makes sense. However, if the client must consult the data frequently, such as with a lookup table, you should consider using a DataSet to cache the data so that you do not have to repeat the retrieval more often than necessary.

CONNECTED MODIFICATIONS USING THE SQLCOMMAND

Using SqlCommand, you can also execute queries and stored procedure calls against the server for which you do not expect any return data. This is typical of insert, update, and delete queries. To execute these types of queries, you will not need a data reader—just a connection and a command. The pattern is very similar to the one previously discussed, the primary difference being that you will use the ExecuteNonQuery method of the command object. Again, although the CommandText can be an ad hoc SQL statement or a stored procedure, using a procedure is strongly recommended.

Listing 17.2 illustrates this process. Suppose that you have a stored procedure that updates an order's quantity based on the order number. The stored procedure is called UpdateQuantityByID and has two parameters: @ID, which represents the order ID of the targeted order, and @NewQuantity, which represents the new value that you will provide for the order quantity. Assuming that the ID of the order you want to modify is 123 and the new quantity you want to assign is 20, the procedure call might look like the one in Listing 17.2.

LISTING 17.2   Modifying Data Using a Connected SqlCommand

```
using System.Data.SqlClient;
public void ExecuteUpdateQuantity()
{
    // Declare Variables
    SqlConnection cn;
    SqlCommand cmd;

    // Connect and execute the data modification
    cn = new SqlConnection
      ("Data Source=TestServer;Database=TestDB;Integrated Security=true");
    cmd = new SqlCommand("UpdateQuantityByID", cn);
```

```
cmd.Parameters.AddWithValue("@ID", 123);
cmd.Parameters.AddWithValue("@NewQuantity", 20);
cn.Open();
cmd.ExecuteNonQuery();
cn.Close();
}
```

The example shows one of the most efficient ways to execute a data modification from the client. Although you are maintaining the connection throughout the update, you are holding that connection for the shortest possible time. As long as you use a well-written stored procedure, this will provide the best possible solution to this situation.

It is also possible to modify data through a data cache called a DataSet and merge those changes back into the database later. However, this is not an optimal technique from a performance perspective and you should avoid it when possible. Instead, rely on good stored procedures to provide the necessary set-based logic to make the required modifications.

Disconnected Operations

The heart of ADO.NET is its support for disconnected operations. Now that it has the ability to retrieve sets of data from the server and cache those on the client for further processing, ADO.NET is stepping closer in every release to the ideal of a client data processing solution. With the introduction of a technology called LINQ to DataSet, which we will discuss later in the chapter, we now have the ability to query cached DataSets instead of having to examine them using collections.

Remember that when we refer to disconnected operations, we are not suggesting that the client does not need to connect, but rather that the client does not have to maintain the connection while processing the retrieved data. The advantage is that the connection time can be as short as possible, thereby reducing the likelihood of server problems such as blocking and deadlocking.

There are two additional classes to consider in our discussion of disconnected operations. They are the SqlDataAdapter class and the DataSet class. You will use these classes in conjunction with the SqlConnection and SqlCommand to query the data and return it to the client as a cached set (rather than a live cursor).

HAVE YOU NOTICED THE PATTERN?

Most of the ADO.NET classes that we have discussed so far have names that begin with the prefix "Sql." When a class name starts with this prefix, you know that the class is specific to the SQL Server implementation of ADO.NET. We use SqlConnection to connect only to SQL Server databases. The SqlCommand class only queries SQL Server databases. All of the other classes fit the same pattern. Other data platforms, such as ODBCConnection and OracleConnection, have classes that also follow this pattern.

So what should we conclude about the DataSet class? We can infer that because this class does not have a data platform-specific prefix, this class is in fact not specific to any data platform. In fact, this is the case. The DataSet class is defined in the System.Data namespace. This distinguishes it from the other SQL Server-specific classes, which are defined in the System.Data.SqlClient namespace. DataSets are universal data caches. No matter where the application acquired the data from, it can still be stored in a DataSet.

Because the client disconnects from the server after retrieving the data, the manipulation of the DataSet has no performance implications on the server. Therefore, we will not concern ourselves with how to process the data once the application retrieves it. However, we should look at how the application executes the procedures and returns the data to the client.

The process of loading a DataSet from a SQLServer data source requires a SqlDataAdapter instance. The SqlDataAdapter class uses the standard adapter design pattern as a go-between that connects the DataSet to the SQL Server data source. Because the physical storage structure of SQL Server differs substantially from both the Tabular Data Stream and the storage architecture of the DataSet, a translation must occur if the data stream from SQL Server is to be converted to the storage format required by the DataSet. The SqlDataAdapter performs this translation.

The critical method of the SqlDataAdapter is the Fill method. This method executes a command object associated with the select behavior of the adapter and translates the resulting data stream for the DataSet, thus filling the DataSet with data. It is possible for a DataSet instance to contain multiple tables of data, and you can even relate these tables to each other using DataRelation objects, which are similar to foreign keys. It is, therefore, possible for a single DataSet to contain many logical tables, providing a very effective data cache format. Listing 17.3 provides an example of loading a DataSet using the SqlClient classes.

LISTING 17.3   Populating a DataSet

```
using System.Data;
using System.Data.SqlClient;
private DataSet GetOrdersDataSet()
{
    // Declare all variables
    SqlConnection cn;
    SqlCommand cmd;
    SqlDataAdapter ad;
    DataSet ds;

    // Configure connection and command
    cn = new SqlConnection
      ("Data Source=TestServer;Database=TestDB;Integrated Security=true");
    cmd = new SqlCommand("GetOrdersByQuantity", cn);
    cmd.Parameters.AddWithValue("@Quantity", 10);

    // Configure adapter and load dataset
    ad = new SqlDataAdapter(cmd);
    ds = new DataSet("SampleDS");
    ad.Fill(ds, "Orders");

    // Return DataSet
    return ds;
}
```

While a number of different code patterns will work for this task, this listing demonstrates a typical implementation of this process. Notice how the code first configures the command before handing it off to the adapter. Although the adapter can also handle other tasks, such as merging data inserts, updates, and deletes into the source database, the select process is by far the most common.

The Fill method also allows us to name the DataTable object that is contained in the DataSet. In this case, we have named the DataTable *Orders*.

The server-side benefit of using DataSets is that in some cases you only have to query the database once; the client can then use the DataSet as needed without having to requery the database. This works fine as long as some data latency is acceptable to the client. The data begins to age as soon as the server returns it to the client, and because the client does not have an active connection to the server, it cannot automatically detect when another application modifies the data on the server.

DETECTING CHANGING DATA

Although the client does not maintain a connection to the server, the client can still detect changing data in other ways. The two primary approaches use rowversion data types and SQL Notifications, respectively.

The more traditional approach is to use rowversion types to determine if the underlying data has changed. This approach has been around for a very long time. (In fact, the old DBLibrary API, which started out as the proprietary API SQL Server supported in the 4.2 generation, contained a statement called Browse that required rowversion types on every table.)

Today, the rowversion process works like this: Because the server automatically updates rowversion columns whenever it modifies data for a row, you can always compare a current rowversion value with a cached rowversion value. When the client retrieves data, it also caches the rowversion so that if an update must take place, the procedure that performs the update will accept the rowversion as a parameter. The server will make the update only where the rowversions are equal. If they are not equal, zero rows will be affected by the update. The client can detect this situation and then determine how to handle the scenario based in its business rules.

The other option, SQL Notifications, is much newer. We will discuss this approach later in this chapter; however, the basic concept is that you will rely on the server to make callbacks to the client when data changes. These callbacks fire events on the client that it uses to respond to the fact that the data changed.

DataSets are not the only vehicle for data caching. Other alternatives are available. One popular option is to retrieve data using a reader that loads that data into collections. You can then use these collections for data binding, lookups, passing to other tiers, and so forth. As a SQL Server professional, you shouldn't care which approach the client developer takes as long as they minimize the number of calls to the database and use caching effectively.

Special Operations in ADO.NET

You cannot design a feature into an application if you are not aware that the feature exists. A data or enterprise architect is required by the nature of the job to be well versed in the features of the languages and tools that they use. With every new release of ADO.NET, Microsoft introduces more of these extra features, which are meant to provide grater flexibility in the data tier. While a discussion of the specifics of coding for these features is better suited for a book on ADO.NET than a book on SQL Server, it is still important for the database architect to know what options are available and how they impact performance and security on the server. In this section, we will discuss some of the more prominent features and their implications.

Multiple Active Result Sets (MARS)

There is a restriction when working with client-generated cursors. Client developers accept it, but constantly complain about it. You can open only one cursor at a time through a single connection. If you want to open another cursor, you must open another connection, even if the connection parameters are exactly the same as those for the first connection.

The underlying logic that causes this behavior is a deliberate restriction in the API that only allows a single pending request for an operation. This is meant to preserve data integrity. While this is desirable in most cases, there are situations where this behavior is not necessary. For these special situations, we can now use Multiple Active Result Sets (MARS). The application's responsiveness provides an alternative to other approaches such as maintaining multiple connections and using server cursors to simulate multiple concurrent requests.

MARS works by interleaving some specific types of requests, thus allowing multiple requests to execute on a single connection without queuing.

MARS does not allow all operations to interleave before the completion of their execution. There are restrictions. Only the following operations can interleave in a MARS session.

- ◆ SELECT
- ◆ FETCH
- ◆ READTEXT
- ◆ RECEIVE (with XACT_ABORT ON)
- ◆ BULK INSERT (with XACT_ABORT ON)
- ◆ Asynchronous cursor population

Within this list, there are other limitations. Because READTEXT is deprecated in the next release, we can scratch that one off the list. RECEIVE is specific to Service Broker behavior, which we will discuss in detail in Chapter 20, "Service Oriented Architecture and the Service Broker." (In addition, because ADO.NET handles MARS entirely through the client, this behavior is not limited to SQL Server.)

It is also important to consider what MARS does not do (or does not do so well). MARS does not provide for parallel processing of multiple operations. Because the operations are interleaving on the same connection, they are multitasking on that same connection. For example, if you have two processors, they can each execute a query on separate connections. Setting processor affinity on the server will determine the total number of processors that can execute SQL Server code.

PARALLEL THIS AND THAT

There is a common confusion between the concepts of processor affinity and Maximum Degrees of Parallelism (MaxDOP). *Processor affinity* refers to the binding of processors in a server to SQL Server execution. This allows SQL Server to ensure that it can execute without starving any other services.

MaxDOP is a different creature altogether. The MaxDOP setting specifies how many parallel execution plans SQL Server can use to execute a single query. A very complex query might be broken up into multiple execution processes. These processes can execute in parallel if adequate resources are available. The result is a more complete utilization of processor resources and better performance when executing complex queries.

No good thing comes without a cost. Although it sounds good on paper, the real cost of the MaxDOP option is its potential to deadlock multiple parallel plans. You might want to experiment with this option; however, if you notice errors stating that you have deadlocks with intra-query parallelism. The best solution is to set the MaxDOP option to 1, thus preventing query parallelism and the problems that can come with it.

Enabling MARS is a simple process. Because the client API handles everything, no server configuration is necessary to enable this behavior. Simply add an option to the connection string for multiple active result sets, and the client will automatically interleave any statements that it can through this connection.

A connection string configured to support MARS would look like this:

```
String sCon =
    "Data Source=TestServer;Database=TestDB;Integrated Security=true;MultipleActiv
eResultSets=true";
SqlConnection cn = new SqlConnection(sCon);
```

Interleaving requests through MARS can benefit the server by not requiring as many connections to perform multiple operations. It can also be extremely convenient for the client-side developer. However, MARS is more prone to deadlocking and can cause additional blocking on the server. You should only use it in situations where you can verify that the benefits of MARS outweigh the potential hazards.

Using SQLBulkCopy

In the early days of SQL Server, we used a command-line utility called the *bulk copy program* to bulk load data from one location to another. The strength of the bulk copy program was in its flexibility. All you needed was a text file. A text file extracted from any source could be bulk loaded into SQL Server, just as SQL Server could output its data into a text file through the same command line. The problem with the bulk copy program was that it was tedious to use, especially from within a client application. Although Transact-SQL supported a BULK INSERT operation, what was needed was a client class that could do bulk loading of data with the same efficiencies as the bulk copy program.

The SQLBulkCopy class fits this requirement and is very easy to implement. You have full control over the source and destination, including column mapping, batch size, and connection properties. If the client goal is to migrate large amounts of data from one SQL Server to another, the SQLBulkCopy class should be the option of first preference.

The class is easy to use. You must define the connection and query that you will use for data extraction, the connection and table destination along with column mappings if necessary, and any other additional information such as a batch size. Then simply execute the operation. Listing 17.4 provides an example of the SQLBulkCopy program in action. Note that this code assumes that the destination table is already present upon execution of the operation. You can use this script to create the table if needed.

```
USE SandboxDB;

CREATE TABLE BulkCopyTarget(
    Title nvarchar(8) NULL,
    FirstName nvarchar(50) NOT NULL,
    LastName nvarchar(50) NOT NULL
    );
GO
```

LISTING 17.4   Using the SQLBulkCopy Class

```
using System.Data;
using System.Data.SqlClient;
using System.Windows.Forms;
private void ProcessBulkInsert()
{
    // Declare variables
    SqlConnection cnSource;
    SqlConnection cnDestination;
    SqlCommand cmdExtract;
    SqlCommand cmdCount;
    SqlDataReader rdSourceReader;
    SqlBulkCopy sbcPerson;
    String sConSource =
        "Data Source=(local)\\MasteringSQL;Database=AdventureWorks2008;Integrated
Security=true";
    String sConDest =
        "Data Source=(local)\\MasteringSQL;Database=SandBoxDB;Integrated
Security=true";
    String sCmdExtract = "SELECT Title, FirstName, LastName FROM Person.Person;";
    String sCmdCount = "SELECT COUNT(*) FROM dbo.BulkCopyTarget;";
    Object sReturnCount;

    // Display the count of records in the target table before the insert
    cnDestination = new SqlConnection(sConDest);
    cmdCount = new SqlCommand(sCmdCount, cnDestination);
    cnDestination.Open();
    sReturnCount = cmdCount.ExecuteScalar();
    MessageBox.Show(sReturnCount.ToString());
```

```
// Extract the data from the source
cnSource = new SqlConnection(sConSource);
cmdExtract = new SqlCommand(sCmdExtract, cnSource);
cnSource.Open();
rdSourceReader = cmdExtract.ExecuteReader(CommandBehavior.CloseConnection);

// Setup and perform bulk insert
sbcPerson = new SqlBulkCopy(cnDestination);
sbcPerson.BatchSize = 100;
sbcPerson.DestinationTableName = "BulkCopyTarget";
try
{
    sbcPerson.WriteToServer(rdSourceReader);
}
catch (Exception ex)
{
    MessageBox.Show("Error writing rows \n " + ex.Message);
}
finally
{
    rdSourceReader.Close();
}

// Display the count of records in the target table after the insert
sReturnCount = cmdCount.ExecuteScalar();
MessageBox.Show(sReturnCount.ToString());
cnDestination.Close();
}
```

SQL Query Notifications

As we mentioned previously, latency is a common issue when working in a disconnected environment.

Without an active connection, there is simply no way to identify directly if another application has changed data since your application retrieved that data from the server. SQL Server 2008 allows ADO.NET Windows applications to send a command to SQL Server and request that a notification be generated if executing the same SQL command would produce result sets different from those initially retrieved.

This notification works as a call back to the client application. The infrastructure that supports this behavior is the SQL Server Service Broker. We will discuss Service Broker in more detail in Chapter 20; this is just a quick preview now of what it has to offer. Because setting this up is a multistep process, we will walk you through that process and then discuss the effects of query notifications when we are finished.

The first step is to enable the Service Broker. You can control this database-level option in two different ways. You can set the option through Transact-SQL code by using the command ALTER DATABASE SandBoxDB SET ENABLE_BROKER and substituting the name of your database for SandBoxDB. You can also use the SQL Server Management Studio interface and change the setting through the Database Properties window, as pictured in Figure 17.2.

FIGURE 17.2

Enabling the
Service Broker

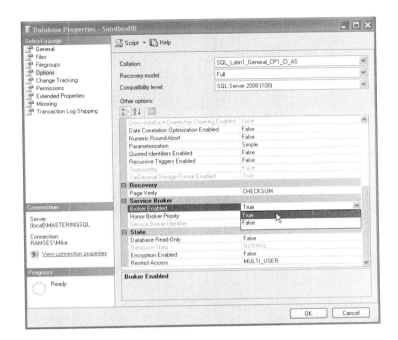

Next, you must ensure that the user requesting the notifications has the permissions to receive those notifications. Users who execute commands requesting notification must have Subscribe Query Notifications database permission on the server. Client-side code that runs in a partial trust situation requires the SqlClientPermission.

Now it is time to code. If you coded the previous example using the SQLBulkCopy class, you can use this to trigger changes to the underlying table. To make sure that you are starting fresh, you may want to truncate the BulkCopyTarget table before you continue.

Our sample application will be a Windows application. You will need two CommandButton instances, one Label and one DataGridView on your startup form. You can lay these out any way you like. One button will execute the code to do the bulk load, while the other will set up the query notification. If you are not familiar with how to set up and code for a Windows interface in C#, don't worry about it. Just read through the code. That is the most important part.

We will begin by declaring the variables so that they are visible to the entire form. We will use these declarations.

```
delegate void UIDelegate();
SqlConnection cnNotification;
SqlCommand cmdNotification;
DataSet dsNotification;
String sCon =
    "Data Source=(local)\\MasteringSQL;Integrated Security=true;Database=SandBoxDB
;";
String sSql =
    "SELECT * FROM dbo.BulkCopyTarget " +
    "WHERE LastName ='Anderson' and FirstName='Nancy'";
```

For this example, we will assume that the code for the first button will handle the bulk load, so you can take that code from Listing 17.4. We will use the second button to set up the query notification. That code will look like this:

```
private void button2_Click(object sender, EventArgs e)
{
    SqlDependency.Stop(sCon);
    SqlDependency.Start(sCon);
    if (cnNotification == null)
        cnNotification = new SqlConnection(sCon);
    if (cmdNotification == null)
        cmdNotification = new SqlCommand(sSql, cnNotification);
    if (dsNotification == null)
        dsNotification = new DataSet();
    GetSandBoxData();
}
```

This code begins by clearing out any existing dependency and then setting up a new one. This will prevent you from accidentally subscribing to multiple dependencies. Notice that the dependency is based on the connection string. Because the SqlCommand object uses that connection data to execute its queries, any changes to the data that would affect this command will be valid for notification.

At the bottom of this snippet is a call to GetSandBoxData. It looks like this:

```
public void GetSandBoxData()
{
  // Clear out the DataSet
  dsNotification.Clear();

  // Ensure the command object does not have a notification object.
  cmdNotification.Notification = null;

  // Bind the SqlDependency object to the command object.
  SqlDependency dependency = new SqlDependency(cmdNotification);
  dependency.OnChange += new OnChangeEventHandler(dependency_OnChange);

  // Populate the DataSet
  using (SqlDataAdapter adapter = new SqlDataAdapter(cmdNotification))
  {
    adapter.Fill(dsNotification, "People");
    dataGridView1.DataSource = dsNotification;
    dataGridView1.DataMember = "People";
  }
}
```

The OnChangeEventHandler procedure is an *event callback*. When the data modification takes place on the server, the Service Broker will send a notification message to the client, which then raises the event on the client side.

The event handler looks like this.

```
private void dependency_OnChange(object sender, SqlNotificationEventArgs e)
{
  UIDelegate uidel = new UIDelegate(RefreshData);
  this.Invoke(uidel, null);

  //Remove the handler as it is used for a single notification.
  SqlDependency dependency = (SqlDependency)sender;
  dependency.OnChange -= dependency_OnChange;
}
```

The callback method uses a *delegate* (a function pointer) to refresh the grid when a client raises the event. The callback cannot refresh the grid directly, because there is a limitation in Windows applications that do not allow a callback event to interact directly with the UI. This is because the callback event is not executing on the UI thread.

So what happens when the delegate calls the RefreshData method? That code looks like this.

```
private void RefreshData()
{
  // Since the code is executing on the UI thread,it is safe to update the UI.

  label1.Text = "Data Modified and Grid Updated";

  // Reload the dataset that is bound to the grid.
  GetSandBoxData();
}
```

This may seem complex when you look at the code, but the concept is quite simple. This is a publisher/subscriber model where the SQL Server Service Broker is the publisher and the client application is the subscriber. By registering a SQLDependency object to the command, the client is subscribing to any notifications indicating that data within the bounds of the command have changed.

In this example, the following events will occur.

1. Click button 2. The grid will appear, but it will be empty.

2. Click button 1 to execute the bulk load process, which will modify the underlying data.

3. The server fires the notification.

4. The client event handler executes.

5. This handler then refreshes the grid by clearing the DataSet and reloading it with the new data.

6. This updates the data in the grid.

For the database administrator, what are the effects of query notifications? First of all, this is only a SQL Server-supported feature. It requires a client software layer called the SQL Native Client. This client provides the address for the callback.

This also requires that you enable the Service Broker for the database that you want to watch. While the overhead is not outrageous, it does all add up. The notification is handled by creating a Service Broker queue on the server for this notification. Each notification queue provides only a single notification. After the server sends the notification to the server, it removes the queue and the client must request the same notification again if it wants to continue the process.

When it is used appropriately, this technique can provide a real benefit to the disconnected application. It works best when the underlying data modifications are infrequent but the client must respond immediately upon change and cannot wait—for example, for a polling interval to elapse before the client action takes place.

If you plan to design query notifications into your applications, we recommend that you perform some stress testing on the system with a production level of notifications, especially if you have many clients and many applications all requesting notifications. This should help you to assess the performance implications specific to your application environment.

Introducing Language Integrated Query (LINQ)

If this is your first look at Language Integrated Query (LINQ), you are in for a surprise. LINQ represents a quantum shift in the way we approach data access in client applications and data access layers. LINQ is clear evidence of the morphing boundaries between data stores, data caches, and, most importantly, the languages and technologies we use to access each layer. For example, consider this code.

```
// Create and load generic list
List<string> beatles = new List<string>(4);
beatles.Add("John");
beatles.Add("Paul");
beatles.Add("George");
beatles.Add("Ringo");

// Execute LINQ query on list
var favoriteBeatles =
        from b in beatles
        where b.StartsWith("P")
        select b;

// Iterate through results of LINQ query
foreach (var b in favoriteBeatles)
        MessageBox.Show(b);
```

If you are a developer, this code is very exciting because it blurs the line between programmatic data structures and databases. If you are a database administrator, this can be a little unsettling—for exactly the same reason . We need to re-evaluate the concept of a queryable data structure in the context of LINQ.

Traditionally, the database developer would view a queryable data source from the context of the data engine. SQL code provides the instructions that the data engine uses to perform the data operation. While modular data service design can provide interchangeability between data engines and data stores, these two components are companions that are never separated.

In this example, where is the data engine and what is the data store? Let's take a look.

This code begins by creating a data store from a generic List collection class. Previously, extracting data from this list would require iterations, comparisons, or searches. With LINQ, we have the elegance of being able to use SQL-like query logic instead.

As its name implies, .NET programming languages such as C# and VB.NET integrate LINQ directly through the .NET Framework.

This means that LINQ can use an existing API rather than requiring new ones. Let's look at our sample code snippet again. Notice that the WHERE clause in this query uses standard string methods to provide a criterion for the query. Transact-SQL does not have a "StartsWith" function. We could accomplish the same task through other means, but the client developer does not need to know that. They can continue to use the methods and API with which they are familiar. In other words, LINQ is integrated into the existing API to minimize the learning curve for the client developer.

We could rattle on and on about how cool this is for developers, but since our audience here is SQL professionals, it would not be relevant. Our primary concern in this chapter is how LINQ affects SQL Server, so in this section we will start by introducing you to the different forms that a LINQ query can take in an application. Next, we will look specifically at LINQ to SQL functionality, and finally we will assess the impact that LINQ can have on SQL Server performance, security, and coding practice.

Different Flavors of LINQ

The intention of LINQ is to be universal; it is a single query structure that you can use in applications to query data from a variety of data sources and structures. To accomplish this, LINQ appears in a variety of different flavors. The primary flavors of LINQ are

- LINQ to SQL
- LINQ to XML
- LINQ to objects
- LINQ to DataSet
- LINQ to Entities

Some of these forms of LINQ are not relevant to SQL Server. Link to XML, which lets you query an XML document without the complexity of XQuery or requiring Document Object Model (DOM) code, is a very cool concept. Client and data access layer (DAL) developers love it, but it is not relevant to SQL Server. The only way that SQL Server might get involved in this scenario is to produce the XML that LINQ is querying.

We could say the same about LINQ to objects. You might execute SQL queries for extracting data to populate into objects. In our previous example, we could have loaded the generic List instance with the data retrieved from SQL Server using a SqlDataReader instance. However, once you have retrieved the data and brought it back to the application or DAL, SQL Server no longer plays a role.

Using the same logic, LINQ to DataSet would also not affect SQL Server beyond the process of originally populating the DataSet. Once the application populates the DataSet from the data source, it disconnects and no longer affects the server unless it attempts to reconnect and merge its changes back into the data source.

It seems that the two flavors of LINQ that will most affect SQL Server are LINQ to SQL, formerly known as DLinq, and LINQ to Entities, which is governed by the ADO.NET Entity Framework. We will discuss the entity framework in a later section of this chapter.

LINQ to SQL

LINQ to SQL is nothing more than a basic Object-Relational Mapping (ORM) layer. We must place an emphasis on "basic." It is not intended to be a full-scale ORM layer. The purpose is to create an object layer that represents data structures in SQL Server so that you can manipulate the data by manipulating the objects. LINQ provides the language for this manipulation as well as the infrastructure that manages this object to data relationship. Because of the nature of LINQ to SQL as an ORM layer, LINQ places certain restrictions on LINQ to SQL. (These restrictions don't appear in other flavors of LINQ.)

IMPORTANT NOTICE ABOUT COMPATIBILITY

The release of Visual Studio 2008 significantly preceded the release of SQL Server 2008. As a result, Visual Studio 2008 is not compatible with SQL Server 2008 with respect to many features, such as creating data connection objects or database projects. You, therefore, have two options.

First, you can use SQL Server 2005 for all of the following examples. Everything that we do in this chapter should work fine on SQL Server 2005, but you will have to translate a little here and there.

Second, you can download the required compatibility patch from Microsoft. This will most likely be included in a Visual Studio 2008 service pack after the final release of SQL Server 2008, but until that time, you will have to download and install the necessary hotfix to provide compatibility. Search at http://www.microsoft.com/downloads for the text "Visual Studio 2008 Support for SQL Server 2008" to find the right fix for the build of SQL Server 2008 that you are using.

LINQ to SQL only works with SQL Server.   You can use any version of SQL Server, including SQL Express, but LINQ to SQL Server does not work with other relational databases such as Oracle. LINQ to SQL depends on the SQL Server provider to provide the necessary support for this technology. If you want to use LINQ with other databases, you will have to look at the other LINQ flavors to provide the required interface.

LINQ to SQL is tightly coupled.   LINQ to SQL requires that you generate an Entity to Object mapping layer. LINQ tightly couples this layer to the database, so any schema changes to the database will require you to regenerate the entity layer. If the changes are significant, you might also have to modify existing code that depends on the entities that you modified.

DOWNLOADING THE NORTHWIND DATABASE

The examples that we will use of LINQ to SQL require that you install the Northwind sample database provided by Microsoft. You should be able to find this download at http://www.microsoft.com/downloads. Search for "Northwind and pubs Sample Databases for SQL Server 2000." Even though the databases are intended for SQL Server 2000, they will install just fine in SQL Server 2008. You will be downloading an .msi file. Executing the .msi will create a folder with the installation scripts. Run the instnwind.sql script on your SQL 2008 instance to create the Northwind database.

CREATING THE OBJECT RELATIONAL MAPPING LAYER

The first step in LINQ to SQL is creating the entity classes that represent the Object Relational mapping layer. You can do this in the Visual Studio 2008 Object Relational Designer. The Designer application saves its data to a database mapping layer (.dbml) file, which is an XML file. Follow these steps to create the .dbml file for the Northwind database.

1. Open Visual Studio 2008 and select File➤ New➤ Project form the menu. Create a new Windows Forms application using the Visual C# language. Name the project **LINQ_ Samples** and store it in a location of your choosing.

2. To add the .dbml file to your project, select Project ➤ Add New Item from the menu. Select LINQ To SQL Classes from the list. Name the new file **Northwind.dbml** and click the Add button. You should see an empty Object Relational Designer on the screen.

3. To add mappings, you will need a database connection. Select View ➤ Server Explorer from the menu. Right-click on the Data Connections node and select Add Connection from the menu. Fill out the Add Connection window so it looks like the one in Figure 17.3, replacing the value in the Server Name textbox with your server and instance. Then click the OK button.

FIGURE 17.3
Creating the database connection

4. In the Server Explorer window, expand the connection that you created to the Northwind database. Then expand the Tables folder. Drag both the Customers and Orders tables from the Server Explorer to the left pane of the Designer. This will create a Customer entity and an Order entity. In the Designer, you will see that because the two tables are bound by a foreign key constraint on the SQL Server, that relationship is recognized in the entity model.

5. Take a moment to look at the entities in the Designer. Click on an entity in the Designer and you will see that the Properties window in the bottom right of the screen will update, giving you full control over the entity. You can change the name of any entity or property, alter its data mappings, and even add new properties that are based on data computations and custom logic.

6. Expand the Views folder in the Server Explorer. Drag the Sales by Category view to the left pane of the Designer. You will see that the Designer treats the view as an entity and it generates an entity class from the structure of the view.

7. Expand the Stored Procedures folder. Drag the CustOrderDetail procedure to either the left or the right pane of the Designer. No matter where you drop it, the result will be that it created a data function in the model. Currently, the object-relational mapping model that the Designer created looks like the illustration in Figure 17.4.

FIGURE 17.4
The Northwind sample entity model

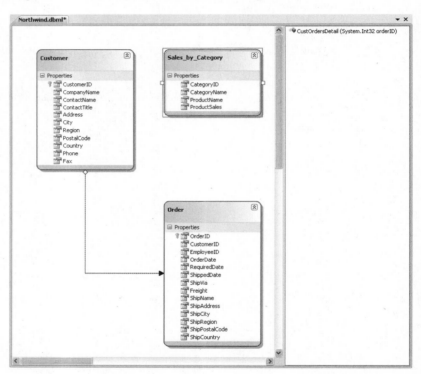

Let's look at a few key points in this model. First, if you go to the Solution Explorer window on the right of your screen and expand the Northwind.dbml node, you will see a Northwind.designer.cs file. Double click this icon to open the file. You will see the code that supports the model. The first class in the code file is called NorthwindDataContext. This class is your entry point into the model. This class knows how to connect to the underlying database and it has properties and methods that provide access to the other entities in the model. The Customers and Orders properties are references to the Customer and Order entities, respectively. You will see a Sales_By_Category property as well.

You will also see that the NorthwindDataContext class has a function called CustOrderDetail. This function represents the stored procedure of the same name. The return value of this function is a class type called CustOrderDetailResult. This class, also defined in the model, defines properties for all the individual data values that the stored procedure returns.

QUERYING SQL SERVER WITH LINQ

Now that we have the entity classes with all of the required connectivity information, the next step is to use the classes to query the database. Suppose that we want to return a list of all the customers located in the United States of America and load the results in a data grid. You can follow these steps to accomplish this task.

1. Open the Visual Designer for Form1 in your application. From the toolbox, drag a DataGridView control and a Button control onto the surface of the form so that they look like the example in Figure 17.5.

FIGURE 17.5
Designing the
Windows form

2. Double-click on the button in the Designer window to open the code stub for the button-click event. In this event stub, add the following code.

```
// Establish the context
NorthwindDataContext db = new NorthwindDataContext();

// Execute the LINQ query agains the data source
var usCustomers =
  from c in db.Customers
  where c.Country=="USA"
  select new
    {
      CompanyName = c.CompanyName,
      City = c.City,
      Country = c.Country
    };
```

```
// Bind the results to the DataGridView control
dataGridView1.DataSource = usCustomers;
```

3. Press the F5 key to run the application. When the form appears on the screen, click the button. This will populate the grid with data by executing the query. If you want to try out the stored procedure, add another button and use this code in its click-event handler.

```
// Bind the results of the stored procedure to the DataGridView control
NorthwindDataContext db = new NorthwindDataContext();
dataGridView1.DataSource = db.CustOrdersDetail(10660);
```

4. This code should return a single row of data for Order Number 10660 to the grid. Save your work.

You should be aware that there are many features available in LINQ to SQL that we have not even hinted at. There are too many to cover in this book, but be aware that LINQ to SQL is quite flexible. LINQ to SQL can support transactional data modifications and will even allow you to map stored procedures to the insert, update, and delete operations. You can also override the default connection properties with alternative connection parameters when you create the DataContext object. These are just a few of the capabilities that LINQ to SQL provides.

The SQL Server Implications of LINQ to SQL

As a database professional, you probably had a much different reaction to the code that you just saw than most client developers will have. The client developers love it. It makes things so easy. There is no more worrying about making connections and retrieving DataSets, and it is simple to provide criteria in a where clause or parameters for a stored procedure. What could be better?

As a SQL professional, you might have different thoughts.

◆ How are the connections made and how long are they held?

◆ What mechanism does LINQ use to query the database?

◆ What are the security implications of LINQ?

AND IN THIS CORNER …

We promise that we are not trying to start a fight here. Our intention is not to "spoil the party" with regard to LINQ to SQL. It is extremely important, however, to be fully aware of the implications of this kind of code. Every tool has its place, and only you and your colleagues can determine the best place for every technology in your environment. It is best to be informed before making those decisions, so that you will not be carried away by the excitement of using new and groovy technology.

The best thing that you can do to assess the impact of this approach on your database is to write some sample LINQ to SQL code and run some traces using SQL Profiler to determine the actual behavior of the tool. We highly recommend that you take the time to do this and evaluate the results. (This is sound advice to follow whenever you are investigating any new technology. Find out what is actually happening before you either put up roadblocks or jump on the bandwagon.)

If you run some traces, you should notice the following issues:

Connections   LINQ does an admirable job of reducing connection overhead. It fully utilizes ADO.NET connection pooling and when the application uses consistent connection properties, it pulls and releases connections to and from the pool effectively.

Execution Process   LINQ to SQL works through the SQL Native Client, which means that it adopts the standard behavior of the client when executing statements against the server. This default behavior is to pass dynamic SQL to the server, which it then executes using the sp_ executesql system stored procedure. A trace on the previous example (the one that loaded the grid with customers in United States) would show us a TextData value for the command that looks like this:

```
exec sp_executesql N'SELECT [t0].[CompanyName], [t0].[City], [t0].[Country]
FROM [dbo].[Customers] AS [t0]
WHERE [t0].[Country] = @p0',N'@p0 nvarchar(3)',@p0=N'USA'
```

This means that you have to contend with permissions issues relating to the execution of dynamic SQL, as well as the possibility of SQL injection issues, if the client developers are not properly scrubbing their parameters before passing them to the server. While not as exposed as using **EXEC,** there may still be some problems.

Schema Dependence   Although it is possible to override the connection parameters when instantiating the DataContext object, the schema from which you generate your entities is the schema you will be stuck with when coding to those entities. Any change of database schema would require you to generate your entities again. This could mean significant recoding for both the client as well as the customization work already done to those entities. The other option is to make the changes by hand. Neither approach is very appealing.

Schema Requirements   The quality of the generated entities depends on how well you are enforcing integrity on the server. (This is a best practice that you should be following anyway.) Primary keys, foreign keys, and other constraints are implemented into the entity structure. The quality of what you get out of the structure depends on what you put in it. For example, you will not be able to write LINQ queries that automatically perform entity correlation unless there are foreign keys present in the database that tell the entity generator how to correlate the data structures together.

Again, we do not want to imply that LINQ is something you should fear. However, you should go into this model with your eyes wide open.

Finally, we should address one more area of concern that deals with LINQ in general and not specifically to the LINQ to SQL model. Be careful that LINQ does not entice your developers to adopt coding practices that diverge from good database-coding standards. One of the hallmarks of good database-coding practice is that your query should only return the data that you will need and use. LINQ can seriously disrupt this standard.

No matter what flavor of LINQ you might be using, you will be tempted to be more aggressive about the quantity of data that you return. Because it is so much easier now to requery the DataSet or XML document to retrieve the data that you want, you are likely to see more of an attitude among developers that if they retrieve more data now, they can avoid round trips to the server later. While this can be a good practice if you know that you will need and use that data, often this practice is little more than "storing nuts for winter," or bringing back additional data "just in case." Avoid the temptation and do not let the practice take root in your organization or in your own development habits.

LINQ and the Entity Framework

The ADO.NET Entity Framework is the logical successor to the LINQ to SQL model. What started in LINQ to SQL as a lightweight Object Relational Mapping (ORM) tool has begun to flesh out with the entity framework, including key issues such as support for multiple data sources through data providers, integration with business intelligence (BI) services, and a higher level of decoupling with the data tier than was available with LINQ to SQL.

The entity model that you create using the ADO.NET Entity Framework supports two query approaches. You can either use LINQ to Entities or Entity SQL. LINQ to Entities should look very familiar now that you have been exposed to the LINQ to SQL model. Entity SQL is an attempt to use a more ad hoc SQL-like structure to query the entities. You are not actually performing ad hoc SQL, because everything will be processed by the entities, but the language does have that general appearance.

The details of using the entity framework are very similar to the LINQ to SQL model. Instead of interacting with entity classes created through the LINQ to SQL Entity Designer, we will use the entity classes generated by Entity Framework Designers. The Entity Framework Designer relies on a new modeling environment that Microsoft calls the Entity Data Model (EDM). Microsoft patterned EDM after the Entity Relationship Model (ERM) that we use almost universally for relational database design. The intention is to take the best parts or ERM as it relates to data and apply it to Entity Modeling.

Similar to LINQ to SQL, the Visual Studio project stored the entity information in an XML file. This time the file has an `.edmx` extension. We can create this by hand, which is the painful way, or we can use a wizard to create the initial bindings and then customize the model from there. In this section, we will once again walk through the process of setting up the entity model and then demonstrate how to query that model. Finally, we will look at the impacts of this technology on the SQL Server from the perspective of the DBA.

WHERE IS THE ENTITY FRAMEWORK?

When the feature list for Visual Studio 2008 (VS 2008) was first released, Microsoft touted the ADO. NET Entity Framework as one of the substantial new additions to VS 2008. We had been able to do LINQ to SQL against SQL Server 2005 for quite some time in VS 2005, but it was time for the next step. Unfortunately, the entity framework was not ready for release when the release date came for VS 2008, and rather than delay the release of the entire product, Microsoft cut the framework from the product for release later. This feature has, however, been fully included in Visual Studio 2008 Service Pack 1.

If you are walking through any of these examples with a release build of VS 2008 with no service packs or patches, then you will not see the options we will present. You must install Service Pack 1 first.

Creating and Querying the Entity Data Model

The result of the model generation in the entity framework case is similar to the LINQ to SQL model, but the process is much different. We will not cover all of the nuances of the entity framework, but if you want to walk through the process of creating a simple model, follow these steps.

1. Start VS 2008 and create a new Windows Form project in Visual C#. Name the project **NorthwindEDM** and save it to a location of your choosing.

2. Add a new Entity Framework model by selecting Project ➤ Add New Item from the menu. Select the ADO.NET Entity Data Model from the list. If you do not see this item in the list, then you must install the service pack (SP1) before you can continue. Name the model **NWindCustomers.edmx** and click the Add button.

3. In the Entity Data Model Wizard, select the option to generate the model from a database and click the Next button.

4. In the next screen, select the Northwind database connection that we created in the previous walkthrough. Notice on the bottom of the wizard form that it specifies the app.config settings name that it will use to save these settings. Click the Next button.

5. In the Object Selection screen, expand the Tables node and select the boxes next to the Customers and Orders tables. You could add many objects to your model, but we will use just these two. Notice that the namespace for the model classes is NorthwindModel. Click the Finish button.

You should see a visual representation of the model in your Designer. Because the underlying tables are related through foreign keys, the model is automatically aware of the correlation and includes this in the model.

On the right side of the screen, you should see the Model Browser window. If you do not see this, select View ➤ Other Windows ➤ Model Browser from the menu. This window allows you to see the details and properties of your entities, as well as the underlying data store. If you expand the Model Browser so that you can see the properties in the entities, it should look like the one in Figure 17.6.

If you select the Customers entity in the Model Browser window, you should now see the properties of the entity in the Properties Window as well as the mapping information in the Mapping Details window. If the Mapping Details window does not appear, select View ➤ Other Windows ➤ Mapping Details from the menu. The mapping details are important because this is where you relate the entities to their underlying data source. If you want to remap an entity property to a different data structure, add a property, or remove a property, you would do it here.

MAPPING FOR REUSE AND MAINTAINABILITY

Entity mapping is a very important part of this process. We wish that we had more time to cover all of its intricacies here. At this point, all of the entities are mapped directly to data structures, but this does not have to be the case. You can remap entities using expressions. You can also add new entities based on existing ones but with different filter criteria. In the end, you can create an entity model that matches your business tier rather than your data structure, and that is the whole idea behind the entity framework. At that point, the EDM becomes a reusable transformational model that negotiates the differences between your logical business structure and physical data structure.

FIGURE 17.6
The Model Browser
window

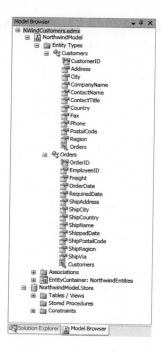

Querying the EDM is very similar to the LINQ to SQL code that we used previously. You have two options. You can either use LINQ to Entities or Entity SQL. Let's take a look at both approaches.

1. In your Windows form, add a DataGridView control similar to the previous walkthrough. We will use this again for data binding. Also, add two buttons under the grid on the form. We will use one of these for the LINQ to Entities query and the other for the Entity SQL code.

2. Double-click the first button in the Designer to take you to the code stub for the click event. We will put a simple query here to return all data for all customers located in the United States. To do this, use the following code.

```
// Create entity context
NorthwindEntities context = new NorthwindEntities();

// Query entity model with LINQ
var USCustomers =
from customers in context.Customers
where customers.Country == "USA"
select customers;

// Bind query results to grid
dataGridView1.DataSource = USCustomers;
```

3. Run the application and click on the first button. The data grid should load with data. These will only be the customers located in the United States.

4. Code the second button to do the same thing with Entity SQL using the following code. Note that the ObjectParameter class is in the System.Data.Objects namespace.

```
// Create entity context
NorthwindEntities context = new NorthwindEntities();

// Query entity model with Entity SQL
var USCustomers = context.Customers.Where
  ("it.Country = @arg",
  new System.Data.Objects.ObjectParameter("Arg", "USA")
  );

// Bind query results to grid
dataGridView1.DataSource = USCustomers;
```

5. Run the application and click the second button. Your grid should load with the same data as before. These will only be the customers located in the United States.

In the Entity SQL code, you should note that the logic makes use of a "where" method. This is called a "builder" method and you use it to build the underlying query. You could have also used the argument `"it.Country = 'USA'"` and that would have worked as well, but parameterization is a better practice as it enforces type safety and is less prone to SQL injection attacks. Also, be aware that the "it" in `it.Country` is an alias intended to reference the contextual entity, in this case Customers.

The SQL Server Implications of the Entity Framework

Although this technology is still new and it is certain to develop further, we can already see some interesting trends as it relates to SQL Server performance and security. Again, as with LINQ to SQL, the questions that a typical DBA would have deal with issues of connectivity, efficiency, performance, etc. The code that we just saw looks very similar to the LINQ to SQL model, but when you peel off the outer layers and look inside, you are really in a different world. The difference is that you have a significantly greater amount of control.

INTEROPERABILITY

One of the great points about the entity framework is that it has significantly more interoperability with other database systems than the LINQ to SQL model. Because LINQ to SQL is dependent on the SQL Native Client, it suffers from the limitations that this defines.

There were the issues with the default query-execution methods, over which you had no control. You also had to contend with the fact that the SQL Native Client provided support only for SQL Server. These two restrictions mean that you had little control and that there was little extensibility in the model.

The entity framework functions much differently. Instead of the SQL Native Client, it uses a data source-provider model, much like standard ADO.NET. This makes it possible, and much more likely, that any database vendor can open up to the entity framework. Because the EDM is not vendor specific, you can reuse the same models again and again, mapping to a variety of different data platforms.

CONTROLLING THE PROCESS

The entity framework is based on a layered model. Figure 17.7 illustrates this layered architecture. The client application only sees the object layer, while the database is only concerned with the storage layer and does not really care about what happens upstream. The magic happens in the middle, in the logical layer where the mapping and transformation take place.

FIGURE 17.7
The entity framework layers

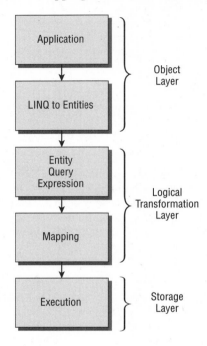

The interesting aspect of this as it relates to the concerns of the typical DBA is that it gives you control over the process at any layer. For example, consider the Object layer. The application sees only this layer of the stack. In the previous example, we returned a set of customers that were located in the United States. We did this by using a `where` statement in our LINQ code that filtered out the other countries from the results.

If the client developer wanted to process these results further, they could use the query as a source in yet another query, maybe adding a criterion for state as an example. This is possible because, by default, the return value of every query implements an interface called IQueryable. That means that every query can be further queried and refined through LINQ.

This process is called *query composition*. Every additional query based on a query is translated into a single logical query expression, no matter how many times the query object has been further processed. The effect of this behavior is to minimize the data that is returned from the server by executing more restrictive and dynamic SQL. As a DBA, however, you may want to prevent this.

If you want to restrict this behavior, you can modify the query objects in the model by casting them to the IEnumerable interface instead. The developer can still use LINQ to query IEnumerable objects, but because they are not IQueryable objects, the actual query expressions cannot be composed. The result is that LINQ will use fixed logic in the initial query to pull the data from the server and any further processing done by additional queries is done on the client.

The good part of this process is that although you have control over exactly what the framework executes on the server, to the client developer it makes no difference. Their code will look the same regardless. The only difference is the interface type that the queries assume.

On the negative side, however, you might return more data to the client than is needed. Be careful that in your zeal to exercise control, you don't force more expensive operations on the server—operations that could be done on the server more cheaply using the right query.

At the data-store level, you can also use stored procedures for all processing. In the entity framework, you already have the ability to map stored procedures to insert and update operations for entities. That can be done directly in the mapping interface. You can also use stored procedures for all data extraction too, if you like, but when you do this, you lose the ability to support composable query behavior at the object layer due to the nature of stored procedure execution.

The theory about stored procedures in general is that in the entity framework, stored procedures are much less important because the entity framework provider can handle all security-related problems and all query plans can be cached on the server to provide the same performance benefits as stored procedures. We are not necessarily advocating that you should drop all stored procedures in deference to the entity framework today, but be aware: this is definitely where Microsoft is going with the entity framework.

THE DBA PARADIGM SHIFT

If you do not feel the earth moving under your feet, then we have not explained the entity framework properly. The database world is definitely about to shift. In the past your work as a DBA has been primarily confined to the database server. You make sure that things are as secure and as efficient as possible on the server, but your concern really stops there as soon as the bits are out of your servers. With the entity framework, this will change.

In the context of the entity framework, the DBA and database developer roles must expand to include logical architecture as well as physical data storage architecture. The DBA or database developer must take a more active role in defining the mapping layer, controlling the physical execution process from the logical layer to the physical layer, and ensuring that the logical layer is constructed with the greatest degree of abstraction possible.

For some database professionals, this is an exciting prospect. After all, living in that silo that is the database world can lead to feelings of isolation. The entity framework will require the database professional to emerge from that silo and think about data resources in terms of business processes, rather than just data services. Imagine a world where instead of spending your time creating and modifying stored procedures, you are creating entity models and managing the process of how those entities interact with your data. That is the future when the entity framework is a part of your architecture.

For other database professionals, this is a frightening prospect. There are so many unknowns when we are dealing with new technologies. Not only do we have concerns about the database itself, but also about how we expand our skill set from TSQL into .NET and from ERM to EDM. Take comfort in the fact that this is an evolutionary and not a revolutionary process. All of the skills that you have today are still valid. Now it is time to expand them a little and take the next step into the future.

The Bottom Line

Connect and query a SQL Server database using ADO.NET connected and disconnected techniques. Understanding how client developers make connection and query your databases will help you manage database resources better. Knowing the differences between connected and disconnected query strategies and how they affect the database is critical to effective database tuning.

Master It For each class in the following list, determine whether you would use it for connected operations, disconnected operations, or both.

1. SqlConnection

2. SqlDataAdapter

3. DataSet

4. SqlCommand

5. SqlDataReader

Use prominent special features of ADO.NET and the SQL Native Client. As ADO.NET matures, Microsoft continually adds special features to the API. As a database professional, it is critical that you understand what these features are so that you can assess their impacts on your databases.

Master It For each of the statements below, specify True or False based on whether the statement will interleave in a MARS connection.

1. SELECT

2. RECEIVE

3. UPDATE

4. INSERT

5. GRANT

6. BULK INSERT

Understand and implement simple examples using the new Language Integrated Query (LINQ) environment. LINQ is actually a collection of technologies. You can use LINQ to query a variety of different data structures. Your ability as a developer to leverage LINQ will depend on your understanding of the different environments where LINQ can operate.

Master It For each of the following scenarios, specify whether you can use LINQ to address the situation, and if so, which variation of LINQ you would use.

1. A data access layer has passed an array of strings to your application and you must identify the string members that are over 10 characters in length.

2. You are connecting to an Oracle server and want to query the data from your data access layer through ADO.NET directly without returning a DataSet.

3. You are connecting to an Oracle server and want to query the data from your data access layer through ADO.NET directly by returning a DataSet.

4. You have created a web application that allows a client to upload sample Simple Object Access Protocol (SOAP) messages. You want to query the SOAP message to show the user what the parameters of their call will be in that message.

Understand and implement simple examples using the ADO.NET Entity Framework. Although it is new technology, the entity framework promises to change the way that we look at distributed solutions. Understanding the general architecture of the framework will be helpful as you decide where this technology fits into your enterprise solution.

Master It   Answer the following questions relating the entity framework.

1. What two query options are supported by the entity framework?

2. In which architectural layer of the framework does the database server exist?

3. Is the entity framework only usable by SQL Server?

4. What is a composable query?

Chapter 18

SQL Server and the Common Language Runtime

Beginning with SQL Server 2005, Microsoft added integration with the .NET Common Language Runtime (CLR) as one of its features. Including the CLR in SQL Server has provided both a bane and a benefit to the SQL developer and administrator. It provides an incredible source of power and potential to your server applications, but it also comes with costs that include resource consumption and additional security complications. This feature is not intended for every application and not every kind of server application can benefit from this capability. Those that can, however, have a new tool at the ready.

This chapter addresses the concepts behind the CLR and its essential architecture, particularly how it interfaces with SQL Server. We will also look at the specifics of how to create and deploy CLR-based artifacts such as stored procedures and functions using C#.

In this chapter, you will learn to:

◆ Enable and configure the CLR in SQL Server 2008

◆ Create managed objects for the SQL Server CLR

◆ Deploy managed objects into the SQL Server CLR

◆ Manage security for the SQL Server CLR

CLR Concepts

Being a Transact-SQL expert is not enough anymore. Although Transact-SQL continues to work well, you have additional options now. With the integration of the .NET CLR into SQL Server, now you can create all of the artifacts that you know in a whole new way. Stored procedures, views, triggers, and functions are just some of the artifacts that you can now create with any .NET language and deploy into SQL Server. It's a whole new world.

Microsoft's intent with CLR integration is not to make Transact-SQL obsolete. TSQL is still the best choice for many operations on the server that perform data services as their primary operations. If anything, the intent is to eliminate the need for extended stored procedures in SQL Server. CLR objects can do all of the things that extended stored procedures do, such as execute processor-intensive code more efficiently than TSQL and provide a mechanism for interacting with the platform.

OBSOLESCENCE CAN BE A GOOD THING

With the impending deprecation of extended stored procedures in SQL Server, CLR objects are more important than ever. If you rely on custom extended stored procedures for your applications, this might be a good time to start evaluating how they can be rewritten in a .NET language utilizing the CLR. If you need to create new extended stored procedures today, you should consider the CLR as your best option now.

The good news is that creating objects for the CLR is a much easier process than creating extended stored procedures. This provides a greater degree of accessibility for applications that could benefit from the features that these extended procedures could provide but did not have the resources to create.

In Chapter 17, "SQL Server and the .NET Client," we discussed how to write C# code for interacting with SQL Server. What is different about this chapter is that we will be writing .NET code that will run within SQL Server as opposed to in a separate client application or component tier. This is an important distinction, and one that requires more background in the CLR and its integration with SQL Server.

CLR Terminology

First, let's cover some definitions that you will see frequently in this chapter. Once we have the framework of common definitions, we can look at the specifics of how the CLR is implemented.

Common Language Runtime   The Common Language Runtime (CLR) is the operating environment for .NET code. Instead of the operating system directly executing the code, in the .NET world, all code is executed by the CLR. You can think of it as a sandbox in which the .NET code runs, isolated from the operating system and other non-.NET code. This includes numerous components such as the just-in-time (JIT) compiler, security engine, debug engine, and execution engine.

Managed Code   All Microsoft .NET code created in languages like VB.NET or C# is called *managed code*. Microsoft calls it managed code because the CLR manages all resources as opposed to the developer writing code to do it. For example, the CLR manages all memory allocation and garbage collection so the developer does not need to write code to allocate and destroy memory. All SQL Server CLR artifacts are managed objects.

Application Domain   Also called an *app domain*, this is an isolated execution environment within a CLR instance. When managed code loads, it does so within an app domain. It is possible for a single CLR to contain many app domains. The purpose is to isolate managed objects into their own operating space for security and stability reasons, preventing failures in one app domain from adversely affecting the processing in another app domain.

Code Access Security   Often called CAS, this is a managed code security feature that allows an administrator to assign execution policies to code. The intention is to be able to control which code elements have permissions to call other code elements. This can prevent an unauthorized process from calling a sensitive piece of code by controlling the policy for the called code. SQL Server uses CAS to control the level of access that managed objects have in SQL Server and the platform as a whole.

Class   A class, as it relates to SQL Server managed objects, is a structure that defines a set of related managed operations such as functions or stored procedures. Although in the true object-oriented mindset, a class is a type that represents an artifact in your application design, it is easier to think of a class in this sense as simply a collection of managed artifacts that you can call from your SQL Server code.

Assembly   An assembly is the basic unit of packaging and deployment in .NET. You can create multiple classes and deploy them in a single assembly. The TSQL code has a CREATE ASSEMBLY statement that you can use to import the assembly metadata into the SQL Server catalog, making the members available for other SQL Server code. You must package any .NET code that you want to use in SQL Server into an assembly and deploy that assembly to SQL Server before the server can use the code.

Framework Class Library   To provide a basic set of functionality for managed applications, Microsoft ships a library of classes that provide basic application functionality, including things like string management, threading, data access and web development. The class library is very large. You do not have to know the entire library to be able to create objects for SQL Server. You will, however, need to use some of the classes in the library to create meaningful managed objects.

Don't Panic! This is Just an Overview

Some of you may have significant experience in writing .NET code in C#, and for others this may be a brand new experience. Our goal for this chapter is not to force you to wade through a ton of C# code. This is not a C# book. But we do want to at least provide some exposure to how the CLR works in SQL Server 2008 so that we can lift the veil of mystery, if only a little.

For this reason, please be aware that our intention here is not to provide exhaustive coverage of CLR-based objects. Most of you who are database administrators probably will not be writing a lot of that code anyway, and some of these objects can be a little involved to create. We will cover only the most common scenarios—hopefully, at a sufficient level of depth so that the next time you are at a party and topic comes up, you will be able to speak intelligently about SQL Server CLR integration. It will undoubtedly make you the most popular person in the room.

Enabling the CLR

For security reasons, the CLR in SQL Server 2008 installs as a disabled feature. If you want to be able to deploy and use managed objects in SQL Server, you must enable this option. This is an advanced option in SQL Server. The code to perform this operation looks like this.

```
sp_configure 'show advanced options', 1;
GO
RECONFIGURE;
GO
sp_configure 'clr enabled', 1;
GO
RECONFIGURE;
GO
```

The effect of this code is to allow the CLR to activate an app domain, hosted by SQL Server 2008, which provides a container in which the managed code can run. If you disable the CLR integration, it will terminate all executing routines and unload all app domains. You must have appropriate ALTER SETTINGS permissions to enable this option. This permission is implicitly held by the serveradmin and sysadmin roles.

YOU CANNOT ENTIRELY DISABLE THE CLR

Be aware that this option only controls whether the CLR is usable for your custom content. The CLR in SQL Server is always available for internal use. There are SQL Server 2008 features, such as the spatial datatypes, that are implemented in the CLR as managed objects. They are always available regardless of the CLR Enabled setting on the server.

After enabling the CLR, all managed code will automatically have access to a limited set of assemblies in the framework class library. Because many element of the .NET framework, such as windowing operations, are not relevant to SQL Server, they are not implicitly supported. The assemblies that SQL Server implicitly supports are

Microsoft.VisualBasic	System.Deployment
Microsoft.VisualC	System.Security
mscorlib	System.Transactions
System	System.Web.Services
System.Configuration	System.Xml
System.Data	System.Core.dll
System.Data.OracleClient	System.Xml.Linq.dll
System.Data.SqlXml	System.Deployment

Any assemblies that SQL Server does not implicitly support are still available for you to use if you register the necessary assemblies in SQL Server using the CREATE ASSEMBLY statement. There may still be some security limitations, however, as not all code is accessible through CAS in SQL Server.

Creating Managed Objects in SQL Server

Microsoft Visual Studio 2008 is the preferred tool for creating managed objects for SQL Server. This development environment simplifies the process of creating classes and assemblies for SQL Server 2008. Using one tool, you can create the objects and deploy them in SQL Server for testing. In this section, we will look at the process of setting up a Visual Studio project for creating managed objects and then look at how to create the most common managed objects for SQL Server, namely the functions and stored procedures.

Setting Up the Project Environment

The first step is to create a Visual Studio SQL Server project.

1. Begin by starting Visual Studio 2008. From the main menu in Visual Studio, select File ➤ New ➤ Project. This will give you the New Project dialog.

2. Drill into the Visual C# tree and locate the node for Database Projects. You should see a dialog like the one illustrated in Figure 18.1. We filled out this dialog to create a new SQL Server project called AWManagedCode. After filling out the dialog, click the OK button.

FIGURE 18.1
Creating a new SQL Server project

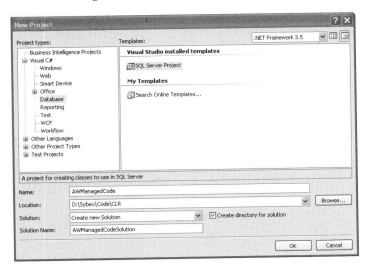

3. After clicking the OK button, you will be presented with the New Database Reference dialog, as pictured in Figure 18.2. (If you already have any data connections defined, you will see a list of connection options and will have to click the Add New Reference button to open the dialog in Figure 18.1.) This dialog allows you to define a connection between the project and a SQL Server instance, and it allows your project to deploy managed

objects to SQL Server directly from Visual Studio for testing purposes, which is very convenient. We are connecting to an instance with an AdventureWorks2008 database, which we will use for our examples.

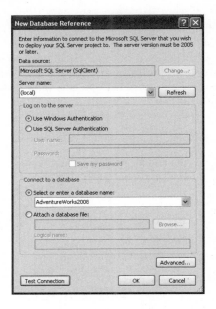

FIGURE 18.2
Configuring
the database
connection

4. After you advance beyond this dialog, you may see a message box asking you if you want to enable SQL Server debugging for this connection. In this example, we will turn this on, as we may want to step through the managed code running in the SQL Server hosted app domain. If you do not turn this on now, you can always enable it later in Visual Studio through the Server Explorer window.

5. You should now have an open project in Visual Studio. The Solution Explorer window in the right portion of the screen ought to look like the illustration in Figure 18.3.

FIGURE 18.3
The Solution
Explorer window

6. In this image, you will see a folder called Test Scripts. This folder will contain the tests that you will use for your managed objects. When you run a test script, Visual Studio performs a deployment of the assembly into the registered SQL Server instance and executes the test script on that server.

7. Right-click any test script in this folder and select a menu option to set that script as the default debug script. Visual Studio will then run that script when you start the project debugger in Visual Studio by clicking the Run button in the toolbar or pressing Alt+F5 on your keyboard.

You can also create additional test scripts if you like. Right-click the Test Scripts folder and select Add New Test Script from the menu. This will add a file to the Test Scripts folder. To debug a test script other than the default, right-click that script in the list and select Debug Script from the menu. Using this approach, you can have a wide array of different test options and can execute any of them whenever you like.

Creating Managed Functions

The simplest managed object that you can create in Visual Studio is a function. Remember that SQL Server functions come in two varieties, scalar and table-valued. Visual Studio supports these same two options.

Scalar functions return a single value. They are the most common types of functions and are very typical in most programming languages. Table-valued functions return a table structure that you can select from and use in place of a table in many situations. We will start by looking at scalar functions and then see how to implement table-valued functions.

MANAGED SCALAR FUNCTIONS

Managed scalar functions are very similar to their TSQL counterparts. They can accept parameters and will return a single scalar value as a result. If you have ever written a function in C# or any other programming language, the process will look very familiar.

1. To begin, you must add a class to the project that will contain your function. To add a class that is preconfigured for a function, go to the Solution Explorer window in Visual Studio. Click on the project in the solution to which you want to add the function, and select Project from the main menu in Visual Studio.

2. At the top of this menu, you will see a list of artifacts that you can add to your SQL Server project. Locate User-Defined Function in the list and select it from the menu.

3. In the Add New Item dialog, you will need to provide a name for the function. Our sample function will be a simple mathematical function that will calculate the cube of an integer by raising it to the power of 3 and returning the result. Set the name as **CubeValue.cs** and click the Add button.

4. You should see the following code in the body of the listing.

```
public partial class UserDefinedFunctions
{
    [Microsoft.SqlServer.Server.SqlFunction]
    public static SqlString CubeValue()
    {
        // Put your code here
        return new SqlString("Hello");
    }
};
```

This code defines a class called UserDefinedFunctions. Visual Studio 2008 supports a concept called *partial classes*. This means that a single class can be distributed across multiple files in a Visual Studio project. As long as all the files are present when the project compiles, Visual Studio will assemble the files into a single class. This is helpful because you can define each function in its own file, but the compiler can still aggregate them into a single class, which makes deployment easier.

You will also notice an attribute tag on top of the function that marks this as a SqlFunction. This attribute is actually a class in the framework class library. It provides instructions to the compiler to tell it to compile it as a SqlFunction as opposed to a regular managed function. Only SqlFunction objects are callable as functions inside SQL Server from TSQL code.

You will need to rewrite this code a bit to suit your purpose. Notice that the function currently accepts no parameter and returns a SqlString as its return value. This is not what we want. We can do much better than a simple "hello world" function, right? You can use any SQL Server datatypes in your function except the following:

varchar	image
char	timestamp
roversion	table
text	cursor
ntext	

WHY NO char OR varchar?

At first glance it seems ridiculous that you can't use char or varchar types in your functions, but there is a reason. Managed code uses Unicode strings and the char and varchar datatypes are not Unicode. The SqlString class in the System.Data.SqlTypes .NET namespace represents a variable-length collection of Unicode characters, essentially equivalent to an nvarchar datatype in SQL Server. You may want to look at the type list in the Visual Studio 2008 documentation for the classes in the System.Data.SqlTypes namespace to get more familiar with your typing options.

After rewriting our procedure to accept an integer as its parameter and returning an integer as a return value, the code would look like this. Note that we have also modified the logic of the function to provide the desired implementation.

```
public partial class UserDefinedFunctions
{
    [Microsoft.SqlServer.Server.SqlFunction]
    public static SqlInt32 CubeValue(SqlInt32 value)
    {
        return (SqlInt32)Math.Pow((Int32)value, 3);
    }
};
```

This function now accepts a SqlInt32 as a parameter and returns the same type. Because the SqlInt32 type is different in structure from the .NET datatype for Int32, we had to do some datatype conversion. For example, the syntax `(Int32)value` converts the parameter named `value` from a SqlInt32 type to a standard .NET Int32 type.

You will also see that we used a framework library class called Math in this example. This class has a method called Pow that you can use to raise a base value to an exponent. One of the advantages of using managed code is that you have almost the complete framework library at your disposal, which allows you to develop more complex routines than you can in TSQL.

To test this function, you will need to add a test statement to the test script. You can either use the one that Visual Studio created for you or create your own.

1. On the desired test script, add the following statement:

```
SELECT dbo.CubeValue(10) as CubeResult;
```

2. Assuming that there are no other test statements in your test script, executing this script should open an Output window in Visual Studio that looks something like the one pictured in Figure 18.4.

FIGURE 18.4
The Test
Output window

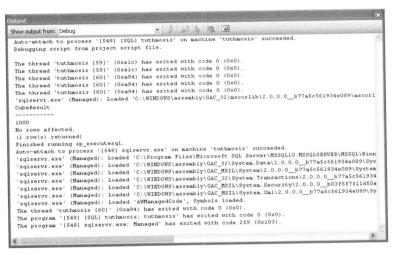

When you debug the test script, it will compile the project and deploy the managed assembly to the referenced server. Notice the results of the function are provided in the middle of the output surrounded by diagnostic and status information.

3. Open SQL Server Management Studio and connect the Object Browser to the instance of SQL Server referenced by the project. You should be able to see the managed assembly in the list for the target database, as illustrated in Figure 18.5. You should also be able to execute the previous test statement in a new Query window connected to the database.

FIGURE 18.5
Viewing
the deployed
assemblies

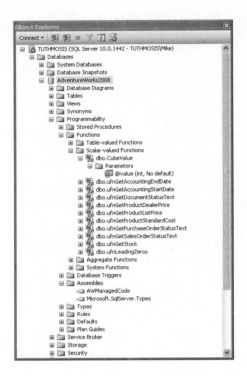

Now the managed assembly is fully deployed. Although you will not use Visual Studio to perform production deployments, this capability is very convenient when developing and testing managed objects.

IT LOOKS THE SAME TO ME

The nice thing about the managed objects is that once you have registered the assembly and added the object metadata to your database, you can call them in your TSQL code just like any other TSQL object. This makes it entirely transparent to a TSQL developer or client developer. They do not need to know if the target object is a native TSQL object or a managed object. The call is the same.

MANAGED TABLE-VALUED FUNCTIONS

Unlike a scalar function, a table-valued function (TVF) requires two methods per function. This is because each function must have multiple methods, each of which marks a separate activity or step in the process of returning the table data to the caller. Each TVF requires at least the following:

An Init Method The entry point into the TVF, which returns the .NET type IEnumerable. This method can accept parameters to be passed to the TVF. Decorate this method with the SqlFunction attribute.

A FillRow Method   This method executes once for each row to be populated into the results using output parameters to populate the output table.

To get a feel for the structure of a TVF, look at the code in Listing 18.1. This example shows a function that selects data from the Person.Person table in the AdventureWorks2008 database based on a range of BusinessEntityID values.

LISTING 18.1   A Managed Table-Valued Function

```
using System;
using System.Data;
using System.Data.SqlClient;
using System.Data.SqlTypes;
using Microsoft.SqlServer.Server;
using System.Collections;
public partial class UserDefinedFunctions
{
    [SqlFunction(Name = "PersonTable",
    FillRowMethodName = "FillRow", TableDefinition = "FirstName nvarchar(100),
LastName nvarchar(100)",
    DataAccess = DataAccessKind.Read)]
    public static IEnumerable InitPersonTable(SqlInt32 StartID, SqlInt32 EndID)
    {
        using (SqlConnection cn = new SqlConnection("context connection=true"))
        {
            SqlCommand cmd = new SqlCommand

("SELECT Firstname, LastName FROM Person.Person WHERE BusinessEntityID BETWEEN @
start and @end");
            cmd.Parameters.AddWithValue("@start",StartID);
            cmd.Parameters.AddWithValue("@end", EndID);
            cmd.Connection = cn;
            DataSet ds = new DataSet();
            SqlDataAdapter ad = new SqlDataAdapter(cmd);
            ad.Fill(ds);
            return ds.Tables[0].Rows;
        }
    }
    public static void FillRow(object row, out SqlString FirstName, out SqlString
LastName)
    {
        DataRow currentRow = (DataRow)row;
        FirstName = currentRow["FirstName"].ToString();
        LastName = currentRow["Lastname"].ToString();
    }
}
```

There are a number of points that you should observe in this code. First, note that the InitPersonTable() method is decorated with the SQLFunction attribute and includes the name of the function. When you deploy this function in SQL Server, you will use the configured function name. There is also an attribute that identified the FillRow method for this function. You can name these methods anything you like as long as they are decorated correctly with attributes.

There is also a DataAccess attribute on the Init method. This attribute allows you to execute ADO.NET in the Init method as needed using a context connection.

Notice the line of code that creates the connection object. The connection string simply states that it should use the context connection, which is a connection to the database in which the function is deployed and executing. Without this attribute, you would not be able to use the context connection.

The Init method returns an enumerable object, which in this case is the rows collection of the data table. For each element in the collection, the function calls the specified FillRow method. This method evaluates the data row, extracts the data to be loaded into the returned table object and loads that data into output parameters. To test this function, add a statement like this to the test script and debug as before.

```
SELECT * FROM dbo.PersonTable(1,100) as PersonList;
```

The parameters passed into the function are then passed into the SQL code in the body of the function, which provides the boundaries for the execution. Once again, you can also execute this function from the SQL Server Management Studio if you like.

Creating Managed Stored Procedures

Stored procedures are extremely common and most SQL Server applications have a significant number of stored procedures that do the real work of the application. Not all stored procedures can benefit from executing in the CLR. Most stored procedures that do simple data access are better off to remain as TSQL operations. But for those cases where a stored procedure does significant processor-intensive operations, must interact with the platform outside of SQL Server, or contains logic that is too cumbersome to write in TSQL code, a managed procedure may do the trick.

Stored procedures are implemented as a single method in the class. Adding a new stored procedure object through Visual Studio will add a new file in a partial class called StoredProcedures. The stored procedure can accept parameters as needed, including output parameters. You can also use stored procedures to send tabular data back to the client. The techniques are a little different from one another, so we will look at each individually.

Using Output Parameters

Conceptually, this is just the same as a parameter marked as OUTPUT in a TSQL stored procedure. A parameter to a C# method that is marked with the out keyword must be initialized in the procedure before the procedure returns. The calling procedure then captures the data in the arguments that is passes to the procedure.

Suppose that you wanted to get a count of persons from the Person.Person table that were between a specific beginning and end value for BusinessEntityID. You could use an output parameter to provide that information to the caller. Listing 18.2 illustrates the use of output parameters as described.

LISTING 18.2   Output Parameters in a Managed Stored Procedure

```
using System;
using System.Data;
using System.Data.SqlClient;
using System.Data.SqlTypes;
using Microsoft.SqlServer.Server;

public partial class StoredProcedures
{
    [Microsoft.SqlServer.Server.SqlProcedure]
    public static void GetPersonCount(SqlInt32 StartID, SqlInt32 EndID, out SqlInt32
PersonCount)
    {
        using (SqlConnection cn = new SqlConnection("context connection=true"))
        {
            SqlCommand cmd = new SqlCommand

("SELECT Count(*) as PersonCount FROM Person.Person WHERE BusinessEntityID BETWEEN
@start and @end");
            cmd.Parameters.AddWithValue("@start", StartID);
            cmd.Parameters.AddWithValue("@end", EndID);
            cmd.Connection = cn;
            cn.Open();
            PersonCount = (int)cmd.ExecuteScalar();
            cn.Close();
        }
    }
};
```

Notice that the method marks the `PersonCount` parameter as out, while the body of the stored procedure assigns a value to this parameter based on the count from the underlying table. You will also notice that it is not necessary to use the DataAccess attribute in the stored procedure as we had to do in a function. This is because it is much more common that a stored procedure will interact with stored data than a function will, so this feature is assumed with stored procedures whereas it is not assumed with functions.

This procedure is called the same way as any other stored procedure call that contains output parameters. To test your code, include the following in your test script and begin the debugger.

```
DECLARE @vCount    int;
EXEC dbo.GetPersonCount 100, 250, @vCount OUTPUT;
SELECT @vCount;
```

In your Output window, you should see the scalar value reported. Again, you can also execute this code from SQL Server Management Studio in exactly the same way.

ACCESSING TABULAR DATA

Many stored procedures return result sets, so this is a common feature that you will need to support in your managed stored procedures. If you know how to write ADO.NET code, then the job is simple. You need only create a command object that represents the code that you want to send back to the client. You can easily send this data using a pipe object that is accessible through the implicit context object. Look at Listing 18.3 for an example.

LISTING 18.3   Returning Tablular Data from a Managed Stored Procedure

```
using System;
using System.Data;
using System.Data.SqlClient;
using System.Data.SqlTypes;
using Microsoft.SqlServer.Server;
public partial class StoredProcedures
{
    [Microsoft.SqlServer.Server.SqlProcedure]
    public static void GetPersonList(SqlInt32 StartID, SqlInt32 EndID)
    {
        using (SqlConnection cn = new SqlConnection("context connection=true"))
        {
            SqlCommand cmd = new SqlCommand

("SELECT FirstName, LastName FROM Person.Person WHERE BusinessEntityID BETWEEN @
start and @end");
            cmd.Parameters.AddWithValue("@start", StartID);
            cmd.Parameters.AddWithValue("@end", EndID);
            cmd.Connection = cn;
            cn.Open();
            SqlContext.Pipe.ExecuteAndSend(cmd);
            cn.Close();
        }
    }
};
```

You will note that even though the stored procedure returns a result set, the method that defined the procedure still returns void. The return data is sent back to the client through the pipe exposed by the SqlContext object. The ExecuteAndSend() method is very convenient. Although the pipe has a Send() method that can pass a data reader or a string message back to the client, the ExecuteAndSend() method eliminates the need to cache the data reader in a variable and send it through the pipe. In this case, the pipe object takes care of executing the command and piping the results directly back to the caller.

Executing this procedure, again, is just like any other procedural object. This code in your test script should do the trick.

```
EXEC dbo.GetPersonList 100, 250;
```

There's nothing to it, right? Once you have created the managed object in Visual Studio and deployed it to the SQL Server, you can use it in SQL Server just as you would any other object.

Create Managed Datatypes

This feature is one of our favorites. When you create managed datatypes for SQL Server, you are not really creating a new type, nor are you duplicating the concept of the user-defined type (UDT) in SQL Server, which is nothing more than a subtype. Using Visual Studio, you have the ability to create compound types for more complex data interactions.

For example, suppose that you wanted to store information about locations on a geometric point system. If you were working with plane coordinates, you would have both an X-value and a Y-value to identify the point. Using SQL Server types, your database would have to have a column for the X-value and another column for the Y-value. Additionally, the client would have to pass these values to an INSERT statement as two separate values. It would be nice if we could have a single type called Point that could store this ordered pair as a complex value. This is exactly what the managed type offers.

> **MANAGED TYPES IN ACTION**
>
> SQL Server 2008 includes support for a new feature called *spatial data*. This feature allows you to store information about geometric or geographic objects in the database. Because these artifacts are complex, often requiring more than a single data point, SQL Server uses .NET managed types for these data elements. Chapter 19, "Using Spatial Data," discusses these types in more detail.

To begin, you need to add a new item to your Visual Studio project. This item will be a user-defined type. The filename will be Point.cs, and this will create a struct called point, which implements the INullable interface. The entire struct is needed to provide support for the type. You will notice that a number of methods have been provided for you already. We will look at the completed code for this type and walk through these methods one at a time. The code is provided in Listing 18.4.

LISTING 18.4   Creating a Managed Type

```
using System;
using System.Data;
using System.Data.SqlClient;
using System.Data.SqlTypes;
using Microsoft.SqlServer.Server;
[Serializable]
[Microsoft.SqlServer.Server.SqlUserDefinedType(Format.Native)]
public struct Point : INullable
{
    private  int _x;
    private  int _y;
    private bool m_Null;
    public override string ToString()
    {
```

```csharp
            return X.ToString() + "," + Y.ToString();
        }
        public bool IsNull
        {
            get
            {
                return m_Null;
            }
        }
        public static Point Null
        {
            get
            {
                Point h = new Point();
                h.m_Null = true;
                return h;
            }
        }
        public static Point Parse(SqlString s)
        {
            if (s.IsNull)
                return Null;
            Point p = new Point();
            string sVal = (string)s;
            string[] pair = sVal.Split(new char[] { ',' });
            p.X = int.Parse(pair[0]);
            p.Y = int.Parse(pair[1]);
            return p;
        }
        public int X
        {
            get {return _x;}
            set {_x = value;}
        }
        public int Y
        {
            get { return _y; }
            set { _y = value; }
        }
    }
```

WHAT IS A STRUCT?

Unless you are a hard-core .NET programmer, you really don't need to know the difference between a class and a struct. For right now, just consider the struct as a lightweight class. It can do almost everything a class can do, but its memory mapping in .NET is a little different than you get with a class. Don't worry about the details. Let your .NET programmers sweat the details.

The first thing we did in this code sample was define the variables. You will need storage for all of the data that the type can manage. In this case, there is a variable for both the X- and Y-value and a variable to store a flag for null if the user attempts to assign a value of null to the datatype. Notice that the variables are private.

At the bottom of the code you will see properties for X and Y. These properties read and write the values of the private variables. All access to the variables will go through these properties. You could also add additional methods to the type if you like, such as a calculation based on the compound data. These methods are callable through the SQL Server variables.

The ToString() method indicates what you will return when the complex type is selected. In this case, we take the two integers and concatenate them with a comma, creating the ordered pair from the individually stored data.

The Parse() method goes the other way around. When an ordered pair is assigned to the datatype as a string, the Parse() method breaks the pair into pieces and assigns the appropriate values to the properties. The remaining methods do null handling and null testing, reading and assigning null values as necessary. To test this code, add the following snippet to the test script. Notice that you assign the value as a string and access the public properties using standard "dot" notation.

```
DECLARE @vPoint Point;
SET @vPoint = '1,4';
SELECT
  @vPoint.X as X,
  @vPoint.Y as Y;
```

If you followed through all of the examples so far, your project, which will become your assembly, should have two classes with two objects each plus the struct for the Point type. We have been deploying these through Visual Studio, but you may not always have that option. To give you more choices, we'll make deployment our next topic.

Deploying Managed Objects in SQL Server

In this section, we will look at the complete deployment process including registering the assemblies and adding the managed objects to the database. Deploying the managed objects in SQL Server is a two-step process. You must first register the assembly with SQL Server and then add the functions and stored procedures from the assembly. Conceptually, it is very much like adding references to extended stored procedures. After deploying the DLL file to the server, you must add the metadata to SQL Server that references the functions in the DLL.

Creating Assemblies

Before you can use the managed objects in the assemblies that you just created, you must first register those assemblies in SQL Server. When you register an assembly in SQL Server, it copies the content of the assembly to the system catalog, making it available to any caller from any location, whether that assembly is registered on their computer or not. This also removes the dependency to a physical file, so after you have registered the assembly on the server, you do not need to retain the physical file or maintain a connection to the computer from which the physical file deployed.

There are two ways to register the assembly, either with the SQL Server Management Studio or through TSQL code. Each approach has its advantages. We will look at both methods.

CLEAN UP BEFORE YOU CONTINUE

If you are following along with these examples, you will need to remove the assembly and objects from the AdventureWorks2008 database before you will be able to continue with these examples. Running the test scripts in Visual Studio performed a temporary deployment, so you are going to have to remove those objects. For right now, just drop the objects. You can use this script if you like.

```
USE AdventureWorks2008;
DROP PROC dbo.GetPersonCount;
DROP PROC dbo.GetPersonList;
DROP FUNCTION dbo.CubeValue;
DROP FUNCTION dbo.PersonTable;
DROP TYPE dbo.Point;
DROP ASSEMBLY AWManagedCode;
GO
```

CREATING AN ASSEMBLY WITH TSQL

As you have previously learned, an *assembly* is a unit of deployment in .NET. All .NET code is contained in an assembly. SQL Server projects, when compiled in Visual Studio, will compile into a DLL file. Registering an assembly in SQL Server is nothing more than copying the contents of that DLL file into the system catalog.

.NET assemblies are very strongly versioned, and SQL Server will enforce a requirement that you cannot register the same assembly version in the database more than once. An assembly version is designated by four characteristics that the assembly programmer will control when he or she writes the code. You, as a consumer of the assembly, will not have any direct control over these characteristics, which are

◆ Assembly name

◆ Version number

◆ Culture setting

◆ Public key token

You will need to interact with the component developers to ensure they have followed a proper versioning standard and that the assembly in question has not been previously registered in the target database. Because the registration process copies the file content into the system catalog, it is not necessary for the assembly to be formally deployed on the target platform.

The assembly from the previous exercises is ready for deployment.

1. To locate the assembly file, go back to the location in the file system where you created the Visual Studio project files. If you did not change any of the project settings, there should be a *bin\debug* path in that location where the assembly now resides. Make a note of this path or copy it to another more convenient location.

2. Register the assembly, using this code and replacing the assembly path in the example with the location of your assembly.

```
USE AdventureWorks2008;
CREATE ASSEMBLY AWManagedCode
FROM 'D:\AWManagedCode\bin\Debug\AWManagedCode.dll';
GO
```

At this point, you are free to add the stored procedures, functions, and any other managed objects that you may have created to SQL Server using the techniques that we will show you later in this chapter. Note that the previous pathname can also be replaced with a Universal Naming Convention (UNC) name, so the assembly file does not have to be local. It can be on any visible network resource as well.

CREATING AN ASSEMBLY WITH SQL SERVER MANAGEMENT STUDIO

You can also drop and create the assembly with the Management Studio interface if you like. This is a very convenient option if there is no need for a script that you might have to maintain for process or versioning reasons.

1. To begin, connect the Object Explorer to the target server and drill into the database, to the Programmability node. In this node you will see an Assemblies node. This node contains all registered assemblies. If you can't find this, look back to Figure 18.5 for an illustration.

2. If you have previously registered an assembly through TSQL, you may not see it in this list until you refresh the node. Right-click in the Assemblies node and select Refresh from the menu. If the assembly is registered, you should see it now.

3. To drop the assembly, right-click the assembly in the list and select Delete from the menu. This will open a dialog like the one pictured in Figure 18.6.

FIGURE 18.6
Dropping
an assembly

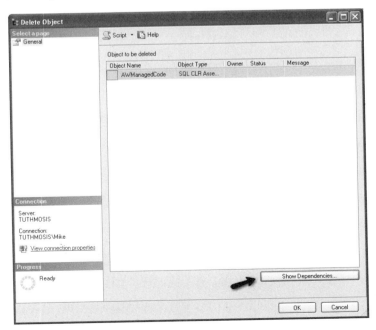

In this image, notice the button labeled Show Dependencies. This is an important consideration. Every managed object is schema bound, which means that it is tied to the assembly. You cannot drop the assembly until you drop all the managed objects created from the assembly in the database. In our example, we had not yet added any managed objects from the assembly. This is why our previous script that dropped the assembly did a drop on all functions and procedures first before dropping the assembly itself.

4. To add the assembly again, right-click the Assemblies node in the Object Explorer and select New Assembly from the menu. This will present a dialog like the one illustrated in Figure 18.7.

5. Complete the dialog as illustrated, substituting the path with the location of your assembly. You should use the path of wherever your assembly file is currently located.

FIGURE 18.7
Registering
an assembly

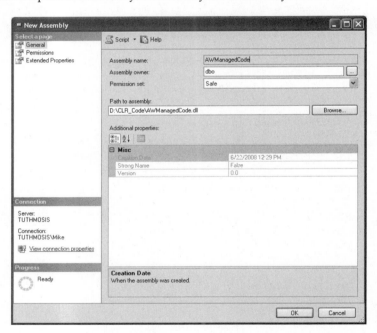

Notice in the dialog that in the dimmed properties section at the bottom, there is a property for the version number. It is currently set to 0. If we had explicitly versioned our assembly before we compiled it, this property would show the version number.

There is also a property called Strong Name. This property refers to status of the strong name key for the assembly. To prevent tampering and to provide stronger versioning, a developer can compile a string name key into the assembly. If this is present, the public key token of that strong name key is part of the version data of the assembly. The assembly in this exercise is not strong named, so no token is present.

6. Click the OK button to commit this action and add the assembly to the database.

You are now ready to add the managed objects within the assembly to the database catalog.

Creating Managed Objects

Before you can call a managed object with TSQL code or from a client application, there must be something in the database catalog to call. Simply registering an assembly with the database doesn't provide the catalog data necessary to call the objects stored in the assembly. We still have to create the catalog data for each element.

The process is simple. We will use the appropriate data definition language statement to generate the object in the catalog. These statements have an option to point the catalog object to an external source instead of providing the code in TSQL. As an example, to add the CubeValue function to the catalog, you would use code like this.

```
USE AdventureWorks2008;
CREATE FUNCTION dbo.CubeValue
(
   @value int
)
RETURNS int
AS
EXTERNAL NAME [AWManagedCode].[UserDefinedFunctions].CubeValue;
GO
SELECT dbo.CubeValue(100);
GO
```

This statement has all of the characteristics of a standard CREATE FUNCTION statement except that the reference to the assembly replaces the code of the function. The result is that whenever a user calls the function in SQL Server, as in the last statement in the snippet, it makes a call to the managed object instead of executing TSQL code.

Notice that the external name of the function is broken into three parts. The first is the name of the assembly, followed by the fully qualified class name that contains the functions, including any namespaces, and finally the name of the function itself.

The TVF is a little different, because the external name is the name of the Init method that represents the entry point to the function. Remember that every TVF requires both an Init method and a FillRow method. Although no specific name is required for these methods, you must know the name of the Init method because this will be required for creating the function in the catalog. Here is an example.

```
USE AdventureWorks2008;
CREATE FUNCTION dbo.PersonTable
(
   @startID      int,
   @endID        int
)
RETURNS table
(
   FirstName nvarchar(100),
   LastName nvarchar(100)
)
AS
EXTERNAL NAME [AWManagedCode].[UserDefinedFunctions].InitPersonTable;
```

```
GO
SELECT *
FROM dbo.PersonTable(100,200);
GO
```

Stored procedures follow the same basic pattern. You will use a standard data definition statement, replacing the TSQL code of the procedure with the external name of the procedure. This script adds and tests the two remaining procedural objects from the assembly to the database catalog.

```
USE AdventureWorks2008;
GO
CREATE PROCEDURE dbo.GetPersonCount
(
  @startID int,
  @endID   int,
  @count   int OUTPUT
)
AS
EXTERNAL NAME [AWManagedCode].[StoredProcedures].GetPersonCount;
GO
CREATE PROCEDURE dbo.GetPersonList
(
  @startID     int,
  @endID       int
)
AS
EXTERNAL NAME [AWManagedCode].[StoredProcedures].GetPersonList;
GO
DECLARE @vCount int;
EXEC dbo.GetPersonCount 100,200,@vCount OUTPUT;
SELECT @vCount;
EXEC dbo.GetPersonList 100,200;
```

The user-defined types also follow the same pattern. This simple statement created the type in the target database.

```
CREATE TYPE POINT
EXTERNAL NAME [AWManagedCode].[Point];
```

You Can Be Selective

As you can see from these examples, just because a registered assembly contains a managed object definition, it does not mean that the managed object is callable in your database. You can be selective. There may be times when all of the managed objects that ship with an assembly are not necessarily appropriate for your application, either from functionality or a security perspective. You only need to add the ones you need. Only someone with the authority to execute the data definition statement in the production database can create these managed objects in the catalog. As an administrator, if you control this permission, you will be able to control the managed objects in your database.

Real World Scenario

A TIME AND PLACE FOR EVERYTHING

The need for managed objects in a database is specialized. Not every application or organization will use this feature, but for those that need it, it can be a life saver. This story about a scenario where managed objects fit well into the overall architecture is from the case files of Michael Lee.

Creating effective application architecture is always full of trade-offs, but following general guidelines and best practices will often make the difference in the long-term health of an application. One of the architectural practices that you should try to be diligent in following is to divide application functionality into appropriate tiers. Using a general Model-View-Controller pattern as a guide—separating application functionality into data tiers, data access layers, business layers, and so forth—can significantly aid in maintenance by decoupling application components.

In one situation, a consulting client had designed an architecture that did some order-processing by pulling orders that had been placed into a database and returning that data to a middle tier through a stored procedure. The process worked quite well until there was a change in the business that caused a modification to the way that the data was presented to the application. In the new model, there was a need to pull data from flat files as well as database tables to properly resolve the orders. The critical issue, however, was that the business tier could not be modified. Everything had to be done through a call to the same stored procedure, or at least a procedure with exactly the same name and parameter list.

We evaluated a variety of approaches. The flat file data could be added to SQL Server tables through bulk inserts and then the stored procedure could be modified to use that data. We could have used a link to the data file and accessed the data in the stored procedure in that manner. For a variety of business reasons, the client rejected these options, leaving us with a quandary regarding how we could access file system resources as part of a data service.

The answer was a managed stored procedure. We created a procedure in .NET that had the same parameter list as the original procedure. This managed code had the resources available to search for, open, and process the files necessary. The data was then correlated as needed to the data resident in SQL Server tables and a result set, which was equivalent in format as that previously returned by the stored procedure, was piped back to the business layer as before.

Because the name of the procedure did not change, and neither did the parameter list or result set format, we were able to substitute the managed procedure directly in place of the TSQL procedure with no changes to the middle tier. We were also able to maintain the separation of business and data logic by not requiring a change to the business layer for processing of the flat file data, which is a data tier responsibility. While there are certainly other approaches that we could have used in this scenario, this one allowed us to achieve our business objectives without compromising our overall architecture.

Managing CLR Security

There are two levels of security for managed objects. As an administrator, you have control over both user security and code access security.

User Security   User security refers to the standard security setup in SQL Server that allows you to control who can access and execute the managed objects that you add to the catalog. With just a few exceptions, this security process is essentially identical to the user security that was discussed in Chapter 8, "Managing User Security."

Code Access Security   Code access security (CAS) relates to the permissions that assemblies have to access each other. For example, you may not want to enable a CLR assembly to have full unrestricted access to SQL Server and platform resources. Even with the best security design, a hacker could potentially exploit this weakness. Following the principle of least permissions, you should never authorize a user to do any more than is needed, and the same should go for the code. It makes no sense to allow an assembly to access platform resources that it does not need to do its work.

Managed Objects and User Security

User security relates to what users can do with the artifacts. There are user security permissions for both the assemblies themselves and the managed objects contained in the assemblies. Once you create an assembly, you can assign user permissions to that assembly as illustrated in Figure 18.8. This allows selected users or roles to interact with the assemblies in specific ways, including taking ownership of the assembly, which gives that user all rights over the assembly.

FIGURE 18.8
Assembly
permissions

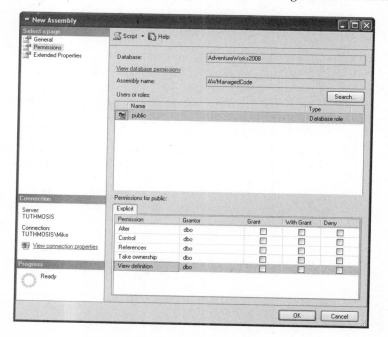

This figure shows permission assignments in the visual interface, but you can also use standard GRANT, REVOKE, and DENY statements to control all permissions programmatically as well as in this statement.

```
USE AdventureWorks2008;
GRANT CONTROL
ON ASSEMBLY::AWManagedCode
TO public;
GO
```

Because the managed objects in the assemblies utilize standard data definiton code, they support the same user security described in Chapter 8. This includes the EXECUTE AS clause that allows the object to execute under the permission structure of any impersonated account or the account of the owner of the object. Please refer back to that chapter if you have any questions about this process.

Assemblies and Code Access Security

If the managed object model has a weakness, it is that these objects can be too powerful if they are not properly controlled and secured. This is not a new issue. Extended stored procedures also suffered from the same problem, and if you have been around SQL Server for very long, you certainly have had experience in locking down extended stored procedures, specifically xp_cmdshell.

Instead of an "all-or-nothing" model where the assembly is either enabled or disabled, the CLR integration model allows the assembly to run under three different security modes called permission sets. These permission sets state what level of access the assemblies will have to SQL Server and to the platform as a whole. While most assemblies will need very limited access to resources, occasionally there may be some requirements for more unrestricted access. The available permission sets are SAFE, EXTERNAL_ACCESS, and UNSAFE.

SAFE   This is the default permission set. When you do not specify any permission set as you create an assembly, it will assume this mode. In safe mode, the managed code is only allowed to do internal computations and data access to the local database resource. Most managed objects do not need access beyond safe mode; therefore, you should not modify the permission set unless the code requires additional resource access.

EXTERNAL_ACCESS   This mode allows access to local resources plus other external resources such as the file system, network resources, registry settings, environmental variables, and the event log. Because these resources could potentially be misused to compromise security and integrity, you must ensure that you tightly control permissions to these managed objects. Only an administrator can create an assembly with the permission set at the level of external access and above, and this permission cannot be granted to nonadministrator users.

UNSAFE   This is the most lenient permission set, and it extends the permissions the full trust level. There are no restrictions on what these assemblies can do, including interacting with services and managing environment options. You should use this permission set with extreme caution, and only when absolutely necessary. This level of access is rarely required and usually indicative of a design inconsistency.

Table 18.1 presents a summary of permission set features.

TABLE 18.1   Permission Set Summary

	SAFE	**EXTERNAL _ ACCESS**	**UNSAFE**
Code Access Security Permissions	Execute Only	Execute + External Access	External Access + Native Code
Programming Model Restrictions	Yes	Yes	None
Local Data Access	Yes	Yes	Yes
Ability to call Native (nonmanaged) code	No	No	Yes

You can set the permission set for your assembly either as you create the assembly in the database or afterward by altering the assembly. You can do this with either the Management Studio or using the TSQL code. As you can see in Figure 18.7, there is a dropdown list for "Permission set." If you use the visual interface, you can set the permission set of the assembly using this dropdown list.

CONFIGURING THE DATABASE FOR EXTERNAL ACCESS

If you tried to set your assembly for external access or unrestricted (unsafe) in the dialog, you probably received an error. This is because you must ensure that some preconditions are met before you will be able to make the permission set more liberal. This is a security measure to ensure adequate protection for all resources. One of two different conditions must exist before you can take this action.

The first option is to mark the database as trustworthy. To do this, you must be an administrative user. Also, if you take this route, you must also be a dbo user when altering or creating the assembly. Consequently, the first condition is that you must be logged into the database as a valid dbo user.

To mark the database as trustworthy, which means that the instance of SQL Server fully trusts the database and all of the objects inside the database, you will use the Trustworthy database property. To view the current setting for the Trustworthy property, use the Database Properties window as illustrated in Figure 18.9. Notice that the option is disabled by default. You cannot modify the property from here.

To enable this option, use the following code.

```
ALTER DATABASE AdventureWorks2008
SET TRUSTWORTHY ON;
```

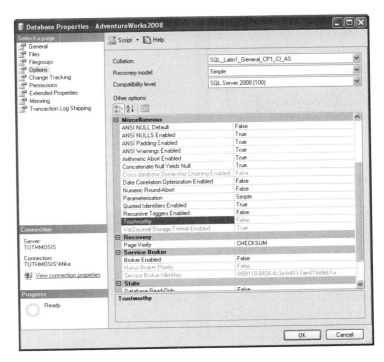

FIGURE 18.9
Database
properties

The other option, which is preferable, is to sign the assembly with an asymmetric key and give the key the appropriate level of permission. The key will ensure that the assembly is intact and has not been altered since it was registered, thus guaranteeing the integrity of the underlying codebase. This is a much more secure option than marking the database as trustworthy. The process requires the following steps.

1. Sign the assembly with a strong name key.

2. Generate an asymmetric key in SQL Server based on the contents of the assembly.

3. Create a login in SQL Server that maps to the asymmetric key.

4. Grant the new login external access or unsafe permissions as needed.

5. Register the new assembly with the permission set that matches the permission set granted to the login.

LOCK IT DOWN

Even though it is very easy to mark the database as trustworthy and be done with it, we strongly recommend that you use a key-based approach. This approach to enabling increased access is significantly more secure. Because the code is signed and more tamper resistant, it also gives you an increased level of granularity. If you mark the database as trustworthy, any assembly in the database can be reset to a higher permission set. The key-based approach allows you to control the specific exposure at the assembly level.

The first step is to sign the original assembly. To do this, you will have to go back to Visual Studio. If your developers already have a key generated that they are using to sign their artifacts, you can use that one. Otherwise, you will need to generate a key. Visual Studio allows you to generate a key within the UI.

1. In the Visual Studio Solution Explorer, right-click on the project and select Properties from the menu.

2. From the tabs on the left of the dialog, select Signing. You should see a dialog like the one in Figure 18.10.

FIGURE 18.10
Signing the assembly

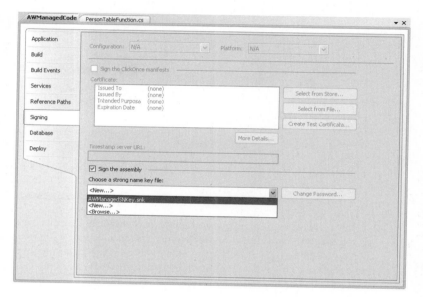

In this dialog, you can choose from a list of already registered key files, or you can browse for or create a new one. If you create a keyfile, you have the option of providing a password, which is recommended. This will help you secure the keyfile, which will represent your signature.

3. After setting the keyfile in this screen, save your project and build it. You must build it before the assembly will be strong named. To build the assembly, click Build ➤ Build Solution from the menu.

4. The next step is to generate the asymmetric key. This process uses the strong name key used to sign the assembly and generates from that a key that it will store in the database. The asymmetric key must be created in the `master` database so that the server login can map to the key. You will then create the login and add the necessary permissions. Step 4 is implemented in the following code.

```
USE master;

CREATE ASYMMETRIC KEY AWManagedKey FROM EXECUTABLE FILE = 'D:\CLR_Code\
AWManagedCode.dll';
CREATE LOGIN AWManagedLogin FROM ASYMMETRIC KEY AWManagedKey;
GRANT EXTERNAL ACCESS ASSEMBLY TO AWManagedLogin;
GO
```

Be sure that the path refers to the assembly that you just signed and not a location to which you copied the assembly at a previous step. Also, make sure that you set the appropriate permission to the login that represents your desired access level. They must match in order for this process to work.

5. The final step is to register the assembly in the database. If you registered this assembly before it was signed, you must drop the assembly and reregister it. This is because the signing of the assembly modifies the assembly metadata, and if you do not add the signed version to the assembly, the key data will not match. If the registered assembly has already been signed, then you can simple alter the permission set.

If using the visual interface to register the assembly, use the Permission Set dropdown list to select the desired level of permissions. If you are using the TSQL code to create the assembly, the code will look like this.

```
USE AdventureWorks2008;
CREATE ASSEMBLY AWManagedCode
FROM 'D:\CLR_Code\AWManagedCode.dll'
WITH PERMISSION_SET = EXTERNAL_ACCESS;
GO
```

Security Considerations

Most of the resistance that the CLR integration in SQL Server encounters relates to security. It is true that the CLR integration creates the opportunity for very powerful and potentially destructive artifacts, but if you manage your environment appropriately, you can mitigate this exposure significantly.

The most important principle to follow is that of least privilege. We mentioned this earlier in this chapter, but it is very important to understand that the majority of the security exposures that cause problems are those when permissions and authority are granted without a requisite need. If you follow the principle of least privilege, you will be able to control much of your exposure.

It is also very important that if you are going to elevate the permission set of an assembly beyond safe level, you should plan very carefully. Remember that when you give an assembly a permission set, it is granted to the entire assembly. If a particular functionality in a managed object will require a higher permission level, those features should be separated from those that do not need this level and packaged in their own assemblies. If you plan for security early, it will be easier to manage later.

The most important advice that we can give is that you should not be afraid of this feature. The power that the CLR provides to your server can be significant, and when this power is properly harnessed, it can allow the server developer to do amazing things.

The Bottom Line

Enable and configure the CLR in SQL Server 2008.   For security reasons, the CLR installs as a disabled feature and you must enable it before you will be able to create assemblies in your database. You can control this feature at the database level, and each database will host its own application domain, which gives you the ability to enable the CLR on some databases but not all databases in a SQL Server instance.

Master It   The CLR integration option is an advanced option that you can only set through code. The code to do this is very specific. Write the statements that you will use to enable this option.

Create managed objects for the SQL Server CLR.   Managed objects mimic standard TSQL objects in a database. Unlike standard procedural objects, however, the code for these managed objects is contained in a .NET assembly. You can create managed object in Visual Studio using any .NET-compliant programming language, including C# and VB.NET.

Master It   For each of the following situations, identify the attribute or code characteristic that you would use in Visual Studio to provide the needed functionality to a managed object.

1. You want to use ADO.NET code in a user-defined function.

2. You need to identify a method for a managed TVF to execute for each populated row in the returned table.

3. You need to execute a command and return the results back to the caller of a stored procedure.

Master It   Write a script that registers a managed assembly called Demo located at C:\demo.dll. The script should then add a function from the script called DemoFunction that takes no arguments and returns an integer. Assume that DemoFunction is in a class called UserDefinedFunctions.

Manage security for the SQL Server CLR.   Because these objects are very powerful, you must manage the security risk appropriately. You can implement user- and role-based security to control access to the managed objects. Additionally, you can use code access security through permission sets to ensure that the managed code is not allowed to execute actions outside of permitted and reasonable boundaries.

Master It   For each of the following situations, indicate whether you would use user security or code access security to achieve the desired result. Also, specify which object's permissions must be modified and which permissions you should use.

1. An assembly called Demo contains a managed function called DemoFunction. You want to secure access to DemoFunction in the database.

2. An assembly called Demo contains a managed function called DemoFunction. Demo function performs database access to the local database.

3. An assembly called Demo contains a managed function called DemoFunction. This function accesses the file system.

4. An assembly called Demo contains a managed function called DemoFunction. You need to allow a backup administrator to take ownership if necessary.

Chapter 19

Using Spatial Data

One of the new features of SQL Server 2008 is the support for spatial data. This exciting feature gives you the ability to store data representing positions and geometric structures natively in SQL Server. This can provide significant opportunities for data mining based on previously difficult metrics such as location, distance, and space. With the prevalence of spatially oriented applications and devices in our society—from cartographic applications to global positioning system (GPS) appliances—being able to store spatial data natively in SQL Server can simplify the data services that these systems require.

SQL Server supports the current standards for spatial data storage and functionality; therefore, much of what you will see when dealing with spatial data might look a bit foreign at first, because it is not implemented using typical Microsoft patterns. However, once you become accustomed to the process, you should find spatial data simple to implement. In this chapter, you will learn to:

- ◆ Define spatial storage in SQL Server
- ◆ Implement geometry data
- ◆ Implement geography data
- ◆ Implement spatial indexes

Spatial Data Concepts

The spatial datatypes in SQL Server adhere to the Open Geospatial Consortium (OGC) specification version 1.1.0. The goal of this standard is to provide a consistent way to describe and manipulate spatial and geospatial data to facilitate the integration of spatially oriented devices and applications. It sounds impressive, but it is really quite simple. You are simply describing where an entity is in your spatial universe, what its shape is, and how it relates to other objects around it. To get a better understanding of these concepts, consider some of the simple plane geometry that you have probably been exposed to in the past.

The Foundation

Plane geometry is the description of shapes in two-dimensional space. Positions in this space are typically described using an ordered pair of numbers indicating their position on an axis. With this in mind, the diagram in Figure 19.1 should look familiar.

FIGURE 19.1
Identifying a
point on a plane

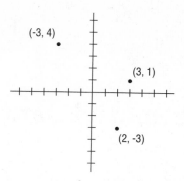

The three points on the plane in this diagram are identified based on their X-coordinate positions (left and right) and their Y-coordinate positions (up and down). The X- and Y-values make up the ordered pair. Using this system, you can identify any point in two-dimensional space.

Note that the diagram does not account for the units of the axes. The type of unit used is irrelevant. It does not matter if the units are meters, feet, or pixels. The math is the same. Any superimposition of units on the positioning system should happen in the business tier of an application and not at the database. In the database, this would be metadata at best, and irrelevant to most data-centric operations.

THINGS I FORGOT FROM SCHOOL

Remember when you were in school and the geometry teacher was going on and on about diagramming figures on a plane? You most likely said to yourself, "When will I ever use this in the real world?" That day has come. The good news is that you do not have to remember all of the awful equations that Mr. Jones tried to teach you in geometry class. However, you might want to brush off the dust from that old geometry book in the closet, just in case. Don't panic. We will keep it simple.

At first glance, this seems to be a very simplistic improvement. Storing a single point on a plane in a database doesn't seem like a very big deal. But take a closer look and it is more complicated than it seems. There are two points in the ordered pair. How will you store these two points? Each number in the ordered pair represents a discrete value, but the two points are aggregated to provide an additional meaningful value. There are a number of ways that you could store this data. If you have ever tried to do this in a relational database, you know that it is not as simple as it sounds.

You could store each value individually in the database. A table that contained data representing a point on a plane could have a column for the X-coordinate and a column for the Y-coordinate on that plane; however, technically this violates best practice because the smallest meaningful value is the pair, not the individual values in each pair. In contrast, you could store the pair in its own column. This would ensure that the pair is always together in a set, but what happens when you need to use the values in the pair for calculations? You would have to store the value as a string and parse the value to get any meaningful information.

As the shapes get more complex, these problems become more complicated. Suppose the shape in question is a line instead of a point. Then you would need to have two ordered pairs of data representing the endpoints of the line. Continuing, the shape could be a polygon, which could have an unlimited number of points in the shape, which would be impractical to model at the data level.

Additionally, suppose that you need to pass this spatial data as a parameter of a stored procedure or function, or you need to store it as a variable. It would be impractical to manage multiple sets of variables or use table variables just to manipulate a set of lines or polygons. The solution is to use the spatial data structures in SQL Server. These structures are implemented in SQL Server as managed .NET datatypes. They are not native SQL Server simple types, but rather they are complex types implemented in .NET code.

Depending on the type of object you are describing, multiple values might need to be stored and manipulated. The managed type takes care of all of the redundant and standardized tasks, such as parsing string data representing the complex structure and storing that data into simple types. These managed types also handle all of the calculations that are common to the data in question, such as determining the length of a line or the distance between two points.

YOU CAN RUN, BUT YOU CAN'T HIDE FROM .NET

If it suddenly seems as though .NET is everywhere in SQL Server and you can't get away from it, there is some truth to that. In Chapter 18, "SQL Server and the Common Language Runtime," we discussed how you can create your own .NET objects for SQL Server. The managed datatype is just one of those objects classes. If you need a refresher, refer back to Chapter 18. If you review the section on creating datatypes, the whole concept of spatial data will be easier to understand.

Geometry Versus Geography

There are actually two spatial datatypes in SQL Server; they are the geometry type and the geography type. Although they do share many common characteristics, there are some differences between them. Each has its own specific purpose that is targeted to different kinds of applications.

The geometry type stores data based on a flat-plane assumption. Every point is defined in two-dimensional space. All of the standard plane geometry you learned in school relates to the geometry datatype, as there is no curvature of space in this model. There is no assumption of a third dimension, so no solid masses, such as conic structures or other intersecting planes, intersect with the planes.

The geography datatype describes an ellipsoidal Earth-mapping model. Contrary to common belief, Earth is not a ball; it is an ellipsoid, more like an egg. There is no actual fixed diameter measure for Earth, because taking the diameter measure at different points would return slightly different values. Because of this shape, a planar approach to position is inexact. The solution is to have a positioning system that can take this curvature into consideration. The classic measures of latitude and longitude are a perfect example of such a system. Although the distance between latitudes remains constant, longitudinal variances occur depending on how far north or south you are; the variances being greater at the equator and lesser at the poles.

Both the `geometry` and `geography` datatypes support a variety of subtypes that represent specific shapes. You configure these shapes using a structure that the OGC calls Well-Known Text (WKT). WKT is simply a text-based format for describing the geometric shapes in question, usually using a set of ordered pairs, which the managed type then parses and manipulates.

Shapes Supported by Spatial Data

The `geometry` and `geography` datatypes are abstractions for specific types of geometric shapes. To create a specific shape, you must provide the appropriate WKT format to the function that creates the type. The specific shapes are basically the same for the `geometry` and `geography` types; the only difference is whether the specific shape exists in a plane or ellipsoidal space. The specific shapes are

- Point

- MultiPoint

- LineString

- MultiLineString

- Polygon

- MultiPolygon

- GeometryCollection

Each shape also has a corresponding collection version. You can store a single point, for example, in a Point type or an entire collection of points in the MultiPont type. The GeometryCollection type is an abstraction of these "multi" types that provides the collection behavior and aggregates the other specific types. The object model for these types is illustrated in Figure 19.2. Only the previously listed types are directly usable in SQL Server. All other types in this diagram are abstract and provide inherited structure only.

FIGURE 19.2
The spatial type
hierarchy

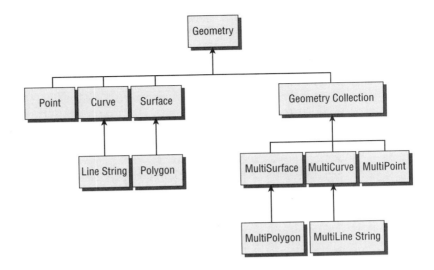

Point The Point type represents a single one-dimensional reference identified by an ordered pair. You can use a single point as a position of reference or as an identifier to a single location on the surface.

MultiPoint This represents a collection of zero or more points, usually representing a set of location identifiers. This is a collection object that can contain only points. You generate the type by using a WKT expression that represents all the points, not by adding points to the collection programmatically, which is the more typical Microsoft-based approach.

LineString A LineString is a one-dimensional object consisting of two or more identifying points and their connecting line segments. Lines can be simple or complex. Figure 19.3 illustrates several LineString objects that, left to right, are simple, complex, and closed. Complex LineStrings have crossing points; closed figures use the same point to begin and end the shape.

FIGURE 19.3
LineStrings

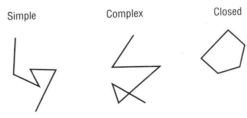

MultiLineString This is a collection of LineString objects. Similar to the MultiPoint object, you create this collection by providing a WKT expression that identifies all the LineStrings in the collection. The contained LineStrings can be simple, intersecting, or closed. Using the different types of individual line strings, you can create a variety of structures. Figure 19.4 illustrates some of the options.

FIGURE 19.4
MultiLineStrings

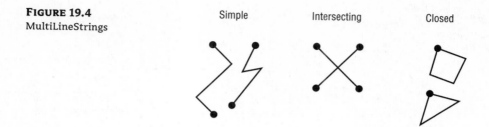

Polygon   A Polygon is a closed shape, referred to as a *ring*. The Polygon consists of a single ring that can have zero or more contained rings within it. The line segments that make up the rings of a Polygon can never intersect. Figure 19.5 illustrates both valid and invalid Polygon structures.

FIGURE 19.5
Polygons

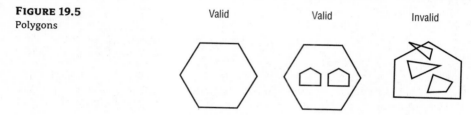

MultiPolygon   This type represents a collection of valid Polygon shapes. If any one Polygon in the collection is invalid, then the entire collection is invalid. The outer ring of any polygon cannot intersect with any other outer ring or the entire collection is invalid.

GeometryCollection   While the previous collection types can store only objects of a specific type, the geometry collection can store multiple objects of various types. For example, you can store both a point and a polygon in a single GeometryCollection type. This gives you the flexibility to aggregate many shapes together.

Defining Spatial Storage

Just as with simple datatypes, spatial types can be used in table definitions or as variable types. You can also set them as parameter types for functions and stored procedures and use them as return values for functions.

Assume that you have a table that requires special data storage. Depending on whether you want planar or ellipsoidal manipulation, you can use either the geometry or geography datatype in much the same way that you would use a standard datatype. Consider the following table as an example. This code assumes that you have already created a sample database called Sandbox.

```
USE Sandbox;

CREATE TABLE dbo.Locations
(
  LocationID    int         PRIMARY KEY CLUSTERED,
  LocationName  nvarchar(30),
  Position      geometry
);
```

In this example, every position is recorded as a value using a `geometry` type. Notice that this code does not specify "Point" as the type. The table is unaware of the existence of the Point type. All spatial data will simply be stored as a `geometry` or `geography` type. This value will be identified as a Point, LineString, or Polygon when you store the value in the table.

THE CONTENTS WILL COME LATER

Loading the data into the type is somewhat complex and we need to introduce the WKT format before it will be clear, so we will illustrate how to do it later in the chapter.

You can also use variables and parameters in the same way. Consider the following incomplete snippet from a function. You will see how spatial data plays an important role in process data as well.

```
CREATE FUNCTION dbo.LocationInfo
(
  @location          geometry
) RETURNS int
AS
BEGIN
  DECLARE @globalLocation  geography;
  – Remainder of function
  return 0;
END;
```

This function does not do anything constructive, but from this illustration you should be able to see the mechanics of using both the `geometry` and `geography` types as parameters and variables. The important element of note here is not the striking difference between this and standard datatype implementation, but rather that the implementation is virtually identical.

Implementing the *Geometry* Type

Now that you have seen the kinds of data that you can store into the `geometry` type and how to define the storage, you are ready to implement the type and load values accordingly. This process is a little bit different from what you are used to with standard types, but it does follow a standard formula, so it is easy to get comfortable with quickly.

In this section, we will begin by learning how to load data into a `geometry` type based on the specific subtypes in question. Then we will look at how to manipulate that data using the methods associated with the .NET types.

Loading Geometry Data

Because spatial data utilizes .NET managed types as opposed to simple SQL Server datatypes, loading values into a spatially typed table or variable is not as simple as assigning the value directly. Instead, you will need to use methods associated with the spatial types to define this storage. The arguments that you provide to these methods are text-based and use a format defined by the OGC called Well-Known Text (WKT). Here is an example of using WKT to assign a point value at position (0,0) to a geometry variable.

```
DECLARE @point geometry;
SELECT @point = geometry::STGeomFromText('POINT (0 0)', 0);
```

WE ARE NOT ELEVATING THIS DISCUSSION

All shapes are created from points. These points can contain, in addition to the X- and Y-coordinates, a Z-value indicating elevation. Although the Z-value is storable, it is ignored in calculations and is, therefore, little more than metadata. All manipulations of spatial types are assumed to be based on just the X- and Y-values alone. For this reason, we will not discuss the Z-value in detail in this chapter.

Additionally, you can include an M-value, which is a measure from a common point of reference. The M-value is used to provide positional context. These values are beyond our scope, but if you want to read more about the role of the Z- and M-values in the specification, please visit the OGC website at http://www.opengeospatial.org.

The STGeomFromText method is defined by the OGC and implemented by Microsoft as a member of the geometry datatype. The method has two arguments. The first is the WKT of the described geometric shape. The second argument is a Spatial Reference ID (SRID), which represents the identifier of the spatial reference system that you are using as a point of reference for your geographic data. This SRID will default to 0 for geometry types, and we will discuss the purpose of this value in greater detail when we address geography later in this chapter.

Parse is an alternative method of storing a value into a geometry type. This method is equivalent to the STGeomFromText method except that it always assumes a SRID of 0, which is a safe assumption for the geometry type. The same operation using the Parse method would look like this:

```
DECLARE @point geometry;
SELECT @point = geometry::Parse('POINT (0 0)');
```

Using this approach, inserting data into the dbo.Locations table that was previously illustrated would look like this. Assume in all of these examples that you are using the Sandbox database.

```
INSERT INTO dbo.Locations
VALUES(1,'Origin', geometry::Parse('POINT(0 0)'));
```

Once inserted, the .NET code converts the text into a binary format representing the geometric object. This value is meaningless if you select it directly from a table, so you must use properties of the geometric typed value to extract the meaningful pieces of data that interest you. For example, suppose you want to return the X- and Y-coordinates of the point that was just inserted into the database. The code to do this would be as follows:

```
SELECT
  Position.STX as XCoordinate,
  Position.STY as YCoordinate
FROM dbo.Locations;
```

Depending on the stored figure, there are a variety of different pieces of information that you can pull from the type such as areas, lengths, and endpoints.

WELL-KNOWN BINARY

SQL Server data is stored in a format called Well-Known Binary (WKB), which is a format defined by the OGC. The WKB format provides a viable storage format that can also be used to exchange data with other applications and data services that are WKB-compliant. Although this chapter focuses on creating spatial artifacts using the WKT format, SQL Server also supports the instantiation of all of these artifacts using WKB with OGC standard methods.

Working with Points and MultiPoints

In the previous example, you saw how to store a point into a `geometry` type. The illustrated method used the generic methods STGeomFromText and Parse. You can use additional methods to create each type of geometric object, which will clarify the code significantly. To create a point directly at the origin of a matrix (position 0,0), you could use this code as well.

```
DECLARE @point    geometry;
SELECT @point = geometry::STPointFromText('POINT (0 0)',0);
```

Using this statement, the argument is verified to ensure that the WKT creates a point as opposed to any other geometric type. If the WKT represents any shape other than a point, the statement will fail. There are numerous methods for getting information about the points that you create. Some of those methods include:

- STX: Returns the X-coordinate of a point

- STY: Returns the Y-coordinate of a point

- STDistance: Returns the shortest distance between two points

- STEquals: Determines if two geometries are identical

For example, if you have two points in a grid and you want to find the distance between those two points, as shown in Figure 19.6. The following code will return the desired value.

FIGURE 19.6
Calculating
distances

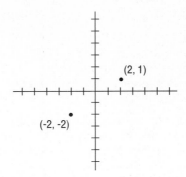

```
DECLARE @point1 geometry;
DECLARE @point2 geometry;
DECLARE @distance numeric(10,2);

SELECT @point1 = geometry::STPointFromText('POINT (2 1)',0);
SELECT @point2 = geometry::STPointFromText('POINT (-2 -2)',0);
SELECT @distance = @point1.STDistance(@point2);

SELECT @distance;
```

You can also store a collection of points in a MultiPoint object. If you want to store these two points into a single datum in SQL Server, the WKT format will require you to list all of the coordinates in order. Loading these two points would require code that looks like this:

```
DECLARE @pointCollection geometry;
SELECT @pointCollection =
       geometry::STMPointFromText('MULTIPOINT ((2 1),(-2 -2))',0);
```

To work with any individual point in the collection, you can access it using an index number based on the position in the collection using the STGeometryN method. This method returns an individual geometry element in a collection based on an index number. The following code returns the X-coordinate of the first point in the collection.

```
SELECT @pointCollection.STGeometryN(1).STX;
```

You can also assign an individual element of the collection to a variable for further processing if you like. This example loads one of the points in the collection into a geometry instance, which is then queried to return its X-coordinate.

```
SELECT @point = @pointCollection.STGeometryN(1);
SELECT @point.STX;
```

WHAT'S THE POINT?

Points are the basis for all geometry. As you will see later in this chapter, you can extract points from other geometric shapes and store those in point instances. Then, using these and other techniques, you can manipulate those points to get additional information about the geometries involved. If the concept of data mining based on geometry is suddenly leaping to the front of your mind, you are on the right track.

Working with LineStrings and MultiLineStrings

In the strictest sense, the LineString does not exist in plane geometry. In geometry, a *segment* is the line fragment that exists between two points on a line. The line itself extends into infinity in both directions. In this sense, a line string is actually a set of connected segments. With the exception of the endpoints, each point in the LineString represents the beginning of one segment as well as the end of another. You might find it easier to think of the LineString in this way, as a set of segments.

The WKT for a LineString is, therefore, nothing more than a set of points. The segments represent the shortest distance between each of these points in the order that they are provided in the WKT expression. A LineString, therefore, needs at least two points in its definition; it can contain additional points if additional segments are added to the structure.

Refer to the diagram in Figure 19.7. This figure illustrates a LineString structure based on a set of two points. There is only one segment in this line string. Because you have already seen how the WKT syntax handles points, this should look very familiar.

```
DECLARE @line geometry;
SELECT @line = geometry::STLineFromText('LineString (-1 -1,3 2)',0);
```

FIGURE 19.7
A LineString

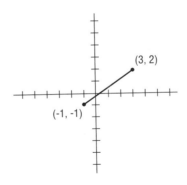

You can add additional line segments to the LineString by adding pairs of values to the list of values in the WKT expression. The first and last point in the list will always be the endpoints of the LineString. If the first and last points in the list are the same, the shape is closed and represents a ring. Now that you have a valid line string, you can extract information about the shape such as its endpoints and length. The following code returns the length of the LineString, which is the sum of the length of all segments.

```
DECLARE @length numeric(10,2);
SELECT @length = @line.STLength();
SELECT @length;
```

There are additional methods that you can use to get information about the LineStrings. The most common of these are

STNumPoints: Returns the number of points that comprise an instance

STPointN Returns a specific point in an instance

STPointOnSurface Returns an arbitrary point that lies on an instance

STStartPoint Returns the start point of an instance

STEndPoint Returns the end point of an instance

If you have more than one LineString instance, you can also use the geometry type to identify relationships between them, such as if they are disjoint or they intersect. Look at Figure 19.8, which illustrates two line strings. The code that follows the figure would identify to the developer that these two LineStrings intersect each other.

FIGURE 19.8
Intersecting
LineStrings

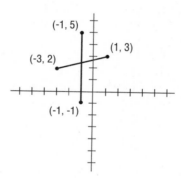

```
DECLARE @line1 geometry;
DECLARE @line2 geometry;
SELECT @line1 = geometry::STLineFromText('LineString (-3 2,1 3)',0);
SELECT @line2 = geometry::STLineFromText('LineString (-1 5,-1 -1)',0);
SELECT @line1.STIntersects(@line2);
```

The MultiLineString is similar in concept to the MultiPoint; it is merely a collection of LineStrings and the WKT expression will match that accordingly. Taking the two preceding LineString structures and loading them into a MultiLineString object would require code like this. Notice how you can interact directly with the elements of the collection. In this example, we determine the two instances.

```
DECLARE @lineStringCollection geometry;
SELECT @lineStringCollection = geometry::STMLineFromText('MultiLineString((-3 2,1
3),(-1 5,-1 -1))',0);
SELECT @lineStringCollection.STGeometryN(1).STEquals(@lineStringCollection.
STGeometryN(2));
```

🌐 **Real World Scenario**

THE PATH TO RICHES

Because this is such new technology, we dug through some proof-of-concept code rather than production code for a case study. For an example of the things you can do with geometric data, consider this application that is current in design. The names and a few circumstances have been changed to protect the parties involved.

The client is a retailer of specialty goods. This particular client has invested in technology to track the customer's movement through their facility. The system tracks their customers' interactions with various kiosks throughout the facility and each interaction is recorded. The facility has hundreds of these kiosks, and customers must interact with them to purchase the desired goods. Although customers do not have to identify themselves to interact with the kiosks, a series of rewards and promotions are offered to carded customers, so most of them choose to take this extra step.

The application in question is a data-mining application that will track an individual customer's movement throughout the facility. Each point of contact that the customer makes is a point in a matrix. From the start of their visit to the end, the set of points can be combined to form a LineString. Some of these LineStrings are simple, consisting of just a few segments. Others are very complex and often cross back on themselves. All of this geometric data is stored in a SQL Server 2008 database. Now comes the fun part. The important part of this application mines this data for patterns. We can ask numerous questions from the data, including:

Which paths are the most common?

Are there commonalities based on the number of points in the path?

Where are the common intersection points of these paths?

If we superimpose qualitative data onto these patterns, such as what kinds of products are available along the most common paths and intersections, then we can plan for better product placement.

For example, if there are one or two points in the facility that everyone walks through, or if people who use certain paths through the facility end up spending larger amounts of money, we can place the best products along those paths to appeal to customers based on their demographics and buying habits. The proof of concept is beginning to show some fruit. What initially seemed like random flows through the facility are, in fact, patterns of behavior and that behavior can be predicted to a certain degree based on demographics.

In an exercise like this, geometric data is not some abstract exercise. It is concrete and can be used to make very valuable business decisions. The moral of the story is that you should not immediately discount spatial data structures as "that stuff that the GPS developers use." There is more to it than that, and you can use this kind of data to your advantage if you know how to manage it.

Working with Polygons and MultiPolygons

The last basic shape in our set is the Polygon. A Polygon is a closed figure with zero or more closed figures inside. Similar to the LineString, the Polygon is made up of set points with segments connecting those points. Because it is a closed figure, the first point and the last point will always be the same. Because it must be a ring, the figure segments are not allowed to intersect with each other, a condition which is allowed with a LineString.

The WKT format for a Polygon is very similar to a LineString. The Polygon illustrated in Figure 19.9 is a simple shape with only an exterior ring. Note that the starting and ending points are the same, at position (3,-2) in the grid. The code that follows the figure creates the Polygon.

FIGURE 19.9

A simple Polygon

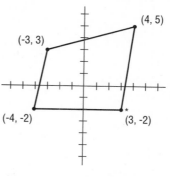

*Starting Point

```
DECLARE @polygon1 geometry;
SELECT @polygon1 = geometry::STPolyFromText('POLYGON((3 -2,4 5,-3 3,-4 -2, 3
-2))',0);
```

Using a simple method called STArea, you can calculate the area of the polygon. The Polygon in Figure 19.9 has an area of 41 units, which can be determined by using this code:

```
SELECT @polygon1.STArea();
```

If you like, you can also include one or more interior polygons inside the exterior shape. These interior Polygons are considered to be "holes" in the exterior shape. Therefore, they cannot overlap the exterior structure, although they can touch each other inside at a single point. Because these interior shapes are considered holes in the outer shape, their areas are deducted from the external shape when calculating an area on the Polygon as a whole.

Consider the shape in Figure 19.10. The external shape is identical to the one pictured in Figure 19.9, but this one contains an internal Polygon as well. It follows all of the rules in that it does not intersect with the external shape at any point. The code following the figure illustrates how to create this shape as well as how to calculate the entire figure.

```
DECLARE @polygon1 geometry;
SELECT @polygon1 = geometry::STPolyFromText('POLYGON((3 -2,4 5,-3 3,-4 -2, 3 -2),(2
2,-1 -1,2 -1,2 2))',0);
SELECT @polygon1.STArea();
```

The area of this figure is 36.5 units, which is the total area of the figure less the area of the internal figure. If you want these figures to be separate overlapping figures as opposed to a single figure with a hole, you must use separate Polygon shapes for each figure. You cannot use a MultiPolygon type to store the entire set because the MultiPolygon shape requires that the elements do not overlap. They are allowed to touch only at a single point.

FIGURE 19.10
A Polygon with
an interior ring

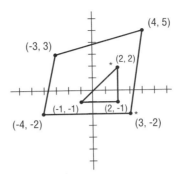

*Starting Point

If you do have separate Polygon instances for each shape, you can get other interesting information about those shapes as well as the total area of each shape. Consider the following code that stores each of the shapes in Figure 19.10 as a separate object.

```
DECLARE @polygon1 geometry;
DECLARE @polygon2 geometry;
SELECT @polygon1 = geometry::STPolyFromText('POLYGON((3 -2,4 5,-3 3,-4 -2, 3
-2))',0);
SELECT @polygon2 = geometry::STPolyFromText('POLYGON((2 2,-1 -1,2 -1,2 2))',0);
SELECT @polygon1.STArea();
SELECT @polygon2.STArea();
SELECT @polygon2.STOverlaps(@polygon1);
SELECT @polygon2.STWithin(@polygon1);
```

The preceding code gives you the individual area of each shape. You can easily add the individual areas together to give you a total area for both figures. The code also determines if the figures overlap or if one figure is entirely within another. This could be very important information if you are determining whether or not these figures could be loaded into a MultiPolygon collection or could be used to create a single Polygon with a hole.

The MultiPolygon shape can contain multiple Polygons. Because each of these Polygons can also have holes, the resulting WKT expression can be very complicated. The WKT convention is very deliberate in its use of parentheses to keep things organized. The following code creates a MultiPolygon shape. The first Polygon in the collection is the figure pictured in Figure 19.10 with the hole. The second is another nonintersecting shape with no hole. Pay close attention to the parentheses as you evaluate this syntax.

```
DECLARE @mpolygon1 geometry;
DECLARE @area numeric(10,2);
SELECT @mpolygon1 = geometry::STMPolyFromText('MULTIPOLYGON(((3 -2,4 5,-3 3,-4 -2,
3 -2),(2 2,-1 -1,2 -1,2 2)),((5 5,10 5,5 10,5 5)))',0);
SELECT @area = @mpolygon1.STGeometryN(1).STArea() + @mpolygon1.STGeometryN(2).
STArea();
SELECT @area;
```

You can also compare objects of different types. One very useful technique is to use the STContains method to see if a Polygon contains another object such as a LineString or a Point. This is useful in determining if one figure is a component of another figure. Also, the STWithin method previously illustrated is very convenient in determining if a point of reference is within the boundaries of a Polygon.

Using the GeometryCollection

Unlike the other collections, such as MultiPoint and MultiPolygon, the GeometryCollection does not require all members of the collection to be of a specific type. This can be very convenient when you want to aggregate elements of varying types into one structure, which can then be stored or passed as a single element.

To create a GeomtryCollection object, you must have elements to place within it. Assume that you wanted to store a point at (4,5) and a LineString from (-3,4) to (3,2) in the same collection. You could use a GeometryCollection with code like this:

```
DECLARE @geomColl geometry;
SELECT @geomColl = geometry::STGeomCollFromText('GEOMETRYCOLLECTION(POINT(4
5),LineString(-3 4,3 2))',0);
```

Remember that the GeometryCollection type is actually the base type for all of the other "Multi" types in the model, which means that this type has less functionality than the other types because it is less specific. What it loses in functionality, however, it gains in flexibility. The GeometryCollection can aggregate shapes together in much the same way as you can pass table-valued parameters in SQL code, allowing you to aggregate larger amounts of data together in a single parameter.

Implementing the *Geography* Type

Unlike the geometry type, which exists only in a two-dimensional plane, the geography type is earthbound in an ellipsoidal projection. The geography type is used more frequently for GPS or cartographic applications, especially those that are more macro-oriented where Earth's curvature might have an overall impact on application implementations.

Although the geography type is almost identical in implementation to the geometry type, there are a few important differences. In this section, you will learn about the role of the Spatial Reference ID in geography and then overview the differences between the geometry and geography implementations.

Understanding the Spatial Reference

Those of you who have worked with GPS applications or who have advanced degrees in geography or cartography have seen this concept before. The essence of the SRID is that, unlike a grid where we can agree on a universal point of reference at position (0,0), earthbound applications are a little different. We must all have a common point of reference.

In school you probably learned that the standard point of reference is the prime meridian, which runs through Greenwich, UK. However, the truth is that many different reference points are in common use today. If we are going to compare metrics from one application to another, or even one observation to another, those metrics are meaningless if they do not use the same point of reference. This is where the SRID comes in.

The SRID is nothing more than an integer that uniquely defines a system of reference. You have many options for the standard point of reference you use, and different kinds of applications ranging from GPS to mapping systems might use different references depending on the application, industry, or even national origin.

One of the important distinctions between geometry and geography types is that geography data requires a SRID. Geometry types default to 0 because a geometric shape can exist in an undefined planar space, but a geography type cannot. SQL Server used a default SRID of 4326, which maps to the World Geodetic System (WGS) 84 spatial reference system. If you want to use any other reference system, you must provide the SRID when you create your geography type.

GETTING A VALID SRID

The SRID that you use must be a valid, defined reference ID and it must also be in the list of reference ID values defined in the SQL Server system catalog. The sys.spatial_reference_systems catalog view contains brief descriptions of the valid reference ID values that SQL Server recognizes. You may want to browse through this list to get an idea of the options available and their relevance to your applications.

If you want to create a geographic entity, the code is essentially the same as the geometry type. The difference is that the point of origin is determined by the SRID. Note that the SRID also indicates the units of measure, which is usually meters, but not always. Therefore, the meaning of any geographic value is entirely dependent on the SRID used when you create the shape. Consider these four lines of code:

```
DECLARE @geog1 geography;
DECLARE @geog2 geography;
SELECT @geog1 = geography::STPointFromText('POINT(1 1)',4326);
SELECT @geog2 = geography::Parse('POINT(1 1)');
```

Based on the defaults for the SRID in SQL Server, these two variables would store the same position based on the same point of reference and are, therefore, comparable data. If you were to execute this statement now, it would indicate that the two Points were equal by returning the value of 1.

```
SELECT @geog1.STEquals(@geog2);
```

If you were to modify one of the points to identify a position other than (1,1), the previous statement would return 0, indicating that the two Points are not equal. If these Points were not using the same SRID, the result would be very different. Consider this code as an example:

```
DECLARE @geog1 geography;
DECLARE @geog2 geography;
SELECT @geog1 = geography::STPointFromText('POINT(1 1)',4326);
SELECT @geog2 = geography::STPointFromText('POINT(1 1)',4120);
SELECT @geog1.STEquals(@geog2);
```

In this case, the two points are using a different point of reference because the SRID values are different. This means that the data is not comparable in any way. Any comparison of these values would be meaningless. Our result for the STEquals is, therefore, also meaningless. Executing this code would result in a selected value of NULL. It cannot return either 0 or 1, as it cannot determine at all if these positions are equivalent or not. Be sure that you keep this in mind if you work with geographic data. You must choose and be consistent with a single point of reference.

Geometry Versus Geography

As we previously mentioned, the geometry and geography types are almost identical in terms of their functionality. The concepts are essentially the same; the basic patterns that you learned with the geometry datatype also apply to the geography datatype. The primary differences lie in their internal implementations and not their external interface. That said, there are a few areas where they are distinctly different and these are worth addressing.

The SRID Requirement   The geometry type can use an SRID if it is relevant, but using it is not required. If you do not provide an SRID for the geometry type, it will default to 0, which represents undefined planar space. The geography type requires an SRID and 0 is not a valid value. The default of 4326 can be overridden in your code, but any shapes are comparable only if they have the same SRID.

Polygon Instances   Because the geography type is a round-Earth model, there are restrictions to the size and structure of shape instances. A Polygon, for example, is restricted to exist within a single hemisphere. Also, point order in geography is strictly enforced. When creating Polygons, all points must be listed counter-clockwise.

Methods   Numerous methods are supported by geometry that are not supported by the geography type. These methods are those that handle objects that exist only in flat planar space. These include but are not limited to:

- ◆ STTouches
- ◆ STOverlaps
- ◆ STCrosses
- ◆ STWithin
- ◆ STContains
- ◆ STRelate

There are also some methods that do essentially the same thing in geography and geometry, but they are named differently because the implementation between planar and ellipsoidal space is so different. For example, the STDistance method of the geometry type is replaced by the STDifference method for the geography type.

This is logical if you think about what the methods do. STDistance will determine the shortest distance between two points. In the case of planar space that is just fine, but in a round-earth space the shortest distance could slice right through the center of the Earth! The information might be useful, but not if you are trying to calculate the distance you would have to travel on the surface of the Earth to go from one point to another. The STDifference method requires that travel occur across the surface of the Earth, instead of taking a shortcut through the Earth's core.

Again, for the most part, the geometry and geometry types are the same in practice, so all of the code you used to create instances and load collections will be the same, the only substantive difference being the use of an appropriate SRID.

Spatial Indexes

Whenever you store data in SQL Server, you have to be able to extract that information efficiently. With spatial data, however, traditional indexes will not work. This is because the values that you must index are stored within the WKB data, and they are often stored deep within that data. In this regard, these spatial indexes are very similar in concept to XML indexes, where traditional column-based indexes provide no practical benefit.

To understand the need for spatial indexing, consider the following code. Notice how the WHERE clause in the final query does not follow a pattern that can benefit from a traditional index due to the lack of a search argument.

```
USE Sandbox;

CREATE TABLE dbo.Locations
(
  LocationID    int           PRIMARY KEY CLUSTERED,
  LocationName  nvarchar(30),
  Position      geometry
);

INSERT INTO dbo.Locations
VALUES (1, 'origin', geometry::STPointFromText('POINT(0 0)',0));

INSERT INTO dbo.Locations
VALUES (2, 'point1', geometry::STPointFromText('POINT(1 1)',0));

INSERT INTO dbo.Locations
VALUES (3, 'point2', geometry::STPointFromText('POINT(-5 -5)',0));

GO

DECLARE @polygon geometry;
SELECT @polygon = geometry::STPolyFromText('POLYGON((2 2, -2 2, -2 -2, 2 -2, 2
2))',0);
```

```
SELECT *
FROM dbo.Locations
WHERE Position.STWithin(@polygon) = 1;

GO
```

This query should only return the `origin` and `point1` as valid responses. `Point2` is outside of the Polygon and, therefore, does not return. However, the only way to determine this fact would be to evaluate every point in the table. If you have a very large table with numerous points, this would be impractical.

A standard search argument in a query requires that the column be isolated on one side of the comparison with an expression on the other side. This is not possible in this case because you are querying based on geometric relationships, not data-based relationships. The solution is to create a spatial index on the Position column in the table that the expression can use to better search through the matching data.

Spatial Index Architecture and Restrictions

Spatial indexes are organized as b-tree structures in SQL Server, so when yore create an index, SQL Server must convert the data from a spatial structure in a grid to a linear tree-based structure. It does this by determining which points exist in which cells in the grid and using this information to create the index of grid locations.

You have the option of controlling the granularity of the grid. For example, if you use an index that breaks the geometry into only a few grid spaces, your index will consume less space but will be useful, because more points will exist in the same cells in the grid. For example, if you have 20 points and they are spread over a 2 × 2 grid with four cells, there will be an average of five points per cell. If the index determines that the query is requesting a point from that cell, it must evaluate all five points.

By contrast, if the grid is a 4 × 4 grid with 16 cells, the density of points per cell will decrease, meaning a large index but a smaller point density. You must decide where this trade-off makes the most sense for you as you design your indexes. Table 19.1 provides a listing of your options. If you do not specify a grid structure to overlay your index, SQL Server will assume a medium level of density.

TABLE 19.1   Spatial Index Grid Structures

KEYWORD	GRID STRUCTURE	NUMBER OF CELLS
LOW	4 × 4	16
MEDIUM	8 × 8	64
HIGH	16 × 16	256

By default, the index is divided into four levels in the tree structure. You can select a grid configuration for each of the four levels in the index. This allows you to aggregate at a lower density at one level but increase the density at another level.

To keep the system from indexing empty space in a grid, you also use what is called a *bounding box*. This is a set of X,Y-coordinates that represents the boundaries of the indexed space.

AVOIDING THE DETAILS

If you really want to know all of the internals on how spatial indexes work and the algorithms they use, you can read the details in the SQL Server Books Online. Because the details are readily available there, we will not repeat them here. The grid density is the only thing that you can control, so it is the only concept you really need to understand now. However, if you want to get the most from spatial indexes, a little extra reading will be worth the time. Understanding how the indexes work will help you structure your queries and select the right granularity for your indexes.

Just as with XML indexes, there are some restrictions on spatial indexes. If you attempt to create a spatial index without following the rules, the process will fail. The important restrictions are

◆ You can create spatial indexes only on spatial columns of type `geometry` or `geography`.

◆ You cannot create a spatial index on a parameter or variable.

◆ Every table that has spatial indexes must have a Primary Key constraint defined.

  ◆ A composite primary key cannot contain more than 15 columns.

  ◆ The total length of all columns in a composite key cannot exceed 895 bytes.

◆ Once you define a spatial index on a table, you cannot modify the primary key unless you drop the spatial index.

Creating Spatial Indexes

If you can create a regular index, spatial indexes will look very familiar. You can create them by using the SQL Server Management Studio (SSMS) interface or by using Transact-SQL (TSQL) code. Either approach will yield the same result.

To use SSMS, open the studio interface and connect the Explorer to the service instance that contains the target database. Expand the database node of the target database. Locate and expand the tables node. In the list of tables, locate the table that contains the spatial data column. Expand this node and locate the indexes node. To create the index, right-click the indexes node and select New Index from the menu. This will open the dialog pictured in Figure 19.11.

This figure shows the complete dialog. To add a column to the spatial index, click the Add button and select the column from the list that appears. Remember that you will only be able to select columns that are typed as spatial data. If you click the Spatial page selector on the left of the dialog, a dialog like the one pictured in Figure 19.12 will appear.

FIGURE 19.11
Creating a
spatial index

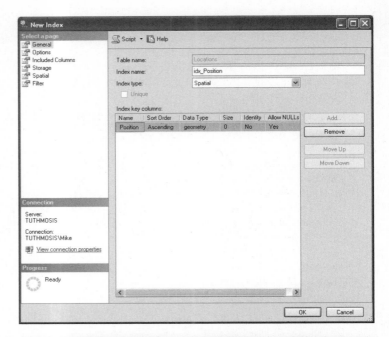

FIGURE 19.12
Setting the spatial
properties

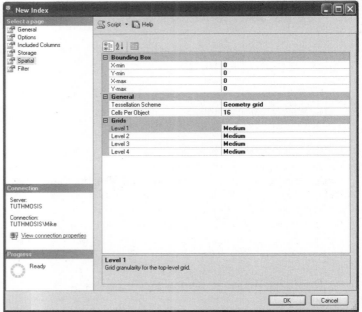

This dialog allows you to control the grid granularity and specify the configuration of the bounding box. You can also adjust the indexing algorithm, known as tessellation, to use either a geometric or geographic scheme.

WHAT IS TESSELLATION?

Tessellation is a fancy word meaning the arrangement of shapes into a pattern. When you were three years old and were arranging your blocks on the kitchen floor, you were practicing the art of tessellation. In the context of spatial data, the concept is that a plane and an ellipsoid are two very different surfaces, so the algorithms used to place objects on the surface to locate them again later will be very different. Make sure that the Tessellation setting for your index matches the datatype upon which the index is built.

You can also create this index using TSQL code. An example is listed here. Note the similarity to standard indexes.

```
USE Sandbox;
CREATE SPATIAL INDEX idx_Position
  ON dbo.Locations(Position)
  USING GEOMETRY_GRID
  WITH (
  BOUNDING_BOX = ( xmin=0, ymin=0, xmax=10, ymax=10 ),
  GRIDS = (LOW, MEDIUM, MEDIUM, HIGH),
  CELLS_PER_OBJECT = 64);
```

You should be able to compare this code to the SSMS dialogs in the previous two figures. This code generates and index called idx_Position on the Position column of the dbo.Locations table. The `USING GEOMETRY_GRID` statement identifies the tessellation algorithm that the index will use. Note how the `WITH` block also identifies the special values, such as the bounding box and the level granularity.

Although spatial indexes are useful, not all methods will take advantage of them. For the geometry datatype, the spatial indexes are used by these methods in the following forms. Note that you cannot invert the form and put the result before the method or it will return false positives.

- geometry1 . STContains (geometry2) = 1
- geometry1 . STDistance (geometry2) < number
- geometry1 . STDistance (geometry2) <= number
- geometry1 . STEquals (geometry2) = 1
- geometry1 . STIntersects (geometry2) = 1
- geometry1. STOverlaps (geometry2) = 1
- geometry1 . STTouches (geometry2) = 1
- geometry1 . STWithin (geometry2) = 1

The **geography** type is similarly constrained. Only the following **geography** methods can utilize spatial indexes and only in these forms.

◆ geography1 . STIntersects (geography2) = 1

◆ geography1 . STEquals (geography2) = 1

◆ geography1 . STDistance (geography2) < number

◆ geography1 . STDistance (geography2) <= number

Use this information as you plan your indexes so that you don't create spatial indexes on columns when the operations you perform in your applications do not support those indexes. Planning ahead can conserve significant resources.

The Bottom Line

Define spatial storage in SQL Server.   As a new feature of SQL Server 2008, you can store information on a variety of geometric shapes directly in SQL Server tables, variables, and parameters. The data storage conforms to accepted standards for geospatial storage, and Microsoft provides support to manipulate and query these values using standards-based methods. Both planar and ellipsoidal space are supported.

Master It   For each of the following scenarios, indicate which of the **geometry/geography** subtypes would be best suited to address the scenario.

1. You need to pass position locations to a procedure to calculate the distance between them.

2. Your client application defines a boundary, and you need to return a list of all stored locations that are contained within that boundary.

3. You need to add a position location to a database table.

4. Your application must calculate the total distance traveled along a set of line segments that connect stored points.

Implement geometry data.   The **geometry** type represents shapes on a flat planar surface. You can use the **geometry** type to define points, line segments, and Polygons on this planar surface. Standards-based methods allow you to query objects based on relationships to other objects as well as to get information about the objects themselves.

Master It   Based on the following figure, write the code statement that calculates the distance between these two points on a flat planar space in a SRID neutral environment.

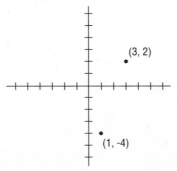

Implement geography data. Useful for GPS and Earth-mapping applications, the geography type provides an ellipsoidal surface for managing geometric shapes. This type is similar to the geometry type in most respects.

Master It Based on the following figure, write the code statement that creates the shape in an ellipsoidal space using the WGS 84 spatial reference system and calculates its area.

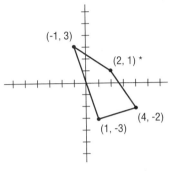

*Starting Point

Implement spatial indexes. To improve the performance of spatially driven queries, you can create spatial indexes on spatial datatyped columns. These indexes break geometric data into linear structures based on grid coordinates. When properly implemented, they can significantly increase the performance of spatial queries.

Master It Write the TSQL statement that would create a spatial index meeting the following criteria:

- The index name is idx_Location.
- The spatial data is stored in a table called Equipment.
- The spatial data column is Location.
- Use geometric tessellation.
- The index levels 1 and 2 are low density.
- Index level 3 is medium density.
- Index level 4 is high density.
- There are 64 cells per object.
- The bounding box is min 0 for x and y and max 200 for x and y.

Chapter 20

Service-Oriented Architecture and the Service Broker

A revolution is going on in the business software industry. Applications are out and services are in. The shift this can cause in application architectures is substantial. SQL Server is an important cog in the enterprise system machine; as such, it certainly must be affected by this architectural transformation. But SQL Server 2008 is well-equipped for this transition. The service-based features of SQL Server can simplify the implementation of a service-oriented architecture substantially.

Of course, everything comes with a cost. What services give us in flexibility we pay for in performance—especially when those services are poorly designed or inappropriately implemented. This balancing act is nothing new in system optimization. It represents a classic performance/functionality trade-off. When properly planned and implemented, however, services can provide benefits that far outweigh the costs. In this chapter, you will learn to:

- ◆ Describe service-oriented architecture

- ◆ Design a solution using SQL Server Service Broker

- ◆ Implement Service Broker artifacts

The Essentials of Service-Oriented Architecture

The concepts are not radical. It's really more the implementation of the concepts that are different. The best-practices domain of the object-oriented architecture world have almost always focused on loose-coupling and reusability. Service-oriented architecture (SOA) is merely the next evolutionary step down that road. More than a fad, however, SOA gives the architect and infrastructural administrator the logical framework they need to design effective service-based solutions. SQL Server 2005 and 2008 have introduced features that make the data service implementation of SOA a true possibility.

You may have had some exposure to SOA concepts, but for the benefit of those who have not, a quick review is in order. In this section, you will learn the basics of SOA theory in general, followed by the application of that theory to SQL Server 2008.

SOA Distilled

You can define a service as a task that is performed for the benefit of another requesting party. Your life is full of services. If you develop software for a company, you are providing a service. Other parties, such as the local post office and your neighborhood dry cleaner, also provide services to you. The services you design into your software actually have a lot in common with these real-life examples of services.

First, the provider of the service makes the service available through a strongly defined and well-know interface. For example, we, the authors, are both consultants, which means that we travel quite a bit. Therefore, we frequently need laundry and dry cleaning services. No matter where in the country we travel, our basic experiences with dry cleaning are always the same. There seems to be a universal "dry cleaner" interface, because the process never seems to vary from one cleaner to another. This means that because the interface is the same, the services provided are essentially interchangeable.

Second, the interface abstracts the implementation. Most people have no idea what actually happens after they drop their clothes off at the dry cleaner. Their clothes mysteriously come back fresh and clean, but the physical process of how they became that way is not known. This is an important aspect of a good service. It should not matter to the consumer of the service how the provider performs the task. Nor should the consumer ever need to have any knowledge whatsoever of the internal processes involved before they can utilize the service interface.

Finally, service implementations may differ in quality. It is up to the consumer of the service to determine whether the quality of the task performed meets the needs of the requestor at the price that is being paid. Some services may require the use of more expensive resources than others. The outcome of the service should reflect the increased cost with increased quality.

In this section, you will learn how software-based services follow these standards and examine some of the characteristics of a good software service. You will also see how to apply SOA concepts to software design using services as a building block.

SOFTWARE SERVICES

Software services mimic their real-world counterparts in that they are programs or components that provide a task-based benefit to other programs or components. Similar to real-world services, their interfaces are strongly defined but their implementation is abstract. Good software developers create their components like this anyway, following the object-oriented development principle of dependency inversion.

THE DEPENDENCY INVERSION PRINCIPLE

One of the most annoying aspects of maintaining and extending applications and components is dealing with the collateral damage. When you change one part of your code, it can break other parts of your code that you must also repair. If each of the fixes breaks something else, you can be patching forever while making little forward progress. This is usually due to dependency problems in your code, where objects have direct dependencies on each other.

Typically, if you write code in one class that uses the functionality of another class, the class that you are writing now has a dependency on the target class specifically. This tight coupling is unacceptable. But if your code were to bind to an interface implemented by the target code instead of the target code itself, you would leave yourself free to switch implementations and decouple your code from the target. Instead, define the interface in your client so that the implementing class depends on the caller. You have inverted the dependency to a contract instead of an implementation. This can save you significant headaches when you try to maintain the code later.

If you think along these lines, there are numerous examples of software components that could be designed as services including:

◆ COM objects

◆ .NET objects

◆ Message queues

◆ Web services

◆ Windows Communication Foundation (WCF) Services

For example, a .NET library that exposes a collection of interfaces and a set of functional classes that implement those interfaces could be thought of as a *service library*. If all of the client objects bind to the interfaces exposed by the service, other service providers could provide their own classes that implement the interfaces and provide concrete services to the client. This is a common practice when designing a framework.

Although this implementation meets the essential definition of a service, it suffers from one weakness in that it is based on a proprietary interface. Although .NET is a common library for implementing components, it is not standards-based and may not be fully supported on all platforms or all runtimes. For example, although there is currently significant effort being made to create a stable .NET runtime on the Linux platform thanks to the effort of the Mono project, technically, there is not a native .NET runtime on Linux and there is no standard that Linux distributions should or could follow, as .NET is not a standards-based API.

When you narrow the field down to standards-based technologies, your options are fewer, but a few technologies quickly leap to the forefront, specifically HTTP and XML using Simple Object Access Protocol (SOAP). These technologies form the basis of the Web Services specification, which provides a standards-based distributed service strategy that is fully platform interoperable.

CLEAN UP YOUR CODE WITH SOAP

SOAP is an XML specification that defines a text-based structure for a remote procedure call. SOAP is based on the idea that good services are message-based. The caller of the service sends a message to the service provider, which then uses the information in the message to perform the actions supported by the service. The message can pass parameter data while a return message can send a confirmation of execution, return data, or a fault. SOAP defines a schema for the envelope, head, and body of the message, but does not dictate the contents of the body, otherwise known as the *payload* of the message. This is up to the parties trading messages, or another specification, such as the web services specification, to provide.

CHARACTERISTICS OF A GOOD SERVICE

There are often misunderstandings about what makes a good service-oriented architecture. It is much more than just throwing services out to the enterprise and hoping people will use them. There are a number of opinions about what makes a good service, and as an extension, a good service-oriented architecture. The following are a few suggestions that you will want to consider as you design your services.

Services are reusable. One of the most important reasons organizations migrate to a service-based model is that it is a practical way of leveraging already existing code for broader reusability. However, it is not enough to simply put a service wrapper around existing code. You must write the code so that it is as decoupled as possible from the implementation environment and requires no knowledge about the code that will ultimately call the service. Tight coupling is the problem we are trying to solve with a service, so you must write your code to reflect that fact.

Services expose only a contract. The implementation details of how the service accomplishes its work should be completely abstracted from the caller of the service. The only thing that the caller should see is the formal contract. This means that the service must not expose any dependency on concrete objects. For example, if a service call requires the client to pass a parameter such as a data connection, the signature of the service method must not expose the argument type as a SqlConnection object, but rather use the abstract type DbConnection, which can represent any ADO.NET-compliant connection object.

Services are composable. Good service methods are responsible for one and only one task. A typical problem in service design is the temptation of having a service do too much. If a service performs only one task, it can be combined with other services to do more complex process. In other words, more elaborate processes are composable from granular services. Often, if the larger processes have common elements, you can create orchestration services, whose responsibility is to manage the composition process with the other more granular services. This allows you to recombine your services in a variety of different ways as needs require.

Services are stateless. One of the drawbacks of a service-oriented architecture is performance. A common performance problem with any reusable component-based architecture is state management. If a component must remember the state of a previous call so that it can respond to a subsequent call, you either have to contend with the overhead of having a component or service instance for each individual caller or you must provide code for maintaining a separate state dictionary for each caller that a singleton service can use. Either way, it makes for performance and maintenance problems. If services are completely stateless, this problem is significantly reduced.

Services are discoverable. A good service should be easily accessible. Additionally, it should also announce that it is available and open for business. You can handle this in a variety of different ways, but the most common is to provide a service directory. You can also provide an interface that the services implement so that when a client crawls the enterprise and looks for available services, it will be able to discover the services and identify their function interfaces.

Services are message-based. Although there has been significant chatter about component architectures over the years, the element of a service-oriented architecture that really separates it from simple component-based architectures is its support for standards. You can design the best .NET component architecture in the world, but what good is that if the client applications are Linux-based Java applications? However, if you use simple text messaging as the communications conduit for the services, you are now wide open. As long as the client can understand text and the appropriate application protocol, such as HTTP, it is completely interoperable, and that is a very low standard to have to meet.

Service Architecture

There are a number of architectural options that utilize a service design. Again, it is important to be selective. Just because a specific design worked in one scenario, it does not necessarily mean that it will work in every scenario. You must evaluate the trade-offs before you walk down a particular architectural path. As a point of reference, if we mention a traditional distributed architecture, we are talking about something that looks like the model in Figure 20.1. Notice the separation of presentation, business, and data logic.

FIGURE 20.1
Traditional distrib-
uted architecture

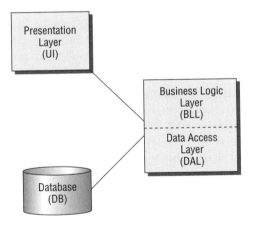

The presentation layer/user interface layer (UI) is the client application or web page structure. This contains little, if any, logic and its focus is on accepting data from the user and reporting results back to the user. A developer would typically implement this as an executable in the case of a Windows-based client application or as a website.

The next level down is the component tier, usually consisting of a business logic layer (BLL) and a data access layer (DAL). The BLL contains the majority of the application logic. This the functional heart of the application. If the BLL needs to interact with database resources, however, it will interact with a separate layer called a data access layer. The DAL provides all of the actual interaction with the database and, therefore, abstracts the database implementation from the BLL. This gives the developer the flexibility to substitute any database resource without having to recode any of the logic in the BLL. The component tier is usually implemented as dynamic link libraries (DLL).

Finally, at the bottom of the architecture stack is the database (DB). In our case, we are assuming that the database implementation will be SQL Server 2008; however, any database could be substituted because the database is entirely abstracted by the DAL.

One of the more popular uses of a service-oriented architecture is to provide an extra level of abstraction that allows business services to interact with each other. For example, suppose that you have an application that uses a traditional distributed architecture. What would happen if you found out that you needed to integrate your application with another currently independent system? The assumption is that your BLL must make calls to and use information from the other system, and the reverse is also true.

One architectural solution is to exchange component interface information with the developers that maintain the other system. You could add references to the other BLL in your code, which would enable you to call into the other BLL and use the services it provides. This approach suffers from some significant problems, however. First, what if the platforms and systems are not compatible? Second, and more important, this would create a very tight coupling to a BLL architecture over which you have no control. If the other developers make breaking changes to their BLL, you will be in trouble.

One solution is to use a service integration layer. Instead of binding directly to the BLL of the other system, both applications would create a service tier. Whenever you need to call the other system, your application calls your local service, which in turn calls the service that wraps the BLL of the other application. As long as the developers of both applications agree to keep the service interfaces immutable, there should be no exposure to a breaking change or component versioning. Additionally, you do not have to expose your entire BLL to the other system; rather you can selectively choose which BLL operations to expose with service calls while encapsulating everything else. Figure 20.2 illustrates this architecture.

FIGURE 20.2
The Service
Integration layer

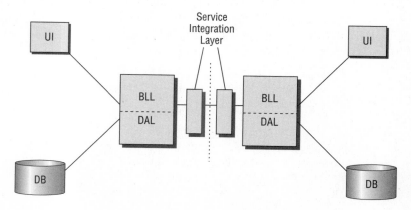

Another popular service-based architecture, which maps more directly to the SQL Server 2008 implementation, is to abstract the database interface though service points. Currently, if you want to call a SQL Server database, you use the native .NET interface (ADO.NET). But what if you are not calling from a .NET application? Additionally, what if you want to expose the database directly to other resources outside of your application, but do not want to allow those callers to interact directly through .NET? One option is to use service interfaces for your database as illustrated in Figure 20.3.

FIGURE 20.3
Services accessing the database

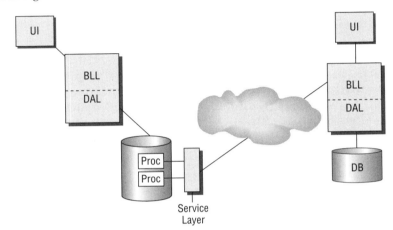

In this scenario, it does not matter what the architecture of the external application is. Because the service interface is message-based, it can be called from anywhere that it is discoverable. SQL Server can then manage the security of the process by ensuring that the calling clients are properly authenticated using other standard means, such as X.509 certificates.

SOAP ENDPOINTS ARE DEPRECATED

If you are familiar with SQL Server 2005, you may have run into a feature that supports the previous architecture called an *HTTP endpoint*. Although that feature is still supported in SQL Server 2008, it has been officially deprecated in this version. This means that in future releases of SQL Server, this feature will be available only when using an earlier server compatibility mode. For this reason, although this is a viable application architecture, we will not discuss it in detail in this chapter. If you have existing SQL 2005 code that relies on this feature, we recommend that you consider replacing this code with an alternative, such as using the Service Broker or a component-based service integration tier.

Understanding the Service Broker

When you use another feature of SQL Server 2008, the Service Broker, yet another potential architecture presents itself. One of the important characteristics of a service is that it is message-based—but there is no assumption as to the physical structure of the message. While a service might expose itself through HTTP using a SOAP message structure, as is standard with web services, it might also use a proprietary message structure. As long as the mode of communication is still text, the integrity of the service is not violated.

The basic architecture is based on message queue concepts. The Service Broker exposes a message-based interface that allows messages to be placed in a queue. SQL Server procedures then respond to the messages actions by processing the messages. Everything managed at the data tier is, therefore, reusable by any application that can see the SQL Server and pass messages to it.

The contract of the interface is strongly enforced. SQL Server allows the developer to define message contracts that specify the acceptable structure of a message. The adherence to this structure can then be enforced in the queue, preventing messages from being placed in the queue unless the specific message contract is implemented. Because this represents workflow plumbing as opposed to business logic, it is often a better architectural option to place this workflow in another layer outside the business services.

OTHER OPTIONS

We don't want you to think that the SQL Server Service Broker is the only way to achieve this architectural design goal. There are other options. With the introduction of the Windows Workflow Foundation (WF) in .NET 3.0, the infrastructure is in place in the .NET framework to create very powerful component-based workflow architectures. The SQL Server implementations work best when the workflow is constrained primarily to data flow as opposed to requiring significant human interactions with the workflow components.

Additionally, it would be irresponsible to discuss the concept of application orchestrations and SOA in general without mentioning Microsoft's BizTalk Server. This product serves as a central messaging communications hub and can provide a very robust data messaging, orchestration, and application interoperability layer in a service-based architecture. Through strongly typed messaging, BizTalk's extensible communications architecture provides almost limitless support for varying application communications architectures. If your application needs a truly robust and extensible integration tier, you may want to give BizTalk a look.

Service Broker Terminology

The Service Broker is a SQL Server subsystem, deeply integrated into the SQL Server architecture. If you think of the Service Broker as a message transport subsystem that uses SQL Server data structures for message persistence and recoverability, you have a pretty good idea about what the Service Broker does. Like most Microsoft Technologies, the Service Broker is very terminology intensive, so understanding the terminology is the first step. Here are some of the basic terms that you will have to understand when discussing Service Broker.

Endpoint   An endpoint is the formal communications point for a server-side component. Endpoints are database-level artifacts and are generally associated with an IP port. SQL Server 2008 supports four types of endpoints.

- ◆ HTTP/SOAP: Supports native web service communications with the data engine. Deprecated in SQL Server 2008.

- ◆ TSQL: Standard endpoint for interacting with SQL Server. The SQL Server clients use this endpoint to execute queries.

- ◆ Database Mirroring: Supports communications between the parties in a database mirroring scenario. See Chapter 12, "Data Availability and Distribution," for more information on this feature.

- ◆ Service Broker: Provides the interface for submitting messages to SQL Server for queuing and orchestration.

Before you will be able to implement a Service Broker solution, you will have to first enable the Service Broker and create an endpoint.

Conversation   In Service Broker, a conversation is a persisted interaction between parties exchanging messages. All messages are persisted to the database queues, providing fault tolerance and recoverability of messages if necessary. Standard messaging patterns support numerous types of messaged conversations including:

- ◆ Fire and Forget: A strict one-way message where the sender does not care to ever get a response back from the queue process.

- ◆ Monolog: A one-way message where the sender only gets confirmation from the queue process and does not get any other data, nor will it respond to the confirmation.

- ◆ Dialog: A bidirectional communication, allowing both sender and queue processes to send and receive messages.

SQL Server currently supports only dialog conversations in Service Broker. All queued messages are associated with a dialog. We will, therefore, use the term dialog and conversation interchangeably in this context.

Message Type   A message type is an actual database object that defines the characteristics of the message. Every message sent to a Service Broker endpoint must adhere to a specified message type. A message type can enforce any structure you need, or none at all. Structure enforcement is called validation. You can set the validation to NONE for a message type if you want to allow any message in any format, which is the default. You can also require an empty message, a well-formed XML message, or a schema-enforced message. The stronger the message type validation, the more overhead in processing the message.

Contract   A contract is an object that defines the structure of a conversation. Think of it as a script in a play. There is no improvisation in a Service Broker conversation. Everything is scripted. The contract supplies this script by stating which message types the initiator of the conversation will use and which the target of the conversation will use. This way, you can guarantee that the messages sent and received follow a very specific pattern and you can code the message-processing logic to that pattern.

Queue   A queue is a repository for messages. As a standard data structure, the concept of the queue implies a first-in/first-out process. An important part of any message queuing process is the reliable delivery of messages and the preservation of order of arrival. SQL Server Service Broker queues enforce both of these characteristics.

SQL Server 2008 implements queues as tables. After enabling the Service Broker on a server, you will be able to create queues. The action of creating a queue will automatically create the repository table in the target database.

Service   The service object brings together a contract and a queue. When you create a service, you define a service name, and specify the contract and queue that will be associated with that service. Any party that wants to enter into a Service Broker dialog must reference a service. Because the service defines the contract and queue, there is no ambiguity as to the server artifacts or the contract that the parties will use.

Multiple services can use the same queue, but by doing so, they are agreeing to abide by the contracts enforced by the queue. Because more than one service can use a queue and potentially there may be more than one conversation using the service at any given time, there has to be a way for the message processor on the SQL Server to keep the conversations separate. It does this through the use of a conversation handle, which is a tag that identifies each conversation thread and ensures that they are kept separate.

To reiterate an important point, all of the items in the preceding list are actually persistent objects in the database. Therefore, there is a syntax for creating artifacts such as a message type, queue, service, and so on. Because these are actually database objects, they are persisted in system tables and recoverable. This gives the SQL Server Service Broker model a degree of reliability that is critically important to ensure guaranteed message delivery, persistence, and processing.

The messages are processed from the queue by stored procedures, which extract messages from the queue and perform any necessary subsequent processing on them to meet the logic or workflow needs of the service. Because each processing stored procedure could in turn start conversations with other services, it is easy to build very granular and composable models. For example, the client could send a message to one service, which would in turn parse the message and begin dialogs with other services to do the ultimate processing. The client would be completely unaware that this is happening because they would see only the single service point with which they interact.

Service Broker Workflow Scenario

To better understand what Service Broker provides to the enterprise, let's consider a scenario. Assume that you are the architect for an application for a corporate travel department. When an employee needs to book travel, they may only want an airline ticket or a hotel, but usually more than one service will be required. We will assume that our department supports booking for air travel, hotels, and rental cars.

One of our goals is to ensure that the application operates asynchronously. Because the process of getting confirmations can be quite lengthy, we do not want the employee to have to stay connected to the application to wait for a response. A confirmation will be emailed to their corporate address once it is generated. We will also assume that this will be a web-based application, so that it is available to employees anywhere. Figure 20.4 illustrates the flow of the application.

FIGURE 20.4

A sample flow

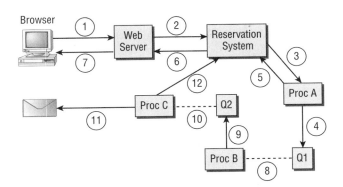

1. The employee uses a browser to connect to the web server and submit a travel request using a web page.

2. The web page extracts the data from the request and sends it to the main reservation system.

3. The reservation system calls a stored procedure in the database and passes parameters extracted from the request.

4. Proc A is responsible for organizing the parameters into a message, starting a conversation with a service, and sending the message, which is placed in a queue labeled Q1.

5. Once the message is sent to the queue, Proc A has completed its work and responds to the reservation system.

6. The reservation system informs the web application that the travel request is in process.

7. The web application sends a response to the browser that the travel request is in process.

8. Concurrently with steps 5 through 7, another procedure on the server, Proc B, is monitoring the queue. When the message is at the top of the queue, Proc B reads and processes the message, performing the requested action.

9. Once Proc B is finished with its work, it places a confirmation message into another queue, labeled Q2.

10. Proc C monitors Q2 and, when able, reads the message.

11. Proc C sends an email confirmation through SQL Server Database Mail to the employee.

12. Concurrent with step 11, Proc C also notifies the reservation system that the travel request has been processed and confirmed.

Although it looks complex, this scenario illustrates some important points about Service Broker. First, the data flow needed to handle the data-side work of processing a request is implemented as an asynchronous service. Proc B is the one handling all of the real processing, but none of the other application components ever talks directly to Proc B. Instead, the procedure is encapsulated behind queues. It gets its workload from a queue and reports its results to a queue. If the logic inside Proc B is time consuming, all incoming and outgoing flows are isolated from this because all interactions with Proc B are placed inside queues.

This is just one example. There are limitless variations on this architecture, and you can define a solution that will satisfy a wide array of needs. If the application requires decoupled components and/or asynchronous processing, the Service Broker model could provide you with the functionality that you require without complicating the architecture with third-party solutions.

 **Real World Scenario**

SERVICE BROKER IN ACTION

We have seen many variations of different Service Broker architecture. Because every client is different, so are the Service Broker implementations that meet their needs. This case study is about one such client. We will call them ABC Corp.

ABC Corp is a manufacturer of injection mold plastics. Their business model requires significant participation in their operations from clients. Although ABC Corp does provide value-added manufacturing services, they could also be considered to be a clearinghouse, matching the needs of clients with the products designed by other clients. Therefore, their clients fall into two categories. Some have developed product designs but have no production facilities, while others are looking to purchase completed products.

ABC Corp wanted to have an application that could automate the process of tracking their process. This process could follow two different paths. In one case, the designer of a product could submit the product specifications to ABC Corp so that they could market the design to their clients. Another option is that a client could identify their product needs to ABC Corp, who could then attempt to locate a design firm who could model the solution. Once a match was found, ABC Corp acted as the intermediary and managed the actual production of the product.

In the past, the process of tracking progress had been a very manual one. Although a variety of collaborative architectural options were available, this was a good opportunity to design a Service Broker solution. The most important aspect of this solution was that it must be asynchronous and completely reliable. Clients must be able to submit progress reports to ABC Corp at any time; ABC Corp would then in turn update schedules internally within the ABC system and send update messages to the corresponding client.

The solution consisted of three main queues. One was for inbound messages from clients. There was a specific message type that indicated a progress update from a requester versus a designer. Both of these message types were dropped into the same queue via a web page that called a stored procedure to place the message into the queue.

The second queue was for internal processing. This queue had a variety of message types that were used to represent specific stages of design and production. The final queue was an outbound queue that was used to trigger a response to a client concerning the progress of the process. This was all integrated with their production system and project management system, but because a Service Broker solution was used instead of direct component communications, the system was extremely fault tolerant of outages at any point in the solution.

While this solution could have been designed using a variety of different technologies such as BizTalk, MSMQ, and SharePoint, the fact that all of the plumbing already existed in SQL Server was compelling. With very little code to glue it all together, the client got a very tolerant and decoupled system that took advantage of all of the features and benefits that SQL Server had to offer.

Implementing Service Broker

Before you can create any Service Broker artifacts, you must first enable the Service Broker. You can do this using either a Transact-SQL (TSQL) statement or using the SQL Server Management Studio (SSMS) interface. Assuming that you wanted to enable the Service Broker for the AdventureWorks2008 database, you would use the following TSQL statement.

```
USE master;
GO
ALTER DATABASE AdventureWorks2008 SET ENABLE_BROKER;
GO
```

Alternatively, you can use SSMS. Access the Database Properties window with a right-click on the database in the SSMS Object Explorer and select Properties from the menu. Go to the Options page and change the value of the Broker Enabled option, as illustrated in Figure 20.5.

FIGURE 20.5

Enabling the
Service Broker

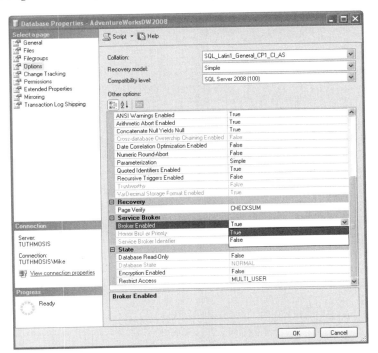

Creating Service Broker Components

Because the components of Service Broker are persistent database artifacts, you must create them before you can use them in a conversation. In this section, we will walk through the process of creating the artifacts necessary to implement a Service Broker solution.

CREATING MESSAGE TYPES

A message type is a template for a message. It can be very simple or it can require compliance with a very strict XML schema depending on your application requirements. This statement creates two simple nonvalidated message types owned by the dbo user.

```
USE AdventureWorks2008;
GO
CREATE MESSAGE TYPE ProductRequest
  AUTHORIZATION dbo
  VALIDATION = NONE;
GO
CREATE MESSAGE TYPE ProductResponse
  AUTHORIZATION dbo
  VALIDATION = NONE;
GO
```

You can also configure message type validation if you like. To validate the messages, use the following values for the VALIDATION clause of the previous statement:

◆ NONE: This is the default. No message validation is performed.

◆ EMPTY: The body of the message must be empty. This is useful for acknowledgement messages that contain no data.

◆ WELL_FORMED_XML: The body of the message must be a well-formed XML document.

◆ VALID_XML WITH SCHEMA COLLECTION <collection_name>: Requires the body of the message to be a well-formed XML document that complies with the named XML schema collection.

HANDLING XML VALIDATION

Validation rules for XML documents are typically stored in schemas. These schemas are XML files that describe the valid contents of the target document. You can store schemas in SQL Server using an XML Schema Collection. This process is discussed in more detail in Chapter 7, "SQL Server and XML."

You can view existing message types in the SSMS Object Explorer. If you open your database node in the explorer interface, you will see a Service Broker node. Expanding this node will present a list of the supported Service Broker artifacts. Open the desired list to see your artifacts. Remember that you may have to refresh the node to see any objects created since the last connection or refresh.

You will also notice a list of system message types in this list as well. If you expand this list, you will see some very useful message types defined at the system level to do things such as end a dialog, report an error, or handle conversation timeouts.

CREATING CONTRACTS

A contract is the message script. It indicates which party in the conversation can send which messages. You must create the message types before you can create the contract because the contract will reference the message types. A contract that uses the two previous message types might look like this:

```
USE AdventureWorks2008;
GO
CREATE CONTRACT ProductInformationContract
  AUTHORIZATION dbo
  (
    ProductRequest SENT BY INITIATOR,
    ProductResponse SENT BY TARGET
  );
GO
```

If a conversation is based on a particular contract, only those message types can be exchanged in that contract. However, regardless of the contract, any conversation can include the following system message types:

- http://schemas.microsoft.com/SQL/ServiceBroker/DialogTimer

- http://schemas.microsoft.com/SQL/ServiceBroker/Error

- http://schemas.microsoft.com/SQL/ServiceBroker/EndDialog

ANOTHER CONVENTION

Notice the names used for the system messages. They are in a URI format. If you think about it, this makes sense. Because a message type can enforce a particular XML schema, it would make sense to use the URI of the schema as the message type. This is certainly not required, as you will note from the example that we used, but it can make it easier to relate the message type back to its correlating schema.

CREATING QUEUES

A queue is the repository for the messages that are sent via a contract. When a message is sent from an initiator to a target, it is not actually sent directly to a target process, but rather to a target queue. Service Broker can then activate a procedure to process the messages in the queue when they arrive, or a scheduled/manual process can extract the messages from the queue and process the messages as required. When creating the queue, you will provide information such as:

- Queue name

- Active status

- Message retention

- Procedure activation

In this example, we will create two queues, a request queue and a response queue. Messages from the service initiator to the target will go into the request queue, while messages from the target back to the initiator will go in the response queue. Additionally, the target procedure could act as initiator to send messages to another queue, as in the travel scenario previously described. This flexibility is what provides the requisite service isolation. The following code creates these two queues.

```
USE AdventureWorks2008;
GO
CREATE QUEUE dbo.ProductRequestQueue
WITH
        STATUS = ON,
        RETENTION = OFF;
GO
CREATE QUEUE dbo.ProductResponseQueue
WITH
        STATUS = ON,
        RETENTION = OFF;
GO
```

These queues are started when created. You can enable and disable the queues by using an ALTER QUEUE statement and changing the STATUS value. These queues also delete the messages after the service processes them. They are not retained in the queue. Destructive reading helps keep a stateless service and a good service should never require that a message is read more than once.

When you create the queue, you are actually creating a SQL Server table. These tables do not appear in the SSMS tables list, but they are there and you can select from them if needed. This is a convenient way to verify that messages are being sent to the queue. If you execute the following statements, you should see two empty tables that correspond to the queues.

```
USE AdventureWorks2008;
GO
SELECT * FROM dbo.ProductRequestQueue;
SELECT * FROM dbo.ProductResponseQueue;
GO
```

It is also possible for a queue to be configured so that a procedure will activate anytime a message enters the queue. This is called activation, and you can control this behavior using an optional ACTIVATION section in the CREATE QUEUE statement. Suppose that you have a stored procedure called dbo.ProcessProductRequest that you want to execute when a message enters the queue. Further assume that you expect a somewhat active queue and would like up to five instances of this stored procedure running at any given time to process incoming messages. The queue code would now look like this:

```
USE AdventureWorks2008;
GO
CREATE QUEUE dbo.ProductRequestQueue
WITH
     STATUS = ON,
```

```
        RETENTION = OFF,
        ACTIVATION (
                STATUS = ON,
                PROCEDURE_NAME = dbo.ProcessProductRequest,
                MAX_QUEUE_READERS = 5,
                EXECUTE AS OWNER
        );
    GO
```

One important feature of this code is the EXECUTE AS statement. You must specify an execution context. Your options are SELF (the default), OWNER, and an explicitly provided user identity. If you use automatic activation, be sure to think through the security context of the procedure that will handle the queue and make sure that the user identity has the rights to perform the actions required by the service.

CREATING A SERVICE

Now we finally have all of the pieces in place to create a service. The service is the union of a queue and a contract. The service TSQL is very simple. To create a service using the previously created objects, you would use the following code:

```
USE AdventureWorks2008;
GO
CREATE SERVICE ProductInfoRequestService
     AUTHORIZATION dbo
     ON QUEUE dbo.ProductRequestQueue (
             ProductInformationContract
     );
GO
CREATE SERVICE ProductInfoInitiatorService
     AUTHORIZATION dbo
     ON QUEUE dbo.ProductResponseQueue;
GO
```

Notice that in this code, only the request service implements a contract. That is because the conversation is restricted to being started by the initiator of the request. In this case, the response queue would simply accept confirmation messages. This will become clearer as we look at the code that processes the messages.

CREATING ENDPOINTS AND ROUTES

SQL Server uses endpoints for remote communications. What this means to you is that if you are going to have the initiator and target of a service in the same server, you do not have to create an endpoint. The messages will automatically be locally routed. However, if you want a stored procedure on one server to initiate a conversation with a procedure on another server, you will have to define an endpoint for the communication.

You cannot create endpoints with the SQL Server Management Studio. Your only option is to use TSQL. Although the illustrations in this book will not require endpoints, as all communications will take place on a single server, we will walk you through this process so you can see all of the steps involved. When you create a Service Broker endpoint, you will define the following.

◆ Owner

◆ Initial state

◆ Protocol

◆ Authentication mechanism

◆ Encryption mechanism

◆ Message forwarding behavior for messages received that are intended for other services

As an example, the following script creates a Service Broker endpoint called SampleEndpoint, which is owned by the sa login. This endpoint listens on port 10000 for any IP address on the machine. Its initial state will be "started" immediately upon creation. Authentication to this endpoint will be Windows-based NTLM by default, but you could have also used Kerberos authentication or an X.509 certificate. This endpoint also supports, but does not require, encryption. Any encryption will require the AES algorithm. Message forwarding is disabled, meaning that if a message is delivered to the endpoint for a service that does not reside behind that endpoint, the message will be deleted rather than forwarded. Here is the code:

```
USE master;
GO
CREATE ENDPOINT SampleEndpoint Authorization sa
STATE = STARTED
AS TCP (
        LISTENER_PORT = 10000
)
FOR SERVICE_BROKER (
        AUTHENTICATION = WINDOWS,
        ENCRYPTION = SUPPORTED ALGORITHM AES,
        MESSAGE_FORWARDING = DISABLED
);
GO
```

The DROP and ALTER statements work just like standard Data Definition statements. For example, assuming that you have permissions to do so, the statement DROP ENDPOINT SampleEndpoint will drop the endpoint. The ALTER statement uses the same syntax as the CREATE statement.

When you send a message to a service, SQL Server assumes that the message is directed to a local service unless there is a specific route configured to direct the message to an alternative location. Therefore, if you need to send a message to a remote server, you will need to configure a route that specifies where messages for a specific service will be sent. The following is an example of static route code. Because these artifacts do not exist in our samples, this code will execute, but it provides no useful function at this time.

```
USE AdventureWorks2008;
GO
```

```
CREATE ROUTE SampleRoute
     AUTHORIZATION dbo
WITH
     SERVICE_NAME = 'SampleService',
     BROKER_INSTANCE = 'BD8CA34B-1409-4AD9-A57A-08CFA96AE283',
     LIFETIME = 1200,
     ADDRESS  = 'TCP://192.168.1.1:10000';
```

In this example, we see a route called SampleRoute created in the context of the AdventureWorks2008 database. Any service message that is sent from this database to a service called SampleService will use this route. The address clause specifies the address of the remote service. Note that there must be an endpoint explicitly created at this IP address and listening on this port number or the message delivery will fail. This example also uses a LIFETIME clause indicating how long SQL Server will consider this route active. This value is measured in seconds. When the route times out, SQL Server purges it from the system. Omitting this clause will create a permanent route in the system.

There is also a clause called BROKER_INSTANCE in the preceding code. Remember that when you enable Service Broker, you do it at the database level. That means that every database can have its own Service Broker instance. If the same service name exists in multiple databases on different Service Broker instances, there may be problems matching to the correct service when the server endpoint receives the message. This clause uniquely identifies the Service Broker instance on the target server to which the message will be directed. You can get this information by running the following query in the target database:

```
SELECT service_broker_guid
FROM sys.databases
WHERE database_id = DB_ID()
```

Getting It Straight

This can all get very confusing when you start routing services together in a many-to-many relationship across multiple services, so it is very important that you understand exactly what you are executing and at which location. Here is a quick reminder list:

◆ Endpoints are server level and exist on the server that is the target of a message.

◆ Routes are database level and exist in the imitator database; they include the values that indicate the location of the target service.

◆ All other objects are database level and refer to local resources used to define repository or contract characteristics of the service.

If you have been doing these exercises as you follow along, you should have numerous Service Broker objects in your AdventureWorks2008 database. For the next examples, we will be using a simplified version of this script with different names to distinguish these objects from the versions that we previously created. Listing 20.1 contains the complete script that the next section assumes. Please note that there is no need to enable the Service Broker if you have already done so. Trying to execute the statement again can cause the query to hang.

LISTING 20.1   A Service Broker Setup

```
-- Enable Service Broker
USE master;
GOALTER DATABASE AdventureWorks2008
  SET ENABLE_BROKER;
GO
USE AdventureWorks2008;
GO
-- Create the Message Types
CREATE MESSAGE TYPE
  [//Sample/RequestMessage]
  VALIDATION = WELL_FORMED_XML;
CREATE MESSAGE TYPE
  [//Sample/ReplyMessage]
  VALIDATION = WELL_FORMED_XML;
GO

-- Create the Contract
CREATE CONTRACT [//Sample/SampleContract]
  ([//Sample/RequestMessage]
  SENT BY INITIATOR,
  [//Sample/ReplyMessage]
  SENT BY TARGET
  );
GO

-- Create the Queues and Services
CREATE QUEUE TargetQueue;
CREATE SERVICE
  [//Sample/TargetService]
  ON QUEUE TargetQueue
  ([//Sample/SampleContract]);
GO

CREATE QUEUE InitiatorQueue;

CREATE SERVICE
  [//Sample/InitiatorService]
  ON QUEUE InitiatorQueue;
GO
```

Constructing a Service Broker Dialog

It's time to wire these objects together. In our examples, we will be using scripts that you will execute yourself so that you can see the results of your actions. In the real world, it is more likely that you will do this inside stored procedures that are called by various application components.

The process consists of three major steps. First, you send the message from the initiator to the target service. Second, you process the request on the target service and send a response. Finally, you will capture the response message in the initiator service and act accordingly.

INITIATING THE CONVERSATION

The first step is to send the initial message to the target service. Although the messages could contain any kind of data, they typically will contain a message body consisting of XML data. The code to perform this operation looks like Listing 20.2.

LISTING 20.2   Initiating the Conversation

```
USE AdventureWorks2008;
GO

DECLARE @hDialog UNIQUEIDENTIFIER;
DECLARE @message NVARCHAR(100);

BEGIN TRANSACTION;

BEGIN DIALOG @hDialog
  FROM SERVICE
  [//Sample/InitiatorService]
  TO SERVICE
  N'//Sample/TargetService'
  ON CONTRACT
  [//Sample/SampleContract]
  WITH
    ENCRYPTION = OFF;

SELECT @message = N'<ProductID>506</ProductID>';

SEND ON CONVERSATION @hDialog
  MESSAGE TYPE
  [//Sample/RequestMessage]
  (@message);

SELECT 'Message Sent to Target'
COMMIT TRANSACTION;
GO
```

The first thing that this code does is define some variables. The @hDialog variable represents the conversation handle. This is a unique identifier that Service Broker uses to keep track of each individual conversation. Because a single service may be participating in multiple conversations at the same time, this ensures conversation identity. The @message variable will store the content of the message that will enter the queue.

Next you begin a transaction. This is not required, but the send message process can be transactional. Note, however, that if the target service is unavailable for delivery, this does not constitute an error. Instead, the message will be held in the initiator queue until it can be sent. This behavior is critical to the asynchronous nature of the Service Broker. You do not want to have to wait for a response; that would be considered synchronous behavior.

The next section begins the dialog. Because the contract states that the initiator of the dialog must begin with a message of type //Sample/RequestMessage, the message that you send must adhere to this requirement. In this case, the only requirement for the message type is that it is a well-formed XML document. Remember that you can, however, require that the message adhere to a specific schema contract. Because the server called "TargetService" is not identified in any specific route as a remote service, the assumption that SQL Server makes is that it is a local service. As a result, this message never actually leaves this SQL Server, so there is no need for encryption.

You might also note that the statement that begins the dialog does not actually mention the queues by name. The queues are abstracted by the contract. When you send a message in a specific contract, the queues are assumed as they are part of the contract definition. When you process a message, as you will see in the next code sample, you will read the message directly from the queue.

The next statement loads the body of the message into the @message variable. Again, this message is a well-formed XML document. The intention is to send a ProductID to the service and have the service return the name of the product associate with that ID. The message represents a packet of information needed to execute the task. This example is hard-coded, but if this were a stored procedure you could easily pass the value in as a parameter.

Finally, you can send the message. Notice that you reference both the dialog handle and the message type. This statement must comply with the previous code that began the dialog. It was that code that defined the dialog handle and the contract that the message would use. At this point, assuming that you can at least successfully persist the message to the local queue for transmission, the transaction will commit and the process is complete. Unlike synchronous requests, this process is not going to actively wait for the service to reply. It is unknown how long that might take. Instead, it can go about its business until a message arrives in its queue from the target service.

Because the queue is implemented in a table structure, you can easily verify that the message has arrived by selecting from the queue. In this way, you could interpret the send message operation as an insert into the queue. The message is now persisted and is just as fault tolerant as all the rest of your SQL Server data structures.

A TABLE, BUT NOT REALLY

The queue is essentially a table, but SQL Server is a little stubborn about presenting it to you that way. If you look in the Object Explorer in the Tables node, you will not see the queue in the list. You can select from it using TSQL, but the editor will underline the name of the queue in red, saying that it is not a recognized object—yet the query executes just fine. You cannot perform other standard table operations. If you try to do a truncate table operation on the queue, you will get a very curt error message stating that you are trying to perform a table operation on a queue. Even with all of this, at the end of the day, the queue is still just a table.

Processing the Message

Now that the message has been entered into the target queue, it is time for the target service to take over. If you created the target queue using activation with a stored procedure, it should automatically fire when the message arrives. Otherwise, you can use a procedure or script that is scheduled or runs manually to process the content of the queue.

In our example, we want to extract the ProductID from the inbound message and use it in a query to select the corresponding ProductName from the database. The script in Listing 20.3 will perform this processing. Note that the extraction of the ProductID value from the message uses an XQuery expression. These are documented in Chapter 7, so refer there if you need help understanding that code.

LISTING 20.3   Processing the Message

```
USE AdventureWorks2008;
GO

DECLARE @hDialog UNIQUEIDENTIFIER;
DECLARE @message NVARCHAR(100);
DECLARE @messageType sysname;

BEGIN TRANSACTION;

WAITFOR
( RECEIVE TOP(1)
  @hDialog = conversation_handle,
  @message = message_body,
  @messageType = message_type_name
  FROM TargetQueue
), TIMEOUT 1000;

IF @messageType =
  N'//Sample/RequestMessage'
BEGIN
  DECLARE @messagexml xml;
  DECLARE @ProductID int;
  DECLARE @ProductName nvarchar(100);
  SET @messagexml = @message;

  SELECT @ProductID = @messagexml.value('(//ProductID)[1]', 'int');
  SELECT @ProductName = [Name] FROM Production.Product
    WHERE ProductID = @ProductID;

  DECLARE @ReplyMsg NVARCHAR(100);
  SELECT @ReplyMsg =
  N'<ReplyMsg>' + @ProductName + '</ReplyMsg>';
```

```
SEND ON CONVERSATION @hDialog
  MESSAGE TYPE
  [//Sample/ReplyMessage]
  (@ReplyMsg);

END CONVERSATION @hDialog;
END

COMMIT TRANSACTION;
GO
```

This script also begins with the declaration of variables. We will need to reference the dialog handle, the message content, and the message type. Because the message type is a system object, it uses a sysname datatype. The Receive method is the opposite of Send and is used to extract a message from the queue. In this example, we are loading data from the queued message into the variables previously declared. The WAITFOR statement indicates that the query is authorized to wait for a message to arrive if no message currently exists in the queue. The TIMEOUT option specifies how long it will wait. Express this duration in milliseconds.

Because we are explicitly receiving only one message, only the first message in the queue will return. If you do not use the TOP(1) expression, all of the messages that meet the criteria will return. Make sure that you either use TOP(1) or write code that can handle multiple messages safely.

You can also use a WHERE clause if you want to restrict the messages returned based on some criteria such as the conversation handle or the message type. This allows you to handle the possibility of multiple conversations, and even multiple contracts, in the same queue gracefully.

The body of this script is just plain TSQL. After extracting the ProductID from the message, you use that information to write a database query to get the return value that you need. The procedure then embeds this value in the response message and sends it back to the client. Now you should see why the initiator service does not require a contract. All of the contract-based enforcement is happening at the target queue. The initiator queue simply acts as a forward queue and a reply queue.

At the end of the script, the processor formally ends the dialog by using the END CONVERSATION statement. Remember that this is one of the system messages supported by all services regardless of the contract. This action informs the initiator that the target considers the work to be completed and the matter closed. As a result, the initiator will actually get back two messages. The first is the response required by the contract, while the second is the end dialog message that the system handles internally.

COMPLETING THE CONVERSATION

Once the target service completes its work and ends the dialog, the initiator queue has the information returned by the service. In our case, this should contain the name of the product embedded into an XML message. Because this is the data that you wanted all along, you must now receive the message from the queue and extract the required information. Listing 20.4 demonstrates how this is done.

LISTING 20.4   Completing the Conversation

```
USE AdventureWorks2008;
GO
DECLARE @message NVARCHAR(100);
DECLARE @hDialog UNIQUEIDENTIFIER;
BEGIN TRANSACTION;
WAITFOR
( RECEIVE TOP(1)
  @hDialog = conversation_handle,
  @message = message_body
  FROM InitiatorQueue
), TIMEOUT 1000;
END CONVERSATION @hDialog;
DECLARE @messagexml xml;
DECLARE @ProductName nvarchar(100);
SET @messagexml = @message;
SELECT @ProductName = @messagexml.value('(//ReplyMsg)[1]','nvarchar(100)');
SELECT 'The Product Name is ' + @ProductName as Result;
COMMIT TRANSACTION;
GO
```

This code is very similar to the previous example of processing the target queue, except in this case the script extracts the data from the initiator queue instead. Similarly, the return message is XML-based and contains a payload with the relevant information that you must extract. Also like the target, you do not have to process the response immediately. SQL Server persistently stored the messages, and you can extract them whenever convenient or necessary.

It is also important to note that the process that responds to the message does not have to be the same one that sent the original message to the target service. Any process that can see the initiator queue and understands how to interpret the data it contains is capable of processing the response message. This makes the entire sequence completely asynchronous. The original sender of the message is not required to check for a response at all, but rather it might submit the message solely for the benefit of another application than can manage the response.

GOOD SERVICES REVISITED

The fact that the original initiator does not have to be the ultimate handler of the response is very important. All parties involved in this process are completely independent of each other and the entire architecture is decoupled. The initiator does not need to know how the target service stores or accesses the needed data. As long as it adheres to the message contract, all is well. The target service also does not have to know anything about who will respond to the action, or how. As long as the contracts remain the same, the internal processing can change over time and each player goes on completely unaware that any alteration took place. Good services must be loosely coupled.

The Bottom Line

Describe service-oriented architecture.   Services are everywhere and almost all modern business applications provide at least some service structure. Some services are better than others, though. It all depends on how they are designed and implemented. It is important to understand the characteristics of a good service.

> **Master It**   For each of the following scenarios, identify which characteristic of a good service is being violated.
>
> 1. Joe creates a service that accepts a message containing numeric data from a client, calculates values from the numeric data, and prints the output on a local printer.
>
> 2. Mary creates a service that accepts login information from a user and then extracts user preference information from a database. Whenever the user connects again to the service, it reuses the preference information retrieved.
>
> 3. Bill creates a service that accepts a serialized SQLCommand object as a parameter. This command is then used by the service to select information from a database.

Design a solution using SQL Server Service Broker.   Service Broker uses message queuing architecture to decouple data services from each other. As opposed to other options such as linked server queries, the caller does not have to know anything about the implementation of the service at the target. Designing good service architecture takes practice, however. Different scenarios lend themselves to different solutions.

> **Master It**   For each of the design requirements listed here, specify which feature of Service Broker meets the architectural requirement in the design, or identify if Service Broker cannot meet this requirement.
>
> 1. Data tiers must be loosely coupled and should not expose any internal details outside of the data tier.
>
> 2. Message processing must be automated, ensuring that messages are handled as quickly and efficiently as possible.
>
> 3. The service must be able to handle multiple clients and must ensure its ability to identify each one.
>
> 4. The services must operate across multiple platforms and accept messages from clients running any operating system.

Implement Service Broker artifacts.   All of the components of a SQL Server Service Broker application are persisted database objects. They become part of the system dictionary of the initiating or target process. The dialogs that send and receive messages will use these artifacts for all data processing.

Master It For each of the following, identify the Service Broker artifact that satisfies the definition.

1. A special table structure where all messages are persistently stored.

2. The object that defines the required structure of a message.

3. Information regarding the location of a remote service.

4. A point of contact that accepts messages from remote clients.

5. An object that provides a script for the message pattern.

Full-Text Search Services

Storing large amounts of text in a database is becoming more common. When Microsoft introduced the MAX option for character datatypes as a replacement for the text datatype, they also significantly simplified the process of storing and retrieving large volumes of text data in a database. The challenge now is dealing with all of that data. As the amount of data grows, the data becomes more cumbersome.

SQL Server Full-Text services provide the ability to work with large text-based data blocks more easily and efficiently. These services include special indexes that allow more efficient access to data within large blocks of text, as well as query structures and keywords that you can use to take advantage of the indexes. Together, they provide a much more robust vehicle for working with text data than can be provided with standard indexes and queries.

Although this feature it not new, SQL Server 2008 has significant improvements to the full-text service set that provide substantial benefits in performance, maintainability, and storage efficiency as compared with earlier versions. In this chapter, you will learn to:

- ◆ Explain and apply full-text architecture in SQL Server 2008

- ◆ Implement full-text indexes

- ◆ Write queries utilizing full-text features of SQL Server 2008

Full-Text Architecture

The Full-Text Engine in SQL Server provides two services, indexing and querying. These two services go hand-in-hand to provide text-based query support. Tightly integrated with the SQL Server query engine and query optimizer, the full-text architecture in SQL Server 2008 provides an integrated and transparent text service for searching through large amounts of text and retrieving data based on those searches. Although the Full-Text Engine executes under a separate daemon (background) process, it is entirely transparent to the user thanks to this integration.

To best understand the functionality and implementation of the full-text service, you must first get a feel for its architecture. In this section, you will be introduced to the terminology of the full-text service, examine the underlying architecture, and see how that architecture supports the querying infrastructure.

Full-Text Terminology

The full-text infrastructure augments the standard SQL Server query architecture, and as a result uses a number of terms that are specific to text-based searching. Some of these terms are industry standards and others are specific to the Microsoft implementation. The following is a list of the most important concepts and terms.

Full-Text Index A full-text index is a token-based index that SQL Server uses to track the occurrence of words and word-forms in blocks of unstructured text. You are allowed to create only one full-text index per table. You are required to have a unique, single-column index on the table that contains the full-text index so that the indexed text data associates correctly with a row identity.

Full-text indexes are shreds of the text data for each row in the table. The text-patterns correlate to the unique key value for each row, thus enabling the query processor to filter rows based on text patterns embedded within the data. Full-text index structures are, therefore, very different from standard indexes.

Full-Text Catalog The catalog is a collection of full-text indexes. A single database can have one or more full-text catalogs. A catalog both aggregates indexes together for administration and provides common property values for the elements in the collection. For example, by rebuilding an entire catalog, you will be rebuilding each index associated with the catalog, using the properties that are common to that catalog. The catalog also aggregates permissions, allowing you to set access permissions at the catalog level and thereby control access to the indexes themselves.

Search Filter You can store text and/or binary data in a variety of ways and using many alternative formats. Usually a file extension or some other metadata identifier will inform any person or service that interacts with the data about the format and structure. Data stored in a text field is the same way. It could be XML data or some other text-based structure, or even a binary representation.

Search filters are full-text components that interpret binary data based on its structure and format. You can create a special column in your table called a type column that will store an identifier for the data in the form of a file extension that the Full-Text Engine can use to process the data. For example, if the type column stores the value "doc," this would indicate a Microsoft Word file type and the engine would process the data stored in the associated VarBinary(MAX) column using an MSWord Filter. For security reasons, this filter processing is done out-of-process in SQL Server using a filter daemon called `fdhost.exe`, which runs under a separate user identity specified on installation.

Stopwords Many words in any language are common and provide no meaningful benefit for searching. In the English language, for example, the articles "the," "a," and "an" are commonly found in text passes, but they provide no real benefit for searching or implying context. They are called stopwords because they bloat the index and can interfere with the query processing. By excluding stopwords, the resulting index is more efficient.

Stoplist A collection of stopwords is a stoplist. SQL Server Full-Text services allow you to create and customize your own stoplists. This is extremely convenient if common usage in your business requires that new words receive the same treatment as traditional stopwords. For example, if your company manufactures widgets, then everything in your product catalog will probably use the word widget. Although this word might be a useful filter term in some cases, if it is too common and is not a basis for further selectivity, you might consider "widget" to be a stopword. In SQL Server 2008, you would simply add the term to the custom stoplist, thereby excluding it from the index.

Word Breakers Every language has certain characters or structures that delimit the words in the language. When you read a written passage, your eye passes by them automatically, but your brain processes the fact that you are now reading a new word. These characters or structures are called breakers. Because they are particular to the language, they are automatically loaded for each supported language in SQL Server. In SQL Server, the full-text component that is responsible for identifying words in a stream of text is also called the Word Breaker.

Word Stemmer Most language comes from a core base of common words or concepts, and through word-forms or conjugation, new words form. For example, the infinitive verb form "to walk" is the common stem for all forms of the word such as "walked" or "walking" as well as a noun form as in "going for a walk." Finding the common stems of these words is critical for determining context. The set of rules that determine how these word forms are identified are called stemmers. Likewise, the SQL Server service that performs this process is also known as the Stemmer.

Population The process of loading a full-text index structure is called population. SQL Server 2008 supports three modes of population. They are full, incremental, and update. Full population will repopulate the entire index. Incremental population only increments modified rows based on timestamp values, and update will populate the index using a change tracking record of modified data since the last index population. Unlike standard SQL Server indexes that are automatically maintained whenever a data modification occurs, full-text indexes can be populated in a batch using a manual Transact-SQL command or a scheduled job to alleviate real-time pressure.

Architecture

Executing a query using a full-text clause initiates a series of events that are somewhat different than standard query processing. Although every database is enabled by default for full-text handling, you must first create full-text indexes before you can use the associated query statements that perform text-based searches. Architecturally, these indexes are very different from standard indexes. Table 21.1 illustrates the primary differences between the two index forms.

TABLE 21.1   The Differences Between Standard and Full-Text Indexes

FEATURE	STANDARD INDEXES	FULL-TEXT INDEXES
Number of indexes per table	One clustered index and over 200 non-clustered indexes allowed per table	Only one full-text index is allowed on any table
Index Currency	Dynamic index updating with every data modification	Static or dynamic index updating allows population automatically or on request
Organization	Uses SQL Server allocated disk space but is not otherwise aggregated	Also uses SQL Server allocated disk space and aggregated into catalogs

---

NEW FEATURE ALERT

The following features may be different from the full-text implementation you are working with now.

First, the Full-Text Engine is now automatically installed. Depending on how far back you go with earlier versions of SQL Server, you may remember doing an additional installation for SQL Server Full-Text Search Services. In SQL Server 2008, as with the two versions before it, the Full-Text engine is part of the standard installer. You simply have to include it as part of the installation process. If you install Full-Text with the standard installer, you will have to configure the service account that SQL Server uses for the out-of-process daemons that do the work of filtering the text.

Second, the full-text indexes are now part of the SQL Server database, as opposed to being external structures. In earlier versions of SQL Server, you would have to locate full-text indexes on disks structured outside of the database, meaning that they would have to be backed up separately from the database itself. This complicated recovery planning and implementation. Now, full-text indexes are backed up with every SQL Server backup process because they are included in the standard catalog. This is convenient, but it does mean that you need to manage your stoplists to keep the index from bloating and wasting SQL Server allocated disk space.

EXECUTION ARCHITECTURE

To this point, we have alluded to the fact that queries using full-text indexes will include special keywords to indicate that the query should be resolved using the full-text infrastructure. These keywords, including CONTAINS and FREETEXT, are implemented as filter operators, typically included in the WHERE clause of a query. When SQL Server sees these words, it flags the query as requiring additional compilation by the full-text compiler. The standard query execution can then occur in tandem with the full-text execution of the query.

If the index includes a column that stores binary data instead of simple text, the Full-Text Engine must rely on a filter to interpret the data appropriately. When you create the index, you will indicate the column in the table that stores the file-type extension. The index will also indicate which language or code page the data uses. This information provides the filter application with the information necessary to apply the correct filter and Word Breaker to the text data. Figure 21.1 illustrates this process.

INDEX ARCHITECTURE

The Full-Text Engine requires a standard index based on a unique key. This can either be a primary key on the table or another key that is a uniquely constrained or indexed column. The engine uses this key to correlate the filter results that the standard query engine and the full-text query engine generate.

As we previously mentioned, all full-text indexes are associated with a catalog. A database can have one or more catalogs. Each catalog defines shared properties, such as a population schedule. When you create a full-text index, you can specify the containing catalog. A full-text index cannot exist outside a catalog.

Because each table contains only one full-text index, that index must include all columns that contain text data that the engine will include in the search. You can only reference columns with a full-text operator if you have previously included the columns in a full-text index.

Loading an index with data is called *population*. This is also often referred to as a "crawl." The default population mechanism is to update the index as client queries make modification to the underlying data structure. While this is ideal from a concurrency perspective, ensuring that the index is always up-to-date, it can cause problems with update performance. For this reason, you also have the option of turning off automatic population and performing the process manually. The catalog contains a population schedule option that allows you to configure when this population occurs.

FIGURE 21.1

Full-text execution

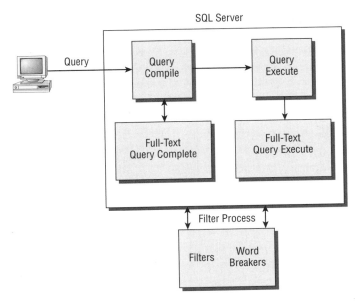

Creating Full-Text Indexes

The full-text infrastructure in SQL Server 2008 is significant, and it requires numerous artifacts to operate effectively. These artifacts include catalog indexes and stoplists. You must create and configure these artifacts before you will be able to take advantage of any full-text indexing features.

In this section, we will describe the process of creating these artifacts. You can create each of them with Transact-SQL (TSQL) code, or in many cases you can also use the SQL Server Management Studio (SSMS) interface. Where SSMS is an option, you have a combination of both dialogs and wizards included with SSMS to accomplish the tasks in question. We will discuss each of those approaches in the pages that follow.

Creating Stoplists

You should never introduce full-text indexing into a solution without some serious process planning. While a full-text index can provide an extra level of flexibility when working with unstructured text, the performance degradation and increased storage requirement can offset much of your gain if you do not properly plan your implementation. One of the resources that you can use to manage the performance of your full-text indexing infrastructure is the stoplist.

The stoplist is a collection of stopwords; these are language-specific words that the engine considers noise (nonrelevant) and are not included in the index. Every language implementation of full-text indexing in SQL Server has a system stoplist, which the engine uses if you do not provide a custom stoplist when you create an index. You can create stoplists either using TSQL code or with SSMS.

CREATING STOPLISTS WITH SSMS

The following example shows how to create a stoplist in SSMS. You will see from the example that a stoplist can extend an already existing stoplist. This is a very common practice. This way you can capture all of the words in a language-specific system stoplist and simply add to them. Alternatively, you can also base your new stoplist on another list located on this or another database.

1. Open the Object Explorer window and connect to the target database. As you drill into the database, you should see a node labeled Storage in the Folder list. Remember where this is located because from this point forward, we will simply refer to this as the storage node.

2. Expand the storage node. You should see a node underneath labeled Full Text Stoplists.

3. Create a new stoplist by right-clicking on this node and selecting New Full-Text Stoplist from the menu. The dialog in Figure 21.2 will appear. As the dialog shows, the basic configuration is very simple.

FIGURE 21.2

Creating the custom stoplist

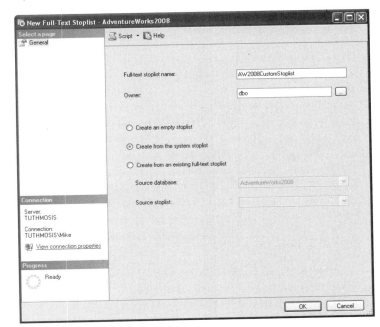

4. Give the stoplist a unique name, preferably something descriptive of the stoplist's purpose in the application. Specify the owner of the stoplist. At this point you can also assign rights to the stoplist to allow other users to modify the stoplist in the future if necessary.

5. Once you have configured the stoplist, click OK.

> Our stoplist is based on the system stoplist so that we will have a relevant starting point. Please note that the relationships between stoplists are static. If you base your stoplist on another stoplist, changes to the original stoplist will not modify your new list in any way.

6. The next step is to add stopwords to the list. Once you have created the stoplist, you can access the stoplist properties by right-clicking on that stoplist in SSMS and selecting Properties at the bottom of the menu. This will present a dialog like the one pictured in Figure 21.3. In our example, we will use the stoplist to filter words from an index that we will build on job applicant resumes stored in the database. (This may mean that words like "work" might be noise in a query.) Add the desired word and click OK in the dialog. This will add the word to your stoplist.

FIGURE 21.3
Adding stopwords

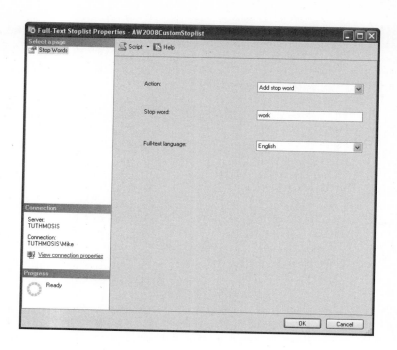

Unfortunately, SSMS does not display the stopwords; however, you can get this information by querying the `sys.fulltext_stopwords` system view. This view lists the stopwords based on the stoplist_id and the language. The English language ID is 1033, so if you were using English, you would execute the following query:

```
SELECT sw.stopword
FROM sys.fulltext_stopwords as sw
INNER JOIN    sys.fulltext_stoplists as sl
  ON sw.stoplist_id = sl.stoplist_id
WHERE language_id = 1033
  AND sl.name = 'AW2008CustomStoplist';
```

You can also use the Properties window pictured in Figure 21.3 to delete a stopword, delete all stopwords associated with a single language in the stoplist, or clear the entire stoplist. You do this by selecting an alternative verb in the Action dropdown list. Note that because this interface does not provide a list of stopwords, you will have to enter the stopword you want to delete if you want to remove a single entry. The preceding query is very convenient for this.

CREATING STOPLISTS WITH TSQL

The syntax for creating a stoplist is simple, but it varies a bit based on the source of the stoplist. The simplest form creates an empty stoplist that is not based on any other list. That syntax looks like this:

```
USE AdventureWorks2008;
CREATE FULLTEXT STOPLIST AW2008CustomStoplist;
GO
```

You can also base your stoplist on the system stoplist. This system stoplist contains the stopwords for all installed language options, which enables a single stoplist to be used with multiple language implementations. That syntax would look like this:

```
USE AdventureWorks2008;
CREATE FULLTEXT STOPLIST AW2008CustomStoplist
  FROM SYSTEM STOPLIST;
GO
```

Finally, you can also create the stoplist based on a stoplist located in this or any other database. The syntax is similar to basing the stoplist on the system and looks like this:

```
USE AdventureWorks2008;
CREATE FULLTEXT STOPLIST AW2008CustomStoplist
  FROM databasename.stoplistname;
GO
```

USING BASE STOPLISTS

If you find yourself adding the same words to custom stoplists over and over again, you may want to consider creating template lists. This procedure works very well in an environment where you may have many databases but they all use the same list. Create a stoplist in a reference database that is visible to all other database. Then whenever you need to create a new stoplist, base it on this reference list as opposed to the system stoplist. Although the relationship is not dynamic—meaning that adding a new word to the reference list will not automatically add the word to the referring lists—it will still provide a good starting point and ensure consistency among all stoplists in your infrastructure.

Of course, sometimes you want the stoplists to be different because they service different applications. If this is the case, you will have to decide if it takes more time to use the base list and make alterations or create a new list for every situation. Planning ahead can save you a lot of time in creating the lists.

Adding or dropping a word in the stoplist requires an ALTER statement as you are making a modification to the existing stoplist. The ALTER statement has two clauses, one for add and one for drop. The following code adds a word to the stoplist and then immediately drops that word in the subsequent statement.

```
USE AdventureWorks2008;
GO
ALTER FULLTEXT STOPLIST AW2008CustomStoplist
ADD 'Aardvark' LANGUAGE 'English';
GO
ALTER FULLTEXT STOPLIST AW2008CustomStoplist
DROP 'Aardvark' LANGUAGE 'English';
GO
```

If you want to drop this stoplist, use the following standard data definition statement:

```
DROP FULLTEXT STOPLIST AW2008CustomStoplist;
```

Creating a Full-Text Catalog

Because a catalog is simply a set of indexes, you should consider it similar to any other kind of aggregation object. The catalog aggregates the indexes and defines characteristics that are common to all of the indexes in the aggregation. Like any other aggregation, it also implements the "propagation of functionality" principle, which states that whatever action you take on the aggregation will be propagated to the members in the collection. For example, dropping the catalog will have the effect of dropping all of the indexes in the catalog.

As before, you can create the catalog either by using SSMS or using TSQL code. Because the artifact is a simple aggregation, both the dialog and code-based approaches reflect that simplicity.

CREATING CATALOGS WITH SSMS

The node for full-text catalogs is also in the storage node. To create a sample catalog, follow these steps.

1. Locate the Full Text Catalogs node in the Object Explorer and right-click the node.

2. Select New Full-Text Catalog from the menu, which will present the dialog pictured in Figure 21.4. This dialog is already completed for our sample catalog.

FIGURE 21.4
Creating the catalog

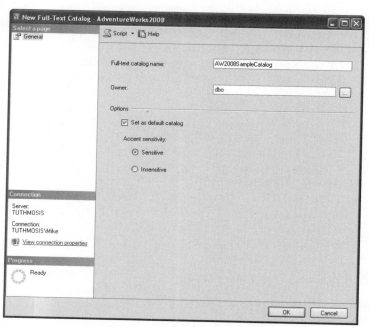

3. Specify whether the catalog will be considered the default. This is marked as the default, which means that if you create an index without specifying the catalog location of the index, it will assume that the index will be part of this catalog.

4. If desired, enable the Accent Sensitivity of the indexes in the catalog. If you are indexing data using languages that implement accent-specific behavior, you may want to enable

this option, because the same spelling of a word varied only by the accent can change the meaning or context of the word.

5. To create the catalog, click OK when you are done.

Now that you have created the catalog, you can specify the other catalog properties and modify the existing properties.

1. To access these properties, locate the new catalog in the list in the Object Explorer. Either double-click on the catalog name, or right-click and select Properties from the bottom of the menu to open the Catalog Properties dialog. This dialog contains three pages.

Figure 21.5 illustrates the content of the General page of the dialog. Most of these properties are read-only; however, you can modify the owner, accent sensitivity, and default properties. Other properties such as counts and population status are informational only and cannot be updated.

FIGURE 21.5

The General page of the Catalog Properties dialog

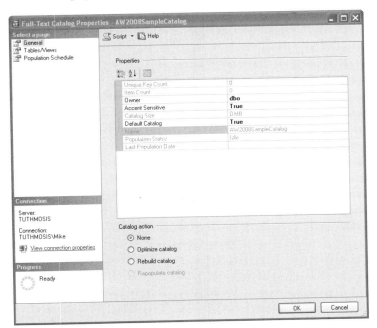

2. At the bottom of the dialog, you will also see a section labeled Catalog Action. Use this section if you want to perform an operation on the catalog, such as rebuilding the catalog or performing a repopulation. Notice that in our example, the option to repopulate is unavailable. This is because our catalog does not currently have any indexes to populate.

3. The third tab is labeled Population Schedule. (We will skip the Tables/Views tab for the time being, as that is the tab we would use to create the actual indexes in the catalog.) The Population Schedule tab, illustrated in Figure 21.6, provides a list of all registered schedules and allows you to enable and disable each schedule. You can also create a new schedule by clicking the New button at the bottom of the dialog.

THE SQL AGENT SERVICE

If you click the New button in the dialog box in Figure 21.6, you will see a very familiar-looking dialog—the SQL Agent Scheduling dialog. As you might expect, the full-text index population process, when scheduled, uses the SQL Agent service for all of its scheduling. Although this is good for you because you are already very familiar with the SQL Agent scheduling process, it also means that you must ensure that the service is running or the index crawls will not take place. We recommend configuring the service to autostart when the server starts. If you need a refresher on the SQL Agent service and its configuration, refer to Chapter 11, "Using the SQL Server Agent Service," which covers the service in detail.

FIGURE 21.6
Setting the index population schedule

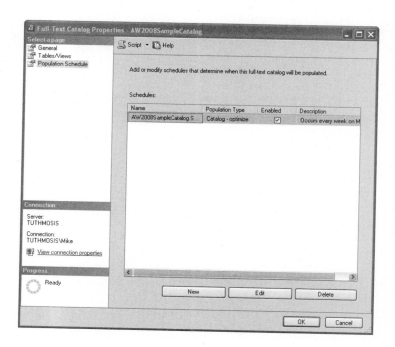

CREATING CATALOGS WITH TSQL

You can also create a catalog through code. You have a few more options available to you if you create the catalog this way. The syntax structure for creating a catalog looks like this:

```
CREATE FULLTEXT CATALOG catalog_name
  [ON FILEGROUP filegroup ]
  [IN PATH 'rootpath']
  [WITH <catalog_option>]
  [AS DEFAULT]
  [AUTHORIZATION owner_name ]
<catalog_option>::=
  ACCENT_SENSITIVITY = {ON|OFF}
```

As you look at this syntax, you will see two options that the graphical UI does not support. The first is the FILEGROUP option and the other is the IN PATH option. Staring with SQL Server 2008, these two statements have no effect. This is why they are not available in the graphical UI. They are deprecated and should be removed from any existing scripts or applications if you are upgrading the full-text components from an earlier version of SQL Server.

Using the preceding syntax, you would create a catalog identical to the one that we created in the previous example by using this code:

```
USE AdventureWorks2008;
GO
CREATE FULLTEXT CATALOG AW2008SampleCatalog
WITH ACCENT_SENSITIVITY = ON
AS DEFAULT
AUTHORIZATION dbo;
GO
```

There is no code for creating the schedule specific to full-text indexing. Because all scheduling is performed using the SQL Agent service, you would use the DDL code associated with the SQL Agent service to create the appropriate schedule. You can also use the SQL Agent UI or create the schedule from the full-text catalog as previously described.

Creating Full-Text Indexes

Now that the supporting artifacts are in place, it is time to create the actual indexes. Once again, you can do this using either SSMS or TSQL code. If you choose to use SSMS, you have two options available to you. The UI provides a page in the Catalog Properties dialog called Tables\Views that allows you to create an index directly in the catalog. There is also a wizard that walks you through the process of creating the index and the catalog at the same time. This is one of many wizards and administrative tools that are available directly through the Object Explorer.

CREATING FULL-TEXT INDEXES WITH SSMS

If you have already created the catalog, the simplest way to create the full-text index is to go back to the catalog entry in the Object Explorer.

1. Double-click on the catalog node in the list to display the Catalog properties. The page of the catalog that supports the full-text indexing is Tables/Views. It is somewhat misnamed. This page will actually create the index rather than merely associate the table with the catalog. Figure 21.7 illustrates this page of the dialog.

In this dialog, the HumanResources.JobCandidate table is in the list of indexed tables. Because you are allowed only one full-text index per table, it is not necessary to name the index. You can simply refer to the table that contains the index.

2. Use the Unique Index dropdown list to select which index will be used for correlating the table structure with the full-text index.

3. If more than one index is available, select the index that is least likely to contend with other table operations. Note that a table is not eligible for full-text indexing unless there is a unique key on the table.

FIGURE 21.7
Adding an index
to a catalog

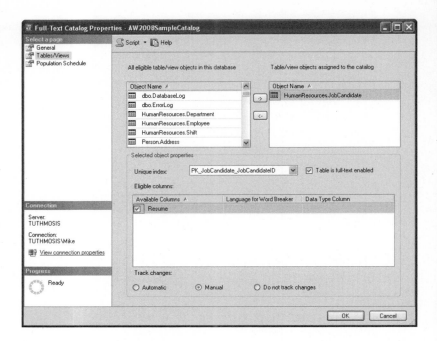

4. Choose the columns in the list that will be included in text-based queries using the full-text search operators. All of the columns that are eligible for full-text indexes are in the list immediately below the Unique Index dropdown. One index will cover all the selected columns. Do not include a column if you will not include it in a full-text search predicate because that will unnecessarily bloat the index.

5. Go to the bottom of the dialog and select the change tracking scheme for the index. Your selection here will determine which population options you can use. The different change tracking options are as follows.

Automatic   All changes are automatically tracked, allowing the index to be automatically updated whenever the underlying text data structure is modified through an insert, update, or delete operation. This is the default behavior, but it can cause performance problems in databases where the text columns are highly volatile.

Manual   Changes are tracked, but the index is not automatically updated. An administrator must update the index manually or a scheduled job can update the index, which will include updates to all tracked entries. This is called "update population."

Do Not Track Changes   The changes are not tracked by the system. Updating the index must be done manually using a full or incremental population; update population is not allowed. Full population will repopulate the entire index while incremental population requires a timestamp column on the data and only updates rows that have been modified since the latest timestamp.

6. Continue to add and configure tables until you have included all of the desired tables into the catalog, and then click OK. Note that because catalogs are database resources, all of the included table indexes must be in the same database as the catalog. You can also include indexed views in this structure if they contain qualifying text data.

Now that you have created the index, you can view the properties of the index by using the Tables node in the Object Explorer.

1. Open the Tables node at the root of the database in the Object Explorer and locate the table that you just indexed. In our case that would be the HumanResources.JobCandidate table.

2. Right-click on this table and select Full-Text Index from the menu. This will open a sub-menu with a list of options based on the structure on the index. In this list, you will see options to disable or delete the index. You can also start or stop index population and manage change tracking for the index.

3. Select Properties at the bottom of the menu to open the Full-Text Index Properties dialog, which is illustrated in Figure 21.8. As is true of the Catalog Properties window, most of the elements of this dialog are informational.

FIGURE 21.8
Configuring
the index

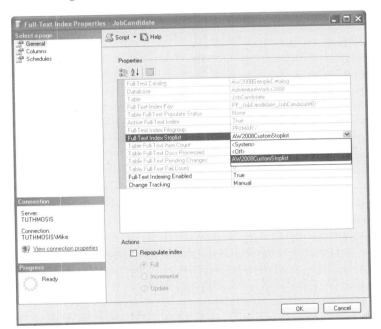

4. One important feature of the index that you can change from here is the associated stoplist. By default the system will generate the index using the system stoplist. If you want to disable the stoplist completely or associate the index with a custom stoplist, as pictured in Figure 21.8, you can use the dropdown list in the dialog. You can also disable the index and modify the change tracking behavior here.

5. Use the Actions section at the bottom of the dialog to repopulate the index using a full, update, or incremental update processes. Your alternatives will depend on the change tracking behavior you are using as well as the structure of the table, because incremental population requires the table to have a timestamp column.

6. Go to the Columns page of the dialog, illustrated in Figure 21.9. It allows you to configure the details of the column. From here you can specify the appropriate Word Breaker that the filter process will use. If the data column is binary and stored as formatted text, you can also identify which column in the table acts as the "type" column. This is the column that stores the file extension as text, thus informing the filter process which format filter it should use when processing the data.

FIGURE 21.9

Configuring the index columns

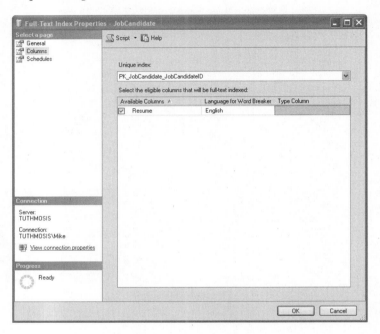

The other page of this dialog, the Schedules page, is similar to the corresponding section in the Catalog dialog and is, therefore, not illustrated here. If you wanted to modify the index-specific schedules, you would use the appropriate page in this dialog .

You can also create indexes using the wizard interface, which is also accessible from the Tables node. Assume that you wanted to place a full-text index on the document column of the Production. Document table. This table stores Microsoft Word documents in a binary format directly in the database. Because these documents are not clear text, they can't be crawled without some help. The filter provides that support.

To create the index, navigate to the Production.Document table in the Tables list in the Object Explorer. Right-click the table in the list and select Full-Text Index ≻ Define Full-Text Index from the menu. Advance past the first page of the wizard. The second page, which is illustrated Figure 21.10, allows you to select which qualifying index on the table it will use as the qualifying index for the full-text infrastructure.

FIGURE 21.10
Choosing the
unique index

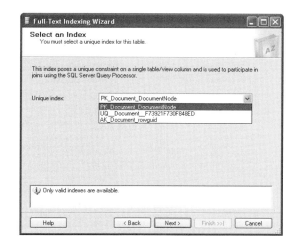

7. Proceed to the next page of the dialog to configure your columns. Each column that is potentially valid will be in this list. However, just because a column is in the list does not mean that it should be included in the index. Only select those columns included in full-text predicates. If the column datatype is varbinary(max) or image, the Type Column option will enable and you will be able to select a column form the list that stored the file extension for the data structure. In the example shown in Figure 21.11, only the Document and DocumentSummary columns are included in the index.

FIGURE 21.11
Configuring the
index columns

8. Go to the next page and configure change tracking for the index. In this example, we will use Automatically, which is the default. Remember that you are not stuck with this. You can alter this setting later by using the Full-Text Index Properties dialog. This dialog is illustrated in Figure 21.12.

FIGURE 21.12
Configuring
Change Tracking

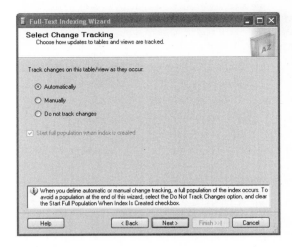

9. The next page allows you to configure the catalog. You can either use an existing catalog or create a new catalog at this point. The options at the bottom of the page will also let you specify the filegroup and the stoplist for the index. Please note that while the filegroup option is no longer supported at the catalog level, it is supported at the index level. This page of the dialog is pictured in Figure 21.13.

FIGURE 21.13
Configuring
the catalog

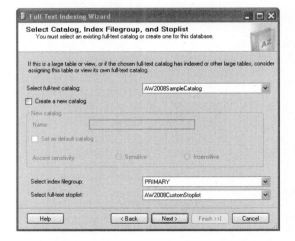

10. The last page, illustrated in Figure 21.14, is the Schedule page. Any schedules that you have already created will be listed here. Additionally, you can use this dialog to create new schedules as needed. Because schedules are not required, you can advance beyond this page without failing the process. You can also configure the schedules later, so it is not important that you fully configure this right now. The Schedule page is illustrated in Figure 21.14.

FIGURE 21.14
Configuring
the schedules

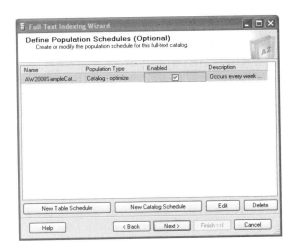

11. The final pages are summary and process pages, and they require no input from you. Click through them to complete the process.

CREATING FULL-TEXT INDEXES WITH TSQL

Now that you understand the options for creating a full-text index, we will look at the TSQL code to perform similar actions to that the ones you just saw in SSMS. If you were to create a full-text index on the HumanResources.JobCandidate table, using the custom stoplist and automatic change tracking, the syntax would look like the following. Assume in this and all subsequent snippets that you are already using the AdventureWorks2008 database.

```
CREATE FULLTEXT INDEX
ON HumanResources.JobCandidate (resume LANGUAGE 'English')
KEY INDEX PK_JobCandidate_JobCandidateID
ON AW2008SampleCatalog
WITH CHANGE_TRACKING = AUTO,
      STOPLIST = AW2008CustomStoplist;
GO
```

Although the syntax is similar, notice the subtle changes for the second index on the Production.Document table. This index tokenizes two columns and includes a binary data filter. If you built this index with the default stoplist and manual change tracking, the syntax would look like this:

```
CREATE FULLTEXT INDEX
ON Production.Document
```

```
(
        Document TYPE COLUMN FileExtension LANGUAGE 'English',
        DocumentSummary LANGUAGE 'English'
)
KEY INDEX PK_Document_DocumentNode
ON AW2008SampleCatalog
WITH CHANGE_TRACKING = MANUAL,
        STOPLIST = SYSTEM;
GO
```

Once you have created the index, you can alter its properties by using the ALTER FULLTEXT INDEX statement. This is a versatile statement that you can use to:

◆ Enable or disable the index

◆ Add a column to the index

◆ Drop a column from the index

◆ Change the stoplist association

◆ Change the tracking behavior

◆ Start or stop index population

For example, if you want to disable the full-text index on the Production.Document table, use the following code:

```
ALTER FULLTEXT INDEX
ON Production.Document
DISABLE;
```

Use the same code with the ENABLE option to re-enable the index. If you want to modify the change tracking behavior so that the index uses automatic change tracking, use this code:

```
ALTER FULLTEXT INDEX
ON Production.Document
SET CHANGE_TRACKING AUTO;
```

A somewhat less obvious use of this statement is to start or stop index population. Now that you have created the index, if you want to perform an update index population, use the following code:

```
ALTER FULLTEXT INDEX
ON Production.Document
START UPDATE POPULATION;
GO
```

As you can see from these examples, once you know the concepts that form the base of full-text indexing, the syntax follows those concepts very well. Whether you use SSMS or code it yourself, the end result is an index structure that is ready to service the full-text query structure.

Real World Scenario

WE'RE DROWNING IN TEXT

It seems that almost all of our clients need to manage text, and that need is growing. Databases have become an increasingly popular tool for managing large amounts of data, whether that be structured text as in a document file, a document image stored in a binary format, or simply Character Large Object (CLOB) storage directly in the database. If you are going to store it in the database, however, you have to have the means to manage it.

TSQL is not well-suited for text-based storage and text manipulation. Although you can use it to perform simple wildcard searches, taking this approach is very inefficient, as one client discovered. This client, a legal consultancy firm, stored large amounts of text in their database; they didn't realize that they had no effective plan for retrieving that text until it was too late. Moreover, there was no practical way they could effectively mine the data in the data tables because the process of querying that text using standard TSQL techniques was far too time-consuming and processor intensive. To make matters worse, the amount of text they needed to store and process was constantly increasing. As the IT director said in one meeting, "We're drowning in text and it is still raining."

There are many options for dealing with text indexing; however, this client already had made a substantial investment in Microsoft infrastructure, and although they were using SQL Server, they were not using it to its full potential. The proposal was to try full-text indexing and see how that worked.

The initial phases were struggles. Setting up indexing and planning an effective key architecture can take time. Doing it incorrectly requires significant refactoring later. We discovered how important it was to have lean base table indexes that we could use to tie the full-text architecture to. We also saw how important it was to perform regular maintenance on the full-text indexes, especially if you are making additions to the index with every update.

The end result of the proof of concept was positive, however. Additional disk resources were needed to store the index, and a few additional responsibilities were imposed on the administrators. The in-house developers needed more training so that they could see when to apply the full-text operations and to what end, but overall the implementation was successful in the sandbox in which we worked. The solution was ultimately rolled out to other operations within the company.

This project could have been a failure, however, if we had not taken special care to ensure that the proposed infrastructure specifically addressed their needs. In particular, making sure that the index architecture matched their data extraction requirements and that the base table indexing model was conducive to the full-text model were critical.

Writing Full-Text Queries

Utilizing full-text indexes is a simple matter of including full-text filter predicates in your query. As we noted in the previous section, the standard query processor and the Full-Text Engine work in tandem. The query engine in SQL Server still processes the standard TSQL statements, but any logic that implements full-text keywords is transferred to the Full-Text Engine. There are keywords that will cause this behavior; there are two functions and two predicates as follows. In this section, you will learn how to implement each of these keywords:

◆ CONTAINS

◆ CONTAINSTABLE

◆ FREETEXT

◆ FREETEXTTABLE

PREDICATES VERSUS FUNCTIONS

Functions return values while predicates operate on values. This is the basic difference. While both the function (table-based) and the predicate (select-based) forms of the keywords use full-text indexing, they approach this process in very different ways.

Full-text implements the functions as rowset functions. Each one returns a temporary or dynamic table that you can join to other tables. The predicates perform filtering actions, but they do not expose the results as table structures, rather they operate on the data identified in the FROM clause of the query. Understanding the differences between the two and the advantages of each will help you construct better text-based searches.

Implementing the *CONTAINS* Predicate

The CONTAINS predicate provides text-based filter processing of data extracted from target table structures identified in the FROM clause of a query. You would typically implement this predicate in the WHERE or HAVING clauses of a TSQL statement. Using this predicate, you can do the following searches:

◆ A specific word or phrase

◆ A prefix term used in a word

◆ One word generated from another word, such as different conjugations of the same verb

◆ One word near another word in a proximity search

◆ A synonym of another word

When using the CONTAINS predicate in a WHERE or HAVING clause, the keyword acts as a Boolean function, returning all of the data rows where the condition specified by the predicate is met. This is similar to other TSQL keywords, such as IN and BETWEEN. The basic syntax structure looks like this:

```
CONTAINS
    ( { column_name | * }
        , '< contains_search_condition >'
  [ , LANGUAGE language_term ]
    )
```

This syntax shows that you must provide two required arguments and one optional argument.

Column Name You must provide a column name. Alternatively, you can use the asterisk to search all indexed columns.

Search Condition   You must provide a search condition. The syntax of this search condition will be different depending on what kind of search you are doing.

Language Identifier   The language identifier is optional. Remember that the stoplists, as well as the filters and stemmers, are all language specific. If you do not provide this argument, SQL Server will assume that you are using the current default language, but providing a language or culture identifier (LCID) allows you to perform the searches using alternate language structures.

SIMPLE SEARCHES

The simplest query form compares the search column with a value for which you are searching. For example, if you wanted to find all documents in the Production.Document table that include the word "repair" in the DocumentSummary field, the code would look like the following. Note that the search string is an nvarchar datatype, so the literal string is prefixed with the Unicode identifier for performance reasons.

```
USE AdventureWorks2008;
GO
SELECT DocumentSummary
FROM Production.Document
WHERE CONTAINS(DocumentSummary, N'repair');
GO
```

You could have used a standard TSQL statement to do this, but it would have been terribly inefficient. For example, instead of using the CONTAINS predicate, your WHERE clause could read WHERE DocumentSummary LIKE '%repair%'. However, because this query cannot use a standard index, the I/O cost could be very high. Even though this is a simple search, full-text indexes provide a much better way to look for this information.

If there are multiple words for which you are searching and you want to use compound logic with AND and OR statements, put them into the search condition string like this.

```
USE AdventureWorks2008;
GO
SELECT DocumentSummary
FROM Production.Document
WHERE CONTAINS(DocumentSummary, N'repair AND reflector');
GO
```

You can also use a variable in place of the search string. The following code is an alternative implementation of the previous code. Notice the use of the variable as well as the alternative representation of the AND logical operator. You can use either presentation of the AND operator at any time.

```
USE AdventureWorks2008;
GO
DECLARE @searchString nvarchar(50) = N'repair & reflector';
SELECT DocumentSummary
FROM Production.Document
WHERE CONTAINS(DocumentSummary, @searchString);
GO
```

The OR operator also has multiple representations. If you were using the above search argument with OR logic instead of AND logic, you could either write `N'repair OR reflector'` or `N'repair | reflector'` because they both yield the same result.

If you are looking for a phrase of multiple words delimited with spaces, you must enclose the phrase in double quotes. For example, searching for the term "Adventure Works" would require the following code.

```
USE AdventureWorks2008;
GO
SELECT DocumentSummary
FROM Production.Document
WHERE CONTAINS(DocumentSummary, N'"Adventure Works"');
GO
```

WATCH YOUR QUOTES

Often the quotation of the search string can have a significant impact on the results of the query. For example if you used the argument `N'"guidelines and recommendations"'`, you would get a match only when this exact phrase occurs. However, the search argument `N'"guidelines" and "recommendations"'` would return any case where these two words were both found in the data field. Be careful when you construct your search arguments.

SEARCHING PREFIXES

You can use wildcards to replace characters followed by a prefix if you want to search for words that begin with a specific prefix pattern. Note that you cannot use the wildcard in the place of the first characters. The index required that a prefix be provided to enable a contained search. For example, to locate any rows where the document summary contains a word that begins with the prefix "bi," you would use the following code.

```
USE AdventureWorks2008;
GO
SELECT DocumentSummary
FROM Production.Document
WHERE CONTAINS(DocumentSummary, N' "bi*" ');
GO
```

You can also combine these searches. For example, to search for all occurrences of the phrase "Adventure Works" that also includes a word that starts with the prefix "bi," you would use this code.

```
USE AdventureWorks2008;
GO
SELECT DocumentSummary
FROM Production.Document
WHERE CONTAINS(DocumentSummary, N' "Adventure Works" AND "bi*" ');
GO
```

SEARCHING GENERATIONS

SQL Server Full-Text Search services supports two forms of word generation. Each uses the key term FORMSOF to search for different forms of a specific word. First, you can do word-form searching with the INFLECTIONAL keyword. Using this term allows you to find different forms of the same word stem. For example, to find text that contains any form of the word "replace," you could use this code.

```
USE AdventureWorks2008;
GO
SELECT DocumentSummary
FROM Production.Document
WHERE CONTAINS(DocumentSummary, ' FORMSOF(INFLECTIONAL, replace)');
GO
```

The returned rows will contain text phrases such as "replaced" and "replacing" because they are all forms of the same stem. Note that this operation is language dependent because each language will use its own stemmers to find word forms.

The second approach uses the THESAURUS key term to find synonyms of a provided word structure. If you wanted to return a list of rows that contain the word "repair" or any other word that is synonymous, you would use this code.

```
USE AdventureWorks2008;
GO
SELECT DocumentSummary
FROM Production.Document
WHERE CONTAINS(DocumentSummary, ' FORMSOF(THESAURUS, repair)');
GO
```

Please note that the default thesaurus files are very rudimentary and will likely need to be edited to allow you to find the terms upon which you will search. The default install location of the thesaurus files is at SQL_Server_install_path\Microsoft SQL Server\MSSQL10. MSSQLSERVER\MSSQL\FTDATA\. There you will find a thesaurus file for each language as well as a global file called tsGlobal.xml. Your ability to perform synonym searches will only be as robust as the content of these files.

PROXIMITY SEARCHES

Another useful technique is to be able to locate words based on their proximity to other words. For example, perhaps the word "repair" has a different meaning when near the word "good." You could search for the pattern "good repair" specifically, but that would return only the specific pattern and not something like "repair is a good" or any other proximal structure. To perform a proximity search, you can use either the operator NEAR, or alternatively you can use a tilde (~) in place of the key term. Performing a search based on this scenario would look like this.

```
USE AdventureWorks2008;
GO
SELECT DocumentSummary
FROM Production.Document
WHERE CONTAINS(DocumentSummary, N' repair NEAR good ');
GO
```

Implementing the *FREETEXT* Predicate

The FREETEXT predicate is much less structured than the CONTAINS predicate. Instead of providing specific relationships among terms that provide structure to the search, the FREETEXT predicate takes a simple list as a parameter and searches for all relationships using those terms. Anything using the provided terms or forms of the provided terms will result in a positive match.

For example, the following code accepts the terms "vital" and "repair" as parameters. Any data rows that contain text in the searched fields that have anything to do with the terms should appear as positive matches. Here is the code to implement this logic.

```
USE AdventureWorks2008;
GO
SELECT DocumentSummary
FROM Production.Document
WHERE FREETEXT(DocumentSummary, N'vital repair');
GO
```

As you can see from this example, the syntax is very simple. There are no structural rules such as those found with the CONTAINS predicate. As a result of this, however, the results are much less precise and you are far more likely to get false positive hits. On the other hand, you are also less likely to miss matches that represent relationships that you did not predict or specifically code for when using the CONTAINS predicate.

Because these two predicates provide mechanisms for accomplishing essentially the same thing, it is important to know the difference and the potential impact of each. Select the option that makes the most sense to your solution: either a highly structure solution or a freeform solution. The choice is yours.

Implementing the Full-Text Functions

If you are comfortable with the concepts underlying the FREETEXT and CONTAINS predicates, you will find that the implementation of the table-valued function versions of these same key terms is not much different. The primary difference is in where you will use them.

While the predicates act as filters, the functions create tables. This can be extremely useful when you need to join the results of a table that uses text-based indexes with other standard tables. It alleviates the step of having to use temporary or derived tables with predicates to accomplish the same result. Otherwise, all of the syntax that you saw in the discussion of the predicates still applies.

To test this out, we will need to create a new index on the Sales.Store table. This table has a column called Demographics. Execute the following code to create the index.

```
USE AdventureWorks2008;
GO
CREATE FULLTEXT INDEX
ON Sales.Store (Demographics LANGUAGE 'English')
KEY INDEX PK_Store_BusinessEntityID
ON AW2008SampleCatalog
WITH CHANGE_TRACKING = AUTO,
   STOPLIST = AW2008CustomStoplist;
GO
```

Suppose that you wanted to write a query that returned the store name and address of any store that specialized in touring bikes. The information about the store specialty is embedded in the XML data field called Demographics rather than being a field itself, which makes it difficult to query without using SQL Server Full-Text Search services. However, using the CONTAINS predicate could be very inefficient because the address information is in another table. Since this will require a join, anything that we can do to filter the rows that will join would have a positive impact on performance by reducing I/O. Unfortunately, the full-text predicates are applied after the query optimization process is complete. However, if you could filter the data before the join optimization begins, you might get better performance.

The full-text functions help us deal with this by providing filtering of the standard query by returning the keys of the satisfying rows in the full-text portion of the query. Consider the following query.

```
USE AdventureWorks2008;
GO
SELECT *
FROM CONTAINSTABLE(
   Sales.Store,
   Demographics,
   N'touring');
GO
```

There are over 700 rows in the Sales.Store table, but only about a fifth of those rows satisfy the condition in the CONTAINSTABLE statement. Executing this query will give you a table with two columns, namely Key and Rank. The key is the configured unique key for the index, in this case the BusinessEntityID. The rank is a measure of how well the row satisfies the criteria. In this case the ranks should be all the same.

So for our benefit, what this function does is return a list of BusinessEntityID values that satisfy the condition. This list, presented as a table, can then join to other tables to get the information that you are seeking. Because it eliminates rows in advance, it significantly improves the I/O performance of the join by requiring joins to fewer rows. If the key is clustered, it is even better for the I/O score. To get the names of qualifying stores, you could use the following query.

```
USE AdventureWorks2008;
GO
SELECT s.Name
FROM CONTAINSTABLE(
      Sales.Store,
      Demographics,
      N'touring') as sKey
INNER JOIN Sales.Store as s
ON s.BusinessEntityID = sKey.[Key];
```

Now that you have joined the full-text table to the standard table to eliminate the nonqualifying rows, you can use any field in the Sales.Store table to join to any other table in the database. Returning the address of a store would require a query like this. Because the only filter criterion in this query relates to the full-text filter, this query would produce significantly less I/O than would a query that used a CONTAINS predicate in the WHERE clause.

```
USE AdventureWorks2008;
GO
SELECT s.Name, a.AddressLine1, a.AddressLine2, a.City
FROM CONTAINSTABLE(
        Sales.Store,
        Demographics,
        N'touring') as sKey
INNER JOIN Sales.Store as s
        ON s.BusinessEntityID = sKey.[Key]
INNER JOIN Person.BusinessEntityAddress as bea
        on s.BusinessEntityID = bea.BusinessEntityID
INNER JOIN Person.Address as a
        ON bea.AddressID = a.AddressID;
```

All of the options that you previously saw relating to the CONTAINS predicate apply to the function as well. The only syntactical difference is the requirement that you provide the name of the table that you are using as the first argument in the function. The same rule applies to the FREETEXTTABLE function.

TUNING FULL-TEXT PERFORMANCE

Because full-text indexes are directly related to standard indexes, most of the performance processes are very similar to performance tuning of standard indexes. Any good practices dealing with standard indexes will most likely transfer to the full-text world. Here is a list of some of the most substantial performance policies that you will want to consider.

◆ Use a small integer-based key as the base key for the full-text index. If the index is clustered, that is even better.

◆ Use the functions instead of the predicates whenever you can restrict table structures and optimize I/O. This is particularly useful when there are no search arguments in the where clause.

◆ Combine multiple search criteria into a single CONTAINS statement instead of using multiple statements.

◆ Eliminate full-text index fragmentation by using the ALTER FULLTEXT CATALOG <catalogname> REORGANZIE command.

◆ Monitor memory use, especially on a 32-bit system. Full-text searches require extensive memory and this can frequently be the bottleneck, especially on 32-bit systems.

The Bottom Line

Explain and apply full-text architecture in SQL Server 2008. SQL Server full-text indexes are architecturally different from standard indexes in SQL Server 2008. In addition to the physical storage format, they are also organized differently. Prior versions of SQL Server organized the indexes completely outside of the database, which required separate backup operations for the indexes, but today they are also database resident. Understanding the architectural differences between standard and full-text indexes is an important step to properly maintaining the application.

Master It Describe the primary differences between standard indexes and full-text indexes in SQL Server 2008.

Implement full-text indexes. You can implement a full-text index using TSQL code or with the SSMS interface. No matter which approach you use, you will have to be familiar with the terminology that is specific to full-text indexing.

Master It Define each of the following terms used in creating full-text indexes.

1. Type column

2. Language

3. Key index

4. change_tracking

5. Stoplist

Write queries utilizing full-text features of SQL Server 2008. Once full-text indexes exist on a table, you can use special statements in your TSQL code to access these indexes. There are four key terms in total, each one differing slightly in its implementation and return structure.

Master It List the four full-text keywords that you can use in your code, identify if that keyword is a function or a predicate, and provide a brief description of its behavior.

Appendices

In this section you will find:

Appendix A

The Bottom Line

Each of The Bottom Line sections in the chapters challenges your understanding of the chapters' concepts and improves your skills.

Chapter 1: Overview of Microsoft SQL Server 2008

Utilize the Architect SQL Server services in the typical IT environment.   SQL Server provides more than just simple data services to the IT infrastructure. SQL Server is packed with so many features that it quite literally has become a data suite in a box. The key is making sure that you know what SQL Server can do and how to use the appropriate feature once you identify the need for it.

Master It   Which SQL Server feature would you use to meet each of the following business requirements?

1. Your company has been collecting sales data for over 10 years. The director of marketing has noticed that over the last two years, sales have been dropping in North America while they have been increasing in Central and South America. You need to see if you can find a reason for the trend.

2. Your company must comply with industry regulations that require the company to provide specific information in a specific format for regulatory inspectors. The inspectors must be able to get the information any time they choose, it must always be organized the way that they want to see it, and it must always contain current data.

3. A significant portion of your firm's sales is handled through the Internet. The marketing department would like to have a mechanism that allows users to search for a product, and if the product is not in stock, they can log in to the system and request to receive an email when the product is available.

4. Much of your company's data is stored as large text fields. This text data must be searchable as efficiently as possible using very fuzzy logic including word forms and proximity searches.

Solutions

1. SQL Server Analysis Services let you define multidimensional data structures that can slice through data in a variety of ways. Using Data Mining Models, you can do trend analysis and look for hidden relationships in the data that might exist.

2. SQL Server Reporting Services allows you to define report formats and make them available through secured web interfaces. If you like, you can also create report models that allow for ad hoc reporting by the user.

3. Using SQL Server Notification Services, you can define notification rules tied to data events. When the data event is recognized, the notification is sent through appropriate formatting extensions.

4. SQL Server's full-text search service allows searching through large text fields. Enhancements to this service in SQL Server 2008 simplify the maintenance of full-text indexes and ease the administration burden of this service.

Install SQL Server 2008.   While the installation process itself is wizard-driven, SQL Server installation takes some planning to make sure that you have an appropriate installation with the right resources in place for the right purposes.

Master It   SQL Server needs the right balance of resources to handle the demands of the data service. What are the four primary resources that SQL Server uses and how do they interact with each other?

Solution   SQL Server uses the following four primary resources:

◆ CPU

◆ Memory

◆ Network

◆ Disk

CPU architecture (32-bit or 64-bit) determines the amount of memory that is accessible by SQL Server and how to configure the server to access that memory. Data must be brought into memory before it can be sent to a client. Without enough memory, more swapping will occur between memory and disk, putting additional strain on the disk I/O subsystem. Inadequate network bandwidth creates an outward pipe bottleneck, requiring data to be stored in memory longer until it can be served out to the client application.

Use the Microsoft SQL Server toolset.   Microsoft ships a number of high-quality tools with the SQL Server product that suit many different purposes. The key is to use the right tool for the job.

Master It   Which of the SQL Server tools would you use for each of the following goals?

1. Writing and executing a query.

2. Identifying the optimal indexing structure.

3. Performing routine security administration tasks.

4. Performing a security audit in which you try to identify failed login attempts.

5. Identifying the interaction between SQL Server and a compiled client application.

6. Configuring the network protocols that SQL Server can use.

Solution

1. SQL Server Management Studio

2. Data Engine Tuning Wizard

3. SQL Server Management Studio

4. SQL Server Profiler

5. SQL Server Profiler

6. SQL Server Configuration Manager

Implement other useful third-party tools. With all the tools out there, it is important that you select the right ones. There are a lot of tools from which to choose.

Master It What is the best third-party tool for creating entity-relationship diagrams?

Solution This is a trick question! The best tool is the one that makes you the most productive. Some experienced users still program in Java using a text editor and compiler macros, because they don't want to get bogged down with the overhead of more elaborate tools. You should use whatever makes you the most productive and helps you create the cleanest possible code.

Chapter 2: Understanding SQL Server Architecture

Apply your understanding of SQL Server internals to implement good logical architecture. It's not enough to simply understand SQL Server internals; you must also be able to apply the information to the implementation of a stable and extensible architecture. The better you understand how SQL Server works, the more likely you will be to avoid the pitfalls and design problems that often plague the novice administrator.

Master It Your SQL Server seems to be running slowly in response to some queries that process large amounts of data. As you investigate the situation more closely, you notice that there is a significant amount of disk activity. There also appears to be a significant amount of LazyWriter activity. Based on your knowledge of SQL Server internals, where should you look next to identify the problem?

Solution Based on this scenario, the problem is likely to be either the amount of memory installed in the server, or the memory configuration. There does not seem to be enough memory in the server to handle the data load that is required for the query, so SQL Server is required to swap data from memory to disk to free up buffers. The LazyWriter activity in conjunction with this indicates that there is significant data modification activity as well that must be captured to disk before the buffers can be reused.

You should evaluate how much memory you have in your server. If you have over 3 GB of RAM, you should check your boot.ini file to see if the /3GB switch is set. This can give you another 1 GB of RAM. If you have over 16GB of RAM but the server is not configured to use AWE, you are not getting the benefit of the extra memory. In this case, remove the /3GB switch (if it is set) because this will prevent the server from seeing memory over 16GB. Make sure that the /PAE switch is set in the boot.ini file, enable the Lock Pages in Memory profile setting, and enable AWE in the server configurations.

Utilize the SQL Server catalog to get more information about the system and your application. All of the information that you need about the SQL Server configurations and settings is available if you know where to go to get it. When properly mined, the SQL Server catalog can provide extensive information that can be invaluable as you diagnose, tune, and maintain your servers.

Master It What SQL Query query would you use to get the following information?

1. Details on the files used in the AdventureWorks database.

2. A list of all the user tables in the AdventureWorks database.

3. A list of all the user tables and their schema names for the AdventureWorks database.

Solution

1.

```
USE AdventureWorks2008;
SELECT *
FROM sys.database_files;
```

2.

```
USE AdventureWorks2008;
SELECT name
FROM sys.objects
WHERE type=''U'';
```

3.

```
USE AdventureWorks2008;
SELECT s.name as SchemaName
,o.name as TableName
FROM sys.objects as o
INNER JOIN sys.schemas as s
on s.schema_id=o.schema_id
WHERE type=''U'';
```

Effectively implement datatypes, including user-defined datatypes. As the foundation for all SQL Server applications, datatypes define how SQL Server will store every piece of information it receives. If this storage is efficient or inefficient, fast or slow to retrieve, or large or small in its storage, you can't always blame SQL Server. Sometimes it's up to you to provide appropriate storage definitions.

Master It Which of the SQL Server datatypes would you use to store each of the following data values?

1. A United States Postal Service zip code with five digits.

2. The first name of a customer.

3. A memo field that stores freeform comments and may contain a lot of data.

4. The total cost of an order.

5. The date of an order (assuming that you process all orders daily and all orders placed on the same day are treated the same).

Solution

1. You could use an integer, but the best choice would probably be to use a char(5) datatype. The value is always fixed to five characters in length, and you will never do any mathematical manipulation with the value.

2. You could use either a varchar or nvarchar type, depending on your need to use Unicode data. You must decide what maximum length would be reasonable. If you expect no first names greater than 20 characters and you don't plan to use Unicode, chose a varchar(20).

3. Because you might have a very long field, choose varchar(max) or nvarchar(max), depending on your need for Unicode. Do not use the text datatype, because this will be deprecated in later releases of SQL Server.

4. Any fixed precision datatype will work, but do not use real or float because doing so could expose you to accuracy problems. You should consider either the small money or money datatypes because they were made specifically for this purpose.

5. Because you do not need to store a time component, look at the date datatype. This stores the date value with no time.

Chapter 3: Databases, Files, and Resource Management

Create new databases.   Creating new databases is a common and fundamental operation. Understanding what happens when a new database is created is a critical step.

Master It   What system database is used as a template when creating a new database on SQL Server? How could you create an object that would exist in any new database on the SQL Server?

Solution   The model database is used as a template when creating a new database. Create objects in the model database that you would like to have exist in new databases.

Planning databases.   Adequate planning for user databases is very important. From choosing the appropriate recovery model to properly placing files, these choices will prepare the database for future operations.

Master It   What is the most appropriate recovery model for a mission-critical database that needs the ability to restore to a point in time?

Solution   The full recovery model allows the transaction log to accumulate all changes until it is backed up. Because all changes are stored in the transaction log, the database can be restored to any point in time in the backup process.

Discovering information about existing databases.   There are many ways to retrieve information about existing databases and their files. Management Studio can be an easy place to view information about individual database options; however, it's important to remember that this information can be retrieved using system catalog views.

Master It   What catalog view displays information about every database and database file on the server, including sizes and file options?

Solution   The sys.master_files view returns information about every database file, for every database on the server. This can be a very useful view to query information across multiple databases. To view similar information for a single database, query the sys.database_files view.

Chapter 4: Tables and CRUD Operations

Plan and implement appropriate normalization strategies.   With a little planning, a database can be designed for efficiency and future growth. Using good normalization practices now can save a lot of headaches later as you try to maintain your application.

Master It   Which normal form is being enforced in each of the following situations?

1. You create a CustomerID column in the Customer table to uniquely identify the customer.

2. A row in the Product table is identified by its ProductCode field and its VendorCode field. You also include the cost that each vendor charges for the product in the same table.

3. A row in the Product table is identified by its ProductCode field and its VendorCode field. The ProductColorCode is also in this table. You need to provide special processing instructions for products that are ordered in the color red. You choose to put those instructions in a separate ProductColorCode table.

4. In the Employee table, you choose to split the employee name into a separate FirstName and LastName column.

Solution

1. This is an example of a primary key, which supports the first normal form.

2. Because the cost can be different for each vendor and product combination, the cost is included to comply with the second normal form, indicating that a non-key field must relate to all primary key fields.

3. The special instructions are specific to the color code, not to either of the primary key fields. The third normal form states that non-key cannot relate to any other non-key field. Since ProductColorCode is not a key field in the Product table, the data belongs in the ProductColorCode table.

4. The first normal form states that all data must be in a non-decomposable form. Breaking the name data into separate fields satisfies this requirement.

Design and create tables using all of the SQL Server table features.   Tables define the structure for all of the data that you will store in your database. With the exception of filestream data, everything will be in a table. Good table design is critical to efficient data storage.

Master It   Which table design feature would you use in each of these scenarios?

1. You need to provide an auto-incrementing key for a table.

2. A deterministic value is frequently calculated when you select from a table and you would prefer to store the data in the table.

3. You want to force a specific column to have a value for every row.

4. You want to separate some data into an archive structure and facilitate the process of keeping the archive current.

Solution

1. An Identity column will provide this feature.

2. A computed column can be used to store the calculation in the table. Because the value is deterministic, this can be marked as persisted to store the value in the table.

3. Explicitly marking the column as NOT NULL will ensure this behavior. This is the default behavior in SQL Server but it can be changed through a configuration setting, so the only way to guarantee this behavior is to mark the column as NOT NULL when you create your table.

4. Creating a partitioned table can facilitate this. If the index is also partitioned, the query will only have to process the active partition for a query, effectively separating the archived data from the main query activity.

Write SELECT statements from simple to complex for returning data to the client.   A database is useless without a mechanism to extract the data once entered. In SQL, this is done with the SELECT statement. Because these statements are very flexible, a good Transact SQL developer should be able to use the SELECT statement to manipulate the data to tell exactly the story that is needed.

Master It   In the AdventureWorks2008 database, there are tables that provide every employee's pay history. Write a SELECT statement that will return the first and last name of each employee from the Person.Person table and their current pay rate from the HumanResources.EmployeePayHistory table. Assume that the current pay is the record with the latest ModifiedDate.

Solution   This solution performs a join from Person.Person to HumanResources. EmployeePayHistory to capture the name information. It then uses a correlated subquery to locate the maximum ModifiedDate value for each BusinessEntityID.

```
USE AdventureWorks2008;

SELECT p.BusinessEntityID, p.FirstName, p.LastName, eph.Rate
FROM HumanResources.EmployeePayHistory as eph
INNER JOIN Person.Person as p
      ON eph.BusinessEntityID = p.BusinessEntityID
WHERE eph.ModifiedDate = (
      SELECT MAX(ModifiedDate)
      FROM HumanResources.EmployeePayHistory
      WHERE BusinessEntityID = eph.BusinessEntityID);
```

Perform data modification operations using the INSERT, UPDATE, DELETE, and MERGE SQL DML statements. The statements that we use to modify data are not difficult to master, but they are critical. Any time that you need to make a modification to your database, you will be using one of these statements.

Master It Write the necessary code to insert the first name, last name, and phone number of every person in our database to a temporary table called #TempPerson.

Solution

```
USE AdventureWorks2008;
-- Create the temp table
CREATE TABLE #TempPerson
(
        FirstName           nvarchar(50)   NOT NULL,
        LastName            nvarchar(50)   NOT NULL,
        PhoneNumber         nvarchar(25)   NOT NULL
);

-- Insert data into the temp table
INSERT INTO #TempPerson (FirstName, LastName, PhoneNumber)
SELECT p.FirstName, p.LastName, pp.PhoneNumber
FROM Person.Person as p
INNER JOIN Person.PersonPhone as pp
     ON p.BusinessEntityID = pp.BusinessEntityID;

-- select to test
SELECT * FROM #TempPerson;
```

Chapter 5: Procedural Programming

Create stored procedures. Stored procedures provide powerful mechanisms for encapsulating database processes. Understanding how stored procedures are created and executed is an important goal for the DBA.

Master It Can a stored procedure reference objects that don't exist? How about columns that don't exist in tables that do?

Solution Yes, a stored procedure can reference objects that don't exist through the process of deferred name resolution. A stored procedure cannot access non-nonexistent columns if the table does exist. Deferred name resolution only applies to non-nonexistent objects, not pieces of objects.

Create views. Views are queries stored as objects and referenced as tables. Creating views allows flexibility in building and storing database queries.

Master It What are three advantages of using views?

Solution Any three of these:

◆ Simplifying data retrieval

◆ Focusing users on specific data

◆ Providing abstraction from change

◆ Providing performance benefits

◆ Separating securable objects

Create user-defined functions.   Creating user-defined functions allows flexibility, both in processing of scalar values, and in processing of result sets.

> **Master It**   What advantage does a table-valued function have over a stored procedure that returns a result set?
>
> **Solution**   A table-valued function can be referenced in the FROM clause of a SELECT statement. To join the result set of a stored procedure to another table in a query, the results must first be inserted into a temporary table.

Chapter 6: Managing Data Integrity

Choose appropriate methods to enforce data integrity.   For a given data integrity rule, there can be several options to enforce that rule. Choosing the appropriate data integrity enforcement mechanism is important for performance.

> **Master It**   What category of data integrity is being enforced by each of the following situations?
>
> 1. A unique constraint that is defined on a combination of two columns.
>
> 2. A Check constraint that only allows values between 1 and 10.
>
> 3. A Check constraint that forces a Bill Date column to be between period start and period end.
>
> 4. A Foreign Key constraint that references another table.
>
> **Solution**
>
> 1. Entity integrity
>
> 2. Domain integrity
>
> 3. Domain integrity and referential integrity
>
> 4. Domain integrity and referential integrity

Create and manage constraints.   Constraints provide declarative integrity enforcement. Creating and managing constraints is important to ensure that integrity rules are enforced by the database.

> **Master It**   When you add a Check constraint to an existing table, is the data verified by default? Can you control this verification? What problems could you encounter?
>
> **Solution**   A Check constraint verifies existing data by default. Turning off a Check constraint can be accomplished by using the WITH NOCHECK option. If rows exist that don't conform to the Check constraint, and the NOCHECK option is used, the constraint will be created, but any modifications to those rows will result in a violation of the Check constraint, even if those modifications didn't affect columns referenced by the Check constraint.

Create and manage DML triggers. Triggers provide a more robust, procedural method of enforcing data integrity rules than constraints. Choosing the appropriate type of trigger is important to properly enforce complex integrity rules.

Master It It's important to choose the appropriate type of trigger in a given situation. Would it be more appropriate to use an AFTER trigger or an INSTEAD OF trigger if you want the trigger to:

1. Maintain aggregate values in a separate summary table?

2. Ignore updates for a column?

3. Modify data to conform to constraints?

4. Audit record modifications?

Solution

1. An AFTER trigger is most appropriate. Using an INSTEAD OF trigger for this operation would require code to be written to perform the modification as well as to maintain the aggregate value.

2. An INSTEAD OF trigger is best for this scenario because modifications to the column don't need to be undone.

3. An INSTEAD OF trigger is required because it executes before constraints are checked. An AFTER trigger won't execute if constraints are violated.

4. Unless certain modifications need to be ignored, an AFTER trigger will work better, because the only code that needs to be written is to audit the change. An INSTEAD OF trigger would need to do the modifications as well as audit the change.

Chapter 7: SQL Server and XML

Implement the FOR XML Transact-SQL structure. Even if you store data relationally in a database, that doesn't mean you cannot retrieve it as XML. In some cases, it makes sense to do just that. Using the FOR XML clause in the Transact-SQL, you can retrieve data in a variety of XML formats and structures.

Master It Explain the difference between the following types of FOR XML statements.

1. RAW

2. AUTO

3. EXPLICIT

4. PATH

Solution

1. Performs little additional formatting. By default, RAW mode outputs RAW row content as attributes. By default, the output is fragment based. This option gives you the most control for simple output.

2. Performs automatically configured XML output. You have fewer options and less control, but much simpler code.

3. EXPLICIT can create much more complex XML structures than RAW or AUTO, but it can be difficult to use. It utilizes a universal table format, which includes all hierarchical information.

4. PATH can produce the same results as EXPLICIT, but it is much easier to use because you will depend on XPath statements instead of the universal table format.

Implement the xml datatype. In SQL Server 2008, the xml datatype is a full datatype at peer with other character datatypes such as nchar and nvarchar. SQL Server implements the type as an nvarchar(max), but it also associates an xml parser with the datatype to ensure that all data stored in an xml data-typed container is well-formed.

Master It List the steps and the code structures that you would use to shred a relational data structure from data stored in an xml data type.

Solution

1. Parse the document in memory using the sp_xml_preparedocument stored procedure.

2. Generate a rowset from the XML using the OPENXML Transact-SQL function.

3. Destroy the memory tree using the sp_xml_removedocument stored procedure.

Validate XML in SQL Server with XSD schemas. Because the XML specification does not define the tags you can use in your documents, there must be a mechanism for ensuring that XML data has the right tags and in the right order. You can use schemas to do this. You can create a schema by using an XML schema collection object in SQL Server.

Master It Write statements that will do the following:

1. Declare a variable called @xmlData as untyped xml.

2. Declare a variable called @xmlData as typed xml using the SampleCollection XmlSchemaCollection that can store fragments.

3. Declare a variable called @xmlData as typed xml using the SampleCollection XmlSchemaCollection that can store only well-formed documents.

Solution

1. DECLARE @xmlData xml;

2. DECLARE @xmlData xml(SampleCollection); or DECLARE @xmlData xml(CONTENT SampleCollection);

3. DECLARE @xmlData xml(DOCUMENT SampleCollection);

Implement basic XQuery structures.   The XQuery standard, which is defined by the W3C, is supported in SQL Server through the xml datatype. The SQL developer can use the xml datatype to query data in a variety of ways, and even modify XML data if necessary.

Master It   For each of the listed scenarios, specify the xml datatype method you would use to address the issue.

1. You want to return a single scalar value from an XML document.

2. You want to return a subset of XML from the document.

3. You want to make a change to an existing XML document.

4. You want to see if a particular note is present in an XML document.

Solution

1. `value()`

2. `query()`

3. `modify()`

4. `exist()`

Implement XML indexes for performance.   Data stored as XML is not stagnant. You don't have to return the entire XML document structure in your query. Using XQuery, you can return individual subsets or values from an XML document. This versatility makes it much more reasonable to store data as XML because you know that you can actually get to it and use it after it is stored.

Master It   You want to create a PATH index on an XML column called OrderXML in a table called Orders. What do you have to do to create the index? Include any actions that are prerequisites to creating the index.

Solution

1. Create a primary key clustered constraint on the Orders table if one does not already exist.

2. Create a primary XML index on the OrderXML column.

3. Create the PATH XML index on the OrderXML column.

Chapter 8: Managing User Security

Describe the components of the SQL Server security infrastructure.   The SQL Server security model is typical of other Windows-based security infrastructures. Principals, securables, and permissions provide a complete environment for protecting your assets and allowing flexible database interactions for authenticated parties.

Master It   In the following list, identify whether the entity is a principal, securable, permission, or scope. In some cases, an entity can exist in multiple categories.

1. Database

2. Select

3. User

4. Application Role

5. Schema

6. Table

Solution

1. Scope and/or Securable

2. Permission

3. Principal

4. Principal

5. Scope and/or Securable

6. Securable

Implement authentication and principals.   There are different forms of authentication that you can choose based on your infrastructure and requirements. Once authenticated, principals represent these authenticated parties and are the basis for all access control in SQL Server.

Master It   For each of the following scenarios, specify which authentication mode would be the best fit for the facts.

1. You want to provide a single sign-on environment for your Active Directory-based Windows Infrastructure.

2. Most of your clients are Windows workstations that are members of a domain, but you do have a few Linux workstations.

3. All of your clients are external to your organization. You do not know what operating systems that they use, and they have no accounts in your network.

Solution

1. If you are Windows inside and out, you should use a Windows-only authentication.

2. You should use a Mixed authentication scheme, allowing the Windows users to connect using integrated security and the Linux workstations to connect through SQL Server standard security.

3. You could use a SQL Server Standard security mode, but then you would have to create a SQL Server account for each user. This might be a good opportunity to explore authenticating through a certificate in a nontrusted mode. If every client is external and you have no control over their platforms, a standard tool such as an X.509 certificate might be the perfect fit.

Manage permissions.   A permission is the right to perform an action or to interact with an object in a specified way. Permissions are the connecting points between principals and securables in a SQL Server security model, which you will use to control access to all of your database assets.

Master It   Write a statement that will perform the desired permissions action based on each of the following requirements.

1. Database-user Pam requires the right to add new rows to the sales.stores table.

2. The MonitorApp Application role should be explicitly prevented from executing the banking.deposit stored procedure.

3. Database-user Bill needs the right to create new tables in the database.

4. The DemoLogin principal requires permissions to make alterations to the SampleLogin principal.

Solution

1. `GRANT INSERT ON sales.stores TO Pam;`

2. `DENY EXECUTE ON banking.deposit TO MonitorApp;`

3. `GRANT CREATE TABLE TO Bill;`

4. `GRANT ALTER ON LOGIN::SampleLogin TO DemoLogin`

Chapter 9: Data Recovery

Understand SQL Server's transaction architecture.   It's important to study the transaction architecture of SQL Server in order to understand what is going on during backup and restore operations.

Master It   What would happen to each of the following transactions during database recovery?

1. A transaction that began and committed prior to the last checkpoint.

2. A transaction that began before the last checkpoint and committed after the last checkpoint but prior to system failure.

3. A transaction that began after the last checkpoint and never committed prior to system failure.

Solution

1. Nothing. The transaction was already committed to the database at the last checkpoint.

2. The transaction would be rolled forward during the recovery process because it committed prior to system failure.

3. The transaction would be rolled back during the recovery process because it did not commit prior to system failure.

Understand the impact that a database recovery model has on backup and restore strategies. The recovery model that you choose for a database impacts the options available for backup and recovery. Choosing an appropriate recovery model is critical to ensure proper recoverability of your databases.

Master It   What recovery model would be most appropriate for the following situations?

1. A development database that only requires full database backups.

2. A production database that must minimize its work loss exposure, and must be able to be recovered to a point in time.

3. A production database that has bulk operations performed on a schedule.

Solution

1. Simple recovery

2. Full recovery

3. Full recovery, combined with the Bulk-logged recovery model. Switch to Bulk-logged recovery before bulk operations occur, and switch back to Full recovery once the bulk operations are completed.

Choose an appropriate backup and data recovery plan for the databases in an organization. Choosing the appropriate backup strategy for a database is an important step in creating a disaster recovery plan for any database.

Master It   What kind of backups should be performed on the following databases?

1. A read-only database.

2. A mission-critical database that is constantly changing, and must be restored with a minimal amount of data loss and recovery time.

3. A development database that can tolerate some data loss.

Solution

1. Full database backups should be made whenever the data is changed (which shouldn't be often since the database is read only).

2. A combination of full, differential, and transaction log backups would be appropriate. You might consider backing up individual database files, if possible, to minimize the amount of time required for recovery.

3. A full backup should be made periodically, but the database could be left in Simple recovery mode so that the transaction logs don't need to be maintained.

Perform regular database backups to prevent data loss.   Performing the appropriate backups is critical to ensuring database recoverability in the event of a failure.

Master It   Write a Transact-SQL statement to perform the following operations:

1. Full database backup of a database named DB1 to a backup device named DB1_Backup. Overwrite any backups that already exist on the DB_1 backup device.

2. A differential backup of a database named DB1 to a disk-based backup device stored in the E:\Backups folder. Overwrite any backups that exist in the file.

3. A transaction log backup of the tail of the transaction log on a database named DB1 to a backup device named DB1_Log. Append the backup to any existing backups on the device. Assume that the database files are unavailable.

Solution

1.
```
BACKUP DATABASE DB1
TO DB1_Backup
WITH INIT;
```

2.
```
BACKUP DATABASE DB1
TO DISK = 'E:\Backups\DB1_Diff'
WITH INIT, DIFFERENTIAL;
```

3.
```
BACKUP LOG DB1
TO DB1_Log
WITH NO_TRUNCATE;
```

Perform database restores using a variety of recovery strategies.   When you're confronted with a situation that requires the recovery of a database, it's important to know the proper procedure to restore the database with a minimal loss of data.

Master It   The disk containing the data files for a database named CriticalDB has failed. The disk containing the transaction log is still available. CriticalDB uses the Full recovery model, and a backup device named CriticalDB_Backup contains the five backups listed here:

1. Full backup of CriticalDB

2. Transaction log backup of CriticalDB

3. Transaction log backup of `CriticalDB`

4. Differential backup of `CriticalDB`

5. Transaction log backup of `CriticalDB`

After replacing the disk that housed the data files, what procedure would you use to restore the database? Provide the appropriate Transact-SQL statements to recover to the point of failure.

Solution   The steps for recovering the `CriticalDB` database are as follows:

1. Back up the tail of the transaction log with the `NO_TRUNCATE` option.
```
BACKUP LOG CriticalDB
TO CriticalDB_Backup
WITH NO_TRUNCATE;
```

2. Restore the full backup of CriticalDB without recovery.
```
RESTORE DATABASE CriticalDB
FROM CriticalDB_Backup
WITH FILE=1, NORECOVERY;
```

3. Restore the differential backup of CriticalDB without recovery.
```
RESTORE DATABASE CriticalDB
FROM CriticalDB_Backup
WITH FILE=4, NORECOVERY;
```

4. Restore the fifth transaction log backup of CriticalDB without recovery.
```
RESTORE DATABASE CriticalDB
FROM CriticalDB_Backup
WITH FILE=5, NORECOVERY;
```

5. Restore the tail-log backup created in step 1 and recover the database.
```
RESTORE DATABASE CriticalDB
FROM CriticalDB_Backup

WITH FILE=6, RECOVERY;
```

Chapter 10: Monitoring SQL Server Activity

Use System Monitor to identify performance bottlenecks.   System Monitor allows you to evaluate the performance of Windows and SQL Server components in order to identify bottlenecks.

Master It   What three main resources are commonly monitored by System Monitor counters?

Solution   CPU utilization, disk I/O performance, and memory usage

Design appropriate traces to monitor events on SQL Server.   SQL Server Profiler allows you to monitor many different types of events occurring on a SQL Server instance.

Master It What guidelines should be followed in order to ensure that a trace has a minimal impact on the server being monitored?

Solution Only monitor for relevant events and columns. Eliminate unneeded columns from monitoring. Use filtering to limit the amount of information recorded by the trace.

Build DDL triggers. Data Definition Language (DDL) triggers make it possible to execute Transact-SQL statements and control transactions.

Master It What function is used to retrieve information about the event that caused a DDL trigger to fire?

Solution The EVENTDATA() function returns an XML document describing the event that caused the trigger to execute. The schema for the XML document can be found at: C:\Program Files\Microsoft SQL Server\100\Tools\Binn\schemas\sqlserver\2006\11\events\events.xsd

Use event notifications to asynchronously capture events occurring on your SQL Server. Event notifications allow Service Broker messages to be sent in response to DDL and trace events.

Master It Can an event notification cause a transaction to be rolled back?

Solution No, an event notification only sends a Service Broker message. It isn't a part of the transaction, therefore the event notification can't roll it back.

Chapter 11: Using the SQL Server Agent Service

Configure Database Mail for email notification. Database Mail allows us to send email from SQL Server Agent and stored procedures. Database Mail uses SMTP servers, where SQL Mail uses extended MAPI calls.

Master It If you're having problems sending email messages using SQL Server Agent, which table can you query to retrieve detailed information about the error messages?

Solution You can query the sysmail_event_log table in the msdb database.

Create jobs to automate routine tasks. Jobs allow us to automate routine tasks using the many available step subsystems.

Master It Imagine you've created a job, and you've tested its execution. The job executes periodically, until one day it stops executing. This occurs right after a reboot of the server. What's the most likely problem?

Solution SQL Server Agent must be started for jobs to execute. It's common to see SQL Server Agent started when it is first used, but you also need to configure the service to automatically start using SQL Server Configuration Manager or the Services console in Administrative Tools.

Create Alerts to detect and respond to various situations. Alerts can respond to performance conditions, error messages, and WMI events, by executing jobs and notifying operators.

Master It If you're executing a job in response to an alert that uses replacement tokens, and the replacement tokens aren't being populated properly, what's the first thing you should check?

Solution Replacement tokens aren't used by default in jobs that fire in response to alerts. You should check the "Replace tokens for all job responses to alerts" option in SQL Server Agent Properties.

Chapter 12: **Data Availability and Distribution**

Identify the elements and benefits of RAID and clustering. RAID and clustering are fault-tolerance techniques that provide an increased uptime when properly implemented. The objective is to ensure that disk or other non-disk failures will not prevent clients from accessing needed data.

Master It For each of the following items below, specify whether RAID or clustering would be the best solution for the described situation.

1. You're concerned about your I/O system having the ability to scale to additional traffic.

2. You want to protect against possible exposure to disk failure.

3. You are concerned that if the network card in your server fails, you will have too much down time.

Solution

1. Anything having to do with I/O is the realm of RAID. If you are concerned strictly with performance and not fault tolerance, consider RAID level 1.

2. Disk faults can also be addressed with RAID. Based on projected performance constraints, you should evaluate combinations of RAID striping, parity striping, and mirroring that will provide the needed protection without unnecessary performance degradation.

3. Clustering can address non-nondisk fault tolerance issues. The partner server in the cluster can take over if the primary server goes down.

Implement transaction log shipping. Log shipping provides an easily maintainable solution to both availability and distribution. With minimal effort, the warm standby server can be brought online and, when properly configured, provide reporting capabilities at the same time.

Master It Describe each of the following log shipping roles.

1. Primary Server

2. Target (Secondary) Server

3. Monitor Server

Solution

1. The primary server stores the production database that accepts the transactions. It is the log of the primary server that is shipped to the secondary server.

2. The target server receives the shipped logs and restores them to the target database. When marked as a standby server, it is also available for reporting.

3. The monitor is a central event monitor. It watches the log shipping event on each server and acts as a central clearing house for all log shipping event information.

Implement database mirroring. With the hallmark of database scope automatic failover, database mirroring is an availability solution that addresses many critical recovery problems. Although not effective for a data-distribution strategy, database mirroring can provide the needed protection against individual database failure.

Master It Which database mirroring mode would you use for each of the following situations?

1. You want the principal server to be able to commit its transactions as quickly as possible, even if that means a slight delay in committing the changes to the mirror.

2. You want to provide an auto-failover capability.

3. You want a high degree of synchronization between the principal and the mirror, but you do not want the overhead of using auto-failover.

Solution

1. Asynchronous (high-performance) mode

2. Synchronous (high-safety) mode with a witness

3. Synchronous (high-safety) mode without a witness

Implement SQL Server replication. With very flexible implementation architecture, replication can address most data-distribution requirements with minimal maintenance. Replication is not suited for availability solutions because there is no guarantee of timely and consistent data delivery at the level required for an availability solution, but it is a very effective approach for distributing selected pieces of data where they are needed.

Master It Which replication role provides each of the following services in a transactional replication model?

1. Distribution in a push subscription

2. Distribution in a pull subscription

3. Executes initial transactions

4. Stores replication transactions ready for delivery

5. Final store of replication transactions

Solution

1. Distributor

2. Subscriber

3. Publisher

4. Distributor

5. Subscriber

Chapter 13: SQL Server Data Security

Create and manage encryption keys.   There are many possibilities when it comes to encryption in SQL Server. Before encrypting data, you should create an appropriate key structure.

Master It   What is used to protect each of the following keys?

1. Database master keys

2. Certificates

3. Asymmetric keys

4. Symmetric keys

Solution

1. Database master keys are protected by both a password and by the service master key to automatically enable decryption. You can remove encryption by the service master key if needed, but this will require that you open the database master key using a password before you can use anything protected by the database master key.

2. Certificates are protected either by a password, EKM device, or by the database master key.

3. Asymmetric keys are protected either by a password, EKM device, or the database master key.

4. Symmetric keys may be encrypted multiple times by different keys. A symmetric key may be encrypted by a certificate, asymmetric key, symmetric key, password, or EKM device. More than one copy of a symmetric key may be encrypted to allow multiple ways to access it.

Transparently encrypt a database.   Transparent Data Encryption allows us to automatically encrypt a SQL Server database and log files without needing to modify applications that use the database.

Master It   Before enabling Transparent Data Encryption, what objects need to be created first?

Solution

1. A database master key in the master database.

2. A certificate or asymmetric key in the master database.

3. A database encryption key for the database protected by either the certificate or asymmetric key in master.

Encrypt data using SQL Server functions. SQL Server provides several functions for encrypting and decrypting data using the encryption keys. Knowing the appropriate use for each function is critical.

Master It! What functions are available for encrypting and decrypting data using a symmetric key?

Solution

1. EncryptByKey

2. DecryptByKey

3. DecryptByKeyAutoCert

4. DecryptByKeyAutoAsmKey

Sign code modules to elevate permissions and prevent modifications. SQL Server allows us to sign modules to grant permissions, rather than relying on ownership chaining. Knowing how this process works will allow you to design and implement more secure database structures that are resistant to modification.

Master It Where can you view information about signed code modules?

Solution Sys.crypt_properties

Chapter 14: Indexing Strategies for Query Optimization

Explain the different indexing architectures and the best uses for each. SQL Server supports a variety of indexing options and a very flexible index implementation model that you can use to optimize query performance. It is critical that you, as a database professional, understand these architectures so that you can create the best indexing strategy to meet your performance goals.

Master It For each of the following query scenarios, identify which indexing architecture you think would be the best suited. For now, disregard maintenance costs and evaluate the indexes only on their merits. There are no definitively right answers. Explain your reasoning.

1. Uniquely selective query (one row returned)

2. Very selective query (few rows returned)

3. Range-based filter

4. Query with no SARGS

Solution

1. If the query always returns just one row, the SARG is probably based on a unique column. If the index is unique, the optimizer does not have to score any other indexes. You should consider creating a unique index. Although you will get better I/O on an absolute basis with a clustered index, you may want to consider a nonclustered index. The overall I/O will not be that much greater and, comparatively speaking, you might benefit more by using the clustered index elsewhere.

2. Similar to question 1, except that you do not have the benefit of a unique index.

3. The more data you select, the less useful a nonclustered index becomes because the data is not grouped on the data page, which requires more pages of I/O to read the data page level. Ultimately, the optimizer will choose a scan. Clustered indexes could prevent this behavior and are better suited.

4. If there are no SARGS at all, no indexes will be useful for filtering unless you can support a covering situation with a nonclustered index. You can still look at the Group By or Order By clauses for additional hints, as an index might be useful in preventing SQL Server from creating temporary result tables (worktables) to resolve these clauses, but this would require a clustered index unless the query is covered.

Create and manage indexes. The CREATE INDEX is simple but very comprehensive. You have many options to make sure that the index implementation is optimal for your performance scenario.

Master It Identify which clause of the CREATE INDEX statement you would use to implement each of the following features.

1. Set the maximum degrees of parallelism to create two parallel query plans.

2. Allow indexes to be created while users are using the table.

3. Configure the index to leave 20 percent of the leaf-level pages free.

4. Drop and rebuild the index in one statement.

5. Add the lastname column to the index leaf-level as a nonindexed field.

Solution

1. MAXDOP = 2

2. ONLINE = ON

3. FILLFACTOR = 80

4. DROP_EXISTING

5. INCLUDE (lastname)

Use special optimizer behaviors to boost performance. The query optimizer is very flexible, but to get the most out of it, you must play by its rules. Understanding how the optimizer will react to special situations gives you a greater ability to capitalize on advantages or avoid pitfalls.

Master It   Write a CREATE INDEX statement that will give you the best index performance for the following query. Assume that @param is an input parameter in a stored procedure that could differ in value with each execution.

```
SELECT ProductName, Price
FROM Orders
WHERE Price > @param
ORDER BY Price DESC;
```

Solution

```
CREATE NONCLUSTERED INDEX NC_Orders_Price
ON Orders(Price DESC)
INCLUDE (ProductName);
```

Price is the only column that is filtered and, therefore, the only one needed in the index. However, if we can include the ProductName in the index, it will cover and we can avoid reading the data page. Because the data will be returned to the client in descending order by price, constructing the index this way will allow the query to begin returning the data immediately to the client and avoid the extra sorting step and the overhead of a worktable.

Chapter 15: Transactions and Locking

Understand and utilize server locking architecture.   Understanding locks and their relationships to transactions is a critical part of managing a SQL Server data environment. Although SQL Server handles all locking automatically for you, you can also get information about locks and transactions through the visual interface and through Transact-SQL code. Knowing why certain locks are held at certain times and being familiar with their compatibility with other locks will also help you manage concurrency.

Master It   For each scenario, identify the lock type that will most likely be used to satisfy the scenario.

1. Select a few rows from a table.

2. Restore a database backup.

3. Rebuild a clustered index.

4. Rebuild a nonclustered index.

5. Delete all rows in a table.

6. Select a range of rows in a table using serializable isolation.

Solution

1. Shared locks on the RID.

2. Exclusive lock on the database.

3. Exclusive lock on the table.

4. Shared lock on the table.

5. Exclusive locks on the RIDs, likely escalating to an exclusive lock on the table.

6. Shared locks on the RIDs with range locks to prevent inserts into the range.

Implement an effective transaction management strategy. Effective transactions make the difference between a consistent database and a heap of junk. The SQL language supports a strict transactional construct and through the SQL Server transaction log, complete ACID transactions are a reality.

Master It Describe the SQL Server auto-commit behavior and explain why it is important in designing a transactional solution.

Solution Auto-commit behavior describes the characteristic of a SQL statement that forces a commit as soon as it is able to complete without error, not waiting for a formal commit instruction. For example, if a single DELETE statement affects 100 underlying rows, all of these rows would be deleted as a transaction. If the rows can be deleted without error, the DELETE will automatically commit. If an error occurs in even one row, all DELETEs will roll back.

This is important to remember as you design your queries because if you want multiple statements to be grouped together as a transaction, you must use explicit transactions to prevent this auto-commit behavior.

Implement an effective distributed transaction strategy. In the larger enterprise, data will be distributed and so, therefore, transactions must also be distributed. Ensuring the integrity of distributed transactions is an important part of any enterprise data architecture.

Master It Explain the difference between the following approaches for querying a remote server:

1. OpenRowset()

2. OpenQuery()

3. Linked server query with four-part name reference

Solution `OpenRowset()` is used for ad hoc queries to a distributed server. They are pass-through queries that contain all authentication and target information in the body of the function call.

If you are going to be using the target server frequently, configure it as a linked server. You can then use a four-part name to reference any object such as a table, view, or stored procedure. If you select from a table using a four-part name, it will return the entire table contents back to the primary server, which is not very efficient.

Using the `OpenQuery()` function, you can execute pass-through queries on a linked server. The function takes the name of the linked server and the query as parameters. This can often be more efficient than using a four-part name when using a linked server.

Get transaction and locking information. Even though SQL Server manages the locking infrastructure for you, it is still frequently necessary to extract information about current transaction and locking status to troubleshoot transaction or locking problems. There are numerous tools available for accessing this information.

Master It What are some of the tools that you can use to extract transaction and locking information from SQL Server?

Solution

1. Use the `sp_lock` system stored procedure.

2. Use the `sp_who` system stored procedure.

3. Use the Activity Monitor in SSMS.

4. Select from transaction-related system views such as `sys.dm_tran_locks` and `sys.dm_tran_active_transactions`.

Chapter 16: Using the Resource Governor and Policy-Based Management

Use the Resource Governor to manage and balance varying workloads. The Resource Governor provides powerful capabilities for monitoring and tuning varying workloads on a SQL Server. Utilizing the Resource Governor can help you better understand and balance workloads across your SQL Server.

Master It What steps must you follow to configure and use the Resource Governor?

Solution

1. Create resource pools, if needed.

2. Create required workload groups.

3. Create a classification function to allocate user sessions into workload groups.

4. Configure the Resource Governor to use the classification function.

5. Monitor the Resource Governor performance counters to better understand the workloads.

Tune the resource pool and workload group settings as required. Use policy-based management to define, evaluate, and enforce a desired configuration. Using policy-based management makes it much easier to configure a server according to best practices and defined policies.

Master It In order to evaluate a policy against a previous version of SQL Server, how must the policy be configured?

Solution It must have an evaluation mode of On Demand, and its conditions must reference facet properties that are valid for that SQL Server version.

Chapter 17: SQL Server and the .NET Client

Connect and query a SQL Server database using ADO.NET connected and disconnected techniques. Understanding how client developers make connections and query your databases will help you manage database resources better. Knowing the differences between connected and disconnected query strategies and how they affect the database is critical to effective database tuning.

Master It For each class in the following list, determine whether you would use it for connected operations, disconnected operations, or both.

1. SqlConnection

2. SqlDataAdapter

3. DataSet

4. SqlCommand

5. SqlDataReader

Solution

1. Both

2. Disconnected

3. Disconnected

4. Both

5. Connected

Use prominent special features of ADO.NET and the SQL Native Client. As ADO.NET matures, Microsoft continually adds special features to the API. As a database professional, it is critical that you understand what these features are so that you can assess their impacts on your databases.

Master It For each of the statements below, specify True or False based on whether the statement will interleave in a MARS connection.

1. SELECT

2. RECEIVE

3. UPDATE

4. INSERT

5. GRANT

6. BULK INSERT

Solution

1. True

2. True

3. False

4. False

5. False

6. True

Understand and implement simple examples using the new Language Integrated Query (LINQ) environment.   LINQ is actually a collection of technologies. You can use LINQ to query a variety of different data structures. Your ability as a developer to leverage LINQ will depend on your understanding of the different environments where LINQ can operate.

Master It   For each of the following scenarios, specify whether you can use LINQ to address the situation, and if so, which variation of LINQ you would use.

1. A data access layer has passed an array of strings to your application and you must identify the string members that are over 10 characters in length.

2. You are connecting to an Oracle server and want to query the data from your data access layer through ADO.NET directly without returning a DataSet.

3. You are connecting to an Oracle server and want to query the data from your data access layer through ADO.NET directly by returning a DataSet.

4. You have created a web application that allows a client to upload sample Simple Object Access Protocol (SOAP) messages. You want to query the SOAP message to show the user what the parameters of their call will be in that message.

Solution

1. Yes, use LINQ to Object.

2. No, Oracle does not directly support LINQ through ADO.NET. LINQ to SQL is only available for SQL Server.

3. Yes, you can use LINQ to DataSet.

4. Yes; because SOAP is an XML dialect, you can use LINQ to XML.

Understand and implement simple examples using the ADO.NET Entity Framework. Although it is new technology, the entity framework promises to change the way that we look at distributed solutions. Understanding the general architecture of the framework will be helpful as you decide where this technology fits into your enterprise solution.

Master It   Answer the following questions relating to the entity framework.

1. What two query options are supported by the entity framework?

2. In which architectural layer of the framework does the database server exist?

3. Is the entity framework only usable by SQL Server?

4. What is a composable query?

Solution

1. LINQ to Entities and Entity SQL.

2. The storage layer.

3. No; because the entity framework uses a provider model, any database with a valid entity framework provider can use the functionality.

4. A query object generated by the entity framework that is typed as IQueryable, thus enabling it to be further queried by additional client operations. All activity in a composable query is performed on the server.

Chapter 18: SQL Server and the Common Language Runtime

Enable and configure the CLR in SQL Server 2008.   For security reasons, the CLR installs as a disabled feature and you must enable it before you will be able to create assemblies in your database. You can control this feature at the database level, and each database will host its own application domain, which gives you the ability to enable the CLR on some but not all databases in a SQL Server instance.

Master It   The CLR integration option is an advanced option that you can only set through code. The code to do this is very specific. Write the statements that you will use to enable this option.

Solution

```
sp_configure 'show advanced options', 1;
GO
RECONFIGURE;
GO
sp_configure 'clr enabled', 1;
GO
RECONFIGURE;
GO
```

Create managed objects for the SQL Server CLR.   Managed objects mimic standard TSQL objects in a database. Unlike standard procedural objects, however, the code for these managed objects is contained in a .NET assembly. You can create managed objects in Visual Studio using any .NET-compliant programming language, including C# and VB.NET.

Master It   For each of the following situations, identify the attribute or code characteristic that you would use in Visual Studio to provide the needed functionality to a managed object.

1. You want to use ADO.NET code in a user-defined function.

2. You need to identify a method for a managed TVF to execute for each populated row in the returned table.

3. You need to execute a command and return the results back to the caller of a stored procedure.

Solution

1. Decorate the function name with the DataAccess attribute.

2. Decorate the Init method of the function with the FillRow attribute which you will set to the name of the populating method.

3. SqlContext.Pipe.ExecuteAndSend(cmd);Deploy managed objects in the SQL Server CLR.

You must deploy managed objects before you can use them. Start by registering the assembly with the target database. Then you can use standard data definition statements to create the actual artifacts such as stored procedures and functions.

Master It Write a script that registers a managed assembly called Demo located at C:\demo.dll. The script should then add a function from the script called DemoFunction that takes no arguments and returns an integer. Assume that DemoFunction is in a class called UserDefinedFunctions.

Solution

```
CREATE ASSEMBLY Demo
FROM 'C:\Demo.dll';
GO
CREATE FUNCTION DemoFunction()
RETURNS int
AS
EXTERNAL NAME [Demo].[UserDefinedFunctions].DemoFunction;
GO
```

Manage security for the SQL Server CLR. Because these objects are very powerful, you must manage the security risk appropriately. You can implement user- and role-based security to control access to the managed objects. Additionally, you can use code access security through permission sets to ensure that the managed code is not allowed to execute actions outside of permitted and reasonable boundaries.

Master It For each of the following situations, indicate whether you would use user security or code access security to achieve the desired result. Also, specify which object's permissions must be modified and which permissions you should use.

1. An assembly called Demo contains a managed function called DemoFunction. You want to secure access to DemoFunction in the database.

2. An assembly called Demo contains a managed function called DemoFunction. Demo function performs database access to the local database.

3. An assembly called Demo contains a managed function called DemoFunction. This function accesses the file system.

4. An assembly called Demo contains a managed function called DemoFunction. You need to allow a backup administrator to take ownership if necessary.

Solution

1. You will implement user security on the function by granting execute permissions to the desired users to roles.

2. This is a scenario of code access security; however, access to the local database is provided by default using the permission set of safe, so you need take no action.

3. You will use code access security to change the permission set on the assembly to External access.

4. You will implement user security on the assembly by granting the take ownership permission to the backup administrator.

Chapter 19: Using Spatial Data

Define spatial storage in SQL Server. As a new feature of SQL Server 2008, you can store information on a variety of geometric shapes directly in SQL Server tables, variables, and parameters. The data storage conforms to accepted standards for geospatial storage, and Microsoft provides support to manipulate and query these values using standards-based methods. Both planar and ellipsoidal space are supported.

Master It For each of the following scenarios, indicate which of the geometry/geography subtypes would be best suited to address the scenario.

1. You need to pass position locations to a procedure to calculate the distance between them.

2. Your client application defines a boundary, and you need to return a list of all stored locations that are contained within that boundary.

3. You need to add a position location to a database table.

4. Your application must calculate the total distance traveled along a set of line segments that connect stored points.

Solution

1. If you are passing a set of locations to a procedure, it makes the most sense to use a MultiPoint type. This can contain multiple positions, and you can easily calculate relationships between them.

2. A boundary indicates a closed shape, which means that you should probably use a Polygon type. The Points are stored in the database, so a query can easily return the list of points that fall within the boundary.

3. A single position indicated a Point. You should create the instance of the Point type and add it to the database into a column of a spatial type.

4. A set of line segments is a LineString. Using the LineString type, you can sum up the total length of the entire line across all segments.

Implement geometry data. The geometry type represents shapes on a flat planar surface. You can use the geometry type to define points, line segments, and Polygons on this planar surface. Standards-based methods allow you to query objects based on relationships to other objects as well as to get information about the objects themselves.

Master It Based on the following figure, write the code statement that calculates the distance between these two points on a flat planar space in a SRID neutral environment.

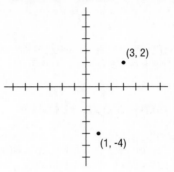

Solution The variable @distance contains the solution value

```
DECLARE @point1 geometry;
DECLARE @point2 geometry;
DECLARE @distance numeric(10,2);
SELECT @point1 = geometry::STPointFromText('POINT(3 2)',0);
SELECT @point2 = geometry::STPointFromText('POINT(1 -4)',0);
SELECT @distance = @point1.STDistance(@point2);
```

Implement geography data. Useful for GPS and Earth-mapping applications, the geography type provides an ellipsoidal surface for managing geometric shapes. This type is similar to the geometry type in most respects.

Master It Based on the following figure, write the code statement that creates the shape in an ellipsoidal space using the WGS 84 spatial reference system and calculates its area.

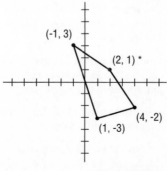

*Starting Point

Solution   The variable @area contains the solution value

```
DECLARE @poly1 geography;
DECLARE @area float;
SELECT @poly1 = geography::STPolyFromText('POLYGON((2 1,-1 3,1 -3,4 -2, 2
1))',4326);
SELECT @area = @poly1.STArea();
```

Implement spatial indexes.   To improve the performance of spatially driven queries, you can create spatial indexes on spatial datatyped columns. These indexes break geometric data into linear structures based on grid coordinates. When properly implemented, they can significantly increase the performance of spatial queries.

Master It   Write the TSQL statement that would create a spatial index meeting the following criteria:

◆ The index name is idx_Location.

◆ The spatial data is stored in a table called Equipment.

◆ The spatial data column is Location.

◆ Use geometric tessellation.

◆ The index levels 1 and 2 are low density.

◆ Index level 3 is medium density.

◆ Index level 4 is high density.

◆ There are 64 cells per object.

◆ The bounding box is min 0 for x and y and max 200 for x and y.

Solution

```
CREATE SPATIAL INDEX idx_Location
  ON dbo.Equipment(Location)
  USING GEOMETRY_GRID
  WITH (
    BOUNDING_BOX = ( xmin=0, ymin=0, xmax=200, ymax=200 ),
    GRIDS = (LOW, LOW, MEDIUM, HIGH),
    CELLS_PER_OBJECT = 64);
```

Chapter 20: Service-Oriented Architecture and the Service Broker

Describe service-oriented architecture.   Services are everywhere and almost all modern business applications provide at least some service structure. Some services are better than others, though. It all depends on how they are designed and implemented. It is important to understand the characteristics of a good service.

Master It For each of the following scenarios, identify which characteristic of a good service is being violated.

1. Joe creates a service that accepts a message containing numeric data from a client, calculates values from the numeric data, and prints the output on a local printer.

2. Mary creates a service that accepts login information from a user and then extracts user preference information from a database. Whenever the user connects again to the service, it reuses the preference information retrieved.

3. Bill creates a service that accepts a serialized SQLCommand object as a parameter. This command is then used by the service to select information from a database.

Solution

1. Good services should be composable. Don't create services that do too much. This service both calculates and prints. Good service design would separate these two unrelated activities into two different services.

2. Good services should be stateless. Never store data in a service if you can help it. A good service should never have to remember anything about a caller between calls to function correctly.

3. Good services should expose only a formal contract. Concrete class implementations restrict the flexibility of the service and couple it too tightly to implementation details. Use interfaces or XML schemas instead of specific object types.

Design a solution using SQL Server Service Broker. Service Broker uses message queuing architecture to decouple data services from each other. As opposed to other options such as linked server queries, the caller does not have to know anything about the implementation of the service at the target. Designing good service architecture takes practice, however. Different scenarios lend themselves to different solutions.

Master It For each of the design requirements listed here, specify which feature of Service Broker meets the architectural requirement in the design, or identify if Service Broker cannot meet this requirement.

1. Data tiers must be loosely coupled and should not expose any internal details outside of the data tier.

2. Message processing must be automated, ensuring that messages are handled as quickly and efficiently as possible.

3. The service must be able to handle multiple clients and must ensure its ability to identify each one.

4. The services must operate across multiple platforms and accept messages from clients running any operating system.

Solution

1. The Service Broker message-based architecture abstracts all implementation details from the parties involved in the service scenario. The messages are simply data packets and do not assume any specific implementation requirements.

2. Activation in queues provides the ability to automate the processing of arriving messages. When a queue is configured with an activating stored procedure, that procedure will automatically respond when a new message arrives in the queue.

3. Dialog handles are included in all message communications. These handles are the identifiers of a particular conversation between the target service and one of its initiator instances.

4. SQL Server does not directly support this behavior. The only way to enqueue a message is to use a TSQL statement, which requires running SQL Server on a Windows platform. You could, however, create a web interface that makes the call to SQL Server; the web page could be available to a client running on any platform.

Implement Service Broker artifacts. All of the components of a SQL Server Service Broker application are persisted database objects. They become part of the system dictionary of the initiating or target process. The dialogs that send and receive messages will use these artifacts for all data processing.

Master It For each of the following, identify the Service Broker artifact that satisfies the definition.

1. A special table structure where all messages are persistently stored.

2. The object that defines the required structure of a message.

3. Information regarding the location of a remote service.

4. A point of contact that accepts messages from remote clients.

5. An object that provides a script for the message pattern.

Solution

1. Queue

2. Message type

3. Route

4. Endpoint

5. Contract

Chapter 21: Full-Text Search Services

Explain and apply full-text architecture in SQL Server 2008. SQL Server full-text indexes are architecturally different from standard indexes in SQL Server 2008. In addition to the physical storage format, they are also organized differently. Prior versions of SQL Server organized the indexes completely outside of the database, which required separate backup operations for the indexes, but today they are also database-resident. Understanding the architectural differences between standard and full-text indexes is an important step to properly maintaining the application.

Master It Describe the primary differences between standard indexes and full-text indexes in SQL Server 2008.

Solution

1. You can create numerous standard indexes on each table. Only one full-text index is allowed per table. All text tokenization for included columns will occur in that one index.

2. Standard indexes are always automatically updated when you modify data. Full-text indexes give you a choice. After initial population, you can update the index after each data modification, or do the index maintenance in batches either manually or on a schedule.

3. Full-text indexes are organized into catalogs, an artifact at the database level. This is not true with standard indexes. Catalogs allow you to take aggregate actions on indexes to perform actions such as dropping or rebuilding on the entire set.

Implement full-text indexes. You can implement a full-text index using TSQL code or with the SSMS interface. No matter which approach you use, you will have to be familiar with the terminology that is specific to full-text indexing.

Master It Define each of the following terms used in creating full-text indexes.

1. Type column
2. Language
3. Key index
4. change-tracking
5. Stoplist

Solution

1. A column in a table that contains metadata, usually a file extension, that identifies the format of text data stored in another column.

2. Indicator of the language set used by the filters and stemmers when processing data using the index.

3. The unique index on the base table to which the full-text index is related. The key is used to maintain entity consistency in the full-text index.

4. Describes how changes to the underlying data will be tracked so that the index can be updated accordingly. The population options available will depend on this setting.

5. A set of words that are considered noise and ignored when crawling the index. Stoplists are implemented in the system catalog and can be customized.

Write queries utilizing full-text features of SQL Server 2008.   Once full-text indexes exist on a table, you can use special statements in your TSQL code to access these indexes. There are four key terms in total, each one differing slightly in its implementation and return structure.

Master It   List the four full-text keywords that you can use in your code, identify if that keyword is a function or a predicate, and provide a brief description of its behavior.

Solution

1. CONTAINS (Predicate): Used in a WHERE or HAVING clause of a query. Provides the ability to filter based on the existence of specific words or word forms and the relationships between words in the data structure.

2. CONTAINSTABLE (Function): Used in a FROM clause. Performs the same function as CONTAINS, but returns a table consisting of the standard keys and ranks of all qualifying rows.

3. FREETEXT (Predicate): Used in a WHERE or HAVING clause. Provides for a free form query, testing all general relationships instead of specific conditions and relationships.

4. FREETEXTTABLE (Function): Used in a FROM clause. Performs the same function as FREETEXT, but returns a table consisting of the standard keys and ranks of all qualifying rows.

SQL Server Analysis Services Overview

Introduced originally in SQL Server 7.0, the Analysis Services package provides business intelligence capabilities that are tightly integrated with the SQL Server toolset. Storing data is not enough. If you are not using that data to make intelligent business decisions, you are missing a significant potential that SQL Server offers. Unfortunately, many SQL Server professionals are not aware of the power of the Analysis Services package and what it can offer their businesses. Our goal is not to cover the intricate details on data warehousing and Analysis Services. Entire books have been devoted to those subjects. We do, however, want to familiarize you with the tools available so that you can make an effective decision as to whether or not you should explore these issues further.

There are many aspects to data warehousing and business intelligence. In this discussion, we will address the basic concepts of the data warehouse and multidimensional data model. Then we will look specifically at the Analysis Services toolset to see how to create data cubes and manage data aggregations.

Designing the Data Warehouse

If you are creating transactional data structures using more traditional Online Transaction Processing (OLTP) models, you are used to implementing relational designs. The benefit of relational data structures is that they reduce data redundancy and ease maintenance through a single point of change. Not only can this conserve disk space, but more importantly it reduces the probability of error by ensuring that data is singularly maintainable. Managing data will require only one change and not many.

The problem with fully relational designs, however, is that they are not well-suited to reporting and data mining. A fully normalized design reduces redundancy by distributing data throughout the database and joining the entities. The joins are particularly problematic for performance increasing the I/O required to correlate the information. Another problem is that reporting on data often requires aggregation, and in a fully normalized design, data is maintained at an atomically granular level, which requires you to perform aggregations as you request the data.

Still even more problematic is the tendency to use the same relational data structure for both reporting and transactional purposes, thereby creating contention and hotspots in the data. For example, running reports based on tables that are heavily transacted can potentially block transactions from completing. In some cases, this could be very serious because preventing transactions from completing in a synchronous business flow can interrupt business operations at critical and high-volume points in time. Although using locking hints can alleviate some of the pressure, having to use hints such as NOLOCK should be a red flag to any data professional, signaling that there are problems with the current data design and its applicability to the current business process.

Data Warehouse Defined

The concept of the data warehouse addresses these specific issues. Many business-oriented practitioners incorrectly think of a data warehouse as simply a large-scale repository of historical data. In reality, it is much more than that. A data warehouse is a repository, but it is designed specifically to meet the needs of the reporting and data analysis roles. A good data warehouse will usually have the following characteristics:

Integrated   Good data warehouses should be integration points for all relevant data from the business. You may have many different transactional data sources, but the data warehouse provides a single point where all of the data can come together. This allows the data to be correlated across functional areas that might have their own transactional data structures. It may even provide integrations with data from outside the organization that could be useful for the decision-making process.

Consistent   When you integrate data from a variety of different sources, it is likely that different sources will describe data in different terms. Combining the data into a single warehouse will be useless unless the data is consistent in terms of measures and structure. For example, if one data source provides measurements in metric units and another in English units, it could cause a consistency issue when correlating that data.

Read Only   Data warehouses are not transactional. Transactions should be executed in the OLTP databases and then loaded into the data warehouse. Although you may not actually mark the warehouse as read only in SQL Server, you should essentially treat it as read only, with the only exception being the load process. This way you will have no contention between the extraction of data from the warehouse and other transactional activity.

Automated   The process of loading the data warehouse should be automated. Using tools like SQL Server Integration Services (SSIS), you can create components that will connect to all needed transactional data sources and load the data into the warehouse. SSIS also allows you to perform transformations to the data as you load it, thus ensuring the consistency of the data by the time it reaches the warehouse. Loads can either be complete or incremental, depending on your load strategy.

RESTORE OR RELOAD?

Whether you need to back up your warehouses or not is often debatable. Data warehouses can be quite large, and backing them up might take a lot of time. If you can restore your data warehouse simply by reloading it from the operational data stores, do you really need to back up the warehouse? There is no right answer to this question. You must consider all factors, including the potential size and scope of the backup, the time it would take to reload the warehouse, and the future availability of archived operational data. Evaluate all factors and decide what is right for you.

Dimensional Data Models

In light of the specialized needs of the data warehouse, it should come as no surprise that specialized data models exists to handle these needs. After significant research regarding the advantages and disadvantages, the data warehousing industry, lead by great minds like Ralph

Kimball (http://www.rkimball.com) and William Inmon (http://www.inmongif.com), has settled on some best practices for organizing the data warehouse. One of the fundamental design practices includes dimensional data modeling.

In a relational world, you strive for a data structure where all data dealing with a specific described entity is located in a single table. Dimensional modeling takes a different approach. All data is separated into two categories, namely measures and dimensions.

Measures represent quantitative data (for example, the number of units of product sold to a customer, the total value of the sale, or the number of coins played on a slot machine). Each measure gives us a raw datum, but without context. The goal of the measure is to store numeric data that can be aggregated depending on how you select the data. In a dimensional model, measures are organized into fact tables. Each fact table describes a specific set of discrete facts, but those facts are meaningless without context. This is where dimensions come in.

A *dimension* is qualitative data. It is more descriptive than a fact, but again it has no meaning unless there is a fact with which to relate it. A dimension might include information about a customer, such as the customer name and the customer's location. This data is stored in tables called dimension tables. Each field in a dimension table indicates a potential way to slice through and aggregate the fact data.

The fact and dimension tables correlate through a set of keys. These keys are generally contrived, having no inherent meaning other than the value through which the facts and dimensions relate. Figure B.1 illustrates a simple dimensional model. The general shape of this model looks like a star with the fact table in the middle and the dimension tables organized around it. This design is, therefore, referred to as a star schema, and it is the standard structure in data warehouse design.

FIGURE B.1

A simple star schema

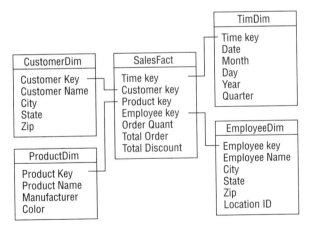

In this illustration, the SalesFact table has keys and measures. The keys relate to the dimensions, and the measures provide the actual data. If you look at the time dimensions, you will notice that the fields are designed to describe a single point in time. Based on the date, information such as the day, month, year, and quarter would populate each row of the TimeDim table such that each row would describe a specific and unique point in time. The same is true with the other dimension tables, each row describing a specific occurrence of that dimensional entity.

As you can see, the advantage of this approach is that with minimal join depth, you can slice through the facts using multiple dimensions at any level of aggregation. For example, if you want to find out the total units sold of a specific product in March of last year. The ProductDim allows you to slice through the fact data by ProductName, while the TimeDim provides the same functionality by month. The query then aggregates the fact data based on these criteria to return the desired value. This elegant solution allows you to slice through the data any way you want while keeping the cost of the operation at a reasonable level.

THE QUESTION OF GRAIN

The granularity of data in a data warehouse is an integral part of the warehouse design. For example, you could create a time dimension that stored an entity for every second of time instead of every day, as in this example. If your business requirements state that you need to be able to extract the data at this level of granularity, then it would be reasonable. However, if you never extract data at a grain finer than a day, it would cause the table sizes of the TimeDim and SalesFact tables to grow unnecessarily while providing no practical benefit. You would have to perform additional aggregation on the data to roll it up to the level of grain that was useful. Although you want to have a grain that supports your business requirements, it is wasteful to warehouse data at a level of grain that is not useful or practical.

Of course, a real data warehouse will have many fact tables. As a result, they will probably share dimensions among them. It is very common for a time dimension, for example, to be shared across most if not all fact tables in a data warehouse. This is one of the reasons that consistency is so important. If the warehouse does not consistently describe the same things in the same terms using the same units, it becomes impossible to effectively integrate the dimensions and results in portions of the warehouse that are stovepipes, or standalone pieces that are not integrated with the rest of the warehouse.

You do not need any special SQL Server tools to create a data warehouse. Although Analysis Services is frequently associated with data warehousing, for reasons which you will see in a moment, you do not need Analysis Services to create a warehouse. Building a data warehouse has much more to do with your database design than it does any special toolset and with no additional tool knowledge, you could design and implement a data warehouse today.

Understanding Analysis Services

Analysis Services is a SQL Server component that adds value to a data warehouse by allowing the database engineer to pre-aggregate data into multidimensional data structures called cubes. A *cube* is nothing more that the intersection of selected dimension fields and facts. The cube processor pre-aggregates the data and stores it in the cube. The goal is to have a data structure that allows significantly faster retrieval of data from the warehouse by performing the aggregations before they are needed so that the data can be returned immediately to the requestor without performing any joins or any aggregations.

For example, consider the previous example of returning the total number of units ordered for a specific product in the month of March. Because the TimeDim table has a granularity to the day, some aggregation must occur to return the sum based on the monthly value because there are multiple fact rows that all satisfy the criteria. Similarly, if you were interested in a result of the total units for a particular product manufacturer in the month of March, then you would have another level of aggregation because one manufacturer may actually produce many products.

The rationale behind data cubes is that if you perform all of these joins and aggregations when you select the data from the warehouse, you will spend a lot of time performing joins and calculating the same aggregates over and over again. By pre-aggregating the data, you will perform this action once when the aggregates are first generated, but from then on, you can retrieve the aggregates directly from the cube.

Because the data warehouse is read only, you never have to worry about the cubes being out of sync with the data warehouse. If, however, you load new data into the data warehouse, you can invalidate the cubes and reprocess the cube to sync it with the warehouse. All of this can be done on a schedule, and cube processing can be included in the SSIS packages that you use to reload the data warehouse.

Creating Data Cubes

The first step in creating data cubes is to create an Analysis Services project. When you install SQL Server 2008, you will get the Visual Studio 2008 environment with some SQL Server Business Intelligence projects, such as Analysis Services, Reporting Services, and Integration Services. Analysis Services is the tool that you will use to set up an Analysis Services data structure.

1. Begin by starting the tool, either by starting Visual Studio 2008 or the BI developer. Select Start ➤ All Programs ➤ Microsoft SQL Server 2008 ➤ SQL Server Business Intelligence Development Studio.

2. To create a new Analysis Service project, select File ➤ New ➤ Project from the menu.

3. In the list on the left side of the dialog, select Business Intelligence Projects. This will give you a list of templates on the right.

4. From the Templates list, select Analysis Services Project as pictured in Figure B.2. Our sample project is called AWSample.

FIGURE B.2
The New
Project dialog

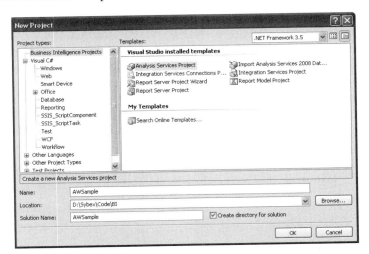

Creating a Data Source

The new project will contain folders in the Solution Explorer that identify the different artifacts in the project, including data sources, dimensions, and cubes. If the Solution Explorer is not visible, click View ➤ Solution Explorer from the menu. We will begin by creating a data source. The data in our example will be based on the AdventureWorksDW2008 database, which is organized into a star schema.

1. Right-click on the Data Sources folder in the Solution Explorer. Select New Data Source from the popup menu. This will start the wizard. The first page of the wizard is only informational. Just click the Next button to advance.

2. You must create a data connection before you can complete the wizard. Click the New button in the middle of the dialog to open the Connection Manager. Complete the dialog as shown in the example in Figure B.3, substituting your server information where appropriate. Test the connection and then click OK.

FIGURE B.3

The Connection Manager

3. This should take you back to the Data Source Wizard, and your new connection should display in the Data connections list box of the dialog. At this point, it should look something like the example in Figure B.4. Click Next to advance.

4. The next screen, pictured in Figure B.5, allows you to set the security structure for how Analysis Services will connect to the underlying database. In our example, we are using the service account, which means we will use the account credentials specified for the service when Analysis Services was installed. Click Next to advance.

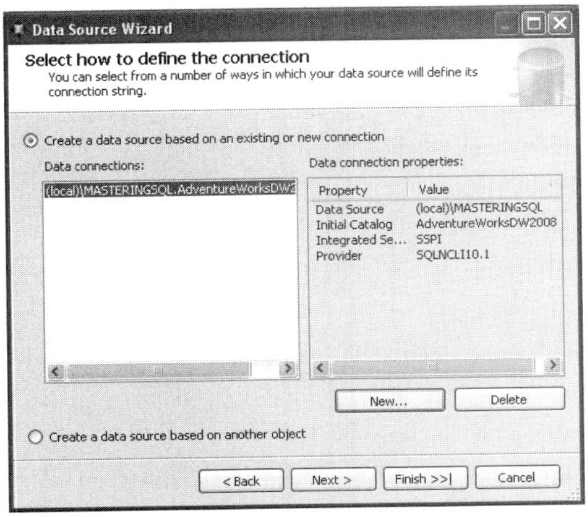

FIGURE B.4

Selecting a
data source

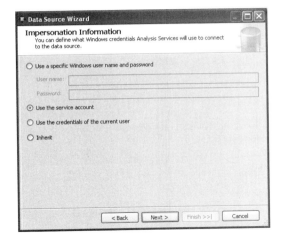

FIGURE B.5

Setting the
service identity

5. Finally, you must enter the name of your data source in the Data Source Name field. The
   example in Figure B.6 uses Adventure Works DW2008, which is the default name based
   on the configurations. Enter Click Finish to complete the wizard.

This should add a new item to the Data Sources list in the Solution Explorer. A data source
provides the connection structure to the database, but it does not identify which of all of the
tables and views in the data source you will use in your application. For that, we need a data
source view.

FIGURE B.6

Configuring the
Data Source Name

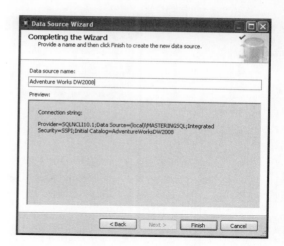

Creating a Data Source View

To create a data source view, use the following steps.

1. Right-click the Data Source Views folder in the Solution Explorer and select New Data Source View from the popup menu. Click Next to advance beyond the informational screen.

2. Select the desired data source in the next screen, as pictured in Figure B.7. Because we have only one data source, it should be the only one listed. You could create a new data source at this step if you wanted. Click Next to advance.

FIGURE B.7

Selecting a data
source for the view

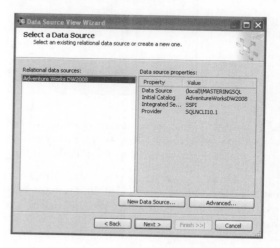

3. The next screen allows you to select tables from the database to use in your data source. In our simple example, we will select the DimDate, DimReseller, and FactResellerSales tables as pictured in Figure B.8. Then click Next to advance.

FIGURE B.8
Select the data
source tables

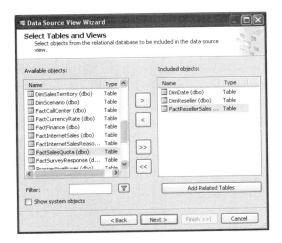

4. The final screen (not pictured) allows you to specify a name for the data source view. The one for this example will be called Reseller Data View. Enter this name and then click Finish to complete the wizard. You should see a new item in the Views list as well as a relational diagram of the selected tables in the Main Client screen.

If you look at the relational diagram created by the wizard, you will notice multiple lines drawn from the FactResellerSales table to the DimDate table. This is because the FactResellerSales table has multiple date values including OrderDate, ShipDate, and DueDate. They can all be queried using the same DimDate table. This is an example of dimension reuse.

Creating a Dimension

The next step is to create the dimensions you will use to aggregate the data into the cube. You will base the dimensions on the dimension tables in the underlying database, but it is not necessary to use all of the dimension fields. In fact, one way to control the quantity of data that results from processing a cube is to restrict the number of hierarchical levels in the dimension, thereby reducing the amount of aggregation that must occur.

1. To begin, right-click the Dimensions folder in the Solution Explorer and select New Dimension to start the wizard. Click Next to advance beyond the informational page.

2. In this example, we are going to base a dimension on the DimDate table in the database; so in the next screen, select Use An Existing Table, as shown in the example in Figure B.9. Click Next to advance.

3. The next screen specifies the source table in the data source view. If you had created multiple views, the Data Source View dropdown list would allow you to select the view. The Main Table dropdown allows you to select a table from the view. In our example, the DimDate table is selected. You will have to select the Key column in the table to relate the facts for cube processing. We will use the standard DateKey. Figure B.10 illustrates the completed dialog. Click Next to continue.

FIGURE B.9
Selecting the
dimension source

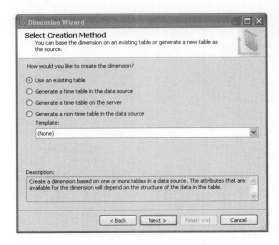

FIGURE B.10
Configuring
the dimension

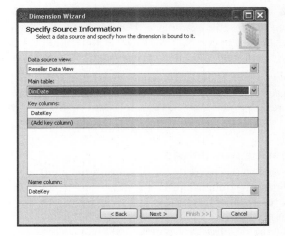

4. Now you must determine which fields to select from the table. Your decision should be based on the desired extraction criteria and acceptable levels of aggregation. Notice in Figure B.11 how the Attribute Type setting helps to establish a hierarchy among values. Select attributes to match the dialog and click Next to advance.

5. The final screen (not pictured) allows you to name your dimension. This dimension is Dim Date. After creating the Dimension, it will appear in the Dimensions folder in the Solution Explorer. Additionally, the Dimension Designer will appear.

6. You will need to define the dimension hierarchy in this designer. Drag the CalendarYear attribute from the attributes list anywhere into the Hierarchies pane. This will create a hierarchy box. Populate this screen like the example in Figure B12 by dragging attributes from the list into the hierarchy.

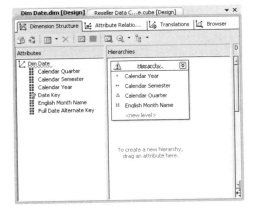

Deploying the Project

You must deploy the project to an Analysis Server before you will be able to view data in the dimension.

1. To configure the deployment, first make sure that Analysis Services is running on the target server. You can use the SQL Server Configuration Manager utility to verify the server state.

2. Then right-click the project name in Solution Explorer and select Properties from the menu.

3. Configure the deployment properties as pictured in Figure B.13, substituting the name of your Analysis Services instance for the one in the dialog.

FIGURE B13

Setting the deployment properties

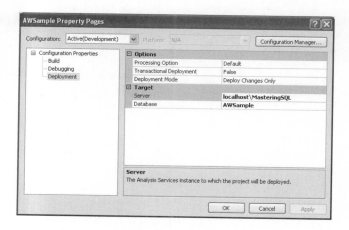

4. Now right-click the project name again and select Deploy from the menu. This will connect to the Analysis Server and deploy the project into an Analysis Server database.

After deployment, you should be able to browse the time dimension data by clicking on the Browser tab in the Dimension Designer. Expand the All level to see the years. Expand a year to see the semesters, and so on.

Creating a Cube

The dimension data is useless unless you have data to aggregate. The next step is to create a data cube. We created the time dimension in advance, but you could also create the dimension on the fly as you create the cube. We will create the Dim Reseller dimension using this approach.

1. Start by right-clicking on the Cubes folder in the Solution Explorer. Select New Cube from the menu. Click Next to Advance beyond the introduction screen.

2. This screen allows you to select the new cube structure. You can base the cube on existing tables in the data source view, or you can create an empty cube. You also have the option of generating new data tables, similarly to way you did with the Dimension Wizard. Our example will use existing tables, as illustrated in Figure B.14. Click Next to advance.

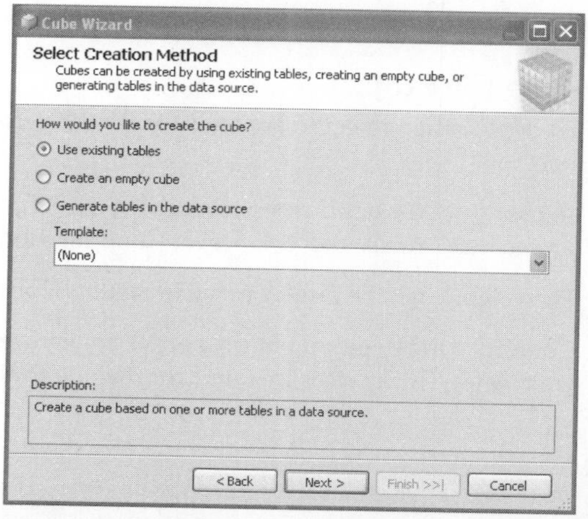

FIGURE B.14

Setting the
cube source

3. This screen allows you to select the Measure Group table, also called the fact table. In our example, FactResellerSales is the fact table. Select this table, as shown in Figure B15, and click Next to advance.

FIGURE B.15
Selecting the
fact table

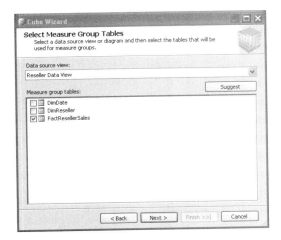

4. Now you must select the measures for the cube. Select only the measures that will be meaningful; including unneeded measures can significantly increase the size of the aggregation. You should also deselect any keys. They are not measures and will never be aggregated. The example in Figure B.16 includes only Order Quantity and Sales Amount. Click Next to advance.

FIGURE B.16
Selecting
the measures

5. If there are existing dimensions designed in the project, you can choose to associate those dimensions with the cube. Pay attention to the keys in the fact table. The keys will tell you which dimensions may be valid choices for processing these aggregations. As you see in Figure B.17, we can select only the existing Dim Time dimension. Click Next to advance.

FIGURE B.17
Associating existing dimensions

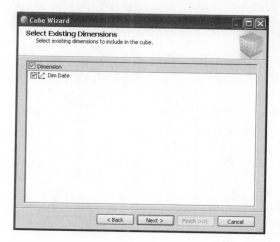

6. The next screen provides a list of tables not covered by existing dimensions for which you may want to create dimensions to cover. In this dialog, shown in Figure B.18, note that the fact table is not selected. This would be pointless as there is no qualitative data in the fact table. The DimReseller table, however, is not currently related to a dimension and, therefore, is included. Click Next to advance.

FIGURE B.18
Selecting new dimensions

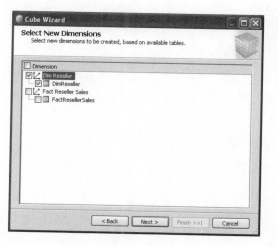

7. The final screen (not pictured) allows you to name the cube. Our example is named Reseller Data Cube. After you name your cube, click Finish in the dialog and the new cube will appear in the Solution Explorer.

Because you created the Dim Reseller dimension concurrently with creating the cube, it is not very useful until you add attributes to the dimension.

1. In the Solution Explorer, double-click on the Dim Reseller in the Dimensions folder to make the Dimension Designer appear.

2. The pane on the far right provides a list of fields in the table. Drag the BankName and ResellerName fields from this list to the Dimension Attributes list on the far left. This will add these two fields as attributes of the dimension.

3. Create the hierarchy in a similar fashion to the way you created the Dim Date dimension. (Because many resellers may use the same bank, there is implied hierarchy.) Drag out the BankName first and then the ResellerName underneath into the Hierarchies panel of the Designer.

4. Then deploy the project and browse the dimension. You should see that resellers are grouped by bank name.

Browsing a Cube

Now that you have created and deployed the cube, you can browse the aggregates in the cube.

1. In the Cubes folder in the Solution Explorer, double-click on the Reseller Sales Cube and click on the Browser tab in the Cube Designer. You will see a screen like the one pictured in Figure B.19. The left pane is a tree view of the available measures and dimensions, and the right pane has drop zones that you can use to drop data into for display.

FIGURE B.19

The Cube Browser

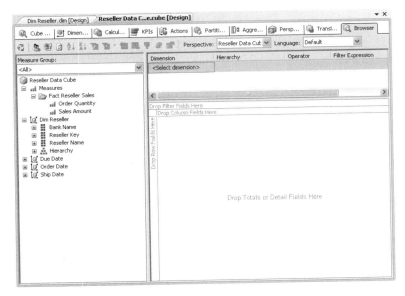

2. Drop the fields into the zones as follows:

   ◆ BankName into the Row Fields zone

   ◆ Order Date into the Column Fields zone

   ◆ Sales Amount into the Detail Fields zone

You should now be looking at a summary of sales data based on Reseller Bank per calendar year. Of course, you could have dragged out any dimension field at any level of hierarchy to change the granularity of the aggregation. The response time should be virtually instantaneous because the data does not have to be extracted from the database but rather is pre-aggregated when the cube is processed.

This has been a very quick overview of the Analysis Services tool, and it only scratches the surface of what it can do. If you think your business and decision-making processes could benefit from having this kind of data readily available, you owe it to yourself and your organization to dig a little deeper into the product. You will find a tool that is very flexible and very powerful, and definitely worth your time to explore.

SQL Server 2008 Reporting Services

Data itself is meaningless without context. As a database professional, a significant portion of your work is devoted to making the masses of raw data that your organization collects more meaningful. You use queries with elaborate filters and grouping statements and stored procedures with both input and output parameters, all to try to organize data so that it tells a meaningful story.

The truth, though, is that even the most meaningful data is of little value if it is not presented in an effective manner. In the past, numerous approaches have been commonly used to organize data to tell a meaningful story. Even with SQL Server 2008, you have numerous choices on how to best deliver data to the intended recipient. One of the most common choices for SQL Server users is SQL Server Reporting Services. This tool provides a complete set of functionality to deliver any content ranging from the simplest data set to extremely complex graphical presentations, all under the SQL Server umbrella.

Almost every database application needs some kind of reporting capability. The problem in the past has been that purchasing a reporting package requires the database professional to learn a whole new product and a new set of paradigms. SQL Server Reporting Services changes that for the SQL Server professional by providing a comprehensive toolset that tightly integrates with the existing SQL Server infrastructure. Reporting Services is a set of tools including a designer, server components, ASP.NET configuration components, and a web services interface.

The subject of SQL Server Reporting Services is certainly vast enough to fill its own volume. In fact, you have to look no further than the Sybex catalog for outstanding resources on Reporting Services. Our goal in this short appendix is, therefore, to walk you through the process of using Reporting Services to set up a connection to database artifacts and create some simple reports. Specifically, in this appendix, we will look at the basic configuration for reporting and creating simple tabular reports. This should at least let you hit the ground running as you begin learning how to implement Reporting Services features in your environment.

Configuring Reporting Services

SQL Server Reporting Services allows for two standard configuration options. When you install SQL Server and Reporting Services, you can decide whether to use a native mode configuration or a SharePoint integrated mode. The difference is primarily how the report libraries are maintained and how you gain access to the reports.

In a native mode configuration, the report server executes on a standard HTTP service. This can be either Internet Information Server (IIS) or it can be a lightweight local web server, usually used for development. As an alternative, you can also integrate the reporting environment with SharePoint, thus creating a SharePoint catalog for the reports and using this SharePoint portal for all access to reports. This also allows the reports to use SharePoint security configurations.

If you install a basic native mode configuration, like the one we will use in this appendix, you will get a local HTTP implementation, most likely resolving to port 8080. This port will expose your report catalog. All reports will deploy to this catalog, and your users will access the reports by navigating to this catalog. Additionally, because the Application Programming Interface (API) of Reporting Services is web service-based, you can also make web service calls to this endpoint to have the server return report content to your application programmatically.

Starting and Locating Reporting Services Ports

Before you can deploy reports to a Reporting Services instance, you must first ensure that the instance is running and you must know the location of that instance. To start Reporting Services, you can go to the SQL Server Configuration Manager utility. Start this utility by going to the Windows Start menu and selecting Start ➤ All Programs ➤ Microsoft SQL Server 2008 ➤ Configuration Tools ➤ SQL Server Configuration Manager. This will open the screen pictured in Figure C.1. Note the instance name, in this case MasteringSQL, next to the Reporting Services node. Each SQL Server installation can have its own Reporting Services instance as well. If you have multiple instances, make a note of which instance you are using.

You can right-click on this node in the Configuration Manager to start and stop the service as well as to access service properties. Make sure that your Reporting Services instance is running before you attempt to connect to the instance in the next step.

You can also configure much of the Reporting Services behavior by connecting to the instance in the SQL Server Management Studio (SSMS). To make this connection, start SSMS and in the connection dialog, specify Reporting Services as the target service as illustrated in Figure C.2. Once connected, you will be able to manage security and report schedules from the SSMS interface. A web-based interface called the Report Manager also provides this same functionality.

FIGURE C.1
Configuring
Reporting
Services

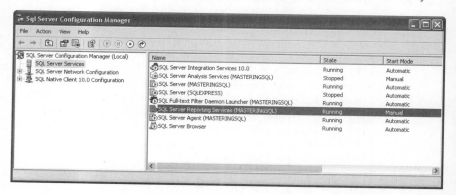

You can get important information about the Reporting Services instance through the SSMS interface. Point to the server instance in the Object Explorer and right-click. From the popup menu, select Properties. This will open the dialog illustrated in Figure C.3. Notice that the URL property contains an HTTP address. This is the location of the web service where the Reporting Services instance is running. In this example, there is a local HTTP service at port 8080. Note that the address includes the instance name as well.

FIGURE C.2
Connecting to the
Reporting Services
instance

FIGURE C.3
Report Server
Properties

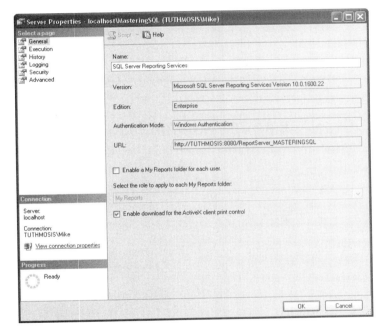

Loading the Report Manager

The Report Manager is a web-based utility that provides much of the same administrative control over the server as the SSMS tool. To access the Report Manager, you will use the address
that we noted in the previous step, except that instead of using **ReportServer** in the URL, you
will use **Reports** instead. Therefore, in this case, the virtual location after the port number
would be /Reports_MASTERINGSQL. This interface is illustrated in Figure C.4.

By default, loading the Report Manager will take you to the Home location of the instance
catalog. If there were reports deployed to this instance, you would see folders here containing
reports and perhaps data sources. You can deploy reports to the Report Server either by upload-
ing them to the catalog in the Report Manager by using the Upload File button, or by pushing
them to the reporting instance from Visual Studio, where you will design the report.

FIGURE C.4
The Report
Manager

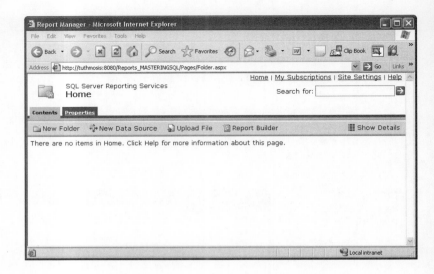

Creating a Simple Report

To give you an idea of the process of putting together a report, let's walk through the process. Creating a report can be distilled to some simple steps. First, you must create the data connection and then define a data set. Once you have the data structure, you can design and browse your report. Finally, you will deploy the report to the report server. We will look at each of these steps in turn.

A report is actually a .NET executable that is compiled by the Visual Studio environment. Although you do not have to know any .NET coding to build a report, SQL Server administrators should be aware that reports are in fact .NET artifacts. First though, you must start Visual Studio, or the Business Intelligence Development Studio. All report development takes place in this environment.

Defining the Report Project

The first step in creating a report is to create a Visual Studio Reporting Services project. This project will act as the container for all required reporting artifacts. The steps for creating the report project are as follows:

1. From the Visual Studio menu, select File ➢ New ➢ Project.

2. In the resulting dialog, select Business Intelligence Projects in the left tree view under the heading Project Types. This will present a set of templates on the right.

3. Select Report Server Project in the list on the right. Do not select the Wizard option. We will be building this report project manually.

4. Provide a name for the report at the bottom of the dialog. In our examples, we will be using the name **AdventureWorksDemo** as the name of the report project.

5. Click OK to finish the dialog and create the report project. In the Solution Explorer on the right of the screen, you should see two folders in the solution: one for Shared Data Sources and one for Reports.

Both data sources and reports are defined in XML files. Data sources use the file extension .rds (report data source), while reports use an .rdl (report definition language) format. Because they are both XML files, you could simply create the XML in a text editor; however, reports are so complex that it is easier to design them using the Visual Studio tool.

Creating a Data Source

A data source is a set of instructions on how a report will connect to its underlying data content. Data sources do not represent live and open connections, but rather connection configurations, very similar to connections strings in traditional data access programming.

Data sources can come in two formats, shared data sources and report data sources. A shared data source represents a set of connection values that many reports can use. The data source can be shared across many reports. The primary advantage to shared data sources is having a single point of change. If you want to change the data source for multiple reports, you only need to alter one artifact and all reports will see the change.

Report-specific data sources are not shared. Each report uses its own data source. This can be useful when you do not want changes in one data source to affect other reports. For example, if you have two reports that use the same underlying data, but you suspect that you may want to redirect one report to another data source without redirecting the other, you should consider report data sources.

Because shared data sources are the most common, we will begin with a shared data source and walk through the simple configuration of this artifact. Use the following steps to configure the data source.

1. In the Solution Explorer, right-click the Shared Data Sources folder and select Add New Data Source from the menu. This will present a new Data Sources dialog like the one pictured in Figure C.5.

FIGURE C.5
Creating a shared
data source

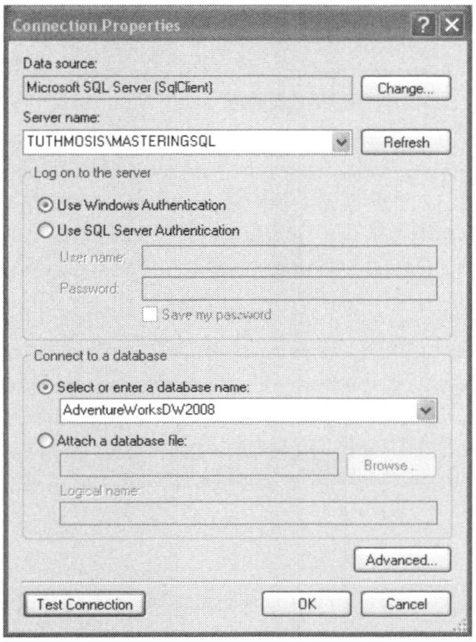

2. Configure the data source by providing a name and identifying the data source type to which you want to connect. Although we are connecting to a SQL Server in this example, if you open the Type dropdown list, you will see that any installed .NET or OLE DB-compliant data source is usable.

3. To configure the connection string, click the Edit button. This will present a standard Connection Configuration dialog that will determine the connection string needed. This example uses the AdventureWorksDW2008 database.

4. You can access the Credentials page of the dialog by using the selector on the left. Figure C.6 shows the default setting for this dialog.

FIGURE C.6
Configuring execution credentials

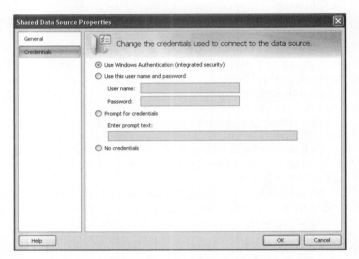

5. Click the OK button to create the data source. You should see the AWDemoSource.rds file in the Solution Explorer. Your data source is ready to use in a report.

AUTHENTICATION SECURITY

In our example, we will use integrated security, meaning that the authority of the executing user will be used to access all database and other resources. In the real world, however, this could cause security problems. Because reports are .NET executables, it is possible that they could contain malicious code and if executed by someone having the appropriate level of authority, could be destructive.

Instead of using Windows Authentication in this case, you should create an account with the permissions necessary to perform the tasks required by the report and no more. You can then configure the connection to use this account as its credential. This implements the Least Permissions security principle to ensure that unintended consequences of executing reports are better managed.

Creating a Report

The next step is to add the report to the project. Creating a report requires you to identify the data source that the report will use. This process will result in a report .rdl file that you can then customize to meet your needs. To create the report, follow these steps.

1. Point to the Reports folder in the Solution Explorer and right-click. From the popup menu, select Add ➤ New Item and select Report from the dialog. Do not select New Report from the menu as this will launch the Report Wizard.

2. At the bottom of the dialog, define a name for the report. Note the file extension of .rdl. In our example, we will use the name ProductDemo.rdl.

3. Click the Add button to add the new report to the project. This will open the report designer.

4. Before you can add fields to the report, you must associate the report with a connection. On the left side of the screen will be a Report Data window. Click the New button at the top left of this window to open a menu of items to add to the report. Select Data Source from this list.

5. This will open the Data Source dialog pictured in Figure C.7. You can either create a report-specific data source or you can refer to an already existing data source. This dialog creates a local data source references called ProductDemoDS that refers to our shared data source. Click OK to add the data source.

FIGURE C.7

Data source configuration

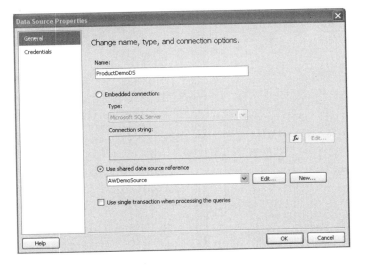

Obviously, you have to select data before you can display it. While the data source defines connection information, it does not specify which data from the data source should be returned in the report. For that, we need a dataset.

For those readers with ADO.NET programming experience, a dataset in Reporting Services is a very different artifact from the System.Data.DataSet class with which you are familiar. The ADO.NET DataSet is a data cache. It represents a disconnected data structure that you can manipulate programmatically in your database application. The Reporting Services dataset is really just a configured query or stored procedure call. It does not represent a data store, but rather the metadata catalog of the data that will return when the configured query is executed by the report. Follow these steps to create a dataset.

1. In the Report Data window, click the New button in the upper left of the window and select Dataset from the menu. This will open the dataset designer illustrated in Figure C.8.

FIGURE C.8
Creating a dataset

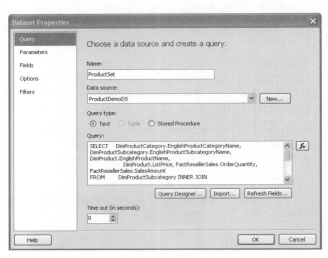

2. You must decide if the dataset will use a query or stored procedure. Most of the time a stored procedure is preferred for security and performance reasons, but in this case we will use a query. You can either create the query by typing the query into the dialog or using the Query Designer by clicking on the Query Designer button. You can also import an existing SQL Script by clicking the Import button. Our query looks like this:

```
SELECT DimProductCategory.EnglishProductCategoryName,
            DimProductSubcategory.EnglishProductSubcategoryName,
            DimProduct.EnglishProductName,
 DimProduct.ListPrice,
            FactResellerSales.OrderQuantity,   FactResellerSales.SalesAmount
FROM DimProductSubcategory
INNER JOIN DimProductCategory
        ON DimProductSubcategory.ProductCategoryKey =
            DimProductCategory.ProductCategoryKey
INNER JOIN DimProduct
        ON DimProductSubcategory.ProductSubcategoryKey =
            DimProduct.ProductSubcategoryKey
INNER JOIN     FactResellerSales
        ON DimProduct.ProductKey =
            FactResellerSales.ProductKey
```

3. Click OK to accept the input and create the dataset. Your Report Data window should look like the dialog illustrated in Figure C.9.

FIGURE C.9
The Report Data window

4. The field names are a little long, and reference to English is unnecessary in this report. To edit the field names, right-click on the dataset in the Report Data window and select Dataset Properties from the menu. This will reopen the dialog. Select Fields from the selectors on the left. Edit the field names as illustrated in Figure C.10.

FIGURE C.10
Editing field names

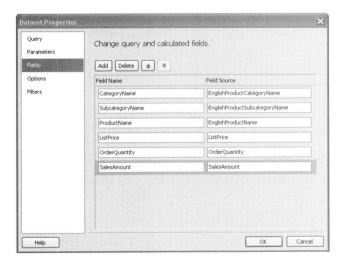

Designing the Report

Now that you have a data connection and a field structure in place, you are ready to start building the report. In reality, there would have to be a significant amount of report design and needs analysis before you actually start building the report. This analysis would tell you which fields you need and how they should be organized. But assuming that is complete, you can now start putting fields on the report.

Before placing a field on a report, you must first define a data region. The region acts as a data repeater. Placing a field in a data region allows the report to iterate over all of the data to populate the report. You can also organize the region into groups with headers and footers for aggregation purposes. There are a number of data region options, but we will demonstrate the most common, which is the Table region.

1. From the main menu, select View ➤ Toolbox. This will display the Reporting Services toolbox on the left side of the screen. Locate the Table control in the toolbox. Drag and drop the table onto the report design surface and resize the control so that it looks like Figure C.11.

FIGURE C.11
Adding a Table region

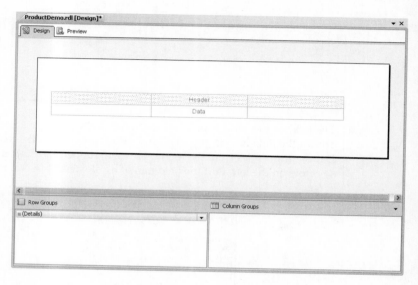

2. Select the cell that contains the word Header and right-click. From the popup menu, select Insert Column ➤ Left to add a new column to the table. There should be four columns in the table.

3. Go back to the Report Data window and drag the following fields from the field list in the window to the Data row on the report.

   ◆ CategoryName

   ◆ SubCategoryName

   ◆ ProductName

   ◆ SalesAmount

4. Notice that as you add the fields to the Data row, it automatically adds corresponding titles to the Header row. Because the fields are prebound to the underlying dataset, you do not have to take any additional steps to bind the report fields to the dataset.

5. Click the Preview tab on the designer to preview the report. Because there is a lot of underlying data, this may take a few seconds to execute and render. The resulting report should look like Figure C.12. As you can see, we would still have a lot of work left to make the report presentable, but the data is there that we want to present to the user.

FIGURE C.12
Previewing the report

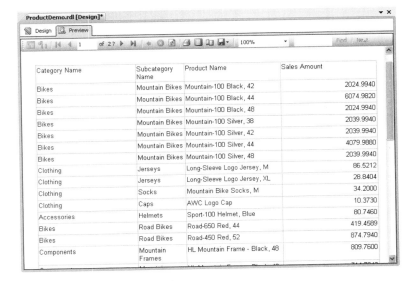

Deploying the Report

So far the report preview has executed the report only within our local Visual Studio environment. Of course, your report users will not all have Visual Studio installed, nor will they likely have direct access to the underlying data sources, so you will have to deploy your reports to the target Reporting Services instance to make them accessible to your users.

To start this process, you must first know the URL of your report server. Look again at Figure C.3 for an illustration of the Properties window in the SSMS that we used to get this information. Make a note of this URL for your own instance as you will need to provide it to the project. To configure the deployment, take the following steps.

1. In the Solution Explorer on the right side of your screen, right-click on the Reporting Services project (not the solution). Select Properties from the menu.

2. You should see a Properties dialog like the one pictured in Figure C.13. In the TargetServerURL property, enter the URL of your server instance that you pulled from the dialog in Figure C.3. Click OK when you are finished.

3. To deploy the project, right-click on the project in the Solution Explorer window and select Deploy. The Output window at the bottom of the screen should show a successful build and deployment. It should be similar to the report illustrated in Figure C.14.

FIGURE C.13
Configuring a
deployment target

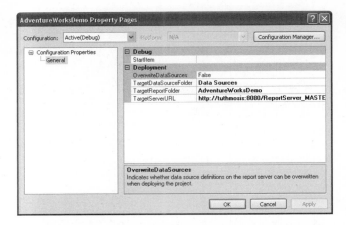

FIGURE C.14
Reporting a suc-
cessful deploy-
ment

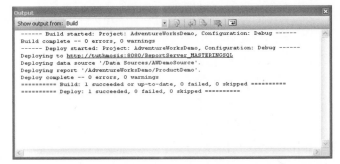

4. At this point you should be able to open the Report Manager, the web-based tool that you were introduced to earlier in this discussion, and view the deployed reports. If you open the Report Manager and navigate to the Home folder now, it should look like the example in Figure C.15.

FIGURE C.15
The Report Man-
ager showing a
Deployed Report
folder

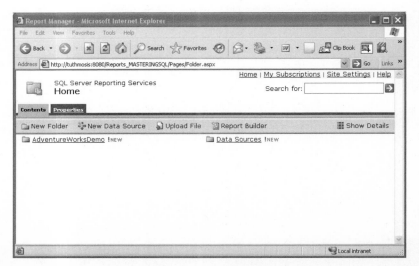

5. Click on the AdventureWorksDemo folder in the Report Manager to view the deployed reports. You should see the ProductDemo report in the resulting screen. Click on the report name link to launch the report. Close the Report Manager when you are finished viewing the report.

Although this walkthrough has only produced a very simple report, we hope that it has been useful for you to see the steps involved in creating a basic report and deploying that report in Reporting Services. For more detailed information, take a look at *Mastering SQL Server 2005 Reporting Services* (Sybex, 2007). This book covers the SQL Server 2005 implementation of reporting services. Also watch for the SQL Server 2008 release of this work that will cover the 2008 version of the tool when it is published.

Index